Also by Nicholas Clee

DON'T SWEAT THE AUBERGINE

Eclip

Eclipse

The Horse that Changed
Racing History Forever

Nicholas Clee

THE OVERLOOK PRESS
NEW YORK, NY

This edition first published in the United States in 2012 by

The Overlook Press, Peter Mayer Publishers, Inc.
141 Wooster Street
New York, NY 10012
www.overlookpress.com

For bulk and special sales, please contact sales@overlookny.com

First published in Great Britain in 2009 by Bantam Press,
an imprint of Transworld Publishers

Cataloging-in-Publication Data is available from the Library of Congress

Manufactured in the United States of America

1 3 5 7 9 10 8 6 4 2

ISBN 978-1-59020-737-6

For Nicolette, Rebecca and Laura

Contents

Prologue

GO TO THE RACES, anywhere in the world, and you'll be watching horses who are relatives of Eclipse. The vast majority of them are descended from Eclipse's male line; if you trace back their ancestry through their fathers, their fathers' fathers, and so on, you come, some twenty generations back, to him. He is the most influential stallion in the history of the Thoroughbred. Two and a half centuries after his imperious, undefeated career, he remains the undisputed paragon of his sport.

The story of this career begins on a spring morning in 1769, at a trial on Epsom Downs. Scorching across the turf towards a small group of spectators is a chestnut with a white blaze. Toiling in his wake is a single rival, who will never catch him – not if they race to the ends of the earth.

Among the witnesses at this awe-inspiring display are two men who, according to the tradition of the Sport of Kings, should not be associated with the horse who will become its greatest exponent. One, Eclipse's owner, is a meat salesman, William Wildman. The second, who wants to own Eclipse, is an Irish adventurer and gambler.

Dennis O'Kelly arrived in London some twenty years earlier, full of energy and optimism and ambition. He has had his ups and downs, including an affair with a titled lady and a spell in prison, but at last – thanks to his gambling abilities and to the remarkable success of his companion, the leading brothel madam of the day – he is starting to rise in the world.

What Dennis does not know is that certain sections of the establishment will never accept him. What he does know, as with quickening pulse he follows the progress of the speeding chestnut, is that this horse is his destiny.

The Chairman

L ONDON, 1748. The capital is home to some 650,000 inhabitants, more than 10 per cent of the population of England.
What image of Georgian metropolitan life comes to mind? You
may have a Canaletto-inspired view of an elegant square.
Bewigged men and women with hooped skirts are strolling; there
are a few carriages, and perhaps a wagon; the gardens are trim; the
houses are stately. Or you may be picturing the London of
Hogarth. The street is teeming, and riotous: drunks lie in the
gutter, spewing; dogs and pickpockets weave among the crowd;
through a window, you can see a prostitute entertaining her client;
from the window above, someone is tipping out the contents of a
chamber pot.

Both images are truthful.[1] London is a sophisticated city of
fashion, an anarchic city of vice, and other cities too. In the West
End are the titled, the wealthy, and the ton (the smart set); in the
City are the financiers, merchants and craftsmen; prostitutes and
theatre folk congregate in Covent Garden; north of Covent
Garden, in St Giles's, and in the East End and south of the Thames,

[1] Canaletto's version may be underpopulated, however, as a result of his use of
a camera obscura, which failed to capture many moving objects.

are the slums, where an entire family may inhabit one small room, and where disease, alcoholism and crime are rampant. 'If one considers the destruction of all morality, decency and modesty,' wrote Henry Fielding, the author of the exuberant comic novel *Tom Jones*, 'the swearing, whoredom and drunkenness which is eternally carrying on in these houses on the one hand, and the excessive poverty and misery of most of the inhabitants on the other, it seems doubtful whether they are most the objects of detestation or compassion.' Among the native populations of these districts is a substantial admixture of Irish immigrants. A new arrival, with some modest savings and a sunny determination to make a name for himself, is a young man called Dennis O'Kelly.

Dennis was born in about 1725. His father, Andrew, was a smallholder in Tullow, about fifty miles south-west of Dublin. Dennis and his brother, Philip, received little education, and were expected to start earning their livings almost as soon as they entered their teens. (There were also two sisters, who made good marriages.) Philip began a career as a shoemaker. Dennis had grander ambitions. Soon, finding Tullow too small to contain his optimistic energy, he set out for Dublin.

The discovery that Dubliners regarded him as an uneducated yokel barely dented his confidence. Charm, vigour and quick wits would see him through, he felt; and he was right, then and thereafter. A few days after his arrival in the city, he saw a well-dressed woman slip in the street, and rushed to her aid. There was no coach nearby, so Dennis offered his arm to support the woman's walk home, impressing her with his courtesy. She asked Dennis about his circumstances and background. Although he gave as much gloss to his answer as he could, he was heard with a concerned frown. You must be careful, the woman advised him: Dublin is a very wicked place, and a young man such as you might easily fall into bad company.

People who give such warnings are usually the ones you need to avoid. But this woman was to be one of several patronesses who would ease Dennis's passage through life. She was a widow in her thirties, and the owner of a coffee house, where she hired Dennis as a waiter. Under her tutelage he lost, or learned to disguise, his rough edges, grew accomplished in his job, and graduated to become her lover. There was supplementary income to be earned by defeating the customers at billiards. It was a pleasant arrangement. It could not satisfy Dennis, though. Once he had amassed a fortune of £50 (about £6,500 in today's money, but then a modest annual income for a middle-class provincial household), he said farewell to his mistress and made his way to London.

This account of Dennis O'Kelly's early progress comes from a sketch 'by our ingenious correspondent D.L.' that appeared in *Town & Country* magazine in 1770, just before the end of Eclipse's racing career. It offered the fullest portrait of Dennis until the publication in 1788, a year after his death, of a racy work entitled *The Genuine Memoirs of Dennis O'Kelly, Esq: Commonly Called Count O'Kelly*. The book belonged to a thriving genre of brief lives, hastily produced and written by hacks (the term 'memoirs' applied to biography as well as autobiography). Their tone was often cheerfully defamatory, and entirely suited to portraying the riotous, scandalous, vainglorious Dennis. But while no doubt legendary in spirit, and certainly unreliable in some details, the *Genuine Memoirs* do tell in outline a true story, verifiable from other sources, including primary ones. It must be admitted, however, that the anecdotes of Dennis's adventures in his younger days seem to be the ones for which 'D.L.' and the author of the *Genuine Memoirs* (who sometimes differ) allowed their imaginations the freest rein.

Dennis arrived in the capital with the qualification only of being able to write his own name. He spoke with a strong accent, which the *Genuine Memoirs* characterized as 'the broadest and the most offensive brogue that his nation, perhaps, ever produced', and 'the very reverse of melody'. (Various contemporary chroniclers of Dennis's exploits delighted in representing his speech,

THE

GENUINE MEMOIRS

OF

Dennis O'Kelly, Efq.

COMMOLNY CALLED

COUNT O'KELLY:

Containing many curious and interefting Anecdotes of that
CELEBRATED CHARACTER, and his COAD-
JUTORs on the TURF and in the FIELD, with
a Variety of authentic, fingular, and entertaining
MILITIA MANOEUVRES, never before publifhed.

———————

LONDON:

Printed for C. STALKER, STATIONERS-COURT,
LUDGATE-HILL.

M DCC LXXXVIII.

With a typo ('commolny') indicating hasty production, The Genuine
Memoirs *appeared shortly after Dennis O'Kelly's death and offered a
racy portrait, uncompromised by notions of accuracy.*

peppering it with liberal exclamations of 'by Jasus'.) He was five feet eleven inches tall, and muscular, with a rough-hewn handsomeness. He was charming, confident and quick-witted. He believed that he could rise high, and mix with anyone; and, for the enterprising and lucky few, eighteenth-century society accommodated such aspirations. 'Men are every day starting up from obscurity to wealth,' Daniel Defoe wrote. London was a place where, in the opinion of Dr Johnson's biographer James Boswell, 'we may be in some degree whatever character we choose'. Dennis held also a native advantage, according to the coiner of a popular saying: 'Throw an Irishman into the Thames at London Bridge, naked at low-water, and he will come up at Westminster-Bridge, at high water, with a laced coat and a sword.'

In the *Town & Country* version of Dennis's early years in London, he relied immediately on his wits. Dennis, the ingenious D.L. reported, took lodgings on his arrival in London at a guinea a week (a guinea was £1 1s, or £1.05 in decimal coinage), and began to look around for a rich woman to marry. Needing to support himself until the provider of his financial requirements came along, he decided that gambling would earn him a living, and he frequented the tables at the Bedford Coffee House in Covent Garden and other smart venues. In the convivial company of fellow Irish expatriates, he played hazard – a dice game. Very soon, his new friends took all his money.

'By Jasus,' Dennis said to himself, 'this is t'other side of enough – and so poor Dennis must look out for a place again.' ('D.L.' had some fun with this story.) He got a position as captain's servant on a ship bound for Lisbon. Sea journeys were hazardous, but could be lucrative if they delivered their cargoes successfully. Dennis was lucky, and got back to London with sufficient funds to support a second stab at a gambling career. This time he avoided hazard, and his expatriate chums, and stuck to billiards.

Another new friend promoted his marital ambitions, suggesting that they form a partnership to court two sisters, each of whom had a fortune of £1,000 a year. It was the work of a week. The partners did not want their marriages to be legally binding, so they hired John Wilkinson, a clergyman who specialized in conducting illegal ceremonies at the Savoy Chapel (and who was later transported for the practice). Before the honeymoon was over, Dennis had managed to persuade his friend to entrust his new wealth to him. Then he absconded. He spent time in Scarborough, attended the races at York, and cut a figure in Bath and in other watering-places. It was some time before he returned to London, where he found, to his satisfaction, that his wife – with whom he had no legally binding contract – had become a servant, and that his former friend had emigrated to India. They could not touch him.

However, Dennis again struggled to earn his keep. The genteel façade that was necessary in the gambling profession was expensive to maintain. And he still had a lot to learn. In order to dupe 'pigeons', as suckers or marks were known, he employed a more experienced accomplice, with whom he had to share the proceeds. Before long, Dennis fell into debt again.

Version two of Dennis's story, from the *Genuine Memoirs*, has come to be the more widely accepted. In this one, he made use of his physical prowess. Leaving behind several creditors in Ireland, he made his way to London and found a position as a sedan chairman. Sedan chairs, single-seater carriages conveyed by horizontal poles at the front and back, were the taxis of the day. There were public, licensed ones, carried by the likes of Dennis and his (unnamed) partner; and there were private ones, often elaborately decorated and carried by men who were the antecedents of chauffeurs. The chairs had hinged roofs, allowing the passenger to walk in from the front, and they could be brought into houses, so that the passenger need not be exposed to the elements. Dennis, who was never shy or deferential, took advantage of the access to make himself known above and below stairs: 'Many and oftentimes,' the *Genuine Memoirs* reported, 'has he carried great personages, male

The Covent Garden Morning Frolick *by L. P. Boitard (1747). Betty
Careless, a bagnio proprietor (a bagnio was a bathing house, usually a
brothel too), travels to work in a sedan chair. Hitching a ride, without a
thought for the poor chairmen, is one of her lovers, Captain Montague.
Dennis O'Kelly was the 'front legs' of a chair.*

and female, whose secret histories have been familiar to his knowledge.'

The physical burdens were the least of the trials of the job. Chairmen carried their fares through London streets that were irregularly paved, and pockmarked with bumps and holes. There was dust when it was dry, and deep mud when it was wet. The ingredients of the mud included ash, straw, human and animal faeces, and dead cats and dogs. The winters were so fierce that the Thames, albeit a shallower river than it is now, sometimes froze over. Pipes burst, drenching the streets with water that turned rapidly to ice. Illumination was infrequent, as the duty of lighting thoroughfares lay in part with the inhabitants, who were not con-scientious; people hired 'link-boys' to light their journeys with firebrands. In daylight, too, it was often hard to see far ahead: London smogs, even before the smoky Victorian era, could reduce visibility to a few feet. There was intense, cacophonous noise: car-riages on cobbles; horses' hooves; animals being driven to market; musicians busking; street traders shouting.

The chairmen slalomed through this chaos with the ruth-lessness of modern bike messengers. They yelled 'By your leave, sir!', but otherwise were uncompromising: a young French visitor to London, taking his first stroll, failed to respond to the yells quickly enough and was knocked over four times. Chairmen could set a fast pace because the distances were not huge. A slightly later view of the city from Highgate (the print is in the British Library) shows the built-up area extending only a short distance east of St Paul's (by far the most imposing landmark) and no further west than Westminster Abbey. To the north, London began at a line just above Oxford Street, and ended in the south just beyond the Thames. Outside these limits were fields and villages. The chair-men carried their customers mostly within the boundaries of the West End.

Dennis was in St James's when he met his second significant patroness (after the Dublin coffee house owner). Some three hundred chairs were in competition, but this November day offered plenty of custom: it was the birthday of George II. Horse-drawn coaches could make no progress through the gridlocked streets, and the chairmen were in demand. A lady's driver, frustrated on his journey to the palace (St James's Palace was then the principal royal residence), hailed Dennis from his stalled vehicle. Dennis leaped to the lady's assistance, accompanying her to his chair and scattering the onlookers who had jostled forward to view such a fine personage. He 'acted with such powers and magnanimity, that her ladyship conceived him to be a regeneration of Hercules or Hector, and her opinion was by no means altered when she beheld the powerful elasticity of his muscular motions on the way to the Royal residence. Dennis touched her ladyship's guinea, and bowed in return for a bewitching smile which accompanied it.'[2]

You may conclude that this mock-heroic description is an acknowledgement that the story is preposterous. But the eighteenth century was a period of great social, and sexual, intermingling. In some ways (ways that Dennis would learn about, but never respect), the class structure was rigid; in others, it mattered little. Important men conducted open affairs with prostitutes and other humble women, and from time to time married them. Not so many grand women took humble men as lovers, but a few did. Lady Henrietta Wentworth married her footman. Adventurous sex lives were common. 'Many feminine libertines may be found amongst young women of rank,' observed Lady Mary Wortley Montagu, the renowned letter writer. Lady Harley was said to have become pregnant by so many lovers that, the historian Roy Porter recorded, her children were known as the 'Harleian miscellany'.

The day following Dennis's encounter with Lady — (the

___

[2] From the *Genuine Memoirs*. I have amplified some of the details of the story of Dennis and Lady —.

Genuine Memoirs gives no name or initials), he was loitering outside White's Chocolate House, musing on her smile, when an elderly woman asked him the way to Bolton Row in Piccadilly. She offered him a shilling to escort her there. When they arrived, she invited him in from the cold to take a drink. The mistress of the house greeted Dennis and asked him whether he knew of any chairmen looking for a place. 'Yes, Madam,' Dennis answered, 'an' that I do: I should be very glad to be after recommending myself, because I know myself, and love myself better than any one else.' Well, then, the woman replied, he should go to the house of Lady — in Hanover Square, mention no name, but say that he had heard of the vacant position. 'God in heaven bless you,' Dennis exclaimed, draining his substantial glass of brandy.

The next morning, Dennis dressed himself as finely as he could, and presented himself in Hanover Square. He made the right impression, got the job, at a salary of £30 a year, and started work the next day. Standing in the hall, self-conscious in his new livery and excited at this access to grandeur, he looked up to see his mistress descending the staircase. She was of course the same Lady — whose teasing smile had occupied his thoughts since their journey to the palace. But she offered no hint of recognition. She hurried into her chair, making it known that she wished to be conveyed to the Opera House. Her expression on arrival was more encouraging; and when, at the end of her appointment, she came out of the theatre, she blessed Dennis with another smile, more provocative than before. Taking his hand, she squeezed it gently round a purse. He felt his strength liquefy; a tremendous effort of concentration was required to force his trembling limbs to carry the chair safely home. Alone, he opened the purse, to find that it contained five guineas.

The next day was busy. No sooner had Dennis returned from an errand to the mantua maker (a mantua was a skirt and bodice open in the front) than he was off again to the milliner, and then to the hairdresser, and then to the perfumer. Last, there was a parcel to deliver to Bolton Row – specifically, to the house where he had received the tip-off about his job.

Again, he was invited in, but this time ushered into a back parlour, where – as the *Genuine Memoirs* described the scene – a giant fire was roaring and where the only other illumination came from four candles. Dennis sat himself close to the blaze, the delicious heat dispersing the cold in his bones. A young woman, with shyly averted face, brought him a tankard of mulled wine. He drained half of it in a gulp. More warmth suffused him; he did not want to move from this room. He looked at the girl, who for some reason was loitering by the door, and got a general impression of comeliness. He asked her what she was called. She replied obliquely: she had been asked to entertain Mr Kelly[3] until her mistress should return, 'and indeed I am happy to be in your company, Sir, for I do not like to be alone'.

This was promising, Dennis thought. 'Upon my soul,' he asserted, 'I am equally happy, and wish to be more so. Come sit by me.'

The girl approached, sat, and turned towards him. She was Lady ––. They fell on each other; bodices, and other garments too, were ripped. As evening turned to night, and as the fire subsided, they enjoyed mutual happiness. At last, Lady –– said she must leave. Exchanging her servant's clothes for her usual ones, and leaving Dennis with another purse, she sought her coach, which had been waiting a few doors away.

Dennis, more dazedly, reassembled his attire. Returning to the workaday world was a wearying prospect. But there was another surprise, less welcome, in store. The door of the parlour opened, and the old woman whom he had conducted to the house three days earlier entered. You have done well for yourself, she observed; such fortune would never have befallen you had it not

[3] Dennis styled himself 'Kelly' – the anglicized version of his name – during his early years in London.

been for my assistance. No doubt you would want to reward me accordingly – my mistress and I depend on taking advantage of such eventualities. Your mistress gave you a purse earlier, and, as a man of honour, you should share it.

Dennis was nonplussed. Surely this woman had no claim on him? 'By Jasus,' he replied, 'but she never gave me a single guinea.'

The woman smiled complacently. 'Come, my dear creature,' she said (pronouncing it 'creter'), 'come along with me, and I'll show you the difference.'

She took him by the hand, and led him to the front parlour. On the wall was a small looking glass. She removed it, revealing an aperture, and invited Dennis to look through. He got a fine view of the back parlour, and particularly of the part of it near the fire. Resignedly, he reached for the purse, looked inside, and saw that it contained an enormous sum: twenty-five guineas. ''Tis only my right that I take ten,' the woman told him, 'as I must account for it to my mistress.' Dennis knew when he was cornered. He handed over the money.

This dampener did not submerge his enthusiasm for the affair, which continued happily for several months. It was both delightful and profitable. But Dennis was not Lady —'s only side-line. The *Genuine Memoirs* said that she took lovers among her own set, too; and, unfortunately, Lord — was not as liberal in his atti-tudes to such behaviour as were some eighteenth-century husbands. He threw her out of doors, and divorced her. With Dennis's mistress went Dennis's job.

After a taste of life in Hanover Square, Dennis was not inclined to return to hauling a licensed sedan chair. He might con-tinue to enjoy the high life, he reasoned, if he lived by his wits. He frequented the Vauxhall pleasure gardens, where, for a shilling a ticket, people gathered to walk, eat, listen to music, and stare at one another. He spent many hours in coffee houses, at tennis courts, and at billiard tables, where he picked up some money as both marker (keeper of the score) and player. He made notable friends, among them the Duke of Richmond and Sir William Draper, the soldier. Everyone was clubbable — while he had money.

As the money ran out, Dennis continued to spend. He had discovered an addiction to extravagance, and he thought he could charm, or dupe, his creditors. But there was a way of taking revenge on people who did not honour the money they owed: you could get them jailed. Dennis's creditors sued, and saw him confined to the Fleet, the debtors' prison.

The year was 1756. Five years would pass before Dennis regained his freedom. It was the disaster of his life. But it led him to the woman who would be both his lifelong companion and his partner in making his fortune.

The Whore's last Shift.

The Whore's Last Shift. *A once-fashionable 'Cyprian lass' (one of the arch phrases by which Charlotte Hayes and her contemporaries were known) is down on her luck. On the table is* Harris's List of Covent Garden Ladies, *first compiled by Charlotte's sometime lover, Samuel Derrick.*

2

The Bawd

CHARLOTTE HAYES FLOURISHED in what one writer described as the 'golden age' of prostitution. It was golden for the clients, perhaps, particularly for the ones who could afford to frequent the splendid serails (harems – French terms and practices were fashionable in this world) that adorned eighteenth-century London. It was golden for a few, a very few, of the prostitutes. But there were ten thousand of them in the capital, according to Roy Porter; Johann Wilhelm von Archenholz, a contemporary visitor, put the figure at fifty thousand. For most of these women, beginning their careers in a kind of slavery and ending up in destitution and disease, gold was elusive.

You could not miss them. Von Archenholz wrote, 'At all seasons of the year, they sally out towards the dusk, arrayed in the most gaudy colours, and fill the principal streets. They accost the passengers, and offer to accompany them: they even surround them in crowds, stop and overwhelm them with caresses and entreaties. The better kind, however, content themselves with walking around till they themselves are addressed.' It was a happy hunting ground for James Boswell, who, like a bat or an owl, would set out as darkness fell. Sex in the open air gave him a particular frisson. He disported with a 'strong, plump, good-humoured girl called Nanny Baker' in St James's Park, and, armed with a condom, 'At the bottom of the Haymarket I picked up a strong, jolly young damsel, and taking her under the arm I conducted her to Westminster Bridge, and then in armour complete did I engage her upon this noble edifice. The whim of doing it there with the Thames rolling below amused me very much.'

What a rogue! We might regard Boswell's lusty antics indulgently, as mere boisterous transgression, from our vantage point two and a half centuries later. This was not a jolly industry, though. Von Archenholz saw the seamy side: 'I have beheld with a surprise, mingled with terror, girls from eight to nine years old make a proffer of their charms; and such is the corruption of the human heart, that even they have their lovers.' He also observed, without much sympathy, the fate of prostitutes later in life: 'Towards midnight, when the young women have disappeared, and the streets become deserted, then the old wretches, of 50 or 60 years of age, descend from their garrets, and attack the intoxicated passengers, who are often prevailed upon to satisfy their passions in the open street with these female monsters.'

In *A Harlot's Progress* (1732), William Hogarth depicted one method of recruitment to the profession. Moll Hackabout, young and fresh of face, arrives in London on the York wagon, to be met by an ingratiating woman. The woman offers lodging and a position; but in fact Moll's immediate future is to be raped by the leering man in the background.[4] The woman in Hogarth's print has been identified as the bawd Mother Needham (madams were often, ironically, 'mother'), and the leering man as Colonel Francis Charteris, who bore the unappetizing sobriquet Rape-Master of Great Britain. Both had died the year before the print appeared, Charteris of unknown causes and Needham following an appearance in the pillory, where she had received an enthusiastic pelting

[4] I am sorry to say that Charlotte Hayes, some years later, would not be above such stratagems.

by the mob. In Hogarth's subsequent prints, Moll Hackabout tastes a brief period of prosperity as the mistress of a rich Jewish merchant before declining into poverty, the workhouse and death.

Charlotte Hayes was (like Dennis O'Kelly) born in about 1725, possibly in Covent Garden — one historian has found a Joseph Hayes living in Tavistock Street at the time. She rose from obscurity alongside two other beauties, Nancy Jones and Lucy Cooper, whose fans congregated at venues including the Bedford Arms on the Strand and Ben Jonson's Head on Little Russell Street. Nancy's and Lucy's stories illustrate the precariousness of their calling. Nancy lost her looks, along with her ability to command admirers, to smallpox, and died of syphilis at the age of twenty-five. Lucy, 'lewder than all the whores in Charles's reign', found a rich protector in Sir Orlando Bridgeman, a wealthy baronet. Thanks to him, she was 'exalted from a basket to a coach' (a basket was a cheap seat on a stagecoach). But in 1765 Bridgeman died, leaving Lucy an annuity with the stipulation that she quit her profession. She ignored his wishes, with decreasing success. After several periods of imprisonment, she died impoverished in 1772.

The trick was to find a wealthy lover, be kept by him in style, but to hold other men in reserve should he go off you, or die. If you had the entrepreneurial skills, you could try setting up as a madam. Both routes offered golden rewards for the most skilful and the luckiest, in an era when keeping paid mistresses and visiting brothels were stylish activities, as long as they were conducted in the manner of a gentleman. Beautiful and charismatic courtesans such as Nancy Jones (briefly) and Lucy Cooper, as well as the likes of Fanny Murray, Kitty Fisher and Harriet Powell, were celebrated figures of the day, and had many aristocratic admirers. Nancy Parsons was the lover of the Duke of Grafton, Prime Minister during the 1760s — although the Duke went beyond the bounds of propriety by entertaining her in his box at the theatre, just a few seats away from his estranged wife. A few years later,

Mary Robinson and Elizabeth Armistead were lovers of the Prince of Wales, the future George IV. Sometimes these affairs ended in marriage. Elizabeth Armistead became the wife of Charles James Fox, the Whig politician, while Harriet Powell bagged the Earl of Seaforth.

Charlotte found no such happy outcome to her career as a courtesan, but, blessed with great entrepreneurial and marketing skills, she picked herself up, to go on to triumph as a madam.

She came of age as the protégée of one Mrs Ward, whose methods of keeping her girls subservient she would emulate. She received an education, because a patina of culture would be an asset in her destined career.[5] When Charlotte reached maturity, she came up for sale. Mrs Ward would have been able to charge up to £50, maybe even £100, for brokering a night with a beautiful young virgin; and she may have done it several times. Refreshing her charges' maidenhoods was another ploy that Charlotte would copy.

Although a young woman might claim to be deflowered more than once, she could not keep doing so indefinitely, and the time came when the ambitious and talented hoped to find wealthy lovers. A mistress could expect lavish apartments and the equivalent of a platinum credit card. She insisted on acquiring the finest clothes, jewels, hats, gloves and other accessories, and on mixing with people of fashion and position. But she maintained this lifestyle only for as long as she continued to bewitch her lover. Fortunately, Charlotte was bewitching. She had brown hair and grey eyes; her features were rounded and girlish, and at their most alluring with very little make-up. Hers was 'a countenance as open as her heart', and her deportment was dignified without affectation.

A bawd is necessarily a cold and sometimes a cruel person, but Charlotte earned indulgence even from chroniclers of the most scandalous episodes of her career. Looking back at the

---

[5] Charlotte did not sign her name with the éclat of Dennis O'Kelly, but she was more literate than he.

contemporary records, one wishes that they contained a little more venom, which might have drawn out more of her personality. Dennis O'Kelly leaps off the pages of those who describe him, while Charlotte – perhaps because she suppressed true feeling, or perhaps because she is portrayed only by men – is unfathomable.

Her greatest conquest was Robert Tracey, usually given the moniker 'Beau', applied to the most dashing bucks of the era. Tracey had accomplishments. 'Abstract him from women, and he was a man far above mediocrity'; he possessed a good library, and felt that reading was so important that he would always take a book to study while having his hair cut. He was also a libertine, and, from Charlotte's point of view, a delightful spendthrift. Still more delightful was his submission to her. Hitherto a man of fleeting affections, he found in Charlotte the love of his life. 'She had him so much at her command that she could fleece him at will' – in the words of the ribald chronicle *Nocturnal Revels*. Craving some extra cash, she would call on Tracey at his chambers in the Temple, tell him that she would not stay unless he play dice with her at a guinea a throw, take his money at each throw she won, and neglect to pay up at each throw she lost. After about a quarter of an hour, once she had amassed a reasonable sum, she would 'bounce away and laugh at him'.

Her other lovers included the poet Samuel Derrick, who offered no pecuniary attractions, as he never made a living from his verse. His most profitable venture, and his magnum opus, was *Harris's List of Covent Garden Ladies*, a publication with a distinctively eighteenth-century flavour. Appearing each year in a style we associate with more conventional guidebooks, it offered Derrick's intimate and witty pen-portraits of the finest prostitutes in London, along with warnings about ones to avoid.[6] But his

---

[6] Two examples: 'A smart little black gypsy [Miss Cross], with a very endearing symmetry of parts; has an odd way of wriggling herself about, and can communicate the most exquisite sensations when she is well paid'; 'She [Pol Forrester] has an entrance to the palace of pleasure as wide as a church door.'

involvement with the bestselling annual came after his affair with Charlotte had ended. While it was going on, he was simply a man 'of a diminutive size, with reddish hair and a vacant countenance', and with no funds. Perhaps Charlotte loved him. Certainly he was always fond of her, referring to her as 'my old friend and mistress Charlotte Hayes'. And no wonder he was grateful. In addition to enjoying her charms, he received entertainment from her 'in the most sumptuous manner' at the Shakespeare or Rose taverns, with Tracey picking up bills of up to £40.[7]

For unknown reasons, Charlotte and Tracey separated. Thanks to his own and Charlotte's efforts, Tracey's finances were in disarray; and then his health went. He died in 1756, leaving Charlotte merely £5 with which to buy a mourning ring. She was unable to find anyone to take his place, and soon she too fell into debt. On 14 June 1758, the Court of King's Bench sent her to the Marshalsea jail; three days later, she transferred to the Fleet. A Fleet record lists an outstanding sum of £45, and separate debts of five shillings (25p) and ten shillings, to a certain Jane Bateman.

Charlotte Hayes and Dennis O'Kelly took their reverses well, refusing to allow their circumstances to cramp their styles. While in the Fleet, Charlotte, in the words of *The Genuine Memoirs of Dennis O'Kelly*, 'did not forget to perform her midnight orgies, or sacrifice to the powers of love and wine'. Dennis was reduced to impoverishment, alleviated only slightly by a job in the tap room (bar), but he never lost his jovial manner. The Fleet was a place where, albeit in depressing and limited surroundings, you could try to lead some semblance of a normal life.

The prison had been built in 1197, near the Fleet river. It adjoined what is now Farringdon Street (to the north-east of Fleet Street). By the mid-eighteenth century it housed mostly debtors –

---

[7] As we have seen, that was £10 more than Dennis O'Kelly's annual salary as Lady —'s chairman.

about 110 of them in Charlotte's and Dennis's time, although sometimes there were up to three hundred, along with their families.

Again, Hogarth – whose father had a spell in the Fleet – gives us a flavour of the scene. Tom Rakewell, hero of *The Rake's Progress*, sits gloomily beneath a meagre grilled window, in a small room shared with two other debtors but containing, in the picture, ten people. One of them is Tom's wife, who is berating him; on his other side, a boy runner and a gaoler are demanding money. A note on the table is from the manager of Covent Garden Theatre, and says: 'Sir, I have read your play and find it will not do.' (For some writers, this print has particular power to chill.)

Tom is not a prisoner in the sense of one enduring punishment for crimes. Rather, he is in confinement until he settles his debts or reaches agreement with his creditors, and, in common with his fellow inmates, he has a key to his room. Some debtors went to the Fleet voluntarily: it offered a way of avoiding payment. Taking to the life there, they would remain inside to spite the people demanding money from them. A Mr Yardley, who had an income of £700 a year, spent ten years in the Fleet owing £100; on his death in 1735 he left in his room items valued at £5,000.

The Fleet boasted a number of distinguished inmates. John Donne, the poet, did time there, at the instigation of his father-in-law. William Wycherley, author of Restoration comedies, was in the Fleet for seven years. William Penn, the founder of Pennsylvania, got into financial trouble and lived for a while in the Rules of the Fleet – an area outside the walls. In fiction, the inmates included Tobias Smollett's Peregrine Pickle (1751), who was waited on by a former Guards officer, and, alliteratively, Charles Dickens's Mr Pickwick (1836–7).

One of the sadder declines of Dennis's and Charlotte's era was that of Mrs Cornelys, impresario of theatrically staged promenades at Carlisle House in Soho. They were, in the words of diarist and rake William Hickey,[8] 'quite the rage'. Each Sunday evening, an immense crowd, 'from the Duchess of Devonshire down to the little milliner's apprentice from Cranbourn Alley', would saunter through the Carlisle House rooms, meeting, greeting and ogling. The decorations might be in Indian, Persian and Chinese styles, with illumination from '9,000 candles', according to one account; the next week, there would be a different theme. 'The magnificence of the rooms, splendour of the illumination and embellishments, and the brilliant appearance of the company exceeded anything I ever saw,' the eighteen-year-old Fanny Burney wrote. But Mrs Cornelys faced competition from attractions such as Almack's Assembly Rooms in St James's and the Pantheon on Oxford Street. When these venues became quite the rage instead, she responded by increasing her expenditure. It did not work. She sank into obscurity, and died in the Fleet in 1797, dreaming of a comeback. Her 'melancholy end holds forth a warning to the imprudent', the *Gentleman's Magazine* observed.

The prison building had four storeys. In the cellar were a kitchen and a dining room, which was known as Bartholomew's Fair. (The original Bartholomew Fair was a summer jamboree at Smithfield.) On the ground floor were a hall and the tap room. The upper floors contained 110 rooms off central corridors. Most of the rooms were 14½ by 12½ feet, and 9½ feet high – the largest in any prison in Britain. A coffee room provided newspapers and journals; in the grounds, you could play games including skittles and tennis. There was a wine club on Mondays, and a beer club on Thursdays, often lasting into the early hours and prompting complaints from those trying to sleep.

On arrival, you paid a commitment fee of £1 6s. The Fleet staff commanded various other sums, and there was rent of 2s 6d (12½p) a week for the share of a furnished room. Hogarth's Tom

[8] From the 1930s to the 1980s, the pseudonym 'William Hickey' appeared under a diary column in the *Daily Express*.

Rakewell shares with two others; some rooms housed six, and dependants too. More prosperous inmates were able to live alone, and to decorate rooms according to their own tastes. One Elizabeth Berkley furnished her chamber with two cane and two stuffed leather chairs, an easy chair, a looking glass, elegant curtains, a chocolate mill and various items of silverware. This was the 'master's side'. The 'common side' was the southern wing, where prisoners slept in dormitories. No stuffed leather chairs and elegant curtains here, in what was probably Dennis's home. He did not earn enough in the tap room to afford better accommodation, but nevertheless became known for his 'jolly song'. And, as when he was a sedan chairman, he managed to insinuate himself into the company of his social superiors.

Delivering drinks for Charlotte's entertainments, he caught her eye; and so began a lifelong relationship, both affectionate and mutually profitable, and never compromised by Charlotte's way of life. 'Charlotte had many friends, it is true, but policy induced her to see them with complacency,' the *Genuine Memoirs* insisted. 'Her affections were still [always] centred in our Hero.' Dennis was both Charlotte's lover and the promoter of her professional affairs. In return, she paid him, financing a resumption of his former ostentation and swagger. He also earned a kind of honour in the jail. A man known as the Sovereign of the Fleet – the informal title belonged to a senior resident, and carried about as much authority as that of Father of the Marshalsea in Dickens's *Little Dorrit* – dubbed him 'Count' O'Kelly. Dennis flaunted the title, unwisely. It was to stick, as the symbol of his upstart status.

Charlotte also subsidized Dennis's transfer to the Rules of the Fleet, where debtors could lodge provided they compensated the prison staff for loss of earnings. During the day they could roam wherever they liked – a leniency that allowed Dennis to be 'as constantly seen in all public places, as if he had not owed a shilling', *Town & Country* magazine reported, with a hint of disapproval. He immediately returned to his old haunts – a potentially disastrous move. But, having endured a painful initiation as a gambler, Dennis was a master practitioner now.

Despite her lucrative enterprises during this period, Charlotte continued to get into trouble, as she would at various times during her long life. In January 1759, John Grinfield took her to court. On 13 April 1761, her accuser was Samuel Wilkinson; and four days later, Joseph Lessly claimed from her £15 10s in damages for her failure to fulfil 'certain promises and undertakings'. Charlotte may have enjoyed episodes of freedom, but in execution of the last debt the court sent her to the Fleet again.

This sentence did not last long. To advertise the generosity of George III, who had come to the throne the previous year, Parliament passed an act 'For the Relief of Insolvent Debtors'. In September 1761, Charlotte and Dennis each filled in and signed the appropriate form, headed 'A true schedule and account of all the real estate, either in possession, reversion, remainder, or expectancy'.[9]

They were free.

---

[9] Dennis's form claimed that several people owed *him* money.

3

The Gambler

ENGLAND IN THE mid-eighteenth century was mad about gambling, and had been for years. Charles II, brought back from exile to assume the throne on the collapse of the Commonwealth in 1660, set a very different tone from the Puritan one that had prevailed in the country under Oliver Cromwell. At Newmarket, where Charles established a court devoted to pleasure and high jinks, the fast set spent fortunes on horses, cock fights, dice and cards. In her history of Newmarket, Laura Thompson reported a story that Nell Gwynn, the King's mistress, once lost 1,400 guineas in an evening, and quoted Samuel Pepys's observation that Lady Castlemaine was 'so great a gamester as to have won £15,000 in one night, and lost £25,000 in another night, at play'.

The Merrie Monarch was succeeded by less breezy characters. But the kingdom of the Hanoverian Georges was no less playful than his. George II was himself the subject of wagering, when he led his troops at the Battle of Dettingen in 1743: you could get 4-1 against his being killed. A similarly ghoulish opportunity for the sporting arose when a man collapsed outside Brooks's club in London. The members staked money on whether he was dead. Perhaps, someone said, they should see if the man could be revived; that suggestion was bad form, the outraged members cried, because it might affect the bet. At another club, White's, the twenty-year-old Lord Stavordale lost £11,000 in an evening, then won it back in a single hand at hazard, exclaiming, 'Now, if I had been playing *deep*, I might have won millions!'

Stavordale's adventure was recorded by Horace Walpole, who was too fastidious to take part in such activities. Walpole's letters also featured another great gambler, the statesman Charles James Fox, characterized as 'dissipated, idle beyond measure'. Fox – at one time effectively the joint leader of the country – lost £140,000 at cards by the age of twenty-five. His escapades were careless and brilliant. Having entered into a wager about a waistcoat that was available only in Paris, he set off in the middle of the night to get hold of one. Mission accomplished, he returned to Calais, where he suddenly recalled that Pyrrhus and Trentham, horses owned by Lord Foley and himself, were carrying wagers to beat another horse at Newmarket; he commandeered a fishing smack, steered for East Anglia, and arrived at the races just in time. A witness reported: '[Fox] eyed the horses advancing with the most immovable look; he breathed quicker as they accelerated their pace, and when they came opposite to him he rode in at full speed, whipping, spurring, and blowing, as if he would have infused his whole soul into his favourite racer.' The instant the horses were past the post, Fox turned his attention elsewhere – a gentleman may sport full-bloodedly, but he is above showing exultancy in victory or dismay in defeat.[10]

Later, he set off with some companions for London, but on a whim stopped off at another friend's house. Dinner was served, the cards and the dice came out, and there was about £5,000 on the table by dawn, when there was a rapping on the door: it was a messenger, chasing Fox to remind him that he was due to speak in the House of Commons that afternoon. Fox swept away the empty

[10] He won the bet. Trentham was first, Pyrrhus second, and their rival, Pincher, third.

July 1782   J. Bretherton f

Charles James Fox, the brilliant Whig politician, whose girth and features at the age of thirty-three were evidence of his self-indulgence. A reckless gambler and womanizer, he ended up happily married to Elizabeth Armistead, a former 'nun' at the establishment of Charlotte Hayes's forerunner, Mrs Goadby.

bottles, threw the dice one last time, and rushed to the stables for his horse. Lacking sleep, underprepared, and with a good deal of alcohol still coursing through his system, he nevertheless 'answered both Lord North and Burke, ridiculed the arguments of the former, and confuted those of the latter', as Walpole reported.

This anecdote comes from Theodore Cook's *Eclipse and O'Kelly*, published in 1907, and the standard work on the great horse and his owner. Cook observed, 'Philosophic foreigners might well have imagined that England was little better than a vast casino from one end of the country to the other.' The Duke of Queensberry ('Old Q'), a notorious rake, once bet someone that he could convey a letter fifty miles in an hour. He won by inserting the letter into a cricket ball and hiring twenty-four men to throw it to one another around a measured circle.

Horsemen not only raced, they also contrived more exotic equestrian activities on which they and their circle could bet. On 29 April 1745, Mr Cooper Thornhill rode from Stilton in Cambridgeshire to London, from London back to Stilton, and from Stilton back to London again, covering the two hundred-plus miles in eleven hours, thirty-three minutes and fifty-two seconds. 'This match was made for a considerable sum of money,' reported William Pick in his *Authentic Historical Racing Calendar* (1785), 'and many hundred pounds, if not thousands, were depending on it.' More fancifully, Sir Charles Turner made a 'leaping match' with the Earl of March for 1,000 guineas: Sir Charles staked that he would ride ten miles within an hour, and that during the ride he would take forty leaps, each of more than a yard in height. He accomplished the feat 'with great ease'. At Newmarket in June 1759, Mr Jenison Shafto backed himself to ride fifty miles in under two hours, and came home in one hour, forty-nine minutes and seventeen seconds. 'To the great admiration of the Nobility and Gentry assembled, he went through the whole without the least fatigue,' Pick noted. For an even more gruelling challenge, Shafto commissioned a Mr Woodcock to do the riding on his behalf. He made a match with Mr Meynell for 2,000 guineas that Woodcock would ride a hundred miles a day for twenty-nine consecutive days, using no more than one horse a day. Woodcock started early each morning, his route illuminated by lamps fixed on posts. His only crisis came on the day when his horse, Quidnunc, broke down after sixty miles; he had to requisition a replacement and start again, and he did not cover the 160-mile total until eleven o'clock that night. But he went on to complete his schedule.

Gambling was not only a sport for grandees. The middle classes and the lower orders loved it too. Horse race meetings, cricket matches, boxing matches and cock fights all offered wagering opportunities, both at the main events and at various side shows – stalls and tables with dice, cards and roulette wheels. There was a national lottery, raising money for such causes as building bridges across the Thames, with a draw staged as a dramatic spectacle at Guildhall. You could – as you cannot today – place side bets on what numbers would appear, paying touts who were called 'Morocco Men' after the leather wallets they carried.

There were many gaming houses in London. Like brothels, they operated openly, but suffered occasional crackdowns. The *Gentleman's Magazine* reported one such incident: 'Justice Fielding [London magistrate, and half brother of novelist Henry], having received information of a rendezvous of gamesters in the Strand, procured a strong party of guards who seized forty five at the tables, which they broke to pieces, and carried the gamesters before the justice, who committed thirty nine of them to the gatehouse [overnight prison] and admitted the other three to bail. There were three tables broken to pieces . . . under each of them were observed two iron rollers and two private springs which those who were in the secret could touch and stop the turning whenever they had any youngsters to deal with and so cheated them of their money.'

These venues were both dodgy and the haunts of people of

Sir John Fielding, the 'Blind Beak of Bow Street', presiding at Bow Street Magistrates' Court. Dennis O'Kelly came before Sir John following a fight at the Bedford Arms; and escaped with a fine, thanks only to the intercession of a friend.

all classes. They were therefore ideal settings for Dennis O'Kelly, who was by now a master 'blackleg'. The origin of this term is obscure, although it may have come from the black boots that were the standard footwear of professional gamblers; or possibly the derivation was the black legs of the rook, a word that also meant sharpster. Another term was 'Greek', first used to indicate a wily character by Shakespeare. Whatever the derivation, Dennis personified the meaning: a person practised in the art of cheating others out of their money. His assiduous apprenticeship 'had reduced to a system of certainty with him, what was neither more or less than a matter of chance with his competitors'.[11]

Opportunities for making a profit were everywhere – even on his feet. Dennis, on achieving a level of affluence, wore gold buckles on his shoes, while also owning a pair of buckles made of pinchbeck, an alloy that resembles gold. If he wore the gold ones, he kept the pinchbeck buckles in his pocket, and vice versa. In company, one of his companions would strike up a discussion about whether the Count's buckles were gold, and encourage the pigeon (dupe) to bet on the question. Dennis would simply perform a bit of sleight of hand, no doubt during some distracting activity initiated by the companion, to produce the buckle that would take the bettor's money.

He continued to get into trouble. At the Bedford Arms, he won money from an American officer who, probably with good reason, suspected that chicanery had taken place, and refused to pay. There were scuffles, and eventually Dennis came before Sir John Fielding.[12] Sir John was inclined to be harsh, but Dennis was rescued by the actor, playwright and fellow Fleet graduate Sam

[11] From Pierce Egan's *Sporting Anecdotes* (1804).
[12] Knighted in 1761, Sir John was known as the Blind Beak of Bow Street. He had lost his sight in a naval accident, and was reputed to have been able to recognize three thousand criminals from the sounds of their voices. He had taken over as chief magistrate of London on the death in 1754 of his half brother Henry.

Foote, who persuaded the magistrate to accept a fine. Dennis's relief, according to *Nocturnal Revels*, was overwhelmed by his sense of ill treatment.

'By Jasus,' he exclaimed, licking his wounds at Tom's Coffee-House, 'he [the American officer] has ruined my character, and I will commence an action against him.'

'Poh, poh,' said Foote, 'be quiet. If he has ruined your character, so much the better; for it was a damn'd bad one, and the sooner it was destroyed, the more to your advantage.'

Mortifyingly, this riposte earned hearty laughter from Tom's clientele. Dennis had to prove that he was a sport by laughing too, especially as he was in Foote's debt.

At least he had the good spirits to rise to this challenge. His cohorts at the gambling centres of London included Dick England, in whom good spirits were entirely absent. England was a version of Dennis with the charm removed, and brutality added. Like Dennis, he was an Irish expatriate. Emerging from an 'obscure, vulgar and riotous' quarter of Dublin, he took an apprenticeship to a carpenter; but the only manual activity for which he showed an aptitude was fighting. Like Dennis, he became the protégé of a businesswoman – his was a bawd. England was rumoured to be involved in highway robbery, and when one of his companions was found shot at the scene of a crime he decided that it was time to decamp to London, setting himself up at a house of ill repute called the Golden Cross. He soon rose in the world, to an address in Piccadilly, where he acquired a manservant, a pair of horses and a smattering of French. There was an awkward moment when his former mistress, who 'could not boast of a single attribute of body or mind to attract any man who had the use of his eyes and ears',[13] turned up on his doorstep, but he got rid of her with a hefty pay-off. Back in Dublin, she used the money to drink herself to death.

[13] *The Sporting Magazine* (December 1795).

Contemporary magazines offer various dismal accounts of the outcomes of England's tricks. At the rackets courts, he cultivated the Hon. Mr Damer, a decent player, before going off to Paris in search of a better one, hiring him to play regularly against Damer, and instructing him to start off by losing. He pretended to back Damer; and Damer, encouraged by the support and by belief in his superiority, backed himself as well – thereby losing up to 500 guineas at a time. With debts of (according to *The Sporting Magazine*) 40,000 guineas, Damer threw himself upon the mercy of his father, but despaired of getting help. Even while his father's steward was on the way to town with the money, Damer was in Stacie's hotel, sending out for five prostitutes and a fiddler called Blind Burnett. He watched them cavort for a while, put a gun to his temple, and fired.

England's most notorious swindle, recounted in Seymour Harcourt's *The Gaming Calendar* (1820), was one of his rare failures. While passing some time in Scarborough, he got into company with Mr Da——n (hereafter called Dawson),[14] a man of property. At dinner, England refilled Dawson's glass assiduously, softening him up for the card game to follow, but he overdid it, causing Dawson to complain that he was too drunk to play. Sure enough, once the cards came out, he descended into a stupor. The conspirators, though, soon devised a fall-back plan to part him from his money. Two of them wrote notes, one recording 'Dawson owes me 80 guineas', the other 'Dawson owes me 100 guineas'; England wrote a note saying, 'I owe Dawson 30 guineas'. The next day, he met Dawson, apologized for his drunkenness and rough behaviour of the previous evening, said he hoped he had given no offence, and handed over thirty guineas.

'But we didn't play,' Dawson pointed out.

---

[14] Eighteenth-century reports often gave only initials, or initials with a few other letters. In formulas such as En——l——d, the attempt at concealment was feeble.

'Get away wit' ye,' England assured him. 'An' these be your fair winnings an' all.'

What an honest gentleman, Dawson reflected as the pair parted 'with gushing civilities'. Soon after, he bumped into England's companions. Further comparisons of sore heads ensued, and Dawson commented on the civility of their friend Mr England, who had honoured a bet that would otherwise have been forgotten.

'As you mention this bet, sir,' one of the companions said, 'and very properly observe that it is gentlemanly to honour debts incurred when intoxicated, I hope we may be forgiven for reminding you of your debts to us'; and the fictitious notes were flourished.

'This cannot be so,' Dawson protested. 'I have no recollection of these transactions.'

'Sir,' came the reply, 'you question our honour; and did not Mr England lately pay you for bets made at the same table?'

Defeated, Dawson promised to pay up the next day.

His own friends came to the rescue. With the help of a five-guinea gift, they encouraged the waiter at the inn to recall that Dawson had been paralysed by drink, and had not played cards. Dawson, with some contempt, returned England the thirty guineas, adding five guineas as his portion of the supper bill. England and his cronies left Scarborough the next day.

Dennis O'Kelly may have spent some time in Scarborough,[15] but there is no suggestion that he was involved in this attempted theft. He was, though, implicated with England – and fellow blacklegs Jack Tetherington, Bob Walker and Tom Hall – in the ruination of one Clutterbuck, a clerk at the Bank of England. Clutterbuck, as a result of playing with this crowd, fell heavily into debt, attempted to defraud the bank of the sum he needed, was caught, and hanged.

[15] See chapter 1.

Although the divisions between the classes in the Georgian era were as wide as they always have been, gambling threw together lords and commoners, politicians and tradesmen, the respectable and the disreputable. Some years later, eminent witnesses would testify on Dick England's behalf at his trial for murder. At the rackets courts, England's companion Mr Damer 'would not have walked round Ranelagh [the pleasure gardens in Chelsea] with him, or had him at his table, for a thousand pounds'.[16] One writer referred to 'Turf acquaintanceship', and offered the anecdote of the distinguished gentleman who failed to recognize someone greeting him in the street.

'Sir, you have the advantage of me,' the gentleman said.

The other man asked, 'Don't you remember we used to meet at certain parties at Bath many years ago?'

'Well, sir,' the gentleman told him, 'you may speak to me should you ever again meet me at certain parties at Bath, but nowhere else.'[17]

The fortunes of Charlotte Hayes, too, began to look up on her departure from the Fleet. Her newly won freedom from debtors' prison received ironic celebration in Edward Thompson's 1761 edition of *The Meretriciad*, as she took advantage of the new King's clemency to begin her ascent to the pinnacle of her profession:

See Charlotte Hayes, as modest as a saint,
And fair as 10 years past, with little paint;
Blest in a taste which few below enjoy,
Preferr'd a prison to a world of joy:
With borrow'd charms, she culls th'unwary spark,
And by th'Insolvent Act parades the Park.

---

[16] *The Sporting Magazine* (January 1796).
[17] From Seymour Harcourt's *The Gaming Calendar and Annals of Gaming* (1820).

Her opportunities in courtesanship may have closed — as Samuel Derrick gently put it in *Harris's List of Covent Garden Ladies*, 'Time was when this lady was a reigning toast . . . She has been, however, a good while in eclipse' — but other opportunities were opening. The brothel-keeping business, she saw, was going up-market, and was ready to boom.

Jane Goadby was showing the way. Back in the 1750s, Mrs Goadby had been on a fact-finding mission to Paris, touring the stylish brothels of the city. They were not known as brothels: they were 'nunneries', populated by 'nuns' under the charge of the 'Lady Abbess', or, in pagan terminology, the 'High Priestess of the Cyprian Deity' (a reference to Aphrodite, goddess of love). The abbess selected beautiful nuns from diverse backgrounds and faiths. They were required to submit entirely to her authority, and to behave in a demure manner, avoiding excesses of eating and drinking. But they were to show no such restraint in the bedroom, where their brief was to demonstrate 'le zèle le plus sincère pour les rites et les cérémonies de la déesse de Cypros' (the most devoted zeal in the rites and ceremonies of the Cyprian goddess). At a time when venereal diseases were widespread, the nunneries offered some degree of security to their patrons by ensuring that the nuns received weekly medicals. A gentleman, who was also expected to behave with decorum, could pass entire evenings there, eating a fine meal, enjoying musical performances, and at the end retiring with his chosen nun. As a bonus, it was all very reasonably priced.

On her return to London, Mrs Goadby set about reproducing these attractions, except the pricing. At her establishment in Great Marlborough Street, Soho, you could spend up to £50 – £20 more than Dennis's annual salary as Lady —'s chairman – for just the sex. But gentlemen who had been on the Grand Tour, and who had experienced the splendours of continental brothels, were delighted to find such services on their doorsteps. The *Covent Garden Magazine* announced excitedly: 'Mrs Goadby, that celebrated Lady Abbess, having fitted up an elegant nunnery in Marlborough Street, is now laying in a choice stock of virgins for the ensuing season. She has disposed her nunnery in such an uncommon taste, and prepared such an extraordinary accommodation for gentlemen of all ages, tastes and caprices, as it is judged will far surpass every seminary of the kind yet known in Europe.' Elizabeth Armistead (Charles James Fox's future wife) started her career as one of Mrs Goadby's nuns.

Charlotte Hayes saw this market as her opportunity too, and Dennis was able to help. Their relationship was one of true partners, sharing the rewards of their labours. In the Fleet, she had provided the funds to get him back into circulation; now he was in a position to reciprocate, and, through his sporting connections, to bring her a classy clientele. She opened a serail near Mrs Goadby's in Great Marlborough Street, and attracted regulars including the Duke of Richmond, the Earls of Egremont and Grosvenor, Lord Foley and Sir William Draper. Not only did these men bring prestige to Charlotte's establishment, they also – being gamblers as well as philanderers – offered synergy, as we say nowadays, with Dennis's business interests.

4

The Duke

POSTERITY HAS DECIDED that William Augustus, third son of George II, was on the whole a bad man. *BBC History Magazine* named him the Worst Briton of the 18th Century. He was cruel in battle, earning the nickname 'Butcher' for his conduct at the Battle of Culloden; he was physically unattractive; and he was self-indulgent. Nevertheless, the racing world, taking what may be a blinkered view, is inclined to view him generously. 'No man can fairly be said to have done more for English racing' is a typical verdict.[18] This was the man who created the finest stud farm of the eighteenth century. He bred Herod, one of the most influential of all Thoroughbred stallions. And he bred Eclipse.

He was born in 1721. His eldest brother, Frederick, Prince of Wales, was fourteen; another brother, George, had died three years earlier, aged only three months. It was William Augustus who became his parents' favourite, while George II and Queen Caroline grew actively to dislike Frederick, who was arty.[19] At four, William was made a Companion Knight of the Bath. That was

---

[18] From Theodore Cook's *Eclipse and O'Kelly* (1907).
[19] One report has Caroline on her deathbed reflecting unmaternally about Frederick: 'At least I shall have one comfort in having my eyes eternally closed. I shall never see that monster again.'

a mere taster for what was to come a year later: the five-year-old prince became Duke of Cumberland, a title that took in Marquess of Berkhamstead, Earl of Kennington, Viscount Trematon, and Baron of Alderney. Marked out for a career in the forces, he joined the navy, did not take to it, but showed precocious enthusiasm and aptitude in the army. By twenty-one, he was a major-general.

The War of the Austrian Succession, one of the immensely complex conflicts in which this period of history specialized, was in progress, and in 1743 Cumberland fought against the French at Dettingen, serving under his father. It was the last occasion on which a British monarch led his troops into battle. As noted in the previous chapter, there was betting that George II would not survive. He did; but Cumberland got a grapeshot wound below his knee, and would be plagued by the injury for the rest of his life. Nevertheless, the battle was a personal as well as a national triumph. Cumberland had given his orders 'with a great deal of calmness and seemed quite unwearied',[20] and was hailed as a hero.

His standing did not diminish two years later when, as captain-general and leader of the allied forces at Fontenoy in Flanders, he suffered defeat. It was a noble defeat, everyone thought, and the King was inclined to share Cumberland's view that the blame lay with the 'inexpressible cowardice' of their Dutch allies. 'Now he will be as popular with the lower class of men as he has been with the low women for the past three or four years,' Horace Walpole wrote. So, when danger arose at home, Cumberland was the obvious man to deal with it.

Ever since the Catholic James II had been ousted from the throne in 1688, he and his descendants had been trying to regain it. In 1689, James landed in Ireland, but was eventually defeated by the forces of William of Orange at the Battle of the Boyne (July 1690).[21]

---

[20] Quoted in *Bred for the Purple* (1969) by Michael Seth-Smith.
[21] We shall visit this scene again, because one of William's men, Colonel Robert Byerley, rode into battle on a horse who was to become one of the foundation sires of the Thoroughbred.

James's son, James Francis Edward, led a second rebellious invasion in 1715, and was also defeated. Thirty years later, the Jacobite cause was in the hands of James's grandson, Charles Edward Stuart – Bonnie Prince Charlie. He landed in Scotland in July 1745, raised an army of supporters, but failed to increase his following when he marched south, and retreated north of the border.

Cumberland caught up with him on 16 April 1746 at Culloden Moor. The battle lasted only about an hour. When the outnumbered Jacobites retreated, they left behind more than a thousand dead, as many wounded, and some six hundred prisoners. This was when Cumberland earned his Worst Briton tag. Ordering the wounded and the prisoners to be executed, he followed up the battle by hunting down the rest of the defeated army and their sympathizers, jailing and deporting thousands of them, and bayoneting and hanging more than a hundred. The policy was 'to pursue and hunt out these vermin from their lurking holes'[22] – language that encouraged the English troops to go on a spree of raping and pillaging. Bonnie Prince Charlie escaped, over the sea to Skye ('Speed bonnie boat . . .', as the song has it) and then back to France. He died, unfulfilled, in 1788.

Cumberland's destruction of the Jacobites got a mixed press. For many, the bloody suppression of a threatened Catholic coup was a glorious act. Parliament voted him an additional income of £25,000 a year; Handel wrote the oratorio *Judas Maccabaeus*, which included the march 'See, the Conquering Hero Comes', in his honour; many English inns changed their names to the Duke's Head; Tyburn Gate, in the area of London – now Marble Arch – where executions took place, became Cumberland Gate (the area now houses the Cumberland Hotel, on Great Cumberland Place). For others, he was 'Butcher' Cumberland. The nickname gained currency, with the encouragement, some suspected, of the Prince of Wales, who had always been jealous

[22] Quoted in the *Dictionary of National Biography*.

42

of his brother's superior place in his parents' affections. In Scotland, the Duke is the Butcher irrevocably. The flower that the English call the Sweet William is, north of the border, the Stinking Billy.

Within a few years, the bad odour had spread. Cumberland did not confine inflexible brutality to his enemies: he also showed it, when they betrayed any hint of poor discipline, to his own troops. When, in 1751, Frederick, Prince of Wales died, leaving behind a son who was heir to the throne but only twelve years old, Cumberland wanted to be named Regent,[23] but Parliament refused. Then Cumberland's military fortunes reached their nadir in another highly complicated conflict, the Seven Years' War, which broke out in 1757. Leading a Hanoverian force, he was defeated at the Battle of Hastenback, and in September 1757 he signed the Convention of Klosterzeven, releasing Hanover to the French. He agreed to this settlement with the sanction, he believed, of George II; but he returned home to be informed by his father that 'he had ruined his country and his army, had spoilt everything and hurt or lost his own reputation'.[24]

Cumberland took the rebuke with dignity. He resigned his military posts, and retired to concentrate on the one pursuit in which he left an indisputably beneficial legacy: horseracing.

Cumberland may have been the first Hanoverian to take an interest in the Turf, but the status of racing as the Sport of Kings – a sport defined by royal patronage – had been embedded in British society since the Middle Ages. King John (reigned 1199 to 1216), who was 'not a good man' as A. A. Milne put it, was another controversial figure to benefit the sport, importing Eastern horses and setting up a royal stud at Eltham. Richard II (1377 to 1400)

---

[23] In the event of the King's death, the Regent would reign until the future George III came of age.

[24] Quoted in *Royal Thoroughbreds* (1990) by Arthur FitzGerald.

raced in a match against the Earl of Arundel; the outcome is not known, but some years later Arundel was beheaded. During the reign of Henry VIII (1509 to 1547), horses came to England from Spain, Morocco and Mantua, two of them as valuable gifts from Ferdinand of Aragon, whose generosity was ascribed to madness resulting from an aphrodisiac dinner fed him by his wife. Henry founded another royal stud, at Hampton Court, and kept an establishment exclusively for what were then known as 'running horses' at Greenwich, where there were a stable jockey and a trainer. He introduced a law designed to improve England's warhorses, also improving the racing stock: he outlawed the grazing of small horses, and he empowered rangers each Michaelmas to make a cull, including among their targets fillies and mares that 'shall not be thought able, nor likely to grow to be able, to bear foals of reasonable stature, or to do profitable labours'. It was the kind of ruthlessness he also applied to his marital affairs.

Elizabeth I (1558 to 1603) went to the races in Salisbury, and paid four visits to meetings in Croydon, where her host, the Archbishop of Canterbury, had great difficulty in finding suitable accommodation for the court. (The town would present him with a similar challenge today.) Elizabeth's successor, James I (1603 to 1625), was not a racing man, but he was a keen promoter of horsemanship, and very committed to hawking and hunting. 'The honourablest and most commendable Games that a King can use are on Horseback, for it becomes a Prince above all men to be a good Horseman,' he wrote. Alas, he lacked the skills to live up to these ideals. There is a story – probably exaggerated in order to emphasize his ineptness – that James once shot over his horse, falling head-first into a river through a sheet of ice, above which only his boots could be seen. His courtiers yanked on them and hauled him to the bank, where 'much water came out of his mouth and body'.

James's great contribution to the sport was to develop the place that was to become the headquarters of racing. Newmarket was a town of fewer than three hundred inhabitants when the King chanced upon it, realizing that it offered access to ideal sporting country. He built a palace there that collapsed, and then in 1613 commissioned Inigo Jones to design a second, where the court enhanced its reputation for profligacy. Some notables thought that the pleasures of Newmarket were a distraction, and Parliament dispatched twelve members to the town to call to the monarch's attention the affairs of state that required his gracious attention. He sent the delegation packing. Nor did he consider his queen's death in 1619 a sufficient reason to suspend the Newmarket sporting schedule.

The doomed Charles I (1625 to 1649) maintained these lavish standards. 'There were daily in his court 86 tables, well furnished [with 500 dishes] each meal,' an observer noted. Regular spring and autumn race meetings began at Newmarket in 1627. In 1647, Charles was held captive in the town before being moved to various other locations, and eventually to the scaffold.

Emphasizing the royalist nature of racing, Oliver Cromwell's republican government banned it. However, race meetings resumed, and flourished as never before, under Charles II (1660 to 1685). Or, as Alexander Pope put it,

Then Peers grew proud in Horsemanship t'excell,
Newmarket's Glory rose, as Britain's fell.[25]

Having established the Newmarket Town Plate, the new King first visited the town in 1666, bought a house there two years later, and, with the previous palace in disrepair, expanded his property to become a new home for himself and his court. His various

[25] Explaining these aberrant lines, the eighteenth-century racing writer B. Walker reassured his readers that Pope's jaundice stemmed from 'an infirm state of health, a figure he was not thoroughly satisfied with, and in consequence an unsocial tendency to lead a recluse life, detached from those splendid meetings instituted in almost every country'. It was certainly impossible to imagine a well-adjusted person frowning on the sport so.

mistresses, Nell Gwynn among them, lodged nearby. Charles conducted sporting, state and amorous affairs during two extended visits each year, coinciding with the spring and autumn meetings. Everyone had a gay time, as the diarist John Evelyn recorded: 'I found the jolly blades racing, dancing, feasting, and revelling, more resembling a luxurious and abandon'd rout, than a Christian court.' An accomplished horseman, Charles would sometimes ride races himself, and win – entirely on merit, according to the courtier Sir Robert Carr. 'I do assure you the King won by good horsemanship,' Sir Robert insisted. Charles rode about the town on his hack, Old Rowley. The name came to be applied to him, and later to the Rowley Mile course.

William III (1689 to 1702) owned a horse with the proud name of Stiff Dick. In a celebrated match in 1698, Stiff Dick defeated the Marquess of Wharton's Careless, hitherto considered invincible. William's sister-in-law and successor, Queen Anne (1702 to 1714), was one of the most enthusiastic of all racing monarchs, and founded the racecourse at Ascot. (The Queen Anne Stakes is run on the first day of the Royal Meeting.) Anne was pregnant eighteen times, suffered numerous miscarriages and stillbirths, and saw no child live beyond the age of eleven. She consoled herself with horses and food. The two pursuits proved incompatible: she grew too heavy for any horse to carry, but she continued to ride to hounds in a specially constructed horse-drawn carriage. Following her death, an ungallant vice-chamberlain noted that her coffin was 'almost square'.

George I (1714 to 1727) and George II (1727 to 1760) took little interest in the Turf. But Prince William Augustus, Duke of Cumberland, did. In addition to military affairs, Cumberland's great enthusiasms were gambling, hunting and racing. As a boy, he would play cards with the ladies of the bedchamber, winning or losing up to £100 in an evening. His appointment on returning from Culloden as Ranger of Windsor Great Park, where he employed demobilized soldiers to construct the lake known as

William Augustus, Duke of Cumberland *by George Townshend. Horses of this era had to put up with a number of notably fat men, among them Cumberland, Dennis O'Kelly and the future George IV.*

Virginia Water, gave him a base from which to develop all three pursuits. The park contained 1,200 red deer, which Cumberland and his guests would hunt on Tuesdays and Saturdays, those present at the kills qualifying for tickets that entitled them to enter their horses for certain races at Ascot (the fortunes of which, moribund since Anne's death, revived under his patronage). During lulls in the hunt, Cumberland and friends such as the Earl of Sandwich – he who liked to snack while working at the Admiralty on a piece of meat between two slices of bread – would get out their dice. Members of the public, who previously had entered the park to collect firewood, were barred, on the grounds that they would disturb the deer that the royal parties wished to pursue. It was an unpopular edict.

From his base at Cumberland Lodge, the Duke began to develop the Windsor Forest Stud, at nearby Cranbourne Lodge. In 1750, he acquired a brown horse from a Yorkshireman called John Hutton in exchange for a chestnut, and named the new arrival Marske.[26] It did not appear to be a momentous deal: Marske's sire, Squirt, had at one time been considered so worthless that he was saved from execution at Sir Harry Harpur's stable only as a result of a groom's pleading. Marske himself turned out to be a good, but not outstanding, racer. As a four-year-old he won a 100-guinea plate at Newmarket in the spring, and a 200-guinea match against Lord Trentham's Ginger in the autumn. He had just one race the following year, and came third. In 1756, he lost two expensive matches worth 1,000 guineas each to the Earl of Sandwich's Snap, one of the fastest horses of the day. He may have got injured after that, as in October he failed to keep a date to race against Thomas Panton's Spectator, with Cumberland paying a forfeit. Instead, Marske went to stud. This second career did not prove illustrious either, and by the time of Cumberland's death in 1765 Marske was commanding a covering fee – the fee that

[26] After the Yorkshire town where Hutton lived.

48

breeders would pay for their mares to mate with him – of only half a guinea.

Another purchase, from Sir Robert Eden in Durham, was a chestnut filly called Spilletta. She, too, saw the racecourse for the first time at the 1754 Newmarket spring meeting. Against three opponents, she finished last, and that was the end of her racing career. She retired to stud, where she also failed to shine. By 1763, she had produced only one foal.

Marske and Spilletta – not, from a breeder's point of view, a marriage made in heaven – mated in 1760, without issue. Three years later, they gave it another go. This time, Spilletta became pregnant.

Cumberland, meanwhile, was pursuing his own pleasures. Unlike current members of the royal family, he would travel about with substantial amounts of cash, a lot of which ended up in the pockets of Dennis O'Kelly, Dick England and their fellow gamblers. When someone came up to him with a pocket book he had lost at the races, he insisted that the finder keep it, even though it contained several hundred pounds. 'I am only glad that it has fallen into such good hands,' Cumberland said, 'for if I had not lost it as I did, its contents would now have been scattered among the blacklegs of Newmarket.' After his death, a soldier in his employment gained permission to wear one of his suits as mourning clothes, and found a concealed pocket containing banknotes to the value of £1,751. But Cumberland also gave away his money to more worthy recipients, donating £6,000 a year to charities.

His increasing disability as a result of the wound he had received at Dettingen, and his prodigious weight (thought to have been up to twenty stone), did not blunt his taste for high living.[27] But his health deteriorated. He required regular medical

[27] Horace Walpole observed him at a dinner party: 'He was playing at hazard with a great heap of gold before him. Somebody said he looked like the prodigal son and the fatted calf both.'

attention; during one operation, he held a candle to assist the surgeon hacking away at abscesses in the wounded leg. His father, George II, died in 1760 (he was on the lavatory at the time), repenting that he had treated Cumberland harshly and acknowledging him as 'the best son who ever lived'. At George's funeral, Cumberland, who had suffered a stroke, cut a sorry figure. According to the report of Horace Walpole, 'The real serious part was the figure of the Duke of Cumberland . . . his leg extremely bad, yet forced to stand upon it near two hours; his face bloated and distorted with his late paralytic stroke, which has affected, too, one of his eyes; and placed over the mouth of the vault into which in all probability he must himself so soon descend; think how unpleasant a situation! He bore it all with a firm and unaffected countenance . . . sinking with the heat, he felt himself weighed down, and turning round found it was the Duke of Newcastle standing on his train to avoid the chill of the marble.'

Cumberland was, however, enjoying some success on the Turf. In 1758, his mare Cypron had given birth to a foal named at first Dapper Tartar, later King Herod, and later still simply Herod. In a match at Newmarket in 1764, Herod met Antinous, owned by the Duke of Grafton. Both owners were formidable gamblers, and by the time the race got underway bets worth more than £100,000 were depending on the outcome. Herod won. He defeated the same opponent again the following year, this time in a match worth 1,000 guineas.

However, the thrill of betting huge sums of money at Newmarket on Herod's first match against Antinous may not have been what the doctor ordered. Cumberland suffered two fits, and was in such a bad way that the London papers announced his death. He recovered, but death was on his case. On 31 October 1765, he arrived home in Upper Grosvenor Street, London, and ordered coffee. When it arrived, he complained of a pain in his shoulder, and began shivering. The King's physician, Sir Charles Winteringham, was sent for. As physicians then were wont to do, he advised bleeding.[28] This treatment had no effect, of course, and Cumberland died soon after. He was forty-four.

'When the melancholy news of the Duke of Cumberland's death reached Windsor,' the *London Chronicle* reported, 'it was received with the utmost concern by all ranks of people, and especially by the labourers on His Royal Highness's works, who cried out they had lost their greatest benefactor.' One is inclined to soften a little towards Butcher on reading this account. But the historian Theodore Cook, writing 140 years later, was unmoved: 'To the common people he was invariably indifferent, and they were his sincerest mourners after he was dead.' Cumberland lay in state in the Painted Chamber at the Palace of Westminster, and on 10 November was buried, following a twenty-one-gun salute, in the royal vault at Westminster Abbey.

Cumberland left plate, pictures, furniture and other effects valued at £75,000, as well as the most significant collection of bloodstock ever to be assembled. There were private sales (among them one for Spilletta, to the Duke of Ancaster), and two auctions. On 19 December, at Hyde Park Corner, the racehorses came under the hammer of John Pond. Herod fetched the largest sum, going to Sir John Moore for 500 guineas. The lots included another horse who will re-enter our story: Milksop, so named by Cumberland because he was nursed by hand, his dam (mother) having refused to suckle him.

On 23 December, Pond supervised the sale of the Cranbourne Lodge stud. Marske was lot number 3, knocked down to Lord Bolingbroke for twenty-six guineas. Several of Marske's offspring were also in the sale. One of them was lot 29, a chestnut yearling. The colt had a white blaze on his face and a white 'stocking' – white colouring below the knee – on his off (right) hind leg. His name was Eclipse.

---

[28] Bleeding was based on the theory of the four humours: black bile, yellow bile, phlegm and blood. The aim was to restore the humours to their proper balance.

5

The Meat Salesman

SUNDAY, 1 APRIL 1764 was a grey day in London. The cloudiness was disappointing, as it obscured a rare astronomical event that had not been visible from southern England for more than a hundred years: an annular eclipse of the sun. One amateur enthusiast rose early to get to a vantage point on Hampstead Heath, taking various smoked glasses with him, but soon realized that the phenomenon would fail to achieve its proper impact. He abandoned the glasses, and resorted to the homespun device of a wafer with a pinhole, sandwiched between two pieces of white paper. At 10.32 a.m., he observed despondently, the moon was at its central point in its path across the sun, but 'wanted many degrees of being annular'.[29] He looked with envy towards the north-west, where the land appeared to be in much greater shadow. Still, as he noted in his letter to the press, he did get the eerie thrill of experiencing a significant drop in temperature.

Unlike total eclipses, annular eclipses do not obscure the entire sun, but leave visible a ring of sunlight around the intervening moon.[30]

[29] From *Lloyd's Evening Post*, 30 March – 2 April 1764
[30] The last annular eclipse above Britain was visible from north Scotland, Orkney and Shetland in 2003. The next one will be in 2093. The last total eclipse in Britain took place in 1999, and the next one is due in 2090.

A correspondent for the *London Chronicle* in March 1764 had offered advance counsel for those suffering 'fears and apprehensions at so awful a sight. It will be very commendable in them to think at that time of the Almighty creator and Governor of the Universe.' There were no such fears for their royal highnesses Prince William Henry and Prince Henry Frederick (the sons of the Duke of Cumberland's late older brother; Henry Frederick was to inherit Cumberland's title, as well as his Turf enthusiasms), who were guests at the Royal Observatory at Greenwich and behaved 'with the most remarkable condescension and affability'. The princes concluded, perhaps on taking expert advice, that the predictions of the extent of the eclipse by the astronomer Mr Witchell had been only one tenth of a digit awry. They offered him 'their approbation'.

To the west, the paddock below the tower at Cranbourne Lodge in Berkshire lay in greater darkness. While the sun was obscured, did Spilletta give birth to a foal with a white blaze and a white off hind leg? So we like to believe. Or did the Duke of Cumberland, the foal's owner, simply appropriate the name of an event that had taken place during the same season? Or perhaps the birth was at the time of the lunar eclipse earlier that year, on 17 March? There is no contemporary record to tell us, although Cranbourne Lodge does have a later monument, commissioned by Cumberland's successor as Ranger of Windsor Great Park, Prince Christian of Schleswig-Holstein, stating that the paddock below the tower was Eclipse's birthplace. The horse was unlikely ever to have been stabled, as one story has it, in Newham in East London, although he is commemorated in the area with an Eclipse Road and a Cumberland Road. Still less likely is it that Eclipse entered the world at what the racing writer Sir Walter Gilbey described as 'the Duke of Cumberland's stud farm on the Isle of Dogs'.

The Royal Stud Book has no birth record, but it does contain a race entry for the new arrival. Following what was common practice at the time, when owners regularly offered such hostages to fortune, Cumberland paid 100 guineas to enter the son of Marske and Spilletta in a match to take place four years later at Newmarket, against horses owned by the Duke of Grafton, Lord Rockingham, Lord Bolingbroke, Lord Gower, Lord Orford and Mr Jenison Shafto. A note of the match also appeared in the 1764 *Racing Calendar*. The Stud Book record says that the colt is '[By] Mask [*sic* – spellings in the eighteenth century were erratic], out of Spilletta a chestnut colt, with a bald face, and the off hind leg, white up to the hock'.

These notes are the best evidence we have to solve one of the enduring mysteries in racing. When Eclipse became the most famous racehorse in the land, rumours began to circulate that his pedigree was fraudulent. His real father, some said, was not Marske but a stallion called Shakespeare. A painting by J. N. (John Nost) Sartorius showed Shakespeare and Eclipse together – though, to my inexpert eye at least, it is hard to spot the implied likeness between the bulky stallion and the fine-boned racehorse. John Lawrence, an equestrian writer who had seen Eclipse in the flesh, was told by Dennis O'Kelly's groom that Shakespeare, as well as Marske, had covered Spilletta in 1763; others told Lawrence that this double covering was 'well-known fact', and hinted that bribery had taken place to ensure that Shakespeare be expunged from the story. The connections of Marske, sceptics hinted, had a great deal to gain by promoting their horse as Eclipse's father. Lawrence himself observed that Eclipse 'strongly resembled' members of Shakespeare's family.

Shakespeare was a good horse, the winner of two King's Plates, and would certainly have been a worthy mate for a mare of Cumberland's. For the 1763 covering season, he moved from Catterick in North Yorkshire to stables belonging to Josiah Cook at Epsom in Surrey, near to where Eclipse would be stabled; he was advertised as '15 hands 2 inches high, very strong, healthful, and as well as any horse in England; as to his performances tis needless to mention them here, he was so well known in his time of running to be the best running horse in England'. Perhaps the attempted deception was not by the connections of Marske, but by members of the Surrey racing fraternity? There was certainly no reason – unless he made a mistake – for the Duke of Cumberland, ignorant as he was of the astonishing potential of his colt, to enter a false parentage in his stud book. O'Kelly's groom told John Lawrence the Shakespeare version, but a certain Mr Sandiver of Newmarket, citing the authority of Cumberland's groom, assured him that it was nonsense.

The question, as Lawrence concluded, is of real significance only to those concerned with the accuracy of Thoroughbred records. Parentage by Shakespeare would not devalue Eclipse's pedigree. It is Eclipse, the supreme racer and progenitor, who defines the value of the pedigree.[31]

Just over a year after Eclipse's birth, Cumberland was dead. The royal racing stable and stud went to auction, and at the 23 December sale of the Cranbourne Lodge stud the chestnut colt (or chesnut, as was the usual spelling) was again ascribed to Marske (the description of lot 29 was 'A chesnut Colt, got by Mask . . .').[32] The bidder with the most determination to get him was William Wildman.

Described as a butcher in his marriage record of 1741, William Wildman (born in 1718) was not a retailer but a livestock middleman, operating as a grazier and as a salesman at Smithfield, the largest cattle market in the world. His business, which turned over between £40,000 and £70,000 a year, was solid, as was he: he sat on parish committees, and supported charities. And, thanks no doubt to his contacts with the sporting landowners

[31] There are further uncertainties in Eclipse's pedigree. See Appendix 2.
[32] The auctioneer went on to confuse Eclipse's pedigree with that of another horse. See Appendix 2.

whose cattle he sold, he became a man of the Turf. He leased a stud farm, Gibbons Grove,[33] at Mickleham, about ten miles from Epsom. A substantial place, it consisted of 220 acres, a farmhouse sporting a clock tower and parapet, and stabling for sixty horses.

This prosperity notwithstanding, Wildman was a lowlier person than was the norm among leading racehorse owners in the mid-eighteenth century. Yet he achieved a feat that almost all his illustrious competitors failed to match: he attained ownership of three outstanding Thoroughbreds. One gets the impression of a man who was decent, determined and energetic, but essentially cautious. Having acquired these horses, he sold them all.

The first of them was Gimcrack. Commemorated each August by the Gimcrack Stakes at York, Gimcrack was a grey horse no bigger than a pony. Wildman bought him in 1763, for about £35. At first he thought he had made a bad deal, and offered, unsuccessfully, to offload his acquisition for fifteen guineas (or £15 15s). But then Gimcrack started racing. He won seven times in 1764 (when the *Racing Calendar* placed him in the ownership of a Mr Green, who makes no further appearances in any volume). He also won his first race in 1765, a £50 plate at Newmarket, before Wildman, taking a course he was to repeat with Eclipse, sold him. Gimcrack went to Lord Bolingbroke, a prolific racehorse owner and ferocious gambler, for 800 guineas, and was to continue to shuttle between owners. He moved next to Sir Charles Bunbury, whose wife Sarah (née Lennox, and later to elope with Lord William Gordon, an army officer) described him (Gimcrack, not Bunbury) as 'the sweetest little horse that ever was'; then to the Comte de Lauraguais, for whom he won a wager by covering twenty-two miles in an hour; and then to Lord Grosvenor. He retired

---

[33] Now the Givons Grove estate.

to stud at the age of eleven in 1771, having won twenty-six of thirty-six races.

Another reward of Wildman's prosperity was his commissions from George Stubbs, Britain's greatest equestrian artist – and, you might argue, one of the greatest British artists in any genre. Stubbs painted *Gimcrack with John Pratt Up* for Wildman, showing Gimcrack on Newmarket Heath. Horse and jockey are next to the Beacon Course rubbing-house, where horses were saddled and otherwise groomed, and where Stubbs would later set his most celebrated painting of Eclipse. Gimcrack shows only a grey sheen on his coat, which whitened as he got older; he and his jockey are turning their heads in the same direction, with the lonely look that athletes assume on contemplating exertions to come. The picture hangs in the Fitzwilliam Museum, Cambridge. A subsequent Stubbs portrait of Gimcrack, one of the painter's best, has the narrative technique you sometimes see in early religious paintings, with different parts of the story appearing on different parts of the canvas: in the background, Gimcrack races several lengths clear of his rivals;[34] in the foreground, he is at the rubbing-house, with his jockey dismounted and two stable lads attending to him. (A version of *Gimcrack on Newmarket Heath, with a Trainer, Jockey and a Stable-Lad* is in the Jockey Club Rooms at Newmarket.)

Wildman, then, was well in profit on his recent racing transactions when he turned up at Cranbourne Lodge on 23 December 1765, looking to buy inmates of the late Duke of Cumberland's stud.

Eclipse's early life comes to us as legend. Accounts of his birth, his sale, his training, his first race – these, like a good many of the stories about Dennis O'Kelly and Charlotte Hayes, have the flavour of anecdotes that have gained embellishments with circulation. At some point, a historian has written them down. Subsequent

---

[34] There is no crowd and the stand is shuttered, indicating that the race is a trial.

historians have repeated them. We might be tempted to accuse eighteenth-century chroniclers of lax standards, had we reason to be complacent about our own regard for historical accuracy and truthfulness. Nevertheless, given the inclination, twenty-first-century reporters can try to gain access to people with memories of actual events, and they have a great deal more documentation to examine. Documentation on Eclipse's connections is sparse, and laconic. In only a few instances are there records to provide correctives to widely published accounts. One of these instances is the Cumberland dispersal sale.

The story goes that William Wildman arrived at Cranbourne Lodge late. Eclipse, his sole reason for attending, had gone through the ring and been claimed by someone else. Brandishing his watch ('of trusty workmanship'),[35] Wildman proclaimed to the auctioneer and assembled bidders that the sale had taken place before the advertised hour, and that every lot should be put up again. John Pond, who was in charge of proceedings, did not fancy doing this; so, to try to pacify the awkward customer, he offered him a lot of Wildman's choosing. This was exactly the compromise Wildman had been angling for. He chose the colt with the white blaze, and paid, according to the first published version of these events, seventy or seventy-five guineas.

It is a nice anecdote, but is it accurate? Wildman may well have missed the start of the auction: one advertisement stated that the proceedings would begin at 10 a.m., while another gave the starting time as 11 a.m. It is very likely that he was aiming particularly to buy the Marske yearling.[36] The advice to do so may have come from Lord Bolingbroke, to whom Wildman had sold

---

[35] From Bracy Clark's *A Short History of the Celebrated Race-horse Eclipse* (1835).
[36] Racing people use the name of the sire (father) as a kind of adjective. They might describe contemporary horses as a 'Kingmambo colt' or a 'Montjeu filly'. The sire, for reasons to do with how breeding operates rather than with the science of genetics, gets more credit for a racehorse's prowess than the dam (mother).

Gimcrack; the connection between the two is suggested by the Stubbs portrait, which shows Gimcrack in Wildman's ownership but with Bolingbroke's jockey, John Pratt, on his back. Bolingbroke was at the sale too, of course: he bought Marske, for twenty-six guineas. But Wildman made bids for other horses. He bought a nutmeg-grey colt by (sired by) Moro, for forty-five guineas, and a bay foal by Bazajet, for six. We know of these transactions because the sale document survives; it is in the possession of the Royal Veterinary College. It is that document that tells us Eclipse was the twenty-ninth lot to come under the hammer that day, and that his price was not seventy or seventy-five guineas, but forty-five. The sale raised 1,663½ guineas in total.

To recap: the legends we have questioned or dismissed so far in this chapter are that Eclipse was born on the day of the 1764 annular eclipse; that his father was Shakespeare, not Marske; that he was born or was stabled in East London; that William Wildman bought him alone at the Cumberland dispersal sale; and that Wildman paid seventy or seventy-five guineas for him. There is another to consider: that the auction was conducted by Richard Tattersall. Then a thrusting young man at the start of his career, Tattersall, who came from a modest background in Lancashire, went on to found, in 1766, the firm of Tattersalls (without an apostrophe), which soon became, and remains today, the largest bloodstock auctioneers in Europe. He also went on to buy, from Lord Bolingbroke, the champion racer Highflyer (a son of Cumberland's great horse Herod), and created numerous further champions by mating Highflyer with daughters of Eclipse. Reports cited Tattersall as one of the promoters of the rumour that Shakespeare was Eclipse's sire. His motive for doing so is obscure. One can see, though, why he was credited with involvement in what was, in hindsight, the most significant bloodstock sale of the era. But there is no evidence that he was anywhere near it. Certainly the advertisements for the sale mention only John Pond.

*

We have now met the four most important people in Eclipse's life: a gambler from a humble background in Ireland; a prostitute from Covent Garden; a royal prince; and a prosperous representative of the middle classes. The most famous of all Thoroughbreds is also the most representative of horseracing, the example of how a highly bred animal with a regal background can nevertheless bring into proximity disparate members of society. Racing is still thought of as a toffs' pursuit, yet it offers more varied material for the social historian than any other sport.

Look at the scene at Epsom on Derby day. The Queen surveys the Downs from her box in the Royal Enclosure. In a nearby box are the Dubai royal family, the Maktoums, who have significant racing interests. Their neighbours in the enclosure are grandees, trainers, racehorse owners, tycoons and celebrities; the men here are in top hats and tails, and the women are in designer dresses and hats. In the next enclosure, where lounge suits and high-street fashions are the order, congregate the professional classes, some of them enjoying corporate entertainment. On the other side of the course, packed into double decker buses, are rugby club members on a day out, and women on hen parties. Further away, in front of the cheaper stands, are families with picnics, and men and women who have come mostly to enjoy a sustained drinking session in the sun. Amid the funfair rides and market stalls on the Downs swarm gypsies and other travellers, touts and card sharps, bookmakers and hucksters.

There is proximity here, but very little interaction. Commingling across the social strata was greater in Dennis O'Kelly's day. Dennis and the Duke of Cumberland probably met on the racecourse, and in other gambling venues too; Dennis and Cumberland's great-nephew, the Prince of Wales (later George IV), were certainly racing acquaintances, and might almost be said to have been close, because 'Prinny' was a regular at gatherings at Dennis's Epsom home. Charlotte Hayes's business also brought her into contact with a great many esteemed clients, and William Wildman came to racing through transactions with Lord Bolingbroke and others.

Nevertheless, eighteenth-century Englanders needed to have sharper antennae than the man in Seymour Harcourt's anecdote (chapter 3) who confused his Bath acquaintance with a social equal. You did not presume that, because a gentleman or lady might condescend to socialize with you on certain occasions, he or she was your new best friend. Wildman shot game on the Duke of Portland's estate, but he did not join the Duke's shooting parties: he went at other times, with a companion from his own circle.[37] We think of the memoirist and rake William Hickey as belonging to the Georgian smart set, but Hickey, the son of a prosperous lawyer, did not move in aristocratic company. Dennis O'Kelly owned the greatest and most celebrated racehorse of the age, and many other fine horses besides; he was a prominent personage at the leading race meetings; and he was himself a celebrity, much discussed in the public prints. But beyond certain portals he could not go. Lacking the sense of deference that comes more naturally to the English, he was enraged by the exclusion.

Relationships on the racecourse between owners, trainers, jockeys, stable staff and members of the public give the most comprehensive picture of class relationships that a single location can show. It is a picture that has changed only superficially since the 1760s. As the Queen, from her supreme vantage point at Epsom, surveys the variegated scene, she can see too, through the woods on the other side of the course, the house where Dennis O'Kelly stabled his racers. The present merges with the past in this panorama: with all the other Derby days she has witnessed; with the Derby days before that, of Hyperion, Persimmon, Gladiateur and Diomed; and before that, with a day in May 1769, when five horses rode on to the Downs from nearby Banstead, and leading them was a chestnut with a white blaze.

[37] The general point stands even if Wildman is not the figure in Stubbs's portrait of the gentlemen's outing on the estate – see chapter 18.

The Young Thoroughbred

THE QUALITIES THAT William Wildman and Lord Bolingbroke saw in Eclipse were not obvious. He was leggy, and possessed, experts thought, an ugly head. His croup was as high as or higher than his withers,[38] a characteristic that was reckoned to be undesirable in a racer. He was 'thick-winded', breathing at disconcerting volume as he exercised. And his pedigree, on his sire's side, seemed to be no more distinguished than his appearance. Marske, his father, was worth only twenty-six guineas, and had been covering mares at the derisory fee of half a guinea.

Moreover, Eclipse was bad-tempered and unruly, so much so that his handlers at William Wildman's stables at Mickleham considered gelding him. Castration, a common procedure in the racing world, has a calming effect – but of course you avoid doing it to an animal who might become a valuable stallion. Fortunately for the history of horseracing, the Mickleham team entrusted Eclipse instead to a 'rough-rider', whose speciality was taking charge of untrained horses. George Elton, or 'Ellers', would don stout leathers to protect his legs and ride Eclipse into the woods

---

[38] The croup is the highest point of a horse's hind quarters. The withers are at the base of the neck above the shoulders.

on night-time poaching expeditions. It was good discipline for the horse, though a dangerous transgression for the rider. Later, Ellers was prosecuted for poaching, and transported.[39]

The Mickleham team had time on their side. Eclipse and his contemporaries belonged to the last generation of racers who were not expected to see a racecourse until they were four or five years old. (Many of their sons and daughters would begin racing at the age of two.) The tests they faced demanded physical maturity. Races were over two, three or more commonly four miles, and many events involved heats. Horses might have to run, in a single afternoon, four races of four miles each, with only half-hour intervals in which to get their breath back. To emerge triumphant at the end of that, they had to call on great reserves of courage and stamina – what the Georgians admiringly called 'bottom'.

During the winter and spring of 1768 and 1769, as Eclipse enters his fifth year, he begins to be subjected to an ever harsher training regime. As contemporary manuals show, he spends his nights, and the portions of each day when he is not at exercise, in an enclosed, windowless, heated stable. It is warm in winter and suffocating in summer, and he wears thick rugs. Sweating is good, believe the early trainers, who regularly turn up the heating and subject the horses, rugged and hooded, to saunas. As the racing season approaches, Eclipse is given purgatives, consisting of aloes or mercury.

Eclipse has his own 'boy', or groom, John Oakley, who sleeps in lodgings above the stable. Oakley gets up at about four each morning, sometimes earlier. After a breakfast of porridge, with perhaps cold meat from the previous day as well as cheese, bread and beer, he mucks out the stable, removes Eclipse's rugs and rubs him down, gives him a breakfast of oats, clothes him again, puts on his saddle and bridle, and mounts him. The pair then join the rest of the string for morning exercise on the Downs.

---

[39] Transportees at this time were usually sent to Maryland or Virginia.

They are under the supervision of the trainer, who is also commonly described as a groom.

Or perhaps Oakley was the trainer? It is a sign of the humble roles of trainers and jockeys at this time that we know so little about the handlers of even so famous a horse as Eclipse. By the end of the century, training was recognized as a specialist role, and trainers were ascending the social ladder. Men of the Turf in the eighteenth century would be surprised to discover that modern trainers, such as Sir Michael Stoute, are rather grand.

Once on the Downs, Oakley and Eclipse start off at an easy gallop.[40] After half a mile or so they come to an incline, and Oakley begins to urge Eclipse to go faster. They race uphill for another half mile before Oakley pulls on the reins. They walk back, and Eclipse gets a moderate drink of water – the Georgians do not believe that horses should be allowed very much refreshment. They gallop gently again, and then walk. Then they have another fast gallop, and then another walk. All this while, Eclipse has been burdened by heavy rugs. Every week or ten days, he wears this clothing on a 'sweat', a gallop of four miles or more. But even on less gruelling days he is sweaty enough.

At about nine o'clock, they return to the stables. Oakley leads him back to his stall, ties him up, rubs down his legs with straw, removes his rugs, and brushes and 'curries' him (with a metal currycomb). He clothes the horse again, and gives him some more oats or hay.[41] The stables are then shut up.

---

[40] Oakley has probably ignored the pre-exercise tip of Gervase Markham: 'Then do yourself piss in your horse's mouth, which will give him occasion to work and ride with pleasure.' (From *How to Choose, Ride, Train and Diet, Both Hunting-Horses and Running Horses*, 1599).

[41] The equestrian expert John Lawrence, writing in the early nineteenth century, thought that oats and hay were a sufficient diet for racehorses. Gervase Markham had recommended also bread, malt and water mash, and the occasional raw egg; and from time to time, Markham said, you should season the horse's meal with aniseed or mustard seed.

Jockeys, too, had to be hardy individuals. When Oakley joined the stable, and was about to ride his first race, he went through a fearful initiation. His colleagues told him that the best way to get his weight down to the eight and a half stone required was to borrow as many waistcoats as he could, go on a three-mile run, strip naked on his return, and immerse himself in the hot dung hill outside the stable boxes. He dutifully obeyed. As he emerged, caked with ordure, he heard a chorus of laughter. Suddenly he was surrounded by his gleeful fellow grooms, all carrying pails; they drenched him in freezing water.

Today, as Eclipse nears his racecourse debut, that episode is far enough in the past for Oakley to have had the fun of playing the same joke on several new recruits. He is an established member of the Mickleham team, and a valued rider of William Wildman's horses at race meetings. From now until mid-afternoon he and the other boys have time off. They play gambling games, many of them now obscure: fives, spell, null, marbles, chuck-farthing, spinning tops, and holes.[42] At four o'clock, they return to the stables and take the horses out for another round of exercise. Then there is more rubbing down, brushing and combing; feeding, of horses and boys; preparing the horse's bed. The stables are shut up again, with horses and boys inside, at nine.

Albeit physically demanding, lowly in status and derisorily paid, working in an eighteenth-century stable is not a bad job. In an enlightened establishment such as Wildman's, Oakley is well looked after, and enjoys the responsibility of being the most important person in the life of a horse he realizes may be special. Eclipse trusts him as he does no other human. Oakley knows that the horse requires special treatment: he will respond only to the most deferential of suggestions, and will rebel against the whippings and spurrings that are normal practice in race-riding.

[42] The temptation for present-day stable staff is to spend their free time in betting shops.

For the horses, however, the regime is brutal. It is not surprising that early racing paintings show animals that are etiolated and apparently long in the back: they are trained until every ounce of 'condition' — spare flesh — is sweated away. Twenty-five years after Eclipse was in training, a jockey called Samuel Chifney wrote a memoir with the modest title of *Genius Genuine*, and showed himself to be ahead of his time both in his attempt to market himself as a racing personality (while holding a job regarded as socially insignificant), and in his view that the accepted training practices of his era were 'ignorant cruelty'. Chifney described a horse returning from a sweating exercise: 'It so affects [the horse] at times, that he keeps breaking out in fresh sweats, that it pours from him when scraping, as if water had been thrown at him. Nature cannot bear this. The horses must dwindle.' In spite of his words, most racehorses continued to be trained in this way until well into the nineteenth century.[43]

Yet Eclipse thrives. He has an unusual way of galloping: he carries his head low, and he spreads out his hind legs to such an extent that, one observer said later, a wheelbarrow might have been driven through them. Even so, he eats up the ground. Oakley has never sat on a horse so fast. Eclipse is — though Oakley does not describe him in these terms — the most brilliant representative to date of a new type of running horse, the fastest the world has ever seen: the Thoroughbred.

During the previous half a century, some mysterious alchemy had been taking place in the breeding sheds of England. The horses that were emerging were blessed with an unprecedentedly potent combination of speed and stamina. How these qualities came

[43] Taking care not to 'overcook' a horse is one of the key skills of the modern trainer. In particular, the trainer does not put a horse through vigorous exercise too close to a race. As I write, one of the favourites for a sprint race at Royal Ascot, ten days away, has had his last serious gallop. He will gallop again in five days, but will not be asked to stretch himself.

about is the subject of much debate, hampered (though not dampened) by the haphazard standards of early record keeping. If you want to take a patriarchal view, you can give most of the credit to just three stallions. Their status has brought to their biographies various fanciful and romantic accretions; what is a matter of historical fact is that every contemporary Thoroughbred descends in the male line from the Byerley Turk, the Darley Arabian or the Godolphin Arabian.

The horse known as the Byerley Turk may not have been a spoil, as the early histories relate, of the Siege of Buda (1686), because recent research suggests that Colonel Robert Byerley of the Sixth Dragoon Guards was not there. The Turk may rather have been captured at the Siege of Vienna (1683) – the 'browne' horse, the least valuable among three Vienna captives, that John Evelyn saw parade in St James's Park in 1684: 'They trotted like does as if they did not feel the ground. Five hundred guineas was demanded for the first; 300 for the second and 200 for the third, which was browne. All of them were choicely shaped but the last two not altogether so perfect as the first. It was judged by the spectators among whom was the King, the Prince of Denmark, Duke of York and several of the Court . . . that there were never seen any horses in these parts to be compared with them.'

Colonel Byerley certainly owned the Turk by 1689, when he took him to Ireland. In spring 1690, they won a silver bell at a meeting held by the Down Royal Corporation of Horsebreeders. That July, Byerley fought at the Battle of the Boyne against the Jacobite forces of the deposed James II, riding the Turk on reconnaissance missions and narrowly escaping capture thanks to the horse's speed. After his side's victory, Byerley returned to England, retired from the army, married, sat as the MP for Knaresborough in Yorkshire, and put his horse to stud. Despite covering what historians consider to have been indifferent mares, the Byerley Turk established an enduring bloodline. He is the great-great-grandfather of the Duke of Cumberland's

Herod. And he appears three times in the pedigree of Eclipse.[44]

The second of the three lauded founding fathers of the new breed was by repute a pure-bred Arabian. He was descended on his mother's side – for Arabs, *this* is the important part of the pedigree – from a mare called the Mare of the Old Woman.[45] While few Englishmen at this time were bothering with the pedigrees of their horses, the Arabs had long been punctilious about them. The Duke of Newcastle wrote, 'The Arabs are as careful and diligent in keeping the genealogies of their horses, as any princes can be in keeping any of their own pedigrees.' Giving false testimony about a horse's background would bring ruin on oneself and one's family.

We have to assume, then, that the patter given to Thomas Darley, a merchant and British Consul in Aleppo, was genuine. Darley bought his Arabian from Sheikh Mirza II in 1702, and in a letter to his brother a year later described the horse's three white feet and emblazoned face, adding that he was 'of the most esteemed race among the Arabs both by sire and dam . . . I believe he will not be much disliked; for he is highly esteemed here, where I could have sold him at a very considerable price, if I had not designed him for England'. The problem was that the War of the Spanish Succession was raging, and Darley was having trouble securing a sea passage for his purchase, although he was hopeful that his friend Henry Brydges, son of Lord Chandos, would be able to take the horse with him on board a ship called the *Ipswich*. Then another problem emerged: the Sheikh changed his mind about the sale. Nevertheless, Brydges made off with the Arabian, who arrived in England at roughly the same time as a letter from the Sheikh to Queen Anne furiously alleging that his possession had been 'foully stolen'. The protests had no effect. The Darley

---

[44] He appears once eight generations back in Eclipse's pedigree, and twice nine generations back. The formula to describe this inbreeding is 8 × 9 × 9.
[45] Both sides of the family belonged to the valued strain called, in Darley's spelling, Manicha (also sometimes Managhi).

Arabian stood at the family estate, Aldby Park near York, until his death in 1730.

Like the Byerley Turk, the Darley Arabian covered mostly unexceptional mares. One of the few good ones was called Betty Leedes, owned by Leonard Childers – pronounced with a short 'i', not as in 'child' – of Cantley Hall, Doncaster. Betty Leedes returned to her paddock in Doncaster, and eleven months later gave birth to 'the fleetest horse that ever ran at Newmarket, or, as generally believed, the world', Flying Childers. Here was the horse that demonstrated what this new breed, the descendants of Eastern stallions on British soil, could do. His portrait by James Seymour shows a prancing, compact, muscular colt, of a type we would assess as a sprinter. But Flying Childers had to race over long distances. In a match against two horses called Almanzor and Brown Betty at Newmarket, he was reported to have completed the three-and-three-quarter-mile Round Course in six minutes and forty-eight seconds – about a minute faster than par. He later ran the four miles-plus Beacon Course at Newmarket in seven and a half minutes, 'covering 25 feet at every bound'. These reports come from the early 1720s, before the publication of John Cheny's first racing calendar (an authoritative record of race results), and may be exaggerated; but we do know that Flying Childers beat Fox, one of the best racers of the day and a winner of three King's Plates, by a quarter of a mile, despite carrying a stone more on his back than did his rival.

By this time, Flying Childers had passed from Leonard Childers's hands to the Duke of Devonshire, and he retired to the Duke's stud at Chatsworth. However, the best racehorses are not necessarily the ones who make the most significant contribution to the breed.[46] Flying Childers sired some good horses, but his

[46] For example, Brigadier Gerard, rated by John Randall and Tony Morris in *A Century of Champions* as the best British horse of the twentieth century, achieved little success at stud.

younger brother, who never raced, continued the male line that dominates the bloodstock industry today. Bartlett's Childers, also known as Bleeding Childers because he would break blood vessels in hard exercise, sired Squirt, who sired Marske, who sired Eclipse.

On the maternal side of Eclipse's pedigree is the third of these famous stallions, the one with the most colourful story of all — although some of the colour may be the result of artful tinkering. The Godolphin Arabian was foaled in the Yemen in the mid-1720s, exported to Tunis, and given as a present by the Bey (Governor) of Tunis to Louis XV of France. The horse failed to please the King, and had been reduced (legend has it) to pulling a water-cart through the streets of Paris when he was spotted by a man called Edward Coke, who paid £3 for him. Coke returned to England, but did not enjoy the company of his acquisition for long, dying at the age of only thirty-two. The horse then passed to Francis, the second Earl of Godolphin. The Godolphins were a racing family. Of the first Earl, a prominent politician who died in 1732, it had been said, 'His passion for horse racing, cock-fighting, and card-playing, was, indeed, notorious, but it was equally notorious that he was seldom a loser by his betting transactions, which he conducted with all the cool calculation and wariness of a professional blackleg.'

The indignity of pulling a water-cart may have been in his past, but there were further indignities for the Arabian at the Godolphin stud at Gog Magog in Cambridgeshire. He was employed as a 'teaser', the horse with the job — it remains an important though unglamorous role in the breeding industry today — of perking up a mare before the main man, the stallion, came along. The main man at Gog Magog was Hobgoblin, a grandson of the Darley Arabian. But when Hobgoblin met a mare called Roxana, he decided that he did not fancy her. So the Godolphin Arabian, no doubt gratefully, covered her instead, and Roxana duly gave birth to Lath, the best racehorse since Flying Childers.

The parents, having hit it off, met again, this time producing Cade – not as good a racehorse, but the sire of the outstanding Matchem, through whom the Godolphin Arabian male line continues to the present. The Godolphin Arabian also got (sired), this time with a mare called Grey Robinson, Regulus, who won eight royal plates and retired undefeated to stud. There, with a mare called Mother Western, he sired Spilletta – Eclipse's mother.[47]

Later, in about 1793, George Stubbs painted the Godolphin Arabian, working from an original by David Morier. In the background, next to the barn, is the Godolphin Arabian's friend, Grimalkin the cat. There are various stories about Grimalkin; again, you can take your pick. One is that when the Godolphin Arabian died, in 1753, Grimalkin placed herself on his carcass, followed the body to the burial ground, and after the interment crawled miserably away, never to reappear until found dead in the hay loft. Another version, even sadder, is that the Godolphin Arabian accidentally crushed Grimalkin; furious with grief, the horse would attempt to savage any other cat that came across his path.

The horse in Stubbs's portrait has the thick neck characteristic of a horse at stud, to an exaggerated extent: his crest – the top of his neck – is so high and convex that his back appears to begin halfway between his legs. What kind of horse is he? Some equestrian writers think that he resembles a Barb, a breed of horse from North Africa, and indeed he has been known as the Godolphin Barb.

Is every contemporary racehorse descended, in male line, from a stallion of one of three different breeds, or were the Byerley Turk, the Darley Arabian and the Godolphin Arabian all in fact, as some historians have argued, Arabs? We cannot be sure. The early owners applied the terms 'Turk', 'Arab' and 'Barb' with

[47] But see Appendix 2.

little concern for breeding; they meant only a horse of Eastern blood.

Eastern horses were not renowned racers, and of these three, only the Byerley Turk, with his cup at Down Royal, saw a racecourse. Why, then, did the early breeders – grandees and substantial landowners, largely based in Yorkshire – import them? They did so because they esteemed Eastern horses for a quality known as 'prepotency': the ability to breed true to type, and to maximize in their offspring the attributes of the mares with whom they mated. The theory worked too, getting its most spectacular early demonstration in the career of the Darley Arabian's son Flying Childers.

In the years following the Restoration and in the early years of the eighteenth century, these breeders imported some two hundred stallions who were to appear in the first *General Stud Book* of 1791. Examination of pedigrees shows that the Byerley Turk, the Darley Arabian and the Godolphin Arabian should not get all the credit, and that many others made significant contributions, even though their male lines expired. You can easily see, for example, the influence of Alcock's Arabian: he was grey, and appears in the pedigrees of every grey Thoroughbred.[48] And of course half of the credit is due to the early mares, although, as is so often the case with females in history, they are obscure figures, many of them nameless. It seems that they, too, had a good deal of Eastern blood; how high a proportion is a contentious matter. At the end of the bottom, maternal line of Eclipse's pedigree is a mysterious 'Royal mare'.[49]

What we do know is that the Thoroughbred, this cross of

[48] A grey horse must have a grey parent, of either sex.
[49] Only about twenty foundation mares feature widely in contemporary Thoroughbred pedigrees. At one time, it was said that the 'royal mares' were imported during the reign of Charles II. Now it is thought more likely that most of them lived at the Sedbury stud of James Darcy, who employed them to breed '12 extraordinary good colts' each year for the King.

Eastern stallions with English mares, transcended its parentage. In the century when the English refined the rules of cricket, and a century before they compiled the rules of football and rugby, they created a new breed of sporting horse, a racer that was bigger, more powerful, and faster.[50] Soon after, Thoroughbreds emigrated and founded dynasties in every horseracing country.

Flying Childers had shown what this new breed could do. But Eclipse became the horse who, in his own time and ever since, represented the Thoroughbred's abilities *in excelsis*.

[50] I am told that Arabs are gentle creatures. Thoroughbreds tend to be less amiable, and more highly strung.

Coup de Foudre

WILLIAM WILDMAN DID NOT get where he was in business without the talent of foresight. If, he reasoned, Eclipse turned out to be the superstar that the Mickleham team thought he was, the horse's unfashionable sire, Marske, would suddenly become a valuable property. Breeders would pay good money to send their mares to Marske, hoping to produce Eclipse mark two. So Wildman travelled down to a farm near Ringwood in Hampshire, where Marske's progenitive worth had risen to three guineas a covering, and offered to buy the stallion for twenty guineas. At eighteen, Marske was getting on a bit and might not have many fertile years left; his owner accepted Wildman's offer. Wildman returned to Mickleham with his purchase, and advertised him in the 1768 *Racing Calendar* at five guineas – a fee that would soon rise.

The window of opportunity for taking advantage of such inside information was not open for long. Others saw the chestnut with the white blaze speeding over the Downs. It is likely that these observers included Dennis O'Kelly.

Dennis by this time had graduated from blackleg to race-horse owner. In 1768, he entered his horse Whitenose in a £50 plate at Abingdon, and there he met Wildman, who had a chestnut filly in the same race. In spring 1769, Dennis owned four horses in training at Epsom, and made regular visits to the town to check on their progress. As he watched them go through their paces, he spotted another horse, head held low, galloping with awesome power.

It was as momentous an occasion in Dennis's life as his first meeting with Charlotte Hayes, and probably more romantic. For an owner or trainer, the first sight of a young and exceptionally talented horse is very like falling in love. You know that this is the real thing; you know, too, that what you recognize is potential, and that much can go wrong. Adrenalin courses through your system; you are exhilarated, insanely hopeful, and scared. 'He really filled my eye,' trainer Vincent O'Brien said of the yearling Nijinsky, who two years later, in 1970, would win the 2,000 Guineas, Derby and St Leger.[51] 'When he was working, you would just see that he would devour the ground,' Simon Crisford of Godolphin said of the two-year-old Dubai Millennium, who went on to win the 2000 Dubai World Cup. This is what Dennis saw on the Epsom Downs. A recently established owner, ambitious to acquire champion racers, he had found the embodiment of his hopes.

He learned that the chestnut belonged to William Wildman. Dennis, the boisterous adventurer, and Wildman, the solid member of the middle classes, became friendly. Wildman outlined Eclipse's history: how the horse had been bred by the late Duke of Cumberland, had got his name because a solar eclipse had taken place at the time of his birth, had come up for sale following Cumberland's death. Dennis congratulated his neighbour on such a splendid acquisition, and offered to help prepare Eclipse for his first race: he would lend a competitor for a trial.

William Wildman and Dennis O'Kelly were interlopers in the upper levels of horseracing. The men who bred the Thoroughbred

[51] The English Triple Crown. Nijinsky was the last horse to achieve this feat.

in the late seventeenth and early eighteenth centuries, and whose names were to be immortalized in racing bloodlines, were the likes of the Lords Godolphin and Fairfax (the Fairfax Morocco Barb); the distinguished soldier and MP Byerley; the royal stud master Darcy (the Darcy Yellow Turk, the Darcy White Turk); and the landowner Leedes (the Leedes Arabian). All these stallions appear in the pedigree of Eclipse; and Eclipse was bred, as was fitting, by a royal duke. He was not, in the normal scheme of things, the kind of possession suited to a commoner. But society was changing. As the eighteenth century wore on, humbly born, entrepreneurial tradesmen were acquiring the means to take part in pursuits that had belonged exclusively to the gentry. When Eclipse came up for sale, Wildman had the contacts and the money to take advantage. His ownership of a horse who was to win five King's Plates in his first racing season was curious enough; what really astonished the Turf establishment was the champion horse's connection with an Irish adventurer whose companion was a brothel madam.

Dennis's progress to Epsom Downs would have seemed even more improbable eight years earlier, when he and Charlotte Hayes emerged from the Fleet prison. Yet by spring 1769 they had reportedly amassed £40,000 – a colossal sum, worth, if the website Measuring Worth is a guide, nearly £4.5 million in today's money. You have to back an awful lot of winners, and sleep with an awful lot of men, to earn that sort of cash. Still, there is no doubt that the couple did extraordinarily well. Charlotte set up a brothel in Soho, and moved on to the fashionable environs of St James's. Dennis hit the coffee houses and the racecourses.

There were – historians' figures vary – between five hundred and two thousand coffee houses in London, and men spent substantial portions of their days in them. The rudimentary spaces, murky with pipe smoke, contained communal benches and tables, counters, and fires above which coffee bubbled in giant pots; the overbrewed beverage must have tasted disgusting. Some had booths, as well as private rooms upstairs. Coffee houses offered

The Coffee-house Politicians *by an anonymous artist (1772). This is an elegant establishment. Dennis O'Kelly's favourite haunt, Munday's, was probably more rough-and-ready.*

newspapers to their customers, and so contributed to the rise of the press. They had particular clienteles: marine insurers met at Lloyd's, the clergy at Child's, authors at Button's, actors and rakes at the Bedford. And blacklegs congregated at Munday's.

Munday's was at New Round Court, near the Strand, until in the late 1760s or early 1770s it moved nearby to number 30, Maiden Lane. It became notorious briefly in the mid-1760s as a source of sedition, when a writer styling himself 'Junius' left at the counter the latest instalments in a series of letters satirizing George III and members of the Grafton administration. But it was more lastingly notorious for its association with Dennis O'Kelly, Dick England, Jack Tetherington, and their gang. Anyone inexperienced in gambling was advised to stay clear of Munday's. One day, a butcher at the table made the mistake of accusing England of thievery, and the even bigger mistake of referring disparagingly to the blackleg's background. England, who was as prone to violent rages as a psychopathic Mafioso in a Martin Scorsese film, beat him up until he recanted.

In spite of this edgy atmosphere, professional men and 'persons of quality' would also drop in, knowing that they would be able to find sportsmen willing to bet to hundreds of pounds. The equestrian writer John Lawrence was, some years later, among these more refined regulars. He found the proprietor, Jack Medley, an amusing fund of sporting anecdotes, though he sensed that Medley's knowledge of racing was not deep. The proprietor was popular with his customers, providing a four-shilling dinner each Sunday at 4 p.m., after some of them had been for their ride in Rotten Row. On Munday's closure, Medley lived on a retirement income of £50 a year provided by, according to Lawrence, the coffee house regulars.[52]

Medley's general line, that his customers' racing conduct

---

[52] Medley's obituary in the *Gentleman's Magazine* in 1798 stated that the sum had come from the Jockey Club.

was not entirely scrupulous, was well informed enough. When he heard that O'Kelly's horse Dungannon had been well beaten in a race, after starting at odds of 7-4 and 6-4 on, he exclaimed, 'Pshaw, tis false it was *not three*, the horse has only *two pails of water* before starting!' This anecdote, which appeared in *The Times*, is not entirely transparent (what has 'three' got to do with it?), but in general alleges that the water was meant to hinder Dungannon's progress. Dennis, Medley is implying, wanted either to bet against Dungannon, or to ensure that the horse would, on the back of a loss, start at longer odds next time.

That was in the future. Meanwhile, Dennis was growing wealthy from gambling, on horses and on cards. We can be sure that his sportsmanship was often dubious, but also that mostly he made money from horses because he understood them. He could spot the good ones to back, and he could spot ones that were not ready to run their best – ones that he could lay (a layer takes others' bets). Once he and Charlotte had started to make money, he was confident that he could use his knowledge to get wealthier still, and to acquire social status. He determined to become a race-horse owner, and not in a small way: he wanted to own the stables and the stud too.

Dennis's aim was not simply to acquire a few racehorses and to land prizes and betting coups with them. The real money, he saw, was in breeding. He would send his best racers to stud, hype up their achievements, and promise owners of mares the prospect of breeding offspring of similar ability. A fashionable stallion might cover forty mares or more in a season, at fees for his owner of upwards of twenty-five guineas a time. The owner might also mate his own mares with the stallion, and then sell the offspring, or – with a view to finding further stallions and mares for the stud – race them. In pursuing this ambition with dedicated profession-alism, Dennis was ahead of his time. His methods anticipated the business philosophy of Coolmore, the Irish bloodstock empire that is the most powerful force in the racing world today. Coolmore has a training centre, Ballydoyle, run by Aidan O'Brien; but the real money rolls in when O'Brien's champions (and other horses in Coolmore ownership), such as Galileo and Montjeu, transfer to the firm's stud farms. Winning races is merely the means to an end, as it was for Dennis.[53]

The base Dennis was considering for his stud was in Epsom, Surrey – then, as now, one of the racing centres of the south of England. Like Newmarket, Epsom is a racecourse with a raw quality. It does not belong to a park, an area of regulated space; it is a route through a landscape. The horses gallop over downs that, beyond the course, roll into the distance. The running rails describe a horseshoe: one tip is past the finishing post below the grandstand; the other, opposite, is where the runners set off at the start of the Derby, the most famous horse race in the world.

The starting stalls clang open, and the Derby runners begin their mile-and-a-half journey with a steep uphill climb. There are thick canopies of trees on their right until, after two furlongs, a gap reveals Downs House, once Dennis O'Kelly's stables. The course continues to climb until beyond the mile marker; then it curves left and descends towards Tattenham Corner, where during the 1913 Derby the suffragette Emily Davison stepped in front of King George V's horse Anmer, with fatal consequences. Some horses hate this bend. The 1986 Derby favourite Dancing Brave, later to prove himself one of the greats, raced downhill so awkwardly that by the time he had entered the finishing straight he was at the back of the field and many lengths behind the leaders. He came storming down the outside, but just failed to catch the winner, Shahrastani. Five years earlier, Shergar had put up a similar performance in the straight, but with the advantage of starting his

[53] Dennis would covet today's stud earnings. Fifty guineas, Eclipse's initial fee, is the equivalent of about £6,000 today. Montjeu's covering fee is 125,000 euros – and he covers a hundred mares in a season.

acceleration from near the front of the field: he won by ten lengths, the biggest margin in Derby history. The ground here has a camber, sloping down to the far rail, and, with just over a furlong to go, it begins a final ascent. Only at this point, having coolly delayed, did Lester Piggott urge his mount Sir Ivor to chase and overtake Connaught to win the Derby of 1968.

There is grandeur about a classic race in such a setting. History is a presence here. The horses racing for the Derby join that history, and indeed represent bloodlines tracing back through Sir Ivor and other great winners to Diomed, who won the first Derby, in 1780, and further back still, to a time before the Derby course was laid out, when Eclipse galloped to the Epsom finishing post from nearby Banstead, with his rivals a distance behind.

In the dry summer of 1618, a herdsman called Henry Wickes, or Wicker – those unreliable early spellings again – stopped with his cattle at a spring on Epsom Common, but found that the animals would not drink. The water was loaded with magnesium sulphate. Wickes and the cows had chanced upon Epsom Salts.[54] Soon, Epsom was famed as a spa town, and visitors were swarming in to take the waters, experiencing the natural distaste that Wickes's cows had shown but suppressing it in the name of health. Samuel Pepys managed to force down four pints of the stuff when he stayed in 1667. He had returned to Epsom despite having found the society there rather vulgar four years earlier, and enjoyed himself a lot more this time: there was 'much company', and next door to his lodgings at the King's Head a party including Nell Gwynn – soon to be Charles II's mistress – kept a 'merry house'.

The patronage of the smart set was fickle. In the early eighteenth century, a man called Livingstone damaged the town's reputation by setting up his own well as a rival to the original,

---

[54] One local history spoils the story by telling us that Dr Nehemiah Grew of the Royal Society had made the discovery some thirty years earlier.

which he managed to close; visitors decided that Livingstone's water was less invigorating, and they began to stay away. There was hope of a revival of fortunes when Mrs Mapp, also known as Crazy Sally but nevertheless in strong demand for her marvellous powers as a bone-setter, lodged in the town. But Epsom's worthies could not persuade her against moving to London, and when, in the 1750s, Dr Richard Russell promoted the benefits of bathing in the sea, he put an end to the career of Epsom as a resort, inspiring health-conscious pleasure-seekers to head for Brighton instead. Epsom Salts endure of course, even though ingesting them has unsurprisingly gone out of fashion, and even though the name no longer indicates provenance. The Epsom Salt Council, an American organization, recommends dissolving the crystals in your bath, with advertised benefits including an improvement in heart and circulatory health, and a flushing away of toxins.

While visitors were arriving in large numbers, Epsom needed to provide more than salty water to keep them amused. It staged athletics competitions, in which the grand folk watched their footmen race. There were concerts and balls, hunting and gambling; and there was horseracing. The first mention of the sport in the local archives is a sad one: the burial notices for 1625 include the name of William Stanley, 'who in running the race fell from the horse and brake his neck'. The next record helps to explain why Oliver Cromwell banned horseracing: in 1648, during the English Civil War, a group of Royalists met on the Downs 'under the pretence of a horse race . . . intending to cause a diversion on the King's behalf'. The sport got going again immediately after the Restoration, and Charles came, with mistresses, before transferring his sporting activities to Newmarket. A poet called Baskerville recalled a visit by Charles, in lines worthy of the master of bathos William McGonagall:

Next, for the glory of the place,
Here has been rode many a race —

King Charles the Second I saw here;
But I've forgotten in what year.

By the early eighteenth century there were regular spring and autumn race meetings at Epsom. Another piece of doggerel portrays the scene:

On Epsom Downs, when racing does begin,
Large companies from every part come in.
Tag-rag and Bob-tail, Lords and Ladies meet,
And Squires without Estates, each other greet.
Bets upon bets; this man says, 'Ten to one.'
Another pointing cries, 'Good sir, tis done.'

Less polite in tone was this reflection on Epsom and its neighbouring towns:

Sutton for mutton, Carshalton for beeves [cattle],
Epsom for whores, Ewell for thieves.

A rather better writer, Daniel Defoe, also observed the scene: 'When on the public race days they [the Downs] are covered with coaches and ladies, and an innumerable company of horsemen, as well gentlemen as citizens, attending the sport: and then adding to the beauty of the sight, the racers flying over the course, as if they either touched not or felt the ground they run upon; I think no sight, except that of a victorious army, under the command of a Protestant King of Great Britain, could exceed it.'[55]
Epsom had horseracing, gambling and whoring, as well as incursions during race meetings by pleasure-seeking Londoners: it

[55] Defoe's lines give you an idea of the atmosphere in which, a few years later, the Protestant Prince William Augustus, Duke of Cumberland, would be greeted as a hero for destroying the Catholic Jacobites.

was Dennis's kind of town. He took lodgings in the town, and looked round for a house to buy.

It would not be his first property. For unclear motives, in 1766 Dennis had bought a house about six miles from the centre of London, in the village of Willesden, paying £110 to a Mr Benjamin Browne. He found his Epsom house, on Clay Hill,[56] some time in 1769, and that year he borrowed £1,500 against three properties: Clay Hill; a house in Clarges Street, Mayfair, where a Mr Robert Tilson Jean was living; and a house in Marlborough Street, Soho, where Dennis was living, conveniently next door to Charlotte's brothel. Dennis arranged this loan from Mr John Shadwell, giving him in return an annuity of £100; he repaid the sum in 1775. The evidence suggests that he was constantly exposing himself, financially, and that bloodstock purchases and gambling setbacks would occasionally leave him naked. Charlotte, too, was apt throughout her life to get into financial difficulty, although by the end of the 1760s her affairs were thriving. She had opened up a new establishment at a prestigious address off Pall Mall, and she was turning it into the most celebrated serail in London.

Dennis was buying horses as well as property. His name appeared for the first time, as subscriber and owner (and as 'Dennis Kelly'), in the 1768 *Racing Calendar*, the book recording the Turf results of that year. The entry gave no hint of the triumphs to come. Dennis owned a single horse, Whitenose, who ran in a single race (the previously mentioned one at Abingdon), and came last. The winner of the £50 prize was Goldfinder, though not the horse of that name who was to play a small role in Eclipse's career; third was the chestnut filly belonging to William Wildman.

By the time of publication of the 1769 *Calendar*, however, Dennis, now sporting his 'O', owned Whitenose, Caliban,

[56] Now West Hill.

Moynealta and Milksop – the horse rejected by her mother and nurtured by hand at Cumberland's stud. Milksop, formerly owned by a Mr Payne, was little, and specialized in 'give-and-take' races, in which weight was allocated on the basis of height. He proved to be a money-spinning purchase. In 1769, he won £50 races at Brentwood, Maidenhead and Abingdon, meeting his only defeat on his home turf at Epsom. He won at Epsom in 1770, and also at Ascot, Wantage and Egham. But by then Dennis owned another horse, who, living up to his name, put the others in the shade.

Eclipse ran his trial against the opponent supplied by Dennis a few days before he was due to contest his first public race. Such trials were common, as a means of getting horses fit and of assessing their abilities. They were popular with the touts – gamblers and their associates who would invade gallops and racecourses in search of intelligence. Sir Charles Bunbury, first recognized head of the Jockey Club and owner of horses who competed against Eclipse, disliked the practice. 'I have no notion of trying my horses for other people's information,' he grumbled.

Trials have gone out of fashion, but the acquisition of inside information never has. Nowadays, journalists and other 'work-watchers' scrutinize horses on the gallops, and stable staff earn a few bob to add to their ungenerous incomes by disclosing news about their charges. This horse is so speedy that he is catching pigeons in exercise, they might report; this one has suffered a setback and will not be fully fit on the day; this one will not be 'off' (primed to do his best) for his next race, but is being laid out for a later contest. By the time horses get to the racecourse, the betting market is well primed, and offers a fair reflection of their chances of success.

One would assume that Dennis, with his gambling interests, wanted to keep this trial quiet. If so, he failed: Eclipse's early biographers report that touts, no doubt members of Dennis's circle, travelled down from London to see Eclipse in action. But, like

Wildman (reputedly) at the Cranbourne Lodge auction, they arrived too late. Scanning the Downs for a chestnut with a white blaze, and unable to spot one, they asked an elderly woman, who was out walking, whether she had seen a race. The woman replied that 'she could not tell whether it were a race or not, but that she had just seen a horse with white legs, running away at a monstrous rate, and another horse a great way behind, trying to run after him; but she was sure he would never catch the white-legged horse, if they ran to the world's end'. The touts returned to the capital. By that evening, the prowess of Eclipse was the talk of Munday's coffee house.

The Rest Nowhere

O N WEDNESDAY, 3 MAY 1769, Dennis O'Kelly set out on horseback for the two-mile journey from Epsom to the race-course on the Downs. An imposing man in his mid-forties, Dennis wore a thick overcoat, which emphasized his increasing bulk; perched on his bewigged head, above blunt features tending to fleshiness, was a battered tricorn hat. Observers would have sym-pathized with the beast of burden beneath him. Dennis was on his way to watch the Noblemen and Gentlemen's Plate, a good but not top-class contest open to horses who had not previously won £30, and carrying a £50 prize. He may already have backed Mr Wildman's Eclipse; he certainly fancied that the afternoon would offer further betting opportunities. But his interest in Eclipse would not be satisfied by betting alone.

The racecourse was roughly at the site it occupies today, with a finishing straight running from near Tattenham Corner – the downhill bend on the Derby course – and stretching towards the rubbing-house, now the site of the Rubbing House pub. At about this time, a Frenchman called Pierre-Jean Grosley visited Epsom while researching a book called *A Tour to London* (1772), in which he described the scene: 'Several of the spectators come in coaches, which, without the least bustle or dispute about precedency, were

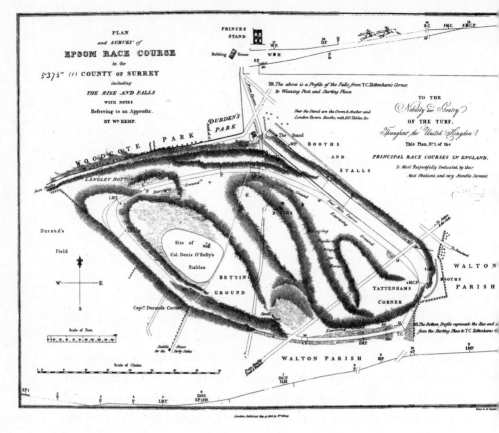

This map of Epsom racecourse shows Dennis O'Kelly's stables inside the course. The course now runs inside the site, and Downs House. Eclipse's first race may have started from near Banstead, off the map to the right.

arranged in three or four lines, on the first of those hills; and, on the top of all, was a scaffolding for the judges, who were to decree the prize.' Some courses, such as Newmarket, were marked by posts. When the future Charles I visited Lincoln races in 1617, he ordered that rails be set up a quarter of a mile from the finish, 'whereby the people were kept out, and the horses that runned were seen faire'.[57] At Epsom, there were no barriers. The crowd towards the finishing post pressed forward from either side, allowing only a slender passage for the racers. There was no betting ring either, on this or on any other course; gamblers congregated at betting posts, shouting out the prices of horses they were prepared to back or lay. The betting post was Dennis's first port of call.

When he arrived, he realized that the blacklegs from Munday's coffee house had got wind of Eclipse's ability, as Eclipse was the only horse in the race that anyone wanted to back. In response, his odds had contracted severely, and no layer was pre- pared to take bets on him at longer than 4-1 on. In other words, you would have to bet £4 to win £1; or, to put it another way again, if a horse trading at that price were to compete in five races, the betting says that he would win four times and lose only once. Eclipse had, the betting said, an 80 per cent chance of victory. Those are extraordinary odds for a debutant, and they did not interest Dennis. He had another idea for making money on the race.

Meanwhile, Eclipse's groom, John Oakley, was walking his horse to the start, four miles away in Banstead. The field were due off at 1 p.m., and Oakley was to ride. This doubling up as groom and jockey was normal. Until the early eighteenth century, owners – from Charles II, winning by 'good horsemanship', down – often rode their own horses in matches. Otherwise, they employed stable staff, who were not yet recognized as 'trainers' or 'jockeys' (the latter term might mean, as it did in the context of the Jockey Club, anyone associated with the Turf).

[57] Charles, in an ironic prefiguring of his fate, viewed the action from a spe- cially erected scaffold.

The riding groom was a humble figure. But a groom from Oakley's era who managed to transcend the role was John Singleton, who worked for the Marquis of Rockingham. After Singleton had ridden the Marquis's Bay Malton to victory at Newmarket over a field including Herod, Rockingham commissioned for him an engraved gold cup, gave him several paintings showing him mounted on the stable's best horses, and generally treated him 'more as a humble friend than as a servant'. Singleton went on to acquire several farms and stables – a rare ascent. But it was not until the next generation, when the roles of trainer and rider split into specialities, that jockeys became noted figures, and even so they remained lower in social rank than training grooms had been. It is a class structure that persists. Jockeys such as Frankie Dettori in Britain and Garrett Gomez in the US may be jet-setting millionaires, but they are nearer in status to stable lads and lasses than they are to the leading trainers.

All we hear of Oakley (c.1736–1793) is that he was 'a very celebrated rider, in great repute'; we cannot even be sure, because the racing calendars do not tell us,[58] that he was Eclipse's regular partner. John Lawrence, who saw Eclipse at stud, stated, 'We believe, Oakley, a powerful man on horseback, generally, or always rode Eclipse', and there is a J. N. Sartorius painting entitled *Eclipse with Oakley Up*. But a catalogue entry for George Stubbs's portrait of Eclipse at Newmarket identifies the jockey as 'Samuel Merrit, who generally rode him'. This was written more than twenty years later, when Stubbs made a copy of his original work, but it presumably reflects an accurate memory for such details. Merriott (as he is more usually spelled), who has in the painting the long, lugubrious face of the comic actor and writer Eric Sykes, is also associated with Eclipse's two 1770 races at York. Nevertheless, the earliest report we have asserts that Oakley was Eclipse's jockey on 3 May 1769.[59]

[58] They did not list jockeys' names until 1823.
[59] For further discussion of Eclipse and his jockeys, see Appendix 1.

Jockeyship required nervelessness and aggression. Some contests permitted 'cross and jostle', meaning you could hamper your opponents. At a race at York, 'Mr Welburn's Button and Mr Walker's Milkmaid, in running the last heat, came in so near together, that it could not be decided by the Tryers [stewards]; and the riders showing foul play in running, and afterwards fighting on horseback, the plate was given to [the owner of the third horse] Mr Graham.' Jockeys wore spurs, and used them; in the days before whip rules, they beat their mounts without restraint. But no jockey ever spurred or whipped Eclipse.

There were four rivals for the Epsom Noblemen and Gentlemen's Plate: Mr Castle's Chance and Mr Quick's Plume, both six-year-olds; and the five-year-olds Gower (Mr Fortescue) and Trial (Mr Jennings). There was no starting tape, or even a flag; there was simply a starter, who shouted 'Go!'

The five set off, well out of the viewing range of the Epsom crowd, and with only a gathering of local spectators lining their route, as at an early section of a stage of the Tour de France. Oakley and Eclipse took the lead, galloping easily and waiting until they approached the Epsom Downs, with about a mile to go, to pick up the pace. From their perspective, the banks of people swelling forward on either side of the course ahead formed converging lines, narrowing at the finishing post almost to a point.

While his rival jockeys began to wield their spurs and whips, Oakley, who wore no spurs, sat motionless in the saddle. He knew that his mount would rebel against any urging. The racers sped through the banks of spectators, and Eclipse, seemingly cantering, eased further ahead. As the field went by, local gentlemen on horseback peeled away from the crowd and galloped behind, braying encouragement.[60] Eclipse passed the post first without having

[60] Early representations of horse races are confusing at first sight. The course is not clearly delineated; various horses and riders are in motion, and it is not obvious whether all or some of them are racing. Gradually, you realize that the posse behind the leading horses consists of sporting gentlemen, not contestants.

at any point stepped up from a low gear; Gower, Chance, Trial and Plume followed, in that order. Oakley offered his mount a tactful hint that they should pull up. But this was not the end of the contest. It was only the end of the first heat.

Plate races – the most important contests – were usually staged in heats, and if three different horses won three heats, they would meet again in a decider. The way to settle the matter earlier was to do what Eclipse did several times, and win two heats; or to take advantage of another rule, centring on the distance post, 240 yards from the finish: as the winner passed the finish, horses that had not reached the distance post were declared to have been 'distanced', and were eliminated. Adding to the ordeal of up to four races in an afternoon, each was a marathon by modern standards, two, three and more commonly four miles in length, and had been so ever since medieval times.[61] Most Flat races in Britain today are contested at distances between five furlongs (five-eighths of a mile) and twelve furlongs (the Derby distance). The Ascot Gold Cup distance of two and a half miles is unusual. The Queen Alexandra Stakes, which also takes place at Royal Ascot, is the longest race in the Flat calendar, at two miles and six furlongs. In the US, the emphasis on speed is greater still. The twelve-furlong Belmont Stakes, the third leg of the Triple Crown,[62] is regarded as a stamina-sapping anomaly.

Why did the Georgians subject their horses to these gruelling tests? The answer is their admiration for 'bottom'. If men

[61] There is a reference to a three-mile race in the medieval romance of Bevis of Hampton. The earliest chronicler of British horseracing is Fitzstephen, who during the reign of Henry II described a contest at Smithfield market: 'The horses on their part are not without emulation; they tremble and are impatient and are continually in motion. At last, the signal once given, they strike, devour the course, hurrying along with unremitting velocity. The jockeys, inspired with the thought of applause and the hopes of victory, clap spurs to their willing horses, brandish their whips, and cheer them with their cries.'
[62] Following the Kentucky Derby and the Preakness Stakes.

had bottom, they were sound fellows; if horses had bottom, they were sound horses. Dennis O'Kelly was remarkable, in the fond words of John Lawrence in *The Sporting Magazine* in 1793, 'for his attachment to horses of bottom'. In other words, Dennis valued staying power; and, Lawrence may also have meant, he profited in his betting from horses with the ability to cope with racing in heats. If they lost one heat, by design or otherwise, they could win the next. Eclipse had superlative bottom, and never lost either a heat or a race.

However, within ten years of his racing career – and thanks in part to his siring of speedier, more precocious racers – the priorities of men of the Turf started to change, and heat racing died out. New types of races, run over shorter distances, were introduced, the most prestigious ones acquiring the status of 'Classics'. Breeders aimed to produce horses that might win these races, and no longer wanted stout stayers, unless they were breeding for the emerging sport of steeplechasing.

Eclipse was speedy, and would have excelled, as his sons and daughters were to do, at these new contests. But on 3 May 1769, and throughout his career, he needed stoutness too. After heat one, he and John Oakley retired to the rubbing-house for a break of just half an hour. Perhaps William Wildman joined them there, to check on the well-being of his horse. Oakley got on the scales, with his saddle, to assure the stewards that he had ridden with the required weight, while another 'boy' tended to Eclipse with a special sponge or cloth – special in that it had been soaked in urine and saltpetre, and then dried in the sun. At some meetings, but probably not at a reputable one such as Epsom, the horses enjoyed tots of alcoholic refreshment, as long as no one in authority was about. The rules from 1666 at the Duke of Newcastle's course at Worksop stated, 'If any other relieve their horses with any thing but faire water . . . the offender shall lose the Cup.' The five horses were then walked back to Banstead. This retracing of a four-mile course seems an odd arrangement, and one would be inclined to suspect that the plate was run over a different, circular Epsom course were it not for the fact that local historians imply that the Banstead one was in more common use.[63]

Meanwhile, the Epsom crowd may have been entertained by boxing matches. There were probably cock fights, the enjoyment of which by people 'of all ranks' bemused Monsieur Grosley, who considered them to be 'after all, no more than children's play'. Gypsies, who had set up an encampment on the Downs for race week, offered to tell your fortune. Other attractions at the course included food and drink stalls, and gambling booths at which you could play EO, an early form of roulette (the wheel consisted of compartments marked 'E' and 'O'), as well as card and dice games, which the inexperienced were well advised to avoid. At Doncaster in 1793, the EO tables, which had been producing results suspiciously biased towards the operators, were seized and burned in front of the Mansion House. Six years later, at Ascot, a gentleman's servant who had lost all his money, as well as his watch, denounced those who had got the better of him as rogues and thieves; a brawl ensued, and then a riot, which was quelled only by the arrival from Windsor of a party of the Light Horse Brigade. Racegoers also had to keep their eyes open for pickpockets, who themselves had to take care that they were not caught: they risked summary judgment by the crowd, who would cut off their pigtails, duck and beat them. A report from 1791 described a pickpocket's death 'from the severe whipping the jockey boys gave him'.

Dennis O'Kelly thought that there was more gambling to be done on the Noblemen and Gentlemen's Plate, in spite of the apparently foregone conclusion of the contest, and returned to the betting post. You get a flavour of the scene from a caricature by Thomas Rowlandson featuring Dennis as well as his later

[63] At Newmarket, matches were run over the dog-legged Beacon Course, but races run in heats were staged on the Round Course.

acquaintance the Prince of Wales. Mounted men crowded round. They roared, pointed and waved their arms, somehow in the confusion hoping to find layers or backers at their chosen prices.[64] Dennis, who knew how to make himself heard, got the assembly's attention when he put in his bid: he would name, he shouted in his rough Irish accent, the finishing positions of the horses in the second heat. He tempted three layers, who offered him even money, 5-4 and 6-4. Then he made his prediction: 'Eclipse first, and the rest nowhere.'

It is the most famous quotation in racing, the line that summarizes Eclipse's transcendent ability. It was not a simple piece of hyperbole, of the 'the other horses won't know which way he went' or 'they'll have to send out a search party for the others' kind: it had a precise meaning. Dennis was predicting that Eclipse would pass the post before any of his rivals had reached the distance marker; they would not receive placings from the judge, who would make the bare announcement 'Eclipse first.' Gower, Chance, Trial and Plume would be, in the context of the official result, 'nowhere'.

Dennis's words have proved telling in other contexts too. Reviewing a new (1831) edition of James Boswell's *Life of Johnson*, the historian Thomas Macaulay wrote, 'He [Boswell] has distanced all his competitors so decidedly that it is not worth while to place them. Eclipse is first, and the rest nowhere.' As ever in our story, however, there are alternative versions. One has Dennis saying, 'Eclipse first, and the rest in no place'; another, 'Eclipse, and nothing else.' There are also reports that he made the bet before a race at Newmarket. It was a neat piece of blackleg's trickery: an interpretation of the letter, if not the spirit, of the bet. At the later, Newmarket race, Eclipse faced only one rival after the first heat,

---

[64] You cannot lay horses in a modern betting ring unless you are a licensed bookmaker, and you are supposed to offer prices about an entire field. But the internet has revived the Georgian way of gambling: customers of betting exchanges such as Betfair can back or lay individual horses.

and was backed heavily to win heat two by a distance. Dennis is certain to have been among the backers. He would not have referred to 'the rest' then, but he may have predicted something along the lines of 'Eclipse first, the other nowhere'.

Over at the Banstead start, Eclipse, Chance, Plume, Gower and Trial set off in the second heat. Once again Eclipse set a steady gallop, and after three miles, as the horses came into distant view, the layers may have been feeling confident: the field was tightly grouped. Then Eclipse began to draw clear. Reports say that Oakley was pulling back the reins 'with all the strength [he] was master of'. Dennis, who needed Eclipse to put more than an eighth of a mile of daylight between himself and his rivals within the next mile, cannot have been pleased at these efforts at restraint. But he had no cause for concern. Eclipse continued to extend his lead. He raced through aisles of bellowing spectators, head low, his long stride devouring the ground. When he passed the post, his nearest pursuer was more than a distance away.

The judge's summary was terse: 'Eclipse first!' A mass of people surged towards horse and jockey, cheering. 'The victor,' Pierre-Jean Grosley wrote, 'finds it a difficult matter to disengage himself from the crowd, who congratulate, caress, and embrace him, with an effusion of heart, which it is not easy to form an idea of, without having seen it.' (How the temperamental Eclipse responded to this adulation, we do not hear.) It is like this today at the Cheltenham Festival, particularly when there is an Irish winner. The 'effusion of heart' unites the racegoers: owners, trainers, jockeys, gamblers; royalty, grandees, middle classes, working classes. William Wildman felt it. Dennis O'Kelly felt it too. In the latter's case, there were unsentimental reasons for the excitement: he had just won a good deal of money. And he had set his sights on the means of making a good deal more.

1-100 Eclipse

A T EPSOM ON THAT early May day, William Wildman and his team at Mickleham saw for certain that they had a potential superstar in their stable. Their tasks now were to maintain his form, to keep him sound, and to plan a programme of races that would prove his greatness.

Modern trainers would have let Eclipse take it easy for a while. Following the race, they would have given him no more than gentle exercise, only by gradations building up to a stiff gallop or two; finely tuned, he would have returned to modest workouts in the days before his next race. It is a regime that would have struck Georgian trainers as namby-pamby. At Mickleham, Eclipse was back to the uphill gallops and 'sweats' right away.

Getting to race meetings was tougher then as well. There were no horseboxes: you had to walk. Setting off, with his groom beside him, in the small hours of the morning, a horse could cover about twenty miles in a day. So Eclipse and Oakley probably made their journey from Mickleham to their next race, thirty miles away at Ascot, in two stages, with an overnight stop at an inn. They would have arrived about five days before the race, and continued training on the racecourse, where they may have run a trial against their prospective opponents. Perhaps Eclipse's performance at the trial explains why just one other horse braved turning up for the race itself.

Eclipse's rival at Ascot on 29 May 1769, for another £50 Noblemen and Gentlemen's Plate, was called Cream de Barbade. Eclipse was quoted at 8-1 on. He won the first heat as easily as the betting had suggested he would. But Cream de Barbade was not a distance behind him, so they raced again. It seemed an unnecessary exercise, and it was: Eclipse won again.

This was when Dennis O'Kelly stepped in to make William Wildman an offer. He asked for a share in Eclipse, and Wildman accepted. Why did Wildman give up any portion of this exciting horse to a man such as Dennis? No doubt Dennis was very charismatic and persuasive, and he certainly offered a generous sum, 650 guineas, for a share that was, according to *The Genuine Memoirs of Dennis O'Kelly*, 'half a leg'. Six hundred and fifty guineas (assuming the sum was reported correctly) must have been worth more than that, even in a horse of Eclipse's potential: Herod, a proven champion, had cost 500 guineas at the Cumberland dispersal sale, and his buyer got all of him. Whether Dennis's share was half a leg or a whole one or even two or three, his intention was clear: having bought property in Epsom, with land for racehorse stabling, he wanted the star inmate to be Eclipse. The horse would make his name and his fortune – he knew it. With hindsight, one is tempted to describe Wildman's decision to take the money as one of the biggest mistakes in the history of horseracing, but one can see why the price at that time, for a horse with victories in just two moderately significant races, was irresistible.

Eclipse's next race was a greater challenge. King's Plates, instituted by Charles II, were the most prestigious contests in the racing calendar, worth 100 guineas. To add to the test of 'bottom' that heat racing set, they usually stipulated that horses should carry twelve stone.[65] For the King's Plate at Winchester on 13

[65] Horses are rarely asked to carry more than ten stone in modern British Flat races. In the championship National Hunt races at the Cheltenham Festival, the horses carry 11st 10lb.

June, Eclipse faced five opponents, including Slouch, who already had a King's Plate under his belt, and a decent horse called Caliban, who belonged to Dennis. Caliban was 2-1 in the betting, one report stated. The short price is a mystery, because Dennis, knowing Eclipse, cannot have fancied Caliban's chances. One possible explanation suggests itself: Dennis and his associates backed Caliban in order to lengthen Eclipse's odds. Eclipse was available to back for the plate at even money – the longest price at which he would ever start a race.[66]

The backers of Caliban knew by the end of the first heat that they had, as the punters say, done their money: the horse trailed in a distance behind, and was eliminated. Did Dennis bet on this result? Did he instruct Caliban's jockey not to offer serious opposition? One can get carried away with conspiracy theories, particularly when someone such as Dennis is involved. In any event, Eclipse needed no help from him. He won the first heat, and the second too, this time at odds of 1-10. Even less effort was required two days later, when he turned out for the £50 Winchester City Plate. There were no opponents. It was a walkover, literally: Oakley mounted Eclipse, and they walked over the course to collect the prize.

Rivals were either scared off by Eclipse's growing reputation, or by his performances against them in pre-race trials. At his next engagement, the King's Plate at Salisbury on 28 June, he walked over again. At the same course the following day, Eclipse started at 1-8 for a thirty-guinea City Plate, and won after two heats. He journeyed down to Canterbury on 25 July for the King's Plate there – another walkover. A painting by Francis Sartorius (father of J. N.) commissioned by Dennis a few years later shows the Salisbury or the Canterbury King's

[66] The rules of the race put Eclipse at an apparent disadvantage. The contest was for six-year-olds; younger horses did not get the weight concessions available in other types of contest. Eclipse, who was five, carried the same weight – twelve stone – as his older rivals.

Plate:[67] Eclipse and Oakley, in isolation, are walking over a sloping cross-country course marked with white posts.

A new jockey, John Whiting, enters reports of the King's Plate at Lewes in Sussex on 27 July. Whiting was 'up' (in the saddle) when Eclipse defeated a sole rival, Kingston, over two four-mile heats. (The next day, Kingston won a race worth £50.)

Eclipse had one more race in 1769, meeting another of his several opponents with jocular names. 'Eclipse' is itself a fine name for a racehorse, suggesting how he overshadowed his contemporaries. 'Milksop', also one of Cumberland's choices, is less glamorous. We have already met Stiff Dick – it is not clear whether his owner, William III, first called him that. Queen Anne suffered the indignity of seeing her horse Pepper finish behind an opponent called Sturdy Lump. The names of foundation sires and mares were often strikingly descriptive: Old Bald Peg, in reference to a white blaze; and, indicating reddish tints, the Bloody-Shouldered Arabian and the Bloody Buttocks Arabian. Some owners and breeders went for irony, choosing names that they hoped their horses would belie in performance. There was Slouch, among the runners-up at Winchester; later, Eclipse would compete against Tortoise. At Lichfield on 19 September, he faced Tardy. The result: Eclipse's fifth King's Plate of the season; odds: 1-7. He was undefeated in nine races, and it was time for his winter break. At last, he was allowed to rest from daily gallops, and to enjoy the freedom of a paddock. He would pick up the routine again the following February.

Some time over the winter, or possibly after Eclipse's first race in the spring of 1770, Dennis O'Kelly fulfilled the ambition he had cherished since first catching sight of the chestnut with a white blaze scorching

---

[67] The title is *Eclipse with Jockey up Walking the Course for the King's Plate*. The identification of Eclipse as a five-year-old is the clue pointing towards one of his two 1769 walkovers.

across the Epsom Downs: he bought Eclipse outright, taking owner-ship of the three and a half legs still in Wildman's possession – or whatever Wildman's outstanding share was – for a sum generally agreed to have been 1,100 guineas; he also appropriated Wildman's racing colours of scarlet with black cap. Eclipse moved the seven miles from Mickleham to Dennis's new Epsom stables in Clay Hill.

Another story, plausible in its portrayal of Dennis but hard to believe in this context, is that Wildman and Dennis gambled over the share. Dennis put two £1,000 notes in one pocket, and one £1,000 note in another, and invited Wildman to choose. Wildman plumped for the pocket with the single £1,000. Would Dennis have risked arousing ill feeling over this important trans-action? Perhaps. A less hypothetical question is this: why did Wildman sell a horse who was clearly a superstar? One theory is that there may have been threats to 'nobble' Eclipse. In fact, Wildman would not have had to receive specific threats to be aware that his champion was at risk: villains were known to break into stables and dose horses with opium; one poor horse died after being fed balls consisting of duck shot. You can see why Wildman may have decided that Dennis and his associates were the men to handle such difficulties.

But there is a pattern to Wildman's bloodstock transactions. His ambition and astuteness led him to acquire fine horses, and his caution prompted him to offload them as soon as they showed their worth. He might have earned a lot more money if he had held on to Gimcrack, his first outstanding racer. He was starting to earn good money from Marske, Eclipse's sire; but a few years later, before Marske's market value had reached its peak, Wildman would sell him too. And he might have earned a small fortune, as well as a more prominent role in racing history, if he had not sold Eclipse to Dennis O'Kelly.

After his legendary debut at the 3 May 1769 Noblemen and Gentlemen's Plate at Epsom, Eclipse never raced again at his home course. In April 1770, at the beginning of his second season,[68] he had more prestigious dates on his schedule. Newmarket, ninety miles to the north-east in East Anglia, hosted a spring meeting that occupied the sporting set, as well as those who visited the town merely for the society, for a week at the end of April. You needed to be there, even if you did not care for racing. Horace Walpole, with magnificently languid insouciance, declared, 'Though . . . [I] have been 50 times in my life at Newmarket, and have passed through it at the time of the races, I never before saw a complete one. I once went from Cambridge on purpose, saw the beginning, was tired and went away.'

Eclipse made the five-day journey to the Suffolk town to face his sternest test yet. He was to race in a match against Bucephalus, the finest horse in the stables of Peregrine Wentworth, a Yorkshire MP and landowner with substantial racing interests and a reputation for sartorial elegance. Bucephalus was another five-year-old chestnut, and he came to the match unbeaten; his prizes included the 1769 York Great Subscription, which was among Eclipse's future engagements. He had the same parentage as Spilletta, Eclipse's mother,[69] and thus was Eclipse's uncle.[70] Wentworth had made the match with William Wildman, contributing 600 guineas to Wildman's 400 — another way of expressing odds about Eclipse of 4–6.

The prelude to this famous race, which took place on 17 April 1770, is the subject of George Stubbs's *Eclipse at Newmarket, with a Groom and Jockey*. Eclipse and his human companions are at the rubbing-house at the start of the Beacon Course, four miles

[68] He was still, officially, a five-year-old. Racehorses in this era celebrated their birthdays on 1 May. Now, they all become a year older on 1 January.
[69] By Regulus, out of Mother Western — but see Appendix 2.
[70] Horses are described as related if they have ancestors in common on their dams' sides. Horses are half brothers or sisters if they have the same mother; but they are not described as such if they have the same sire, perhaps because sires are so prolific.

away from the Newmarket stands. The groom looks apprehensive; the jockey is purposeful and confident; the horse is fit and alert. The scene is quiet, but pregnant with the implication of the superlative performance to come.[71]

Eclipse and Bucephalus, nephew and uncle, set off from the Beacon Course start, Eclipse assuming the lead as usual. They galloped for more than two miles before taking a dog-leg right turn and heading towards the finish. As they came within sight of the stands, Bucephalus moved up on Eclipse's flank to challenge, goading Eclipse into the most determined gallop of his career. Eclipse surged ahead. Bucephalus strained to keep in touch until, broken, he fell away, leaving Eclipse to arrive at the line well in front. Bucephalus never raced again. Eclipse, by contrast, shrugged off his exertions to race again two days later.

The records of the match in the racing calendars list Eclipse as Mr Wildman's. But Dennis commissioned the Stubbs painting to mark the victory. And the horse was certainly in Dennis's ownership on 19 April, the date of the Newmarket King's Plate. The race was in four-mile heats over the Round Course (a vanished feature of the Newmarket landscape adjoining what is now the July Course), and Eclipse's opponents were a fellow five-year-old, Pensioner, and two six-year-olds, Diana and Chigger. Diana was the winner of previous King's Plates at Newmarket, York and Lincoln. Chigger had already lost once to Eclipse, at the 1769 King's Plate at Winchester. He was owned by the Duke of Grafton, who had resigned recently as Prime Minister and who a few years earlier had scandalized certain sections of society by flaunting his mistress, the courtesan Nancy Parsons. Grafton, later to own three Derby winners, once skipped a Cabinet meeting because it

[71] For a fuller discussion of Stubbs's painting, see chapter 18. Stubbs later identified the jockey as Samuel Merriott. Perhaps John Oakley, if Eclipse's ownership had already changed, was no longer involved. One report describes Oakley as Eclipse's 'constant groom'; another asserts that he was a jockey riding for various owners. It is hard to know what to conclude. See Appendix 1.

clashed with a match involving one of his horses. In common with the sport he patronized, he was despised by Horace Walpole (he who had got 'tired' halfway through watching a race), with the result that his reputation is locked to Walpole's description of him as 'like an apprentice, thinking the world should be postponed to a whore and a horserace'.

Chigger got no closer to Eclipse at Newmarket than he had at Winchester, and was withdrawn after Eclipse won the first heat. Mr Fenwick, owner of Diana, decided that his mare had no chance of adding another King's Plate to her tally. Only Pensioner maintained a challenge to Dennis's horse. Dennis made his way to the betting post, where he found Eclipse quoted at 7-4 and 6-4 to distance his single rival. This is the moment, in some accounts, when he announced, 'Eclipse first, and the rest nowhere', or, 'Eclipse, and nothing else.' But if the Newmarket race is the source of the legendary prediction, the phrasing must have been tampered with, because 'the rest' was a single horse. So it seems more likely that he uttered the words at Eclipse's Epsom debut. Nevertheless, Dennis, and no doubt his cohorts too, backed Eclipse to distance Pensioner, placing 'large sums' at 7-4 and 6-4. Eclipse landed the gamble.

As noted earlier, King's Plates were the most valuable races in the Turf calendar, private matches apart. Even so, owners were starting to see little point in challenging for them if it meant racing against Eclipse. He walked over the course for the 100-guinea prize at Guildford (5 June); he journeyed north, to Nottingham, and walked over there (3 July); then he headed further north, to York, for the hat-trick (20 August). We can picture him on his journey, perhaps with two grooms by his side. He is a national celebrity, and as he and his companions pass by inns on the route, proprietors and their customers come out to see him. At the inns where they stop each night, the senior groom gets a bed while the junior sleeps with the horse, to keep him safe.

At last, at York on 23 August, Eclipse met some competition, and recorded his most impressive victory. It should have been one of Dennis's finest hours. Instead, he was in disgrace.

Late one night at Blewitt's Inn in York, Dennis was apprehended after disturbing in her bed a certain Miss Swinburne, whose screaming had wakened the house. Miss Swinburne was the daughter of a distinguished local citizen, a Catholic baronet. To compromise her honour was a serious affront.

The August issue of *Town & Country* magazine carried the tit-illating news, dating it 27 July: 'A certain nominal Irish count, it is said, forced himself into a young lady's bedchamber in the night, at York, in the race-week, for which offence he has been appre-hended and committed to York castle.' In its next issue, *Town & Country* amplified the story. 'The renowned Count K', owner of 'the celebrated Eclipse', had passed the evening, and early hours of the morning too, at the coffee house, playing the dice game hazard. Returning tipsily to his hotel, he found his room locked. His solution to this problem was to barge the door open, only to discover, in what he had expected to be an empty bed, Miss Swinburne, terrified out of sleep by his crashing entrance. Typically, Dennis saw this as a delightful opportunity, and made a soothing overture.

'Tis all one to me, my dear,' he gallantly averred. 'Sure we may lie here very cosily till morning.'

This proposal was the opposite of soothing for Miss Swinburne, who leaped out of bed and fled into the corridor, 'naked as she was', yelling in horror. Fellow lodgers came to her aid. Realizing at last that to salvage this situation was beyond his powers of charm, Dennis retreated to his room, where he con-structed a makeshift barricade. Miss Swinburne's rescuers gathered outside the door, broke through his defences, and seized him.

The author of *The Genuine Memoirs of Dennis O'Kelly* enjoyed himself when he got to this episode. His account had Dennis, on

A Late Unfortunate Adventure at York. *Dennis O'Kelly (centre — note the portrait of Eclipse above the bed) tries to get out of trouble with both bluster and cash, while Miss Swinburne swoons.* 'Honi soit qui mal y pense' *says the motto — rough translation:* 'Shame be on him who makes a scandalous interpretation of this.'

arriving in his room, drawing back the silken curtain of his bed, finding Miss Swinburne there, and gazing 'with astonishment and delight' on her countenance. 'The chisel of Bonerotto! [*sic*] The pencil of Corregio! [*sic*] Never formed more captivating charms. For some time our hero stood, like Cymon, the celebrated clown, when he first beheld the beauties of the sleeping Ephigenia.' Dennis looked around for some means of identifying the intruder, but found only 'a fashionable riding-dress, a watch, without any particular mark of distinction, and the other common accommodations of women'. Then, in what is one of the less credible passages of a generally unreliable book, Dennis became suspicious: what if this woman had heard about his vast winnings at the meeting and was out to use her feminine wiles to rob him? Drink exacerbated the dark thoughts typical of the late hour, and Dennis began shouting accusations at Miss Swinburne. When she shouted in return, Dennis immediately sobered up. He tried to calm her, but a crowd had already gathered at the door. He escaped out of the window. No dishonour was done to Miss Swinburne, 'who was altogether as chaste as she was charming'.

The fact that the York meeting had not yet started and Dennis's winnings were still to arrive dents the credibility of this account of his behaviour. The *Town & Country* version rings truer: you can picture the ever-bullish and well-oiled Dennis hoping to seduce the terrified young woman, still trying to win her round as she flees into the corridor, and conceding defeat only when rescuers appear on the scene.

How extraordinary it was, the *Memoirs* added, that Miss Swinburne should have been given Dennis's room. 'The cause of the young lady's nocturnal invasion could never be rightly accounted for. Beds were, no doubt, scarcely to be obtained by fair means . . .' Yes; or Dennis's avowal that it was his room was a desperate attempt to soften the offence.

Anyway, there was a stink. A prosecution was mooted. But Dennis, thanks to representations by influential friends, escaped with a payment of £500 to local charities and an advertisement in the press. On 2 October, the *York Courant* ran the following notice on its front page:

> I do hereby acknowledge that I was (when in liquor) lately guilty of a very gross affront and rudeness to a young lady of a very respectable family, which I am now very much concerned at, and humbly beg pardon of that lady and her friends for my behaviour to her, being very sensible of her lenity and theirs in receiving this my public submission and acknowledgement; and, as a further atonement for my offence, I have also paid the sum of five hundred pounds to be disposed of for such charitable purposes as that lady directs; and am content that this may be inserted in any of the public newspapers. Witness my hand this 25th day of August 1770. D. O'Kelly

Dennis may have had to prostrate himself before another. *Town & Country* amused itself in this respect, inventing a letter to Dennis from Charlotte Hayes:

> Sir,
> Your behaviour at York, which is in every body's mouth, strongly merits my resentment, that the condescension of writing to you is more than you ought to expect. After the many repeated vows you have made, and oaths you have sworn, that I, and I alone, was the idol of your heart, could so short an absence entirely efface me from your remembrance? And was I to be abandoned for the accidental rencounter of a new face? Had she yielded to your embraces, your amour would probably have remained a secret to the world, and I only from your behaviour might have made the discovery. But you are justly punished, did I not share in the loss.
> Oh! Dennis, are my charms so faded, my beauty so decayed, my understanding so impaired, which you have so often and so highly praised, as to destroy all the impressions you pretended they had

made upon you! But if love has entirely subsided, surely gratitude might have pleaded so strongly in my behalf as to have excluded all other females from your affections. Remember when in the Fleet, when famine stared you in the face, and wretched tatters scarce covered your nakedness – I fed, clothed, and made a gentleman of you. Remember the day-rules I obtained for you – remember the sums you won through that means – then remember me.

But why do I talk of love or gratitude! Let interest plead the most powerful reason that will operate on you. What a wretch! To fling away in a drunken frolic – in the ridiculous attempt of an amour – more money, aye far more money,[72] than I have cleared by my honest industry for a month – or even your horse Eclipse, with all his superior agility, has run away with in a whole season.

This last reflexion racks my soul. Write to me, however, and tell me of some capital stroke you have made to comfort me, for I am at present,

Your most disconsolate

Charlotte Hayes

Marlborough Street

September 4th

A print appeared, with the title *A Late Unfortunate Adventure at York*. It shows a crowded bedroom, with a portrait of Eclipse above the bed; in the centre of the room Dennis is making emollient gestures, holding out notes marked '500' and '1000', while a man threatens him with a pikestaff. An angry woman is holding a swooning Miss Swinburne, beneath a sign reading 'The Chaste Susanna'. From behind a door peeks another woman, bare-breasted.

---

[72] An amusing rhetorical emphasis. In fact, Eclipse earned £2,157 that year. Charlotte's monthly turnover – if not her profit – from her 'honest industry' was probably greater than that.

Nearly twenty years later, following Dennis's death, *The World* reminded its readers of the adventure, alleging that Dennis had commented bitterly – and untruly – that he would never donate another penny to charity. It was also said that he gave an undertaking never again to set foot in Yorkshire. The 1770 York meeting (if he was there) was the last he attended in the county – where, the *Genuine Memoirs* related, 'he was considered, by the ladies, as satyr; and by the gentlemen, who very laudably entertained a proper sense of female protection, a ruffian'. This was Dennis's reputation outside Yorkshire too, and the 'unfortunate adventure' helped to cement it. Miss Swinburne recovered her good name; Dennis, among the people who mattered, did not.

One of the people who was to matter most was the owner of a rival to Eclipse for the York Great Subscription (worth £319 10s to the winner). Sir Charles Bunbury, single again after his wife Lady Sarah (née Lennox) had eloped the previous year, was the steward of the Jockey Club, and was on his way to establishing himself as 'The First Dictator of the Turf'. His entry for the York race was called Bellario. A second rival, Tortoise, came from the stables of Peregrine Wentworth, winner in 1769 with Bucephalus (defeated by Eclipse at Newmarket in April). Bellario and Tortoise had fine reputations, which counted for little in the betting: Eclipse's starting price was 1-20.

The race was run over four miles on the Knavesmire, a stretch of common land that was once the site for executions. York racing week was the north's answer to the big meetings at Newmarket, and the huge crowd at the course included the Duke of Cumberland (nephew of the Cumberland who bred Eclipse), the Duke of Devonshire, the Dukes and Duchesses of Kingston and Northumberland, and the Earl and Countess of Carlisle. One would like to know whether the disgraced Dennis O'Kelly had the brass neck to join them. It would have been a shame to miss this race.

Eclipse set off in his customary position at the front of the field, and this time never allowed his rivals, as he had done briefly at Epsom and Newmarket, to get close to him. Head low, raking stride relentless, he powered further and further clear. At the betting post, a layer shouted that he would take 100-1 *on* Eclipse.[73] After two of the four miles, Eclipse was already a distance (240 yards) ahead of the others, and he maintained the gap, coming to the line 'with uncommon ease'. In one account, Dennis gave a group of men the scary task of standing to form a wall beyond the finishing line to encourage Eclipse to pull up.

Sir Charles Bunbury took the defeat with the lack of grace of a modern football manager. Jibbing at the loss to the upstart O'Kelly, he never accepted that Eclipse was his horse Bellario's superior. And he seems never to have been willing to accept Dennis as his equal – an attitude that was to blight Dennis's Turf ambitions.

Eclipse's 1770 schedule included four further engagements. But he raced only once. At Lincoln on 3 September, he walked over for his tenth King's Plate. Then he returned to Newmarket, where on 3 October he met another of Sir Charles Bunbury's horses, Corsican, in competition for a 150-guinea plate. In the view of the betting market, there was no competition: Eclipse was 1-70. You might have offered those odds about his getting from one end of the Beacon Course to another. He managed it, as did Corsican – only somewhat more slowly. On 4 October, Eclipse yet again scared off the opposition for a King's Plate, and walked over the Newmarket Round Course.

He was due to meet Jenison Shafto's unbeaten Goldfinder

---

[73] Betting in running is another feature of the eighteenth-century betting market that has made a comeback in the internet era. The same odds with a betting exchange such as Betfair would be 1.01. A winning bet would return a one penny profit on a £1 stake.

(son of Shafto's Snap, who had twice defeated Eclipse's sire Marske), prompting jokes from O'Kelly about how the rival connections would be 'gold losers'. But Goldfinder broke down at exercise, and the match did not take place.[74]

That was the anti-climactic end of Eclipse's career as a racer. He had won eighteen races, including eleven King's Plates. His prize money totalled £2,863.50 – the equivalent of about £304,000 today. It is a relatively modest sum: for winning the 2008 Epsom Derby, New Approach won for his owner, Princess Haya of Jordan, more than £800,000.

However, Eclipse's money-making days were far from over.

He had defeated all the best horses of his day. 'He was never beaten, never had a whip flourished over him, or felt the tickling of a spur, or was ever, for a moment, distressed by the speed of a competitor; out-footing, out-striding, and out-lasting, every horse which started against him,' the equestrian writer John Lawrence said. John Orton, in his *Turf Annals*, wrote, 'The performances of Eclipse . . . have always been considered to exhibit a degree of superiority unparalleled by any horse ever known.' The racing historian James Rice put it more fancifully: Eclipse 'never failed in a single instance to *give them all their gruel*, and the need of a spyglass to see which way he went, and how far he was off'. Eclipse was without dispute – except possibly by Sir Charles Bunbury – the champion of his era. Horsemen agreed that he was 'the fleetest horse that ever ran in England, since the time of [Flying] Childers'.

It was time to set about transmitting that ability to future generations.

---

[74] Jenison Shafto, perhaps to escape gambling debts or perhaps to escape the pain of gout, shot himself in 1771.

10

The First Lady Abbess

SEX FOR A LIVING IS a pursuit that Eclipse and Charlotte Hayes had in common. As Eclipse embarked on his remunerative second career as a stallion, Charlotte was already the undisputed 'first lady abbess of the town'. Her Marlborough Street establishment in Soho, though thriving, had not satisfied her ambition, which was to set up a brothel that was still more lavish, and that would adorn the most prestigious district of London. So, in the late 1760s, she set up in a street in St James's called King's Place,[75] a narrow thoroughfare within sight of the royal residence St James's Palace. Fashionable clubs such as White's and Boodle's were nearby. The grandest members of society had their homes in the parish, and were all – including a few of the women – potential customers, who might visit a brothel as they would a gambling club, as part of an evening's entertainment.

Number 2, King's Place was a smart town house of four floors. You could pass a complete evening there: listening to musicians and watching dancers, conversing with the delightful residents, gambling, dining and drinking, before repairing upstairs. A night with one of the 'nuns' might set you back £50,

[75] The road is now Pall Mall Place.

sometimes more; if you had enjoyed all the extra amenities as well, you were looking next morning at a bill of at least £100. That kept out the riff-raff. It was at least a third of what many professional London men, such as lawyers and civil servants, earned in a year.

Cheaper options were available, however. A 'bill of fare' for an evening at Charlotte's — as reported in *Nocturnal Revels*, a scandalous account of the lives of Charlotte and her contemporaries — included the hiring of 'Poll Nimblewrist' or 'Jenny Speedyhand' for 'Doctor Frettext, after church is over' (the doctor's fee for this brief business was a modest two guineas). 'Sir Harry Flagellum' was down to pay ten guineas for the severe attentions of 'Nell Handy', 'Bet Flourish' or 'Mrs Birch herself': it was gruelling work, as the woman eventually entrusted with it complained. 'Two long hours,' she groaned, 'have I been with this old curmudgeon; and I have had as much labour to rouse the Venus lurking in his veins, as if I had been whipping the most obstinate of all mules over the Alps.'

Nocturnal Revels alleged that the most valuable customer of the evening was 'Lady Loveit, just come from Bath, much disappointed in her amour with Lord Atall'. Keen to be 'well mounted', her ladyship was assigned a fee of 50 guineas for the services of 'Captain O'Thunder, or Sawney Rawbone'. For the evening dramatized in the book, O'Thunder got the job. He and his lady neglected to lock their door, and were interrupted *in flagrante* by one Captain Toper, who was reluctant to leave. 'By Jasus,' O'Thunder exclaimed, 'this is very rude and impartinent to interrupt a Gomman and a Lady in their private amusements!' He set about the interloper, but when the question of a duel came up, declined to test his honour. Lady Loveit, dismayed by his lack of gallantry, favoured Sawney Rawbone thereafter.

According to E. J. Burford, author of several books set in this milieu, Lady Loveit was Lady Sarah Lennox, and Lord Atall was Lord William Gordon, for whom Lady Sarah had abandoned her marriage to Sir Charles Bunbury. It is tempting to imagine that Captain O'Thunder was Dennis O'Kelly (who was a captain in the Middlesex Militia by this time), performing stud duties for Charlotte and relishing a liaison with the former wife of the first Dictator of the Turf, the man who was to be responsible for excluding him from the inner circle of horseracing. But the author of *Nocturnal Revels* seems not to have been making this connection, and later introduced 'the Count', a new figure, to the scene.

Nocturnal Revels portrayed Dennis as a general man about the house, and credited him with dreaming up 'elastic beds', specially designed for the delight of Charlotte's customers, who experienced on them 'the finest movements in the most ecstatic moments'. When Charlotte retired, a bawd called Mrs Weston bought these beds, winning for her house great popularity among 'peers and peeresses, wanton wives, and more wanton widows', for whose satisfaction she provided 'some of the most capital riding masters in the three kingdoms'. Charlotte employed males in various capacities too. A satirical sketch in the *London Magazine* reported an auction for 'Cream-coloured Tommy – In plain English, a pimp deep in the science of fornication and intrigue . . . He will cringe, fawn and flatter like a Parisian. A guinea for him! Well spoke Charlotte! A true whore's price! Charlotte Hayes has got him, to be chaplain at her nunnery.'

Charlotte's name appeared in the public prints, in memoirs, and in topical verses – a level of fame that her modern counterparts would prefer to avoid. Cynthia Payne, who held 'parties' at her house in Streatham, and Heidi Fleiss, 'the Hollywood madam', became celebrities who appeared on chat shows, but they did so after scandals and court cases had ended their sex industry careers. Charlotte was a celebrity when she was in her prime. As would be the case in our own age, her status quelled moral considerations; that she provided titillating copy was the main thing. But, entertaining as her story is, it cannot be dissociated from its basis in exploitation and its association with misery.

Consider Charlotte's employees. Although well-known molls catered to Doctor Frettext and Sir Harry Flagellum,[76] the chief attractions of Charlotte's establishment were her own protégées, whose recruitment often involved distressingly underhand methods. One, tried and tested in the business, was to lurk at register offices, dressed modestly and purporting to be in search of a young woman to attend to a lady. On snaring an appropriate candidate, Charlotte would take her to a house that, under a false name, she had rented specially, and wine and dine her. The young woman, perhaps up from the country, would retire to bed, only to find her sleep interrupted by one of Charlotte's customers. 'In vain she laments the fraud that has been played upon her,' *Nocturnal Revels* explained, with a mixture of prurience and compassion. 'Her outcries bring no one to her relief, and probably she yields to her fate, finding it inevitable; and solaces herself in the morning with a few guineas, and the perspective view of having a new gown, a pair of silver buckles, and a black silk cloak. Being once broke in, there is no greater difficulty in persuading her to remove [from] her quarters, and repair to the nunnery in King's Place, in order to make room for another victim, who is to be sacrificed in the like manner.'

For the privilege of raping this virgin, 'Lord C-N, Lord B—ke, or Colonel L—e' would have paid a handsome sum. Deflowerment was a highly prized pleasure, and was the subject of a certain amount of fraud. 'A Kitty Young or a Nancy Feathers . . . could easily be passed off for vestals, with a little skilful preparation.' Charlotte seemed to be happy to convince herself that she was operating with essential honesty, arguing that, 'As to maidenheads, it was her opinion, that a woman might lose her maidenhead 500 times, and be as good a virgin as ever. Dr O'Patrick had assured her, that a maidenhead was as easily made

---

[76] Burford was unable to identify Frettext, but claimed that Flagellum was the Earl of Uxbridge.

as a pudding; that she had tried herself, and though she had lost hers a thousand times, she believed she had as good a one as ever . . . She had one girl, Miss Shirley, just come from the play with Counsellor Pliant, who had gone through 23 editions of vestality in one week; and being a bookseller's daughter, she knew the value of repeated and fresh editions.'

Charlotte would also place advertisements in the press, seeking young women to go into service, and would meet the applicants herself at the specially rented house. Sometimes, the nuns would come, or be brought, to her. Betsy Green arrived in the care of a Captain Fox, who clearly thought that he was doing his charge a favour. A sickly girl in her early teens, Betsy had been soliciting on the street when Fox found her, and had been placed by him in the care of his friend Lord Lyttelton. Since Lyttelton was later to earn the title 'The Wicked Lord Lyttelton', Fox's arrangement showed a lack of insight. However, when he learned of Betsy's mistreatment at Lyttelton's hands, he rescued her and entrusted her to Charlotte. 'Under [Charlotte's] care and tuition her wonderful beauty was brought out,' Burford quoted. 'No age or clime has ever produced such a perfect model of voluptuous beauty.' Betsy became the mistress of Colonel John Coxe, who doted on her. When Coxe (whose name Betsy assumed) was away, though, she regularly summoned 'all her most abandoned companions of either sex and converted his house into a temple of debauchery'. Reports of these orgies got back to Coxe, who threw Betsy out. Later, she acted in Drury Lane, and boasted lovers including Lord Falkirk, the Earl of Craven and the Earl of Effingham. But the relationships did not endure, and she eventually returned to brothel life.

Betsy's decline was the fate of most prostitutes, even when they had the contacts that employment by Charlotte afforded them. Nevertheless, some had the beauty, charm and determination to make good lives for themselves, above all enjoying the luck to find men who did not suddenly abandon them to poverty. A gentleman of means might take one of the 'nuns' as his mistress, setting her up (after compensating the madam) in fine apartments, with servants and a carriage. As long as he did not vulgarly flaunt her, as the Duke of Grafton did Nancy Parsons, it was a dashing way to behave. In that respect, Captain Fox had taken Betsy Green to a woman who offered her better prospects of advancement than almost any other employer in London.

A 'shaggy-tail'd uncomb'd unwash'd filly of 14 . . . bought from her industrious painstaking mechanick of a father for a song' blossomed, under Charlotte's care, to become Kitty Fredericks, 'the veritable Thais[77] amongst the *haut ton*, the veritable flora of all London'. Harriet Lamb, seduced by an aristocrat and abandoned at Charlotte's, became another favourite: 'Kind Charlotte Hayes,' wrote the poet Edward Thompson, 'who entertains the ram / With such delicious, tender, nice house-lamb!' Though well trained in how to behave in society, these women were usually bereft of education. A possibly apocryphal story about Polly Vernon, who adorned the parties that Captain Richard Vernon ('Old fox Vernon') held for his racing chums, told how she reacted to Wicked Lord Lyttelton's enquiry about whether she knew Jesus Christ: indignantly, she protested that 'she wondered at his Lordship's imperence [sic] . . . she never had no acquaintance with foreigners'.

In the modern era, prominent mistresses such as Antonia de Sancha (who had an affair with the Conservative minister David Mellor) and Bienvenida Buck (whose lover was the Chief of the Defence Staff, Sir Peter Harding) achieve tabloid celebrity. In the eighteenth century, you could be a courtesan (the paid mistress of a grand figure) and former prostitute, and become a subject for the most prominent artist of the day. Emily Warren was walking the streets with her father, a blind beggar, when she met Charlotte; she was then twelve years old, and illiterate. Charlotte

[77] The courtesan who travelled with the army of Alexander the Great.

did not correct that deficiency, but taught Emily deportment and manners that 'attracted universal admiration wherever she appeared abroad'. Emily modelled for the painter Sir Joshua Reynolds, who portrayed her as Thais and declared that 'he had never seen so faultless and finely formed a human figure'.[78]

It was 'to the great astonishment of all beholders', Town & Country magazine reported in an archly ironic tribute to the 'Monastery of Santa Charlotta', that Charlotte was able to transmute 'the basest brass into the purest gold, by a process as quick as it is unaccountable'. Charlotte provided her nuns not only with tutoring in ladylike skills, including dance and music as well as deportment, but also with fine dresses, luxurious underwear, jewellery and other adornments. She did not do so out of a spirit of lavish charity, however. She was investing in the monastery, as well as ensuring that the women, who were indebted to her for these donations, and for board and lodging too, were chained to the place unless wealthy admirers bought them out. Customers who attempted to persuade nuns to leave Santa Charlotta's without compensation for the proprietor were committing a grave breach of decorum, while those who offered presents to their favourites were in fact giving them to Charlotte.

Charlotte advertised her pampered charges by strolling with them in parks and pleasure gardens, and by gracing fashionable venues. At the opening in 1772 of the Pantheon,[79] the grand Oxford Street hall devoted to masquerades and concerts, she and several nuns were among the crowd of 1,500 in spite of an announcement by the Master of Ceremonies that actresses and courtesans would not be admitted. The edict failed, but the MC still tried to bar the dance floor to Betsy Coxe and her then lover, Captain Scott, who observed, 'If you turn away every woman who

[78] The painting hangs in the morning room at Waddesdon Manor in Buckinghamshire.
[79] Now the site of the Oxford Street branch of Marks & Spencer.

is not better than she should be, your company will soon be reduced to a handful!' Today, if a man took an 'escort' to a party, he would probably try to disguise her occupation; his eighteenth-century counterparts were not so squeamish.

The fashion-consciousness of Charlotte's profession is apparent in a picture entitled *A Nun of the First Class* (1773). The nun wears a tight hairdo, ascending to a point bearing a small bonnet, from which descends a row of orbs. She has a choker, a flower in her bodice, and a cheek patch[80] – these patches were originally coverings for smallpox scars, but became desirable adornments. In *A Saint James's Beauty* (1784) (which appears in this book's colour section), the nun wears a dress of some rich, heavy material; her hat sports feathers and a bow. She looks out of a window towards the palace – she is expecting a royal visitor. He may be the Prince of Wales (the future George IV), or his brother the Duke of York.[81]

In addition to royalty and lords, Charlotte's most favoured customers were Jewish merchants and financiers. The print *One of the Tribe of Levi, going to Breakfast with a Young Christian* shows an elderly gentleman at a breakfast table in a large reception room. Above him, a painting portrays a scene of seduction. A smiling, liveried black servant boy holds a seat for the nun, who stands richly dressed for the gentleman's inspection. E. J. Burford speculated that the woman observing them from the sofa – a rather crone-like figure – is Charlotte. Jewish men, he quoted her as saying, 'always fancy that their amorous abilities never fail'; they were civil, and spoke gently.

---

[80] E. J. Burford said that the cheek patch was there; it is invisible in the print I have seen.

[81] The previous Duke of York, brother of George III, had once, at the end of a visit, insulted the celebrated Kitty Fisher by leaving her only £50. Kitty, whose usual charge for a night was 100 guineas, illustrated her contempt by placing the banknote between two slices of buttered bread, which she ate for her breakfast.

One of the Tribe of Levi, going to Breakfast w:th a Young Christian.
London, *Printed for* R. Sayer & J. Bennett *Map & Printsellers* N.º 53 Fleet Street, *as the Act directs* 27 M. 1778.

One of the Tribe of Levi, going to Breakfast with a Young Christian *(1778). A scene from a King's Place nunnery. E. J. Burford thought that the crone-like figure in the background was 'probably' Charlotte Hayes. She was to live for another thirty-five years.*

Eighteenth-century men rarely allowed their enthusiasm for sleeping with prostitutes to wilt at thoughts of the risks involved. Gonorrhoea was widespread; worse, you might get syphilis (though the distinction between the diseases was not understood), guaranteeing a terrible decline and death. Charlotte's good name depended on healthy experiences for her customers. She employed a doctor, Chidwick, to give her nuns weekly check-ups, and she provided 'Mrs Phillips' famed new engines' – condoms, made of dried sheep's gut and tastefully presented in silk purses, tied with ribbon. Mrs Phillips owned a shop in Covent Garden that offered 'implements of safety for gentlemen of intrigue', in three sizes. A woman of advanced marketing skills, she promoted her wares with this advertising jingle:

To guard yourself from shame or fear
Votaries of Venus, hasten here;
None in wares e'er found a flaw
Self-preservation's nature's law.[82]

However, Charlotte's principles weighed lightly in the scales against commercial opportunities. In this business, you had to be flexible. *Nocturnal Revels* carried the anecdote of a nobleman who arrived at the nunnery with a plan to win a bet of 1,000 guineas against a rival, who was cuckolding him. The bet was that the rival would be afflicted with 'a certain fashionable disorder' within the next month, and the plan was this: Charlotte would provide an infected woman; the nobleman would sleep with the infected woman; the nobleman would infect his wife; the wife would infect the rival. Charlotte's first reaction to this scheme was a show of outrage. 'Heavens, you astonish me!' she cried. 'And I think you use me very ill, my Lord, considering the constant care I have

[82] Mrs Phillips retired to Jamaica, where she was elected to the appropriate post of mistress of the revels at carnivals.

always paid to your Lordship's health and welfare. I know of no such rotten cattle as you talk of; they never come under my roof, I assure your Lordship.' In response, his lordship produced a bank-note for £30. Charlotte said that she would see what she could do. The next time the nobleman met his rival in public, he demanded payment of his bet; the rival handed over the money.

James Boswell was, despite his careful use of 'armour complete', a frequent sufferer from the pox. So was the young William Hickey, who recalled treating himself with mercury (the standard medicine for the ailment) and enduring the unpleasant side-effect – exacerbated by his unwillingness to stop drinking – of 'salivation': black saliva flooded his mouth, and his tongue swelled up to prevent his ingesting anything other than fluids. Thus poisoned, he must have had a strong constitution to pull through and survive to the age of eighty.

In his entertaining account of his rackety life, Hickey noted that he was a frequent visitor to the 'house of celebrity' kept by 'that experienced old matron Charlotte Hayes'. However, he has caused confusion by referring also to 'Mrs Kelly and her bevy of beauties in Arlington Street'. A passage in the *Memoirs of William Hickey* recalled an episode from 1780. Hickey was in Margate, dining with his brother and two friends, when a sumptuous landau arrived, bearing Mrs Kelly, 'two nymphs' and a girl of twelve or thirteen. The girl, Mrs Kelly explained, was her daughter, off to a convent school in Ostend. At dinner, Hickey's brother got very drunk and made leering advances to the girl, offering such gracious observations as 'the young one's bosom had already too much swell for a nun' and 'no canting hypocritical friar should have the fingering of those plump globes'. He lunged at her, but fell to the floor, insensible. Mrs Kelly rushed the girl away, and roundly abused the whole company. Hickey, undeflected by the acrimony and farce into which the evening had descended, retired to bed with one of the nymphs.

Charlotte did start to style herself Mrs O'Kelly, and the 'O' was often treated as optional. But it is misguided to speculate that she and Dennis had a daughter and sent her abroad for a convent education.[83] Hickey's Mrs Kelly is clearly someone else, who is introduced only a few pages after a mention of Charlotte Hayes and her house of celebrity; and Burford wrote about Mrs Kelly of Arlington Street (not King's Place) – her first name, according to him, was also Charlotte – as a different person. In any event, the young girl in Hickey's anecdote may not really have been Mrs Kelly's daughter, but a ward of some sort – though one who got a more sheltered education than did Charlotte's Betsy Green and Emily Warren.[84]

Several of the nuns we have met in this chapter did well for themselves, escaping their cloisters to become the mistresses of wealthy men; some, such as Harriet Powell, made good marriages too. But of course they were exceptional. Most prostitutes, including those who spent their careers in the environs of St James's, endured miserable declines, which would begin before they were thirty years old. And although they were more likely to find grand lovers and husbands in Georgian London than at any other period of the capital's history, they did not enjoy complete social movement. Stigmas endured. Emily Warren became the mistress of a friend of William Hickey's, Captain Robert Pott, who on being posted to India commissioned Hickey to secure a passage for her to join him. Pott's father was dismayed. 'The unthinking boy,' he complained to Hickey, 'has taken that infamous and notoriously abandoned woman, Emily, who has already involved him deeply as to pecuniary matters, with him to India, a step that must not only shut him out of all proper society, but prevent his being employed in any situation of respect or emolument.' The story ended sadly.

[83] She is assigned a daughter and a role in the Margate episode in Hallie Rubenhold's *The Covent Garden Ladies*.
[84] The teenage Emma Lyon, later to become Lady Hamilton, may have danced at Mrs Kelly's.

The couple made a 'great impression' in Madras (Chennai), and set sail for Calcutta (Kolkata); but Emily died on board, mysteriously succumbing to fever shortly after drinking two tumblers of water mixed with milk.[85]

Charlotte, meanwhile, continued to prosper. In 1771, she opened a second King's Place brothel, at number 5, entrusting number 2 to a Miss Ellison. She also had an establishment in King Street, for the King's Place overspill. The German visitor Johann Wilhelm von Archenholz noted that King's Place was clogged with carriages in the evenings, and observed of the nuns, 'You may see them superbly clothed at public places; and even those of the most expensive kind. Each of these convents has a carriage and servants in livery; for the ladies never deign to walk anywhere, but in the park.'

Charlotte was in her pomp. Edward Thompson, who had followed her progress, wrote in the 1770 edition of his poem *The Meretriciad*:

> So great a saint is heavenly Charlotte grown
> She's the first lady abbess of the town;
> In a snug entry leading out Pell Mell
> (which by the urine a bad nose can smell)
> Between th'hotel[86] and Tom Almack's house
> The nunnery stands for each religious use;
> There, there, repair, you'll find some wretched wight
> Upon his knees both morning noon and night!

However, no businesswoman could afford to be complacent. Rivals were always threatening to challenge one's status as London's most fashionable hostess, and the entertainments at Mrs

---

[85] Hickey was to suffer a similar loss. In 1782, he travelled to India with his mistress, Charlotte Barry; she died the following year.
[86] The Golden Lion, at the corner of King's Place and King Street.

Cornelys's soirées or at the Pantheon might lure away customers. One had to innovate.

Accounts of James Cook's voyages in the Pacific had found an enthralled audience in England. When in 1774 Commander Tobias Furneaux returned from Cook's second voyage, he brought with him Omai, a young Tahitian, who made a great impression on society. An ode entitled *Omiah* was addressed to Charlotte Hayes, whom for some reason the poet enjoined to coax Lord Sandwich ('Jemmy Twitcher') to secure Omai's homeward passage.

> Sweet Emily, with auburn tresses,
> Will coax him by her soft caresses,
> And Charlotte win the day;
> Old Jemmy's goatish eyes will twinkle;
> Lust play bo-peep from every wrinkle;
> But first bribe madam Ray.[87]

What fired Charlotte's imagination were the sexual rites of the Pacific islanders. One ceremony involved the deflowering of a young girl in front of an audience of village notables, with a venerable woman called Oberea presiding. Charlotte decided to recreate the spectacle in King's Place, but to introduce more variety to it: there would be not one virgin, but a dozen (as her definition of virginity was loose, the casting did not present a challenge). She hired a dozen lusty young men, with whom the 'unsullied and untainted' nymphs would perform under the tutelage of Queen Oberea, 'in which character Mrs Hayes will appear on this occasion'. Charlotte's invitation advised that the rites would begin 'precisely at seven'. Twenty-three men accepted, mostly including 'the first nobility', along with a few baronets, and five commoners.

---

[87] Martha Ray was Sandwich's mistress. In 1779, she was assassinated by a jealous former lover, James Hackman.

The spectacle entertained these dignitaries for two hours, and 'met with the highest applause from all present'. When a collection came round for 'the votaries of Venus', there was a generous response. Their blood up, the distinguished gentlemen now got their own opportunity to perform with the young women. The evening ended on a festive note, with champagne and musical entertainment in the form of catches and glees. In the account in *Nocturnal Revels*, an exhausted but exultant Charlotte, her last guest having departed at four in the morning, 'threw herself into the arms of the Count, to practise, in part at least, what she was so great a mistress of in theory'.

It was the greatest triumph of Charlotte's career, her equivalent of the moment in April 1770 when Eclipse galloped clear of Bucephalus. She was established, and rich, recognized as the nonpareil of her profession. She was the companion of the owner of the greatest racehorse of the day. Charlotte and Dennis were at the summits of two of the most important leisure industries in Britain.

11

The Stallion

Fifty guineas, the sum Lady Loveit paid for her romp with Captain O'Thunder, was also the cost of sending a mare to Eclipse. In 1771, it was the highest stud fee in England. Like the modern champions Nijinsky and Secretariat, Eclipse had achieved fame that transcended his sport, and his transfer to a role as a begetter of future champions generated huge interest.[88] His sexual attention, Dennis O'Kelly could assume, was a privilege for which owners of mares would fork out an expensive premium.

Eclipse, who had spent most of his racing career in dark stables, now began to enjoy more of the open air. He passed a happy, idle winter in 1770–71, grazing in his paddock at Clay Hill. He put on condition – the equestrian equivalent of a paunch; his neck began to thicken too, slowly transforming him into the imposing, high-crested figure that features in the later portrait by George Garrard (see this book's colour section).

His new career probably began in February 1771. There were sixty or more mares to impregnate in time to enable them to give birth, after an eleven-month pregnancy, in the early months

---

[88] In the TV sitcom *Cheers*, a husband whose broody wife was demanding constant sex complained, 'Even Secretariat gets a break now and again!'

of the following year. The foals' official birthdays would be on 1 May. Today, when horses have their birthdays on 1 January, a foal born after 1 May is considered late. Stallions have to pack a lot of virile activity into a short space of time.

Breeders in the eighteenth century did not know a great deal about when their mares would ovulate.[89] Then, as now, they brought the horses to the stud and left them there, perhaps for a month. Stallion owners advertised in the *Racing Calendar* that the mares would get 'good grass', at a weekly fee of about five shillings. The mare enjoyed this grass for a day or so before her rendezvous.

One of the first mares to meet Eclipse was not a visitor. Clio, a great-granddaughter of the Godolphin Arabian, was one of several mares bought by Dennis to breed to his stallion; by the time of his death, he had amassed a broodmare band of thirty-three. Clio faced an experience that was little different from what would happen at a contemporary stud farm – the central act is the same, after all. A stable boy led her to the breeding shed, or perhaps to a fenced-off area of a paddock. She would not simply allow the stallion to turn up and ravish her: she required foreplay, a task from which, on a stud farm, the stallion is exempted. In his place, the horse with the unfulfilling job of 'teaser' arrived and nuzzled Clio's hindquarters for a while, until she lifted up her tail and released a small stream of urine. It was a signal that she was in season, although the procedure might go ahead even if she did not give such encouragement. It was also the teaser's only reward: once Clio had given it, he was led away. Now Dennis's staff took steps to protect their stallion, binding Clio's hind legs or tying them to posts, because mares in this circumstance were apt to kick out, and had been known to deal fatal blows to their valuable would-be paramours.

[89] The breeder is not the provider of the stallion. To breed is to own brood-mares, and to produce a foal by sending a mare to a particular stallion.

Eclipse and his stud groom approached. Inexperienced as he was, the stallion knew what was on the menu, and as he got close to Clio he let out an unearthly bellow, a neigh transformed into something deep and resonant and scary. He reared, and the staff moved into panicky action. One tried to soothe the mare; another lifted her tail; another two, one of them pushing from the rear, guided the half-ton Eclipse towards docking. Once there, he did not hold back, and was done in a few seconds. He rested on Clio for a couple of moments longer, before withdrawing. As Dennis's was a well-managed stud with a regard for hygiene, Eclipse had his penis and testicles washed before he returned to his paddock – the importance of this procedure would be demonstrated a few years later when the great stallion Herod, bred like Eclipse by the Duke of Cumberland, died following an inflammation of his penis sheath. Eclipse was probably due to be on duty again later in the day.

The mare, calm now, returned to her paddock. Everyone hoped that Eclipse's sperm was fusing with Clio's ovum to produce an embryo, but, as this was 1771, they could not scan to check. The best that the stud managers could do was try to maximize Clio's chances of getting pregnant. They may have arranged for Eclipse to cover her again, the same day or within a day or two. Over the course of the next month, they presented her to the teaser a couple of times more; when she showed no interest, they assumed that she had conceived. While Clio remained in her own paddock, visiting mares would return home at this stage. Their grooms and other staff from their studs would arrive, pay the fees (fifty guineas, a guinea for the groom, and grazing fees) and take them away. If any mares turned out not to be 'in foal', Dennis would offer a special deal next season.[90]

The greater frequency of double coverings is the main dif-

[90] Today, when the science of breeding is more accurate, stud owners usually give a live foal guarantee, offering a free subsequent mating if the first one is unproductive.

ference between the eighteenth-century stud and a modern farm. Now that scanning has reduced the reliance on double coverings, stallions are able to cover more mares. Eclipse, in his first season, covered sixty mares, as well as those owned by Dennis; a leading contemporary sire such as Montjeu, standing at the Coolmore stud in Ireland, covers a hundred mares or more each spring. In 2007, the National Hunt sire Oscar managed, with unflagging virility, 367 different coverings. Some stallions do not even get a holiday. At the end of the season, 'shuttle stallions' travel to the southern hemisphere and put in another stint there. It is a busy job; but they have to do it, because the Thoroughbred industry, wishing to preserve the integrity of the breed, has never contemplated the introduction of artificial insemination.

In spring 1772, Clio gave birth to a male foal, named Horizon. By the time Horizon was a yearling, Dennis faced the quandary of all owner-breeders: whether to sell the horse, or train him for racing. If he sold, he earned instant money. If he raced the horse, and other home-bred colts and fillies, he might find that they would show the ability to become valuable stallions and broodmares of the future; on the other hand, he could not afford to give the impression that he was holding on to the best ones and selling only the dross. He held on to Horizon. Two years later, Horizon became the first offspring of Eclipse to race, and won a match over a mile at Abingdon, earning 300 guineas. But his subsequent career was moderate, and he did not graduate to become a stallion.

Such is the story of the vast majority of horses in training, including impeccably bred ones. Great racehorses are rare, only a small percentage of that rare group become successful stallions, and only a small percentage of those successful stallions become part of an enduring line in a Thoroughbred dynasty. In 1771, there were three stallions – Herod, Matchem and Eclipse – who were to join this elite group; and the Eclipse line was to dominate those of the other two by a ratio of more than nine to one.

Actually, there were four stallions in this elite group, because Eclipse's sire, Marske, was still in business – indeed, after fifteen years at stud, he was only now, thanks to Eclipse's exploits, coming into fashion. As mentioned earlier, William Wildman had bought him from a Hampshire farmer for twenty guineas, and in 1769 stood the horse at the Gibbons Grove stud in Mickleham at a fee of five guineas. That was the year when Eclipse hit the race-course, winning five King's Plates and suddenly suggesting that his neglected father might be worth something after all. Wildman raised Marske's fee accordingly, to ten guineas; by 1772, he was asking for thirty guineas, and was also taking steps to quash a threatening rumour that was circulating, to the effect that a stallion called Shakespeare, and not Marske, was Eclipse's real father. Wildman's advertisement for Marske in the *Racing Calendar* included the statement: 'Mask [*sic*] was the sire of Eclipse. Witness my hand, B. Smith, stud groom to the late Duke of Cumberland.' Most people believed him, but not everyone.

The believers included the Earl of Abingdon. Once again – following his sales of Gimcrack and Eclipse – Wildman decided to offload an asset once its value started to rise, and he sold Marske to Abingdon, who paid 1,000 guineas for the horse. The Earl, who sported the Wodehouseian name of Willoughby Bertie, bumped up Marske's stud fee and earned back the purchase price within a season. Standing him at Rycot in Oxfordshire, Abingdon set the fee at fifty guineas, and a year later he doubled it. One hundred guineas was the highest sum commanded by any stallion of the era. *The Sporting Magazine* claimed that Abingdon demanded 200 guineas for Marske's services one year, and the equestrian writer John Lawrence trumped that claim with 300 guineas, although there is no corroboration of these figures in the racing calendars of the period. Marske became champion sire[91] in 1775, and again in 1776.

[91] The sire whose offspring earn most money through racing.

His involvement with Eclipse and Marske apart, Wildman remains of interest to us on account of his association with George Stubbs. One of his commissions from the artist was rediscovered recently, and fetched a small fortune. It is a painting of Wildman's horse Euston, a grey son of Antinous bred by the Duke of Grafton and the winner of twelve consecutive races, including two King's Plates, in 1773 and 1774. Euston, alert head turned inquisitively, is tall and fine-framed, and carries a jockey wearing crimson silks, which Wildman presumably adopted on passing his original colours to Dennis O'Kelly. The horse is set against a country landscape, possibly Grafton's estate, with the land behind him falling to a lake with a walled tower on the furthest bank, and beyond that hills rolling into a misty distance. As in many of Stubbs's paintings with country settings, the horse is posed next to trees – in this case, an oak and a willow, of a slenderness to match Euston's physique. What is he doing here, ready to race and with a jockey on his back but far from a racecourse? The answer is prosaic, though the effect of the painting is not. Stubbs was not greatly interested in racing scenes, and quite often plopped down his racehorses against backgrounds chosen simply because his clients would find them pleasing. It gives his work an other-worldly, haunting quality.

Stubbs exhibited the painting at his first, 1775 exhibition at the Royal Academy. After the Wildman dispersal sale, *Portrait of a Horse Named Euston, Belonging to Mr Wildman* passed through several hands, until no one knew, or could discern, the identity of the horse. Only when the painting went for cleaning in the late 1990s was the title revealed. Restored, the portrait went on sale at Sotheby's in November 2000, and fetched £2.7 million – the third highest price ever paid for a work by Stubbs.

The most touching legacy of the relationship between Wildman and Stubbs is the study – some call it a 'conversation piece' – *Eclipse with William Wildman and His Sons John and James*. It is one of the rare Stubbs paintings of a racehorse and owner, leading you to suppose that he was friendlier with Wildman, a fellow self-made man, than with his aristocratic patrons. It shows family members at ease with one another and proud of their horse, and is especially poignant in the light of Robert Fountain's evidence, in his essay *William Wildman and George Stubbs*, that one of these boys and maybe both did not survive their father.[92]

William Wildman – meat salesman, first owner of Eclipse, and art patron – died on Christmas Day, 1784, aged sixty-six. At his dispersal sale at Christie's in 1787, the lots formed, however you count them (there were nineteen paintings according to Fountain's sums, and seventeen according to Judy Egerton's), the most important contemporary collection of Stubbs's work along-side the Prince of Wales's. They depicted racehorses, dogs, a lioness and a panther; a series of four paintings may show Wildman and a friend, two hearty men of middle age, as the visitors from the 'smoaky town' on a shooting expedition at the estate of the Duke of Portland. The sale included some 150 other paintings, including a Rubens and a da Vinci, and fetched, according to Fountain, the very modest-seeming sum of £665 – a figure that, translated to the present-day equivalent of £67,000, is insignificant in the context of subsequent valuations.

Marske, also painted by Stubbs (see colour section) following a Wildman commission, died in July 1779. He had sired 154 winning horses, whose 352 victories earned £72,000. A poet called Samuel Harding, perhaps at the behest of Abingdon, made the following attempt to immortalize him:

Dissolved in tears, ye sportsmen, mourn the loss,
Renowned Rycote bears the heavy cross,
Old MARSK is dead! the King of horses gone,
Sire to Eclipse, who ne'er was beat by none,

[92] There is a fuller discussion of this painting in chapter 18.

Eclipse doth mourn, Transit, Shark, Pretender;
He was their sire. – grim Death made him surrender.

If that effort had been his only memorial, Marske would not have been remembered for long. Fortunately, his descendants did a more eloquent job.

Eclipse stood at stud from 1771 to 1788, and sired, at a rough estimate, 500 colts and fillies. The best of them, and the one who was to continue the male line that is most influential today, came early. In 1772, the Earl of Abingdon, who had not yet bought Marske, sent his mare Sportsmistress from Oxfordshire to Clay Hill. The following spring, Sportsmistress gave birth to a colt, chestnut like both his parents, and with a white blaze like his father's. Abingdon's stable staff referred to the foal as 'Potato', a name, according to legend, that one lad rendered in writing on a corn bin as 'Potoooooooo'. The horse became Pot8os. His later owner, Earl Grosvenor, tickled his audience at White's club by observing, 'Must say the boy could count, even if he couldn't spell.'

In a five-year career from 1777 to 1782, Pot8os won numerous races at Newmarket, including two Jockey Club Plates and two prizes worth 700 guineas each, and he also enjoyed three victories in a race called the Clermont Cup, all by walkovers. At ten, he retired to Grosvenor's Oxcroft Stud in Cambridgeshire. By that age, most twenty-first-century stallions have been at stud for six seasons. Nevertheless, Pot8os had time to sire 172 winning sons and daughters, among them Waxy, who continued the Eclipse male line from which a huge majority of contemporary Thoroughbreds descend.

Pot8os's defeated opponents included another son of Eclipse, King Fergus. Out of a mare called Creeping Polly, King Fergus was sold by his breeder, Mr Carver, back to Dennis, and forged a racing career of moderate distinction, with highlights including several valuable matches at Newmarket. He seemed unlikely to become a prized stallion, and passed an unsuccessful spell at stud in Ireland before returning to England, where he caught the eye of an owner and breeder called John Hutchinson. Like the jockey and trainer John Singleton,[93] Hutchinson was a horseman of modest birth who had managed to climb the social rankings. Starting out as a stable boy to Sir Robert Eden, who bred Eclipse's dam Spilletta, he went on to train for Peregrine Wentworth, owner of Eclipse's defeated opponent Bucephalus, and rose to become an owner and breeder. He took a liking to King Fergus's 'wonderfully clean legs' and 'mak' an' shap' (he meant, one supposes, the horse's conformation), judgements that were to prove sound. The stallion sired numerous good horses, including Hambletonian – the hero of *Hambletonian, Rubbing Down*, widely considered to be George Stubbs's greatest painting. Through Hambletonian, the line continued to the great and undefeated St Simon (born in 1881); the Prince of Wales's Derby winner Persimmon (b. 1893); the Italian champion Ribot, twice a winner (in 1955 and 1956) of the Prix de l'Arc de Triomphe; and Alleged, another dual Arc winner (1977 and 1978).

You can see how rare it is to make an enduring mark in bloodstock breeding. Eclipse is the most influential sire of all time thanks to only two of his hundreds of sons. While some others did well at stud, their male descendants, sooner or later, flopped, and their male lines died out.

Breeders of the era could not foresee these developments. All they had to go on were the performances of Eclipse's sons and daughters on the racecourse. What particularly strikes the contemporary observer is that Eclipse sired three of the first five winners of the Derby: Young Eclipse (1781), Saltram (1783), and Sergeant (1784). But the Derby was not yet the most prestigious

[93] See chapter 8.

George Stubbs's best-known painting of Eclipse
shows him at Newmarket, before the toughest
challenge of his career.

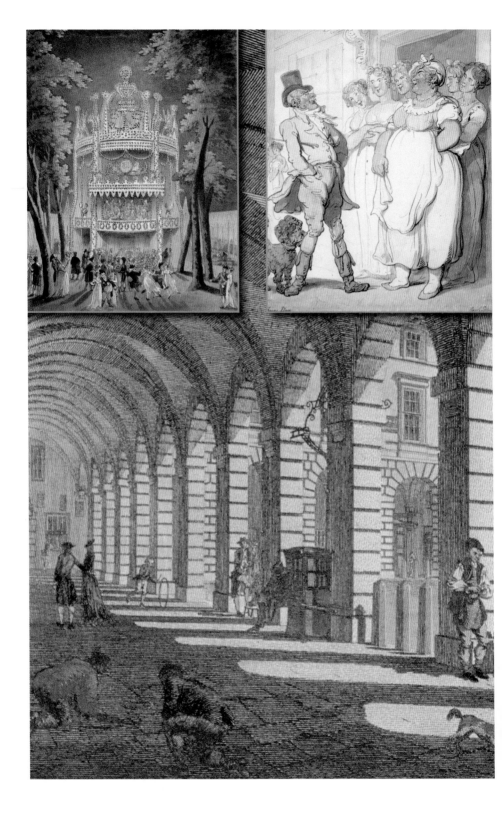

Scenes from the louche London over which Charlotte Hayes reigned: (**main picture**) Covent Garden, her spiritual home; (**left**) the Vauxhall pleasure gardens, where Londoners gathered to see and be seen; (**centre**) a gentleman is the centre of attention for some King's Place 'nuns'; (**right**) a St James's beauty looks out towards the palace, expecting her royal lover.

Above: Eclipse's long-undervalued sire Marske, painted by Stubbs.

Below: J. N. Sartorius's *Eclipse with Oakley Up*, showing the horse's low head carriage while galloping.

The Duke of Cumberland at play, on a surprisingly buoyant horse, on his Windsor estate.

Stubbs's touching portrait of Wildman and his sons.

The Eclipse Macarony, a surely ironic title (a macarony was a dandy) for the gross, bearish Dennis O'Kelly.

Above: caricaturists did not hold back from depicting the Prince of Wales and his jockey, Chifney, as guilty of pulling their horse, Escape.

Below: Thomas Rowlandson's portrait of members of the Jockey Club, an assembly from which Dennis O'Kelly was excluded.

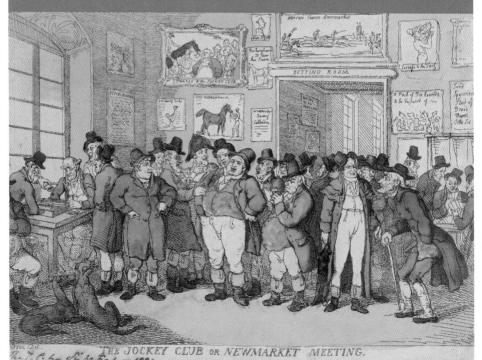

Dennis O'Kelly's nemesis, Sir Charles Bunbury, a.k.a. the first Dictator of the Turf (black coat – though some historians question the identification).

Eclipse by George Garrard, who painted the
horse at stud, with a stallion's high crest.

horse race in the world. It was a new contest, and over what was, by the standards prevalent when Eclipse was racing, a short distance. For breeders, the victories confirmed the impression that although the progeny of Eclipse were speedy, they did not necessarily have 'bottom'.

In the 1770s, Eclipse faced competition as a stallion from highly regarded rivals such as Matchem and Snap, about whom the breeding adage went, 'Snap for speed, and Matchem for truth and daylight' – truth and daylight in this context meaning soundness and stamina. Then there was Marske, Eclipse's own father. Marske was succeeded, following his two years as champion sire, by Herod, who held the title from 1777 to 1784 and who handed over the crown to his son, Highflyer, champion from 1785 to 1796, and again in 1798. (King Fergus managed to intervene in 1797; one historian thinks that Pot8os, another Eclipse son, was the true champion in 1794.) The writer John Lawrence introduced the now-insignificant Goldfinder as another competitor: 'The produce of Eclipse ran too generally and exclusively to speed; and that, in toughness and continuance, they were greatly surpassed by their competitors on the course, the stock of King Herod and Goldfinder.' Eclipse was in fact never champion sire, finishing runner-up to Herod and then to Highflyer every year from 1778 to 1788.

How could this be? Eclipse's celebrity, and the subsequent records of his descendants, make his failure to win a single sire's championship appear extraordinary. Every contemporary reference to Eclipse indicates that he was a household name: the Seabiscuit, the Red Rum, the Desert Orchid of his day, only with a far more awesome reputation as a racer. The flamboyant, dodgy personality of his owner, Dennis O'Kelly, heightened the mystique, as did Dennis's talent for hype. Yet the words of John Lawrence – one of Eclipse's greatest admirers – hint that a few observers may have been able to separate their awe for Eclipse from their assessment of his progeny. There were also class considerations: some men of the Turf preferred not to do business with a scandalous Irish upstart.[94]

Richard Tattersall, who had supported the rumour that Shakespeare was Eclipse's sire, was gleeful when a colt called Noble won the 1786 Derby. Noble, who had started at the huge price of 30-1, was a son of Tattersall's stallion Highflyer, and defeated the favourite, Eclipse's son Meteor. Eclipse had had his day, Tattersall exulted. Described in a nineteenth-century history of the Jockey Club as 'an auctioneer, though of excellent repute' (the same work characterized Dennis O'Kelly as 'a disreputable adventurer'), Tattersall was hugely proud of Highflyer. He built a mansion called Highflyer Hall, and was pictured there, bluff of countenance and sporting a wide-brimmed hat, standing in front of a painting of the horse and with his hand resting on a document bearing the instruction 'Highflyer not to be sold' (see colour section). When Highflyer died, in 1793, Tattersall's tribute to him – more touching than Harding's ode to Marske – was this gravestone inscription: 'Here lieth the perfect and beautiful symmetry of the much lamented Highflyer, by whom and his wonderful offspring the celebrated Tattersall acquired a noble fortune, and was not ashamed to acknowledge it.'

Tattersall and his contemporaries would have expected the Herod and Highflyer male line, and that of Matchem, to have surpassed Eclipse's in later generations. But Eclipse has come out on top – by a distance. It is estimated that 95 per cent of contemporary Thoroughbreds are Eclipse's male line descendants. A check of the lists of top contemporary stallions suggests that the percentage may be even higher than that: the representatives of the Herod and Matchem lines are sparse. How did Eclipse become, in

---

[94] Also, Herod and Highflyer were more local to many of the top breeders. And O'Kelly, not being a member of the Jockey Club, could not race his Eclipse progeny in certain valuable matches that might have boosted the prize money credited to their sire.

the words of racing historian Arthur FitzGerald, 'the most influential stallion in the history of the Thoroughbred'?

Herod and Highflyer have a good deal to do with it. Georgian breeders noted that uniting the Herod and Eclipse lines was a remarkably effective 'nick' – a cross that produced outstanding racers. At his death, Dennis O'Kelly owned nine daughters of Herod, whom he had bought to breed with Eclipse and with Eclipse's sons. The nick also worked the other way round, when Herod covered Eclipse's daughters, and it worked when Herod's son Highflyer covered Eclipse's daughters.[95] 'Send me your Eclipse mares,' Richard Tattersall said, 'and you shall have the best racehorses in England as a result.' It was no vain boast; and it offered a formula for the breeding of champions for years to come.

[95] I apologize for neglecting the female role in my discussion of Eclipse's male descendants. His daughters are also significant presences in pedigrees. Horses, of course, inherit half their genes from their fathers and half from their mothers, so there is no reason to treat the sire as more important. However, a successful sire produces hundreds (these days, thousands) of offspring, whereas a successful dam produces, if she is particularly fertile and robust, about ten. Moreover, the Thoroughbred is an inbred animal, so the male line saturates pedigrees to an ever greater extent as the generations continue. That is why the Eclipse male line is so important.

12

The Most Glorious Spectacle

IN THE LAST QUARTER of the eighteenth century, one world began to make way for another. Concepts of citizenship, alien to Britain's royalist traditions, fuelled revolutions in America and France. Wars transformed the map of Europe. Industrialization gathered pace, bringing with it a more turbulent social structure. The press became a mass medium. There was a new imaginative atmosphere: in place of the earthy humour of Henry Fielding, there was the fine moral discrimination of Jane Austen, and the robust intellectual conservatism of Samuel Johnson was followed by the Romantic idealism of William Wordsworth, Samuel Taylor Coleridge and Percy Bysshe Shelley. Gentlemen and ladies were expected to behave with far greater decorum than had their scandalous predecessors. There was a new notion of personality. Observing the likes of Charles James Fox, William Hickey and even Dennis O'Kelly, you get the impression of a certain self-consciousness, as if these men were playing a game or had adopted roles: the flamboyant statesman, the rake, the sporting dandy. While the ideal of the British sporting gentleman persisted, a new ideal, of sincerity to the true self, came to inspire people's behaviour.

One risks bathos by appending horseracing, aptly described

as the 'great triviality',[96] to this list. But remember the scene on Derby day. No other sport has so many ties to so many levels of society. It was bound to change too.

In essence, the eighteenth-century gentlemanly pursuit became a mass entertainment, and more professional – more industrialized, if you like. Three men were at the heart of the transformation of racing, driving innovations that continue to shape the sport today; and they were all Eclipse's contemporaries.

In about 1750, a group of sporting gentlemen took to meeting regularly in the Star and Garter pub in St James's. Calling themselves the Jockey Club, they established a race to be staged during the spring meeting at Newmarket, where they acquired premises: 'A contribution free plate [the entrants did not have to pay a fee], by horses the property of the noblemen and gentlemen belonging to the Jockey Club at the Star and Garter in Pall Mall, one heat on the Round Course, weight eight stone, seven pound.'

The Jockey Club, which evolved into an administrative body and later moved into estate management, is not what we normally understand by the word club, and it has no jockeys in it. In the eighteenth century, groups of men meeting frequently, such as those taking regular rooms in coffee houses or taverns, tended to call themselves clubs. Jockeys were owners and others connected to the Turf. At first, the noblemen and gentlemen probably thought of the JC as a forum for socializing, drinking, and challenging each other to races, but soon they began giving instructions on how races were to be run, and they gradually assumed the status of the governing body at Newmarket. Later, they were to govern the whole of British racing, with responsibilities such as compiling the fixture list, controlling the rules of the sport, disciplining miscreants, licensing trainers and jockeys and other staff, and ensuring proper veterinary care; they also

[96] By Phil Bull, the founder of the ratings organization Timeform.

acquired a good deal of land, as well as various racecourses.[97]

In 1762, the Jockey Club announced the official colours that members would use consistently thenceforth. The men who registered their colours included a royal duke (Cumberland – riders of his horses wore purple), five other dukes, a marquess, five earls, a viscount, and a baron. A historian of the JC wrote that the members were 'almost to a man, of royal or noble or hereditarily gentle birth; and they were, almost to a man, either hereditary or elective legislators, for nearly all the commoners, or at any rate a large proportion of them, were Members of Parliament'. (That was exactly the profile of the clientele at Charlotte Hayes's King's Place nunnery.) An industrialist commented, perhaps with bitterness, that 'To become a member of the Jockey Club you have to be a relative of God – and a close one at that.'

Such breeding did not mean that JC members were not rackety. They gambled, they drank and they womanized. Their first home, the Star and Garter, was where Lord Byron (great-uncle of the poet) killed a man called Chaworth following an argument about dealing with poachers, and where Lord Barrymore bet successfully that he could find a man who would eat a live cat. (It was also where, in 1774, the rules of cricket were refined.) In 1792, a member called Charles Pigott broke ranks to write *The Jockey Club: Or a Sketch of the Manners of the Age*, a scandalous collection of portraits of contemporaries from the Prince of Wales down. Pigott was expelled.

One member who remained above reproach, however, was

[97] Having argued that horseracing reflects society, I must concede that sometimes the adaptation to wider influences is sluggish. The Jockey Club, a self-selecting body, ran British racing, the tenth largest industry in the country, until 1993, when it transferred its administrative responsibilities to the British Horseracing Board. In 2006, the JC handed over the policing of the sport to the Horseracing Regulatory Authority. A year later, the BHB and HRA merged, to form the British Horseracing Authority. Now, the JC concentrates on the administration of its racecourses and other estates.

the baronet Sir Charles Bunbury, the man who cemented the JC's position as the authority of racing. Uninspiring both as an MP and as a husband, Bunbury did not allow the elopement of his wife Lady Sarah to deflect him from his real passion, Turf affairs. (He had, briefly, entertained the notion of challenging Sarah's lover Lord William Gordon to a duel, until it was pointed out to him that if adultery were to be the grounds, he might have to issue challenges to quite a few other men as well.) He immersed himself in racing and in his role as steward of the Jockey Club, of which he was later recognized as perpetual president, or 'Dictator of the Turf'.

Bunbury's sturdiness was the making of the Jockey Club. When the Prince of Wales became involved in a racing scandal, Bunbury did not hesitate to instruct the heir to the throne on how he was expected to behave.[98] His inflexible nature could cause him to be mean, however. When his colt Smolensko, ridden by Tom Goodisson, won the 1813 Derby, Bunbury and others won a considerable amount of money from a bookmaker called Brograve. Unable to honour the bets, Brograve shot himself. Paying Goodisson, who had ridden Smolensko to three victories, Bunbury handed over just a modest sum; Brograve's drastic default, he explained, meant that it was all he could afford.

Today, Eclipse's peerless status has biblical authority in the racing world. He is one of the rare historical figures to achieve a reputation beyond dispute. Sport, in which achievement is usually measurable, arouses just as much disagreement among aficionados as do more subjective matters such as the arts — tennis fans, for example, differ about the relative merits of Bjorn Borg and John McEnroe, in spite of the existence of records, and even head-to-head results, that might settle the issue. But at least there is a record of Eclipse's achievements: we know the races he won, who

[98] This was the Escape Affair. See chapter 17.

his opponents were, in some cases how easily he won, and how favoured he was in the betting. We can also trace his extraordinary influence as a stallion.

The man largely responsible for introducing authority to racing records, as Bunbury brought it to the sport's governance, was James Weatherby. A Durham solicitor, Weatherby came to Newmarket in 1770 as keeper of the match book – the record of match races arranged and run – and secretary of the Jockey Club. We do not know a great deal about him, except that he was quite an operator.

The first 'racing calendar', John Cheny's *An Historical List of All Horse Matches Run, and of All Plates and Prizes Run for in England*, had appeared in 1727. Before that, when record keeping was in the hands of keepers of private stud books, accounts of races were rare – a fortunate exception being this glimpse, from the Duke of Devonshire's stud book, of the brilliance of Flying Childers: 'Chillders [*sic*] & Fox run over ye long course, Chillders carried 9 stone, Fox 8 stone. Chillders beat Fox a distance and a half.' Cheny's and subsequent calendars included race results, notices of rules, selected records of cock fights, advertisements promoting stallions, and advertisements for medicines such as 'Watson's Cambridge horse balls'. However, when Weatherby arrived on the scene, during Eclipse's second season, there were rival calendars, one edited by Mr B. Walker, the other by William Tuting and Thomas Fawconer.

After Walker withdrew from the market, Weatherby, who had supplanted Tuting as keeper of the match book and Fawconer as Jockey Club secretary, set about supplanting their racing calendar as well. He persuaded Tuting to abandon Fawconer; then he seized and concealed 1,600 copies of Fawconer's calendar before it came out. Why were Fawconer's subscribers not furious with him? Whatever Weatherby's tactics were for deflecting the blame for the disappearance of the books, they worked, and in 1774 he found a healthy collection of subscribers for his own publication (a record of the 1773 season). Fawconer carried on nonetheless, but died in 1777. At this point, Weatherby announced brazenly that Fawconer's 1772 edition, 'having hitherto been distributed to but a few of the subscribers, the rest of the subscribers, and others, are hereby informed that the same may be had of Mr Weatherby'.

Racing results were only half of the records that racing, if it were to be an efficient industry, required. They needed to be supplemented by, and linked to, pedigrees. In the words of a modern historian, a fair market in horses requires accurate pedigrees as surely as the motor market requires vehicle registration documents. Anyone making a commercial decision about bloodstock will ask: what is a horse's breeding, what were the performances of its ancestors, and what does that evidence suggest about the horse's potential? The answers, until Weatherby came along, were usually vague.

Weatherby's nephew, also called James, set about producing a comprehensive account of racing bloodlines, commissioning an author called William Sydney Towers to research in old racing calendars and in whatever private stud books he could lay his hands on. In 1791, *An Introduction to a General Stud Book* (compiled by Towers) began the job of rescuing the Turf 'from the increasing evil of false and inaccurate pedigrees'; it was succeeded by further introductions, until the volume regarded as the definitive first edition of the *General Stud Book* appeared, in 1808.

The *GSB* listed mares with their offspring. Looking for Eclipse in the index, we are directed to Spilletta, 'Bred by Sir Robert Eden, foaled in 1749, got by Regulus, her dam (Mother Western) by Smith's Son of Snake – Lord D'Arcy's Old Montagu – Hautboy – Brimmer.' (These last three names are the damsires in the tail female line – the bottom line of the pedigree, from mother to her mother, and then to her mother's mother, and so on.) Spilletta's foals are a bay filly (foaled in 1759) by the Duke of Cumberland's Crab; Eclipse (1764) by Marske; Proserpine (1766) by Marske; Garrick (1772) by Marske; and Briseis (1774) by Chrysolite.[99] We can trace further male lines in the pedigree by looking for Eclipse's sire Marske (out of the Ruby Mare) in the index, and then for Marske's sire Squirt (out of Sister to Old Country Wench), and so on. A later volume of the *GSB* authorized Eclipse's date of birth as 1 April 1764: 'Eclipse was so called, not because he eclipsed all competitors, but from having been foaled during the great eclipse of 1764.'

Assembling this information, from inconsistent calendars and private records of fitful reliability, must have been a painstaking and frustrating job. But Weatherby and Towers performed it with remarkable accuracy. There were further, even thornier problems for compilers of later editions, as more and more horses came up for inclusion. Who should be in, and who out? The editors explained that 'half-bred' animals were not eligible; and in 1821, they first mentioned the implied contrasting term, 'Thoroughbred'. By it, they meant a horse descended from a particular group of mares, accepted as the foundation mothers of the breed.

One of the earliest quandaries concerned a horse who was, like his grandfather Eclipse, a national celebrity. Copenhagen was Wellington's charger at the Battle of Waterloo. He had inherited the Eclipse temperament: when Wellington dismounted following the battle and gave him a pat, Copenhagen lashed out, nearly achieving the fatal blow that Napoleon's forces had failed to land. Not bearing a grudge, Wellington said of him, 'There may have been many faster horses, no doubt many handsomer, but for bottom and endurance I never saw his fellow.' The problem was Copenhagen's inheritance from Lady Catherine, his mother. Lady Catherine's owner, General Grosvenor, had lobbied to get her included in the *GSB*, and Copenhagen appeared in one edition as well. But the editors later removed them, on the grounds that

---

[99] Eclipse's pedigree is examined in Appendix 2.

among Lady Catherine's ancestors was 'a hunting mare not thorough-bred'.

There were more incendiary issues than this to come, with implications for international diplomacy. The term 'Thoroughbred' evolved to mean, in effect, 'horses granted admission to the *General Stud Book*'. But that caused a problem when racing developed as an international sport and industry, because Weatherbys could not trace back a good many American horses, for example, to the English foundation mares. Much ill feeling ensued: while English bloodstock experts argued that 'the pages of the *Stud Book* should be zealously safeguarded', American breeders thought that the dastardly British were closing off the market by stigmatizing American horses as half-bred. The dispute did not begin to be resolved until the middle of the twentieth century, and a more practical definition of 'Thoroughbred' at last appeared in 1969.[100] More recently, Weatherbys has granted admission to horses traced to sources in the stud books of other countries. The ancestry of the Thoroughbred is no longer exclusively English.[101]

Dealing with such matters is more than a simple publishing job. Weatherbys, which is still in business and still a family firm (and which, after James Weatherby's initial shenanigans, has maintained a fine reputation for integrity), continues to compile the

[100] 'Any horse claiming admission to the *General Stud Book* should be able: 1. To be traced in all points of its pedigree to strains already appearing in pedigrees in earlier volumes of the *General Stud Book*, those strains to be designated "thoroughbred". Or: 2. To prove satisfactorily eight "thoroughbred" crosses consecutively including the cross of which it is the progeny and to show such performances on the Turf in all sections of its pedigree as to warrant its assimilation with "thoroughbreds".'

[101] Or rather, traceable to imported sires and to English-domiciled mares whose precise breeding is unknown, but that may have included a good deal of Eastern blood. British racing, both Flat and National Hunt, has always been open to non-Thoroughbreds: in 1948, two English Classics, the 2,000 Guineas and St Leger, were won by horses (My Babu and Black Tarquin respectively) whom the *GSB* considered unacceptable.

Racing Calendar and *General Stud Book,* and also manages race entries, issues lists of runners and riders, allocates weights, registers horses and owners, and collects and distributes prize money. It is a kind of civil service of British racing.

Our third influential man of the Turf left us the race that was to represent the summit of Thoroughbred achievement, as well as one of the most widely used of all eponyms: Derby.

From the 1770s, racing's organizers began to introduce new kinds of contests, both to encourage the speediness that stallions such as Eclipse were engendering, and to offer better spectacles to the public. Four-mile heats went out of fashion, and in came shorter races, which you might be able to see from start to finish if you had a decent vantage point, and which took a few minutes, rather than a whole afternoon, to decide[102] (they were to heat races roughly what limited-overs cricket matches are to five-day Tests). Racecourses also staged races that encouraged ordinary people to bet. At matches and plates, huge sums were bet by racing insiders and their friends, who felt that they knew what was going to happen. Now handicaps, which assigned weights to horses according to their abilities, created – at least in theory – a more open betting market. In 1791, forty thousand people gathered at Ascot to watch the Oatlands Stakes, in which the bottom weight and officially least able horse carried 5st 3lb (it is hard to form a mental image of his jockey), and the top weight and officially best horse carried 9st 10lb. The winner, at 20-1, was

---

[102] Match racing took longer to decline. One of the most celebrated races of the nineteenth century, drawing a hundred thousand spectators to York in spring 1851, was the match in which The Flying Dutchman (the 1849 Derby winner) defeated Voltigeur (the 1850 winner), avenging a shock defeat the previous autumn. A few matches continued to take place in the twentieth century, most famously – the fame of the contest revived by a hit book and film – between Seabiscuit and War Admiral on 1 November 1938, when Seabiscuit triumphed by four lengths.

Baronet,[103] owned by the Prince of Wales. As a betting magnet, the race was a huge success, with £100,000 staked on the result; as an enricher of punters, however, it was a disaster. So few people had backed Baronet that, a contemporary wrote, 'Horses are daily thrown out of training, jockeys are going into mourning, grooms are becoming EO [roulette] merchants and strappers are going on the highway.'

Some of the most venerable races in the calendar followed the Oatlands Stakes model: the Ebor, the Cambridgeshire and the Grand National are among the examples. The Melbourne Cup, the race that stops Australia, is also a handicap. The Santa Anita Handicap is the event that Seabiscuit's owner, Charles Howard, most wanted to win. However, it is the Classics and prestigious weight-for-age races (older horses carry more weight, but otherwise the weights are level) that reveal the greatest champions: the St Simons, Nijinskys and Secretariats. These races have also revealed the supremacy of the Eclipse line.

The first of these races, which came to be known as the Classics, was the St Leger. In 1776, a group of sportsmen subscribed to a new sweepstakes – a relatively recent innovation, in which several owners advanced entry fees that formed the prize money – at Doncaster. The race was over two miles (later reduced to its current distance of an extended one mile, six furlongs), and it was won by Lord Rockingham's Allabaculia.[104] In 1778, the sportsmen voted to name their race after one of their number, General Anthony St Leger, an Irish-born, Eton and Cambridge-educated former MP who bred and raced horses from the nearby Park Hill estate.

The catalyst for the next two Classics was another Eton and

---

[103] Baronet was a son of Vertumnus, who was standing at the O'Kelly stud. Vertumnus's sire was Eclipse.

[104] By a sire called Sampson, Allabaculia – unnamed, as was the race, in the first records – was a great-granddaughter of Flying Childers. Her dam is unknown.

Cambridge man. Edward Smith-Stanley, the 12th Earl of Derby, began his association with Epsom in 1773, when at the age of twenty-one he took over the lease of a nearby house called The Oaks. A year later, he married Lady Elizabeth Hamilton. The wedding was grand. General John Burgoyne, who had owned the property previously and who three years later was to surrender to American forces at Saratoga, played host and wrote a masque, *The Maid of the Oaks*, for the occasion; David Garrick, the actor and impresario, stage-managed the drama; Robert Adam, the great architect, designed the dance pavilion. But despite this splendid inauguration, and the arrivals of two daughters and a son, the marriage foundered. While playing cricket at The Oaks, Lady Derby met the Duke of Dorset, fell in love, and ran off with him. Lord Derby declined to divorce her, so preventing her from marrying the Duke, but also preventing himself from marrying the woman he loved, the actress Elizabeth 'Nellie' Farren. Lady Derby's death in 1797 cleared the way. This second union was much happier, even though Lord Derby's new bride did draw the line, the historian Roger Mortimer wrote, 'at cock-fights staged in her drawing room'.

In other respects, Derby was a jovial, convivial figure. He hosted regular house parties, and at one of them the company agreed to establish on nearby Epsom Downs a new race, over a distance of a mile and a half, for three-year-old fillies. In tribute to the hospitality that brought it about, they named the race the Oaks. It was a sweepstakes, and the first running, in 1779, attracted seventeen subscribers contributing fifty guineas each to the prize fund, with twelve fillies eventually going to post. One of them, a daughter of Herod called Bridget, was Derby's; she was the 5-2 favourite, and she won. Down the field was an Eclipse filly with the bare name Sister of Pot8os. She was owned by Dennis O'Kelly.

Reconvening at The Oaks, Derby and his guests agreed that their fillies' race had been a great success, and that they should

Lord Derby's house The Oaks, after which the classic race for fillies was named, and where, reputedly, Derby and Charles Bunbury agreed the naming of the Derby Stakes on the toss of a coin.

supplement it with another new sweepstakes, this time for both colts and fillies and over a mile, the following year. But what to call the race? Sir Charles Bunbury was among the party, and he, intent on encouraging speedier Thoroughbreds, had been a great promoter of these shorter races, for younger horses, carrying lighter weights. Perhaps the race should be named after him? And so we come to another racing legend: Bunbury and Derby competed for the honour by tossing a coin, and Derby won.[105] Had Bunbury called the toss correctly, we assume, the great race would have been named the Bunbury; the 'Run for the Roses' at Churchill Downs would be the Kentucky Bunbury; a football match between Arsenal and Tottenham would be a North London bunbury; and motor cars would crash into one another in demolition bunburys. As it is, we remember Sir Charles with the Bunbury Cup, a seven-furlong handicap at the Newmarket July meeting.[106]

A year later, on 4 May 1780, Bunbury gained compensation when his colt Diomed (6-4 favourite) became the first winner of the Derby Stakes. Second was Dennis O'Kelly's Boudrow (4-1), by Eclipse. The nine competitors raced over the last mile of the course that Eclipse had graced eleven years earlier. This race was even more popular than the Oaks, attracting thirty-six subscribers and eventually a field of nine, generating a prize fund for Bunbury of 1,125 guineas.

Diomed, by a son of Herod called Florizel, was not at first a shining advertisement for the Derby Stakes. His subsequent racing record was mixed, and his stud career was so undistinguished that

---

[105] This famous story first appeared in print some 120 years later, in the second edition (1911) of *The History and Romance of the Derby* by Edward Moorhouse, who cited 'tradition treasured by the descendants of Sir Charles Bunbury'.

[106] 'Bunburying', which probably has nothing to do with Sir Charles, is what Algernon does in Oscar Wilde's play *The Importance of Being Earnest*: it is the invention of a friend who must be visited, and who offers an excuse for pursuing one's interests.

by 1798, when he was twenty-one years old, he was commanding a fee of only two guineas for each mare he covered. Bunbury gave up on him, and sold him to America. As the horse crossed the Atlantic, so did a message from James Weatherby's secretary: 'Mr Weatherby recommends you strongly to avoid putting any mares to [Diomed]; for he has had fine mares to him here, and never produced anything good.' Diomed also had a reputation for firing blanks, semen-wise.

However, just as there was a wonderful alchemy when Arab stallions met English mares on English soil, so was there when Diomed met American mares in Virginia. The stallion would emerge from his stable at a gallop, and set about his procreative task with the enthusiasm and vigour of a horse half his age.[107] Diomed sired numerous champions, right up until his thirtieth year, by which time his covering fee was $50. He died at thirty-one. 'Without Diomed,' a US historian observed, 'the most brilliant pages of our Turf story could never have been written.' Four generations down his male line came Lexington, a stallion who by the end of the nineteenth century was to saturate the pedigrees of the best American racehorses – and who created a headache for the compilers of the General Stud Book, because, like Copenhagen, he had dubious ancestry on his dam's side.

Several of Lord Derby's guests, and particularly Sir Charles Bunbury, would have been dismayed if the rogue Dennis O'Kelly had won the first running of the Derby Stakes. But Dennis had come close, and in 1781 he won the second running, with Young Eclipse. 'Jontlemen,' he told the Munday's coffee house crowd in the weeks before the race, 'this horse is a racer if ever there was one.' Alas, the Derby turned out to be Young Eclipse's finest hour, as it had been Diomed's; and Young Eclipse was not a successful stallion. Describing the horse as 'not a bit too honest', a writer – probably John Lawrence – noted in The Sporting Magazine,

---

[107] According to the Thoroughbred expert Peter Willett in The Classic Racehorse.

'O'Kelly on first training this horse for the Derby, which he won, was certainly deceived, having flattered himself that fortune had favoured him with another Eclipse! Vain expectation, that two such phenomena should appear together in the world! Between Flying Childers and Eclipse, there was an interval of between 40 and 50 years, and we shall be in high luck, indeed, if we can produce a third to those – what a trio! – within 50 years of the latter.'

The writer went on to note that it was not always possible to take the inconsistent form of Dennis's horses at face value: 'race-horses, more particularly in hands such as those of Dennis O'Kelly, are extremely apt to run according to the immediate pecuniary interests of their proprietors'. If the owner wanted to lay against a horse, the horse was apt to run slowly; next time, with the owner's money down at a bigger price, the horse would show miraculous improvement. Such practices, or at least suspicions of them, have not gone away.

Dennis's horses were probably all trying in the Derby, though. It was too valuable a race to mess about in. He had the Derby second again in 1783, when Dungannon, later to stand at his stud, lost out to Saltram, also by Eclipse; and he won for the second time the following year, with another son of Eclipse called Sergeant.[108]

Lord Derby triumphed in his own race in 1787. He and Lady Elizabeth were still married, but living apart, and he and Nellie Farren were conducting a relationship of apparently irreproachable propriety. 'The attachment,' James Boswell wrote, 'is as fine as anything I have ever seen: truly virtuous admiration on his part, respect on hers.' One of Nellie's most celebrated roles was Lady Teazle in Sheridan's play *The School for Scandal*. Lord

---

[108] The Derby distance had been extended to a mile and a half, and the runners set off on the opposite side of the Downs to the winning post, taking a course behind Downs House, where Dennis now had his training stables (see map on p. 88). A course on the near side of Downs House came into use in the late 1840s.

Derby ran a filly called Lady Teazle in the 1784 Oaks, finishing second; three years later, Sir Peter Teazle, his only Derby winner, gave Derby's virtuous admiration an enduring symbol in the sporting record books. He later turned down a bid for the colt of 500 guineas from, according to *The Times*, the Duke of Bedford and Dennis O'Kelly.[109]

Sir Charles Bunbury was to win the Derby twice more. There was Smolensko, whose jockey was so meanly rewarded, and before that, in 1801, a filly called Eleanor. Some time before the 1801 race, Bunbury's trainer Cox fell mortally ill. Close to death, with a parson standing by, Cox indicated that he had something to say. The parson bent low; Cox breathed in his ear, 'Depend upon it – that Eleanor is the hell of a mare.' He was right: Eleanor beat the colts in the Derby, and a few days later won the Oaks as well. She is one of only four fillies – 'filly' is a more usual term than 'mare' to describe a horse of three – to achieve the double.[110]

The Derby was not yet the most important race in the calendar, but it was getting there. The founding in 1809 of the 2,000 Guineas (one mile, for three-year-old colts and fillies) and in 1814 of the 1,000 Guineas (one mile, for three-year-old fillies) facilitated the rise in prestige, because these races became preludes to the Derby and the Oaks, which in turn led to the St Leger. The five races became the English Classics, the prizes that all owners dreamed of winning, and that were the highest goals of the breeding industry. By 1850, the Derby was stopping the nation: Parliament adjourned during the week of the race. 'We declare Epsom Downs on Derby Day to be the most astonishing, the most

---

[109] Lord Derby's family was not to record another victory in the race until Sansovino triumphed for the 17th Earl in 1924. The current earl, the 19th, won the 2004 Oaks with Ouija Board, his only horse in training.

[110] The others are Blink Bonny (1857), Signorinetta (1908) and Fifinella (1916). The other fillies to have won the Derby are Shotover (1882) and Tagalie (1912). At the time of writing, the last filly to contest the Derby was Cape Verdi (1998); she went off favourite, but was unplaced.

THE DERBY.—AT LUNCH.

The Derby – At Lunch *by Gustave Doré (1872). 'The Derby is emphatically, all England's day,' wrote Blanchard Jerrold in his accompanying text.*

varied, the most picturesque and the most glorious spectacle that ever was, or ever can be, under any circumstances, visible to mortal eyes,' the *Illustrated London News* asserted.

In the middle of the twentieth century, the owner and breeder Federico Tesio – who bred the champion Nearco – could say, 'The Thoroughbred racehorse exists because its selection has depended not on experts, technicians or zoologists, but one piece of wood: the winning post of the Epsom Derby.' And it was this piece of wood that reinforced Eclipse's dominant role in racing history. Five of the ten Derby winners in the 1850s, when the *Illustrated London News* hailed the glorious spectacle, were from the Eclipse male line. By the first decade of the twentieth century, the figure had risen to nine out of ten. In the past fifty years, all but three Epsom Derby winners have been Eclipse's male-line descendants. The history of racing's greatest race is a tribute to the sport's greatest horse.

13

Cross and Jostle

DENNIS O'KELLY WAS A larger-than-life figure in the world of Sir Charles Bunbury, James Weatherby and the Earl of Derby. He competed against them, often with success. As the owner of Eclipse, he had bragging rights that they could not match. But he was never one of them.

In part, Dennis acknowledged this disparity. Although he referred to himself and his companions as 'jontlemen', he did not make much effort to assume the disguise of a gentleman of the Turf. No top hat, embroidered waistcoat and lace-adorned cravat for him; he went about with battered headgear and an elderly, striped coat. An unmistakeable, bearish figure, he was at the centre of a kind of court at race meetings, gambling on the horses during the day and on dice in the evenings. When he was the caster – the player throwing the dice – at hazard, he demanded generous sums as stakes, and liked to brandish large wads of banknotes. One fellow, seeing Dennis apparently unable to find the note he wanted, asked to help. 'I am looking for a little one,' Dennis told him, flicking through his collection of hundreds. 'I want a fifty, or something of that sort, just to set the caster.' Fifty pounds was more than a year's wages for many people.

Dennis's bravado implied that no pickpocket would dare to

tackle him. One did, in an upstairs room at an inn during Windsor races, and was spotted before fully extracting the notes. The assembly clamoured that they would drag the miscreant before a magistrate, but Dennis grabbed hold of him, hauled him to the door, and booted him down the stairs. ''Tis a sufficient punishment to be deprived of the pleasure of keeping company with jontlemen!' he observed.

The wad of notes also served to put people in their place. At the racecourse, a gentleman placing a bet with him asked, snootily, 'Where lay your estates to answer for the amount if you lose?' 'My estates!' Dennis exclaimed. 'Oh, if that's what you *mane*, I've a map of them here.' He got out his wallet, revealing notes worth many times the value of the gentleman's money – which also went into the wallet, and stayed there.

Dennis liked to bet on boxing matches too. Bare-knuckle fights were sometimes staged among the attractions at race meetings, usually on demarcated patches of ground; spontaneous bouts at venues such as Vauxhall Gardens and Marylebone Fields were also common. Jack Broughton, a boxer and author of the first set of rules for the sport, constructed a boxing amphitheatre on Oxford Street in London, with a rectangular platform for the combatants. Here, in 1750, the Duke of Cumberland was said to have lost a bet of £10,000 when Broughton, amid allegations of match-fixing, suffered defeat at the hands of John Slack. A print of the fight has the title *The Bruiser Bruis'd: or The Knowing Ones Taken-in*. Cumberland, who had sponsored the amphitheatre, was furious, and closed it. Just over twenty years later, Dennis was also involved in a bent fight. The difference between Eclipse's breeder and Eclipse's subsequent owner was that Cumberland lost his money, whereas Dennis made sure not to.

The notorious fight between Peter Corcoran and Bill Darts took place at the Epsom race meeting in the spring of 1771. Corcoran, like Dennis, was born in County Carlow, and like him had been a chairman on coming to London. He had also heaved coal, and was a natural boxer. 'His aim was generally correct, and he scarcely ever missed the object in view,' Pierce Egan later recorded in *Boxiana* (1812), a collection of boxing anecdotes. But Darts was the better known, with a reputation as 'one of the most desperate hitters of the time', and was the favourite for the contest.

When, on entering the ring, Darts fought cagily, and before long threw in the towel, there were jeers and boos from the crowd, and soon reports circulated that Dennis, having backed his countryman Corcoran, had bribed Darts with £100 to lose. In his report of the affair, Egan protested, with a vehemence that may have been ironic, 'Surely, no thorough-bred sportsman could commit such a bare-faced robbery!', adding that there had been no need for fixing, because Corcoran, according to the 'best information', was twice the fighter that Darts was anyway.

Corcoran was not above taking a fall himself. At a fight against an opponent called Sellers, he began by knocking Sellers down; then, strangely, he backed off, put up little defence against a series of blows, and surrendered. 'The poor Paddies were literally ruined,' Egan – writing in the days before political correctness – noted, 'as many of them had backed their darling boy with every farthing they possessed. St Giles was in a complete uproar, with mutterings and disapprobation at [Corcoran's] conduct!' Previously in dire financial trouble, Corcoran was suddenly flush again. But he soon sank back into poverty, 'and was as much despised as he had been before respected; and was so miserably poor at his decease, that his remains were interred by subscription'.

Dennis was never poor again, although he did sometimes run short of funds. Eclipse was earning well; however, Dennis owned only one other stallion, Sultan, whose fee was just five guineas, and he was also paying for the upkeep of some fifteen racehorses, as well as various broodmares. He was acquiring land and properties too. In 1771, he bought nine acres on Epsom Downs next to the racecourse, stabled his racers there, and built a house. Continuing to expand his portfolio of properties in the town, he eventually, in the 1780s, built his own house and stables on Clay Hill. A traveller, describing the 'beautiful and elegant villa', reported that the drawing room at the O'Kelly residence was forty feet by twenty feet, and that there were twenty-five paddocks, as well as a fine garden. 'Here,' the traveller added, 'I was entertained with a sight of Eclipse.' This bare mention dismayed one local historian, who lamented, 'Oh! Casual and unresponsive scribe, who was entertained with a sight of the famous Eclipse and was satisfied to dismiss the subject in nine words.'

Like Lord Derby, Dennis and Charlotte entertained generously during race meetings. Their guest list was prestigious, with, in the 1780s, the Prince of Wales at the head; another royal, the Duke of Cumberland,[111] joined the party, as did nobles such as Lord Egremont and Lord Grosvenor, mingling with a selection of Dennis's less reputable associates, Dick England and Jack Tetherington among them. No doubt Charlotte brought her most lovely King's Place nuns to adorn the gatherings. While the entertainment may have been wild, Dennis insisted upon one rule: that no gambling should take place under his roof – 'Nor would he ever propose or accept the most trifling wager in private company.'[112] Did he think that gambling lowered the tone? It seems, from him, a somewhat hypocritical scruple.

The author of *The Genuine Memoirs of Dennis O'Kelly* pretended, with a rhetorical flourish, that this was when Dennis acquired his 'O':

Who keeps the best house in England? was the frequent question – O! Kelly, by much. Who the best wines? O! Kelly, by many degrees. Whose the best horses? O! Kelly's beat the world. Who the pleasantest fellow? Who? O! Kelly. In short, such was the

[111] Nephew of the Cumberland who bred Eclipse.
[112] From *The Genuine Memoirs of Dennis O'Kelly*.

frequent use of that ejaculatory vowel upon referring to the Count, that at length it became incorporated with his original name, and the harsh guttural of the consonant K was softened by the modest melody of the liquid O. No more humble Dennis Kelly. No more Mr Kelly. No more Count Kelly!

Dennis did not play the grand host with total authenticity, however, and his servants amused themselves with anecdotes about his gaffes. 'John, bring us the apples,' he would say, when referring to pineapples. One servant, ordered to buy fish in Epsom but reporting that he could not procure any, was told, 'Go back, sirrah! Go back; and by Jasus, if you can't get fish, bring herrings.'

Like many wealthy people, Dennis could be generous in some respects, and mean in others. He would spare no expense in entertaining; he would throw money around with apparent care-lessness at the racecourse; and despite the report that he had vowed never to be charitable again after the donation enforced by his misbehaviour with Miss Swinburne at York, he gave to good causes, such as the Benevolent Society of St Patrick. At a Society evening in 1786, Dennis succeeded the Marquis of Buckingham in the chair, and proposed toasts to the Marquis and to 'the inland navigation of Great Britain and Ireland' – this being the period of intensive canal construction, offering work for Irish labourers. At the same time, some of his employees, particularly jockeys, com-plained about his evasiveness over payments. One, Tom Cammell, was very indignant: 'Damn his fat, pampered guts; I have kept mine thin, and rode many a hard race to stuff his, and now can't get my money, without a still harder run over the course at Westminster Hall.' The reporter of this outburst suggested that Cammell was a victim of a temporary, gambling-induced cash flow crisis. Dennis, this reporter (John Lawrence) added, occupied a rare position in between sporting aristocrats and gamblers; though 'not overladen and depressed in his career by scruples', he was no worse a man than his supposed superiors.

Class, however, is not a matter of achievement, nor of morality. While the Duke of Grafton could scandalize society without jeopardizing his Jockey Club membership, Dennis, the partner of a madam, had no prospect of gaining election. Similar, unspoken rules apply today. Current JC members, all upstanding people no doubt, could commit quite a few indiscretions without loss of status. Yet the porn baron David Sullivan, despite ownership of a string of racehorses and a victory at the Eclipse Stakes,[113] is unlikely to be joining any time soon.

Once a blackleg, always a blackleg, was the JC's unbending view of Dennis. Not being what Daniel Defoe called (satirically) a True-born Englishman was another of his demerits, as it has been for many others. His older contemporary, the Jewish financier Sampson Gideon, attained fabulous wealth and converted to Anglicanism, but failed to be awarded a title, only to see his son gain a baronetcy. This pattern, of recognition held over to the next generation, was also to be the O'Kelly story.

Dennis aspired to be a member of the Turf elite; he thought he should be a member. He was one of those people who believe that anything they set their minds to achieving is within their reach. Possessing a mixture of naivety and chutzpah, they often do get what they want, and they rise to a new floor in the social hierarchy; but they have failed to see, and are dismayed and bewildered to discover, that certain rooms on that floor are barred. Using a slightly different metaphor, the historian Roy Porter wrote in his history of the eighteenth century, 'It was easy to rise *towards* the portal of the next status group. Crossing the threshold was more difficult, and required special visas.'

It has been an unvarying feature of society that no matter how successful or eminent you are, you always have to know your place. The late Auberon Waugh, son of one of the great novelists of the twentieth century (Evelyn Waugh) and a self-confessed

---

[113] His horse David Junior won the 2006 running.

member of the 'bourgeois cultural elite', discovered on arrival at Oxford University that he was excluded from the smart set that congregated round the dons Maurice Bowra and Isaiah Berlin. What he lacked, he concluded sourly, was 'an ancient name, a stately home and a couple of thousand acres'. Friends of the late Princess Margaret took care always to address her, in line with royal protocol, as 'Ma'am', while very dear friends called her 'Ma'am darling'. We might conclude, on hearing that Dennis and Charlotte entertained royalty and lords at Clay Hill, that eighteenth-century society was more fluid; but away from Epsom – or from the King's Place brothel – the barriers were up.

Dennis was bitterly uncomprehending that men with no obvious claim to pre-eminence, and who socialized with him and played sport with him, in effect continued to say, 'You are beneath us.' The key man who held that attitude kept the social contact to a minimum as well. During the Epsom races, Sir Charles Bunbury partied at The Oaks, not at Clay Hill. It seems that he would not send his mares there either, and he owned, throughout his racing career, only one horse sired by Eclipse. Bunbury ran the Jockey Club, he determined its rules, and he did not like the cut of Dennis's jib.

Dennis's feelings came out when he offered a jockey[114] a huge salary of £400 to be his retained rider, and promised to double the sum if the jockey agreed never to ride for 'any of the black-legged fraternity'. The jockey asked whom he meant. 'O, by Jasus, my dear,' Dennis shouted, 'and I'll soon make you understand who I mean by the black-legged fraternity! There's the D of G, the Duke of D, Lord A, Lord D, Lord G, Lord C, Lord F, the Right Hon. A, B, C, D, and C, I, F, and all the set of *thaves* that

[114] 'Thormanby' (William Willmott Dixon), writing more than a hundred years later, said that the jockey was Frank Buckle. Born in 1766, Buckle began riding at seventeen, so the story is feasible. He succeeded Sam Chifney as the leading jockey of his era, and was noted, unlike some of his contemporaries, for his unassuming manner and honesty.

belong to their humbug societies and clubs, where they can meet and rob one another without detection!'

One of these 'thaves', Lord A (Abingdon), offered Dennis a classically patrician put-down one evening at Burford races. The company at dinner were proposing matches for the following year, and Abingdon – owner of Eclipse's sire, Marske – offered to race a horse against one belonging to a Mr Baily, who appealed to Dennis for help over the terms. Giving a succinct precis of the English sportsman's attitude that professionalism is infra dig, Abingdon observed loftily, 'I, and the gentlemen on this side of the table, run for honour; the Captain [Dennis] and his friends for profit.'

The match was made, and Baily asked Dennis to stand half of the 300-guinea stake. Dennis, who did not approve of the terms, declined, adding fiercely: 'If the match had been made cross and jostle,[115] as I proposed, I would have stood all the money; and by the powers I'd have brought a spalpeen [young ruffian] from Newmarket, no higher than a two-penny loaf, that should (by Jasus!) have driven his lordship's horse and jockey into the furzes, and have kept them there for three weeks!'

Dennis also made a bid for social cachet through the military. While he happily brandished his bogus rank of 'Count', bestowed by a fellow inmate in the Fleet, he recognized that a more prestigious title might carry more weight. His opportunity came when a noble, to whom he had given some 'secret services' in the course of a legal action, secured him a captaincy in the Westminster Regiment of the Middlesex Militia.

The militias, which were the responsibility of lord lieutenants of counties, were raised with the aim of securing England against enemy invaders. They recruited through a form of national service: your name went into a ballot, and if it was drawn, you had to join up; you also had to make yourself available each year for

[115] A race in which contestants have licence to try to impede the other horses.

training. A typical order stated: 'Every militia man (not labouring under any infirmity incapacitating him) who shall not appear at the time appointed for the annual exercise shall be deemed a deserter and forfeit £20 or six months in gaol, or until he has paid.'

The Genuine Memoirs of Dennis O'Kelly may have been unreliable, but they offered a plausible portrait of a regiment comprising a motley assortment of officers and soldiers – a Georgian Dad's Army. 'Lamb, the Major, was a common mechanic, we believe, a watch-maker; and the Captains and Subalterns were, in general, really so low and obscure, as to be beneath the level of contempt or observation.' By the 1770s, the regiment had found roles for further obscure personages, whom the author of the *Memoirs* gleefully caricatured. There was Burbridge, a farmer, who despite his rank of lieutenant colonel responded to every enquiry about regimental business with the words: 'What do you ask me for? I do not know.' There was Barlow, the major, 'a superannuated mercer', incapable of marching because of gout, but useless on horseback as well. Dennis's fellow captains included a Dutchman called William Hundeshagen, whose frame held 'not six ounces of flesh' and whose misshapen hands and feet were evidence, like those of a castrato, of 'nature diverted from its regular courses'. Our hero, though, 'bore the most soldierly appearance of any officer in the regiment'.

This was the time of the American War of Independence (1775 to 1783), when Britain's enemies also included the French, Spanish and Dutch. Dennis's regiment travelled round the country on manoeuvres. In 1781 to 1782, for example, there were musters in Kent, Liverpool and Lancaster. Dennis journeyed in style, with accompanying carriages and servants, and Charlotte followed, with her own lavish retinue. He also found time – as no doubt did she – for his 'more profitable avocations'. But he was present at every important military exercise, and he stood firm whenever there appeared to be a threat, while his fellow soldiers panicked – or so the *Genuine Memoirs* had it. Resorting to crudity, the author reported that when enemy ships could be seen off the coast, 'the temple of Cloefina [the lavatory] became the alternate and eternal citadel of [Dennis's fellow officers'] prowess'. Dennis petitioned the Lord Lieutenant to dismiss these officers, without result. There would soon be peace, the Lord Lieutenant observed; and the men were old.

By the beginning of 1781, Dennis had risen to the rank of major, in charge of one of the regiment's nine companies, and had led the regiment before the King in St James's Park. He became Lieutenant Colonel Dennis O'Kelly in 1782. He failed to show gratitude to his supporters for his elevation, though. The *Genuine Memoirs*, switching as they often did from eulogy to censure, reported that Dennis did not invite any of his fellow soldiers to a grand entertainment in Lancashire attended by Lord Derby and various other nobles: 'A conduct so ungrateful, and so strongly tinged with upstart insolence, could not fail of producing great enmity and ridicule, and it is a fact, to the honour of those who were of that party, that even they joined in the general censure and disgust.'

Although Dennis's overtures to the Jockey Club made no headway, in other respects his Turf affairs were beginning to thrive. In *Eclipse and O'Kelly*, Theodore Cook recorded some of his impressive transactions. One of Dennis's broodmares, the Tartar mare, proved especially valuable, throwing ten chestnut offspring to Eclipse between 1772 and 1785; and Dennis made good money by selling them. The colts Antiochus and Adonis went to Sir John Lade (1,500 and 1,000 guineas; at the Cumberland dispersal sale, the renowned Herod had fetched only 500 guineas, and Eclipse only 45), Jupiter to Mr Douglas (1,000 guineas), and Mercury to Lord Egremont (2,500 guineas). Mr Graham offered 5,000 guineas for Volunteer, but was turned down. The fillies were in demand too: Venus went to Lord Egremont (1,200 guineas), the dam of a racer called Crazy and a Herod mare went to Mr Broadhurst (300 guineas), Lily of the Valley went to the Duke of

Bedford (700 guineas), Boniface and a Herod mare to Mr Bullock (250 guineas), and Queen Mab to the Hon. George Bowes for 650 guineas. The *Annual Register*, the chronicle of events of the year, reported of the Jupiter transaction that it involved a bonus of £500, payable to Dennis if the colt won on his debut.

Amid these transactions, Dennis was never tempted to part with his most valuable asset. Lord Grosvenor, owner of Eclipse's outstanding son Pot8os, offered 11,000 guineas for Eclipse; Dennis responded to the offer with the impossible demand of 20,000 guineas, a £500 annuity, and three broodmares. When another interested party (the Duke of Bedford, perhaps) asked about the stallion's selling price, Dennis replied, 'By the Mass, my lord, and it is not all Bedford level that would purchase him.'

The fame of stallion and owner are apparent in contemporary references. In a heavy-handed satire entitled *Newmarket: Or an Essay on the Turf* (1771), the author wrote, with galumphing jocularity:

> I think I never met with a stronger proof of this, nor with any thing that ever pleased me better, than the following important article of intelligence. 'On Sunday last arrived in town, Count O'Nelly, master of the famous horse Moonshade.' See how honour, coy mistress as she is, yet mounted this gentleman's horse, and announced his arrival in town.
>
> I only urge, that the following titles, given to an excellent horse, would sound very nobly, and be bestowed with admirable justice. Kelly's Eclipse. Creations: Duke of Newmarket; Earl of Epsom and York; General of the Race-grounds; Baron Eclipse of Mellay; Viscount Canterbury; Lord of Lewes, Salisbury, Ipswich, and Northampton; Marquis of Barnet, and Premier Racer of all England.

14

An Example to the Turf

IN HER PROFESSIONAL LIFE, Charlotte remained Charlotte Hayes or Mrs Hayes. But away from the King's Place nunnery, she was Charlotte O'Kelly. Whether there was ever a Mr Hayes, we do not know, and we have no evidence that Charlotte and Dennis ever became wife and husband. It has been suggested that theirs was an unofficial union, like the 'Savoy Chapel wedding' performed by the impious clergyman John Wilkinson with which the younger Dennis was reported to have duped a young lady of fortune. The *Genuine Memoirs of Dennis O'Kelly* had this to say on the subject: 'Whether the God of love had . . . presented [Charlotte] at the altar of Hymen, we do not presume to ascertain. Certain it is, that if reputation, and cohabitation, were sufficient evidences of matrimony, the performance of that ceremony must have been confirmed in the eyes of the world.' Which is a nice way of saying that no marriage ever took place.

Charlotte was wealthy, successful, extravagant, and careless. An astute and often unscrupulous businesswoman, she was also wayward and nervy, and often landed in trouble. In 1776, the creditors of a bankrupt haberdasher, James Spilsbury, got her imprisoned in the Marshalsea for unpaid debts concerning 'the use and hire of certain clothes and garments . . . let to hire to the said Charlotte at her special interest and request . . . and also for work and labour before that time done performed and bestowed . . . in making fitting adorning and trimming diverse clothes, garments and masquerade dresses'; 'the said Charlotte not regarding her said several promises and under-takings so made as aforesaid but contriving and fraudulently intending craftily and subtly to deceive and defraud . . . hath not yet paid the said several sums of money or any part thereof . . .' The creditors sued for £50. Charlotte spent several months in jail before Dennis secured her release. Whether his delay was a symptom of lack of gallantry or lack of funds is not altogether clear.

The author of the *Genuine Memoirs* certainly showed gal-lantry. 'No woman could have maintained a better conduct,' he insisted. '[Charlotte's] conversation was delicate and agreeable, and her manners conciliating, from gentleness and modesty.' This paragon would never have defrauded anyone: her debt was 'rather neglected than withheld'. Such was the respect due to Charlotte, the *Genuine Memoirs* added, that the arresting officers were inclined to dismiss the claim against her, and they allowed her bail instead so that the true extent of the debt could be revealed and dis-charged. Dennis was in York at the time, and about to land himself in the 'unfortunate adventure' with Miss Swinburne. The evidence belies this account, however. Charlotte did indeed go to prison, and Dennis was not in York. His adventure there had taken place six years earlier.

When at liberty, Charlotte spent much more of her time in London than in Epsom. She lived in a newly acquired property in Half Moon Street, Piccadilly, where, as she began to take life more easily, she delighted especially in the company of her pet parrot. Polley had been procured by Dennis from Bristol, and had cost fifty guineas – the sum that was Eclipse's highest covering fee. (One report says that Dennis paid 100 guineas for Polley.) Owing to her rarity, and to her reputed status as the first parrot to be bred in England,[116] Polley was credited with miraculous abilities. She sang a variety of tunes, on request, beating the time with her wings, and if ever she made a mistake, she would return to the appropriate bar, and resume. According to the *Gentleman's Magazine*, her repertoire included 'the 114th Psalm, "The Banks of the Dee", "God Save the King" and other favourite songs'. What Eclipse was among horses, another report enthused, Polley was among parrots.

In the 1780s, Dennis – born in about 1725 – entered what was considered to be old age. Life expectancy during this period was a little more than thirty-five years. While that figure reflects high levels of infant and child mortality, it also shows why people who lived into their late fifties and beyond were thought to be doing especially well. Not until the twentieth century, and then only in affluent societies, did the biblical lifespan of three score years and ten become a feasible standard. Charlotte Hayes – roughly Dennis's contemporary, and destined to live for another thirty years – was in 1780 'that experienced old matron', in the words of William Hickey.

So, in his late fifties, Dennis began to assume elderly habits. Whatever the Jockey Club thought, he was leaving behind the anarchic life of the blackleg, and he was no longer in tune with some of his old associates, Dick England among them. One evening in the 1780s at Munday's coffee house, Dennis and a certain Lieutenant Richard were comparing notes about what a vile scoundrel England was. An eavesdropper reported the conversation to England, who was elsewhere in the house. England came charging into the room, took on both Dennis and the Lieutenant, and beat them up. Dennis was so bruised that he was unable to leave the premises, and had to accept the hospitality of the proprietor, Jack Medley, who gave him a bed for the night. Unwisely,

[116] Another version has it that she arrived on a ship from the West Indies.

Dennis and the Lieutenant sued. The case came before the King's Bench, where England pleaded guilty; the judge, ruling that the defendant had been severely provoked, awarded only one shilling in damages.[117]

It was inevitable that a man enjoying Dennis's successes would find an extended family popping up and making claims on his charity. For the most part, he did the right thing. In the early 1770s, he had brought his brother Philip over to England, and put him in charge of the stables and stud at Epsom. Philip arrived with his wife, Elizabeth, and son, Andrew Dennis, who received a fine education at Dennis's expense. Although Andrew would inherit the O'Kelly talent for controversy, he gained more ease in society than Dennis ever enjoyed.

The *Genuine Memoirs* said that Dennis also helped two nieces. Who they were is not clear, because they receive no mention in the notes about the family in the O'Kelly papers, lodged at the University of Hull. One of the documents, an importuning letter to Dennis, refers to 'your sister Mrs Mitchell' and her daughter 'Miss Mary Harvey', who had travelled to England with Philip. Again, this is puzzling. Dennis's sister Mary married a man called Whitfield Harvey, so perhaps Miss Mary was the daughter of that marriage (before a second marriage, to Mitchell).[118] The letter writer is Thomas Gladwell, who was married to Dennis's cousin. With what must have been lack of tact, he said that 'friends were not pleased with my marriage', and reported that 'I could have

---

[117] In 1784, Dick England fled the country after shooting a man called Le Rowles (or, possibly, 'Rowlls') in a duel. He returned twelve years later to face trial. After support from the witness box from the Marquis of Hertford and Lord Derby, who surprisingly described him as 'a very civil, well-bred, polite gentleman', England got away with a verdict of manslaughter and a sentence of a year in Newgate. On his release, he enjoyed a comfortable old age, and died 'peacefully in his bed' at eighty.

[118] A second sister, unnamed in the papers, married someone called Sterne Tighe. See Appendix 3.

made a more advantageous match'. Gladwell was struggling to get by on a clerk's wages of £30 a year. 'Hearing of your goodness of heart to all your relations and others who have applied to your assistance emboldened [my wife] to lay this state of our circumstances before you. Be pleased to grant us some relief.' Dennis kept the letter, but whether he responded to it is doubtful: Gladwell mentioned three previous requests that had received no acknowledgement. Another letter in the collection is from a family member recommending one Patrick O'Fallon, and presuming on 'the general good nature of your character' to request that O'Fallon be found some 'small place', perhaps in the Custom House.

By this time, Dennis was considerably, though precariously, affluent. He owned various properties and a good deal of land in Epsom, as well as a substantial racing operation; and he owned, or at least rented, properties in London too. Sometimes, he raised cash through leasing arrangements, and he also went in for subletting. The O'Kelly papers include an aggrieved letter from James Poole, writing to say that he is 'by no means satisfied' with the condition of a house he let to Dennis several years earlier: it 'has been turned into separate habitations for poor persons', who have left it in a state of disrepair. Poole demanded that the house be returned to its original state, and that the overdue rent be paid.

Of the Epsom properties, only a barn from the Downs House stables survives. But Dennis's last and most impressive acquisition still stands. Cannons[119] in Edgware had been, in the early part of the eighteenth century, the site of an ostentatiously grand palace built by James Brydges, Duke of Chandos. A drawing in the British Library shows a colonnaded structure of overweening vulgarity. There were ninety-three servants in the house; in the grounds were storks, flamingos, ostriches, blue macaws, eagles and, at one time, a tiger. By reputation, this was the model for

[119] The current spelling is Canons.

Cannons (now spelled Canons) in Edgware, the villa built by Hallett, the last home of Eclipse and of Dennis O'Kelly. The house is now part of the North London Collegiate School for Girls.

'Timon's Villa' in Alexander Pope's *Epistle to Burlington* ('At Timon's villa let us pass a day / Where all cry out, "What sums are thrown away!"') – although scholars are inclined to accept, at least partially, Pope's denial of the connection. Some of Chandos's expenditure nevertheless resulted in achievements of enduring value. He appointed George Frideric Handel as composer in residence: Handel wrote the eleven Chandos Anthems to be performed in the adjoining church, Whitchurch, where he played the organ; and *Acis and Galatea*, his wonderful masque (or chamber opera), received its first performance in the Cannons grounds.

If you were going to spend a fortune at this time, you did not want that fortune to be secured by South Sea stock. Unfortunately, Chandos was an investor in the apparently booming South Sea Company, and he took a heavy hit when the share price collapsed.[120] He carried on, undaunted, but bequeathed family finances that were seriously in the red. In 1747, the second Duke sold Cannons, with the result that the palace, completed just twenty-five years earlier, was broken up and dispersed. The marble staircase went to Lord Chesterfield's Mayfair house – which was later demolished too. According to a history of Cannons, the eight Ionic columns in front of the National Gallery in London are from the Cannons colonnade. The ornamental gates stand at an Epsom mansion called The Durdans. A cabinet-maker called William Hallett bought the estate, and built a more modest villa there, of Portland stone.

In 1785, Dennis bought Hallett's villa, with some of the grounds, and the following year he struck a deal for the remainder of the estate. A document in the London Metropolitan Archives tells us that the second purchase cost him £10,500. He took

[120] This was 'The South Sea Bubble'. Investors bought into the South Sea Company, and into other companies, with the blind enthusiasm that was to greet internet stock nearly three hundred years later. Then the realization dawned that these companies – like a good many internet ventures – were unprofitable. Panic selling ensued, and fortunes were lost.

possession of a park some two miles round, containing between three and four hundred deer, with lakes and avenues, as well as smallholdings with cows, sheep and horses.

Horace Walpole, that barbed critic, disapproved of Hallett's taste, referring to his decorations as 'mongrel chinoise'. The third Duke of Chandos also had criticisms of the new Cannons house: 'The kitchen [is] not much larger than a Tunbridge kitchen, and smokes and stinks the house infernally. The only way of letting the smoke out, for none goes out of the chimney, is through the window, which lets it in again at the window above it.'

In spite of these drawbacks, the villa Dennis bought and subsequently lived in was a smart place. In the basement were a housekeeper's room, kitchen, scullery, butler's pantry, ice-house, servants' hall, dairy and larder, with cellars for wine, beer and coal. The ground floor contained a library, a breakfast parlour, a dining room, a grand saloon of forty-five feet by twenty-one feet, a drawing room, a stone hall and a stone staircase. There were six bedchambers and a dressing room on the first floor, and a further six bedchambers, for servants, on the attic storey. Today, this house is part of the North London Collegiate School for girls.

Dennis was slowing down, without mellowing. The company he kept at Cannons was 'more select' than that of his former days, consisting of 'people of the first class of his own sex' as well as 'unexceptionable' female friends. He was demanding and difficult with his brother Philip, and he berated his nephew, Andrew, for the kind of behaviour in which he himself, when younger, had specialized. His friends had to endure boorish joshing. With one, O'Rourke, Dennis would bang on monothematically about how he possessed the superior Irish lineage;[121] the *Genuine Memoirs* said

[121] The descent of the clan O'Kelly from Milesius (after whom Dennis named one of Eclipse's sons), the King of the Celts in the sixth century BC, may be apocryphal; but there is a more certifiable line from Cellagh, an Irish chief living in the ninth century AD. The O'Kellys ruled for seven hundred years over a kingdom corresponding roughly with what we know as Connaught.

that O'Rourke ('whose soul was made of fire!') put up with it.

On the racecourse, Dennis's energy was undiminished. In 1786, his racer Dungannon, who had come second in the Derby three years earlier, narrowly defeated the Prince of Wales's Rockingham in a valuable Newmarket match, made more valuable still by the heavy betting on the outcome. The losers, reported *The Times* (then the *Daily Universal Register*), complained about the rough tactics, or 'cross and jostling', of Dungannon's rider. There was a rematch the following spring, when Rockingham was in the ownership of a man called Bullock (the Prince, suffering one of his periodic financial crises, had sold his stable), in a race that also featured the Duke of Grafton's Oberon and Sir Charles Bunbury's Fox. *The Times* contributed to the build-up: 'The grand sweepstakes on Tuesday comprehends more first-rate horses than ever ran together before. Vast sums are depending on this extraordinary contest, and the odds are perpetually fluctuating. Dungannon was the favourite, but the tide is turned towards Rockingham.'

On the eve of the race, Dennis withdrew Dungannon. It was not a popular move. *The Times* said, 'The Duke of Bedford was 1200 [guineas] minus on account of O'Kelly's Dungannon not starting on Tuesday, and the minor betters, who had laid their money play or pay, suffered in proportion. Illness was pleaded, and the horse ordered into the stable. Turf speculation daily becoming more and more precarious, since occasional indisposition is as readily admitted at Newmarket as on the stage.'

Very few racegoers believed in Dungannon's 'indisposition', was the implication. It is the charge that the writer John Lawrence was also to make: that the well-being of Dennis O'Kelly's horses tended to reflect the financial interests of their owner. The Duke of Bedford and others had lost the money they had bet, and others – not named by *The Times* – must have gained. 'Whatever bears the name of Rockingham seems somehow or other to have *dupery* inseparable from it,' the paper observed, casting aspersions both on the horse and on a former Prime Minister, the late Marquis of

Rockingham (who had died in 1782). Yet the paper also reported that Dennis had lost at least one bet on the race, having predicted, incorrectly, that Rockingham would not be able to lead from start to finish. Moreover, he lost money overall at the meeting: 'In the last week's business of Newmarket, according to public report, the Duke of Bedford was minus, Lord Egremont was minus, Mr O'Kelly was minus, even the Duke of Queensberry was a little minus. We should be glad, therefore, to know, who was major on the occasion; – or is it on the turf, as we know it often happens in a gaming table, that when £10,000 have been lost in an evening, not a single person is to be found who has won a guinea?' We should treat this report with a little scepticism – *The Times*'s next mention of the affair certainly indicates that its reporting was fallible: 'The report of O'Kelly's being expelled the Jockey Club, in consequence of not suffering Dungannon to start after being led to the post, is not true. O'Kelly, for a number of years past, has been an example to the turf for fair play, and punctuality in payments.'

The comments on Dennis's character were questionable (if they were not meant ironically), and the implication that he was a Jockey Club member was wrong. Later, the paper suggested that Dennis, plagued by ill health, was planning to quit the Turf. But, controversial to the end, he carried on racing. In 1787, thirteen horses ran in his colours. His colt Gunpowder came second in the Derby, and his filly Augusta, bought at the Prince of Wales's dispersal sale (chapter 17), came second in the Oaks. In October, he and the Duke of Bedford made an unsuccessful bid for the colt that had beaten Gunpowder at Epsom, Lord Derby's Sir Peter Teazle.

Dennis's affliction, which was no doubt the reason why this once vigorous man was beaten up so badly by Dick England, was gout. In this, at least, he joined the upper crust: gout, a.k.a. the 'English malady', was 'the distemper of a gentleman whereas the rheumatism is the distemper of a hackney coachman', in the view of the patrician Lord Chesterfield. Perhaps that observation gave solace to Dennis as he endured his agonies. Gout is an accretion of uric acid that forms crystals in joints, particularly in the feet, so that the slightest movement or touch produces excruciating pain. One pictures Dennis, his swaddled feet resting on a stool, extravagantly complaining of his lot and, frustrated at his immobility, furiously shouting at his family and servants. Only Charlotte got kind treatment.

We are inclined to be callous about gout, and to laugh at the bibulous old man with the inflamed extremities. Like a hangover, gout is a joke ailment, a comic comeuppance for high living. Evidence about its causes certainly suggests a link with the extraordinary indulgences of the eighteenth-century lifestyle. A typical dinner of the time was, in the words of historian Liza Picard, 'a nightmare of meat and poultry', with course upon course of beef, pork, chicken, hare, pheasant and snipe; interludes of seafood such as crayfish and turbot; and heavy puddings to follow. Then there was the drink. One bottle of wine was an almost teetotal quantity. William Hickey, inviting some good-time girls to an evening party at an inn, selected them on the basis that 'each . . . could with composure carry off her three bottles'.[122] Six bottles, of wine that was sometimes fortified with spirits, was not an unusual portion. The wine might be kept in lead casks or sweetened with lead sugar, which probably triggered various illnesses, gout among them.

The eighteenth-century sufferer could console himself with the thought that not only was gout classy, it was also, according to medical theory of the time, a guard against other diseases. This was

[122] Pris Vincent, one of the women, performed her party piece at the end of the evening: urinating from distance at a target. For the particular amusement of another guest, Lord Fielding, she stood on one side of the table, and appointed Hickey to hold a champagne bottle at the other side. Lifting her petticoats, she aimed a stream of piss so accurately 'that at least one-third actually entered the bottle', Hickey admiringly reported. He added, 'Lord Fielding was near suffocation, so excessively did it excite his mirth'.

a sad illusion, particularly in cases of overweight people such as Dennis. Always bulky, Dennis ballooned in later years, although he may not quite have weighed in at the twenty stone that the *Whitehall Evening Post* assigned to him. Obesity would have brought with it additional problems such as diabetes, high blood pressure, and heart trouble.

Shortly after the October 1787 meeting at Newmarket, Dennis's illness attacked him 'with determined violence', the *Genuine Memoirs* said. He repaired to his house in Half Moon Street, Piccadilly, where a physician called Dr Warren attended to him. Warren would have intervened little up to now, prescribing simply oils for the inflamed areas of Dennis's anatomy and recommending that Dennis limit his alcohol intake – to the trifling amount, say, of a pint of wine a day. Now, more drastic measures were called for: bleeding to realign Dennis's humours, quinine to steady the nerves, laudanum to ease the pain, and perhaps some bespoke herbal medicines.

Unsurprisingly, these treatments did not effect an improvement. Dennis sank into a lethargic state, and, showing little apparent discomfort, slipped towards death. He passed away on 28 December. The *Genuine Memoirs* concluded, 'As his career was a lesson of wonder, so was his death an example of imitation.'

The 14lb Heart

DENNIS O'KELLY – ROGUE, madam's companion, and Jockey Club reject – got a distinguished send-off. He was buried with 'great funeral pomp' on 7 January 1788 in the vault of the Cannons church, Whitchurch, where he still lies. Officers of the Westminster Regiment of the Middlesex Militia attended, along with eminent neighbours, who all enjoyed a slap-up dinner afterwards, with a liberal supply of wine.

The farewell from the public prints was, as Dennis might have expected, mixed. Under the heading 'O'Kelly is dead', the *Whitehall Evening Post* announced that it had received two unprintable obituaries, the first overly eulogistic, the second overly hostile. The paper's own verdict leaned towards the second position. One could not expect a man who had made his fortune on the Turf, the paper pronounced, to be morally scrupulous; but one might have hoped that a colonel in the militia would have observed the behaviour of a gentleman. Disaster could not soften Dennis O'Kelly, 'nor prosperity sublime'. He was, though, a generous, undiscriminating host, 'as unambitious in his company, as easily contented, as if he had ended life as he began it – as a chairman in the streets'. On the subject of Charlotte, the *Whitehall Evening Post* held its nose: 'Had [O'Kelly] left the [Fleet] prison a better man than he found it, virtue might have thought it something – but it was not so, unless a man is better by such an addition as Charlotte Hayes.'

The *World Fashionable Advertiser* chose the period of mourning to remind readers of Dennis's embarrassing incident with Miss Swinburne at Blewitt's Inn, York (chapter 9). It had another colourful anecdote to share: that one room of Dennis's villa at Clay Hill was full of portraits of young ladies, 'the most remarkable for their faces and manners – in the seminary which Charlotte Hayes once kept for religious education'.

The Times[123] could not make up its mind. Dennis offered to the poor an example of how they must never despair of gaining wealth, was the paper's conclusion a few days following his death. He had bought Cannons, and then a further portion of the estate, without requiring a mortgage. There, Charlotte Hayes could enjoy 'her pious age'. However, any dissector of Dennis's corpse would find 'all inflammation, all corruption'. On the Turf, where success was synonymous with criminality, Dennis was 'as Sir Isaac Newton was among the philosophers – at the head of his science'.

Then the journalist wrote something puzzling: 'That O'Kelly was a chairman, and afterwards a marker at a billiard table, has been reputed under a very orthodox sanction; but we have every reason to believe that such an assertion is altogether heterodox, though it is to be found in a piece of biography written by myself.'

The claim that stories of Dennis O'Kelly's early life were mythical is not shocking. But was the author saying that he had already written *The Genuine Memoirs of Dennis O'Kelly* (which were certainly published some time that year, 1788)? It would have been fast work – although hacks were expected to turn round such opportunistic books with great speed. The exuberant, cynical tone of the *Genuine Memoirs* tallied with the journalist's cheerful admission in Dennis's obituary that he had reproduced unreliable accounts of our hero's life.

[123] Newly christened; the paper had begun publishing as the *Daily Universal Register* in 1785.

Later, *The Times* decided that it was Dennis O'Kelly's supporter. Referring to the scurrilous stories about Dennis in the *World Fashionable Advertiser*, it lambasted 'A certain affected morning print, remarkable for its incautious, groundless and calumniating assertions', and thundered, 'THE WORLD is a lying WORLD!' 'Is it possible,' *The Times* asked, forgetting its earlier portrait of Dennis, 'that in a country, nay in an age like this, it should be necessary to revive the ancient adage, De mortuis nil nisi bonum [One should not speak ill of the dead]?'

The *Genuine Memoirs* were both satirical and adulatory, both scurrilous and discreet. The anonymous hack commissioned to churn them out may well have haunted the Covent Garden milieu of Dennis, Charlotte and their associates. While offering plenty of evidence of Dennis's bad behaviour, he summarized him as a paragon. While revelling in Dennis's crudities, he advised his tender readers that he had omitted 'uninteresting coffee-house anecdotes; attempts at wit; nocturnal broils; and, the indecent intrigues of public and private brothels. A life so variegated as was that of Colonel O'Kelly, must have abounded with the common occurrences of such scenes; but we hold it highly improper that they should be presented to the general eye. They are fit only for the depraved contemplation of sensual and dissipated minds, and are in our opinion more injurious to virtue and society in general, than even the example of practical immorality.'

All the newspapers were intrigued by Dennis's will. It was a document (dated 11 October 1786) that proved his devotion to Charlotte Hayes. He wanted her to be secure, and comfortable. 'Into the proper hands of Charlotte Hayes, called Mrs O'Kelly [the phrasing is another hint that there was no formal marriage], who now lives and resides with me', Dennis bequeathed an annuity of £400, secured against the rents at Cannons, where Charlotte could live if she wished. He ordered that she should have the run of Cannons, and – suspecting that her parties might be boisterous? – specified that she should not be liable for any damage to the furniture. He left her various personal effects: a large diamond ring and other jewellery, as well as a silver tea pot and a coffee pot, along with silver plates and two silver candlesticks. He gave her his carriage and carriage horses too. Charlotte also inherited, with Dennis's brother Philip and nephew Andrew, Dennis's most valuable possession of all: Eclipse. They were to share the stud fees, as well as any fees generated by the stallions Dungannon, Volunteer and Vertumnus; if these horses were not to enjoy stud careers, they were to be sold, to Charlotte's, Philip's and Andrew's benefit. Philip got the broodmares, with the bonus that ten of them could be covered by the O'Kelly stallions free of charge, after which he would have to pay the market rate.

Dennis's will confirmed the stories that, disillusioned by the refusal of the Turf aristocracy to admit him to their inner circles, he had fallen out of love with racing. He ordered that all his racehorses be sold; moreover, he specified – this detail was widely reported – that if either Philip or Andrew should bet on horses, make matches, train horses or race them, 'or be engaged or concerned in any such matters in any shape or manner or upon any account or pretence whatsoever, then . . . they shall forfeit and pay unto my executors[124] and trustees the sum of £500 of lawful British money to be by them deducted and retained for their own use and benefit out of the property'. Andrew ignored this clause, with impunity.

The dispersal sale, on 11 February 1788, was the final proof that Dennis could match anyone in management of Turf affairs, if not in social acceptability. Conducted by the bloodstock auctioneers Tattersalls, it fetched in excess of £8,000 – some thousand pounds more than had changed hands at the sale of the Prince of Wales's stud the previous year. The Prince, having come to a new financial arrangement with his father George III and wasting no

---

[124] They were William Atkinson of Pall Mall, an apothecary, and Thomas Birch of Bond Street, a banker.

time in returning to the Turf, was among the buyers. He spent as extravagantly as he had before his enforced disposal, paying 1,400 guineas and 750 guineas for two sons of Eclipse, Gunpowder and King Heremon; he also bought the Eclipse fillies Scota (550 guineas) and Augusta (150 guineas).[125] According to Theodore Cook (in *Eclipse and O'Kelly*), there was not to be a racing sale of comparable influence for another seventy years.

The sale was supposed to clear Dennis's debts. But he had not been as flush as he thought.

By now, Eclipse was feeling his age. Like his gout-afflicted late master, he was having trouble with his feet: his coffin bones (they are in the hooves) were 'very much rounded and diminished'.[126] When Andrew decided to transfer the O'Kelly stud from Clay Hill to Cannons, Eclipse was too disabled to make the fifty-mile walk, and became the first horse in Britain to travel by means of others' efforts. Philip O'Kelly devised for him a prototype horsebox, a four-wheeled carriage with two horses to draw it. A groom kept him company, 'and when (like other travellers) he chose to take a glass of gin or aniseed for himself, he was directed to furnish his old friend Eclipse with a lock of hay, and a drop of the pail'.[127]

One of the prints carried a twee account of the move in the form of an epistle from Eclipse to his son, King Fergus:

I set out last week from Epsom, and am safe arrived in my new stables at this place. My situation may serve as a lesson to man: I was once the fleetest horse in the world, but old age has come upon me, and wonder not, King Fergus, when I tell thee, I was drawn in a carriage from Epsom to Cannons, being unable to walk

[125] Augusta travelled to and fro bewilderingly. Bred by O'Kelly, she was sold to the Prince, bought back, and sold at the dispersal sale; but she ended up at the O'Kelly stud at Cannons.
[126] From *A Short History of the Celebrated Race-horse Eclipse* by Bracy Clark.
[127] From William Pick's *The Turf Register and Sportsman and Breeder's Stud Book*.

even so short a journey. Every horse, as well as every dog, has his day; and I have had mine. I have outlived two worthy masters, the late Duke of Cumberland, that bred me, and the Colonel, with whom I have spent my best days; but I must not repine, I am now caressed, not so much for what I can do, but for what I have done.

I am glad to hear, my grandson, Honest Tom, performs so well in Ireland, and trust that he, and the rest of my progeny, will do honour to the name of their grandsire,

Eclipse

Cannons, Middlesex

P.S. Myself, Dungannon, Volunteer, and Vertumnus, are all here. Compliments to the Yorkshire horses.

Andrew saw that Eclipse did not have much time left. In December of that year, 1788, *The Times* reported that 'The French King has sent over an eminent anatomic drawer to Captain O'Kelly's seat at Cannons, in order to make a minute and complete figure of the celebrated horse Eclipse. He is now there, where it is intended he shall remain a fortnight.' This man may have been Charles Vial de Sainbel,[128] a thirty-five-year-old veterinarian who had been a victim of political machinations at the Royal Veterinary College in Paris.

It was Sainbel – now living in a London house once occupied by Sir Isaac Newton – whom Andrew hastened to fetch just two months later when, on the morning of 25 February 1789, Eclipse fell ill with colic. This intestinal affliction often causes terrible pain for horses, and can be fatal. On arrival at Cannons, Sainbel gave the suffering Eclipse laudanum, and tried the generic treatment of bleeding. He would have punctured a vein in the horse's neck, and allowed up to five pints of blood to drain out. Despite this attention (possibly because of it), Eclipse continued to

---

[128] This was how the English styled his surname, St Bel. He wrote later that he had made studies of Eclipse when alive. See chapter 21 for more on Sainbel.

decline, and died on 27 February, at seven o'clock in the evening.[129]

Sainbel performed a post-mortem, and satisfied himself that Eclipse had been beyond the reach of medicine. 'I infer that the reins [kidneys] performed their functions in a very imperfect manner, and that the animal died in consequence of the affections of these viscera, and of a violent inflammation of the bowels,' he wrote later. Eclipse had a large heart, Sainbel noticed. He weighed it: it tipped the scales at 14lb. This unusual size, a good five pounds heavier than standard, has been taken as one explanation for Eclipse's stamina. But Sainbel and Andrew wanted further explanations, and they agreed to offer a detailed anatomical study. The first ever work of its kind, it would confirm Eclipse's status as the paragon of the breed, and it would fix that status for posterity.

So it was a funeral of the flesh only when Eclipse was interred at Cannons. 'A large assembly' enjoyed cakes and ale as they paid tribute to the horse. Eclipse, like his father, received a poetic eulogy. The last line was a dig at Eclipse's rival stallions, and no doubt at Richard Tattersall, owner of Herod's son Highflyer and author of the taunt a few years earlier that Eclipse 'had had his day'.

Praise to departed worth! Illustrious steed,
Not the fam'd Phrenicus of Pindar's ode,[130]
O'er thee, Eclipse, possessed transcendent speed
When by a keen Newmarket jockey rode.

[129] He was nearly if not actually twenty-five (though his contemporaries would have said that he had not reached his twenty-fifth birthday, which they assigned to 1 May). That was a pretty good innings. Herod died at twenty-two, and Highflyer at twenty. Eclipse's long-lived contemporaries included his father, Marske, who survived to twenty-nine, and Matchem, who achieved the great age of thirty-three. Among more recent champions, Nijinsky lived to Eclipse's age of twenty-five, while Secretariat died at nineteen.
[130] Pindar's first Olympic ode refers to this horse, with which Hiero of Syracuse won an Olympic crown.

Tho' from the hoof of Pegasus arose
Inspiring Hippocrene, a fount divine!
A richer stream superior merit shows,
Thy matchless foot produced O'Kelly's wine.

True, o'er the tomb in which this fav'rite lies
No vaunting boast appears of lineage good;
Yet the Turf Register's bright page defies
The race of Herod to show better blood.

Eclipse sired about 165 sons and daughters who were winners on the racecourse; their victories totalled an estimated 863, and their earnings exceeded £132,000. Their prizes put him second in the sires' championship for eleven consecutive years, from 1777 to 1788. Dennis O'Kelly boasted that Eclipse had earned him £25,000 at stud – but that may have been a characteristic O'Kelly blag. A rough calculation suggests that the real figure was no more than half that.[131] The press reported that Matchem – who was the most celebrated stallion when Eclipse started his career, and who eventually commanded a fee of fifty guineas – had earned stud fees of £17,000.

Whether or not Eclipse overtook Matchem's stud earnings, he was to surpass him in another way. For the next fifty years, their male lines were of similar importance to breeders, with Matchem's, if anything, slightly favoured. But that changed, and is a historical curiosity now. In 2007, Matchem was not the tail male (male line) ancestor of any of the top thirty sires in Europe; and of only one, Tiznow, in the US list. The only sire in either list with a male-line descent from Herod was Inchinor. The fifty-eight others all descended from Eclipse.

[131] Based on advertised fees and number of coverings, along with probable conception rates. But perhaps O'Kelly also counted his revenues from selling and racing Eclipse's progeny.

16

The Litigant

ANDREW DENNIS O'KELLY, the guardian of the O'Kelly and Eclipse legacy, was an altogether more refined figure than his uncle Dennis. A portrait from 1784, when Andrew was in his early twenties, shows an urbane young man who has benefited from the education that Dennis, and Philip his father, lacked: fine of feature and of dress, he gazes assuredly at the viewer with almond-shaped eyes.

Unlike his uncle too, he became a figure of the establishment. The Jockey Club, as if compounding the snub to Dennis, accepted Andrew into membership after Dennis's death, and the Jockey Club ruler Sir Charles Bunbury, who had owned only one racehorse sired by Eclipse, sent mares to the O'Kelly stallion Dungannon. Other leading men of the Turf to use the stud included the Duke of Grafton, the Duke of Bedford, Lord Grosvenor, Earl Strathmore and the Prince of Wales. Andrew was a confidant of the Prince's, and had influential political friends. He had cultural interests: he was among the subscribers to a printing of the complete works of Handel, and he held a concert at Cannons with Nancy Storace – who had sung Susanna in the first performances of Mozart's *The Marriage of Figaro* – among the soloists.

Yet Andrew could not cast off the O'Kelly talent for controversy, and he spent a good part of his life enmeshed in disputes and legal complications. One of his earliest tangles with the law concerned his behaviour in the Middlesex Militia, the county force in which Dennis had risen, with the help of patronage and of his wallet, to the rank of lieutenant colonel. Andrew joined the militia's Westminster Regiment too, and was a captain when Dennis died. In 1793, an officer called Thomas Gordon agreed to transfer his lieutenant colonelcy in the regiment to Andrew for £200; Andrew was to pay Gordon a further fifty guineas should the regiment remain embodied a year later. Such clauses were typical of the time. Most sales agreements involved caveats and bonuses of various sorts – the purchase of a horse might require an extra payment if the horse won a particular race, for example. It is no wonder that the Georgians were such a litigious bunch.

Andrew enjoyed his rank for only three years until, in 1796, he faced a court martial. The charge, heard at Horse Guards in St James's, was that, while billeted in Winchelsea, he and fellow soldiers – among them his cousin, Philip Whitfield Harvey[132] – had appropriated government coal from the barracks for the house where Andrew was staying. Andrew's companions swore before the court that they had not realized that the coal was unaccounted for; that they had not realized that the coal was assigned to the men in barracks; that the quantity of coal they had taken was small; and that Andrew was absent for three of the five months when the offences were alleged to have taken place. This testimony did not impress the court. It found Andrew guilty, ruled that he should be dismissed from the regiment, and fined him £100, reserving judgment only on how much compensation he should pay for the coal. A letter from Charles Morgan, writing on behalf of the King, softened the sentence but not the essential blow:

[132] The son of Dennis and Philip's sister, Mary O'Kelly, from her marriage to Whitfield Harvey.

I take the earliest opportunity of acquainting you, that His Majesty, graciously taking into consideration all the circumstances of the case, and noticing, moreover, that of 18 articles of charge preferred against you, only one had been established to the satisfaction of the Court Martial, that very slender evidence had been offered in support of others; and that several had been entirely abandoned, did not think it necessary that the said sentence should be carried into execution; but his Majesty at the same time judging that it will not consist with the upholding of discipline in the said regiment, or tend to promote a respectful attraction from the men towards their Officers, that you should retain your Commission of Lieutenant Colonel in the corps, was pleased to express his Royal intention of giving direction, through his Majesty's Secretary of State, to the Lord Lieutenant of the County of Middlesex, for displacing you from the Westminster regiment of Militia.

I am, Sir, your most obedient, and very humble servant, Charles Morgan.

It was a lofty, conclusive dismissal. But, while the court martial was reported in *The Times*, it made no dent in Andrew's reputation. Ejection from the regular forces was shameful; ejection from a county militia was not so grave.

Another incident shows that Andrew's talent for plunging himself into disputes was not always accompanied by sound insight. He intervened on the road from Epsom to London when he came across a stalled coach in which one of the passengers, a guards officer, was shouting at the coachman. Andrew took up a position on one side of the coach, with a companion on the other, and whipped the coachman and his horses on towards town — actions that resulted, predictably, in the coach's careering into a ditch, with injuries to both the coachman and the officer's female companion. When the coachman sued, the court heard that the guards officer had taken the young woman, Miss Williams, to the races, had got drunk, and on the journey home had become abusive, charging the coachman with being in league with highwaymen. The judge, ruling that the officer's behaviour had been 'barbarous', fined him £100. Andrew escaped censure.

His behaviour may have been barbarous, but the guards officer's fear of highwaymen was not exaggerated. If you travelled regularly in the eighteenth century, you had to accept that there was a high chance of getting robbed. 'One is forced to travel, even at noon, as if one was going to battle,' Horace Walpole wrote. His friend Lady Browne observed, 'We English always carry two purses on our journeys, a small one for the robbers and a large one for ourselves.' Andrew himself, a regular commuter between Cannons and his late uncle's house in Piccadilly, became a victim when his chaise was stopped by two footpads, uttering 'violent imprecations'. Andrew defied them, drawing his sword. One of the thieves tried to shoot him, missed, and the pair ran off. By the time Andrew had roused help at the next turnpike, the thieves had got away.

That was in 1793. Seven years later, at eight o'clock on the evening of 3 December 1800, it happened again, but with three attackers. Having held up the carriage, Robert Nutts stood by the two horses, while James Riley opened the chaise door and threatened to blow Andrew's brains out unless he handed over his money. Andrew thought better of raising his sword this time, and gave up some cash. The thieves, dissatisfied with the modest sum, suspected that he was carrying – as recommended by Lady Browne – a larger purse as well, so Nutts came back and searched him, joined by the third thief, who extracted £50 in banknotes from Andrew's breeches. With that, the footpads made their escape. But a constable, Nibbs, had witnessed the robbery, and ran to the nearby Adam and Eve pub, where he enlisted four men to help. Nibbs and his posse caught up with Nutts and Riley, who ineffectually fired their pistols before being arrested. Their companion, who was never identified, got away. Nutts and Riley were convicted of highway robbery, and hanged at Newgate on 24 June 1801.

As the 1790s progressed, the complications in Andrew's life multiplied, bequeathing us a collection of family papers peppered with convoluted references to financial and legal disputes. Correspondents claim not to have been paid, or send impenetrable reports of their transactions. Every O'Kelly property is subject to complex mortgage and leasing arrangements; every deal includes conditions or provisos or insurance clauses. Bailiffs arrive to remove furniture; a tenant charges that Andrew intercepted him on the road and taunted him with the words, 'The bailiffs are coming, the bailiffs are coming.' At one time, Cannons had liabilities attached to it of some £30,000. Andrew aroused distrust and made enemies, such as an anonymous correspondent who wrote to Andrew's friend, Lady Anna Donegall: 'Beware, O'Kelly is not the man he appears. Duplicity is the chief part of his composition. His first aim is to have the reputation of receiving your favours; his second, to continue to pay his expenses from your husband's pocket. Before the death of Lord Donegall's father he and his family were in the greatest distress. Charlotte Hayes was in the Fleet. I thus have cautioned you, wishing to protect innocence, beauty and virtue.' Lady Donegall paid no attention to this warning, and remained on warm terms with Andrew. So, according to the evidence in the files, did Lord Donegall – a baffling show of loyalty, as the two men spent most of their adult lives suing each other. However, contrary to what the anonymous letter writer implied, it seems to have been Andrew who was the financial loser.

George Augustus Chichester, second Marquess of Donegall, was an inveterate spendthrift and gambler. He first did business with the O'Kellys in 1794, when, aged twenty-five and carrying the title Lord Belfast, he visited Cannons and picked out some horses. Already, he had a significant flaw as a business partner: he was an inmate of the Fleet debtors' prison, though allowed out under the day rules.[133] The contract he struck with Andrew's father Philip involved a post-obit: a commitment to pay a sum on the death of his father, the Marquess. Five years later, the Marquess obligingly died, and his son took possession of his title, along with a substantial chunk of what is now Northern Ireland. It would be a long time, however, before he paid his O'Kelly debts.

Within a few years of meeting, Andrew and the newly created Marquess – whose conduct, according to one of Dennis's friends, was 'most atrocious' – were in disagreement about their finances, while continuing to operate as a team. They may have tried to use the partnership to circumvent authority, as for instance in the case of a horse called Wrangler, listed in the *Racing Calendar* for 1801 under Andrew's name. Two Middlesex sheriffs, Perring and Cadell, seized Wrangler while he was on his way to Newmarket, in execution against the chronically indebted Donegall. Andrew protested that Wrangler was his, and sued, with Sir Charles Bunbury turning up at court to swear that he had sold the horse to him. Donegall, who had leased Cannons from Andrew earlier that year, testified from the stand that Wrangler was not his, but Andrew's. Another witness supported this statement by saying that he had observed Andrew making a match for Wrangler, at a race meeting where Donegall had 'damned [Wrangler] for a bolter,[134] and said he would have nothing to do with him'. So far, so good; but then Andrew's case collapsed embarrassingly. A groom confessed that although he had been paid by Andrew, Wrangler was stabled with other horses belonging to Donegall; and another groom, asked to name Wrangler's owner, replied, 'The Marquess of Donegall.' One would like to have seen Andrew's and Donegall's faces when those words were uttered. Before a crowded court, the judge dismissed the case – which had

---

[133] Which, just over thirty years earlier, Dennis O'Kelly had also enjoyed.
[134] I.e., he was uncontrollable.

surely been a ruse to reclaim a horse that Andrew and Donegall had owned jointly.

Over the next eighteen years, Andrew and Donegall were in and out of court, lobbing claims and counter-claims at each other, all the while offering assurances that it was nothing personal. In 1814, Andrew wrote to Donegall, who was then in Ireland, to remonstrate with him about reports that he and his father Philip had taken 'improper advantage of your lordship'. Donegall replied, 'I beg leave to say that I never fabricated such reports and that they are altogether void of truth, as to the bills filed in chancery against your father and yourself . . . they were contrary to my approbation and without my consent, having always lived on the most intimate footing with you and conceiving you to be a man of the strictest honour and integrity and which was the general opinion of the world when I first had the pleasure of your acquaintance.' This was courteous. The fact was, however, that Donegall owed Andrew some £37,000, from total debts amounting to an eye-watering £617,524 – about £33 million in today's money. Among financial profligates of the era, only the Prince of Wales could rival him. Eventually, Donegall acknowledged the sums he owed Andrew, although whether he followed up the acknowledgement with any cash is not clear. Certainly, in 1819, Andrew's cousin Philip Whitfield Harvey wrote to Andrew from Dublin: 'Lord Donegall is in great distress for even £100. Lady D, that was, is determined to proceed to London immediately without a guinea or even a carriage. She will not allow her noble spouse to quit her apron strings, fearing that he might tie himself to some more deserving object.'[135]

Whether or not the author of the warning letter to Lady Donegall gave a fair report of Andrew's character, he was well informed about Andrew's finances. Dennis's will had implied greater wealth than he really possessed, and his estate turned out

[135] Donegall remained deep in the red until his death in 1844.

to be insufficient to pay his debts and legacies. To compensate, Andrew borrowed money, took out mortgages, and rented properties. But the late eighteenth century was not a good time to stretch your finances. There was revolution in France, followed by European war, and soon everyone was feeling the pinch. From 1787, the year of Dennis's death, to 1800, Philip and Andrew advertised regularly in the *Racing Calendar* that all the thirty-plus mares at Cannons, with their foals, were up for sale. Many of the foals found buyers; but, in those straitened times, no one wanted to pay the high prices that the O'Kellys were asking for the mares.[136] Meanwhile, the value of the O'Kelly stallions was falling. By the turn of the century, Dungannon and Volunteer were covering mares at a modest ten guineas each – fees suggesting that there was not a great deal of confidence in their ability to get outstanding racers.

Charlotte Hayes was another encumbrance on Andrew. She was as scattily profligate as ever, and in 1798 she got herself committed again to the Fleet debtors' prison.[137] Andrew's subventions to her at this time included the hefty sum of £728 to satisfy a debt to one Thomas Pilton, a Piccadilly upholsterer, and £105 to buy her the right to the Fleet day rules, allowing her to live outside the prison walls. The next spring, when Charlotte was released, she satisfied further debts, to Thomas and Mary Potts (£48 15s), and to John Thomas (£235 14s). She and Dennis's brother Philip had already agreed that, in the light of the money that Andrew had raised following Dennis's death, Andrew should be granted sole right to property worth that sum. Now Charlotte signed, in her scratchy hand, a document releasing to Andrew all her portion of the estate, with the exception of her £400 annuity. The good news for her was that she would no longer be responsible for the upkeep

---

[136] There is no record of what happened to the horses in the end. Perhaps Donegall bought them – and never paid for them.

[137] She had been in the Fleet from 1758 to 1761, and in the Marshalsea in 1776.

of the horses – though no doubt she had never assumed that responsibility anyway.

The only transfer that had taken place before this was of 'a very extraordinary and rare bird called Parrot gifted with extraordinary powers of speech and song'. But Polley was to live for only another few years. In October 1802, Philip O'Kelly had sombre news to give to his son, in a letter (original spelling preserved) hinting that Charlotte was a constant worry: 'Polley was taking ill on Saturday night last with a purging and bloody flox and all things that was fit for her was got. She died on Sunday morning. Dr Kennedy go her to have her stuffd so she is no more. Charlett is in the same state as ever.' The death, which sounds unpleasant, was a traumatic family event. A family servant, signing herself E. Wilson, wrote to Andrew: 'My trouble was so great at the death of the bird and I did not know what I was doing, the loss of my children never afflicted me more. I am truly sorry and surprised to hear you attribute to my neglect or want of care her death, as it was impossible if my life was at stake to be more attentive than I was. I could not keep her alive no more than I can my good self when it shall please God to call me.'

Polley got the tribute, surely rare for a bird, of an obituary in the *Gentleman's Magazine*, which reminded readers of her skills: 'Died, at the house of Colonel O'Kelly, in Half-moon-Street, Piccadilly, his wonderful parrot, who had been in his family 30 years, having been purchased at Bristol out of a West-India ship. It sang, with the greatest clearness and precision, the 114th Psalm, "The Banks of the Dee", "God Save the King!" and other favourite songs; and, if it blundered in any one, instantly began again, till it had the tune complete. One hundred guineas had been refused for it in London.' The magazine made the double mistake of announcing that Polley would be interred alongside Eclipse at Cannons. In fact, as Philip wrote, she was stuffed, and continued to reside at Half Moon Street; and Eclipse's skeleton at this time was at a small, private museum in Mayfair.

Charlotte appears to have been willing to give up the annuity bequeathed to her by Dennis as well. Lawyers raised objections, however. One told Andrew, who was hoping to sell Cannons, that any deal should be subject to the £400 yearly charge, 'as [Charlotte] has very much encumbered it and may create some difficulties in the title'. A man called Brockbank held the same view, to Charlotte's dismay — which she expressed to Andrew in one sprawling, minimally punctuated (and, again, idiosyncratically spelled) sentence constituting the only letter of hers we have.

> February, 1801
> My dear Colonel, I am very sorry to find that Mr Brockbank
> makes any objection to my giving you the releace for my annuiteis
> and the acknowledgement of the other sums mentioned in it that
> you and your father have paid and secured to be paid for me but I
> am not surprised at aney thing that such a man as Mr Brockbank
> should say or do after the manner he has conducted himself
> towards me and you — unjust advantage he is attempting to take of
> you against my wishes or concent — if you or any other person has
> the smallest doubtes of the justness of what is contained in the
> releace I shall be ready at any time to com forward and make an
> affidavit of those circumstances which Mr Brockbank must be per-
> fectly well acquainted with as I have at different times stated to
> him monies that you have paid for me and I have give him money
> to keep the transactions of my selling my annuities from your
> knowledg and am my dear colonel yours sincerely C. O'Kelly.

The annuity was still attached to Cannons when Andrew at last sold the estate, to Sir Thomas Plumer, in 1811. Charlotte is described in one document as a 'spinster' (another hint that she never married, although the term may be applied loosely) 'who is now advanced in years'; in another, she is living on the Cannons estate (though not in the mansion house) and 'aged about 85 years'. Plumer, who was the solicitor general, indemnified himself against paying her any money. Cannons cost him £55,000.

It is not certain how many further payments Charlotte claimed. E. J. Burford stated that she died in 1813, though on unclear evidence. She does not appear in the Middlesex burial records that contain Dennis O'Kelly, Philip (who died in 1806) and Andrew; and I could not find her in the Westminster archives either. Her death is as obscure as her birth. But this is not the obscurity of poverty and disease that a huge majority of her fellow prostitutes suffered. Surviving into at least her mid-eighties, and doing so, in spite of her various setbacks, in comfort, Charlotte Hayes achieved an impressive transcendence of her background – thanks to her business flair, and thanks as well to Dennis O'Kelly and Eclipse.

Andrew Dennis O'Kelly died, suddenly, in 1820. He left a mystery surrounding his personal life: did he ever marry? In notes about the family left in the O'Kelly archive, Mary O'Kelly Harvey stated that he did, while Theodore Cook, author of *Eclipse and O'Kelly*, disagreed. Cook found references to a son, Charles, and to a daughter, Eliza, and he quoted a letter from Charles to Andrew dealing with the usual O'Kelly themes of bust-ups over rents and mortgages. ('Mr Michell went down to Grosvenor Place and discovered that Walton the broker was in the act of taking away all the furniture and yours with the rest . . .W Stacpoole says he will bring an action against you and he has no doubt but that he will be able to saddle you with all the taxes and rent of the house since Mr Stacpoole left England.') But Cook did not spot any references to this family in Andrew's will (dated 1820), and assumed that they had all died.

It seems that Eliza had. However, Cook disregarded a bequest to one Charles Andrews, a student in Aberdeen to whom Andrew gave an annuity of £200, with the provision that he must pursue his studies satisfactorily and observe morality in his conduct. In the National Archives, there is a will dated 1826 by one Charles Andrew O'Kelly. The brief document states that the author was described as Charles Andrews 'in the will of my late father Lt Colonel Andrew Dennis O'Kelly', and leaves everything to Charles's mother, named Susanna and with an illegible surname, about which one can be sure only that it is not O'Kelly.

The obvious conclusion to be drawn from this will and from Andrew's, which makes no mention of Charles's status as a member of the family, is that Andrew was unmarried, and that Charles was illegitimate. Andrew's will contains no reference, either, to a wife.

One of Andrew's principal legatees was his cousin, Philip Whitfield Harvey. The two were close: they had been in the Middlesex Militia together, and Andrew introduced Philip to the Prince of Wales and his circle. What is not clear is whether Andrew and Philip were involved in more clandestine activities. Philip's wife, Frances, inherited an Irish newspaper called the *Freeman's Journal* from a man called Francis Higgins, who had risen to newspaper proprietorship from an unpromising early career doing odd jobs for a felon in Newgate prison. In his will, Higgins also left Andrew £300, declaring that 'if I did not know that he, my friend, was in great affluence, I would have freely bequeathed him any property I might be possessed of'. Andrew's connection with Higgins, alleged W. J. Fitzpatrick in *Secret Service Under Pitt* (1892), was shady, and Andrew's role was as a conduit between the British government and various secret agents, among them Higgins (the 'Sham Squire'), who used his position at the *Freeman's Journal* to undermine the cause of Catholic emancipation.[138] If that was the case, Andrew may have approached Philip on behalf of the government too. In the family papers, Mary O'Kelly Harvey – daughter of Philip and Frances – is at pains to emphasize her

---

[138] Though as Fitzpatrick thought that Andrew and 'Count' O'Kelly (Dennis) were the same person, he may not be the most reliable guide.

Detail from Stubbs's great painting of Hambletonian (Eclipse's grandson)
after the horse's gruelling match with Diamond.

Right: a bookmaker and his client at Newmarket, at a time when bets were struck on an ad hoc basis.

Below: in the foreground, two men make a deal over a horse; with his back to us, Dennis O'Kelly instructs (to win or lose?) a jockey.

A race meeting at a country course, where the spectators find their own vantage points, by Rowlandson.

Rowlandson's *The Betting Post*, with the Prince of Wales (pointing) on the left, and Dennis O'Kelly (blue coat and crutches) on the right.

Left: the bloodstock auctioneer Tattersalls was at this time based near Hyde Park Corner in London.

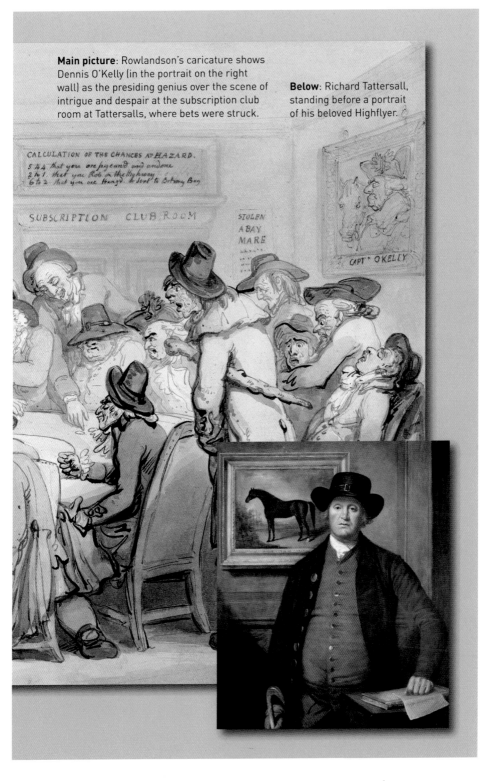

Main picture: Rowlandson's caricature shows Dennis O'Kelly (in the portrait on the right wall) as the presiding genius over the scene of intrigue and despair at the subscription club room at Tattersalls, where bets were struck.

Below: Richard Tattersall, standing before a portrait of his beloved Highflyer.

CALCULATION OF THE CHANCES AT HAZARD.
5 to 4 that you are pigeond and undone
2 to 1 that you Rob on the Highway
6 to 2 that you are Hang'd. & Sent to Botany Bay

SUBSCRIPTION CLUB ROOM

STOLEN
A BAY
MARE

CAPT.ᴺ O'KELLY

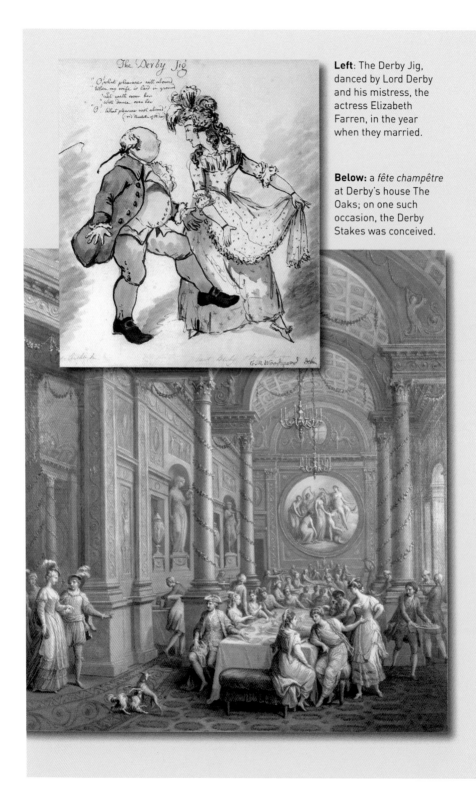

Left: The Derby Jig, danced by Lord Derby and his mistress, the actress Elizabeth Farren, in the year when they married.

Below: a *fête champêtre* at Derby's house The Oaks; on one such occasion, the Derby Stakes was conceived.

J. N. Sartorius's painting of the Derby in the 1790s, before it became the race that stopped the nation.

DERBY DAY

Buses from Morden Station to the Course
Every 30 Seconds   Fare 8d

Left: Vera Willoughby's 1932 poster advertises the bus service of one's dreams.

Below: a scene that might be from Evelyn Waugh or P. G. Wodehouse, at Tattenham Corner in the 1920s.

THIS PIECE OF PLATE with THE HOOF OF ECLIPSE was presented by HIS MOST GRACIOUS MAJESTY William the Fourth to the JOCKEY CLUB May 1832.

ECLIPSE

Eclipse relics (**clockwise from top**): the Jockey Club whip, reputedly containing hair from Eclipse's tail; a framed portion of his chestnut hide; three details of his hoof; and his skeleton. The skeleton is at the Royal Veterinary College, and the other bits of his anatomy are at the Jockey Club Rooms.

father's distance from the government, and says that he turned down money to write anti-Catholic propaganda, suffering discrimination as a result.[139]

Andrew certainly did make himself politically useful. In 1813, we find him investigating the conduct of the Prince's – now the Prince Regent's – estranged wife, Caroline of Brunswick. George Augustus had married Caroline, his cousin, under pressure from his father. His first meeting with her, just a few days before the wedding in 1795, was a shock: he found her revolting, and later described her as 'the vilest wretch this world was ever cursed with'. The Prince, seriously overweight, was far from gorgeous himself; but the unfailing willingness of glamorous women to become his mistresses may have blinded him to that realization. He sought refuge in alcohol on the happy day, and by the evening was so drunk that he collapsed into the fireplace of the bridal chamber, remaining there insensible until the morning. Nevertheless, the union was at some point consummated, and a daughter produced, before the couple separated. The Prince conducted further affairs. Caroline, it was rumoured, took lovers too – a treasonable offence, and one, if proved, that would have given a convenient justification for dispatching her and any descendants to outer darkness. As part of what was known as the 'delicate investigation', Andrew went to Caroline's house and interviewed her servants, but found no incriminating evidence. In 1821, when George Augustus succeeded to the throne, Caroline arrived at Westminster Abbey for the coronation, but was turned away at the doors.

Andrew was also an ally of the Prince in his racing interests. In that role, he got involved in the Escape Affair.

---

[139] The Act of Union of Great Britain and Ireland came into effect in 1801.

A target for caricaturists when he was Prince of Wales, George IV is portrayed more respectfully here, in an Ascot scene by John Doyle.

The Decline of the Jontleman

GEORGE AUGUSTUS FREDERICK, the Prince of Wales, was clever and – before he expanded to seventeen and a half stone in weight – handsome. He was also vain, extravagant and self-indulgent. His secret marriage to the Catholic widow Mrs Fitzherbert, his numerous affairs, his Whig sympathies, and his girth all made him a target for satirists. 'Let us enquire who are the chosen companions and confidential intimates of the Prince of Wales. They are the very lees of society: creatures, with whom a person of morality, or even common decency could not associate,' wrote Charles Pigott in his widely circulated lampoon *The Jockey Club: Or a Sketch of the Manners of the Age*.[140] '[George Augustus] was, however, genuinely fond of racing,' says the *Biographical Encyclopaedia of British Flat Racing*, as if pointing out the one trait that excuses everything.[141] One might point also in mitigation to the architectural splendours – among them the streets, terraces and other buildings of John Nash[142]

---

[140] For writing this attack on many of his fellow members, Pigott, you may recall, was invited by the actual Jockey Club to withdraw.

[141] Much as racing enthusiasts say of the Duke of Cumberland, in effect: 'Yes, he butchered a great many Scots; but he did breed Eclipse and Herod.'

[142] Whose best-known achievements include Regent's Park and Regent Street, as well as the remodelling of the Royal Pavilion in Brighton.

– that are the legacy of the Prince's extravagant patronage.

George Augustus ('Prinny') had his first runners on the racecourse – the jockeys wearing the royal colours of purple jacket with gold lace, scarlet sleeves and black cap – in 1784. By 1785, he already had eighteen horses in training, the winners including Eclipse's son (and former Derby winner) Saltram, Rockingham (later to be a rival to Dennis O'Kelly's Dungannon), and Rosaletta, who in one race finished second to Dennis's Soldier. The two owners – from absolutely contrasting backgrounds, but each frowned upon by certain sections of the establishment – were social acquaintances, and Dennis, had he still been alive when Pigott wrote *The Jockey Club*, would no doubt have got a mention alongside other representatives of the 'lees of society'. Prinny was a regular among the guests at Clay Hill when Dennis entertained during the Epsom spring meeting, and they appear together among the crowd of gesticulating and shouting gamblers in Rowlandson's caricature *The Betting Post*.[143]

By 1786, Prinny had twenty-six horses in training. Naturally, he also had huge debts, and because he got no help in clearing them from his father, he was forced to offload the entire stable. Not going to market from a position of strength, he could not command premium prices. The stud, reported the *St James's Chronicle*, 'was not sold but given away', to purchasers who in some cases sold on their horses immediately, for double what they had paid. Two of the fillies, Annette and Augusta, were to finish first and second in the 1787 Oaks – Augusta in the ownership of Dennis O'Kelly. Another lot, a Highflyer yearling, went to a Mr Franco. Later, the yearling kicked out in his box and got his foot stuck between the wooden boards, until the grooms managed to free him uninjured. He got the name Escape.

A year later, Parliament cleared Prinny's debts. Immediately,

[143] See chapter 18 and colour section.

he splashed out on racehorses again, buying back some of those he had sold, Escape among them. As the disapproving Charles Pigott wrote, 'No sooner had parliament voted this money, than decency was set at defiance, public opinion scorned, the turf establishment revived in a more ruinous style than ever, the wide field of dissipation and extravagance enlarged, fresh debts contracted to an enormous amount, which it is neither in his own, or the nation's power to discharge, and strong doubts entertained that the money voted by parliament was not applied to the purpose for which it was granted.'

In 1788, Prinny became the first royal winner of the Derby, with his colt Sir Thomas. He had thirty-five horses in training in 1789, and the following year he hired the leading jockey of the day, Sam Chifney, famous for the 'Chifney rush': a perfectly timed finishing burst after a quiet ride at the back of the field.

A portrait of Chifney gives him the roughened features of a minor member of Britain's gangland. But he was a dandy. His jockey's attire featured ruffs and frills, and he cultivated 'love locks' that hung down below his jockey's cap. He was also conceited. In his autobiography, to which he gave the frank title *Genius Genuine*, he claimed that 'In 1773 [when he was 18], I could ride horses in a better manner in a race to beat others, than any person I ever knew in my time; and in 1775, I could train horses for running better than any person I yet saw.' He was, in short, an upstart. Riding grooms then were merely promoted stable lads, and were considered to be, essentially, servants. Here was one assuming the trappings of celebrity. Moreover, Chifney did not appear to be honest. Those waiting tactics: were they not a ploy to lose races that he should be winning? Chifney was the kind of person that authorities are only too delighted to punish.

On 20 October 1791, at Newmarket, Prinny's horse Escape started as the hot, 1-2 favourite for a two-mile race worth sixty guineas. He finished last of four. The next day, he turned out again, for a four-mile race over the Beacon Course. Chifney, who had not backed him[144] in the first race, did so this time, at odds of 5-1; so did the Prince. Escape romped home, ahead of a field including two of the horses who had finished in front of him the day before.

As soon as he passed the post, the rumblings of suspicion and discontent started up. Here, surely, was a blatant scam, not only on the part of Chifney, but of the Prince as well, to get better odds in the second race. A Rowlandson caricature, *How to Escape Winning*, shows Chifney pulling Escape's reins and holding his whip in his mouth, while in the foreground Prinny, with a sly look at the viewer, taps his nose. Agitated, Prinny wrote to Sir Charles Bunbury:

> Dear Bunbury, I found on my arrival in London so many infamous and rascally lies fabricated relative to the affair that happened at Newmarket by republican scribblers and studiously circulating the country that I now find it absolutely necessary that these calumnies should be contradicted in the most authentic manner. After having consulted with many of my friends I leave what happened and the manner of contradiction to be discussed between you and my friend Sheridan[145] who has been so good as to undertake the management of this matter. P.s. If you think that any enquiries are necessary respecting Chifney I only beg you will see such steps taken as you think proper – I am very sincerely yours, G.R.

Bunbury did take what he thought were the proper steps. He hauled up Chifney to testify before him and his fellow Jockey Club stewards Ralph Dutton and Thomas Panton. Chifney, in his affidavit, swore that he had bet only twenty guineas on the race that Escape won; that he had not stopped Escape in the first

---

[144] Allowing jockeys to bet invites suspicion at best and corruption at worst. The Jockey Club eventually banned the practice in 1887.
[145] The politician and playwright Richard Brinsley Sheridan, author of *The Rivals* and *The School for Scandal*.

'How to ESCAPE Winning.'

Thomas Rowlandson's view of the Escape affair, How to Escape Winning *(1791). Sam Chifney, Escape's jockey, pulls the horse, who is further hampered by a banner saying,* 'Honi soit qui mal' *(a motto that also appears in* A Late Unfortunate Adventure at York — *page 106). The Prince of Wales taps his nose knowingly at the viewer.*

race; and that he had never profited from the defeat of a horse he had ridden or trained. The stewards were unimpressed. Bunbury paid a visit to Prinny and told him that 'if Chifney were suffered to ride the Prince's horses, no gentleman would start against him'.

Here, in summary, was the new dispensation on the Turf. Just over a century earlier, Charles II had governed at Newmarket; now, the heir to the throne was being shown his place.

Prinny did not like it, and the next year he put his stud on the market again. There are conflicting reports about whether he did so entirely because of Escape (his debts were again serious, and Escape's was not the only controversial race involving one of his horses); what is clear is that, while he was to return to the Turf once more and to race horses at Newmarket, he shunned the town until at least 1805, and probably thereafter as well, in spite of this letter from Bunbury and the Earl of Darlington:

> Sir, We humbly beg leave to represent to your Royal Highness that we are deputed in our official situations as stewards of Newmarket to convey to you the unanimous wish of all gentle-men of the turf now present at Brighton, which we respectfully submit to your consideration.
>
> From serious misconceptions or differences of opinion which arose relative to a race, in which your royal highness was con-cerned, we greatly regret that we have never been honoured with your presence there since that period. But experiencing as we constantly do, the singular marks of your condescension and favour, and considering the essential benefit not only that the Turf will generally derive, but also the great satisfaction that we all must individually feel from the honour of your presence, we humbly request that your Royal Highness will bury in oblivion any past unfortunate occurrences at Newmarket and you will again be pleased to honour us there with your countenance and support.

Reading the riot act to the Prince was one thing, but alienating him irrevocably was another.

Chifney, by contrast, was dispensable. Possibly the jockey had not always been honest in his riding, but on this occasion he looks like the victim of a miscarriage of justice. Everyone knows that jockeys sometimes stop horses, and that trainers leave horses unfit, or run them over inappropriate distances. However, when you look in detail at alleged incidents of these practices, you rarely find unambiguous evidence. The contemporary counterpart of Sam Chifney, certainly in respect of his brushes with the authorities, is the Irish-born jockey Kieren Fallon. In spring 1995, Fallon rode a beaten favourite, Top Cees, in a Newmarket handicap. Three weeks later, he rode Top Cees to an easy victory in the valuable Chester Cup, at the rewarding odds of 8-1. The *Sporting Life*[146] accused Fallon, along with Top Cees' trainer Lynda Ramsden and her husband Jack, of cheating. Fallon and the Ramsdens sued; the paper failed to prove its case, and was forced to pay £195,000 in damages, as well as costs. More recently, Fallon was the most prominent defendant in a race-fixing trial arising from an expensive investigation by the City of London police. The prosecution's evidence had many flaws – among them that, for the races under investigation, Fallon's winning percentage was actually higher than normal. The case collapsed.

In *Genius Genuine*, Chifney recalled that Escape was a 'stuffy' horse – one who needed plenty of exercise – and that the first race had toughened him up for the second. Escape was capable of putting in disappointing runs, and Chifney had shown himself a good judge of when they would take place. In the Oatlands handicap that year, he had chosen to ride Baronet, the eventual winner, instead. There was a horses for courses factor too: Escape had run some of his best races over the Beacon Course. At worst, it appears that Escape's connections were guilty of failing to

---

[146] Later merged with the *Racing Post*.

communicate to the betting public that their horse might not be at his best for the first, 20 October race.

The Prince, albeit after telling Bunbury to deal with Chifney 'as you think proper', stuck by the jockey. According to Chifney, Prinny's words were: 'Chifney, I am perfectly well satisfied with your conduct since you have rode for me, and I believe you have discharged your duty like an honest, faithful servant, and although I shall have no further occasion for you, having ordered all my horses to be sold, I have directed my treasurer to continue during my life to pay you your present salary of two hundred [guineas] a year.' Having received this verbal and financial tribute, Chifney concluded that the Prince was, no matter what others may have been saying, a great man. 'Language cannot describe my feelings on hearing this generous communication. I bowed and retired in silence, beseeching at the same time in my heart the Almighty to pour down his choicest blessings on a Prince whose magnanimity and goodness of heart induced him graciously to condescend to give protection and support to an unfortunate injured man, who but for this act of benevolence must otherwise have starved with his wife and children and who with them are bound to pray for such a generous benefactor.'

Chifney did not conduct his life thereafter with the humility that this encomium implies. Two hundred guineas was a sizeable professional's salary, and Chifney could carry on working as well, because the Jockey Club did not have the power, which it would later assume, to eject ('warn off') miscreants from racing alto-gether. Unfortunately, Chifney had an extravagant nature, and descended into debt. In about 1800, about nine years after the Escape scandal, he asked for and received permission from the Prince to sell the annuity. This was when Andrew Dennis O'Kelly became involved in the affair.

You will have noticed that, despite the stipulation in his uncle's will that he should abandon racing, Andrew continued to take part in the sport. He was never as serious about it as Dennis had been, but he raced up to seven horses during various seasons in the 1790s, and he also owned horses in partnerships – with the Marquess of Donegall, and with the Prince of Wales.[147] One of the mementoes of their continuing relationship is an 1801 letter from Andrew to George Augustus's equerry: 'I have endeavoured to select some venison out of my park at Cannons which I hope will prove worthy the Prince's acceptance. I have sent it by this day's coach directed to you and request you will do me the favour to present it with my most respectful duty to His Royal Highness.'

In 1800, Donegall took on Chifney as a groom. When Chifney sold his annuity to Joseph Sparkes for 1,200 guineas, someone had to offer security that Sparkes would get his yearly payments in return. Donegall said that he, being a marquess, could not do it, and asked Andrew to underwrite the sum instead. What followed was inevitable. The money went to Sparkes for a few years before drying up, and the annuity became another subject for litigation. In 1813, Andrew wrote that 'the holder of the annuity wishes to resume proceedings against me in the Court of Common Pleas'. Two years later, Andrew settled a sum on George Sparkes (to whom Joseph had assigned the annuity); a year after that, he deposed that the annuity was among Donegall's debts. It was another Donegall/O'Kelly mess.

The lump sum of 1,200 guineas gave Chifney only temporary relief. Defaulting on a payment of £350 to a saddler called Latchford, he was sent to the Fleet, where he died in 1807, aged fifty-three. He left behind the design for the 'Chifney bit', ignored by the Jockey Club at the time but later to become standard equipment in racing stables. Aimed at controlling highly strung horses, the bit gives handlers a firm control of the horse's jaw.

[147] A typically complicated arrangement concerned a mare called Scota. Jointly owned by Andrew and Prinny, Scota went to stud on the understanding that Prinny, paying an annuity for the privilege, would breed from her. When he sold his racing interests, he asked for her back.

It was apparent to the press at the time that the 1792 sale of the Prince of Wales's stud marked the end of an era. In its 13 March issue, *The Times* observed:

This was a melancholy sight to the whole kennel of black legs. Here end the hopes of royal plunder. Not even so much as a foal is to remain in his Highness's possession. The Turf is to be considered as a spot no longer tenable; and deserted by the Prince, it will soon be abandoned by every other gentleman in the kingdom.

Indeed, of late years, so much roguery has been practised, that there was no dependance to be placed on the horse or his rider – a pill of compounds given on the morning of running – a jockey purposely losing his weight, and many other tricks which lie in the power of the groom and the rider, without the possibility of detection, laid gentlemen so much at the mercy of their menial servants, that nothing short of ruin could be the consequences of a man of fortune attaching himself to Newmarket. The sale of the Prince's stud, it is therefore to be hoped, will be a good precedent for many more of a similar nature.

The Duke of York [Prinny's brother] was there, and bid for several of the horses. The public, no doubt, would naturally have hoped with us, that at a time when the Prince of Wales had seen the imprudence of keeping up a very large Turf establishment, the Duke of York would have followed his example; especially at a time when the friends of his Highness allege in Parliament that £37,000 a year, added to his other revenues, is not sufficient.

Trends are hard to spot as they begin, but *The Times* was prescient here. The era of Eclipse and O'Kelly – the era when Dennis and the likes of Lord Egremont and the Prince of Wales could be rogues together on the Turf – was over. A new era, of structured and regulated racing, was arriving. That does not mean that skulduggery disappeared. As we shall see, it got worse: more professional, and more vicious. It made one nostalgic for Dennis, the *jontleman* rogue.

In 1793, a *Sporting Magazine* correspondent (probably John Lawrence) was nostalgic already:

> The zenith of racing popularity, when the laurel of victory was disputed, and in eternal competition, among a Duke of Cumberland, a Captain O'Kelly, a Shafto, and a Stroud. There are, tis true, now in health and hilarity, some few of the sportsmen who then graced the turf with their presence and their possessions; they well know how gradually the turf has been declining from the splendour of those days, to its present state of unprecedented sterility. Racing, like cocking, seems to have had its day (at least for the present generation).
>
> Of the late D. O'Kelly, Esq, it may be very justly acknowledged, we shall never see a more zealous, or a more generous promoter of the turf, a fairer sportsman in the field, or at the gaming table. In his domestic transactions he was indulgently liberal, without being ridiculously profuse; and he was the last man living to offer an intentional insult unprovoked, so he was never known to receive one with impunity. In short . . . he was not in the fashion now extant.

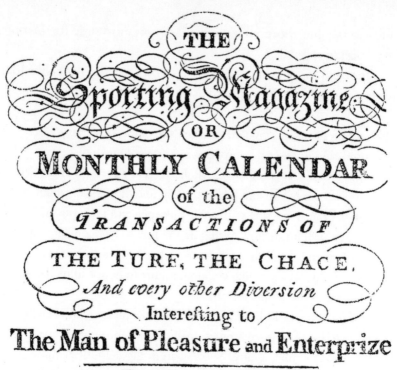

THE
Sporting Magazine
OR
MONTHLY CALENDAR
of the
TRANSACTIONS OF
THE TURF, THE CHACE,
And every other Diversion
Interesting to
The Man of Pleasure and Enterprize

VOLUME THE FIRST.

LONDON.
Printed for the PROPRIETORS, and Sold by J. WHEBLE;
N° 18. Warwick Square. Warwick Lane, near St Paul's.
MDCCXCIII.

The Sporting Magazine, *which contained many anecdotes about Eclipse, Dennis O'Kelly and their contemporaries.*

Artists' Models

THERE WAS ANOTHER COMMON interest in the lives of the O'Kelly family and the Prince of Wales: the painter George Stubbs (1724–1806). It may have brought them together as agents behind a puzzling episode in Stubbs's later career.

Some time after 1790, a 'gentleman' – his identity as guarded as that of the anonymous nobleman who commissioned Mozart's *Requiem* – called on Stubbs with a proposal. It was to paint, in the words of the prospectus that appeared in *The Sporting Magazine*, 'a series of pictures [portraits] from the Godolphin Arabian to the most distinguished horse of the present time, a general chronological history of the Turf specifying the races and matches and particular anecdotes and properties of each horse, with a view to their being first exhibited and then engraven and published in numbers'. The gentleman, identified to the public only as 'Turf', said that he had deposited with a banker the sum of £9,000, on which Stubbs could draw as required.

Stubbs was approaching his seventieth birthday. Born the son of a currier (someone who dresses leather) in Liverpool, he had largely taught himself his artistic techniques, a process that had included dissecting horses for eighteen months in

Lincolnshire. He rented a cottage in the village of Horkstow, where, assisted by his very tolerant common-law wife Mary Spencer, he anatomized a series of equine corpses. He bought each specimen alive, bled the horse to death, injected the arteries and veins with wax or tallow, suspended the body from an iron bar, and dissected and drew it for six or seven weeks, until it was so cut up and putrefied that he needed to move on to the next one. His first biographer, Ozias Humphry, gave an example of Stubbs's technique: 'He first began by dissecting and designing the muscles of the abdomen – proceeding through five different layers of muscles till he came to the peritoneum and the pleura through which appeared the lungs and the intestines – after which the bowels were taken out, and cast away.' Airless, noisome, and thick with bluebottles, that room would have displeased today's health and safety inspectorate.

When Stubbs arrived in London, towards the end of the 1750s, he quickly made his mark. His fine portraits, and his peerless paintings of horses and other animals – far in advance of previous works in the genre – put him in great demand among wealthy patrons. But interest in his work declined towards the end of the 1780s; and Stubbs, who was uncompromising and prickly, had a difficult relationship with the recently established but influential Royal Academy. The offer from 'Turf' of £9,000, attractive in itself, came with the bonus of an opportunity to promote the career of Stubbs's son, George Townly Stubbs.

An advertisement for the *Review of the Turf* appeared in *The Sporting Magazine* of January 1794. Dedicated 'by permission to His Royal Highness, the Prince of Wales', the *Review* would be

an accurate account of the performance of every horse of note that has started from the year 1750 to the present time; together with the pedigrees; interspersed with various anecdotes of the most remarkable races; the whole embellished with upwards of 145 prints, engraved in the best manner, from original portraits of

From The Anatomy of the Horse *(1766) by George Stubbs. Stubbs paid greater attention than had any previous artist to horse anatomy. However, not all experts believe his representations to have been consistently accurate (page 276).*

the most famous racers, painted by G. Stubbs, RA, at an immense expense, and solely for this work.

The whole to be published in numbers, each containing three capital prints, 20 inches by 16, in addition to three smaller, engraved from the same subject.

An elegant house is open in a central situation, under the title of the Turf Gallery, to which subscribers have a free admission.

Stubbs would produce the 145 or more paintings, to be exhibited at a gallery in Conduit Street, off Hanover Square. George Townly would make engravings from them for prints to be exhibited alongside the paintings, and to be available for purchase. The prints would also appear, in large and small sizes and three at a time, in successive numbers – a partwork, we would call it – of the *Review of the Turf*.

Stubbs and his anonymous backer knew all about segmenting the market. They offered various methods of purchase: you could buy the whole lot of pictures in advance, or you could buy single numbers, or single prints. At the time of the advertisement, there were already sixteen paintings on show in the gallery. One of them was of Eclipse, and another of his sire Marske. There were, however, never any more than those sixteen paintings, and just one number of the *Review of the Turf* appeared. Perhaps the subscription figures were disappointing? In any event, the £9,000 promised to Stubbs did not materialize.

The Prince of Wales and Andrew Dennis O'Kelly have both been associated with the *Review of the Turf*. The Prince was already a patron of Stubbs's work. Among his commissions was a portrait, showing him on horseback, with two terriers running ahead, by the Serpentine in Hyde Park. According to Stubbs's biographer Robin Blake, Prinny's obesity is 'carefully concealed'. Judy Egerton, in her magnificent *Catalogue Raisonné* of Stubbs's works, viewed the portrait differently, brusquely summarizing it as 'an overweight bully riding a long-suffering horse'. The two Stubbs experts arrived at varying conclusions too (though amicably) about the funding of the *Review of the Turf*. Blake agreed with the suggestion, advanced by others before him, that 'Turf' was George Augustus, the Prince of Wales; hence the reticence — shown both by Ozias Humphry and by 'T.N.', Stubbs's obituarist in *The Sporting Magazine* — over the patron's identity. The Prince would have wanted to be discreet about his association with a business venture, and following the Escape affair, in which he had been accused of setting up a betting coup,[148] he was not enjoying high esteem among the racing set who would be Stubbs's main customers. His indebtedness would also explain the non-appearance of the funding.

Holders of this theory, Judy Egerton suggested, may have fallen into the '*Great Expectations* fallacy' — the belief that a mysterious benefactor must be a grand personage. She advanced a different notion, with support from David Oldrey, former deputy senior steward of the Jockey Club: that 'Turf' was Andrew Dennis O'Kelly, in a surreptitious ploy to hype his stallions. Oldrey's principal evidence is that Dungannon, Volunteer and Anvil, the three contemporary stallions in the first *Review of the Turf* exhibition, all stood at the O'Kelly stud. Dungannon may have been worthy of an appearance in the *Review* (though eventually his record as a sire was disappointing), but Volunteer and Anvil were unproven, and sat oddly in a collection that also featured indisputable Thoroughbred giants such as the Godolphin Arabian, Marske and Eclipse. Of Anvil, the catalogue copy said that he 'may be ranked amongst the best stallions of the present day, and from the cross of the Eclipse mares in Mr O'Kelly's stud, with the blood of King Herod, much may be expected from this horse'. This was hype, and Andrew, and his father Philip, would have been embarrassed to be revealed as the authors of it.

To back up this view, Egerton pointed out the unlikelihood

[148] See chapter 17.

of the Prince of Wales, with business to transact with Stubbs, leaving his apartments in Carlton House to visit the painter in Somerset Street: he would have issued a summons instead. True; but the Prince could have commissioned an associate – perhaps Sheridan, who acted for him during the Escape affair – to pay the visit on his behalf. In response to Egerton's second argument, that Prinny was in no position to offer advances of up to £9,000, one might point out that an inability to match his expenditure to his financial circumstances was Prinny's regular failing. His racing interests were also represented in the first group of paintings and prints: Anvil had run under his colours; and there was also Stubbs's *Baronet at Speed with Samuel Chifney Up*, portraying the horse and jockey who had won for the Prince the 1791 Oatlands Handicap.

The O'Kelly papers do not help us, so we fall back on speculation. We have seen enough of the O'Kelly way of doing business to suggest a compromise solution to the *Review of the Turf* mystery: that there was a partnership of some kind between the Prince of Wales and Andrew. The arrangements would have been exceptionally complicated, involving breeding rights at the O'Kelly stud and various other considerations. However, subsequent events intervened. The Prince, engulfed in scandal and debt, sold his racehorses; the O'Kellys found that they could not offload the mares at their stud; the outbreak of war with France caused an atmosphere of financial uncertainty. The ambitious project collapsed. Andrew continued to acquire work by Stubbs nonetheless, and by 1809 he owned, according to John Lawrence, one of the largest collections of the artist's work.

Stubbs's portrait of Eclipse for the *Review of the Turf* is a copy of his 1770 *Eclipse at Newmarket, with a Groom and Jockey*, which hangs now in the Jockey Club Rooms in Newmarket. (The 1770 original is in private hands.) In Judy Egerton's expert view, while Eclipse is 'finely modelled' in the later version, 'the handling of the groom and jockey is more awkward', and the paint surface is 'thin'. In *The Sporting Magazine*, the two human figures were described as 'the boy who looked after [Eclipse], and Samuel Merrit, who generally rode him'. Whether the jockey really was Samuel Merriott is discussed elsewhere.[149] The labelling of the adult-looking groom as 'the boy' was a mark of the status of stable staff; today, they remain 'lads' and 'lasses'.

A print of this picture (see this book's colour section) hangs above my desk as I write. Eclipse, saddled, stands before a square brick building with a pitched roof of yellowish tiles. We know, from a landscape study by Stubbs of the same scene, that the building is the four-miles stables rubbing-house at the start of the Newmarket Beacon Course, and can therefore speculate that the scene is the prelude to what may have been Eclipse's toughest race, his match of 17 April 1770 against Bucephalus.[150] Eclipse has a cropped tail and a plaited mane. Light makes gleaming patterns on his chestnut coat. His body is long; he has an athletic elegance. Behind him, the Newmarket heath stretches towards a modest row of trees. The horizon is a quarter way up the picture, and the big sky above is springlike, with massing white and dark clouds.

The 'boy', smartly dressed in a black coat, holds Eclipse's reins, and looks over his shoulder, with what may be apprehension, at the jockey. This groom has had to get Eclipse to Newmarket, keep him fed and watered and healthy and happy, and present him in perfect condition on the day. Now he transfers the responsibility, and all he can do is wait and watch. Eclipse is looking at the jockey too; and Merriott – if it is he – returns the look, calmly. Without that calm, he could not do his job – no matter how good his horse may be. He wears the red colours with a black cap that Dennis O'Kelly had appropriated from William Wildman on buying Eclipse; he carries a whip, but as if reassuring the horse

---

[149] See chapter 8 and Appendix 1.
[150] Eclipse's other race on the Beacon Course took place later that year, on 3 October, against Sir Charles Bunbury's Corsican.

he will not use it, and he does not wear spurs on his boots, reminding us that Eclipse 'never had a whip flourished over him, or felt the tickling of a spur'.[151]

As so often in Stubbs's work, what we witness here is a quiet, contemplative moment apart from the action. Every element of the scene is beautifully placed, so that, in spite of Merriott's striding posture, the painting conveys stillness. The horse and his rider are about to offer a demonstration of greatness, in front of cheering crowds. But Stubbs does not show these jubilant events, either in this or in any other of his paintings. When he does show a race, in his portrait of Gimcrack at Newmarket, the contest is only a trial, climaxing in front of a shuttered stand; it has taken place in the past, and is in the background of the picture, while the foreground has Gimcrack with his stable staff at the rubbing-house. There is in Stubbs's paintings a very British mix, apparent too in the poetry of Tennyson and the music of Elgar, of grandeur and melancholy.

The portrait of Eclipse borrows from a study Stubbs made of the horse, with a plain background behind. The study, donated by the late American collector (and owner of the great horse Mill Reef) Paul Mellon, hangs now in the Royal Veterinary College, facing Eclipse's skeleton.

Stubbs had also used this study for *Eclipse with William Wildman and His Sons John and James* (see colour section). This affectingly informal portrait places Wildman and his sons with Eclipse beneath a giant, forked oak tree. The Surrey downs fall away behind them. Wildman, seated on the trunk of the tree, is pointing – perhaps to his sons, perhaps to the horse. The boys wear tricorn hats as he does, and are finely dressed in blue coats, waistcoats and breeches. The older holds Eclipse's reins; the younger leans casually against the tree, with his hand on the shoulder of his

---

[151] From John Lawrence's *The History and Delineation of the Horse* (1809).

brother, who turns back to say something to him. They look affectionate, and happy, and proud of their horse.[152]

Stubbs's painting stayed in the Wildman family until the early twentieth century, and after various transactions crossed the Atlantic, to be bought in 1929 by William Woodward, chairman of the American Jockey Club. At about this time a clumsy restoration job was done on it. Having since received more skilled attention, it hangs in the Baltimore Museum of Art.

The intimate atmosphere of *Eclipse with William Wildman and His Sons* suggests a close relationship between painter and owner. Wildman may also appear in a series of four Stubbs paintings showing two gentlemen on a day's shooting expedition on the Duke of Portland's estate. Robert Fountain and Judy Egerton discussed the possible identification, though with caveats; the brown-coated man who may be Wildman does not bear a very close resemblance to the figure in the Eclipse portrait. But Wildman did own this series. Other Stubbs works in his collection – at that time, the largest aside from the Prince of Wales's – included portraits of Marske, Gimcrack and Euston; further portraits of horses, grooms and gamekeepers; a painting of a horse frightened by a lioness; and various dogs.

If you cannot afford Stubbs, one collector of the time advised his friend, try George Garrard. Certainly, Garrard (1760–1826) fills the runner-up spot among contemporary painters of Eclipse. His portrait, dated to 1788 (see colour section), shows

---

[152] It is possible that one or both of these boys did not survive William Wildman. The nomenclature and the dates are confusing. Robert Fountain, author of *William Wildman and George Stubbs*, said that the elder son was called William. (Perhaps he was called John William, or William John.) Unable to find any records for William, he speculated that the boy died before his father did (in 1784). Fountain also said that James died in 1827, at the age of fifty-four; so James could not have appeared in *William Wildman and His Sons*, if Stubbs painted it before Wildman sold Eclipse in 1770. See chapter 11.

Eclipse the stallion, with a typically muscly, powerful neck, and a high crest. The horse stands against a background of thick woods – near the ones, we may conjecture, in which he was rumoured to have roamed in his younger days, when his rider Ellers would take him poaching. Garrard's painting is cruder than Stubbs's work, but in compensation conveys Eclipse's strength and power.

The kinds of early representations of the Thoroughbred that one has come to think of as typical of the era are the portraits in which Francis Sartorius (1734–1804) and his son John Nost Sartorius (1759–1828) specialized. Their horses have spindly frames, with long and oddly curved necks; they gallop like rocking horses, with all four legs splayed out at once. The absurdity of this stride was not the painters' fault: no artists then understood how horses moved, because they could not distinguish the motions of the legs with the naked eye. Stubbs may have sensed that something was wrong with the traditional way of representing horses at the gallop, and for that reason – and because he was not an enthusiast for the sport – rarely depicted racing scenes. Of one of the rare exceptions, *Baronet at Speed with Samuel Chifney Up*, a contemporary critic commented, 'There is something very singular in this picture, the horse's legs are all off the ground, at that moment when raised by muscular strength – a bold attempt, and as yet well perfected, this attitude has never been yet described but by Mr Stubbs.'

Stubbs was only half right. A horse *is* airborne briefly during a gallop. But, as the photographer Eadweard Muybridge was to demonstrate some eighty years later, this moment occurs when the legs are tucked under the body. Muybridge's photographic sequence, *The Horse in Motion*, showed that when the legs extended, one rear leg and one foreleg hit the ground first (though not at the same time), and that the others (the 'lead' legs) followed, extending further. For a moment, one leg and then two support half a ton of animal.[153]

---

[153] A 'rotatory' motion, or 'cross-cantering', involves different front and rear leads. For dogs, a rotatory motion when running is normal.

Clearly, Francis Sartorius had no inkling of these mechanics when he attempted to paint Eclipse at full speed. While the result is, in the words of Theodore Cook,[154] 'somewhat impossible', it does at least convey the horse's huge stride, and reveals a distinctive, and rather ungainly, head carriage, level with his body. The title of one picture names the jockey in the scarlet and black as John Oakley, adding to our doubts about whether Oakley or Merriott – named by Stubbs – was Eclipse's usual partner. A further Sartorius is a rare depiction of a walkover: Eclipse and his jockey are making their leisurely way towards a King's Plate. The course, narrow and climbing and marked with white posts, seems better suited to cross-country runs than to horse races.

John Nost made use of his father's studies, in one instance placing copies of Francis's portraits of Eclipse and of the stallion Shakespeare side by side in a single composition. Why he did so is not clear. Perhaps he believed the rumours that Shakespeare, rather than Marske, was Eclipse's sire. It may be relevant that John Nost lived in Carshalton, near to the O'Kelly stud at Epsom and to the farm where Shakespeare had stood for a while. Although Shakespeare's owners – if they commissioned the portrait – could gain no commercial advantage from it (their horse being dead by the time of composition in the 1780s), they may have wanted it for sentimental reasons.

The Sartoriuses were simply in business to give sporting patrons what they wanted, and their paintings reflect no greater ambition than that. Stubbs had to satisfy patrons too, but he created work with a more ambiguous tone. The nobility of his animals is inscrutable, and vulnerable; the humans merely associate with it. A contemporary artist who has recast that ambiguity in more blatant terms is Mark Wallinger, winner of the 2007 Turner Prize. Wallinger invokes Eclipse in his series entitled *Race, Class, Sex,*

[154] In *Eclipse and O'Kelly*.

paintings of four of Eclipse's male-line descendants. The portraits are life-size, in a hyper-realist style, and set against white backgrounds. According to copy in a catalogue of Wallinger's work, they are a 'recasting of a historical painting genre in terms of the rhetoric of the stud book'. Moreover, they 'can be read in terms of a discourse on representation itself'. The only radical quality of these themes is the jargon accompanying them: Stubbs managed all of this, and more.

Like Eclipse, Dennis O'Kelly was immortalized by one of the greatest artists of the day. There is no record of Dennis's acquaintanceship with Thomas Rowlandson (1756–1827), though his presence in a series of Rowlandson prints is a clue that the two were familiar.

Educated at the Royal Academy, Rowlandson started out as a serious painter, but turned to more immediately remunerative caricatures after squandering a £7,000 inheritance – some of it going to Dennis, perhaps – at the gaming tables of London. With a relish for teeming, anarchic scenes, he excelled at depicting racecourses, with their shady gambling booths, riotous beer tents, lecherous men, loose women and conspiring punters.

The dating of these pictures places them after Dennis's death. Dennis appears shabbily dressed, with stomach bulging above his breeches, wearing a tricorn hat containing some sort of leafy arrangement,[155] and – no doubt because of his gout – carrying a crutch. In *The Betting Post* (see colour section), he is weighing down a small, rotund pony. The Prince of Wales, already at this young age (he must be in his early twenties) showing signs of corpulence, is also on horseback, and has his arm outstretched, striking a bet. The tightly grouped pack of men are all clamouring and gesticulating; only Dennis, who sits slightly detached from the crowd, makes no movement. The implication may be that he is

---

[155] It may be, as a badge of the land of his birth, clover.

the knowing one, the man with a sure grasp of how this race will turn out.

In *The Mount*, Dennis stands before a jockey being helped into his riding gear, and gives instructions with an emphatic gesture of his hand. In *The Course*, he is a figure in the boisterous crowd; he is walking on his crutch and holding a hand to his head, as if in despair at some loss. *Colonel Dennis O'Kelly Making a Deal* (shown in this book's colour section) again shows Dennis, this time with his back to us, giving instructions to a jockey. Why is that 'making a deal'? Perhaps there was a case of mistaken identity when the picture was named, and Dennis was taken for the dealer[156] showing off a horse in the foreground. Or perhaps Dennis's deal with the jockey is somewhat shady.

Dennis may also be the gambler in military uniform in Rowlandson's *A Kick-up at a Hazard Table*, published in 1787, the year Dennis died. He has an empty pocket book, and with a pointed pistol is accusing the man opposite him of cheating. The man brandishes his own pistol – less convincingly – in return, clutches his winnings, and cowers. There is a great hubbub round the table: a spectator holds a chair aloft, and is about to bring it down on Dennis's arm; another is about to tackle Dennis's opponent; some gamblers reach for their swords, while others attempt to get out of the way. Joseph Grego, an early authority on Rowlandson's caricatures, said that the incident that inspired this print took place at the Royal Chocolate House in St James's, and was broken up by guardsmen, 'who were compelled to knock the parties down with the butt ends of their muskets'.

An earlier caricature of Dennis, by an artist called Mansergh, is entitled *The Eclipse Macarony*. A macarony (or macaroni) was a dandy – a word that evokes a young, slender, foppish figure. But Dennis, perched on a horse at the betting post and

---

[156] Perhaps Richard Tattersall – he is standing under an advertisement for Highflyer.

again wearing a hat with a leafy motif, is gross. His rounded chin juts out over floppy jowls. A substantial, collared coat emphasizes his bulk.

Thus, in their contrasting styles, Rowlandson and Stubbs paid tributes to Dennis and Eclipse: the burly rogue and the gracious equine athlete. It would be pleasing to claim that Eclipse, the greatest racer Stubbs painted, inspired his greatest work. But, superb though the three pictures are, they yield to a still greater portrait that Stubbs was to paint, at the age of seventy-five, of Eclipse's grandson – Hambletonian.

Eclipse's Legacy – the Eighteenth and Nineteenth Centuries

THIS CHAPTER AND THE next follow the Eclipse male line: a vital thread as racing developed. It tells the stories of the Eclipse descendants who have been at the centre of some of the most significant or dramatic events in the sport. They include the inspirer of the greatest equine painting; the Derby winner that never was; the Derby winner that avenged Waterloo; and the Derby winner that broke a gambler's heart. There is the colt who did not run in the Derby, or in any other Classic, but who became the Eclipse of the nineteenth century. There are two of the fastest fillies on the Turf. There is the supreme steeplechaser, nicknamed simply 'Himself'. There is the colt who was the last winner of the English Triple Crown, but who could not give of his best in the race that was supposed to confirm his greatness. There is the American champion who, in the final leg of the Triple Crown, left the rest nowhere. I might have included many others: the great Italian champion Ribot; Sea Bird, an even greater horse than Secretariat, according to some; Red Rum, the triple Grand National winner; Shergar, winner of the Epsom Derby by a record margin. Through them all, the Eclipse bloodline helped shape racing as it is today. But the horses that follow seem to me to have played important parts in Turf history.

The focus on the male line may appear to be a sexist approach. Certainly, there have been famous horses, such as Seabiscuit, who were not Eclipse's tail male descendants.[157] Some of the horses in the following pages did nothing to perpetuate the line: Running Rein, having given his name to an impostor, disappeared; Arkle was a gelding. The justification for concentrating on the male line is as mentioned earlier: that, as it continues, it multiplies, saturating pedigrees. A successful stallion sires hundreds of sons (and daughters), sometimes thousands. If a few of the sons become successful stallions, continuing the male line, they will have hundreds of sons (and daughters) too. A few generations later, these descendants will cross: multiplication upon multiplication.

According to my count, there are eighty-one instances of Eclipse in the pedigree of St Simon (born in 1881, just under a hundred years after Eclipse's death). Thanks to St Simon's successes as a sire, the increase in that number in succeeding generations was exponential.[158] The Eclipse line thus became the most significant genetic factor in the history of horseracing.

Hambletonian (born in 1792)

Eclipse — King Fergus — Hambletonian

The greatest of all horseracing paintings is a tribute to the Thoroughbred, but not to the Turf. It shows the nobility of a magnificent horse; and it shows us, the spectators, to be exploiters of that nobility.

Hambletonian, stabled in Yorkshire, was a winner of the St Leger, and undefeated in races he had completed (he had once, at

[157] Seabiscuit, the American folk hero of the 1930s, descended on the side of his sire, Hard Tack, from the Godolphin Arabian and Matchem — although his dam, Swing On, was from the Eclipse line.
[158] Though the St Simon male line is less abundant today.

York, veered off the course). He was owned by a hard-drinking, hard-gambling baronet of twenty-eight, Sir Harry Vane-Tempest. In 1798, Vane-Tempest's horse Shuttle lost a 1,000-guineas match to Joseph Cookson's Diamond, the Newmarket champion. Seeking revenge, Vane-Tempest challenged Cookson to race Diamond against Hambletonian, this time for 3,000 guineas. The match would take place on 25 March 1799 (Easter Monday) over the four miles-plus of the Beacon Course at Newmarket, and Hambletonian would carry 8st 3lb, while Diamond would carry eight stone.

The quality of the horses, and the north versus south element of the contest, brought a huge crowd – 'the greatest concourse of people that ever was seen' – to Newmarket. Inns for miles around were packed. Hundreds of thousands of pounds were bet; Hambletonian was the favourite, and went off at 5-4 on. Vane-Tempest, a man of quick and excitable passions, found the tension on race day almost too hard to bear, confessing to Frank Buckle, as the famously unflappable jockey mounted Hambletonian, 'By God, I'd give the whole stake to be half as calm as you!'

At the off, Buckle allowed Hambletonian to settle in behind Diamond. He kicked on ahead after a mile and a quarter, before they reached the dog-leg right turn that took them in the direction of town, towards the finishing post. Hambletonian led by about two lengths, until Dennis Fitzpatrick, Diamond's jockey, spurred his mount forward to challenge. The two, with their riders driving them brutally, charged side by side to the line, Hambletonian just warding off his rival and getting home by 'half a neck'. 'Both horses were much cut with the whip, and severely goaded with the spur, but particularly Hambletonian; he was shockingly goaded.'[159]

[159] From *The Sporting Magazine*, quoted by Judy Egerton in *George Stubbs, Painter*. Different standards of behaviour towards the horse prevailed then. Today, there are no spurs of course, and jockeys get punished for excessive use of the whip.

Vane-Tempest was as exultant after the race as he had been nervous before. He commissioned George Stubbs to paint two pictures recording Hambletonian's triumph, and advertised in *The Sporting Magazine* that 'No artist whatever, except Mr Stubbs, has had my permission to take any likeness of Hambletonian since he was in my possession.' Of this claim, the editor of the magazine sniffed that it 'partakes too much of PUFF for a gentleman's signature to accompany'. Vane-Tempest's puff was evanescent, and he certainly did not behave like a gentleman. He refused to pay Stubbs, went to court to defend himself against the painter's claim for 300 guineas, and lost. One of Stubbs's paintings, of Hambletonian as he won the race, never went beyond the drawing stage, and has since disappeared. That left John Nost Sartorius to portray the scene in traditional fashion: elongated horses stretching for the winning post; gentlemen in top hats in pursuit; roaring crowds.

What we have from Stubbs is *Hambletonian, Rubbing Down* (see colour section). The crowds have gone. Dominating the frame, Hambletonian jerks and twists – improbably balanced on his two left legs – in nervous exhaustion. A squat, dour groom stands at his head, holding the reins; a stable lad rests one hand on the horse's withers, and has a rubbing cloth in the other. Both figures look at us impassively. You have had your fun, they seem to imply; you are intruding now, and it is we whose concern is this battered horse. It is a long way from the celebratory scene that Vane-Tempest thought he had ordered, and one can see why he was disappointed. At the heart of racing are blood, sweat and mystery, never more powerfully depicted than in this masterpiece.

Hambletonian recovered, won more races, and retired to stud. He sired more than 140 winners, and continued an Eclipse line that descended to and beyond the greatest racehorse of the nineteenth century, St Simon.

Whalebone (b. 1807)

Eclipse — Pot8os — Waxy — Whalebone

As well as breeding Eclipse, the Duke of Cumberland owned another great horse, Herod. It was the cross of Eclipse and Herod lines — male and female descendants of Eclipse mating with female and male descendants of Herod — that was 'the strongest single factor in the successful transformation of the Thoroughbred from a typical eighteenth-century weight carrier over long distances to the nineteenth-century carrier of weights over short distances'.[160] Among the first demonstrators of this transformation were the early Derby winners Waxy and his son Whalebone, and they passed on the Eclipse/Herod genius to future generations.

Waxy, whose dam was a daughter of Herod called Maria, was one of six sons of Pot8os among the thirteen runners in the Derby of 1793. He was only fourth favourite in the betting, at 12-1, but he came home with half a length to spare over the odds-on shot Gohanna; and after he and Gohanna had fought a tremendous series of rematches, he spent most of his well-earned retirement at the Duke of Grafton's stud at Euston Hall, Norfolk. Grafton — the undistinguished Prime Minister in the 1760s and the scandalous consorter with the prostitute Nancy Parsons — once ordered that an avenue of trees, through which he might drive to the races, be planted between Euston Hall and Newmarket, twenty miles away. The planters had to stop with six miles to go, when they came up against — Grafton had not considered this obstacle — someone else's land.

The Duke bred Waxy's greatest son by putting Waxy to his mare Penelope. Their offspring, Whalebone, was no looker. He was just over fifteen hands tall — a standard height in Eclipse's day but one that now, just forty years later, was considered modest. A stud groom described him as 'the lowest and longest and most

---

[160] From the *Biographical Encyclopaedia of British Flat Racing*.

double-jointed horse, with the best legs and the worst feet I have ever seen'. Later, the racing writer 'The Druid' (Henry Hall Dixon), who had named Waxy 'the modern ace of trumps in the Stud Book', summed up Whalebone as 'shabby'. In training, The Druid added, Whalebone's chief occupation 'was to rear and knock his hooves together like a pair of castanets'.

Despite these dubious traits, Whalebone went off the 2-1 favourite for the 1810 Derby, and he justified the odds easily, leading all the way. But his subsequent career on the racecourse was chequered, and his initial covering fee on retiring to stud was a modest ten guineas. His performance as a stallion proved that valuation wrong. The line through his son Camel produced numerous champions, among them the great 1930s winner Hyperion. Through another son, Sir Hercules, descend the most valuable horses in bloodstock breeding today. The historian Roger Mortimer wrote of Whalebone, 'A very high proportion . . . of the great horses in racing history include his name in their pedigree.'

Running Rein (b. 1841)

Eclipse — Pot8os — Waxy — Whalebone — Waverly — The Saddler — Running Rein

The judge called Running Rein the winner of the 1844 Derby. The only problem was that Running Rein was somewhere else at the time. Another contestant in the race was also an impostor. A further was pulled by his jockey; yet another was nobbled, and then pulled as well. It was an event of almost farcical corruption.

Turf morals, never impeccable, were at their lowest in the first half of the nineteenth century. In the early 1800s, bookmakers had arrived on racecourses, quoting odds about every horse in a race rather than, as gamblers had done in Dennis O'Kelly's day, striking bets individually ('Eclipse first, and the rest nowhere'). It was during this period too that Tattersalls, the bloodstock auctioneer, opened its subscription rooms, and book-makers who settled bets there formed themselves into a group known as the Ring.[161] Many of them were, in the historian Roger Longrigg's haughtily contemptuous phrase, 'deplorable little men'. They corrupted stable staff and jockeys, and in notorious incidents at Doncaster and Newmarket poisoned horse troughs. One of the most feared was 'Ludlow' Bond, who used to be seen mounted on a grey on Newmarket Heath and who was known as 'death on a pale horse'. Then there was Crockford, 'the second most evil man on the 19th-century Turf' in Longrigg's view[162] and someone of extreme lack of physical attractiveness: 'His cheeks,' the writer Sylvanus wrote, 'appeared whitened and flabby . . . His hands were entirely *without knuckles*, soft as raw veal, and as white as paper, whilst his large, flexible mouth was stuffed with "dead men's bones" – his teeth being all false.' You did not want to meet an angry Crockford. You did not want to meet him cheerful either: his laugh was 'hideous'.

Crockford enjoyed his most rewarding coup when he bribed the starter to ensure that Mameluke, on whom he had taken many bets for the 1827 St Leger, lost. In the Running Rein Derby of 1844, he was the owner of the second favourite, Ratan. Someone got to the horse on the night before the race, however, and next morning Ratan's coat 'was standing like quills upon the fretful por-cupine, his eyes were dilated, and he shivered like a man with ague'.[163] The colt nevertheless started for the race; to make doubly certain that he could not win, his jockey, Sam Rogers, pulled him. Crockford, devastated at being done to as he was in the habit of doing to others, died two days later. Gamblers who had bet with him on the Oaks propped him up in an armchair at his club, to

---

[161] The enclosures that house betting rings on racecourses are often known as Tattersalls, or 'Tatts'.

[162] Longrigg's candidate for the top spot is Henry Padwick. See the essay on Hermit, coming up.

[163] Quoted in *Derby Day 200* (1979).

ensure that he appeared to be alive until after the race – that way, their bets remained valid. Corpse-like in life, Crockford passed for a living person when dead.

The man who set about tackling this corruption was Lord George Bentinck. Sir Charles Bunbury had been the first Dictator of the Turf;[164] Bentinck was the second. Bunbury was a rigid man of integrity; Bentinck was an arrogant, impulsive and not always scrupulous gambler. In 1840, he made £60,000 backing his filly Crucifix, who won the 2,000 Guineas, 1,000 Guineas and Oaks; and then, knowing that she had broken down, he made more money by laying against her for the St Leger.[165] Later, he got into a duel with the best shot in England, George Osbaldeston, after he had accused Osbaldeston of cheating over a bet and had paid his £200 of losses to him slowly, note by note, asking, 'Can you count?' – to which Osbaldeston replied, 'I could at Eton.' Osbaldeston challenged Bentinck and was determined to kill him, but on the intercession of friends he settled for firing his bullet through his opponent's hat. Bentinck survived to reform the starting system, introducing flag starts to replace the previously chaotic procedure in which a man simply shouted 'Go!', and in particular to pursue corrupt gamblers and their associates. The Running Rein affair was his most notable success.

Running Rein was bought as a yearling by Goodman Levy ('Mr Goodman'), a gambler, and entered for his first race, at Newmarket, the following year. But, instead of Running Rein, the horse that ran at Newmarket was Maccabaeus, a three-year-old. What had happened to Running Rein is not recorded: you fear that it was not pleasant. Maccabaeus was backed down from 10-1 to

---

[164] Some historians say that he was the third. The first, by their count, was Charles II, and the second was Tregonwell Frampton, the eccentric 'Keeper of the running horses at Newmarket' under William III, Queen Anne, George I and George II.

[165] According to William Day, son of the trainer John Day. Another version of the story has it that John Day was responsible for the deception.

Lord George Bentinck, who successfully pursued the chief fraudsters at 'the dirtiest Derby in history'.

3-1, won the race, and made Goodman a fair deal of money. The Duke of Rutland, owner of the runner-up, protested against the result without effect. The case – in which Rutland had Bentinck's support – came to trial, but collapsed when a stable lad (for reasons at which we can only guess) swore that the winning horse really was Running Rein.

'Running Rein' (that is, Maccabaeus) was entered for the following year's Derby,[166] before which Bentinck, who had been gathering evidence over the winter, got up a petition against the colt's taking part. But the Epsom stewards made the odd decision to allow him to race, with the proviso that there would be an inquiry if he won. He did win, by three parts of a length.[167] Enter m'learned friends.

'Produce the horse! Produce the horse!' the judge demanded at the trial – the true age of 'Running Rein' could have been determined by an examination of his teeth. But Goodman and his associates did not produce the horse. Rather, they withdrew from the case, and fled the country. 'If gentlemen would associate with gentlemen, and race with gentlemen, we should have no such practices. But if gentlemen will condescend to race with blackguards, they must expect to be cheated,' the judge concluded.

The cheating in the 1844 Derby had not stopped at Maccabaeus and Ratan. The rider of the favourite, Ugly Buck, like Sam Rogers on board Ratan, pulled on his reins to make sure that his mount could not win. The stewards grew suspicious about the appearance of a horse called Leander, and when Leander had to be put down because Maccabaeus had struck into him and broken his

[166] The Derby is for three-year-old colts and fillies. Goodman's cheat was not unprecedented. The stud groom for five-times Derby winner Lord Egremont admitted that he had twice won the race with four-year-olds.
[167] A four-year-old competing against three-year-olds at this time of year would normally carry 11lb more on his back, to compensate for his greater maturity.

leg, they ordered that his jaw be cut off and examined. The vets announced that Leander was a four-year-old. Leander's owners, German brothers called Lichtwald, were warned off English race-courses for life. They took it badly, one of them declaring that the English were liars – Leander was not four, but six!

After all that, the winner of the 1844 Derby was announced as Orlando. His owner was Colonel Peel, brother of the Tory Prime Minister Sir Robert Peel and, unfashionably, an honest sportsman.

Bentinck's lifelong ambition was to win the Derby. Two years later, he sold his racing stud in order to commit himself to politics. One of the yearlings in the sale was called Surplice. In 1848, Surplice won the Derby – for his new owner, Lord Clifden. Bentinck's despair was recorded by his friend Benjamin Disraeli, who had come across him a day or two later in the House of Commons Library.

> [Bentinck] gave a sort of superb groan. 'All my life I have been trying for this, and for what have I sacrificed it?' he murmured. It was in vain to offer solace. 'You do not know what the Derby is,' he moaned out.
>   'Yes, I do, it is the Blue Ribbon of the Turf.'
>   'It is the Blue Ribbon of the Turf,' he slowly repeated to him-self, and sitting down, he buried himself in a folio of statistics.

A few months later, Bentinck died of a heart attack. He was forty-six.

Gladiateur (b. 1862)

Eclipse – Pot8os – Waxy – Whalebone – Defence – The Emperor – Monarque – Gladiateur

By the mid-nineteenth century, England had been exporting Thoroughbreds, to Europe and to the New World, for more than a hundred years. Racehorses went to Ireland, France, Italy, Germany, Austria, Hungary, Russia, Switzerland, the Netherlands and Scandinavia; they went to North and South America; they went to South Africa, Australia and New Zealand. In 1730, Bulle Rock, a son of the Darley Arabian, emigrated to Virginia, and similarly bred racers followed him across the Atlantic, among them the first Derby winner Diomed, who had a grandson called American Eclipse. Sons and daughters of Whalebone, in the Eclipse male line, also made the journey. In France, the Société d'Encouragement pour l'Amélioration des Races de Chevaux en France (Society for the Improvement of French Bloodstock) promoted the importation of English stock, and the French Stud Book referred to the Thoroughbred as the *Pur-Sang Anglais* (Pure-blooded English). The English, meanwhile, continued to assume that their bloodstock was the best. Gladiateur, 'The Avenger of Waterloo', shattered that illusion.

The one claim that the English could make of Gladiateur was that an Englishman, Tom Jennings of Newmarket, trained him. Jennings did a skilful job, because Gladiateur suffered from navicular disease, an inflammation of the bones in one of his front feet, and was often unsound. He was unfit when he raced for the 2,000 Guineas, but won, at odds of 7-1. For the Derby, he was in much better shape, and he came from behind – he was in tenth place as the field rounded Tattenham Corner – to pass the post in front by two lengths. It was a sensational result, and a French newspaper played up the Anglo-French rivalry, reporting that Gladiateur had required protection from six hundred hired bouncers, and that there had been a plot by the English to seize his jockey, Harry Grimshaw, and bleed him, so that he would be too weak to perform at his best.

In fact, Gladiateur's triumph was popular, as triumphs by favourites tend to be. The colt next crossed the Channel to his homeland, and in front of 150,000 spectators won the Grand Prix de Paris. After two victories at Goodwood came the St Leger, the third leg (after the 2,000 Guineas and the Derby) of the Triple Crown, won previously only by West Australian (in 1853). Two days before the race, Gladiateur was lame. But he defied his infirmity to defeat the Oaks winner, Regalia. His only defeat that year came when Grimshaw, who was short-sighted, allowed him to get too far behind the leaders in the Cambridgeshire handicap, in which he was unplaced.

Though increasingly unsound, Gladiateur won all his six races the following season, his greatest victory coming in the Ascot Gold Cup. It was another race in which Harry Grimshaw allowed his rivals – there were just two, Regalia and Breadalbane – to get away from him, and at halfway he was some three hundred yards in arrears. Then he gave Gladiateur his head. The colt, oblivious to the effect on his suspect foreleg of pounding over the bone-hard ground, swallowed up the others' lead, overtook them before the turn into the straight, and passed the post forty lengths clear. Regalia finished exhausted, and Breadalbane was pulled up. 'The Vigilant', writing in *The Sportsman*, described it as 'the most remarkable race I have ever seen, or ever expect to see . . . The style in which the great horse closed up the gap when he was at last allowed to stride along was simply incredible.'

Some great racehorses – Eclipse, Highflyer, St Simon – become great sires. Some racehorses below that rank – Phalaris, Sadler's Wells, Storm Cat – also become great sires. And some great racehorses – Sea Bird, Brigadier Gerard, Secretariat – do not become great sires. Gladiateur, who retired to stud at the end of the 1866 season, fell into this last category. He has, nevertheless, an immortal place in racing history, as the most notable tribute to him, a life-size statue at the entrance to Longchamp racecourse, recognizes.

The erosion of the status of the English as breeders and owners of the best racing stock did nothing but accelerate thereafter. In the next twelve years, there were four further French winners of the Ascot Gold Cup, and French colts and fillies had won five more English Classics by 1880. During the twentieth century, champions came from all over. By common consent, the three greatest horses of the century were Sea Bird, Secretariat and Ribot – respectively, French, American and Italian. The last winner of the English Triple Crown was Nijinsky (in 1970): bred in Canada, owned by an American, and trained in Ireland.

Other racing powers arose. Japan sent over El Condor Pasa to finish second to Montjeu in the 1999 Prix de l'Arc de Triomphe. In 2006, five thousand Japanese fans converged on Paris to cheer on their hero, Deep Impact, in the Arc; they bet on him so enthusiastically that at one stage his price was 10-1 *on*. In a race that was not run to suit him, he finished only third, although he was arguably the best horse in the field.

Today, the two most influential owners on the British Turf are not British. They are Coolmore, the Irish bloodstock operation run by John Magnier, and Darley, owned by Sheikh Mohammed bin Rashid Al Maktoum, ruler of Dubai.

Hermit (b. 1864)

Eclipse – Pot8os – Waxy – Whalebone – Camel – Touchstone – Newminster – Hermit

Henry Weysford Charles Plantagenet Rawdon Hastings, fourth Marquess of Hastings, was a wastrel, and he knew it. 'Money with me oozes away; in fact, it positively melts,' he observed. Unable to be contented, he could divert himself only with the fleeting thrills of gambling and drinking, and of making off with Florence Paget, the belle of her day and the fiancée of Hastings's contemporary Henry Chaplin.

The jilted Chaplin consoled himself by purchasing racehorses. Among them was Breadalbane, left trailing by Gladiateur in the 1865 Derby and the 1866 Ascot Gold Cup; and a chestnut yearling, later named Hermit. After a promising season as a two-year-old,

Hermit emerged as one of the favourites for the Derby of 1867.

Whatever infatuation Hastings may have felt for Florence Paget did not last long. A revealing photograph shows him lying on a chaise longue, languidly perusing a book, while by his side Florence bends her head over some embroidery; in another, Florence is seated, while Hastings lies at her feet, facing away from her, with a newspaper. Neither image conveys marital bliss. Florence was soon sending little notes to Chaplin, and Hastings developed an obsession with inflicting a further defeat on his rival. He bet against Hermit as if, Florence noted in alarm, the colt 'were dead'.

From a week before the race until a few moments before it reached its climax, Hastings appeared certain to collect. On 15 May, Hermit broke a blood vessel on the gallops, and his jockey switched to another colt, with a less celebrated rider taking the mount in his place. Confidence in his chances deteriorated further on the atrociously cold Derby Day, 22 May, when amid a collection of forlorn horses parading in the paddock before the race, Hermit looked the most forlorn of all. You could back him at the desperate price of 66-1. Hail pelted down as the runners and riders prepared to race, and they endured ten false starts before getting underway. As they came round Tattenham Corner into the home straight, the leaders were Marksman, Van Amburgh, and the 6-4 favourite Vauban. With just under a furlong to go, the 10-1 shot Marksman gained a clear lead; then Hermit, coming from way back, swooped, catching Marksman a few strides from the line to win by a neck.

At the unsaddling enclosure, Hastings gave the victorious Hermit a pat. He had lost £120,000 on the race, £20,000 of it to Henry Chaplin.

Hastings's fortunes never recovered. He sold his Scottish estates, and soon fell into the clutches of Henry Padwick, a moneylender dubbed by Roger Longrigg as 'the most evil man of the 19th-century Turf'. Padwick's speciality was destroying the lives of his clients. He and his bookmaking associate Harry Hill, having laid heavily against Hastings's colt The Earl for the 1868 Derby, ensured that the bets would come good by getting Hastings to withdraw The Earl from the race. No matter, Hastings thought. I still have the favourite, the filly Lady Elizabeth. What he did not know was that, because he had over-raced Lady Elizabeth in an effort to claw back his debts, he had ruined her as a top-class racer. She ran unplaced. She ran again, also unsuccessfully, in the Oaks a few days later, when Hastings was hissed by the crowd for putting her through this gruelling schedule. Demonstrating the mistake into which Hastings had been led, The Earl went on to win the Grand Prix de Paris, as well as three races at Royal Ascot. Had he taken part in the Derby and run to that form, he would almost certainly have won.

It was at this stage that the third Dictator of the Turf, Admiral Henry John Rous (1791–1877), entered the story. Rous was vigorous, enthusiastic, opinionated and inflexible. He was the first public handicapper, devising a new weight-for-age scale (under which young horses received weight from older rivals) and assessing the merits of racers with the aid of his notebook and old naval telescope. He was enraged by The Earl and Lady Elizabeth affair, feeling certain that Padwick and John Day (trainer of both horses) had, for their own gain, misled Hastings about the horses' well-being. Without stopping to think about his evidence, Rous wrote to *The Times* to allege that 'Lord Hastings has been shamefully deceived', and, explaining Hastings's compliance, asked the rhetorical question, 'What can the poor fly demand from the spider in whose web he is enveloped?' Hastings denied that he had been deceived, or that he had acted under influence, and Day sued. But the case did not get to court. Rous withdrew his letter, because the principal witness died.

Hastings, aged only twenty-six, suffered a drastic deterioration in health in autumn 1867. At the St Leger, he was walking with crutches. It is not known exactly what was wrong with him; only that he was a broken man. He met his end, like fellow Old

244

Etonian Captain Hook, while reflecting on Good Form. 'Hermit's Derby broke my heart,' he said. 'But I didn't show it, did I?'

St Simon (b. 1881)

Eclipse — King Fergus — Hambletonian — Whitelock — Blacklock — Voltaire — Voltigeur — Vedette — Galopin — St Simon

Like Eclipse, St Simon was effortlessly superior to his rivals on the racecourse, and was never extended; he became a great sire; he was higher at his croup (his rump) than at his withers; and he had a difficult temperament. One day, in an effort to calm him down, his handlers introduced him to a cat. But this was not to be a love affair such as the one between the Godolphin Arabian and Grimalkin.[168] Rather, it was like introducing a mouse to a rattle-snake. St Simon picked up the cat and threw it against the roof of his box; the impact was fatal.

Towards the end of St Simon's two-year-old career, his experienced trainer, Mathew Dawson, predicted that he would 'probably make the best racehorse that has ever run on the Turf'. His jockey, Fred Archer, was similarly impressed. Riding him in a training exercise on an April morning, Archer decided that the colt was performing a little sluggishly, and gave him a touch with his spur. St Simon took off; Archer regained control of him only as they neared the entrance to Newmarket High Street. 'He's not a horse,' the shaken jockey reported. 'He's a steam engine.'

Under the rules of racing, St Simon could not compete in the Classics, because of the death of the Hungarian-born Prince Batthyany, who had bred him and made the entries. Instead, he proved his greatness most vividly in the Ascot Gold Cup. With the field nearing the home turn, St Simon was cantering behind the leader, Tristan (winner of the race the previous year). His jockey, on this day Charlie Wood, merely had to shake the reins for St

---

[168] See chapter 6.

Simon to sail past; he won by twenty lengths, and kept galloping for a further mile. The next day, Tristan won the Hardwicke Stakes. St Simon went on to win races at Newcastle and Goodwood, the latter again by twenty lengths, before retiring to stud.

Fred Archer (1857–1886) won greater fame than has been accorded to any other English jockey. Sir Charles Bunbury and other men of the Turf of Eclipse's day, when jockeys were 'boys' and when the upstart Sam Chifney got his comeuppance, would not have approved of this adulation, and Admiral Rous would have regretted it too. Rous 'was courteous and considerate to jockeys, but nothing would have induced him to invite one to his dinner table'.[169] This, though, was a new era, of mass communication; an era that nurtured celebrity. Horseracing, which had featured only patchily in the public prints until the mid-nineteenth century, was widely reported, and jockeys were the public faces of the sport. Archer was the finest of them, a man of unmatchable talent and willpower. Only Gordon Richards, in the first half of the twentieth century, and Lester Piggott, in the second half, have come close to achieving the same level of public recognition. 'Archer's up!' people would say, to indicate that all was well with the world.

All, however, was not well with Archer. He was obsessively determined, as top jockeys must be, and he earned the nickname 'The Tinman' owing to his relish for making money. In his seventeen seasons, he rode a third of his eight thousand mounts to victory; he won the Derby five times, the Oaks four times, and the St Leger six times. But he put himself through some terrible punishment to gain these successes. A tall man, he could keep himself under nine stone only by restricting his lunch to a biscuit and a small glass of champagne, sometimes resorting also to a fierce purgative known as 'Archer's Mixture'. When, in autumn 1886, he

---

[169] From the *Biographical Encyclopaedia of British Flat Racing*.

contracted a fever after wasting down to 8st 7lb to ride in the Cambridgeshire handicap, he lacked the physical resources to fight the illness. Delirium compounded the depression he had suffered since the recent death of his young wife, and on 8 November he shot himself.

St Simon sired Persimmon, the best horse to be raced by a member of the British royal family. When Albert Edward ('Bertie'), the Prince of Wales, led in the victorious Persimmon after the 1896 Derby, top hats filled the air, and the cheering echoed round the Epsom Downs. A film of the finish of the race was projected in London theatres to thrilled audiences, who demanded several repeats and sang 'God bless the Prince of Wales'. Persimmon went on to win the St Leger, and the following season won the Ascot Gold Cup as well as a new, prestigious race: the Eclipse Stakes. Fabergé later modelled him in silver.

This was the moment at which the supremacy of the Eclipse line was ensured. '[St Simon] and his descendants,' the Thoroughbred Heritage website asserts, '[dominated] global racing at the turn of the 20th century and for decades after.' St Simon's greatness confirmed Eclipse as the greatest sire of all.

Eclipse's Legacy – the Twentieth and Twenty-first Centuries

LISTS OF THE GREATEST horses in history are male-dominated. Does that mean that fillies and mares are not as good? Overall, yes it does. But five fillies have, albeit with weight allowances, beaten the colts to win the Derby. Sixteen fillies, most recently the outstanding Zarkava, have won Europe's richest race, the Prix de l'Arc de Triomphe. Three fillies have won the Kentucky Derby. In 2007, the filly Rags to Riches won the Belmont Stakes, defeating Curlin – and Curlin went on to win the world's two richest races. Fillies and mares are certainly as popular as their male counterparts, and often more so: racing fans tend to ascribe special qualities of pluck and fortitude to females doing battle with male rivals.

Sceptre (born in 1899)

Eclipse – King Fergus – Hambletonian – Whitelock – Blacklock – Voltaire – Voltigeur – Vedette – Galopin – St Simon – Persimmon – Sceptre

Pretty Polly (b. 1901)

Eclipse – Pot8os – Waxy – Whalebone – Sir Hercules – Birdcatcher – Oxford – Sterling – Isonomy – Gallinule – Pretty Polly

Two of the best and most popular female racehorses raced in the early years of the twentieth century. Sceptre won four Classics, but may be best known for a race she lost. Pretty Polly acquired such a formidable reputation that she started favourite for twenty-three of her twenty-four races, and in twenty-one of them was at odds-on.

Sceptre needed a big supply of pluck and fortitude, because she had an owner, a gambler called Robert Sievier, who put her through an exceptionally gruelling schedule. From April to June 1902, she ran in the 2,000 Guineas, 1,000 Guineas, Derby, Oaks, Grand Prix de Paris, and two races at Royal Ascot. In the autumn, she cemented her position as 'the country's sweetheart' with victory in the St Leger. But Sievier, on a winning streak as a punter when he bought Sceptre, hit a losing one that her exploits could not offset, and he sold her the following spring. Under new ownership, she lined up in July 1903 for the ten-furlong Eclipse Stakes at Sandown. Over the next ninety-seven years, only a few contests would challenge this one for the title of race of the century.

The owners of Sandown Park had wanted to stage a race to make a mark with their recently established course. With backing from Leopold de Rothschild, they offered a huge purse of £10,000 (double the prize that went to the winner of the Derby), and appropriated the most prestigious of racing names: Eclipse. The Eclipse Stakes, inaugurated in 1886, was the first contest of the year in which older horses met the Classic generation of three-year-olds. Sceptre's main rivals in 1903 were Ard Patrick, winner of the previous year's Derby – the only one of the five Classics that Sceptre had missed out on; and Rock Sand, winner of that year's 2,000 Guineas and Derby. 'All the rings were packed to suffocation, and everybody was keyed up to the highest pitch of excitement,' a contemporary report noted, and the three rivals lived up to the occasion by staging an epic. Turning into the home straight, Ard Patrick hit the front, and was immediately challenged by Sceptre, with Rock Sand drawing alongside. With two furlongs to go, Rock Sand started to lose touch, and Sceptre edged ahead; but, as the crowd bellowed encouragement at the filly, Ard Patrick timed a last effort to get back up on the line and win by a neck. (In the autumn, Sceptre again defeated Rock Sand – who by then had completed the Triple Crown by winning the St Leger.)

While Sceptre and Pretty Polly had overlapping careers, they did not meet on the racecourse. Pretty Polly won the 'Fillies' Triple Crown' (1,000 Guineas, Oaks, St Leger), and suffered only two defeats – the second, to the consternation of the Ascot crowd, in the last race of her career, the Ascot Gold Cup. Unfashionably bred, she appeared not to be a success at stud, and was not a solicitous mother. Only later did it become apparent that her descendants included an impressive number of outstanding racers.

Phar Lap (b. 1926)

Eclipse – Pot8os – Waxy – Whalebone – Sir Hercules – Birdcatcher – The Baron – Stockwell – Doncaster – Bend Or – Radium – Night Raid – Phar Lap

Like Seabiscuit (who was not an Eclipse male-line descendant), Phar Lap was a hero of the Depression. His tremendous exploits lit up a bleak time, and made him the most famous racer in New Zealand and Australian history. This fame inspired people, as Eclipse's fame had done, to take more than usual interest in his anatomy, their findings offering an interesting theory about the Eclipse legacy.

Phar Lap's story, again like Seabiscuit's, has been well documented in print and on film. Phar Lap – the name derives from a Thai word for lightning – was foaled in Timaru, New Zealand, and was sold for just 160 guineas. He grew into a giant chestnut, standing at over seventeen hands. Probably needing to mature into his frame, he began his career moderately, before running up a tremendous sequence of races, including fourteen in a row without defeat. In Australia's most prestigious horserace, the Melbourne Cup, Phar Lap was third in 1929, first in 1930 (carrying 9st 12lb) and unplaced in 1931 when asked to carry the impossible burden of 10st 10lb. After that, Phar Lap travelled to Mexico for the Agua Caliente Handicap, the richest prize ever given in North American racing. He won, in track record time. Two weeks later he was dead, for reasons about which there is still debate. Some suspect poisoning.

At autopsy, Phar Lap was discovered to have an abnormally large heart – the same weight, 14lb, as Eclipse's. The theory is that it was an inheritance – not through the male side of his pedigree, but through a daughter of Eclipse called Everlasting (and tracing back to a stallion called Hautboy). The large heart characteristic, so the theory goes, is carried by a gene on the X chromosome, which a father can transmit only to a daughter.[170] But this is just a theory. Understanding what the approximately 2.7 billion base pairs of horse genomic DNA do, how they interact with one another, how they are passed on by mare and stallion during reproduction, and how they are expressed in the resulting foal, is going to be the work of the next several decades.

Phar Lap's remains, like Eclipse's, were preserved. His heart is at the National Museum of Australia in Canberra; his hide is at the National Museum of Victoria in Melbourne; and his skeleton is at the National Museum of New Zealand in Wellington.

Arkle (b. 1957)

Eclipse — Pot8os — Waxy — Whalebone — Sir Hercules — Birdcatcher — The Baron — Stockwell — Doncaster — Bend Or — Bona Vista — Cyllene — Polymelus — Phalaris — Pharos — Nearco — Archive — Arkle

[170] If a male passes on his X rather than his Y chromosome, his offspring is female. So Eclipse's daughters – according to the 'X factor' theory – got the chromosome with the gene that expressed a large heart. Some of his sons were pretty good racers – but not because of that characteristic, unless they had inherited it from their mothers.

As we have seen, Eclipse exerted an unparalleled influence on the development of horseracing, around the world. His two principal contributions – speedier, more precocious Thoroughbreds and, indirectly, an industrialized bloodstock industry – are mostly phenomena of Flat racing. But Eclipse's name is all over National Hunt pedigrees too. The line from him through the stallions Phalaris and Nearco that resulted in Nijinsky also produced the greatest horse in the history of steeplechasing.

Steeplechasing has its origins in matches over the country-side towards some landmark, such as a steeple. In the early nineteenth century, aficionados bred greater speed into these contests by mating their stout mares with Thoroughbred racers.[171] Cheltenham, which is to jump racing what Newmarket is to the Flat, first staged its Grand Annual Steeplechase – still a feature of the Cheltenham Festival – in 1834, despite the antipathy of the Rev. (later Dean) F. C. Close, who had deplored the atmosphere of the town during race week. 'It is scarcely possible to turn our steps in any direction without hearing the voice of the blasphemous, or meeting the reeling drunkard, or witnessing scenes of the lowest profligacy,' he expostulated.

Yes, Cheltenham's contemporary inhabitants might agree, that sounds familiar.

The first official Grand National, at Aintree in Liverpool, took place in 1839,[172] when Captain Becher, on Conrad, fell into one of the brooks; he remounted, and on the second circuit fell into it again. Ever after, it was Becher's Brook. Our enduring image of poor Becher, one of the crack jockeys of the day, is of a man lying dazed in a stream while his rivals jump over him.

For many years, the Grand National was the most important

[171] They still do. National Hunt horses do not further the breed, because almost all of them are, like Arkle, geldings. Sometimes, Flat-bred racers turn out to excel at steeplechasing; among them was Red Rum, winner of three Grand Nationals.

[172] Some racing historians argue that the first Grand National was in 1836.

race in the National Hunt (the name indicates the roots of the sport) calendar. But, gradually, the Cheltenham Gold Cup gained recognition as the blue riband event. The race that fixed the Gold Cup in the public consciousness as the Derby of steeplechasing was another candidate for race of the century: the 1964 show-down between the hero of Ireland, Arkle, and the defending champion from England, Mill House.

When Mill House won the Gold Cup in 1963, the English thought that they had a horse who would dominate the event for many years. But the Irish were sure that they had an even better one. Mill House and Arkle first met later that year, in the Hennessy Gold Cup at Newbury, when Arkle slipped on landing three fences from home, and Mill House came out on top. The Irish still said their horse was superior. At Cheltenham the follow-ing spring, the rivals met again, in what was virtually a match: there were only two other horses in the race, and they were left a long way behind. It was what everyone wanted to see: Arkle and Mill House turning for home together, head to head. Then Arkle pulled clear, jumped the last, and accelerated up the Cheltenham hill to the finishing post. 'This is the champion,' Peter O'Sullevan, the commentator, called. 'This is the best we've seen for a long time.'

O'Sullevan was right. The connections of Mill House tried to refute his verdict, but in three subsequent meetings, Arkle gave their horse ever more severe drubbings. Arkle won two more Gold Cups, and put up astonishing weight-carrying performances in handicaps, winning an Irish Grand National, two Hennessy Gold Cups and a Whitbread Gold Cup with up to 12st 7lb on his back.

Arkle ran his last race, the King George VI Chase, at Kempton Park on 27 December 1966.[173] Aged nine, I was there.

---

[173] The King George is usually held on Boxing Day, but had been delayed because of frost and snow.

It was the first time I had seen the already legendary steeplechaser in the flesh. I had ridden a horse once in my life, I had spent no time with horses, but I could tell, as Arkle appeared in front of the stands before the race, that this was the animal at the centre of the day's events: in his deportment, in his alertness, in what one can sum up only as his presence, he stood out from the rest. It was a bearing that the *Irish Times* had described as exhibiting 'the dignity, the look of supreme assurance that marks a President de Gaulle'. In Ireland, Arkle was and still is 'Himself'. He was almost unbeatable, and he was 9-2 on. I thought that I was there to see an exhibition.

I, and my cousin and his girlfriend, were standing by the rails on the inside of the course, near the last fence. We could not see much from there, but we were, briefly, very close to the action. As the field passed a few feet away at the end of the first circuit, all seemed well: Arkle was leading, and travelling comfortably. He maintained his lead, though not by far, on the second circuit. He jumped the final fence about five lengths in front of the second horse, who, I was told afterwards, was called Dormant. As they galloped past, I craned my neck over the rails (did someone lift me?). The two horses' receding backsides now appeared to be level. Something was wrong. The crowd noise had that eerie, muted quality you get at a football ground when the away team scores.

Arkle had lost. We learned later what had happened: he had staggered to the line with a broken bone in his foot. It was, for a nine-year-old boy expecting to return home aglow with the memory of a triumphant performance, a jolting anti-climax.

Once the disappointment had eased, I learned to accept that defeat for Arkle on that December day at Kempton was immaterial. He had nothing left to prove. He had earned the highest rating any chaser had ever received, or is ever likely to receive, and was so superior to his rivals that the rules of handicapping had to be specially adjusted to accommodate him. He was bombarded with letters and presents, and was the hero of poems and songs. Occasionally, a new champion gets mentioned in the same breath as Arkle, but none challenges his position as, in the words of his biographer Sean Magee, 'the presiding spirit of steeplechasing'.

Nijinsky (b. 1967)

Eclipse — Pot8os — Waxy — Whalebone — Sir Hercules — Birdcatcher — The Baron — Stockwell — Doncaster — Bend Or — Bona Vista — Cyllene — Polymelus — Phalaris — Pharos — Nearco — Nearctic — Northern Dancer — Nijinsky

Eclipse, and his descendant St Simon, seemed to those who saw them to be invincible. They were supreme. However, supremacy is not the only definition of greatness; sometimes, greatness is a quality that comes with flaws. It is a poignant syndrome, recognized ever since Achilles' mother neglected to allow the protective waters of the Styx to soak his ankles. I have always been drawn to sporting figures of brilliant talent who at key moments have been unable to prove their superiority: the Australian distance runner Ron Clarke, who broke numerous world records but never won a gold medal; the graceful tennis player Hana Mandlikova, so often betrayed by nerves on the big occasions; and the racehorse Nijinsky, effortlessly in command in all his races, until he ran in the most valuable race of all.

Nijinsky was the discovery of Vincent O'Brien. Few people in racing would disagree with a *Racing Post* poll that named O'Brien, a man of restrained bearing and uncanny judgement, the outstanding trainer of the twentieth century. In National Hunt racing, he sent out the winners of three consecutive Grand Nationals, three consecutive Gold Cups (four in all), and three Champion Hurdles. Turning to the Flat, and setting up stables at Ballydoyle in Tipperary, he had similar success, and eventually won six Derbies. In 1968, the year of his colt Sir Ivor's Epsom victory, O'Brien spotted the year-old Nijinsky on a farm in Ontario, Canada. 'He really filled my eye,' he explained later. He recommended the colt to Charles Engelhard, a jowly industrialist who was one of the leading racehorse owners of the time.[174]

Nijinsky was the champion two-year-old in 1969, won the following year's 2,000 Guineas, Derby and Irish Derby with ease, and put up his finest performance in the King George VI and Queen Elizabeth Stakes at Ascot, cantering past a classy field of older horses. By this time, there was more public recognition for Nijinsky than any British or Irish Flat racer had gained for many years – and more than any has gained since. He looked magnificent; like Arkle, he radiated class. To add to his charisma, there was the impassive presence on his back of Lester Piggott, the most talented jockey of his generation.[175] Piggott was notoriously laconic, apparently no more excited about winning a Derby than he was about victory in a lowly selling race; but he certainly appreciated Nijinsky. 'That day,' he said about the King George, 'he was the most impressive horse I ever sat on.'

What went wrong with Nijinsky is debatable. A bout of ringworm following the King George cannot have helped: the colt lost nearly all his hair. Nevertheless, Vincent O'Brien got him ready for the St Leger, and in September at Doncaster Nijinsky became the first horse since Bahram in 1935 to win the Triple Crown.[176] He seemed to do it as effortlessly as ever, and Piggott did not push him. Only with the benefit of hindsight did one notice that the horse had no energy to spare.

Three weeks later, Nijinsky stepped on to the Longchamp turf for the contest that O'Brien and Engelhard intended to be the glorious conclusion to his career: the Prix de l'Arc de Triomphe, the most valuable race in Europe. There was a huge crowd, and a

[174] Engelhard, who spoke in a gravelly voice produced with almost no movement of the facial muscles, was rumoured to be the model for Ian Fleming's villain Goldfinger.
[175] Liam Ward rode Nijinsky in Ireland. Lester Piggott rode nine Derby winners during his career, a record.
[176] 2,000 Guineas, Derby, St Leger.

good portion of it invaded the Longchamp paddock in an effort to get close to the celebrated horse. Always highly strung, Nijinsky got very worked up; he was sweating and on his toes, and Piggott had a hard job controlling him as they cantered to the start.

Nijinsky was drawn on the outside of the field, a position that forced Piggott, when the race got underway, to drop in behind the other runners. I can still remember Peter O'Sullevan's commentary, my best guide as I watched the race on a tiny black and white television. Nijinsky was near the back of the field, fourth from last; the field was nearing the entrance to the home straight, and still there were only three horses behind him, while a wall of horses was in front. Unable to get an opening, Piggott lost ground and momentum by taking his mount wide. At last Nijinsky got into gear, came charging down the outside, and with the winning post in sight caught the leader, Sassafras, and pushed his nose in front – then he swerved, and the two horses hit the line, seemingly together. The judge called for a photo. The angle of the television cameras at Longchamp, giving a deceptive view of finishes, left viewers uncertain about the result. At the course, O'Brien was surrounded by well-wishers telling him that his horse had won, but he could sense, as we could at home, that the verdict was not going to go the right way. In those days, you had to wait for the photograph to be developed. But soon came the inevitable announcement: Sassafras was the winner, by a head.

Piggott received a lot of stick. He had let Nijinsky get too far behind the leaders; he had waited too long; it was an impossible task to make up that amount of ground in the short Longchamp straight – that was what the critics said, and O'Brien agreed. But even the outstanding trainer of the twentieth century can get things wrong, as O'Brien was immediately to demonstrate. Deciding that Nijinsky was back on form and ready to sign off his career victoriously, he sent over the colt just two weeks later for the Champion Stakes at Newmarket.

'The moment I saw Nijinsky in the parade ring,' Piggott

said, 'I could tell that he had not got over the Arc experience: he was a nervous wreck, and the huge crowd which had turned out to bid him farewell just made matters worse.' Nijinsky ran sluggishly, and finished second again,[177] a performance offering strong evidence that he had been past his best on Arc day too. The Nijinsky of a few months earlier would have had no trouble in winning at Longchamp, even from his backward position in the field.[178] But what happened to him at Longchamp and Newmarket is a common syndrome: since 1970, numerous fine horses have demonstrated how hard it is to maintain scintillating form throughout a long season.[179]

I had wanted Nijinsky to win the Arc very badly. He was the best horse: he should have won. I still get a pang when I think about it, and I find the video of the race painful to watch. But I think that the defeat strengthened Nijinsky's hold on my imagination. The following year, another exceptional colt, Mill Reef, won the Derby, Eclipse Stakes and the King George, and went on to Longchamp and won the Arc as well. Mill Reef was a more durable horse than Nijinsky, and may have been a better one; but he never excited me as much.[180]

[177] The winner, Lorenzaccio, was, as Piggott said, 'not remotely in the same league as Nijinsky in his prime'. But Lorenzaccio did have some importance as a sire, maintaining one of the rare male lines that endures from the Byerley Turk and Herod.

[178] Dancing Brave's brilliant Arc victory in 1986 showed that it was possible to make up ground in the Longchamp straight.

[179] Among them: Troy (1979 Derby, Irish Derby, King George), third in the Arc; Shergar (1981 Derby, Irish Derby, King George), fourth in the St Leger; Nashwan (1989 2,000 Guineas, Derby, Eclipse, King George), third in the Prix Niel; Generous (1991 Derby, Irish Derby, King George), eighth in the Arc; Authorized (2007 Derby, Juddmonte International), tenth in the Arc.

[180] Mill Reef's owner was Paul Mellon, who endowed the Yale Center for British Art. Mellon's collection of work by Stubbs included the painter's first study of Eclipse; he donated it to the Royal Veterinary College. Mill Reef was trained by Ian Balding, father of Clare, the BBC television and radio presenter.

The story is not really sad. Nijinsky enjoyed a contented life at stud at Claiborne Farm in Kentucky, and sired the Derby winners Golden Fleece, Shahrastani and Lammtarra. Moreover, his racecourse performances had an extraordinary effect. They alerted the world to the ability of his sire Northern Dancer, who at his base on Windfields Farm in Maryland went on to set a record, still unbroken, for the highest covering fee in history. And they inspired the growth of racing and breeding empires whose policy, pursued in a more determined way than anyone had seen before, was to corner the market in the best bloodlines.

Nijinsky was syndicated for $5.5 million, following a common practice among owners of top stallions in the second half of the twentieth century. You have to spread the risk, as you would in any corporate venture. While the valuation of stallions is enormous, their failure rate – and this includes some of the best racers – is frightening. So you distribute the ownership, sharing the costs and the profits among, say, forty partners, each getting the right to send one mare to the stallion a season.

Some stallions, such as Dubai Millennium (see below), die young; a few, like the American champion Cigar, turn out to be infertile; most simply get offspring who do not run very fast. The successful ones, however, are by a huge margin the biggest earners in racing. At six-figure fees for each mare they cover, they perform more than a hundred coverings a season, and they can keep it up for twenty years or longer. What they earned on the racecourse was insignificant by comparison. The point of racing, for the heaviest hitters in the industry, is not the actual sport, but what goes on in the breeding shed. The logical strategy, then, is to do systematically what Vincent O'Brien and Charles Engelhard did with Nijinsky: annex the best bloodlines, spot the potential stallions early, race them, and retire them to stud. Dennis O'Kelly would have been at home in the modern bloodstock world.

Engelhard did not see this policy come to fruition, dying at the age of fifty-four in 1971. O'Brien pursued it with two partners:

his son-in-law John Magnier, and Robert Sangster. Magnier, who ran the Coolmore stud and is now in charge of the entire international business, is a fearsome and laconic operator about whom it has been observed that the softest part of his head is his teeth. Sangster, heir to the Vernons pools business, was (he died of cancer in 2004) exuberant, a generous giver of parties and a lover of the jet-setting life that came with international racehorse ownership. O'Brien, who died in 2009, was modest and courteous. In the 1970s and early 1980s, this unusual threesome would descend on the sales in Keeneland and Saratoga and buy up the best yearlings – offspring of Northern Dancer in particular – they could find. Prices rocketed, and Northern Dancer's stud fee rose to $1 million.

There have been several outcomes of the bloodstock boom of the 1970s and 1980s. One is that Coolmore has grown into the most powerful bloodstock operation in the world. Another, that racing, at the very top level, is no longer a pursuit for aristocrats, unless they engage in it with the ambition and ruthlessness required in big business. The Queen was the leading owner on the British Turf in 1954 and 1957; she is nowhere near that position today, and she last enjoyed success in a Classic in her Silver Jubilee year, 1977.[181] There is of course a third outcome: the boom in breeding Classic colts and fillies, who would go on themselves to breed world-class offspring, strengthened the dominance of the bloodline from Eclipse.

Secretariat (b. 1970)

Eclipse – Pot8os –Waxy –Whalebone – Sir Hercules – Birdcatcher – The Baron – Stockwell – Doncaster – Bend Or – Bona Vista – Cyllene – Polymelus – Phalaris – Pharos – Nearco – Nasrullah – Bold Ruler – Secretariat

With Secretariat, we return to the champion as invincible athlete.

[181] The Queen's filly Dunfermline won the 1977 Oaks and St Leger.

Actually, Secretariat was beaten a few times, through bad luck, careless preparation and, once, disqualification. In the races that mattered, though, he was awesome.

The US Triple Crown races take place over five weeks in May and June. They are the Kentucky Derby, over one and a quarter miles at Churchill Downs; the Preakness Stakes, over a mile and one and a half furlongs at Pimlico; and the Belmont Stakes, over one and a half miles at Belmont Park. They are quite unlike the tests that horses face in the English Classics. The course at Newmarket (the 2,000 Guineas) is a straight mile, with a dip and then a rising finish; the contestants at Epsom (the Derby) go on a roller-coaster ride over the Downs; Doncaster (the St Leger) is a park course, but nevertheless has uphill and downhill sections. American tracks are all flat, left-handed ovals, and they have dirt surfaces[182] – turf racing is less important in the US.

Secretariat entered the Kentucky Derby, on the first Saturday in May in 1973, as the favourite, but on the back of a defeat and facing doubts over whether he would stay the distance. When the gates opened, it soon became clear that his stamina would face a proper test, because his jockey, Ron Turcotte, dropped him to the back of the field, from where he was forced to race wide to gain a position. In spite of that disadvantage, the reddish chestnut colt with the blue and white chequered blinkers powered home, in a time that has never been bettered. In the Preakness Stakes, two weeks later, Turcotte again started slowly, and this time drove his mount past the entire field early in the back stretch. Any normal horse would have used up too much energy in that manoeuvre. Secretariat, however, kept on going. His victory margins over the second horse, Sham, and the third, Our Native, were the same as they had been in the Derby. Only the

---

[182] Some tracks, but not the Triple Crown ones, have introduced artificial surfaces such as Polytrack, also in use at the English courses Lingfield and Wolverhampton.

timing was in dispute: unofficial clockers recorded that Secretariat had broken the Pimlico track record, although the official timing device did not.

Secretariat was by now a national figure, a cover star of *Time* and *Newsweek*. His defining race awaited him, and at Belmont Park on 9 June he and Sham went into battle once more, with Secretariat aiming to become the first Triple Crown winner for twenty-five years. It was brutal: the two colts fought for the lead at an apparently suicidal pace. Before the end of the back stretch Sham dropped away, broken, as Bucephalus had been when trying to match strides with Eclipse. Sham finished last, and never raced again. Secretariat carried on galloping relentlessly. 'He is moving like a tremendous machine!' the commentator yelled. In the home straight, Turcotte looked back; he would have needed binoculars to get a proper view of his nearest pursuer. The rest were nowhere. Secretariat passed the post thirty-one lengths in front. He had set a new world record for twelve furlongs, and as Turcotte[183] tried to pull him up, he passed the thirteen-furlong marker in a new world record as well. 'It is hard to conceive,' Tony Morris and John Randall wrote, 'how any horse in history could have lived with him, at any distance, on that magic afternoon of 9 June 1973.'

In 1972, Secretariat had been the first two-year-old to be named Horse of the Year. This award is the climax of a ceremony staged each January in Beverly Hills to honour the stars of horseracing: it is known as the Eclipse Awards. A Triple Crown winner and American sporting hero, Secretariat was a shoo-in as the 1973 Horse of the Year as well.

Secretariat was another of Eclipse's descendants to boast an unusually large heart. How large we do not know for sure, because it was never weighed; the veterinarian who examined him, Dr

---

[183] Five years later, Turcotte fell from his horse in a race at Belmont, and was left a paraplegic.

Thomas Swerczek, thought that it was at least twice as large as normal. A few years after Secretariat's death, Swerczek weighed the heart of Secretariat's rival Sham, discovered it to be 18lb, and decided that Secretariat's had been a whopping 22lb. If there is anything in the 'X factor' theory, which argues that the large heart gene resides on the X chromosome that a father passes on only to daughters,[184] it may explain why Secretariat, a moderately successful sire of male offspring, was a very successful sire of females.

Dubai Millennium (b. 1996)

Eclipse — Pot8os — Waxy — Whalebone — Sir Hercules — Birdcatcher — The Baron — Stockwell — Doncaster — Bend Or — Bona Vista — Cyllene — Polymelus — Phalaris — Sickle — Unbreakable — Polynesian — Native Dancer — Raise a Native — Mr Prospector — Seeking the Gold — Dubai Millennium

Sheikh Mohammed bin Rashid Al Maktoum and his relatives from the Dubai royal family arrived on the international racing scene in the late 1970s. Flush with oil money, they raised still further the heat in the American sales rings. Some of the deals were staggering, and they illustrated how bloodstock was a pursuit only for those who could afford to take huge, scary gambles. In 1983, Sheikh Mohammed[185] paid a world record $10.2 million to outbid Coolmore, as well as the American partnership of trainer D. Wayne Lukas and self-made tycoon Eugene Klein, for a Northern Dancer colt. The colt, Snaafi Dancer, was shipped over the Atlantic to the stables of John Dunlop in Sussex. Dunlop soon discovered that Snaafi Dancer was too slow to race; 'A nice little horse but no bloody good' was his summary. So Snaafi Dancer, who at least boasted a pedigree that might appeal to breeders, went to stud. He

[184] See the essay on Phar Lap.
[185] He became ruler of Dubai in 2006.

was infertile. Goodbye $10.2 million, plus training and stabling fees. Two years later, Coolmore broke the Snaafi Dancer record by paying $13.1 million for Seattle Dancer, a son of Nijinsky. While Seattle Dancer earned some money on the racecourse, he did so only to the tune of about £100,000, and while he was fertile he was nevertheless a moderate stallion.

No doubt Coolmore was bitterly disappointed by this setback, as Sheikh Mohammed had been by the Snaafi Dancer debacle. But they both know that failure is the norm, and that if their judgement is sound – they employ some of the best judges of horseflesh in the business – they will find the rare Thoroughbreds that compensate for the rest. At about the time it bought Seattle Dancer, Coolmore was advertising a young stallion, Sadler's Wells. In spring 2008, Sadler's Wells (another son of Northern Dancer) retired, having broken the record of Eclipse's rival Highflyer to become champion sire fourteen times. If you own Sadler's Wells, you can afford quite a few Seattle Dancers.

Sheikh Mohammed set up his own training operation, Godolphin (named in tribute to the Godolphin Arabian), in 1994. (The overall name of the sheikh's racing empire, Darley Racing, pays tribute to another of the foundation sires, the Darley Arabian – Eclipse's great-great-grandfather. The sheikh's breeding operation is the Darley Stud.) Two years later, he inaugurated the world's richest horse race, the Dubai World Cup, which now has a purse of $6 million. Racing, and other sports including golf and powerboat racing, have been key elements in the sheikh's promotion of Dubai as a glamorous destination for tourism and business. The country's capital is the fastest growing city on the planet.

Dubai Millennium was supposed to be the supreme racing exemplar of Sheikh Mohammed's ambitions. According to the bloodstock writer Rachel Pagones, Sheikh Mohammed 'spent hours alone with Dubai Millennium, going into the colt's box after evening stables to feed him carrots, stroke his shining, sunwarmed coat and simply sit'. Originally called Yaazer, Dubai

Millennium had taken on the burden of high expectation on the day that his trainer told the sheikh that this was the best horse he had ever trained, and got the response, 'In that case I will change his name.'

The colt's new name signified his obvious target as the 2000 running of the Dubai World Cup; but before that, his first big challenge was the 1999 Derby, a race no horse carrying Sheikh Mohammed's colours had won.[186] It went badly. Dubai Millennium, ridden by Frankie Dettori,[187] got worked up in the paddock, pulled too hard, was a spent force by the time the field rounded Tattenham Corner, and finished ninth.

Sent back to trips of a mile, he won three races in a row, climaxing with the Queen Elizabeth II Stakes at Ascot, after which Sheikh Mohammed declared him to be 'the best we have had in Godolphin'. Proving that he had read the script, Dubai Millennium turned up for the World Cup the following March 2000 in stupendous form, pulverizing the field to win by six lengths in record time. 'It is the greatest race in my life,' Sheikh Mohammed said.

Dubai Millennium's next race was at Royal Ascot, where his most dangerous opponent was the French champion Sendawar, owned by the Aga Khan. Sendawar was a very good horse, but the betting market made an insulting mistake in promoting him to favouritism. It was like Bucephalus taking on Eclipse, or Sham taking on Secretariat: Sendawar tried to keep up with Dubai Millennium, was broken, and fell away, leaving Dubai Millennium to win by eight lengths.

Now the racing world wanted to see him face another super-star: Montjeu, winner of the 1999 Prix de l'Arc de Triomphe and

[186] It is still the case. Lammtarra, the 1995 winner, was trained by Godolphin but ran in the colours of Sheikh Mohammed's nephew. In 2008, New Approach raced to victory at Epsom in the colours of the sheikh's wife, Princess Haya – he had given her the horse as a present.
[187] The popular jockey at last broke his Derby duck in 2007, on Authorized.

of the 2000 King George VI and Queen Elizabeth Stakes (in which he had evoked memories of Nijinsky by overtaking the field in a canter). Montjeu was in the ownership of Sheikh Mohammed's great rivals Coolmore, and soon after the Ascot race the Coolmore team challenged Dubai Millennium to come to Ireland, to race against Montjeu in the Irish Champion Stakes. Sheikh Mohammed responded by issuing a counter-challenge, through the *Racing Post*: an old-fashioned match, one on one, $6 million staked by each side. It would have been an early candidate for race of the century, but it was not to be. On the day that the *Post* carried the story, Dubai Millennium broke a leg on the Newmarket gallops, and, after a life-saving operation, retired to stud. He had covered only one book of mares when he contracted grass sickness, an often fatal condition that destroys a horse's nerve endings. He did not survive.

Dubai Millennium's career marked the high point of Sheikh Mohammed's horseracing fortunes. In the first years of this century, Coolmore has gained the upper hand. The Ballydoyle racehorses – now in the care of the boyish-looking, softly spoken Aidan O'Brien (no relation of Vincent) – are dominating Europe's most prestigious races, and the 'Coolmore Mafia' are colonizing the winners' enclosures that had been the regular haunts of the sheikh's Godolphin team. O'Brien seems to produce champions from a conveyor belt.[188]

In breeding, the superiority is even more marked. The leading four sires in Europe in 2007 were all Coolmore's, while the sires from Sheikh Mohammed's Darley Stud were off the pace. Meanwhile, relations between the two operations, for reasons that have been kept extraordinarily well hidden, have broken down, and the rivals have returned to slugging it out in the sales ring.

---

[188] In the past few years alone, they have included Giant's Causeway, Galileo, High Chaparral, Hawk Wing, Rock of Gibraltar, Dylan Thomas, Henrythenavigator and Duke of Marmalade.

Their competing bids pushed up the price of a two-year-old colt, to whom Coolmore later gave the unflattering name The Green Monkey,[189] to $16 million – another world record – while Darley paid $9.7 million for Jalil, a son of leading sire Storm Cat. Both colts conformed to what one might call the Snaafi Dancer syndrome, failing to live up to their valuations.

In the bloodstock world recently, then, it has been John Magnier first, Sheikh Mohammed nowhere, and you get the impression that the sheikh does not find that result acceptable. Recently, he has switched tactics, buying as stallion prospects colts with proven form, such as the 2007 Derby winner Authorized. In 2007, he spent at least $200 million on bloodstock, and he went on to splash out a further $420 million on the Woodlands Stud, the largest stud farm in Australia. Magnier, notwithstanding his estimated personal fortune of £1.3 billion, would be pushed to match those sums.

More than two hundred years after Eclipse's death, the battle to secure the best bloodstock – which one might characterize as the battle over Eclipse's legacy – involves huge egos, business ruthlessness, and national pride. As I said, Dennis O'Kelly was there first.

---

[189] The Green Monkey is a Barbados golf course to which Coolmore has ties.

Anatomical drawings of Eclipse from Charles Vial de Sainbel's An Essay on the Proportions of the Celebrated Eclipse — *the work that helped Sainbel to set up the Royal Veterinary College.*

The Skeleton

ECLIPSE STANDS, SKELETALLY, in a glass case in the small museum of the Royal Veterinary College in Hertfordshire. Opposite him, misdated to c.1750 rather than to c.1769, is his portrait, Stubbs's first study of him. Eclipse has had a tortuous and often undignified journey here, and he has survived questions about his identity as well as several attempts at impersonation. Now, he is back in his rightful, starring role; and he is for the second time at the centre of pioneering research.

The first research took place following his death in 1789, when Charles Vial de Sainbel, the French veterinarian, anatomized him. Sainbel, and his English wife, were back in England – where he had earlier failed to set up a veterinary college – escaping from the dangers of revolutionary France. His friends had gone to the guillotine or had emigrated, and his estates had been confiscated. A tall man with a dark complexion and prominent cheekbones, he was amiable, ambitious, egotistical and punctilious. Getting his college off the ground was now a pressing need. Perhaps he made Andrew O'Kelly an offer to examine Eclipse, having seen that the great horse would be the means of furthering his cause.

Sainbel skinned the body and removed the organs. One of his first services to subsequent researchers was the discovery that

Eclipse's heart was abnormally large, at 14lb.[190] Then Sainbel set about measuring the skeleton. This is not a straightforward job. You cannot do it simply with a tape measure, because you do not know how the angles of the joints would have been affected by half a ton of bodyweight. Sainbel's solution was to take the straightforward measurements and to deduce the rest in proportion to them. The results are odd. He gives the length of Eclipse's head as twenty-two inches, which is short, and the horse's height as three times that figure, sixty-six inches, which is exceptionally tall. It translates to 16.2 hands – a good height for a twenty-first-century racehorse but giant by the standards of Eclipse's era. (Racing historians reckon Eclipse's true height to have been about 15.3 hands.) There are dubious details in Sainbel's portrait of Eclipse too. He shows a white blaze extending down Eclipse's face and covering his muzzle, and a white stocking covering his hock, whereas in the Stubbs and Sartorius portraits the blaze is only on the front of Eclipse's head, and the top of the stocking is below the hock. These discrepancies have led to questions about whether Eclipse really was the horse that Sainbel studied.

Sainbel calculated that Eclipse's stride could cover twenty-five feet, that he could complete two and one-third galloping actions a second, and that he could cover four miles in six minutes and two seconds. That all seems somewhat theoretical. More impressive is the vet's account of the mechanics of the gallop: Sainbel described the motions, involving lead legs and brief elevation from the ground, that Muybridge was to photograph some ninety years later. However, despite his hope of offering 'a surer guide to the brush or chisel of the artist, who commonly only employs them in opposition to nature', he failed to influence the conventions of horse painting. Artists, until visual evidence made

[190] See chapter 20 for more on the theory that the characteristic was passed on, through female offspring, to great racehorses including Phar Lap and Secretariat.

them change their ways, carried on depicting the 'rocking horse' gallop.

Whatever the flaws in Sainbel's study, it impressed the men he wanted to influence. They approved his proposals and came up with his financing, and the Veterinary College, London,[191] the first British school for veterinarians, welcomed its first students in January 1792. Sainbel was the inaugural professor.

He enjoyed the fruition of his campaign only briefly. In August the following year, Sainbel developed a fever, and died at the age of forty. (His symptoms, of severe shivering, hint that his fatal condition was the infectious disease glanders, which can be transmitted from animals.) Sainbel's testament, and one of the few sources of income for his widow, was *Essays on the Veterinary Art: Containing an Essay on the Proportions of the Celebrated Eclipse*. He had concluded that, while Eclipse had 'never been esteemed handsome', the horse's frame was 'almost perfect'. Even if Eclipse's offspring had made no impression on Thoroughbred history, his role as the figurehead in Sainbel's campaign to further animal welfare would have confirmed him as one of the most important of all Thoroughbreds.

Eclipse's skeleton now began its wanderings. Its first owner was Edmund Bond, who was the O'Kellys' vet and who had attended Sainbel's dissection of the corpse. Bond kept it in his own small museum in Mayfair. When he died, he left behind a debt of £500 to a fellow vet called Bracy Clark, who received payment from Bond's widow in the form of Eclipse.

Bracy Clark, while writing the first attempt at a full account of Eclipse's career as well as other studies of equestrian matters, was a man of varied interests, also assembling an insect cabinet that earned him membership of the Linnaean Society, and founding the first cricket club in Worcester. But he lacked ideal facilities

[191] It began styling itself 'Royal' in 1826.

for keeping a skeleton. Eclipse was, literally, Bracy Clark's skeleton in the cupboard – or rather, the limbs were in two adjoining cupboards, with the torso and head stashed on top. At last recognizing that this arrangement was unsatisfactory, he donated Eclipse for display in a cabinet in Egyptian Hall, Piccadilly, where at various times the exhibits also included Egyptian artefacts, a family of Laplanders 'complete with house and reindeer', and a pair of eighteen-year-old Siamese twins.[192] The Royal College of Veterinary Surgeons offered to take the responsibility off his hands for sixty guineas, but got a brusque response – 'a hundred being demanded for this invincible monarch of the racecourse'. Bracy Clark also rebuffed the first rumours ('very ungenerous and ridiculous') that his possession was fake. 'The bones themselves, which are remarkable, would sufficiently evince their genuineness to any person not wilfully blind or prejudiced,' he insisted.

Meanwhile, other parts of Eclipse's anatomy were acquiring the status of religious relics (see colour section). The royal family took possession of a couple of his hooves, and in 1832, at the climax of a grand dinner, William IV presented one of them to the Jockey Club. It was mounted on a salver, and had an inscription carved in gold. The club instituted it as the trophy for an annual race, the Eclipse Foot, staged at Ascot. The hoof is still in the Jockey Club Rooms in Newmarket, along with the Newmarket Challenge Whip – into which are reputed to be woven hairs from Eclipse's mane and tail – and Stubbs's copy[193] of his painting of Eclipse at the Newmarket Beacon Course rubbing-house. So Eclipse has a hallowed place at an institution that never admitted Dennis O'Kelly, his owner.

What happened to the second royal hoof is a mystery. When Theodore Cook was writing *Eclipse and O'Kelly*, he received the following letter: 'Lord Knollys, Balmoral Castle, 1906: Dear Mr Cook, I have submitted your letter to the King, and I find that his

---

[192] Also known as the London Museum, the hall was demolished in 1905.
[193] Made for the *Review of the Turf*. See chapter 18.

Majesty does possess one of Eclipse's hoofs. Yours very truly, Knollys.' However, my enquiries at The Royal Collection drew a blank, with no record showing up on the collection's database — unless for some reason Eclipse's was the unmarked hoof inscribed 'Xmas 1902'. A third hoof, converted into a snuff box, was last recorded in Jamaica. The last report of the fourth placed it in Leicestershire. A William Worley was said to have owned a tie-pin made from material from one of the hooves. In 1910, there was a proposal that the Jockey Club hoof travel to Vienna, so that the Emperor of Austria could take snuff from it at a lunch to mark the opening of a field sports exhibition.[194]

Portions of Eclipse's hide went hither and thither too. Theodore Cook, writing his biography of Eclipse and O'Kelly in 1907, reported that there was a section of chestnut hide, together with a letter saying that it had come from Andrew O'Kelly, at The Durdans, a grand house in Epsom. When the light shone on it, Cook enthused, it produced 'that extraordinary iridescent effect which makes a true chestnut the loveliest colour in the world'. A letter in Cook's possession from a man who was friendly with the son of Thomas Plumer, who had bought Cannons from Andrew, said that the younger Plumer could remember playing with Eclipse's skin in the Cannons loft. Then there was a story that a portion of Eclipse's hide was being kept in pickle at a tanner's in Edgware; another of Cook's correspondents cut off a bit and sent it to him.

In 1860, just three weeks before he died at the age of eighty-nine, Bracy Clark got his 100 guineas. His customer was John Gamgee, who thought that Eclipse would bring lustre to his new veterinary college in Edinburgh. 'The skeleton of Eclipse now in

[194] Eclipse's skeleton, notwithstanding a request from Edward VII that it be part of the exhibition, was not entrusted to the journey. The grand lunch was delayed a week, because news of Edward's death came through on the day it had been due to take place. It is not clear whether the hoof was part of the occasion.

our possession, still connected by its ligaments, is proof that Eclipse was a horse of most perfect symmetry,' wrote Gamgee's father, Joseph, in the *Edinburgh Veterinary Review*, while noting that 'some very important errors' had crept into Sainbel's original measurements. Despite this prize attraction, Gamgee struggled to make an impact with his college. He transferred to London, where he called his venture the Albert Veterinary College, but again got into difficulties. Packing it in, and preparing to head off to America in search of better fortune, Gamgee donated the skeleton to the Royal College of Veterinary Surgeons.

Eclipse's new home was the RCVS museum in Red Lion Square. It was not hospitable. In the early 1900s, a member of the RCVS council noted with dismay 'the dirty and dusty state [the skeleton] is in . . . if it is not kept in a clean state there will soon be no skeleton of Eclipse at all'. Another said, 'I was in the museum this morning and I think it more a place to set potatoes in than anything else.' Nevertheless, the college did not take any remedial action until 1920: converting its dark and dusty museum into a library, it handed over the skeleton to the Natural History Museum, which had first put in a request for it eighteen years earlier.

By this time, there was another point of comparison between bits of Eclipse's anatomy and religious relics: they were unfeasibly numerous. In 1907, when Theodore Cook was trying to unravel the story, 'Six "undoubted" skeletons of Eclipse claimed my bewildered attention. No less than nine "authentic" feet were apparently possessed by this extraordinary animal. The "genuine" hair out of his tail would have generously filled the largest arm-chair in the Jockey Club. The "certified" portions of his hide would together have easily carpeted the yard at Tattersalls.'

Lady Wentworth, the dogmatic Thoroughbred historian, doubted the credentials of the skeleton in the Natural History Museum. She noted the conflicting measurements, as well as the differences between Sainbel's portrait and Stubbs's, and she argued that the task of reassembling a skeleton from separate parts, kept by the vets Edmund Bond and Bracy Clark among the remains of other horses, was akin to 'solving a Greek crossword puzzle'.[195] In her view, the bones were those of 'a common cross-bred horse'. The marketable value of the skeleton was an incentive to fraud, Lady Wentworth alleged. 'Eclipse's skeleton, like Caesar's wife, would have to be above suspicion before we could base any theories on it.'

Nevertheless, this skeleton continued to enjoy official status, if not appropriate prominence. In 1972, the racing paper the *Sporting Life* ran a sad story about how 'The Turf's greatest horse lies forgotten in a museum basement.' That neglect ended eleven years later, when Eclipse travelled to Newmarket to join the exhibits at the new National Horseracing Museum, opened by the Queen. He stayed in Newmarket for twenty years, although his ownership changed in 1991, when the Royal College of Veterinary Surgeons – much to the disappointment of the Natural History Museum, which holds the skeletons of other Thoroughbreds including St Simon, and which had come to regard Eclipse as its natural possession – donated it to the Royal Veterinary College as a 200th birthday gift. At the same time, the American collector Paul Mellon gave the college his Stubbs portrait – the one that Stubbs used as a model for *Eclipse with William Wildman and His Sons* and *Eclipse at Newmarket, with a Groom and Jockey* – as well as a bronze statue of Eclipse by James Osborne.[196] Eclipse completed his travelling in 2003, when he moved from Newmarket to join the portrait and statue at the opening – again by the Queen – of the Eclipse Building at the RVC in Hatfield, Hertfordshire.

[195] She does not appear to have had any evidence that the skeleton was in separate bits when in Bond's care. John Orton, writing in 1844, said that Bond exhibited it.

[196] There is a replica of this statue next to the paddock on the Rowley Mile course at Newmarket.

I glance up from my computer screen, and I see above my desk my print of Eclipse, as painted by Stubbs, preparing to race against Bucephalus. I click on a folder named 'Pics', and there is Eclipse with William Wildman and his sons, or Eclipse at stud painted by Garrard, or Eclipse by Sartorius walking over the course for the King's Plate. Now, it is time to enter the great horse's physical presence.

I take the train to Potters Bar, and a taxi beyond the suburban streets into the Hertfordshire countryside. We pull up at the Royal Veterinary College's Eclipse Building, and I go into a reception area overlooked, from the floor above, by Eclipse's statue. The RVC receptionist, informing a colleague of my arrival, announces herself as 'Pam in Eclipse'. I look to my left; through an open door, at the opposite end of a modestly sized room, is the skeleton. I go in.

Panels on the wall tell the stories of Eclipse and Sainbel. I turn round; there is the Stubbs painting. It requires a conceptual leap to link skeleton and portrait: the bones, fleshless, appear to be those of a smaller animal than a Thoroughbred. Are they linked? Or is the RVC's proudest possession a fake? Dr Renate Weller, of the RVC's Structure and Motion laboratory, joins me, and we look at the skeleton. This certainly seems to be the skeleton of an animal who stayed constitutionally sound into old age, showing only a fusion of the last thoracic and first lumbar vertebrae, and of the fourth and fifth lumbar vertebrae. But did Sainbel anatomize the horse whom Stubbs painted? We look at the portrait. Dr Weller, who has a nicely sceptical sense of humour, is inclined to dismiss Stubbs, despite his reputation for verisimilitude, as a source of anatomical evidence. She points to the angle of the fetlock, and says that it is too steep; the angle of the shoulder is 'much too steep'; the angle of the tarsus (the joint on the hind leg) 'looks bizarre'; and Eclipse's neck appears to be too short. 'I don't like this picture,' she concludes.

We move to Dr Weller's narrow, shared office, where,

weighing down the papers in a tray on a filing cabinet, are two resin models of Eclipse's humerus (the bone at the top of the fore-limb). She tells me about the RVC's research. The college has examined seven hundred horses, and eighteen horse skeletons. Its aims are to further the understanding of equine anatomy, and to gain insights into the relationship between the conformation of a horse and equine injuries.

Dr Weller and her colleagues in the RVC's Structure and Motion team removed Eclipse's right (off) front leg and put it through a CT scanner, taking care that the metal pins used to mount the skeleton did not overheat the apparatus. They loaded the CT images into a program called Mimics, which reproduced them in 3D; a further piece of software, Magics, combined the images of the individual bones to produce a complete 3D image of the leg. The Mimics file guided a laser to carve a replica of the leg in a tank of resin. Yet another piece of software, which had been developed for such uses as simulating the effect of surgery on children with cerebral palsy, depicted the mechanics of the limb.

The Structure and Motion team's conclusions have a ring of bathos. Eclipse, they found, was by contemporary standards a small, light-framed Thoroughbred, 'with average bone measurements without any outstanding features'. But maybe that was the horse's secret? As Muybridge showed with his photographic sequence of the gallop, a running horse, weighing some 500kg, hits the ground first with just one leg; never are the four legs bearing the half-ton or more. Did Eclipse's averageness keep him sound? Dr Weller and her colleagues have since looked at other skeletons, among them the Natural History Museum's St Simon and Brown Jack. Brown Jack: now there, indisputably, was a sound horse. From 1929, he won six consecutive runnings of Royal Ascot's Queen Alexandra Stakes — at two and three-quarter miles, the longest Flat race in the calendar. Dr Weller, unsentimental about the RVC's Eclipse association, says, 'Brown Jack impressed me more.'

This opinion notwithstanding, Eclipse has a key role in the

RVC's promotional and educational activities. In 2004, the college sent its reproduction leg to the Royal Society Summer Exhibition. The leg is also the star prop in the RVC's educational outreach programme to schools and colleges. Seeing a physical specimen, the RVC says, teaches more about anatomy, and inspires more enthusiasm for the subject, than any number of diagrams and textbook explanations. The college, which is lobbying for the financial support to create an entire replica of Eclipse's skeleton, believes that its Eclipse project can be the prototype for the creation of similar teaching aids. The project may also show the way towards modelling of human subjects, so that replicas can give evidence of the likely outcome of surgery.

Eclipse is also at the heart of advanced genetic research. Matthew Binns of the RVC, Paula Jenkins of the Natural History Museum, and Mim Bower of Cambridge University have been leading a project to explore genetic variations in Thoroughbreds. The horses they have examined include, as well as Eclipse, Hermit, whose Derby victory broke Lord Hastings's heart, and St Simon, the 'steam engine' ridden by Fred Archer. Their findings will give us our fullest understanding yet of these great horses, and may also offer information to help trace horses' genetic weaknesses. One of the great worries for the bloodstock industry is that, in an inbred animal, genetic defects may be perpetuated and become widespread.

The researchers started by encasing in wax a tooth from the Eclipse skull, and drilled it. The genetic material they extracted contained bad news. This tooth did not belong to an animal from what, according to the official records, was Eclipse's matrilineal line.[197]

[197] The researchers examined mitochondrial DNA, which is passed down the distaff line and which can therefore identify Thoroughbred 'families'. (In the bloodstock world, the term 'family' indicates the bottom, female line of a pedigree.) Thoroughbred families were first classified by the nineteenth-century Australian historian Bruce Lowe, who gave them numbers. Eclipse belongs to family number 12.

In the light of the convoluted history of the skeleton, a separation of the body from its proper head, and the replacement of the head with a substitute, are not surprising occurrences. The Natural History Museum, when it possessed the skeleton, displayed it headless, and has in its archives a letter from a man who had heard that Eclipse's head was kept in a grotto – destroyed by fire in 1948 – in Weybridge.

As I write, results of tests on the body are yet to appear, though I am hopeful that they will conform to the accepted pedigree and thus indicate, with near incontrovertibility, that the RVC's skeleton really is Eclipse's. If the tests reveal a different pedigree, however, they will not prove fakery. Rather, I should be inclined to suspect that the pedigree was inaccurate. The skeleton seems to be the one that Sainbel studied. How could he have stripped and anatomized the wrong horse? He knew what Eclipse looked like: he said that he had seen him alive.[198] It is hard to imagine a set of circumstances that could have compelled him, with the O'Kellys' connivance or at their instigation, to pass off a fake as the real thing. I remain convinced that the skeleton in the RVC, or most of it, is Eclipse.

No other racehorse has done this much. Eclipse was a supreme champion, who easily defeated the best racehorses of the day. His bloodline was to dominate the bloodstock industry. In alliance with Herod, his genetic influence transformed racing into a spectacle of thrilling speed, for masses of people to enjoy. He is the icon of the sport, its unquestionable symbol of greatness: its Jesse Owens, or Michael Jordan, or Donald Bradman, or Pele. The Eclipse Stakes and the Eclipse Awards, along with various other

---

[198] Dr Weller does not think that the inconsistency between Stubbs's and Sainbel's portrayals of Eclipse's white markings is significant. 'Since horse passports were introduced, vets have had to draw horse's markings,' she says. 'The differences between what two vets will draw are amazing.'

institutions named after him, are tributes to his status. Not only does he endure as ancestor of every Thoroughbred alive today, but as an inspiration to veterinary research and education.

I mentioned Owens, Jordan, Bradman and Pele. But they are only human. There is something otherworldly, as Stubbs knew, about a great horse; something belonging to the realm of legend.

From the distance over the Downs, a chestnut Thoroughbred appears: galloping with head low, jockey motionless, the rest nowhere.

Sources

Chapter 1

Anon., *The Genuine Memoirs of Dennis O'Kelly, Esq*
Anon., *Nocturnal Revels*
Cook, *Eclipse and O'Kelly*
Gatrell, *City of Laughter*
Hitchcock, *Down and Out in Eighteenth-Century London*
Picard, *Dr Johnson's London*
Porter, *English Society in the 18th Century*
Weinreb and Hibbert (eds), *The London Encyclopaedia*
Williams, *History of the Name O'Kelly*
Town & Country magazine (September 1770)
Fleet prison debtors' schedules, London Metropolitan Archives
Papers of Colonel Andrew Dennis O'Kelly, Brynmor Jones Library, University of Hull

Chapter 2

Anon., *The Genuine Memoirs of Dennis O'Kelly, Esq*
Anon., *Nocturnal Revels*
Archenholz, *A Picture of England*
Brown, *A History of the Fleet Prison, London*
Burford, *Wits, Wenchers and Wantons*
Burford and Wotton *Private Vices – Public Virtues*
Clayton, *The British Museum Hogarth*
Hickey, *Memoirs*
Linnane, *Madams, Bawds and Brothel-Keepers of London*

Porter, *English Society in the 18th Century*
Rubenhold, *The Covent Garden Ladies*
Thompson, *The Meretriciad*
Weinreb and Hibbert (eds), *The London Encyclopaedia*
Fleet prison debtors' schedules, London Metropolitan Archives
Fleet records, National Archives
Noble Collection, Guildhall Library

Chapter 3

Anon., *Nocturnal Revels*
Bloch, *Sexual Life in England*
Blyth, *The High Tide of Pleasure*
Burford and Wotton, *Private Vices – Public Virtues*
Chinn, *Better Betting with a Decent Feller*
Cook, *Eclipse and O'Kelly*
Egan, *Sporting Anecdotes*
Harcourt, *The Gaming Calendar and Annals of Gaming*
Linnane, *Madams, Bawds and Brothel-Keepers of London*
Oxford English Dictionary
Picard, *Dr Johnson's London*
Pick, *An Authentic Historical Racing Calendar*
Porter, *English Society in the 18th Century*
Prior, *Early Records of the Thoroughbred*
Rice, *The History of the British Turf*
Rubenhold, *The Covent Garden Ladies*
Steinmetz, *The Gaming Table, Its Votaries and Victims*
Thompson, *The Meretriciad*
Thompson, *Newmarket*
Thormanby, *Sporting Stories* (1909)
The Sporting Magazine (1792, 1795)

Chapter 4

Cook, *Eclipse and O'Kelly*
Duke of Ancaster's Stud Book (1772–78)
FitzGerald, *Royal Thoroughbreds*
FitzGerald, *Thoroughbreds of the Crown*
Heber, *An Historical List* (1754, 1755, 1756)
Kiste, *King George II and Queen Caroline*

Longrigg, *The History of Horse Racing*
Magee, *Ascot: The History*
Mortimer, *The Jockey Club*
Newmarket Match Book (1754)
Oxford Dictionary of National Biography
Pick, *An Authentic Historical Racing Calendar*
Pond, *Sporting Kalendar* (1754, 1755, 1756)
Rice, *The History of the British Turf*
Seth-Smith, *Bred for the Purple*
Thompson, *Newmarket: From James I to the Present Day*
Walker, *An Historical List* (1769)
Lloyd's Evening Post (1765)
London Chronicle (1765)
London Evening Post (1765)
Pacemaker (October 2007)
St James's Chronicle (1765)
The Thoroughbred Record (1924)

Chapter 5

Blake, *George Stubbs and the Wide Creation*
Church, *Eclipse: The Horse, the Race, the Awards*
Clark, *A Short History of the Celebrated Race-horse Eclipse*
Cook, *Eclipse and O'Kelly*
FitzGerald, *Thoroughbreds of the Crown*
Fountain, *William Wildman and George Stubbs*
Heber, *An Historical List* (1764, 1765, 1768)
Lawrence, *The History and Delineation of the Horse*
Lawrence, *A Philosophical and Practical Treatise on Horses*
Lawrence and Scott, *The Sportsman's Repository*
Longrigg, *The History of Horse Racing*
Mortimer, *The History of the Derby Stakes*
Orchard, *Tattersalls*
Taplin, *The Gentleman's Stable Directory*
Williams, *UK Solar Eclipses from Year 1*
The Field (12 June 1937)
Lloyd's Evening Post (30 March–2 April 1764)
London Chronicle (22–24 March 1764; 3 April 1764)
London Evening Post (3–5 April 1764)
The Sporting Magazine (1814)

Chapter 6

Church, *Three Generations of Leading Sires*
Clark, *A Short History of the Celebrated Race-horse Eclipse*
Cook, *Eclipse and O'Kelly*
FitzGerald, *Royal Thoroughbreds*
Holcroft, *Memoirs of the Late Thomas Holcroft*
Lawrence, *A Philosophical and Practical Treatise on Horses*
Lawrence, *The History and Delineation of the Horse*
Lawrence and Scott, *The Sportsman's Repository*
Longrigg, *The History of Horse Racing*
Markham, *How to Choose, Ride, Train and Diet*
Morris, *Thoroughbred Stallions*
Mortimer, *The Jockey Club*
Prior, *Early Records of the Thoroughbred*
Rice, *The History of the British Turf*
Robertson, 'The Origin of the Thoroughbred'
Taunton, *Famous Horses*
Taunton, *Portraits of Celebrated Race Horses*
Thompson, *Newmarket: From James I to the Present Day*
Trew, *From 'Dawn' to 'Eclipse'*
Wentworth, *Thoroughbred Racing Stock*
Willett, *The Classic Racehorse*
The Field (25 December 1920)
Pedigreequery.com
TBHeritage.com

Chapter 7

Bawtree, *A Few Notes on Banstead Downs*
Church, *Eclipse: The Horse, the Race, the Awards*
Clark, *A Short History of the Celebrated Race-horse Eclipse*
Cook, *Eclipse and O'Kelly*
Curling, *British Racecourses*
Epsom Common
Gill, *Racecourses of Great Britain*
Grosley, *A Tour to London*
Heber, *An Historical List* (1766, 1768)
Home, *Epsom: Its History and Surroundings*
Hunn, *Epsom Racecourse*

Lawrence, *The History and Delineation of the Horse*
Lawrence, *A Philosophical and Practical Treatise on Horses*
Lillywhite, *London Coffee Houses*
Longrigg, *The History of Horse Racing*
O'Brien and Herbert, *Vincent O'Brien*
Pagones, *Dubai Millennium*
Picard, *Dr Johnson's London*
Piggott and Magee, *Lester's Derbys*
Porter, *English Society in the 18th Century*
Pownall, *Some Particulars Relating to the History of Epsom*
Rice, *The History of the British Turf*
Salter, *Epsom Town Downs and Common*
Waller, *1700: Scenes from London Life*
West, *Tavern Anecdotes*
Whyte, *History of the British Turf*
The Times digital archive (1787)
Town & Country (August 1770)
Coolmore.com
Epsom Salt Council website
Measuring Worth website

Chapter 8

Bawtree, *A Few Notes on Banstead Downs*
Church, *Eclipse: The Horse, the Race, the Awards*
Clark, *A Short History of the Celebrated Race-horse Eclipse*
Cook, *Eclipse and O'Kelly*
Egan, *Book of Sports*
Egerton, *George Stubbs, Painter*
Gill, *Racecourses of Great Britain*
Grosley, *A Tour to London*
Lawrence, *The History and Delineation of the Horse*
Lawrence and Scott, *The Sportsman's Repository*
Longrigg, *The History of Horse Racing*
Magee, *Ascot: The History*
Mortimer, *The Jockey Club*
Osbaldiston, *The British Sportsman*
Orton, *Turf Annals*
Pick, *An Authentic Historical Racing Calendar*
Porter, *London: A Social History*

Prior, *Early Records of the Thoroughbred*
Rice, *The History of the British Turf*
Salter, *Epsom Town Downs and Common*
Taunton, *Famous Horses*
Tuting and Fawconer, *The Sporting Calendar* (1769)
Walker, *An Historical List* (1769)
Whyte, *History of the British Turf*
The Sporting Magazine (September 1793; January 1794)

Chapter 9

Anon., *The Genuine Memoirs of Dennis O'Kelly, Esq*
Burford, *Royal St James's*
Church, *Eclipse: The Horse, the Race, the Awards*
Clark, *A Short History of the Celebrated Race-horse Eclipse*
Cook, *Eclipse and O'Kelly*
Egerton, *George Stubbs, Painter*
FitzGerald, *Royal Thoroughbreds*
Lawrence, *The History and Delineation of the Horse*
Longrigg, *The History of Horse Racing*
Orchard, *Tattersalls*
Orton, *Turf Annals*
Pick, *An Authentic Historical Racing Calendar*
Rede, *Anecdotes and Biography*
Rice, *The History of the British Turf*
Seth-Smith, *Bred for the Purple*
Thompson, *Newmarket: From James I to the Present Day*
Tuting and Fawconer, *The Sporting Calendar* (1769, 1770)
Walker, *An Historical List* (1769, 1770)
The Sporting Magazine (September 1793)
Town & Country (August 1770; September 1770)
York Courant (14 August 1770; 2 October 1770)

Chapter 10

Anon., *Nocturnal Revels*
Anon. (Charles Pigott), *The Jockey Club*
Archenholz, *A Picture of England*
Burford, *Royal St James's*
Burford, *Wits, Wenchers and Wantons*

Burford and Wotton, *Private Vices – Public Virtues*
Hickey, *Memoirs*
Linnane, *Madams, Bawds and Brothel-Keepers of London*
'OMIAH: An Ode Addressed to Charlotte Hayes'
Rubenhold, *The Covent Garden Ladies*
Thompson, *The Courtesan*
Thompson, *The Meretriciad*
Weinreb and Hibbert (eds), *The London Encyclopaedia*
Annual Register (1774)
The London Magazine (1772)
The Times (September 1815)
Town & Country (February 1769)

Chapter 11

Black, *The Jockey Club and Its Founders*
Cain, *The Home Run Horse*
Conley, *Stud*
Cook, *Eclipse and O'Kelly*
Egerton, *George Stubbs, Painter*
FitzGerald, *Thoroughbreds of the Crown*
Fountain, *William Wildman and George Stubbs*
Harding, *An Elegy on the Famous Old Horse Marsk*
Lawrence, *The History and Delineation of the Horse*
Lawrence and Scott, *The Sportsman's Repository*
Orchard, *Tattersalls*
Orton, *Turf Annals*
Pick, *An Authentic Historical Racing Calendar*
Randall and Morris, *Guinness Horse Racing: The Records*
Taunton, *Portraits of Celebrated Race Horses*
Tuting and Fawconer, *The Sporting Calendar* (1769, 1770)
Walker, *An Historical List* (1769, 1770)
Willett, *The Classic Racehorse*
Willett, *The Story of Tattersalls*
Racing Calendar
Racing Post Bloodstock Review 2007
The Sporting Magazine (January 1794)
TBHeritage.com

Chapter 12

Black, *The Jockey Club and Its Founders*
Curling, *British Racecourses*
Derby Day 200
Gill, *Racecourses of Great Britain*
Longrigg, *The History of Horse Racing*
Magee, *Ascot: The History*
Mortimer, *The History of the Derby Stakes*
Thompson, *Newmarket: From James I to the Present Day*
Towers, *An Introduction to a General Stud Book*
Tyrrel, *Running Racing*
Willett, *The Classic Racehorse*
Willett, *A History of the General Stud Book*
Guardian (21 March 2006)
Racing Calendar
The Sporting Magazine (June 1814)
British Horseracing Authority website
The Cox Library website
The Jockey Club website
TBHeritage.com
Weatherbys website

Chapter 13

Anon., *The Genuine Memoirs of Dennis O'Kelly, Esq*
Black, *The Jockey Club and Its Founders*
Cook, *Eclipse and O'Kelly*
Egan, *Boxiana*
Egan, *Sporting Anecdotes*
Epsom Common
Harcourt, *The Gaming Calendar and Annals of Gaming*
Lawrence, *The History and Delineation of the Horse*
Lawrence and Scott, *The Sportsman's Repository*
Parsons, Philip, *Newmarket: Or an Essay on the Turf*
Shoemaker, *The London Mob*
Steinmetz, *The Gaming Table, Its Votaries and Victims*
Thormanby, *Sporting Stories*
Waugh, *Will This Do?*
White, *Ancient Epsom*

Annual Register (1775)
Independent on Sunday (February 1998)
The Sporting Magazine (September 1793; June 1814)
The Times (March 1786)
Town & Country (September 1770)
HotBoxingNews.com
Clay Hill papers, Surrey History Centre
Papers of Colonel Andrew Dennis O'Kelly, Brynmor Jones Library, University of Hull

Chapter 14

Anon., *The Genuine Memoirs of Dennis O'Kelly, Esq*
Anon., *The Minor Jockey Club*
Buss, *The North London Collegiate School*
Cook, *Eclipse and O'Kelly*
Fraser, *William Stukely and the Gout*
Harcourt, *The Gaming Calendar and Annals of Gaming*
Hickey, *Memoirs*
Picard, *Dr Johnson's London*
Porter, *English Society in the 18th Century*
Shoemaker, *The London Mob*
Steinmetz, *The Gaming Table, Its Votaries and Victims*
Thormanby, *Sporting Stories*
Williams, *History of the Name O'Kelly*
Gentleman's Magazine (1787, 1802)
Racing Calendar
The Sporting Magazine (October 1792; February 1796; March 1796)
The Times digital archive
Whitehall Evening Post (1 January 1788)
Canons records, North London Collegiate School
Papers of Colonel Andrew Dennis O'Kelly, Brynmor Jones Library, University of Hull
Plumer papers, London Metropolitan Archives

Chapter 15

Church, *Eclipse: The Horse, the Race, the Awards*
Clark, *A Short History of the Celebrated Race-horse Eclipse*

Cook, *Eclipse and O'Kelly*
Egan, *Sporting Anecdotes*
Mortimer, Onslow and Willett, *Biographical Encyclopaedia of British Flat Racing*
Orton, *Turf Annals*
Sainbel, *Elements of Veterinary Art*
Taunton, *Portraits of Celebrated Race Horses*
Trew, *From 'Dawn' to 'Eclipse'*
Gentleman's Magazine (1787 supplement)
Monthly Review (1788)
Racing Calendar
Racing Post Bloodstock Review 2007
The Times digital archive
Whitehall Evening Post (2 January 1788; 7–10 March 1788)
World Fashionable Advertiser (7, 8, 12 January 1788)
Pedigreequery.com
St Lawrence, Little Stanmore, burial records, London Metropolitan Archives
Will of Dennis O'Kelly, National Archives

Chapter 16

Burford and Wotton, *Private Vices – Public Virtues*
Cook, *Eclipse and O'Kelly*
Fitzpatrick, *Secret Service Under Pitt*
Picard, *Dr Johnson's London*
Porter, *English Society in the 18th Century*
Weinreb and Hibbert (eds), *The London Encyclopaedia*
Gentleman's Magazine (1802)
The Newgate Calendar (exclassics.com)
Racing Calendar
The Times digital archive
Traceyclann.com
Fleet prison debtors' schedules, London Metropolitan Archives
Papers of Colonel Andrew Dennis O'Kelly, Brynmor Jones Library, University of Hull
Plumer papers, London Metropolitan Archives
Wills of Andrew Dennis O'Kelly and Charles Andrew O'Kelly, National Archives

Chapter 17

Anon. (Charles Pigott), *The Jockey Club*

Cook, *Eclipse and O'Kelly*

FitzGerald, *Thoroughbreds of the Crown*

Longrigg, *The History of Horse Racing*

Magee, *Ascot: The History*

Mortimer, *The History of the Derby Stakes*

Mortimer, Onslow and Willett, *Biographical Encyclopaedia of British Flat Racing*

Thompson, *Newmarket: From James I to the Present Day*

Tyrrel, *Running Racing*

Whyte, *History of the British Turf*

Racing Calendar

The Sporting Magazine (September 1793)

The Times digital archive

Fitzwilliam/Langdale papers, Public Record Office, Northern Ireland

Papers of Colonel Andrew Dennis O'Kelly, Brynmor Jones Library, University of Hull

Chapter 18

Blake, *George Stubbs and the Wide Creation*

Cook, *Eclipse and O'Kelly*

Egerton, *British Sporting and Animal Paintings*

Egerton, *George Stubbs, Painter*

Grego, *Rowlandson the Caricaturist*

Lawrence, *The History and Delineation of the Horse*

Noakes, *Sportsmen in a Landscape*

The Sporting Magazine (January 1794)

Chapter 19

Blake, *George Stubbs and the Wide Creation*

Derby Day 200

Egerton, *George Stubbs, Painter*

Longrigg, *The History of Horse Racing*

Magee, *Ascot: The History*

Mortimer, *The History of the Derby Stakes*

Mortimer, Onslow and Willett, *Biographical Encyclopaedia of British Flat Racing*

Noakes, *Sportsmen in a Landscape*
Randall and Morris, *A Century of Champions*
Thompson, *Newmarket: From James I to the Present Day*
Willett, *The Classic Racehorse*
Annual Register (1844)
Pedigreequery.com
TBHeritage.com
Victorian-cinema.net

Chapter 20

Church, *Eclipse: The Horse, the Race, the Awards*
Lennox, *Northern Dancer*
Longrigg, *The History of Horse Racing*
Mortimer, Onslow and Willett, *Biographical Encyclopaedia of British Flat Racing*
Pagones, *Dubai Millennium*
Randall and Morris, *A Century of Champions*
Guardian (November 2005)
Observer (October 2005)
Ascot.co.uk
Australian Government Culture and Recreation website/ Melbourne Cup
Horsesonly.com (Mariana Haun, 'The X Factor')
National Museum of Australia website
SportingChronicle.com

Chapter 21

Black, *The Jockey Club and Its Founders*
Church, *Eclipse: The Horse, the Race, the Awards*
Clark, *A Short History of the Celebrated Race-horse Eclipse*
Cook, *Eclipse and O'Kelly*
Hall, 'The Story of a Skeleton: Eclipse'
Sainbel, *Elements of Veterinary Art*
Weinreb and Hibbert (eds), *The London Encyclopaedia*
Wentworth, *Thoroughbred Racing Stock*
The British Racehorse (November 1963)
The Veterinary Record (March 1991)
Royal Veterinary College website

Appendix 1

Eclipse's Racing Career

When details differ, I have given the sources:

* Tuting and Fawconer, *The Sporting Calendar* (1769, 1770)
† B. Walker, *An Historical List of Horse-Matches, Plates and Prizes, Run for in Great Britain and Ireland* (1769, 1770)
‡ Bracy Clark, *A Short History of the Celebrated Race-horse Eclipse* (1835)
§ William Pick, *An Authentic Historical Racing Calendar* (1785)
¶ John Orton, *Turf Annals of York and Doncaster* (1844)

1769

3 May, Epsom. Noblemen and Gentlemen's Plate, for horses that have not won £30 (matches excepted). Four-mile heats. Five-year-olds (Eclipse, Gower, Trial), 8st* (8st 7lb†); six-year-olds (Chance, Plume), 9st 3lb; older horses, 9st 13lb. Winner, £50.
Heat 1: **1st Eclipse** (Mr Wildman); 2nd Gower (Mr Fortescue); 3rd Chance (Mr Castle); 4th Trial (Mr Jennings); 5th Plume (Mr Quick).
Heat 2: **1st Eclipse**; distanced Gower, Chance, Trial, Plume.
Betting: (heat 1) 1-4 Eclipse; (heat 2) 6-4, 5-4, evens Eclipse to distance field. (Jockey: John Oakley)

29 May, Ascot. Noblemen and Gentlemen's Plate. Two-mile heats. Four-year-olds, 8st 5lb; five-year-olds (Eclipse, Cream de Barbade), 9st 3lb. Winner, £50.

Heat 1: **1st Eclipse** (Mr Wildman); 2nd Cream de Barbade (Mr Fettyplace).
Heat 2: **1st Eclipse**; 2nd Cream de Barbade.
Betting: 1-8 Eclipse.

13 June, Winchester. King's Plate. Four-mile heats. For six-year-olds; 12st (younger horses carry same weight). (Six-year-olds Slouch, Chigger, Juba, Caliban, Clanvil; five-year-old Eclipse.) Winner, 100 guineas.
Heat 1: **1st Eclipse** (Mr Wildman); 2nd Slouch (Mr Turner); 3rd Chigger (Duke of Grafton); 4th Juba (Mr Gott); distanced Caliban (Mr O'Kelly), Clanvil (Mr Bailey).
Heat 2: **1st Eclipse**; 2nd Slouch; 3rd Chigger; 4th Juba.
Betting: (heat 1) 5-4* (evens†) Eclipse; 5-2, 3-1* (2-1†) Caliban; 2-1, 3-1 Chigger; 5-1, 6-1* (4-1†) Slouch; (heat 2) 1-10 Eclipse.

15 June, Winchester. City Plate. Four-mile heats. Five-year-olds (Eclipse) and six-year-olds; 10st; older horses, 10st 7lb. Winner, £50.
1st Eclipse (Mr Wildman) walked over.

28 June, Salisbury. King's Plate. Four-mile heats. For six-year-olds; 12st (younger horses carry same weight). Winner, 100 guineas.
1st Eclipse (Mr Wildman) walked over.

29 June, Salisbury. City Plate. Four-mile heats. 10st. Winner, silver bowl and 30 guineas.
Heat 1: **1st Eclipse** (Mr Wildman); 2nd Sulphur (Mr Fettyplace); distanced Forrester (Mr Taylor).
Heat 2: **1st Eclipse**; 2nd Sulphur.
Betting: 1-10* (1-8†) Eclipse.

25 July, Canterbury. King's Plate. Four-mile heats. For six-year-olds; 12st* (12st 1lb†) (younger horses carry same weight). Winner, 100 guineas.
1st Eclipse (Mr Wildman) walked over.

27 July, Lewes. King's Plate. Four-mile heats. For six-year-olds; 12st (younger horses carry same weight). (Six-year-old Kingston; five-year-old Eclipse.) Winner, 100 guineas.
Heat 1: **1st Eclipse** (Mr Wildman); 2nd Kingston (Mr Strode).
Heat 2: **1st Eclipse**; 2nd Kingston.
(Jockey: John Whiting‡)

19 September, Lichfield. King's Plate. Three-mile heats. For five-year-olds; 8st 7lb. Winner, 100 guineas.
Heat 1: **1st Eclipse** (Mr Wildman); 2nd Tardy (Mr Freeth).
Heat 2: **1st Eclipse**; 2nd Tardy.
Betting: 1-7 Eclipse.

9 races, 9 wins, including 5 King's Plates. Prize money: £706.50.

1770

17 April, Newmarket. Beacon Course (4 miles, 1 furlong, 138 yards). 8st 7lb.
Eclipse (Mr Wildman) beat Bucephalus (Mr Wentworth). Winner, 1,000 guineas (Mr Wildman contributed 400 guineas; Mr Wentworth contributed 600 guineas).

19 April, Newmarket. Round Course. King's Plate. Four-mile heats. For six-year-olds; 12st (younger horses carry same weight). Six-year-olds Diana (mare), Chigger; five-year-olds Eclipse, Pensioner. Winner, 100 guineas.
Heat 1: **1st Eclipse** (Mr O'Kelly); 2nd Diana (Mr Fenwick); 3rd Pensioner (Mr Strode); 4th Chigger (Duke of Grafton). Diana and Chigger withdrawn.
Heat 2: **1st Eclipse**; distanced Pensioner.
Betting: (heat 1) 1-10* (1-15†) Eclipse; (heat 2) 6-4*, 7-4§ Eclipse to distance Pensioner.

5 June, Guildford. King's Plate. Four-mile heats. For six-year-olds; 12st (younger horses carry same weight). Winner, 100 guineas.
1st Eclipse (Mr O'Kelly) walked over.

3 July, Nottingham. King's Plate. Four-mile heats. For six-year-olds; 12st (younger horses carry same weight). Winner, 100 guineas.
1st Eclipse (Mr O'Kelly) walked over.

20 August, York. King's Plate. Four-mile heats. For six-year-olds; 12st (younger horses carry same weight). Winner, 100 guineas.
1st Eclipse (Mr O'Kelly) walked over.
(Jockey: Samuel Merriott¶)

23 August, York. Great Subscription. Four miles. For six-year-olds and upwards. Six-year-old Eclipse (8st 7lb); seven-year-old Bellario (9st); eight-year-old Tortoise (9st). Winner, £319 10s.

1st Eclipse (Mr O'Kelly); 2nd Tortoise (Mr Wentworth); 3rd Bellario (Sir Charles Bunbury).

Betting: 1-20 Eclipse; 4-7 Tortoise to beat Bellario. 1-100 Eclipse in running.

(Jockey: Samuel Merriott¶)

3 September, Lincoln. King's Plate. Four-mile heats. For six-year-olds; 12st (younger horses carry same weight). Winner, 100 guineas.

1st Eclipse (Mr O'Kelly) walked over.

3 October, Newmarket. Beacon Course (4 miles, 1 furlong, 138 yards). For six-year-olds, 8st 10lb (younger horses carry same weight); older horses, 9st 2lb. Six-year-old Eclipse; five-year-old Corsican. Subscription 30 guineas† (O'Kelly paid 100 guineas*‡). Winner, 150 guineas (one quarter of 20 subscriptions of 30 guineas each†).

1st Eclipse (Mr O'Kelly); 2nd Corsican (Sir Charles Bunbury).

Betting: 1-70 Eclipse.

4 October, Newmarket. King's Plate. Four-mile heats. For six-year-olds; 12st (younger horses carry same weight). Winner, 100 guineas.

1st Eclipse (Mr O'Kelly) walked over.

9 races, 9 wins, including 6 King's Plates. Prize money: £2,157.

Overall record: 18 races, 18 wins, including 11 King's Plates. Prize money: £2,863.50.

Jockeys

Details about Eclipse's jockeys are sparse. The earliest report that John Oakley was in the saddle for Eclipse's Epsom debut comes in William Pick's *Authentic Historical Racing Calendar* (1785). John Lawrence, who did not see Eclipse race but did see him at stud, says that 'we believe' that Oakley 'generally, or always rode Eclipse'. But when in 1793 George Stubbs painted a copy of *Eclipse at Newmarket, with a Groom and Jockey* (the original is dated 1770), the exhibition catalogue identified the jockey as 'Samuel Merrit, who generally rode him'; John Orton wrote that Merriott (the more usual spelling) rode Eclipse at York. Bracy Clark, in his record of the 1769 King's

Plate at Lewes, wrote, 'Eyewitnesses say that John Whiting rode him this time; whether Oakley, his constant groom, always rode him is not certain.' The Turf historian James Christie Whyte asserted that '[Dennis] Fitzpatrick and John Oakley rode him in almost all his races'. According to the dates in Orton's *Turf Annals*, however, Fitzpatrick (the first Irish jockey to ride in England) was the same age as Eclipse – in other words, in 1769 he was five.

Bracy Clark's mention of Oakley as Eclipse's 'constant groom' is arresting. In the days before race-riding became a distinct role, grooms usually doubled as race-riders. If Oakley were the groom, he – knowing the headstrong horse best – would have been a good choice of rider for Eclipse's first race.

Is Oakley the groom – or, as the catalogue copy puts it, 'the boy who looked after him' – in Stubbs's painting? Eclipse may have belonged by this time to Dennis O'Kelly, who commissioned Stubbs; we do not know whether the groom would have changed stables with the horse. John Orton, though, described Oakley as a rider, chiefly for Lord Abingdon.

There is a jockey on board Eclipse in the Sartorius picture of Eclipse and Shakespeare. He looks a bit like the jockey in the Stubbs painting; but you could not swear that he is the same person. Another Sartorius painting is entitled *Eclipse with Oakley Up*. John Nost Sartorius was not painting at the time of Eclipse's racing career, but may have copied studies by his father, Francis.

One is inclined to treat all these reports with caution. The earliest ones, identifying Oakley at Epsom (Pick) and Merriott at Newmarket (Stubbs), may be the most reliable; and Ortan was working from local records when he asserted that Merriott was up at York. Perhaps Oakley often rode for Wildman, and Merriott for O'Kelly.

Appendix 2

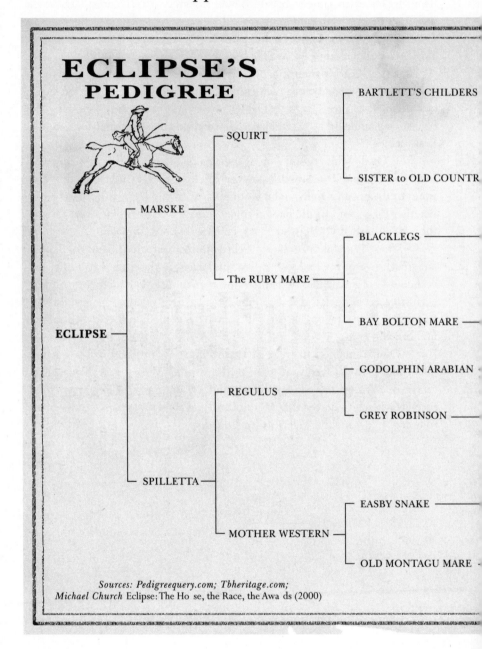

ECLIPSE'S
PEDIGREE

- ECLIPSE
  - MARSKE
    - SQUIRT
      - BARTLETT'S CHILDERS
      - SISTER to OLD COUNTR
    - The RUBY MARE
      - BLACKLEGS
      - BAY BOLTON MARE
  - SPILLETTA
    - REGULUS
      - GODOLPHIN ARABIAN
      - GREY ROBINSON
    - MOTHER WESTERN
      - EASBY SNAKE
      - OLD MONTAGU MARE

Sources: Pedigreequery.com; Tbheritage.com;
Michael Church Eclipse: The Ho se, the Race, the Awa ds (2000)

298

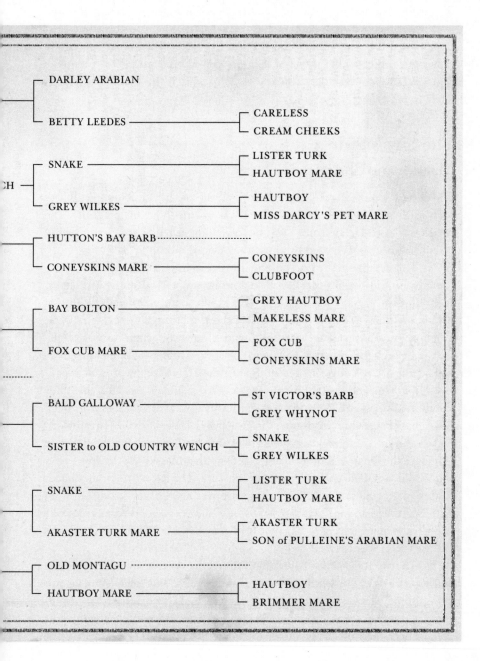

CH

DARLEY ARABIAN

BETTY LEEDES ——— CARELESS
                   CREAM CHEEKS

SNAKE ——— LISTER TURK
              HAUTBOY MARE

GREY WILKES ——— HAUTBOY
                    MISS DARCY'S PET MARE

HUTTON'S BAY BARB

CONEYSKINS MARE ——— CONEYSKINS
                        CLUBFOOT

BAY BOLTON ——— GREY HAUTBOY
                   MAKELESS MARE

FOX CUB MARE ——— FOX CUB
                     CONEYSKINS MARE

BALD GALLOWAY ——— ST VICTOR'S BARB
                      GREY WHYNOT

SISTER to OLD COUNTRY WENCH ——— SNAKE
                                    GREY WILKES

SNAKE ——— LISTER TURK
              HAUTBOY MARE

AKASTER TURK MARE ——— AKASTER TURK
                          SON of PULLEINE'S ARABIAN MARE

OLD MONTAGU

HAUTBOY MARE ——— HAUTBOY
                     BRIMMER MARE

James Weatherby and William Sydney Towers, publisher and author respectively of *An Introduction to a General Stud Book* (1791), did an impressive job of introducing authority to the publication of pedigrees, sorting through previous haphazard compilations. Towers' account of Eclipse's breeding continues to be the one – small updates apart – you will see most commonly reproduced. But doubts, some of them ineradicable, surround the identities of several of the great horse's ancestors. In two instances, the *GSB* version is likely to be wrong.

The Sire's Side
Marske and Shakespeare

Eclipse is a son of Marske, according to all the published pedigrees. But as soon as Eclipse became famous, there was gossip about his paternity. The father was not Marske, some said, but a stallion called Shakespeare, whose claims had been suppressed by conspiracy (see also chapter 5).

These rumours were potentially damaging to William Wildman. Cannily, he had bought Marske as soon as he saw the potential of Eclipse, realizing that Marske's value as a stallion would shoot up once the ability of his son was known. By the time Eclipse had retired from his unbeaten career, Wildman was advertising Marske – whose services, when he was at the Duke of Cumberland's stud, had been considered to be worth no more than half a guinea – at a covering fee of thirty guineas. He had to prevent breeders, hoping to get another Eclipse, from entertaining the idea that they should send their mares to Shakespeare instead. One early attempt to quell the rumours was an advertisement in Tuting and Fawconer's 1771 racing calendar: the ad contained a signed statement by Bernard Smith, the stud groom of the Duke of Cumberland, asserting that Marske was Eclipse's sire. But it did not convince all men of the Turf. The bloodstock auctioneer Richard Tattersall argued, 'for Shakespeare was a large and strong chestnut with white legs and face who got chestnuts and was a good runner. Marske was a bad runner, a brown, who got brown or bay. Mr O'Kelly's groom says Eclipse's dam was covered by both, and first by Shakespeare.'[196]

There are three flaws in Tattersall's reasoning. First, while Shakespeare was the winner of two King's Plates, and while Marske was inconsistent, Marske did win a Jockey Club Plate; his two defeats by the outstanding Snap were no disgrace. Second, fathers do not dictate the hair colouring of their offspring, either in equine or in human breeding; indeed,

[196] Quoted in Theodore Cook's *Eclipse and O'Kelly*.

the same sire and dam may produce variously coloured foals. Marske mated, indisputably, twice more with Eclipse's dam Spilletta: their daughter Proserpine (1766) was bay; their son Garrick (1772) was chestnut. Third, why should Dennis O'Kelly's groom have possessed any authority in the matter? Eclipse was born at the Duke of Cumberland's stud.

William Taplin, in *The Gentleman's Stable Directory* (1791), asserted that the Duke of Cumberland and his groom were uncertain whether Marske or Shakespeare was Eclipse's sire, but resolved the issue by calculating that 'the time of the mare's bringing forth (during the great Eclipse) coming nearest to the day she was booked to have been covered by Marske, to him was attributed the distinguished honour of getting one of the first horses of the known world'. Taplin seems to be saying that Marske's more recent covering of Spilletta is evidence that he was the father. That evidence demonstrates nothing, and perhaps what he means is that Marske covered Spilletta eleven months (a horse's gestation period) before the birth.

This must be the meaning of 'she came to Marske's time' in John Lawrence's account, the fullest summary of this problem. In *The History and Delineation of the Horse* (1809), Lawrence wrote:

It has always been taken for granted, that he [Eclipse] was a son of Marske, a fact, beyond the power of man to ascertain. Eclipse's dam was covered both by Shakespeare and Marske, and she came to Marske's time, so the honour was awarded to him. If I recollect awright, she had missed by him the previous year. But the circumstance of a mare coming regularly to her time, determines nothing, since they are so uncertain in that respect, in which I have repeatedly known variations from a week or ten days, to two or three weeks. Great stress was laid upon the supposed likeness of Basilius, one of the earliest sons of Eclipse, to old Marske, and indeed the resemblance appeared to me strong; but I could discover no common family resemblance between Eclipse and his presumed full-brother Garrick. On the other hand, I think Eclipse strongly resembled the family of Shakespeare, in colour, in certain particulars of form, and in temper. Nothing can be more unimportant than these speculations, and Eclipse's pedigree would suffer no loss of honour or credit, should Shakespeare be placed at the head of it; which horse had more of the Darley Arabian in him, than Marske, and in all respects, was equally well-bred, and full as good a runner. Shakespeare, like Marske, was a great-grandson of the Darley Arabian, through Hobgoblin and Aleppo, and his dam the little Hartley mare, the dam also of Blank, was a grand-daughter of the same Arabian, and out of the famous Flying Whig. One or two of the sons of

Eclipse, still alive, appear to me strongly to resemble the Shakespeare.

It is necessary, however, to subjoin the late intelligence on this subject, with which I have been favoured by Mr Sandiver, of Newmarket, which goes to assert, on the authority of the stud-groom, that Eclipse's dam really never was covered by Shakespeare. On this I can only observe, that in the year 1778, I was frequently in the habit of visiting Old Eclipse, then at Epsom, on which occasions I often discoursed the subject of the disputed pedigree, with Colonel O'Kelly's then groom, who assured me that the mare was covered by Shakespeare, which account I also had from various other persons, as a well-known fact. And to conceal nothing, it had been reported, that a groom had been bribed to ascribe the get of Eclipse to Marske, there being a strong interest in the reputation of that stallion.

You would have thought that the evidence of a groom at the Duke of Cumberland's stud, where Eclipse had been born, would be more authoritative than that of a groom working for Dennis O'Kelly, who acquired the horse six years later. But Lawrence appears to have given the accounts equal weight. He went on to reproduce the J. N. Sartorius picture – presumably commissioned by someone keen to make a point – of Shakespeare and Eclipse. We, no longer believing that a father invariably stamps his appearance on his children, cannot accept likeness to one sire or lack of likeness to another as evidence of paternity.

In 1763, when Eclipse was conceived, Marske and Spilletta both lived at Cranbourne Lodge, where the Duke of Cumberland had his stud. Shakespeare was standing at Josiah Cook's at Epsom. Would Cumberland's staff have sent Spilletta to be covered by Shakespeare, and then put her to Marske; or have put her to Marske, and then sent her to Shakespeare? Either option seems eccentric. But what convinces me that Marske was Eclipse's father is that the earliest records say he was. The Royal Stud Book at Windsor contains a note of the following entry for Cumberland's 'sucker' (foal) in a match at Newmarket:

Mask [sic], out of Spilletta a chesnut colt, with a bald face, and the off hind leg, white up to the hock. First spring meeting. Match against the Duke of Grafton's colt, by Doctor; Lord Rockingham's colt, by the Godolphin Hunter; Lord Bolingbroke's colt, by Damascus; Lord Gower's colt, by Sweepstakes; Lord Orford's colt, by Feather; Mr Shafto's colt, by his Hunter.

The 1764 *Racing Calendar* also noted the forthcoming match for 'RH the Duke's C. [colt] got by Mask, his dam by Regulus'. Cumberland and his competitors, the entry stated, would each advance 100 guineas for the race, to be run on the Duke's course, with the racers carrying 8st 10lb, during Easter week in 1768.

The next document is the catalogue of the sale of the late Duke of Cumberland's stud on 23 December 1765. Lot number 29 is 'A chesnut colt got by Mask', knocked down to William Wildman for forty-five guineas. Eclipse. There were eighteen broodmares in the sale. Of those covered in 1765, seven had been to Marske. None had been to Shakespeare. There is no record of Cumberland's ever having sent a mare to Shakespeare.

In 1764 and 1765, no one had any reason to tamper with the records. Marske was an unfashionable stallion; his siring of an ungainly chestnut yearling was not going to improve his profile. Only when Eclipse started racing did Marske's value soar. *Then*, his connections had a strong incentive to promote him as Eclipse's sire; but not six years earlier. So the match book entry and sale document are probably truthful.

The Shakespeare rumours did not compromise Marske's career. Sold by Wildman to the Earl of Abingdon, Marske went on to command the extraordinary covering fee of 100 guineas. He was champion sire in 1775 and 1776.

Bartlett's Childers

Marske was a son of Squirt, who was a son of Bartlett's Childers. A full brother (by the Darley Arabian, out of Betty Leedes) to the great Flying Childers, Bartlett's Childers (born in 1716) tended to break blood vessels in hard exercise, and was sometimes known as 'Bleeding Childers'. He never raced. There is a tiny doubt that he ever existed. However, contemporary references to him in the racing calendar of John Cheny and in the stud book of Cuthbert Routh, a Yorkshire breeder, argue in his favour. Cheny wrote that 'many gentlemen of honour' asserted that there were two Childers brothers.

Spanker Mare

Betty Leedes, dam of Bartlett's Childers, appears in the *General Stud Book* as the daughter of Cream Cheeks, and as the granddaughter of the Spanker Mare. Bred by James Darcy (son of Charles II's master of the stud), the Spanker Mare (born in about 1665) was the product of a mating between Spanker and his mother, the Old Morocco Mare. The Spanker Mare thus had the Old Morocco Mare as her mother and grandmother; in the formula of bloodstock breeding, she was inbred to the Old Morocco Mare 2 × 1 (two generations back as well as one generation back). (Spanker was also Betty Leedes's grandfather on her sire's side.)

Some historians find this close inbreeding distasteful, and question whether James Darcy would have indulged in it. The Thoroughbred Heritage website suggests that it is 'more likely' that the Old Morocco Mare mated with a horse called Young Spanker – her grandson. But Lady Wentworth, author of *Thoroughbred Racing Stock*, insisted that the mother/son union accorded with 'the Arab principle' – than which, in her book, there could be no higher.

The Spanker Mare, daughter of the incestuous union, supposedly gave birth to a full sister to Cream Cheeks called Betty Percival. In 2002, researchers at the Department of Genetics at Trinity College, Dublin, published their account of tests of two horses tracing back in the female line to Betty Percival, and of one tracing back in the female line to Cream Cheeks. The DNA of the Cream Cheeks descendant did not match that of the Betty Percival descendants. The finding meant that Cream Cheeks and Betty Percival had different dams.

Which was the daughter of the Spanker Mare? There was already evidence that it was not Cream Cheeks. In *Early Records of the Thoroughbred* (1924), C. M. Prior quoted Cuthbert Routh's claim that Cream Cheeks's dam was 'a famous roan mare of Sir Marmaduke Wyvill's'. Routh and Wyvill were neighbours.

Does this finding remove incest from Eclipse's background? Not necessarily. Another of his ancestors is Charming Jenny, a third daughter of the Leedes Arabian and the Spanker Mare.

The Dam's Side
The Cumberland Dispersal Sale Catalogue

The entry, with original spelling, reads: 'A chesnut Colt, got by Mask, his dam by a full brother to Williams's Squirrel, his great grandam by Lord Darcey's Montague, his great great grandam by Hautboy, his great great great grandam by Brimmer.' You will notice that the grandam's generation is missing. The entry should read: 'his dam by Regulus [or should it? – see below], his *grandam* by a full brother to Williams's Squirrel', etc. The compiler of the catalogue seems to have got the pedigree confused with the similar one of a mare in the sale, Miss Western.

Spilletta (sometimes spelled 'Spiletta')

According to the stud book of her later owner, the Duke of Ancaster, she was a chestnut, not a bay as recorded in the *GSB*.

Born in 1749, Spilletta was officially the daughter of the stallion Regulus, and out of a mare called Mother Western. But in 1754, the year of her unsuccessful racing season, she was listed in Reginald Heber's racing calendar as a daughter of Sedbury. John Pond, in his 1754 racing calendar, hedged his bets, listing her as Sedbury's on one page and as Regulus's on another. Our justification for assigning her to Regulus is that this is the more recent version, and the one that became accepted.

Mother Western

Spilletta's breeder, Sir Robert Eden, certainly did mate Mother Western with Sedbury to get a filly called Miss Western (born in 1746). She was also bought by the Duke of Cumberland; it was her pedigree that got confused with Eclipse's in the dispersal sale catalogue.

Mother Western's sire is officially Easby Snake (or 'Smith's Son of Snake'). But in the earliest records of Miss Western's racing career, her dam (Mother Western) is listed as by 'Sir Marmaduke Wyvill's Scarborough Colt'. This is the version in both Pond's and Heber's 1751 racing calendars; Heber maintains it in 1752, but Pond switches to 'a full brother to Mr Williams's Squirrel' – Easby Snake. Again, the later version became the one that was perpetuated.

In this case, there is a reason to doubt the official version. In the 1748 and 1749 editions of Cheny's racing calendar, there are announcements for races involving two of Sir Robert Eden's colts: the colts are out of mares, or more probably a mare, whose sire is the Scarborough Colt. Sir Robert owned only a few horses. It is possible that this mare is Mother Western. If so, one can only be baffled at why the record of her sire changed. As we have seen, however, this sort of thing happened a lot.

Implications

As I have explained, I do not believe that Shakespeare was Eclipse's sire. But what if he were? Like Marske, he was a great-grandson in the male line of the Darley Arabian; he was also a great-grandson of the Darley Arabian in the female line (i.e., he was inbred to the Darley Arabian 3 × 3). His presence in Eclipse's pedigree would increase significantly the number of strains of the Darley Arabian in modern Thoroughbreds. It would also reduce the number of strains of the Lister Turk, who does not appear in Shakespeare's background.

The removal of the Spanker Mare from Eclipse's pedigree would, disappointingly, delete two strains of Old Bald Peg – the Spanker Mare's great-grandmother on the father's side, and grandmother on the mother's side (3 × 2). (Or the Spanker Mare may – see above – have been the daughter of Young Spanker, in which case the inbreeding to Old Bald Peg would be 4 × 3. Young Spanker appears in only one contemporary record, and not in the *General Stud Book*; we know nothing of his female ancestry.)

Old Bald Peg is an iconic horse for historians of the Thoroughbred. Of pure Eastern blood (the *General Stud Book* describes her as the daughter of an Arabian and a Barb mare), she lived at Helmsley in Yorkshire. She was the property of the Duke of Buckingham and then, when Helmsley was seized by the Commonwealth, of Thomas Fairfax, Oliver Cromwell's commander-in-chief. Later, Buckingham found his way back to Helmsley, thanks to a marriage with Fairfax's daughter. By sending Old Bald Peg's daughter, the Old Morocco Mare (born in about 1655), to the Darcy stud to meet the Yellow Turk, Buckingham bred Spanker, the outstanding racehorse of Charles II's reign.

Old Bald Peg is at the root of what pedigree experts call family number six. The numbering system was the invention of an Australian researcher called Bruce Lowe, who at the end of the nineteenth century traced back the tail female lines of winners of classic races, and numbered the lines to reflect their successes. Tail female descendants of Tregonwell's Natural Barb Mare had won the most classics, and went into family number one; the Burton Barb Mare was at the root of family number two, and so on. (Eclipse descends in tail female from a Royal Mare listed as the tap-root of family number twelve.) The list went down to number forty-three. However, the genetic evidence cited above appears to show that Cream Cheeks, Bartlett's Childers's mother and therefore Eclipse's great-great-great-grandmother, may not have been Old Bald Peg's tail female descendant, and therefore was not a member of family number six. Her removal diminishes the influence of that family, and of Old Bald Peg on pedigrees in general.

If Sedbury, not Regulus, were the sire of Eclipse's dam Spilletta, the Godolphin Arabian would disappear from Eclipse's pedigree. The number of strains of the Godolphin Arabian in contemporary Thoroughbreds would be greatly reduced; and the number of strains of the Byerley Turk would be greatly increased. Regulus was the Godolphin Arabian's son; Sedbury was the Byerley Turk's great-grandson. Sedbury was also a descendant of the Helmsley Turk, an important early sire but one who does not appear in Eclipse's official pedigree. However, I am inclined to believe that Spilletta's sire's name changed from Sedbury to Regulus in the early records as a result of proper correction.

I have doubts, though, about Eclipse's damsire, for reasons stated above. The inclusion of the Scarborough Colt in place of Easby Snake in the pedigree would introduce to it a new name, the Thoulouse Barb. He was the Scarborough Colt's tail male grandfather, and had been imported at the end of the seventeenth century by a Cumberland breeder, Henry Curwen, who had bought him from Louis XIV. The Scarborough Colt was also a descendant — as Easby Snake was not — of Old Bald Peg.

Conclusion

Pedigrees of early racehorses are full of question marks, dead ends and questionable attributions. The names — exotic, homely and bizarre — tantalize. Behind them lie histories that are only fragmentarily apparent. We want to know more about them.

Nothing that we may discover has implications for Eclipse's reputation. Eclipse is Eclipse.

The O'Kelly Family

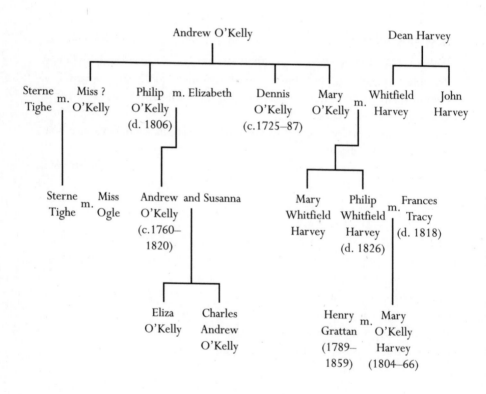

Appendix 4

Racing Terms, Historical and Contemporary

Bay A coppery brown — the most common colour in Thoroughbreds. Other Thoroughbred colours include black, brown (the distinction between black and brown is often fine), chestnut, grey, and roan (grey hairs with a base of a darker colour).

Betting post Where betting transactions took place on a racecourse before the introduction of betting rings. Bets were struck between individuals rather than, as later, between backers and bookmakers.

Black type Victory or a placing in a **Pattern** or Listed race will show in black (bold) type in sales catalogues. It is a valuable qualification for horses seeking a career at stud.

Blackleg A gambler, usually dishonest.

Blinkers A hood with eye-cups that reduces a horse's range of vision. Some horses need them to concentrate. A visor has slits in the cups, allowing a slightly better view.

Breeze-up A sale at which prospective purchasers can watch horses go through their paces.

Broodmare A mare employed for breeding.

By/out of A foal is 'by' its sire, and 'out of' its dam.

Claimer After a claiming race, any runner may be claimed for an advertised sum or more. This sum is reduced if the owner runs the horse with less weight.

Colt A male horse, younger than five.

Conformation The shape and build of a horse.

Cover To impregnate a mare.

Damsire The sire (father) of a dam (mother), or maternal grandfather.

Distance 240 yards. In Eclipse's day, a horse who had not passed the distance post by the time the winner had passed the finishing post was 'distanced'.

Do a tap A jockey dismounting from a horse who has run badly might say, 'He didn't do a tap.' The horse never got going properly.

Dotted up Won easily. Other favourite expressions include 'bolted up', 'hacked up', 'sluiced up', 'won doing handsprings', and 'won with his/her head in his/her chest'.

Each way Two bets: one that the horse will win, the other that the horse will be placed. A £1 each way bet costs £2. To be 'placed' means to finish first or second in races with five to seven runners (but only to finish first in races with four runners or fewer); first, second or third in races with eight to fifteen runners; and first, second, third or fourth in handicaps with sixteen runners or more. The odds with bookmakers are a fifth or (in most handicaps) a quarter of the win odds. Say you place £1 each way on a 10-1 shot in a handicap. The horse wins: you get £10 plus £2.50 (the place return, a quarter of the win return) plus your £2 stake – £14.50. The horse is placed: you get £2.50 plus the £1 of your stake that was the place bet – £3.50.

Exchange A betting exchange is an online version of a betting post: a place where layers and backers find each other to strike individual bets. Exchanges such as Betfair are controversial: critics say that they encourage corruption, allowing people to **lay** horses that they know will not win, or that they have the means of stopping from winning. The earliest indication that a horse is injured before a big race is often when the horse's exchange price lengthens.

Exposed An exposed horse has shown how good he or she is – the implication being, not good enough to win today's race. An unexposed horse may be about to show form in advance of any previously revealed.

Family A horse's ancestors in the **tail female** line. A horse's half brother or half sister has the same mother; having the same sire does not make horses half siblings.

Filly A female horse, younger than five.

Fizzy A fizzy horse is in an excitable state, or inclined to get that way. Also 'buzzy'.

Furlong One-eighth of a mile: 220 yards.

Gelding A castrated male horse. Temperamental horses who are unlikely to become stallions but who might be good racers usually get this treatment; most male horses who race at the age of six and above are gelded. In 2003, the gelding Funny Cide won the Kentucky Derby. Geldings are ineligible for the Epsom Derby.

Giving, receiving It is better to receive than to give. Receiving weight from a rival or rivals means carrying less; giving means carrying more.

Going The state of the ground. On British turf courses, the going descriptions are, in descending order of hardness: hard (a word that clerks of the course use rarely), firm, good to firm, good, good to soft ('soft' is 'yielding' in Ireland), soft, and heavy. It is said of some racehorses that they 'go on any ground', but most have preferences. Horses with economical, daisy-cutter actions usually prefer ground that is fast (on the firm side); those who bend their knees and pound the turf go better on, or perhaps are less disadvantaged by, slow, soft ground.

Greek Same as **blackleg**.

Hand Four inches, a unit of measurement of a horse's height. The measurement is from the ground to the withers – the top of a horse's shoulders. Eclipse is generally agreed to have been about 15.3 hands, which was a good height in the mid-eighteenth century but modest by the standards of Thoroughbreds today.

Handicap A race in which horses carry weights according to ratings allotted by the official handicapper. In theory, they should finish in a dead heat. An example from a handy copy of the *Racing Post*: a five-furlong handicap at Lingfield in which horses rated 72 to 83 took part, won by the 78-rated Zowington. He carried 8st 13lb. A filly called Ocean Blaze finished second; she was rated 76, and therefore carried 2lb less, 8st 11lb.

Handicapper In Britain, the official handicappers work for the British Horseracing Authority, and assign ratings that dictate the weights horses will carry in handicap races. If a horse is a handicapper, he or she specializes in this type of race, not being good enough to run in **Pattern** (Group) or Listed races. In the US, handicappers are racing enthusiasts who study form.

Horse Apart from the obvious, generic definition, the term implies an ungelded male of five years old and above.

Jockey Before it came exclusively to mean 'rider', jockey was a generic term for a racing man.

Lay To lay a horse is to accept the bet of someone backing it. Bookmakers are 'layers'.

Lead (leg) The leg that advances further. (In horses, the side of the lead foreleg and lead rear leg is usually the same.) The other one hits the ground first. A horse may 'change legs' (switching lead legs) while galloping, sometimes when feeling uncomfortable on the ground. Turning left, a horse should lead with the left foreleg; turning right, with the right. A horse turning left but on a right lead is on the 'wrong' leg.

Let down A horse that will not 'let himself down' is reluctant to gallop properly, perhaps because he finds the ground too hard, or too soft.

Maiden A horse who has not won a race. Or a race for horses who have not yet won a race.

Mare A female horse of five years old and above.

Missed out 'He missed out the open ditch.' This expression, which a steeplechase jockey might use, does not mean that the horse ran around the fence to avoid jumping it (a manoeuvre that would result in disqualification), but that he jumped it clumsily.

Nap A tipster's strongest recommendation.

Near/off side A horse's near side is the left; the off side is the right. A rider mounts and dismounts on the near side. Eclipse's white stocking was on his off hind leg.

Nick In breeding, a cross – of, for example, Eclipse with Herod mares, or Eclipse sons or daughters with Herod daughters or sons – that regularly produces good racers.

Nursery A **handicap** for two-year-olds.

Off/not off Primed, or not, to run to full potential.

On the bridle (or bit)/off the bridle (or bit) A horse on the bridle is coasting along, without effort from the jockey; when the horse is off the bridle, the jockey is working away.

Out of the handicap The top weight in the Grand National carries 11st 10lb; the lowest weight a horse can carry in the race is 10st. Let us say that the top weight has a handicap rating of 165. A horse with 10st on his back would, in theory, have a rating of 141 – 24lb (1st 10lb) lower. But what of a horse rated 135? He also carries 10st, but should, to have a chance against the others, carry 9st 8lb. He is 'out of the handicap'.

Pattern The 'Pattern' of racing was introduced in the early 1970s. Pattern races are the most prestigious contests, ranked Group 1, Group 2 and Group 3. Winning or placed form in these races, and in the Listed races that follow them in prestige, shows in **black type** in form guides and sales catalogues.
Pinhooking Buying foals with the aim of selling them on as yearlings.

Rough off To give a horse a holiday from training.
Rubbing-house Where horses in Eclipse's era were saddled, and where they were rubbed down after races or between heats.

Seller After a selling race, the winner is sold at auction, and other runners may also be bought.
Stud A stallion; more commonly, a farm with horses for breeding. A stud may house broodmares only.
Stuffy A stuffy horse needs lots of exercise to get fit.

Tail male, tail female Respectively, the top and bottom lines in pedigrees. The top line ascends through the sire to his sire (the grandsire), and through the grandsire's sire, and so on; the bottom line ascends through the dam to her dam (the granddam), and through the granddam's dam, and so on.
Thoroughbred A horse whose breeding satisfies the criteria of compilers of stud books.
Tote The Tote runs the Totalisator, a pool betting system known in France and the US as the Pari-mutuel. The UK and Ireland are unusual among racing countries in having a tote as well as bookmakers. France, the US, and Japan are among the nations with tote monopolies; Australia has bookmakers on-course; only some states license them elsewhere. The Tote (the company) is state-owned; at the time of writing, plans to sell it are on the shelf.

Bibliography

Books

Eclipse and O'Kelly

Anon., *The Genuine Memoirs of Dennis O'Kelly, Esq: Commonly Called Count O'Kelly* (C. Stalker, 1788)

Blyth, Henry, *The High Tide of Pleasure: Seven English Rakes* (Weidenfeld & Nicolson, 1970)

Church, Michael, *Eclipse: The Horse, the Race, the Awards* (Thoroughbred Advertising, 2000)

Clark, Bracy, *A Short History of the Celebrated Race-horse Eclipse* (London, 1835)

Cook, Theodore Andrea, *Eclipse and O'Kelly* (William Heinemann, 1907)

Hall, Sherwin, 'The Story of a Skeleton: Eclipse' in *Guardians of the Horse: Past, Present and Future* (British Equine Veterinary Association, 1999)

Sainbel, Charles Vial de, *Elements of Veterinary Art: Containing an Essay on the Proportions of the Celebrated Eclipse* (London, 1791)

Trew, Cecil G., *From 'Dawn' to 'Eclipse'* (Methuen, 1939)

Racing and General

Allison, W., *The British Thoroughbred Horse* (Grant Richards, 1901)

Anon., *A General and Particular Account of the Annular Eclipse of the Sun* (London, 1764)

—— *Historical Memoirs of His Late Royal Highness William-Augustus, Duke of Cumberland* (London, 1767)

——— *A List of the Sporting Ladies* (London, 1775)

——— *The Minor Jockey Club: Or a Sketch of the Manners of the Greeks* (R. Farnham, 1792)

Archenholz, Johann Wilhelm von, *A Picture of England* (P. Byrne, 1791)

Bayles, F. H., *Atlas and Review of British Race-Courses* (Equitable Publishing Syndicate, 1911)

Black, Robert, *The Jockey Club and Its Founders* (Smith, Elder & Co., 1891)

Blake, Robin, *George Stubbs and the Wide Creation* (Pimlico, 2006)

Bloch, Iwan, *Sexual Life in England* (Francis Aldor, 1938)

British Sporting Painting 1650–1850 (Arts Council, 1974)

Brown, Roger Lee, *A History of the Fleet Prison, London* (Edwin Mellen Press, 1996)

Buss, Frances Mary, *The North London Collegiate School 1850–1950* (Oxford University Press, 1950)

Cain, Glenye, *The Home Run Horse* (DRF Press, 2004)

Chinn, Carl, *Better Betting with a Decent Feller* (Harvester Wheatsheaf, 1991)

Church, Michael, *The Derby Stakes* (Racing Post, 2006)

——— *Three Generations of Leading Sires* (Racing Post, 1987)

Clayton, Tim, *The British Museum Hogarth* (British Museum Press, 2007)

Coaten, Arthur, 'The Evolution of Racing' in *Flat Racing* (Seeley Service & Co., 1940)

Conley, Kevin, *Stud* (Bloomsbury, 2002)

Curling, B. W. R., *British Racecourses* (Witherby, 1951)

Derby Day 200 (Royal Academy, 1979)

Egan, Pierce, *Anecdotes of the Turf, the Chase, the Ring, and the Stage* (London, 1827)

——— *Book of Sports* (London, 1832)

——— *Boxiana* (London, 1812)

——— *Sporting Anecdotes* (Thomas Hurst, J. Harris, J. Wheble, 1804)

Egerton, Judy, *British Sporting and Animal Paintings 1655–1867* (Tate Gallery, 1978)

——— *George Stubbs, Painter. Catalogue Raisonné* (Yale, 2007)

Ellis, Markman, *The Coffee House: A Cultural History* (Weidenfeld & Nicolson, 2004)

FitzGerald, Arthur, *Royal Thoroughbreds* (Sidgwick & Jackson, 1990)

——— *Thoroughbreds of the Crown* (Genesis Publications, 1999)

Fitzgerald, George, *An Appeal to the Jockey Club* (London, 1775)

Fitzpatrick, W. J., *Secret Service Under Pitt* (Longman, 1892)

Fountain, Robert, *William Wildman and George Stubbs* (British Sporting Arts Trust, 2004)

Fraser, Kevin J., *William Stukely and the Gout* (University of Melbourne, 1992)

Gatrell, Vic, *City of Laughter* (Atlantic Books, 2006)

Gill, James, *Racecourses of Great Britain* (Barrie & Jenkins, 1975)

Grego, Joseph, *Rowlandson the Caricaturist* (Chatto & Windus, 1880)

Grosley, Pierre Jean, *A Tour to London* (London, 1772)

Harcourt, Seymour, *The Gaming Calendar and Annals of Gaming* (London, 1820)

Harding, Samuel, *An Elegy on the Famous Old Horse Marsk* (London, 1780)

Hayes, John, *Rowlandson Watercolours and Drawings* (Phaidon, 1972)

Henderson, Andrew, *The Life of William Augustus, Duke of Cumberland* (J. Ridley, 1766)

Henderson, Tony, *Disorderly Women in 18th Century London* (Longman, 1999)

Hickey, William, *Memoirs* (ed. Peter Quennell, Hutchinson, 1960)

Hillenbrand, Laura, *Seabiscuit* (Fourth Estate, 2001)

Hitchcock, Tim, *Down and Out in Eighteenth-Century London* (Hambledon Continuum, 2004)

Holcroft, Thomas, *Memoirs of the Late Thomas Holcroft* (London, 1816)

Hone, William, *The Table Book* (Tegg & Co., 1827)

Hore, J. P., *History of Newmarket and Annals of the Turf* (Hore, 1885)

Jerdein, Charles and F. R. Kaye, *British Blood Lines* (J. A. Allen, 1955)

Kelly, Bernard W., *The Conqueror of Culloden* (R. & T. Washbourne, 1902)

Kiste, John Van der, *King George II and Queen Caroline* (Sutton, 1997)

Lane, Charles, *British Racing Prints* (Sportsman's Press, 1990)

Lawrence, John, *The History and Delineation of the Horse* (Albion Press, 1809)

—— *A Philosophical and Practical Treatise on Horses* (H. D. Symonds, 1802)

—— and John Scott, *The Sportsman's Repository* (London, 1820)

Leicester, Charles, *Bloodstock Breeding* (Odhams Press, 1957)

Lennox, Muriel, *Northern Dancer* (Mainstream, 1999)

Lillywhite, Bryant, *London Coffee Houses* (Allen & Unwin, 1963)

Longrigg, Roger, *The History of Horse Racing* (Macmillan, 1972)

Lyle, R. C., *Royal Newmarket* (Putnam, 1940)

Lysons, Daniel, *The Environs of London* (London, 1792–96)

Magee, Sean, *Ascot: The History* (Methuen, 2002)

Markham, Gervase, *How to Choose, Ride, Train and Diet, Both Hunting-Horses and Running Horses* (James Roberts, 1599)

Morris, Tony, *Thoroughbred Stallions* (Crowood, 1990)

Mortimer, Roger, *The History of the Derby Stakes* (Michael Joseph, 1973)

——— *The Jockey Club* (Cassell, 1958)

——— Richard Onslow and Peter Willett, *Biographical Encyclopaedia of British Flat Racing* (Macdonald, 1978)

Muir, J. B., *W. T. Frampton and the Dragon* (Sporting Fine Art Gallery, 1895)

Noakes, Aubrey, *Sportsmen in a Landscape* (Bodley Head, 1954)

O'Brien, Jacqueline and Ivor Herbert, *Vincent O'Brien: The Official Biography* (Bantam Press, 2005)

Orchard, Vincent, *Tattersalls* (Hutchinson, 1953)

Orton, John, *Turf Annals of York and Doncaster* (York, 1844)

Osbaldiston, William Augustus, *The British Sportsman* (London, 1792)

Oxford Dictionary of National Biography (Oxford University Press, 2004)

Pagones, Rachel, *Dubai Millennium* (Highdown, 2007)

Parsons, Philip, *Newmarket: Or an Essay on the Turf* (London, 1775)

Percivall, William, *Twelve Lectures on the Form and Action of the Horse* (London, 1850)

Picard, Liza, *Dr Johnson's London* (Weidenfeld & Nicolson, 2000)

Pick, William, *The Turf Register and Sportsman and Breeder's Stud Book* (York, 1803)

Piggott, Lester and Sean Magee, *Lester's Derbys* (Methuen, 2004)

Pigott, Charles, *The Jockey Club: Or a Sketch of the Manners of the Age* (H. D. Symonds, 1792)

Porter, Roy, *English Society in the 18th Century* (Pelican, 1982)

——— *London: A Social History* (Hamish Hamilton, 1994)

Prior, C. M., *Early Records of the Thoroughbred* (The Sportsman Office, 1924)

Randall, John and Tony Morris, *A Century of Champions* (Portway Press, 1999)

——— *Guinness Horse Racing: The Records* (Guinness, 1985)

Rede, Leman Thomas, *Anecdotes and Biography* (London, 1799)

Rice, James, *The History of the British Turf* (Sampson Low, 1879)

Robertson, J. B., 'The Origin of the Thoroughbred' in *Flat Racing* (Seeley Service & Co., 1940)

Robinson, Edward Forbes, *The Early History of the Coffee House in England* (Dolphin Press, 1972)

Seth-Smith, Michael, *Bred for the Purple* (Frewin, 1969)

Shoemaker, Robert, *The London Mob* (Hambledon Continuum, 2004)

Siltzer, Frank, *Newmarket* (Cassell, 1923)

Steinmetz, Andrew, *The Gaming Table, Its Votaries and Victims* (Tinsley Brothers, 1870)

Taplin, William, *The Gentleman's Stable Directory* (J. & J. Robinson and C. & G. Kearsley, 1791)

Taunton, Theophilus, *Famous Horses* (Sampson Low, 1901)

Taunton, Thomas Henry, *Portraits of Celebrated Race Horses of Past and Present Centuries* (Sampson Low, 1887)

Thompson, Jon, *Mark Wallinger* (Ikon Gallery, 1995)

Thompson, Laura, *Newmarket: From James I to the Present Day* (Virgin, 2000)

Thormanby, *Sporting Stories* (Mills & Boon, 1909)

Tyrrel, John, *Running Racing* (Quiller, 1997)

Ulbrich, Richard, *The Great Stallion Book* (Libra, 1986)

Waller, Maureen, *1700: Scenes from London Life* (Hodder & Stoughton, 2000)

Watson, Rev. John Selby, *The Reasoning Power in Animals* (London, 1867)

Waugh, Auberon, *Will This Do?* (Century, 1991)

Weinreb, Ben and Christopher Hibbert (eds), *The London Encyclopaedia* (Macmillan, 1983)

Wentworth, Lady, *Thoroughbred Racing Stock* (Allen & Unwin, 1960)

West, William, *Tavern Anecdotes* (London, 1825)

Whyte, James Christie, *History of the British Turf* (Henry Colburn, 1840)

Willett, Peter, *The Classic Racehorse* (Stanley Paul, 1981)

—— *A History of the General Stud Book* (Weatherbys, 1991)

—— *The Story of Tattersalls* (Stanley Paul, 1987)

Williams, J. D., *History of the Name O'Kelly* (Mercier, 1977)

Williams, Richard, *Egham Eclipses* (Egham-by-Runnymede Historical Society, 1999)

Williams, Sheridan, *UK Solar Eclipses from Year 1* (Clock Tower Press, 1996)

Yuill, Alan, *Thoroughbred Studs of Great Britain* (Weidenfeld & Nicolson, 1991)

Charlotte Hayes

Anon., *Nocturnal Revels* (M. Goadby, 1779)

Burford, E. J., *Royal St James's* (Robert Hale, 1988)

—— *Wits, Wenchers and Wantons* (Robert Hale, 1986)

—— and Joy Wotton, *Private Vices – Public Virtues* (Robert Hale, 1995)

Linnane, Fergus, *Madams, Bawds and Brothel-Keepers of London* (Sutton, 2005)

'OMIAH: An Ode Addressed to Charlotte Hayes', *The New Foundling Hospital for Wit* (London, 1784)

Rubenhold, Hallie, *The Covent Garden Ladies* (Sutton, 2005)
—— *Harris's List of Covent Garden Ladies* (Sutton, 2005)
Thompson, Edward, *The Courtesan* (J. Harrison, 1770)
—— *The Meretriciad* (C. Moran, 1761, 1770)

Epsom

Andrews, James, *Reminiscences of Epsom* (L. W. Andrews & Son, 1904)
Bawtree, Harold, *A Few Notes on Banstead Downs with Some Remarks on Epsom Races* (William Pile, 1928)
Dorling, E. E., *Epsom and the Dorlings* (Stanley Paul, 1939)
Dorling, W., *Some Particulars Relating to the History of Epsom* (Epsom, 1825)
Epsom Common (Epsom Common Association, 1981)
Harte, Jeremy, *Epsom: A History and Celebration* (Francis Frith Collection, 2005)
Home, Gordon, *Epsom: Its History and Surroundings* (Homeland Association, 1901)
Hunn, David, *Epsom Racecourse* (Davis-Poynter, 1973)
Pownall, H., *Some Particulars Relating to the History of Epsom* (Epsom, 1825)
Salter, Brian J., *Epsom Town Downs and Common* (Living History, 1976)
White, Reginald, *Ancient Epsom* (William Pile, 1928)

Racing Records

Cheny, John, *An Historical List of All Horse Matches Run, and of All Plates and Prizes Run for in England* (London, various years)
Duke of Ancaster's Stud Book (1772–78)
The General Stud Book (Weatherbys, 2006)
Heber, Reginald, *An Historical List of Horse Matches Run; and of Plates and Prizes Run for in Great Britain and Ireland* (London, various years)
Newmarket Match Book (1754)
Pick, William, *An Authentic Historical Racing Calendar* (York, 1785)
Pond, John, *Sporting Kalendar* (London, various years)
The Racing Calendar (Weatherbys, 1773–)
Towers, William Sydney, *An Introduction to a General Stud Book* (Weatherbys, 1791)
Tuting, William and Thomas Fawconer, *The Sporting Calendar: Containing an Account of the Plates, Matches, and Sweepstakes Run for in Great Britain* (London, various years)

Walker, B., *An Historical List of Horse-Matches, Plates and Prizes, Run for in Great Britain and Ireland* (London, 1769, 1770)

Newspapers and Journals

Annual Register (various years)

The British Racehorse (George Rathbone, 'Reconstruction of Eclipse', November 1963)

The Burlington Magazine (David Mannings, 'Reynolds and the Shaftos: Three Letters and a Deposition', November 1997)

The Field (December 1920; June 1937)

Gentleman's Magazine (November 1765; 1787 supplement; October 1802)

Guardian (Sean Magee, 'The Day When Arkle Became the Greatest', November 2005)

Independent on Sunday (Fiammetta Rocco, 'Ma'am Darling: The Princess Driven by Loyalty and Duty', February 1998)

Lloyd's Evening Post (1764, 1765)

London Chronicle (1764, 1765)

London Evening Post (1764, 1765)

The London Magazine (1772)

Monthly Review (1788)

Morning Post (1775)

The Newgate Calendar (exclassics.com)

Observer (Clare Balding, 'The Sheikh Is Unstirred', October 2005)

Pacemaker (Tony Morris, 'Sorting Fact from Fiction', October 2007)

Racing Post Bloodstock Review 2007

St James's Chronicle (1765)

The Sporting Magazine (various issues)

The Tatler (July 1927)

The Thoroughbred Record (September 1920; June 1924)

The Times (digital archive)

Town & Country (1769, 1770)

The Veterinary Record (March 1991)

Whitehall Evening Post (1788, 1789)

World Fashionable Advertiser (1788)

York Courant (1770)

Websites

Ascot.co.uk

Australian Government Culture and Recreation website/ Melbourne Cup

Bloodlines.net

British Horseracing Authority website

Coolmore.com

The Cox Library website

Epsom Salt Council website

Horsesonly.com (Mariana Haun, 'The X Factor')

HotBoxingNews.com

The Jockey Club website

Measuring Worth website

National Museum of Australia website

North London Collegiate School website

Pedigreequery.com

Royal Veterinary College website

SportingChronicle.com

TBHeritage.com

Traceyclann.com

Victorian-cinema.net

Weatherbys website

Archives

Canons records, North London Collegiate School

Clay Hill papers, Surrey History Centre

Fitzwilliam/Langdale papers, Public Record Office, Northern Ireland

Fleet prison debtors' schedules, London Metropolitan Archives

Fleet records, National Archives

Noble Collection, Guildhall Library

Papers of Colonel Andrew Dennis O'Kelly, Brynmor Jones Library, University of Hull

Plumer papers, London Metropolitan Archives

St Lawrence, Little Stanmore, burial records, London Metropolitan Archives

Wills of Dennis O'Kelly, Andrew Dennis O'Kelly and Charles Andrew O'Kelly, National Archives

Acknowledgements

Timothy Cox has been extraordinarily hospitable and helpful, allowing me to work at the Cox Library and hunting down information that I would never have discovered on my own. He has also offered many useful suggestions about the text. Any surviving errors are mine.

I got the idea to write this book when I read the passage on Eclipse and Dennis O'Kelly in Glenye Cain's excellent *The Home Run Horse*. She has been very generous in her encouragement. Sean Magee, another writer with far better qualifications than mine for this venture, has given me kind assistance. Michael Church, author of the splendid *Eclipse: The Horse, The Race, The Awards*, also selflessly welcomed me as I stepped on to his territory. I am grateful, too, for the help of the racing writers Tony Morris and Rachel Pagones, and of Martin Stevens of *Pacemaker*.

Caroline Baldock and Gerald Goodman of the Epsom Equestrian Conservation Group took me on a tour of Dennis O'Kelly's and Eclipse's haunts in Epsom. The trainer Philip Mitchell showed me the old stable block at Downs House, home to the O'Kelly racers. I thank John and Rebecca Morton of Thirty Acre Stables, and Jeremy Harte of Bourne Hall Museum.

David Oldrey answered my questions about the O'Kellys, the Jockey Club and the *Review of the Turf*. Dr Renate Weller made time to see me to discuss the Royal Veterinary College's work on Eclipse's skeleton; and I thank her colleagues Professor Matthew Binns and Elspeth Keith. Dr Mim Bower, of the McDonald Institute for Archaeological Research at the University of Cambridge, patiently explained her genetic research.

I thank Judy Burg and Helen Roberts at the archives in the Brynmor

Jones Library, University of Hull; Karen Morgan and the library staff at the North London Collegiate School for Girls; Anne Craig of the Public Record Office, Northern Ireland; Jane Lewis of the Surrey History Centre; Graham Snelling and Alan Grundy of the National Horseracing Museum; Diane Bellis of Waddesdon Manor; Kathryn Jones of The Royal Collection Trust; Wes Proudlock of the Australian Institute of Genealogical Studies; Dermot Mulligan of Carlow County Museum; and the staff at the British Library, National Archives at Kew, London Metropolitan Archives, Westminster City Archives, and Guildhall Library.

I also wish to thank Robin Blake, author of *George Stubbs and the Wide Creation*; Peter Mackenzie and Lindsay Ankers of Mainstream Publishing; John Sharp of Weatherbys; Adam Caplin; and Marion Regan.

My editor, Selina Walker, has been a constant guide, never allowing my knowledge of her faith in the book to settle into the complacent assumption that I could not make it better. I thank Sheila Lee for her expert and resourceful work on the illustrations; and everyone at my friendly, collegiate publisher, Transworld. And I thank my agent, Ros Edwards, a friend and support as always.

Picture Acknowledgements

Images reproduced in the text:

9 *The Covent Garden Morning Frolic* by L. P. Boitard, 1747: Guildhall Library and Art Gallery © Corporation of London.

16 'The Whore's Last Shift', anonymous engraving from *The Covent Garden Magazine*, 1770.

29 Portrait of Charles Fox by J. Bretherton, 1782.

32 *View of the PUBLIC OFFICE, Bow Street, with Sir John Fielding presiding and a Prisoner under examination*, engraving after Dodd, c. 1779.

47 *William Augustus, Duke of Cumberland* by George Townshend, 1751–58: National Portrait Gallery, London.

77 *The Coffee-house Politicians*, engraving, 1772: Guildhall Library and Art Gallery © Corporation of London.

88 *Plan and Survey of Epsom Race Course* by William Kemp, 1823: by permission of the British Library, Maps 5375 (1).

106 *A Late Unfortunate Adventure at York*, engraving, 1770: © The Trustees of the British Museum, Department of Prints and Drawings.

121 *One of the Tribe of Levi, Going to Brakefast with a Young Christian*, engraving, 1770: courtesy of The Lewis Walpole Library, Yale University.

151 The Oaks, Surrey, anonymous engraving.

156 'The Derby – At Lunch' from *London: a Pilgrimage* by Gustave Doré, 1872.

174 A view, in Indian ink, of Cannons, in the parish of Little Stanmore, or

Whitchurch, near Edgeware, the seat of D. O'Kelly, Esq., c.
1790–1810: by permission of the British Library, Maps K Top 30.25.c.

202 *George IV at Ascot*, drawing by John Doyle: © The Trustees of the
British Museum, Department of Prints and Drawings.

207 *How to Escape Winning* satire by Thomas Rowlandson, 1791: © The
Trustees of the British Museum, Department of Prints and Drawings.

217 Dorsal view of the muscle structure of a progressively
dissected horse, study No 7 from 'The Anatomy of the Horse', 1766 by
George Stubbs: Royal Academy of Arts, London/The Bridgeman Art
Library.

237 Anonymous portrait of Lord George William Cavendish Bentinck,
pen and ink, nineteenth century: private collection/The Bridgeman Art
Library.

268 *Elements of the veterinary art, containing An essay on the proportions of the
celebrated Eclipse . . .*, by Charles Vial de Sainbel, 1791: The Huntington
Library, San Marino, California, RB 614264.

Colour sections

First Section

Eclipse, by George Stubbs, 1770: private collection/The Bridgeman Art
Library.

View of the Piazza, Covent Garden, coloured engraving after Thomas Sandby,
1770: Guildhall Library Print Room © Corporation of London; *Vauxhall
Gardens*, aquatint after Thomas Rowlandson and A. C. Pugin, 1808: ©
Mary Evans Picture Library/Alamy; *The King's Place*, watercolour by
Thomas Rowlandson: © Atkinson Art Gallery, Southport, Lancs./The
Bridgeman Art Library; *A St James's Beauty*, coloured engraving, 1784: ©
The Trustees of the British Museum, Department of Prints and
Drawings.

Marske aged 20, oil painting by George Stubbs, 1770: courtesy of Sotheby's
Picture Library; *Eclipse with John Oakley Up*, oil painting by John Nost
Sartorius, 1771: © Christie's Images Ltd; *A Riding Party in a Country
Landscape*, oil painting by Judith Lewis, c. 1755; detail of *Eclipse with Mr
Wildman and his Sons*, after an oil painting by George Stubbs, c. 1770: ©

Mary Evans Picture Library/Alamy; *The Eclipse Macarony*, coloured etching by R. St G. Mansergh, 1773: National Portrait Gallery, London.

A Hint for an Escape at the next Spring Meeting, engraved satire after Isaac Cruikshank, 1792: © The Trustees of the British Museum, Department of Prints and Drawings; *The Jockey Club or Newmarket Meeting*, coloured engraving after Thomas Rowlandson, 1811: Jockey Club Estates; *Sir Charles Bunbury with Cox, his trainer, and a Stable-Lad*, painting by Benjamin Marshall, ?1801, a study for *Surprise and Eleanor*: © Tate, London, 2008.

Eclipse, coloured illustration from *Cassell's Book of the Horse*, 1890, after a painting by George Garrard: © Mary Evans Picture Library/ Alamy.

Second Section

Detail of *Hambletonian*, oil painting by George Stubbs, c. 1800: Mount Stewart, The Londonderry Collection (The National Trust) © The National Trust.

A Bookmaker and his client outside the Ram Inn, Newmarket, pen and water-colour, by Thomas Rowlandson: Paul Mellon Collection/The Bridgeman Art Library; *Dennis O'Kelly with Others, at Newmarket*, ink and watercolour, by Thomas Rowlandson: The Halifax Collection; *The Race Meeting*, ink and watercolour, by Thomas Rowlandson: courtesy of Sotheby's Picture Library; *The Betting Post*, watercolour by Thomas Rowlandson, 1789: copyright © V&A Images.

Tattersall's Horse Repository, coloured aquatint after A. C. Pugin and Thomas Rowlandson, from *Ackerman's Microcosm of London*, 1808: © Historical Picture Archive/Corbis; *The Subscription Club Room*, pen and watercolour by Thomas Rowlandson: private collection/© Agnew's, London, UK/The Bridgeman Art Library; *Richard Tattersall with Highflyer in the background* oil painting by Thomas Beach: private collection/The Bridgeman Art Library.

The Derby Jig, ink and watercolour, by George Moutard Woodward, 1797: courtesy of Sotheby's Picture Library; *Fête Champêtre at The Oaks, near Epsom: the Supper Room*, oil painting by Antonio Zucchi (1726–95): © The Right Hon. Earl of Derby/The Bridgeman Art Library; *Derby Sweepstake*, oil painting by J. Francis Sartorius, 1791–2: Epsom Library, Surrey/The Bridgeman Art Library; *Derby Day,* poster by Vera Willoughby, 1932: © Transport for London; Derby Day, 1928, coloured photo by Francis Frith: Francis Frith Collection/akg-images.

Eclipse relics: Jockey Club Estates; Eclipse skeleton: Royal Veterinary College.

Index

Bahram 256

Baker, Nanny 18

Baronet 148–9, 209, 220

Barry, Charlotte 125n

Barrymore, Lord 142

Bartlett's Childers 70, 308–9, 312

Baskerville (poet) 82–3

Bay Malton 90

Bazajet 59

Becher, Captain Martin 252

Bedford, Duke of 155, 167–8, 177, 178, 189

Bellario 106, 110, 111

Belmont Stakes (USA) 92, 248, 261, 262

Benevolent Society of St Patrick 162

Bentinck, Lord George 236, *237*, 238, 239

Berkley, Elizabeth 25

Berlin, Isaiah 164

Betty Leedes 69, 308, 309

Betty Percival 309

Bevis of Hampton 92n

Binns, Matthew 278

Birch, Thomas 184n

Black Tarquin 147n

Blake, Robin: *George Stubbs and the Wide Creation* 218–19

Blink Bonny 155n

Boitard, L. P.: *The Covent Garden Morning Frolick* 9

Bolingbroke, Lord 51, 54, 56, 58–9, 61, 62

Bond, Edmund 271, 275

Bond, 'Ludlow' 235

Boniface 168

Boswell, James 7, 17–18, 95, 123, 154

'bottom' 63, 92–3, 137

Boudrow 152

Bower, Mim 278

Bowes, Hon. George 168

Bowra, Maurice 164

Boyne, Battle of the 42, 67

Breadalbane 241, 242

Bridgeman, Sir Orlando 19

Bridget 150

Brigadier Gerard 69n, 241

Brilliant 106

Brimmer 145, 310

Briseis 146

British Horseracing Authority 142n

Brograve (bookmaker) 143

Brooks's (club) 278

Broughton, Jack 159

Brown Betty 69

Brown Jack 277

Browne, Lady 192

Brydges, Rev Henry 68

Bucephalus 102, 103, 136, 221

Buck, Bienvenida 118

Buckingham, Duke of 312

Buckingham, Marquis of 162

Buckle, Frank 164 *and n*, 231

Bulle Rock 240

Bunbury, Sir Charles 85, 110, 142–3, 164, 194, 236, 246

and naming of Derby Stakes 151, 152

and Prince of Wales 143, 206, 208–9, 210

as racehorse owner 56, 85, 106, 110, 111, 152–3, 155, 177, 189

Bunbury, Lady Sarah (*née* Lennox) 56, 110, 114–15, 143

Burford, E. J. 114, 116n, 120, 121, 124, 199

Burgoyne, General John 150

Cranbourne Lodge Stud, Windsor 48, 51, 53–4, 55
Craven, Earl of 117
Crazy 167
Cream Cheeks 309, 310, 312
Cream de Barbade 98
Creeping Polly 135
Crisford, Simon 75
Crockford (member of the Ring) 235–6
Cromwell, Oliver 27, 45, 82
Crucifix 236
Culloden Moor, Battle of 42
Cumberland, William Augustus, Duke of 40–41, 42–3, 46, 47, 48, 49–51, 60, 83n, 142, 159, 203n, 233
  dispersal sale 51, 55, 58–9, 76, 98, 167–8, 308, 310
  and Eclipse 51, 53, 54, 55, 307–8
Cumberland and Strathearn, Prince Henry Frederick, Duke 53, 110, 161
Curlin 248
Cypron 50

Damer, Hon. Mr 35, 37
Dancing Brave 80, 258n
Darcy, James 72n, 76, 309
Darcy Yellow Turk 76, 312
Darley, Lord Thomas 68, 76
Darley Arabian, the 67, 68–70, 71, 72, 240, 311
Darley Racing and Stud 242, 264, 266–7
Darlington, Earl of 208
Darts, Bill 159, 160

David Junior 163n
Davison, Emily 80
Dawson, Mathew 245
Dawson, Mr 356
Day, John 244
Deep Impact 242
Defoe, Daniel 7, 83, 163
Derby, Lady Elizabeth 150, 154
Derby, Edward Smith-Stanley, 12th Earl of 149–50, 151, 152, 154–5, 158, 167, 172n, 178
Derby, Edward Stanley, 17th Earl 155n
Derby, Edward Stanley, 19th Earl 155n
Derby, the 80, 87, 92, 141, 148 and n, 151, 152, 154n, 155 and n, 156, 157, 248, 261; **1780** 152; **1781** 136, 153–4; **1783** 136, 154, 177; **1784** 136, 154; **1786** 138; **1787** 154, 178; **1788** 205; **1793** 233; **1801** 155; **1810** 234; **1813** 143, 155; **1844** 234, 235–6, 238–9; **1848** 239; **1849** 148n; **1850** 148n, 155; **1865** 240, 242; **1867** 242, 243; **1868** 243–4; **1896** 136, 247; **1913** 80; **1924** 155n; **1968** 81; **1981** 80–81; **1986** 80; **1999** 265; **2007** 265n
Derrick, Samuel 21, 22
  Harris's List of Covent Garden Ladies 16, 21–2, 38
Dettingen, Battle of 27, 41, 49
Dettori, Frankie 90, 265
Devonshire, Duke of 69, 110, 144
Diamond 231
Diana 103, 104
Dickens, Charles 23, 25

Hautboy 145, 251, 310
Hawk Wing 266n
Haya, Princess of Jordan 112, 265n
Hayes, Charlotte 16, 17, 18n, 19,
    20–22, 37–9, 60, 84, 109n,
    113–20, *121*, 122–3, 125–7,
    169–70, 171, 181–2, 196–9
  and O'Kelly 25–6, 39, 75, 76,
    108–9, 123–4, 127, 161, 166,
    169, 179, 183–4, 198
Heber, Reginald: racing calendar
    310, 311
Helmsley Turk, the 312, 313
Henry VIII 44
Henrythenavigator 266n
Hermit 242–3, 244, 278
Herod (King Herod) 40, 50, 51, 59,
    67, 90, 98, 130, 131, 137, 138–9,
    150, 152, 167, 187n, 188, 219,
    233, 258n
Hertford, Marquis of 172n
Hickey, William 24, 61, 123, 124,
    125n, 140, 171, 179
Higgins, Francis 200
High Chaparral 266n
Highflyer 59, 137, 138, 139, 187 *and*
    n, 204
Hill, Harry 243
Hobgoblin 70
Hogarth, William 3
  A Harlot's Progress 18–19
  The Rake's Progress 23, 24–5
Horizon 131
horsebreeding 128–31
Howard, Charles 149
Humphry, Ozias: *A Memoir of George
    Stubbs* 216, 219
Hundeshagen, William 166
Hutchinson, John 136

Hutton, John 48
Hyperion 61, 234

Inchinor 188

Jalil 267
James I 44–5
James II 41, 67
Japanese racehorses 242
Jenkins, Paula 278
Jennings, Tom 240
Jerrold, Blanchard 156
Jockey Club 85, 89, 110, 138,
    141–3, 163, 164, 178, 189, 210,
    211, 272, 274
John, King 43
Johnson, Samuel 95, 140
Jones, Inigo 45
Jones, Nancy 19
Jupiter 167, 168

Kelly, Mrs 123–4
Kempton Park: King George VI
    Chase (1966) 253–4
Kentucky Derby (USA) 92n, 248,
    261
King Fergus 135–6, 137, 185
King Heremon 185
King Herod *see* Herod
Kingston 100
Kingston, Duke and Duchess of 110
Klein, Eugene 263

Mitchell, Mary (*née* O'Kelly, *formerly* Harvey) 172, 190*n*
Montagu, Lady Mary Wortley 11
Montague 145, 310
Montjeu 80 *and n*, 131, 242, 265–6
Moore, Sir John 51
Moorhouse, Edward: *The History and Romance of the Derby* 152*n*
Morgan, Charles 190–91
Morier, David: *Godolphin Arabian* 71
Moro 59
'Morocco Men' 31
Morris, Tony *see* Randall, John
Mortimer, Roger 150, 234
Mother Western 71, 145, 310, 311
Moynealta 85
Munday's 77, 78, 86, 89, 153, 171
Murray, Fanny 19
Muybridge, Eadweard: *Horse in Motion* 224–5
My Babu 147*n*

Nash, John 203 *and n*
Nashwan 258*n*
National Hunt racing 147*n*, 252, 253, 255
Natural History Museum 275, 277, 278, 279
Nearco 157, 252
Needham, Mother 18–19
New Approach 112, 265*n*
Newcastle, Duke of 50, 68, 93
Newmarket: Or an Essay on the Turf 168
Newmarket Racecourse 27, 28, 30, 44–6, 48, 49, 54, 56, 89, 135, 177, 235, 236*n*
  Beacon Course 57, 69, 94*n*, 102–3,

205–6, 209, 221, 231
  Bunbury Cup 152
  Jockey Club 141, 144, 220
  King's Plate (1770) 103–4
  1,000 Guineas 50, 155, 236
  Round Course 69, 94*n*, 103, 141
  Rowley Mile course 46, 275*n*
  2,000 Guineas 147*n*, 155, 236, 261
  see also under Stubbs, George
Nijinsky 75, 128, 187*n*, 242, 252, 255–9, 264
Noble 138
Nocturnal Revels 21, 34, 114, 115, 116, 122, 127
Northern Dancer 259, 260, 263, 264
Northumberland, Duke and Duchess of 110
Nun of the First Class, A 120
Nutts, Robert 192–3

Oakley, John 63–6, 89, 90, 91–2, 93, 96, 97, 99, 100, 103*n*, 185, 225, 300, 301
Oaks, The (house) 150, *151*, 164
Oaks, the (race) 150, 152, 178; **1784** 155; **1787** 204; **1840** 236; **1844** 235–6; **1868** 244; **2004** 155*n*
Oberea, Queen 126
Oberon 177
O'Brien, Aiden 80, 266
O'Brien, Vincent 75, 255–6, 257, 259, 260
O'Fallon, Patrick 173
O'Kelly, Andrew 4
O'Kelly, Andrew Dennis 172, 176, 184, 185, 186, 187, 189–96, 198, 199–201, 210–11 219, 220

DISPATCHES

FROM

THE

REPUBLIC

OF

LETTERS

IN MEMORIAM

Doris Westheimer Neustadt
(1897–1991)

Walter Neustadt Jr.
(1919–2010)

"We recognize that the power of the written word is one answer to a broader understanding between the peoples of the world and thence to a more peaceful and cooperative life together in this ever-narrowing universe."

—Walter Neustadt Jr., Address at the 1972 Neustadt Banquet

Royalties from the first edition will be donated to the Walter Jr. and Dolores K. Neustadt Scholarship fund for University of Oklahoma students.

DISPATCHES

FROM THE

REPUBLIC

OF

LETTERS

FIFTY YEARS OF THE
NEUSTADT INTERNATIONAL PRIZE FOR LITERATURE
1970–2020

EDITED AND WITH AN INTRODUCTION BY DANIEL SIMON

PREFACE BY ROBERT CON DAVIS-UNDIANO

PHONEME
MEDIA

DEEP
VELLUM

DALLAS, TEXAS

Phoneme Media, an imprint of Deep Vellum
3000 Commerce St., Dallas, Texas 75226
deepvellum.org · @deepvellum

Deep Vellum is a 501c3 nonprofit literary arts organization
founded in 2013 with the mission to bring
the world into conversation through literature.

FIRST EDITION, 2020

ISBN: 978-1-64605-033-8 (hardcover) | 978-1-64605-034-5 (ebook)

LIBRARY OF CONGRESS CATALOGING IN PUBLICATION DATA

Names: Simon, Daniel, (Professor of English) editor author of introduction.
| Davis, Robert Con, 1948- author of preface.
Title: Dispatches from the republic of letters : fifty years of the Neustadt International Prize for Literature, 1970-2020 / edited and with an introduction by Daniel Simon ; preface by Robert Con Davis-Undiano.
Other titles: World literature today.
Description: First edition. | Dallas : Phoneme Media, Deep Vellum Publishing, 2020. | Includes bibliographical references and index.
Identifiers: LCCN 2020010120 (print) | LCCN 2020010121 (ebook) | ISBN 9781646050338 (hardcover) | ISBN 9781646050345 (ebook)
Subjects: LCSH: Literature, Modern—20th century—History and criticism. | Literature, Modern—21st century—History and criticism. | Authors—21st century—Biography. | Authors—20th century—Biography. | Neustadt International Prize for Literature. | Authorship.
Classification: LCC PN771 .D63 2020 (print) | LCC PN771 (ebook) | DDC 807.9—dc23
LC record available at https://lccn.loc.gov/2020010120
LC ebook record available at https://lccn.loc.gov/2020010121

Distributed by Consortium Book Sales & Distribution
Cover design by Jen Rickard Blair
Interior layout by Kirby Gann
Printed in the United States of America

CONTENTS

The Neustadt Prizes and *World Literature Today*

"Norman, Oklahoma, sounded to many a European ear as Persepolis or Samarkand once may have done to Marlowe or to Keats: the name of a remote, half fairy-like city from which the broadest-minded review in the world of letters radiated information, disseminated ideas, and appraised trends of taste."

—Henri Peyre, *Books Abroad*, Autumn 1976

The Neustadt International Prize for Literature

The Neustadt International Prize for Literature is sponsored by *World Literature Today*, the University of Oklahoma's award-winning magazine of international literature and culture, currently in its ninety-fourth year of continuous publication. The prize, conferred every two years, consists of $50,000, a replica of an eagle's feather cast in silver, and an award certificate. An international jury of writers convenes on the University of Oklahoma campus every other year to decide the winner of each prize.

The charter of the award stipulates that the Neustadt Prize be given in recognition of important achievement in poetry, fiction, or drama and that it be conferred solely on the basis of the literary value of the writer's work. The prize may serve to crown a lifetime's accomplishment or to direct attention to an important body of work that is still developing.

Established in 1969 as the Books Abroad International Prize for Literature, then renamed the Books Abroad / Neustadt Prize in 1972 before assuming its present name in 1976, the Neustadt Prize is the first international literary award of its scope to originate in the United States and is one of the very few international prizes for which poets, novelists, and playwrights are equally eligible. Funding for the prize has been ensured in perpetuity by a generous endowment from the Neustadt family of Dallas, Texas; Denver, Colorado; and Watertown, Massachusetts.

The NSK Neustadt Prize for Children's Literature

Since 2003, *World Literature Today* has also sponsored the NSK Neustadt Prize for Children's Literature, awarded every other year to a living writer or author-illustrator with significant achievement in children's or young-adult literature. Made possible through the generosity of Nancy Barcelo, Susan Neustadt Schwartz, and Kathy Neustadt, the NSK Prize celebrates literature that contributes to the quality of children's lives. Candidates for the award are nominated by a jury of writers, illustrators, and scholars, and the jury also selects the winner of each biennial prize. Laureates receive a check for $35,000, a silver medallion, and a certificate at a public ceremony at the University of Oklahoma in odd-numbered years.

www.neustadtprize.org

Laureates of the Neustadt International Prize for Literature
1970–2020

1970	Giuseppe Ungaretti (Italy)
1972	Gabriel García Márquez (Colombia)
1974	Francis Ponge (France)
1976	Elizabeth Bishop (United States)
1978	Czesław Miłosz (Poland / United States)
1980	Josef Škvorecký (Czechoslovakia / Canada)
1982	Octavio Paz (Mexico)
1984	Paavo Haavikko (Finland)
1986	Max Frisch (Switzerland)
1988	Raja Rao (India)
1990	Tomas Tranströmer (Sweden)
1992	João Cabral de Melo Neto (Brazil)
1994	Kamau Brathwaite (Barbados)
1996	Assia Djebar (Algeria)
1998	Nuruddin Farah (Somalia)
2000	David Malouf (Australia)
2002	Álvaro Mutis (Colombia)
2004	Adam Zagajewski (Poland)
2006	Claribel Alegría (Nicaragua / El Salvador)
2008	Patricia Grace (New Zealand)
2010	Duo Duo (China)
2012	Rohinton Mistry (India / Canada)
2014	Mia Couto (Mozambique)
2016	Dubravka Ugrešić (Croatia / The Netherlands)
2018	Edwidge Danticat (Haiti / United States)
2020	Ismail Kadare (Albania / France)

Preface
Robert Con Davis-Undiano

In 1974, when Francis Ponge received the third Neustadt International Prize for Literature, he made comments that have become part of the aura of the prize. He called it "perfectly magnificent," "so original and so unlike any other in the conditions of the deliberations." He was referencing aspects of the prize that traditionally have caught the attention of many, starting with its being housed at the University of Oklahoma, not in Paris, Buenos Aires, Berlin, Tokyo, or another cosmopolitan, literary capital. He celebrated the transparency of the voting process, the unique Neustadt practice of a jury voting *for* rather than *against* nominees. Every fall, for the Neustadt Prize or the NSK Neustadt Prize for Children's Literature, nine of the most important writers in the world join forces as a legislature unto themselves to choose a Neustadt or NSK laureate. Instructed by the Neustadt charters to hold at bay all outside pressures or subtle encouragement to steer the process in a given direction, Neustadt juries famously ignore politics in any form or the political impact of one writer winning over a rival. They focus instead on each writer's literary accomplishments.

Landlocked and far from all world capitals, Norman, Oklahoma, site of the University of Oklahoma, is a small town on the Southern Plains that does not obviously have a cosmopolitan culture that can sponsor the celebration of world literature and internationalism. And yet, against all odds, this is precisely where these amazing prizes originated and launched into fame. That fact has fired the imagination of many writers. The rise and renown of the prizes, as Nobel laureate Czesław Miłosz, the fifth Neustadt Prize winner, notes, are among "those things which should not exist." And why should they not exist? Because these prizes represent rare forces for good pitted against some overwhelmingly strong, negative tendencies in the world connected to commercialism, lassitude, and fashion. The glorious fact of the Neustadt

Prizes, in other words, is welcome and hugely beneficent but not an inevitable development or one that anyone could have predicted. These famous prizes came into existence precisely to push back against what Miłosz calls the "the dark and immutable order of the world," an amazing occurrence, as he allows, that "favors all those who in the game of life bet on improbability."

The wager on improbability is the miracle of the Neustadt Prizes and possibly—as many of the jurors note—of the United States itself. Indigenous peoples and colonial powers originally came to Oklahoma and the Americas searching for new truths and fresh beginnings, and their incessant searching has defined this part of the world in terms of innovation and cultural energy. Dubravka Ugrešić, the twenty-fourth laureate, notes the welcome persistence of this American spirit in the prizes and in Oklahoma itself. "The literary landscape that has greeted me in Norman," she writes,

> has touched me so deeply that I, briefly, forgot the ruling political constellations. I forgot the processes underway in all the nooks and crannies of Europe, I forgot the people who are stubbornly taking us back to some distant century, the people who ban books or burn them, the moral and intellectual censors, the brutal rewriters of history, the latter-day inquisitors; I forgot for a moment the landscapes in which the infamous swastika has been cropping up with increasing frequency—as it does in the opening scenes of Bob Fosse's classic film *Cabaret*—and the rivers of refugees whose number, they say, is even greater than that of the Second World War.

Ugrešić attributes this sense of hope and wonder upon visiting Norman to the unlikely success of the Neustadt Prizes, the wager on literary excellence and celebration. She further credits these prizes as iconic representations of American ideals, the grand experiment dedicated to new beginnings. This understanding that the Neustadt Prizes thrive in an explicitly American context is yet another reason that writers and literati from around the world have been so powerfully captured by the Neustadt tradition.

There is ample evidence that Neustadt laureates, many of the most important writers of the last five decades, commonly see the Neustadt Prize in this vein. Elizabeth Bishop, the fourth laureate, heralds the Neustadt Prize as "a [rarefied] place so far inland" and an icon of possibility and hope far away from traditional literary venues where one must peck "for [mere] subsistence along coastlines of the world." Tomas Tranströmer, number eleven, addresses the difficulty but also the importance of translating poetry today and credits the Neustadt Prize as creating an atmosphere in Norman where translation, with all its risks and imperfections, is simply "what we do here in Oklahoma." Adam Zagajewski, number eighteen, judges the Neustadt Prize, with its traditional tilt toward poetry, as commensurate with "the immense risk involved in writing poetry today . . . perhaps the most daring thing in the world" to do. Mia Couto, number twenty-three, views the Neustadt Prizes as beacons working against "what unites us today, in all countries, on all continents . . . fear," seeing in the prizes a source of hope more powerful than fear.

In effect, these Neustadt laureates are explaining why this prize is regarded among writers at least as second in importance, as the *New York Times* once noted, only to the Nobel Prize itself. Their answer is that the Neustadt Prizes encompass the promise of literature and the model of what America stands for. To this day, the prizes continue to reward and celebrate the best writers anywhere, often the "best" before they are recognized as such anywhere else. It is encouraging that this extraordinary profile of integrity and boldness has been tested repeatedly since the inception of these prizes, and that reputation has survived unblemished to the present day. The fact of these prizes coming into existence in the U.S. heartland, embodying some of the most important of American ideals and continuing to thrive beyond all measure to be a force for good in the world, explains both the audacity and the beauty of this amazing tradition.

Norman, Oklahoma
August 2019

Robert Con Davis-Undiano *is the executive director of* World Literature Today.

Introduction
The Neustadt Prize on the World Stage
Daniel Simon

"UNGARETTI VINCITORE BOOKS ABROAD PRIZE PREGOTI COMUNICARE ANSA"
Telegram from Piero Bigongiari to Romano Bilenchi
February 9, 1970, 11:00 a.m.

In February 1970, with the transmission of a telegram from Norman, Oklahoma, to a correspondent of *La Nazione* newspaper in Florence, Italy ("Ungaretti winner Books Abroad Prize please inform National Associated Press Agency"), news about the winner of a fledgling literary prize made its way into the world. Over the next fifty years, that fledgling's uncertain wings would come to be represented by a magnificent silver eagle feather symbolic of both the flights of literary imagination as well as the writer's traditional quill.

Nothing guaranteed that the initial fledgling would have more durable wings than Icarus, however. The Neustadt International Prize for Literature, which in time came to be known as "the American Nobel," started out as a modest initiative that, in several respects, aimed to remedy what many perceived to be the Nobel Prize in Literature's perennial flaws, a critique still often heard today when the Swedish Academy makes its annual announcement. Formally unveiled as the "Books Abroad International Prize for Literature" by Ivar Ivask at the thirty-sixth congress of PEN International in Menton, France, in September 1969, the spark for this new international prize preceded Ivask's tenure as the longest-serving editor (1967–91) of *Books Abroad* and its successor, *World Literature Today*. A lively discussion surrounding the merits (and demerits) of the Nobel Prize had taken place five years earlier during the annual meeting of the Modern Language Association in New York City in December 1964. At the behest of Robert Vlach, *Books Abroad*'s editor at the time, Herbert Howarth—a British-born translator of Arabic and professor of English from the University of Pennsylvania—convened a panel of scholars to discuss the Nobel's track record at the MLA convention. Those talks formed the core of the subsequent "Nobel Prize Symposium" featured in the Winter 1967 issue of *Books Abroad* that included Howarth's introductory essay, "A Petition to the Swedish Academy," which in turn sowed the seeds of Ivask's 1969 charter. (To read the charter, turn to page 319.) More on that connection in a moment.

Although Ivask didn't realize it when he took over as editor in 1967, *Books Abroad* had almost foundered on the rocks of financial hardship in the mid-1960s. In that same winter of 1964–65 when Vlach and Howarth convened their MLA panel in New York, the very existence of the journal itself was hanging in the balance. During the fall of 1964, Pete Kyle McCarter, the University of Oklahoma's vice president for academic affairs (who would eventually become provost and interim president in 1970–71), apparently called on Vlach to make a case for *Books Abroad*'s continued existence— namely, whether the university could justify funding the journal even as protests over civil rights injustices and the escalating U.S. war in Vietnam increasingly occupied the country's (and the administration's) focus.[1] Vlach responded in an impassioned three-page letter about the indispensability of institutional support, the journal's efforts to expand circulation, the perennial problem of inadequate staffing, and the desirability of paying foreign contributors (two cents a word for articles, three cents a word for book reviews). Vlach challenged McCarter that unless the university could come up with the funding to adequately support the journal, the administration should let it migrate to an institution that would. At the end of the letter, Vlach wrote: "Dr. House's idea is worth a better fate than suicide."[2] Thankfully, the administration ultimately decided that the journal did deserve a better fate.

Dr. House was Roy Temple House, who had served as *Books Abroad*'s founding editor from 1927 to 1949. By the mid-1940s, the journal that House had built during his two-decade tenure achieved such renown that the Nebraska-born scholar was nominated for the Nobel Peace Prize in 1948. House, who also chaired OU's Department of Modern Languages from 1918 to 1942, somehow kept the journal afloat financially during the lean years of the Great Depression and World War II. His successors as editor, three European émigrés—Ernst Erich Noth (1949–58), Wolfgang Bernard Fleischmann (1959–61), and Robert Vlach (1961–66)—each put his personal stamp on the journal, gradually expanding *Books Abroad*'s coverage from an initial focus on the literatures of western Europe (for the most part, those literatures taught by House and his colleagues in the department).

When the Czech-born Vlach took over the helm as editor in 1961, he extended the journal's coverage to include "Books of Asia and Africa," in keeping with the catholicity of his interests and his wide-ranging talents as a poet, translator, journalist, and literary critic. In anticipation of *Books Abroad*'s fortieth-anniversary year (1966–67), Vlach urged McCarter to help underwrite a speaker series that would have brought "nine Nobel Prize winners or other world-famous foreign writers" to the university, and President George Lynn Cross endorsed a $25,000 application to the Ford Foundation to support the series.[3] Like the editors who preceded him, Vlach continually tried to impress upon the administration and his faculty colleagues the value of a journal like *Books Abroad* in bringing prestige to the university, even when the publication could barely make ends meet financially, like so many of the so-called little magazines of the modernist and postwar era. Bringing Nobel laureates to campus would have been an impressive coup for the young editor.

Unfortunately, the Ford Foundation turned down the grant request, then Vlach died suddenly in January 1966, at the age of forty-nine, so his dream never came to fruition.[4] Associate Editor Bernice Duncan, who had worked with every editor from House to Vlach, took over as acting editor in the wake of her predecessor's death. Soon enough, another European émigré would be hired as the journal's sixth editor: the polyglot Estonian-Latvian poet and frequent *Books Abroad* contributor Ivar Ivask, whom Duncan helped recruit for the position from his professorship at St. Olaf College in Minnesota. When Ivask arrived on campus in fall 1967, the issue featuring the Nobel Prize symposium—including Vlach's posthumous contribution on Slavic writers—had recently been published. Howarth's "Petition to the Swedish Academy," the first of nineteen essays in the issue, was frequently damning in its critique. "I would like to see the Swedish Academy less often fix the crown, and sometimes the death-mask, on fulfilled grandeur," wrote Howarth, "more often go ranging for the discovery and reinforcement of genius which is still on the advance."[5]

Howarth—who worked for the British government in Tel Aviv during World War II but resigned in protest over its policies in Mandate Palestine—went on to propose five changes to the academy's procedures, including, notably, a recommendation to "exert itself to discover writers outside the domains of the Big Powers and the current languages of diplomacy." Moreover, "Only with hesitation and restraint," he wrote, "should the Academy endorse a writer already widely recognized and rewarded." Ultimately, the literary world would be better served if the Nobel contributed to "the enlargement of the periphery of international vision."[6] While no doubt such criticisms stung the members of the academy, it nevertheless extended an invitation to four of the issue's contributors—Howarth, Manuel Durán, Albert H. Carter Jr., and Robert E. Spiller—to take part in a symposium in Stockholm in fall 1967 and included their talks in the subsequent proceedings volume, *Problems of International Literary Understanding* (1968).

Having grown up in the Soviet-controlled Baltics during the interwar years and experienced the Cold War as an exile in the West, Ivask knew that living on "the periphery of international vision" had real-world consequences. He took careful note of Howarth's critiques when formulating the original charter for the Books Abroad Prize, and he credited Howarth in the preamble to the 1969 announcement. Ivask signaled his intention that the new prize would rival the Nobel ("To date, there is no competition to the criteria set up by the Swedish Academy, with its attendant perquisites of professional status and monetary compensation"), and he was also careful to avoid the Stockholm model of a permanent jury, choosing instead to empanel a new group of writers every other year. Ivask envisioned a prize "representative of American concern for genuine achievement in world literature"—note the emphasis on "genuine achievement," not Old World perquisites. To the PEN delegates assembled in France, Ivask concluded with a hopeful question: "Is it not faith in the essential creative function of literature that has brought us together from all corners of the globe?"

Almost inevitably, despite such a lofty international vision, not every

pitfall could be avoided. Of the twelve jurors named to the first jury in 1970—
Piero Bigongiari (Italy), Heinrich Böll (Germany), J. P. Clark (Nigeria), Frank
Kermode (Great Britain), Jan Kott (USA), Juan Marichal (USA), Gaëtan Picon
(France), A. K. Ramanujan (India, USA), Allen Tate (USA), Mario Vargas
Llosa (Peru), and Andrei Voznesenski (USSR), plus Ivask—nearly half were
Europeans, with the entirety of Africa, Asia, and Latin America represented
by merely one writer each. And only six of the twelve took part in person
when the panel convened at the University of Oklahoma in February 1970.
The complicated logistics of prize-giving vexed Ivask so much that he would
modify the original charter to account for some of the eventualities that might
disrupt his lofty plans for an award that would compete with the Nobel.[7]

Too, Ivask's announcement of the first prize amount—$10,000—in
September 1969 was something of a wish and a prayer. Earlier that summer,
Vice President McCarter wrote to Ivask to inform him that "there now seems
little or no prospect that the money for the projected *Books Abroad* prize can
be raised this year. I am very sorry to send you this news, for I can understand what embarrassment it will cause you in notifying the distinguished
people who, because of your own prodigious efforts, have agreed to serve on
the Board [i.e., jury], and I can understand your own great personal disappointment, which I share. [Vice President Thurman] White tells me, however,
that the list of prospective donors has now been exhausted, and no likelihood
any longer exists of raising the money within the next two months."[8] Despite
McCarter's dire prediction, Ivask was able to secure contingency funding from
the office of then-President J. Herbert Hollomon Jr., thereby averting disaster.[9]

Ivask could finally breathe a sigh of relief when the jury arrived on the
OU campus in February 1970 and emerged with a winner despite an initial deadlocked vote.[10] Ivask broke the tie, elevating Italian poet Giuseppe
Ungaretti over the leftist Chilean poet Pablo Neruda. After hastily arranging
travel plans for the eighty-two-year-old Italian poet, Ivask welcomed Ungaretti
to Oklahoma on March 13, 1970. (For a fuller account of Ungaretti's visit to
OU, turn to "The Old Captain's Last Voyage" on page 19.) At the banquet
in Ungaretti's honor, President Hollomon echoed Ivask's lofty vision for this
new award emanating from the Southern Plains of the United States:

This land and this place is for Western man, young, vital, unreasoning, irrational, hopeful, lustful, and youthful. We honor today and he honors us, a poet who at any age is young and hopeful, innocent, loving, and rational. It is this combination of the Dionysian and Apollonian that makes life have any hope at all. It does us great honor that he comes to us as the first laureate of a prize based upon a tradition of interest in literature at a university only a little more than half a century old, from a place and a time of great tradition from which all of our art, our music, our poetry, and much of our prose comes. It is, I believe, a signal beginning to what I hope will become a great tradition in Western European America as for the whole world: to award a prize to someone in literature without consideration of his background or ideology and without reference to political boundary.

Flushed with the success of having crowned the prize's first laureate, Ivask soon confronted the inevitable reality of coming up with funding for the next biennial award. Fortunately, a Maecenas—according to 1974 laureate Francis Ponge, evoking the Roman emperor Octavian's friend and adviser who was legendary for his patronage of Horace and Virgil—came to the prize's rescue: the Neustadt family of Ardmore, Oklahoma. The same week that Ivask was in France announcing the debut of the Books Abroad Prize, Boyd Gunning, executive director of the University of Oklahoma Foundation, wrote to Doris Westheimer Neustadt to formalize the Walter Neustadt Memorial Fund in honor of her late husband, Walter Neustadt Sr., who had served as a trustee of the foundation from 1951 to 1965. Gunning outlined his plans to utilize the memorial fund to underwrite acquisitions for the library, art museum, and natural history museum and to endow a professorship.[11] Walter Neustadt Jr., who had received his master's degree from OU in 1941, followed in his father's footsteps as a trustee for the OU Foundation beginning in 1965, joined the advisory board for the University of Oklahoma Press, and served on the OU Board of Regents from 1969 to 1976. Through the intercession of David A. Burr, who had served as President Cross's assistant and became vice president for university affairs in 1968, Neustadt recognized that the Books Abroad Prize presented a natural opportunity to realize his family's philanthropic ideals by endowing an award that would bring international renown to his beloved university.[12] President Paul F. Sharp announced the family's initial gift of $200,000 on May 17, 1972, with Regent Nancy Davies, Doris Westheimer Neustadt, Walter and Dolores Neustadt, and Allan and Marilyn Neustadt as honored guests in attendance.

With the endowment in place that spring, Ivask would publish a glowing "Progress Report" in the summer 1972 issue, in which he somewhat triumphantly claimed that "the faith in impartial literary evaluation on a worldwide scale, which this journal has championed now for forty-six years, has again been vindicated." After receiving the 1972 award, Colombian novelist Gabriel García Márquez wrote: "This is a prize that has taken shape in the fertile imagination of a native of Estonia who has attempted to invent—rather than dynamite—a literary prize that would be dynamite for the Nobel. It is a prize in the mythical Oklahoma of Kafka's dreams and the land of the unique rose rock, and has been awarded to a writer from a remote and mysterious country in Latin America nominated by a great writer from far-off Iceland." By the time French poet Francis Ponge was chosen as the 1974 laureate, it became clear that the Neustadt Prize represented a remarkable convergence between Ivask's global literary vision and the Neustadts' cultural patronage. In his acceptance speech, Ponge remarked:

> This gratitude—how shall I put it—is very complex, because I owe this honor and this award to the University of Oklahoma and to *Books Abroad,* to the chairman of the jury, to the jury itself, naturally, and to the Neustadt family who have made it possible for this prize to become something perfectly magnificent. It is so rare to find this combination that I do not know how to express myself. It is certainly extraordinary that almost fifty years ago the University of Oklahoma decided to support a publication like *Books Abroad* and to continue supporting it. With Mr. Ivask's assumption of the editorship came the creation of this prize, which is so original and

so unlike any other in the conditions of the deliberations, the jury which is renewed with each prize, and all the other very original things connected with it. This initiative is truly extraordinary, as is the family who supports it by playing the role one would expect of a truly cultured Maecenas, that is to say, of one who has a very devoted interest in activities other than sports.

The fledgling's wings had magnificently spread.

*

The twenty-five Neustadt laureates' acceptance speeches in the pages that follow offer five decades' worth of insight into the evolution of world literature since 1970. Moreover, the accompanying essays that introduce each of the laureates' speeches provide an evolving panorama of international literary tastes and critical judgments during that same time frame, distilling the collective will of the more than 250 writers, translators, and scholars who have served on the juries over the years. Each of the special issues of *Books Abroad* or *World Literature Today* devoted to the prizewinner may likewise be viewed as a time capsule offering a wealth of insights into the literary zeitgeist since 1970.

The predominant theme of the laureates' acceptance remarks is literature's relationship to the broader social, cultural, and political world of its time. For some laureates, writing offers an escape from the world into an aesthetic realm purified of worldliness, but for most, writing is inextricably engaged with reflecting or changing the world. Themes of freedom, tolerance, forgiveness, bearing witness, solidarity, justice, and outright revolt appear often in their reflections on the writer's role. Assia Djebar quotes Mario Vargas Llosa: "In the heart of all fiction, the flame of protest burns brightly." For Claribel Alegría, inheriting "the sword of poetry" obligates the writer to wield it on behalf of justice.

While some of the Neustadt winners in the pages that follow remain rooted in their country and language of origin, many of the writers pen their works from a place of geographic or linguistic exile, and even those who never left home (or eventually returned) frequently write from a position apart from the cultural mainstream. According to Duo Duo, "Poetry takes this periphery as a blessing and continues to offer rituals for the sick rivers, to offer readable landscapes for the heart." Often, authors will claim a literary genealogy over a national one: among European poets, an unmistakable line runs through the work of Ungaretti, Ponge, Miłosz, Tranströmer, and Zagajewski. In the New World, another line runs through the work of Bishop, Paz, Cabral, and Brathwaite. Yet both lines readily cross the Atlantic—and Pacific—as well.[13]

Questions of language abound in their meditations. The laureates frequently invoke both an oral tradition as well as scribal legacies and literary histories in their work. Some plumb the depths of their native tongue, while others, like Farah and Malouf, embrace a polyglot English that may be global in expanse but ultimately full of local "coloratura." Issues of translation—not only of linguistic transfer but cultural translatability—often arise. Ultimately, for a novelist like Raja Rao, how we use language reflects our humanity, and the writer engages in "radical questioning" to probe the human condition.

One of the perennial pleasures of that condition is the gift of storytelling, and many of the laureates claim that the enchantment of telling stories drives much of their work. Dubravka Ugrešić quotes Nabokov's *Lectures on Literature* in this regard: "There are three points of view from which a writer can be considered: he may be considered as a storyteller, as a teacher, and as an enchanter. A major writer combines all three—storyteller, teacher, enchanter—but it is the enchanter in him that predominates and makes him a major writer." Writers achieve "major" status by enchanting or challenging their readers, without whom they would be anonymous scribes, describing the shadows on the wall of the cave. For Mia Couto, "Literature and storytelling confirm us as relatives and neighbors in our infinite diversity."

Writers also confront the pressing questions of history in their work, from the Middle Passage (Brathwaite, Danticat), the Cold War (Miłosz, Zagajewski), and civil wars (Alegría, Couto) to the legacies of the postcolonial world. Writing about Patricia Grace's gift to the Māori people of New Zealand, Mvskoke writer Joy Harjo—the first Native American U.S. poet laureate—connects her work to a globalizing sense of pan-indigenous reckoning: "We understand that we have all been colonized, challenged by the immense story we struggle within. We are attempting to reconstruct ourselves with the broken parts." In 1973 Gabriel García Márquez announced that he was giving his $10,000 award to a defense fund for political prisoners in Colombia. And in protest against the Reagan administration's policies in Central America, Max Frisch donated his prize money to a local organization working to build schools in Nicaragua.

While each writer claims the right to absolute freedom in the aesthetic realm of the imagination, their work ultimately connects to the broader moral and ethical concerns of our age. In speaking to "the business of making in all its forms," David Malouf ponders "what we are seeking when we set out there in the world some artefact, some made thing, that was not previously part of nature but is now, so that nature is changed, enlarged by its presence." Such "forms of making," contends Malouf, reflect the power of the writer's craft to remake the world. In turn, 1984 laureate Paavo Haavikko offers a powerful reflection on the writer's task:

> Thus literature is always philosophical and always moral. It asks what is right in the final count, knowing that there is no reply. But it asks and it seeks, and it cannot be shackled by laws, social systems, technology or business. Using all the rich patterns in the world, literature constructs a form in which the following things can be found: the question of injustice and justice, the movement of events in the world, and darkness. The reader is invited, he is given an opportunity—but he may walk past if he will. It is the writer's lot to go on working, in the dark, in motion, free, alone, available. The value of this work is not in immutable, established classics; it is not in any completed book; it is in the endless work itself, the endless effort to remain free and unbound.

Djebar, Alegría, Danticat, and others take up "the question of injustice and justice" at an even deeper level, situating their work in the tradition of bearing witness, emerging from the solitude of writerly preoccupations to claim a sense of solidarity with the powerless. "What does the artist do to move the world?" asks Danticat. "I want to say we can begin by bearing witness. . . . Sometimes we cannot fully move the world, but it can move us with its vastness, its expanse, its limitlessness, its geography or geographies, its beginnings and endings, its injustices." In such a worldview, the writer's impulse is to work toward healing trauma and ensuring our collective survival. For Djebar, that work of healing is reciprocated by her readers, fellow writers, and like-minded artists, who offer her "the power of solidarity [in] the solitude of my exile."

The centrifugal pull of great literature, as embodied by the work of these twenty-five writers, draws us into a fuller realization of our humanity.

*

Looking back on the first half-century of the Neustadt Prize, has Ivask's dream of an award that would be "representative of American concern for genuine achievement in world literature" been fully realized? In his 1978 acceptance speech, Czesław Miłosz replied in the affirmative while at the same time marveling over the improbability of the Neustadt Prize: "The Neustadt literary prize belongs too, in my opinion, to those things which should not exist, because they are against the dark and immutable order of the world. . . . The decision of founding such a prize seems to me a wise one, not only because I am a recipient, but because it favors all those who in the game of life bet on improbability."

Octavio Paz, the 1982 laureate, echoes Miłosz in offering a broad-minded assessment:

> . . . very few literary prizes [. . .] are truly *international*. Among these a place apart is occupied by the Neustadt Prize. Two characteristics lend it a unique face: the first is that each jury is composed of critics and writers belonging to different languages and literatures, which means that it constitutes an *international* body, as international as the prize itself; the second characteristic is that the jury is not permanent but instead changes from one prize to the next—that is, every two years. These two characteristics translate

into two words: *Universality* and *Plurality*. Due to the first word, the prize has been awarded to poets and novelists in Italian, English, French, Polish, Spanish and Czech; due to the second word, Plurality, we find among the laureates not only writers of different languages but also of different literary and philosophical persuasions. In esthetic terms, Plurality is a richness of voices, accents, manners, ideas and visions; in moral terms, Plurality signifies tolerance of diversity, renunciation of dogmatism and recognition of the unique and singular value of each work and every personality. Plurality is Universality, and Universality is the acknowledging of the admirable diversity of man and his works. Considering all this, in the convulsed and intolerant modern world we inhabit, the Neustadt Prize is an example of true civilization. I will say even more: to acknowledge the variety of visions and sensibilities is to preserve the richness of life and thus to ensure its continuity. Hence the Neustadt Prize, in stimulating the universality and diversity of literature, defends life itself.

For Paz, a poet from the ancient cosmopolis of Mexico City who also served as a diplomat in Paris, Tokyo, Geneva, and Mumbai, that such a prize emanated from a small-town university less than a hundred years old must have been even more of a marvel. Decades before he was named a Neustadt laureate, Paz had discovered an Oklahoma-based journal that would open his literary awareness to the world: "In those days the literary isolation of Mexico was almost absolute, to the degree that when I read those pages I felt the opening of the doors of contemporary literature in languages other than my own. For a while *Books Abroad* was my compass, and foreign literatures ceased to be for me an impenetrable forest."

Two decades later, Adam Zagajewski would even make the audacious claim that "Norman, Oklahoma, has established itself as one of the undeclared capitals of modernity."[14] And William Gass, in calling the Neustadt Prize "the most important international award we have," noted that for a writer like Assia Djebar, the award "stands for this priceless connection which literature can

make between distantly separated places and far-off times, between a ceremony in Oklahoma and a city in Algeria." Finally, 2014 laureate Mia Couto
would echo Paz in claiming that "what we are celebrating here, in Oklahoma,
year after year, is more than literature. With the Neustadt Prize we all praise
the cultural diversity of our world and the cultural diversity of each one of us.
That is crucial in a moment where personal and national identities are constructed like fortresses, as protection against the threats of those who are presented to us as aliens."

Combining all these threads into a single appeal, 2016 laureate Dubravka
Ugrešić argues that those in positions of cultural power must preserve our
"Gutenberg civilization" for the generations that follow:

> . . . we should invest all our energies in supporting people who are
> prepared to invest in literature, not in literature as a way to sus-
> tain literacy but as a vital, essential creative activity, people who
> will preserve the intellectual, the artistic, the spiritual capital. I
> couldn't have dreamed that one day a student theater in Norman,
> Oklahoma, would be putting on the first-ever staging of my story,
> written thirty-three years ago. Literary continuity, therefore, does
> exist, and the fact that it describes an unexpected geographical tra-
> jectory only heightens the excitement.
>
> The literary landscape that has greeted me in Norman has
> touched me so deeply that I, briefly, forgot the ruling political
> constellations. I forgot the processes underway in all the nooks
> and crannies of Europe, I forgot the people who are stubbornly
> taking us back to some distant century, the people who ban
> books or burn them, the moral and intellectual censors, the bru-
> tal rewriters of history, the latter-day inquisitors; I forgot for a
> moment the landscapes in which the infamous swastika has been
> cropping up with increasing frequency—as it does in the open-
> ing scenes of Bob Fosse's classic film *Cabaret*—and the rivers of
> refugees whose number, they say, is even greater than that of the
> Second World War.

In a "convulsed and intolerant modern world" that increasingly demonizes "those who are presented to us as aliens," such pleas for cultural patronage and diversity, tolerance, and universality are needed more than ever. Since 1970, the Neustadt International Prize for Literature has helped preserve "the intellectual, the artistic, the spiritual capital" of the world, and one can only hope that the prize will continue to promote it for generations to come.

Norman, Oklahoma
August 2019

Daniel Simon *is* WLT*'s assistant director and, since 2008, editor in chief.*

1. McCarter's opinion was strongly informed by the counsel of Savoie Lottinville, director of the University of Oklahoma Press, which had handled the printing and distribution of Books Abroad since the journal's founding in 1927. While Vlach complained of working 60–70 hours a week in his budget request for 1965–66, Lottinville in turn questioned Vlach's competence in the business of publishing. In an August 1964 letter to McCarter, Lottinville—a former Rhodes scholar who earned a master's degree from Oxford and coached the university's boxing team—offers a lengthy analysis of the journal's editorial formula and circulation woes, then concludes by mentioning the prospect of replacing Vlach. See Savoie Lottinville to Pete Kyle McCarter, December 30, 1963, and August 29, 1964, Presidential Papers of George Lynn Cross, Western History Collections, University of Oklahoma, Norman (hereafter abbreviated WHC).

2. Robert Vlach to Pete Kyle McCarter, November 20, 1964, *World Literature Today* archives, WHC.

3. Robert Vlach to Pete Kyle McCarter, April 21, 1965, *World Literature Today* archives, WHC.

4. Joseph M. McDaniel Jr., secretary of the Ford Foundation, to George Lynn Cross, June 8, 1965, Cross Presidential Papers, WHC.

5. In accepting the 1972 award, García Márquez would comment, "the role of a literary award like the BA / Neustadt Prize is not only to crown the glorious achievements of the living past (or a dying one, even one that may be dead, for that matter) which has quite often been the case with the Nobel Prize, but also to reward and call attention to the remarkable things actually happening and bursting into creation now."

6. Herbert Howarth, "A Petition to the Swedish Academy," *Books Abroad* 41, no. 1 (Winter 1967): 4–7.

7. Ivask's "Revised Charter of the *Books Abroad* International Prize for Literature," with provisions to limit proxy and absentee balloting, appeared in the spring 1972 issue of *Books Abroad*. That charter also formalized the procedures of "elimination balloting," which became the gold standard for other juries in the future.

8. Pete Kyle McCarter to Ivar Ivask, July 10, 1969, *World Literature Today* archives, WHC.

9. See George Lynn Cross, *The Seeds of Excellence: The Story of the University of Oklahoma Foundation* (Transcript Press, 1986), 121–22.

10. Ivask recounts the details of the first jury's proceedings in "Giuseppe Ungaretti: Laureate of Our First International Prize for Literature," *Books Abroad* 44, no. 2 (1970): 191–94.

11. R. Boyd Gunning to Mrs. Walter Neustadt [Sr.], September 25, 1969, OU Foundation archives, University of Oklahoma, Norman.

12. An undated eight-page endowment proposal to Walter Neustadt appears in the 1972 Books Abroad folder, box 7 of the Presidential Papers of Paul F. Sharp, WHC. See also David A. Burr to Paul F. Sharp, "Books Abroad" memo, November 30, 1971, Sharp Presidential Papers, WHC; "Literary Prize Endowed" press release, May 11, 1972, Sharp Presidential Papers, WHC; and Carol J. Burr, *Because They Cared : A Chronicle of Private Support at the University of Oklahoma* (University of Oklahoma Foundation, 1975), 22.

13. The Chinese poet Duo Duo cites the influence of Charles Baudelaire, Federico García Lorca, Marina Tsvetaeva, and Ilya Ehrenburg on his poetry.

14. The French-born literary scholar Henri Peyre once wrote that "Norman, Oklahoma, sounded to many a European ear as Persepolis or Samarkand once may have done to Marlowe or to Keats" (*Books Abroad*, Autumn 1976).

Generic titles such as "Laureate's Words of Acceptance," "Presentation of . . . ," and "Encomium for . . ." have been replaced in this collection with thematic titles. Detailed biliographical information about all the pieces included here can be found in the "Recommended Reading" section that begins on page 329. Elisions to the original texts are marked by bracketed ellipses, and occasional typos, errors in fact, formatting inconsistencies, and stylistic infelicities have been silently emended.

GIUSEPPE UNGARETTI
THE 1970 LAUREATE

Giuseppe Ungaretti (1888–1970) was born into an Italian family in
Alexandria, Egypt, where he was educated in French and began working
as a journalist and literary critic. He moved to Paris in 1912 but enlisted
in the infantry in World War I and fought in the trenches in northern Italy.
World War I served as the catalyst for Ungaretti's venture into poetry,
and he published his first collection in 1916. Among the many literary
affiliations that influenced his work were hermeticism (which he helped to
revolutionize in the 1930s), symbolism, and futurism. Ungaretti's books of
poetry include *L'allegria* (1931), *Sentimento del tempo* (1933), *Un grido
e paesaggi* (1952), and *Vita d'un uomo* (1969; Eng. *The Life of a Man*,
1958).

I am happy to be here not only on
account of the honor, but also for
having seen in a distant land, which
seems isolated from the world, how
much can be done for the support
of culture and for the diffusion
of poetry—with determination,
with grace, and with a well-guided
intuition.

—Giuseppe Ungaretti

The Old Captain's Last Voyage
Ivar Ivask

Balugina da un faro
Verso cui va tranquillo
Il vecchio capitano.

G.U.

Vacationing amidst the solitary Finnish woods and lakes, I am trying to order my impressions of the dramatic events that occurred in connection with Giuseppe Ungaretti between 7 February and 4 June of this year, and in which I was to a certain degree involved. True, I had very briefly met the Italian poet on 17 April 1969 after his highly successful reading at the Poetry Center in New York, where he was presented by Professor Luciano Rebay from Columbia, with English translations of his verse read by Isabella Gardner, Allen Ginsberg, and Louis Simpson. But little did I then surmise that about a year later, Ungaretti would be the first recipient of the just-established international literary award. My reaction to his exaggerated manner of reading—ranging from a barely audible whisper to a hoarse shout; now angelic-looking, now more like the grimace of a Kabuki actor—was ambiguous. This was probably the case because I then honestly preferred the often obscure complexities of Eugenio Montale to Ungaretti's sparse, essential lines. It was for this reason that Montale became one of my candidates when the jury met in Norman, 5–7 February 1970. (My other candidate was Jorge Guillén.) Since Montale had advance support by several other jury members, his chances were quite good. However, when he politely declined to accept any international literary prize at that time, this changed considerably the situation confronting the members of the jury who had gathered for their deliberations. Since the story of the first jury has already been told in these pages (see *BA* 44:2) and in the *Saturday Review* (see the issue of 21 March 1970), suffice it to recapitulate here that it was my vote as chairman which broke the tie between Pablo Neruda and Ungaretti in favor of the latter.

This was the first dramatic event. No less exciting was the visit of the eighty-twoyear-old patriarch of Italian letters to Norman and New York. Ungaretti arrived at Oklahoma City's Will Rogers Airport on Friday 13 March together with Professor Luciano Rebay and John Ciardi who had joined him in New York. The poet was totally exhausted from an uninterrupted flight all the way from Rome. No one had at that time any idea that he had not slept much even before leaving and that he had broncho-pulmonary troubles. I hardly recognized the poet whom I had met only last year in New York; he had let his white hair grow to shoulder-length locks and refused to shave his white stubble with the explanation that it was important to renew one's appearance from time to time. Ungaretti was furious, his cane flailing the air, because he believed that his suitcase had not arrived. Yet the one suitcase from Rome was vehemently disowned by him, and he only grudgingly accepted it when I demonstrated its obvious contents to him: several copies of *Vita d'un uomo* and a tuxedo (among other things).

Came Saturday morning 14 March, the day of the solemn presentation of the award, and Ungaretti said he did not feel up to reading his verse or giving any speeches. Understandably so, what with his prolonged sleeplessness, and the change in time from Rome to Oklahoma, his not too stable health at the advanced age of eighty-two. Yet it was also quite vexing to all organizers who had made infinite preparations, and already the guests were arriving, including a crew of *Radiotelevisione italiana* . . . The success of the evening was far from assured. Fortunately, in the afternoon things began to look up: the maestro had had a good nap and together with Ciardi and Rebay, the four of us sat down around a small table in one of the university cottages where Ungaretti was lodged. He went through his collected poems page by page in order to make a selection for the reading. "This one is not bad, is it?" Ungaretti generously consulted us. Mostly we nodded our "si, si" assent, although worrying a bit that this part of the program might both tire the laureate and exceed the allotted span of fifteen to twenty minutes, since after each original poem, Ciardi or I would read the English version by Andrew

Wylie. Ungaretti's final choice for the occasion was eighteen poems, which spanned half a century of productivity: "Agonia," "Veglia," "Sono una creatura," "Solitudine," "Girovago," "Caino," "Tu ti spezzasti," "Cori descrittivi di stato d'animo di Didone, I, IV, VIII, X, XVIII, XIX," "Variazioni su nulla," "Ultimi cori, nos. 12, 24," "Proverbi I–IV," and "Dunja." (The selection was determined, at least in part, according to which poems happened to be available in Wylie's translation, which Ungaretti obviously preferred.)

The evening program, a black-tie affair, began at 6:00 p.m. I have carefully leafed through the photographs of the poet reproduced in Leone Piccioni's *Vita di un poeta Giuseppe Ungaretti* (Rizzoli, 1970), a moving interpretive biography, but it seems to me that Ungaretti never looked better and more the magician that he always was than during the last months of his life—what with his beard and long white hair; the earlier severity was gone, a compassionate openness marked his face. I had the honor of saying the opening words. One of the real connoisseurs of Ungaretti's oeuvre, Professor Luciano Rebay, pronounced the encomium. Then J. Herbert Hollomon, at that time president of the University of Oklahoma, rose to present the hand-lettered certificate, bound in blue leather, to the first laureate of the *Books Abroad* International Prize for literature, and said:

> This land and this place is for Western man, young, vital, unreasoning, irrational, hopeful, lustful, and youthful. We honor today and he honors us, a poet who at any age is young and hopeful, innocent, loving, and rational. It is this combination of the Dionysian and Apollonian that makes life have any hope at all. It does us great honor that he comes to us as the first laureate of a prize based upon a tradition of interest in literature at a university only a little more than half a century old, from a place and a time of great tradition from which all of our art, our music, our poetry, and much of our prose comes. It is, I believe, a signal beginning to what I hope will become a great tradition in Western European America as for the whole world: to award a prize to someone in literature without consideration of his background or ideology and without reference

to political boundary. But recognizing someone somewhere who brings to man the hopefulness and the despair of man's short time alive. In a very deep sense, Ungaretti has brought to the world a sense of love and of hope and of feeling that lies, unspoken often, within all of us.

It therefore does me honor to be able to present to him, the first laureate, the *Books Abroad* University of Oklahoma Prize for Literature.

Giuseppe Ungaretti responded with the following words (translated here into English):

I am very moved by this ceremony in this distant land. It was exhausting to get here: it was far away, it was farther than I ever would have imagined, but finally I did get here to receive the honor that was bestowed on me this very moment, which is an honor surpassing my merits, and this honor was accompanied by most kind words. I find myself at a university which is a model of a university—a model for encouraging studies, but also for the diffusion of poetry. Hence I am happy to be here not only on account of the honor, but also for having seen in a distant land, which seems isolated from the world, how much can be done for the support of culture and for the diffusion of poetry—with determination, with grace, and with a well-guided intuition.

I was comforted to read in Piccioni's spirited account that microphones hardly ever work when Ungaretti reads his verse since his voice fluctuates so much. We had the same difficulty in Norman. But enough of the man's unusual intensity came through to move his audience, who listened intently to the hunched figure of the old poet seated in the pit of the amphitheater-like modern auditorium of the Oklahoma Center for Continuing Education. (I myself was strongly reminded of Vainamoinen, the Finnish god of song in the *Kalevala,* and indeed Ungaretti's forebears—the name means literally "Little Hungarian"—had migrated centuries ago from Hungary to Tuscany.) Suddenly the complete unity of his life and poetry became clear to me, the perfect overlapping achieved in such lines as "La morte / si sconta / vivendo," "Ora sono ubriaco / d'universo," "In nessuna / parte / di terra / mi posso accasare," "Cereo un paese innocente," or "Fui pronto a tutte le partenze." The immediate truth of "S'incomincia per cantare / E si canta per finire" became clear, alas, only in retrospect.

It was a moment of cordial simplicity in spite of all solemn appearances, potted palms, popping flashlights and whirring television cameras. It was Ungaretti's moment and he placed on it his unmistakably vigorous imprint. The standing ovation seemed so insignificant in the presence of this tiny, stooped, white-haired old man who almost seemed to have come to us from another reality, to which he had witnessed as the prophets of old. Two and a half months later this creature of myth was dead.

No one entertained seriously this possibility at that hour of fulfillment. The reading over, the crowd descended to congratulate the poet, have copies of his books autographed, take more pictures. Tired but obviously pleased, Ungaretti complied. He inscribed for me then and there the copy of *Vita d'un uomo* from which he had just read, combining Italian, Arabic, and French words, thus representing the three cultures which most decisively had shaped him.

At the banquet, toasts were made as candles fluttered: by President Hollomon, the Italian minister plenipotentiary, Giulio Terruzzi, John Ciardi (in the name of the American poets), Professor Lowell Dunham, chairman of the department of modern languages at the university, and Ungaretti was made an honorary citizen of Norman by the mayor's representative, Professor James Artman. I read some of the telegrams and greetings that had arrived for the occasion: from Governor Dewey Bartlett, Jorge Guillén, Francis Ponge, Octavio Paz, Professors Thomas Bergin (Yale), Glauco Cambon (Connecticut), Zbigniew Folejewski (British Columbia), etc. I would like to quote also here some of these messages. Jorge Guillén, hospitalized in Puerto Rico, wrote:

Ungaretti's presence always brings such a sharing of happiness, of vitality generously given, that to be with him always means a celebration and a joy. This time, Ungaretti's celebration will be in Norman, Oklahoma, because he is the poet who is being honored.

With all my heart I am glad that the light of this prize has focused on a truly illustrious figure, abounding in years and merit. The marvelous precision of Ungaretti's language has been for all of us an unsurpassable model of disciplined expression.

Francis Ponge gave this opinion in his letter to me dated 3 March 1970:

J'ai été ravi . . . que mon cher grand ami Ungaretti ait été désigné par votre jury ce qu'il est, effectivement: le plus grand poète vivant. Voilà qui rachète l'injustice stupidement commise par le jury Nobel. . . . Bravo donc!

Octavio Paz in his turn commented:

It was a great joy to know that Ungaretti was the first laureate, a most deserving and welcome choice. For once an international jury did the right thing. I hope you will manage to keep this high level in subsequent choices.

Glauco Cambon's telegram put it succinctly and memorably:

Dear Ungaretti, I wish I could share this happy occasion with you tonight, but your poetry makes it possible for me to be with you anywhere because poetry is the only antidote to exile.

Allen Ginsberg's short poem in tribute, "Ungaretti in Heaven," can be read in this issue; it, too, seems to have acquired a prophetic ring.

The feted poet expressed his thanks very simply, praising the beautiful women near him and again the university that went to such lengths to reward poetry. The mood remained festive and no one wanted to break it. President Hollomon summed it up by saying that it had been a perfect day which nevertheless had to end just as we have one day to die, yet the experience of these hours cannot be destroyed. Said it and extinguished grandly with his palm the candles on the candelabra in front of him. It seems strange that someone would bring up the subject of death at such an occasion, but it seemed right and, looking back, uncannily so. Later Ungaretti commented favorably that the president of a university should have those rarest of talents, wit and style. The poet withdrew to a deserved rest, while the other guests continued to celebrate his victory.

Although we hardly believed that Ungaretti would take up our suggestion to use the next day before returning to New York for a visit to Anadarko, the "Indian Capital of the World," he enthusiastically accepted. So we went there by car, Ungaretti, Rebay, my wife and I. It was a windy, cloudy Sunday afternoon with Ungaretti alternately taking naps and engaging in lively conversation, while the not very varied south Oklahoma landscape rolled by. We went first to the Indian Village, an open air museum of dwellings used by the various Southern Plains Indian tribes, faithfully reproduced by the Indians themselves. It is located a mile out of Anadarko on the Tonkawa hills near the site of an Indian massacre. Ungaretti was too tired to take the full guided tour by Miss Dolores Buffalo, an Otoe Indian, and so he just looked at some of the tepees, observed the landscape with typical stretches of red clay bleeding here and there. It was evident that he felt the almost sacral character of the place belonging to the original inhabitants of this red earth. When a group of Indians performed some of their authentic war dances, Ungaretti was as fascinated and delighted as a child. It later turned out that the leader of the group had been among the first American soldiers to liberate Rome from the Nazis and hoped to return there with his dancers as part of a European tour. In town, we visited the small but well-arranged Southern Plains Indian Arts and Crafts Museum. Ungaretti could not admire enough the exhibited samples of Indian beadcraft and silverwork. He commented that the Indians possessed the best sense of color in the world. This, coming from one who had lived in Paris and known most of the great modern painters there, was no superficial judgment.

He bought samples of bead and silverwork, as well as suede moccasins for his granddaughter Annina. That this encounter appealed strongly to the basically nomadic nature of Ungaretti, always open to new exotic adventures, be they in Egypt, Brazil, or Oklahoma, is reported by several people with whom he later talked about it, and was expressed in the last letter I received from him, dated 6 May: "La ricordo continuamente e ricordo la sua sposa e le loro straordinarie cortesie e gli incontri inaspettati con gli indiani."

Monday morning 16 March, Ungaretti boarded the plane for New York, accompanied by Luciano Rebay. He looked now really ill, complaining about various aches and pains. None of us had been easy about the state of his health during the past strenuous days, but now we were frankly worried. The medical diagnosis in New York confirmed the worst, and the poet was committed to the Presbyterian Hospital at Columbia University with bronchopneumonia and a congested heart. What a sad epilogue to the festive days in Norman! His son-in-law, the architect Mario Lafragola, flew in from Rome, and so did his good friend, Signora Nella Mirone from Milan. Fortunately, the poet's health responded well to the medical treatment, and he was permitted to return to Rome on 26 March—just before the erratic layoffs on account of the sick calls among the air control personnel. During April and May, Ungaretti was recuperating at Salsomaggiore. He sent several letters promising various contributions to the issue I was planning in his honor for the autumn. I was to discuss these matters with him personally during our stay in Rome early in June. We arrived in Rome on Monday, 1 June. 2 June was the day of the Italian Republic, marked by colorful military pageantry. During that day, I phoned the poet, who lived with his daughter Ninon, and was informed that Ungaretti was not at all in Rome, but in Milan; neither was his daughter available. I should call back on Wednesday, at ten in the morning. This sounded strange. The mystery was resolved when I learned Wednesday morning from the housekeeper that I could not see the "professore" because he had died in Milan, Monday night, 1 June, from a lung clot at the home of friends. . . . In my shocked disbelief I could only express amazement that the news had not yet been publicized anywhere. Could it really be true? Yes, yes, the news was to be released later that day and the burial services were to be held Thursday

4 June at the church of San Lorenzo fuori le Mura, the burial following at the cemetery of Verano.

It was still difficult to believe. None of the newspapers carried the front page news that Italy's greatest modern poet had died. I wandered into Rizzoli's bookstore to buy the second, enlarged edition of *Vita d'un uomo,* discovered Piccioni's just-published biography of the poet, and discreetly inquired from the clerks whether they had by chance heard the news. No, indeed, and how could it be true when nobody knew about it? Died on 1 June, and still the fact was unknown on the morning of 3 June? Thus I wandered around Rome, obviously belonging to the very few who were aware that the life of that great Roman poet had ended. Visiting in the afternoon the Spanish poet Rafael Alberti and his wife, the writer María Teresa León, in their Andalusian-looking apartment in the Trastevere district, it was I who had to break the news about their friend to them. Then, the afternoon and evening papers finally carried the news. Why was it withheld for two whole days? It seems to have been the poet's own wish that the announcement of his passing and his actual burial come as close as possible, to avoid elaborate preparations.

One would almost have expected a state funeral, just as de Gaulle ordered for Paul Valéry back in 1945, but the poet got his wish of a simple funeral by ordering the delay of the announcement. The Early Christian basilica of San Lorenzo fuori le Mura, several times rebuilt with its high ceiling of rugged wooden beams, was nevertheless filled with about one hundred of the poet's relatives and friends. Next to us sat the poet and critic Piero Bigongiari, who came to Norman with his wife to present Ungaretti as his candidate and saw him win. Among those who had come to pay their last respects were Carlo Bo, Mario Luzi, Giancarlo Vigorelli, Leone Piccioni, Oreste Macrí, Libero de Libero, Giorgio Bassani, Leonardo Sinisgalli, Carlo Levi, Natalia Ginzburg, Maria Bellonci, Alfonso Gatto, Murillo Mendes, Attilio Bertolucci, Vittorio Sereni, Renato Guttuso, and Guido Piovene. But also a number of students, even hippies, paying last homage to the poet who kept always close to the young and their aspirations, only recently reading a poem, "Greece 1970," at a rally directed against the regime of the Greek colonels. Cardinal Dall'Aqua blessed the casket and then it was carried out into the bright sunlight by Luzi, Piccioni, Bo, Vigorelli. No speeches in church and almost none at the tomb until the critic and longtime friend of the poet, rector of the University of Urbino, Carlo Bo, stepped forward to say a few words. He stressed that Ungaretti had not only been a poet, but poetry itself, and above all a companion, *the* companion. At the same time, he lamented the absence of any high government official. The coffin was placed in the tomb next to that of the poet's wife, Jeanne (who died in 1958), and the opening closed with concrete. Someone advanced and incised with a dry branch in large letters the name Ungaretti, and added a cross. Milena Milani inscribed the word "poet," somebody else wrote the poet's often-repeated self-characterization as "Uomo di pena"—man of sorrows. The crowd dispersed, casting one more look at the plain epitaph—even this spontaneously created, but later probably to be covered with a more finished marble plaque. The huge wreaths sent by the University of Rome, where Ungaretti taught for so many years, the Writers' Syndicate, the Italian premier, the Association of Italian Editors and Authors, the Editions Apollinaire (a friend from his first Paris years), shook in the breeze. I met the daughter of the poet, Signora Ninon Lafragola, who told me that I was probably the first in Rome to learn about her father's death. We walked away in the company of Ungaretti's last secretary, Ariodante Marianni and his wife. He told me how much our award had meant to Ungaretti, who came very close to getting the Nobel Prize in 1969. He returned full of excitement from his last American trip, planning to write down some of his impressions of Oklahoma for the issue of *Books Abroad* in his honor. It turned out to be his last great joy in life. We talked at length about the issue, now in memory of Ungaretti, and went to the railroad station to send off Carlo Bo and Piero Bigongiari with his wife Elena, who were returning to Florence. We did not feel like joining them and going from Florence on to Umbria as we had originally planned. Ungaretti's death had changed everything.

*

I had met Ungaretti briefly in 1969. Then followed those three incredible days spent in his company in Norman during March of this year. Our correspondence had lasted but three months. But never has someone won me over so completely and in so short a time, as a human being and artist, as did Giuseppe Ungaretti. Our encounter was of a rare intensity and openness; the loss the more cruel and real. Fortunately his life and poetry were and still are completely fused, Life of a Man, which communicates to us all that he was and always will be: "Poesia / è il mondo l'umanità / la propria vita / fioriti dalla parola / la limpida meraviglia / di un delirante fermento," as he wrote back in 1916 as a soldier in the trenches of World War I. He wrote and acted out of such a "delirious ferment" which made him travel like a restless nomad, made him try out every new way of poetic expression. Prudence was not part of his character. Who but Ungaretti would have literally risked his life, ill and eighty-two years old, to fly halfway around the globe just not to disappoint those friends who had gathered in Norman to hear him read his poetry and receive a new international literary prize? The present issue praises the poet for his original achievement and mourns the disappearance of an extraordinary human being from our midst: an almost equally grave loss for those who had the privilege to have been his friends of a lifetime and for those who knew him but a few years, months, or even days. For future friends, the man will be the poetry.

Born in Riga, Latvia, in 1927, **Ivar Ivask** *served as editor of* Books Abroad *and* World Literature Today *from 1967 to 1991. He inaugurated the Neustadt Prize in 1969.*

The Perennial Wanderings of the Nomad
Luciano Rebay

Caro Ungaretti, Mr. President, Ladies and Gentlemen:

In the years following the First World War, a group of leading Italian critics and writers expressed the belief that poetry was dead, and that henceforth the only medium through which a poet might communicate was prose. Apocalyptic statements of this kind are not entirely unusual—we have all heard time and again that the *novel* is dead—but the significant fact in this instance is that few predictions of doom uttered in recent times have proved to be so completely incorrect. Our very presence this March 14, 1970, in Norman, Oklahoma, thousands of miles from Italy, proves in the most spectacular manner not only that Italian poetry has managed to survive in our century, but that it has known a period of revival and greatness worthy of a long tradition of poetic excellence. For we are here to honor Giuseppe Ungaretti, a leading protagonist of this revival and in a real sense the father of contemporary Italian poetry, the master who, by daring to explore anew the hidden meanings as well as the most secret potentialities of the Italian language, was the first to revitalize a tradition that had threatened to become stagnant.

Clearly, however, the significance of his work today reaches far beyond the confines of Italy. Now in his eighty-second year, Ungaretti has won world fame for his poetic achievements, at the same time distinguishing himself as a challenging critic and scholar of poetry, ranging from Vergil to Dante, from Petrarch and Leopardi to Mallarmé, from Góngora and Shakespeare to Racine and Blake, from Valéry and Saba to Breton and Saint-John Perse, among others. Also, one must not forget, he has produced superb translations from Shakespeare, Blake, Góngora, Racine, Mallarmé, Perse. And in turn, his poems have been translated into every major Western language. He has been a frequent contributor to *La Nouvelle Revue Française*, where some of his major poems were published even before their appearance in Italy, and to such prestigious journals as *Commerce* and *Mesures*, which during the period between the First and Second World Wars kept alive an interest in what was new and vital in creative literature throughout the Western world. I expect that in the near future a scholar—a comparatist—will study the seminal influence that Ungaretti's poetry has had on his younger contemporaries and on later generations, both in Italy and abroad. The findings of such an investigation, it is easy to predict, will show ramifications throughout Europe and across the Atlantic Ocean as far as Brazil, where Ungaretti lived and taught for six years between 1936 and 1942, and in the United States, where, as he well knows, he has many friends and admirers. To anticipate but one example, I shall refer you to Robert Lowell's "Returning," a poem from *For the Union Dead*, which, as Lowell himself has indicated, could never have been written without the stimulus of Ungaretti's "Canzone" from *La terra promessa*.

The impact of Ungaretti's poetry—his sparing use of words, his capacity to bring language to unusual heights of lyric tension, his power to create illuminating images—has been acknowledged by the leading men of letters of our century. T. S. Eliot, who was also born in 1888, said of Ungaretti: "He is one of the very few authentic poets of my generation." Saint-John Perse has praised him for "having given universal meaning to the voice of European man." Robert Lowell has pointed out that "Ungaretti did something new, and stood like a human rock behind it." And Allen Tate, observing that as a result of the work of poets such as Ungaretti and Montale, the poetic center of continental Europe had shifted from France to Italy, stated: "I consider Giuseppe Ungaretti one of the great modern European poets, who since the death of Paul Valéry has no superior in Europe." But perhaps the best summary of what constitutes the essence of Ungaretti's contribution to modern poetry is to be found in a reflection by André Pieyre de Mandiargues: "If you want to know his equals," he wrote, "you must turn to Berg, Stravinsky, Picasso, men whose art partakes of the nature of lightning and who know, or knew, how to ally in their creations the greatest lucidity with the blind force of un-reason. Each of them has accomplished the prodigious feat of losing his head, yet keeping it."

Prodigious feat, indeed: for poetry is forever an adventure at the limit of reason and logic, "the exploration of a personal continent of hell," says

Ungaretti, in which the poet feels utterly alone, different and at times isolated from his fellow men, as though condemned by the weight of a very special responsibility: to discover a secret, and to reveal it. As far back as 1931 he wrote in the *Nouvelle Revue Française*: "Je suis un 'homme' qui a toujours brûlé sa vie pour quelque chose de bien plus grand que l'homme, et cela, en effet, c'est de la poésie." (I am a "man" who has always burnt his life for something much greater than man himself, and that is poetry.) We should note at this point that Ungaretti's complete works, just published in Italy by Mondadori, are fittingly titled *Vita d'un uomo*—Life of a Man.

Why did Ungaretti adopt for his *opera omnia* this inclusive title? Because, obviously, he does not believe that the poet is an abstract entity, separate from humanity, but on the contrary that even in his necessary, unavoidable, and at times tragic loneliness, he is an integral part, and often the most alive, most vigilant part of humanity. The poet is therefore first and foremost a "man," and his poetry cannot but convey his particular mode of being a man, cannot but express—to quote Glauco Cambon—his "search for the archetypal meaning of personal experience." In the preface to *L'allegria* (Joy), the definitive edition of the first volume of his collected verse, Ungaretti made a statement that is essential to the understanding of his approach to art and that places his entire poetic output in proper perspective. He wrote—and that was again 1931: "This old book is a diary. Its author has no other ambition than to leave a good biography of himself, an ambition which he believes is shared by the poets of all times." And only last year—in the eight-five-page appendix of newly written, candid "Notes," which to me constitutes the happiest surprise of *Vita d'un uomo*—recalling that he had composed his first poems in Milan during the autumn of 1914, he observed: "I wrote those poems in the only natural way known to me, trying to represent in them the environment that surrounded me, what aspects of my personality it reflected at that particular moment, and, as laconically as possible, the variations of my feelings. . . . Those first poems are exactly what all my subsequent poems will be, embedded in a psychological situation closely linked to my biography: never have I known a poetic dream that did not stem from a direct personal experience."

Ungaretti was born in Egypt, in that crucible of different races and religions that was Alexandria, the native city of another great poet, Constantine Cavafy, and also of Filippo Tommaso Marinetti, the flamboyant founder of futurism. Ungaretti's family (he was the younger of two sons) was of humble stock, had emigrated from Lucca, in Tuscany, at the time of the construction of the Suez Canal, where the poet's father had found work as a laborer. He died when his son Giuseppe was only two years old. His widow, a strong-willed, deeply religious woman, raised their two children alone with the income provided by a bakery she and her husband had managed to open in the poor district of Moharrem Bey. Ungaretti spent the first twenty-four years of his life in Alexandria—a crucial formative period that not at all surprisingly left a lasting imprint on his poetry. One of the constantly recurring themes in his work—the desert—is in fact the result of his direct contact with the Sahara. For Ungaretti, the desert means distance, light, freedom, sensuousness, the piercing melancholy of Bedouin songs and, above all, dreams, mirages—the dreams and mirages of the nomad who becomes for him the symbol of the poet in his perennial wanderings in search of innocence, happiness, love. In a three-line poem titled "Tramonto" (Sunset) we read: "Il carnato del cielo / sveglia oasi / al nomade d'amore" (The flesh-colored sky / awakens oases / for the nomad of love). This was written in 1916 on one of the battlefields of the First World War. Although the sunset described here is not an African one, the images it evokes by analogical counterpoint unmistakably are. The nomad reappears later as the protagonist of a longer poem, written in 1918, "Girovago" (Wanderer), a metaphor for the poetic quest. The last lines convey in an inspired synthesis the poet's longing for purity and innocence: "Godere un solo / minuto di vita / iniziale // Cerco un paese / innocente." (To enjoy only one / minute of life primeval // I seek a country / innocent.)

In a 1926 article, "Innocenza e memoria" (Innocence and Memory)—which, incidentally, provided the title for his book of essays in French translation, *Innocence et mémoire*, published last year—Ungaretti characterized poetry as an insatiable longing for innocence ("una speranza inappagabile d'innocenza"), a brilliant definition that Marcel Raymond quoted in his well-known study *From Baudelaire to Surrealism*. Ungaretti later elaborated on it in his fundamental essay, "Ragioni di una poesia" (Reasons for My Poetry, 1949), now to be found at the beginning of his collected works. "Poetry," he wrote, "enables man to create an illusion of youth reconquered, and to believe in this illusion; to become, as Rimbaud wanted, *voyant*—a seer; . . . to bring forth an illusion of innocence, the illusion of the perfect freedom man enjoyed before his fall." This "illusion," this feeling of freedom, lightness, joy is one of the precious gifts that Ungaretti's poetry has to offer, a gift available to any of us if only we open *Vita d'un uomo*.

In 1912 Ungaretti left Egypt for Europe. He did not at first, as one might expect, choose to live in Italy. Rather, he settled in Paris, with friends and schoolfellows from Alexandria who had gone to the French capital to complete their studies. In Paris he enrolled at the Sorbonne, studied under famed professors, such as Henri Bergson, and even began work on a doctoral thesis on the nineteenth-century poet Maurice de Guérin. But most important, he found his way to bohemia and frequented some of the leading exponents of the literary and artistic avant-garde: Picasso, Braque, Léger, Salmon, Jacob, Cendrars, and especially Apollinaire, with whom he quickly developed a deep and devoted friendship.

Ungaretti remained in Paris until the outbreak of the First World War, at which time he moved to Italy to volunteer in the army. He served as a private in the infantry, first on the Italian front in the Carso Mountains and later on the French front in the Champagne region. It was out of that conflict that his first major poetry was born, although it would be most inaccurate to label any of his lyrics "war poems." "In my poems there is no trace of hatred for the enemy, or for anyone," says Ungaretti, "there is simply an acute awareness of the human condition, of the brotherhood of men in their suffering, and of the extreme precariousness of human life." In the trenches, during lulls between battles, or at night in his tent, Ungaretti wrote what later he was to call his "diary," on scraps of paper which he would stuff into his pack. A literary-minded lieutenant, Ettore Serra, one day discovered them by accident and later in 1916 published them at his own expense in an eighty-copy edition. The slender volume—Ungaretti's first book of verse—was called *Il porto sepolto* (The Buried Port) and revolutionized Italian poetry. The title was suggested to Ungaretti by the sunken Pharaonic harbor of his native Alexandria. In the book, however, the buried port is an allegory for poetry itself, whose orphic secrets are brought out from the depths into the light by the poet: "Vi arriva il poeta / e poi torna alla luce con i suoi canti / e li disperde // Di questa poesia / mi resta quel nulla / d'inesauribile segreto." (The poet reaches [the buried port] / and then returns to the light with his songs / and scatters them around. // Of this poetry / there remains to me the nothingness / of an inexhaustible secret.)

Most of the poems of *ll porto sepolto* were short, the lines were not regular ones, there was no rhyme, no punctuation, no attempt at D'Annunzian grandiloquence; the general versification represented a complete break with tradition. Yet those lyrics had a freshness, an intensity, a regenerating strength that was uncannily captivating and moving. Italian poetry was never the same after them. Their compressed power continues to fascinate those who read them today.

ll porto sepolto was incorporated in 1919 into a larger collection of poems, *Allegria di naufragi* (Joy of Shipwrecks). This title, echoing as it does the celebrated last line of Leopardi's "L'infinito" ("E il naufragar m'è dolce in questo mare"—And to shipwreck is sweet for me in this sea), indicates, as later poems revealed, that Ungaretti was then already seeking to get back into the mainstream of Italian lyric tradition (Leopardi had been, with Mallarmé, the poet who had presided over his youth while he was still living and studying in Egypt), and that he was rediscovering for himself the meters of the old Italian masters, especially the hendecasyllabic line and the septenary. It was a new "season"—to use the word Ungaretti has adopted for each progressive stage in his poetic development—that culminated in the publication in 1933 of *Sentimento del tempo* (Sentiment of Time), the book of summer and sensuality, and, in its second part, of a tormenting religious crisis.

Beginning in the mid-thirties, Ungaretti then worked on his next book in which he intended to reflect the autumn of his life, "an autumn," he wrote, "which bids farewell to the last signs of earthly youth, to the last carnal appetites." But the publication of this work, to be called *La terra promessa* (The Promised Land), was delayed until 1950 by supervening tragic events. These events—the death of his nineyear-old son in Brazil in 1939, followed by the horrors of the Second World War—led instead to the printing in 1947 of *ll dolore* (Grief), "of my books the one closest to me," says Ungaretti. "I wrote it during terrible years, half-choking. I cannot speak of it except to say that that grief will never cease torturing me." *ll dolore* includes some of the most powerful poems Ungaretti has written—I have in mind one in particular, "Tu ti spezzasti" (You Were Shattered), in which the cosmic sense of bereavement caused by the loss of his son is recorded in heart-rending, unforgettable lines.

In the course of the last two decades Ungaretti has published three new volumes of collected verse: *Un grido e paesaggi* (A Shout and Landscapes, 1952), which includes "Monologhetto" (Little Monologue), a lyric chronicle of some of the most significant moments in his life, as well as new poems for Antonietto, his dead son; *Il taccuino del vecchio* (The Old Man's Notebook, 1960), a collection of poems in the metaphysical vein of *La terra promessa*; and, in 1967, *Marte delle stagioni* (Death of the Seasons), which many thought was his swan song. But then, in 1968, the year of his eightieth birthday, the unpredictable "vecchio" surprised everyone by bringing out with characteristic coquettishness yet a new book, *Dialogo*, a love dialogue of dazzling verbal virtuosity and youthful confidence, perhaps best epitomized by a single line: "Ancora mi rimane qualche infanzia," which approximately translated means "Some infancy is still left to me." Observed Ungaretti in a recent interview, as reported by Leone Piccioni: "I believe that in the poems of old age the freshness and illusion of youth are gone; but I also believe that they encompass so much experience that if one succeeds in finding the right words, they represent the highest form of poetry one may leave." *Vita d'un uomo*, I may add, does not close with *Dialogo*. The last composition, "Dunja," again a love poem, but inspired—one should note—by a different lady, was begun in Rome on April 2, 1969, and I can still see Ungaretti's triumphant expression when he showed it to me in New York two weeks later.

This makes me realize that I have said nothing of what Ungaretti means to me personally. But tonight is not the time for personal recollections. Were I to follow them, they would take me back to Rome where I first met Ungaretti fourteen years ago while he was still teaching at the University; or to Paris with Jean Paulhan; or to Milan with Jean Fautrier; or, especially, to New York in 1964 when he spent a semester as visiting professor at Columbia and charmed students and colleagues alike with the warmth of his personality. As I conclude this tribute of my affection and admiration, I believe that the paramount fact to be stressed here, on this evening of the award to him of such a distinguished prize, is that, thanks to Giuseppe Ungaretti and his work, Italian poetry early in this century regained a universality of language through which have found exemplary expression the innermost anguish, dreams, and hopes of modern man.

March 14, 1970
University of Oklahoma

P.S. As I reread this encomium two and a half months after Ungaretti's death, I have before me the typewritten text of what I believe to be his last poem, "L'impietrito e il velluto" (The Petrified One and Velvet)—the second inspired by Dunja. He handed it to me after the award ceremony in Norman. This poem was then still unpublished (it has now been included in the second printing of *Vita d'un uomo*), and I remember being struck and very moved by its unmistakable images and visions of death. Ungaretti watched me as I read it; then he took a pen and slowly wrote along the margin a few words, which I translate: "A poem like this I may never be able to write again, perhaps it is my last poem. To Luciano Rebay with great affection. Ungaretti."

Luciano Rebay *(1928–2014), a leading postwar critic of Italian literature, was the Giuseppe Ungaretti Professor (emeritus) at Columbia University.*

GABRIEL GARCÍA MÁRQUEZ
THE 1972 LAUREATE

Gabriel García Márquez (1927–2014) was born in Aracataca, Colombia, where his maternal grandparents raised him for the first nine years of his life. He began his career in writing as a journalist while studying at the University of Cartagena, writing columns for the university's paper. In 1955 García Márquez published his first novella, *La Hojarasca* (Eng. *Leaf Storm*, 1972), a stream-of-consciousness story about a young boy's first encounter with death. But it would not be until the publication of *Cien años de soledad* (1967; Eng. *One Hundred Years of Solitude*, 1970) that he would become the literary figure he remains to this day. García Márquez's publications include the novels *In Evil Hour* (1970), *Love in the Time of Cholera* (1985), and *The General in His Labyrinth* (1989). His novellas include *Chronicle of a Death Foretold* (1981) and *Of Love and Other Demons* (1994), and his nonfiction includes such titles as *The Story of a Shipwrecked Sailor* (1970) and *News of a Kidnapping* (1996).

His final publication was the novella *Memories of My Melancholy Whores* in 2004. García Márquez was the recipient of the 1982 Nobel Prize in Literature and is widely considered one of the most significant authors of the twentieth century.

These circumstances suffice to make of the . . . Neustadt International Prize for Literature the one great international prize for highly deserving writers who are not yet well known.

—Gabriel García Márquez

Allegro Barbaro, or Gabriel García Márquez in Oklahoma
Ivar Ivask

García Márquez has studied and read more English than French or Italian, yet perfectly fluent in the latter two, he is hesitant to speak English. Why? "Because the English sentence is too simple," he explains. As to his tastes in music (he is quite a stereo-buff), he prefers the period from the late Beethoven to the last Bartók. He admires in particular Bartók's way of breaking up the melodious line to which the eighteenth- and nineteenthcentury masters have accustomed us. There is a lesson here for the modern novelist: "The Spanish prose sentence falls almost inevitably into hendecasyllabic or alexandrine verse which I want to avoid. One of the main tasks in polishing the text of my new novel, *El otoño del patriarca*, a complicated work, will be to break this flow of my sentences. By the way, the double meaning in the English translation of the novel's title, 'The Fall of the Patriarch,' is more apt than the original title but unfortunately cannot be duplicated in Spanish."

An aversion to simple sentences, a wish to achieve greater rhythmic complexities in the prose of his fiction: it all fits the complicated, intense, cordial character of the Colombian novelist who had come to Oklahoma to accept his prize (see *BA* 47:1, pp. 7–16). He made his stopover of barely two days, 27–28 June 1973, on his way from New York to Los Angeles and from there to a longer vacation with his entire family in Mexico. The best manner of characterizing this brief encounter would be in terms of one of Bartók's compositions, "Allegro barbaro." However, for Bartók—one of García Márquez's most admired human beings—"everything came too late." Fortunately this is not true in the case of García Márquez, who by forty-five has produced a world-wide bestselling novel and was awarded in 1972 both the prestigious Latin American Rómulo Gallegos Prize as well as the *Books Abroad* / Neustadt International Prize for Literature.

He had come to accept the *Books Abroad* / Neustadt award at an informal presentation "with an absolute minimum of witnesses." Crowds and public spectacles frighten him, hence his insistent request that we dispense this one time with a public ceremony. A few sentences were pronounced by Mrs. Walter Neustadt, who presented the symbolic silver eagle feather (in a box made of three woods native to Oklahoma—cherry, pecan and walnut); Huston Huffman, President of the University of Oklahoma Board of Regents, spoke briefly in Spanish and presented the check for ten thousand dollars along with the hand-lettered leather-bound certificate—in the absence of vacationing University president Paul F. Sharp—while thunder and lightning were raging outside and we looked out to see it raining in Macondo. Two photographers illuminated the scene inside. García Márquez's thanks came later in the form of a short written statement released to the press:

> This is a prize that has taken shape in the fertile imagination of a native of Estonia who has attempted to invent—rather than dynamite—a literary prize that would be dynamite for the Nobel. It is a prize in the mythical Oklahoma of Kafka's dreams and the land of the unique rose rock, and has been awarded to a writer from a remote and mysterious country in Latin America nominated by a great writer from far-off Iceland. These circumstances suffice to make of the *Books Abroad* / Neustadt International Prize for Literature the one great international prize for highly deserving writers who are not yet well known.

To be quite honest, the image of dynamite and dynamiting never would have occurred to me; it belongs to García Márquez's own resourceful imagination. Furthermore, since things are not supposed to be too simple, another news release was simultaneously made in New York by García Márquez's American publishers Harper & Row, explaining that he intends to establish with his prize money a defense fund for political prisoners in his native Colombia.

In retrospect I am still amazed at how many matters we were able to talk about before the presentation! He related to me, for example, that Pablo Neruda, the runner-up for the 1970 *Books Abroad* Prize, had expressed his great satisfaction to him in Paris about Giuseppe Ungaretti winning our award a few months before his death. What would García Márquez do in Los Angeles? Talk about Ray Bradbury. Science fiction aside, he thought Bradbury had written three or four of the most amazing pages in all modern prose. And Borges had dedicated some of his finest pages to a Spanish edition of Bradbury, as García Márquez informed me, immediately adding: "There are very few authors whom I have read completely; Borges is one of them." Spending an evening in the company of two poets, my wife and I, it was inevitable that his expressed dislike of—or better, lack of interest in—poetry had to come up. No, it actually was not quite exact, he considered himself a "clandestine poet," who liked, among twentieth-century poets, most especially Pablo Neruda, Pedro Salinas, Luis Cernuda, and Jorge Guillén. What about the roman nouveau, structuralism? A dead end.

So the hours passed, with García Márquez alert to everything: food and wine being served, music in the background, questions about literature past, present and future. Too bad I thought of playing the record with Bartók's "Allegro barbaro" only long after he had left. By now he is surely in Mexico, where his sons Rodrigo and Gonzalo were born, trying to break the backbone of the all-too-natural Spanish prose sentence. But how can you possibly turn the noun "otoño" of Latin origin into anything resembling the Anglo-Saxon "fall"? And I remembered Borges meditating in a similar vein about the advantages of writing in English. No doubt, the major Spanish-language writers today are less provincial than their English-speaking peers who hardly ponder the subtle shades of meaning offered them by the Castilian tongue.... Yet isn't this what Goethe's world literature is all about: the creative contact between the intensely local and universal relevance and responsibility? García Márquez will stop in Colombia on his way back to Barcelona from Mexico. He promised to return to Oklahoma because of its spaces, silence, and simple sentences.

The Fabulating Gifts of Gabriel García Márquez
Thor Vilhjálmsson

I do not feel inclined to join with those who hold that the poet should be relieved of his shamanistic duties, unburdened of his responsibility and role in enchanting his fellow man. The poet cannot be reduced to the task of merely collecting facts to feed the cybernetic monsters that are taking over, running and rounding our little lives and that are making us all identical moles striving to fill our quota of anthill chain-labor tasks and chain-life functions, where all shades of tergiversation are anathema and high treason, regardless of whether they are impelled by inner needs and nobly motivated; the creed in the shadow of the cybernetic tyrannosaurus rex of the encroaching brave new world is threatening to take over: mole stay mole. What then are our arms against the sea of robotification troubles and mechanization that threaten to suck out our souls and spit them into the void or onto garbage-dumps on the moon, there to wander undancing and bodiless among broken spaceships, surplus H-bombs, cyclonic gas. containers and exiled warfare-germs as spirits ambulating from crater to crater over the lunar sands while the earth-bound bodies continue to do the blind St. Vitus dance to the untuned commands of robots who may one day acquire whims and suddenly delight in crushing legions of our frail kind of ants with their unticklish toes?

One is fantasy. And therefore my choice of candidate in the present race is a writer eminently endowed with a gift of speech animated by dynamic fantasy. Gabriel García Márquez is one of those writers who enchants us as he deals with those perennial forces that rule our lives and cast us hither and thither. He also represents a highly encouraging phenomenon in world literature, which has been designated as the South American boom in literature. In an age when more and more often we hear that the novel is dying or dead, as the fish in the sea and life in Lake Erie, under the threat of *Menschendämmerung* it is worthwhile, I feel, to find such a countercurrent of fantasy and to bewingedly reflect thus upon the human lot awhile, and refreshed, thence to renew our efforts and even gingerly resume taking arms against a sea of troubles, and by opposing. . . .

García Márquez does not fail to deal with the dark forces, or give the impression that the life of human beings, one by one, should be ultimately tragic, but he also shows every moment pregnant with images and color and scent which ask to be arranged into patterns of meaning and significance while the moment lasts.

For: "You are the music / while it lasts." (T. S. Eliot)

It seems to me that García Márquez marries realism and objectivity with a most singular sense of the fantastic and delicious fabulating gifts, often employing surrealistic clairvoyance to paint frescoes full of moral indignation and anger protesting against oppression and violence, degradation and deceit. Extolling pride, he clearly depicts certain ludicrous, even grotesque aspects, such as quixotic bravery and intransigent single-mindedness of purpose. It is a joy to encounter a poet who revels in his seductive powers as García Márquez does. And yet he is so exact in his formulation and precise in his composition. In juxtaposing the twin elements of humor and tragedy García Márquez often achieves contrapuntal heights where language and image are thoroughly fused.

It is my opinion that the role of a literary award like the *BA* / Neustadt Prize is not only to crown the glorious achievements of the living past (or a dying one, even one that may be dead, for that matter) which has quite often been the case with the Nobel Prize, but also to reward and call attention to the remarkable things actually happening and bursting into creation now. I have the impression that in the case of García Márquez we have a writer at the height of his productivity, and I feel it would be fascinating to award this distinction while that creativity is at its full flow. A book such as *Cien años de soledad* (*One Hundred Years of Solitude*), a masterpiece, makes García Márquez indubitably one of the most important writers of fiction today.

In awarding García Márquez the *BA* / Neustadt Prize which he so well merits, I also feel that the great boom of South-American literature is saluted. This is a remarkable phenomenon of contemporary literature which revives optimism about the future of the novel. It is a fascinating body of literature that encompasses such varied and impressive writers as Asturias, Carpentier, Lezama Lima, Julio Cortázar, Vargas Llosa, Guimarães Rosa and Carlos Fuentes, and it induces me to revive the use of the word "South-American" instead of the term "Hispano-American" literature. Not forgetting the great poetry bred in this hemisphere, let me mention Neruda and Octavio Paz. Most of those just mentioned would also qualify for the present prize, but we should bear in mind that two of them have already been given the Nobel Prize, making it an act of redundancy to heap other prizes upon them.

García Márquez has invented a fantastic imaginary country of his own with its pertinent mythology of persons and events, recurrent in all his books, linked by allusion, with themes taken up and carried from one book to the other and elaborated upon, causing García Márquez's mythological world to emerge and expand, addicting readers to a fantasy and humor that titillates the imagination and makes the reader eager for more. Nor should we forget its ubiquitous poetry.

Reykjavík, Iceland

Novelist, short-story writer, poet, essayist, and translator **Thor Vilhjálmsson** *(1925–2011) was a leading exponent of Icelandic modernism. His awards included the Nordic Council Literature Prize and the Swedish Academy Nordic Prize.*

FRANCIS PONGE
THE 1974 LAUREATE

Francis Ponge (1899–1988) was a French essayist and poet. He was born in Montpellier and studied at the world-renowned Sorbonne. His first poems were published as early as 1923, and it would be through these publications that he introduced his distinct poetic style. His style of prose poetry (he often referred to this style as *proêms*) features meticulous descriptions of natural, everyday objects in lyric prose form. Ponge's collections of poetry include *La Rage de l'expression* (1952; Eng. *Mute Objects of Expression*), *Pour un Malherbe* (1965), *Le Savon* (1967; Eng. *Soap*, 1969), and *La Fabrique du Pré* (1971; Eng. *The Making of the Pré*, 1978). In 2005 Gallimard Press published *Pages d'atelier, 1917–1982*, a text encompassing Ponge's entire life's work, including some pieces that had previously never been published. In addition to the Neustadt Prize, Ponge received the French National Poetry Prize in 1981 and the Grand Prix of the Société des Gens de Lettres in 1985.

It is . . . rare to find a university which dedicates itself to and gives what is necessary for culture, for something which is probably more important than sports and does not risk becoming an opiate of the young.

—Francis Ponge

Master of the Still Life in Poetry
Michel Butor

Francis Ponge is certainly one of the greatest living poets. His specialty is the prose poem in the tradition of Baudelaire, Mallarmé, Jules Renard and Paul Claudel. The subject matter is always very commonplace—ordinary things or landscapes—and the idea is not only to describe but to extract a learning, a wisdom from the contemplation of nature. So he writes various kinds of prose fables in many ways reminiscent of Lafontaine. He can be called the master of the still life in poetry; but in that still life, the work, the effort of the painter is always reflected. Each poem, then, is a meditation upon life and art, and especially upon language. His prose style, extremely rich and diverse, is also very controlled, always chaste ("châtié" as we say in French); he is in that regard typically French.

His quiet influence has been decisive on three periods of French literature: existentialism (one remembers the essay of Sartre in *Situations*), the nouveau roman (with the still-life concern) and *Tel Quel* (with the linguistic trend). And through these movements, of course, he has been influential in all the important literatures of the world today. Ponge tries to be as classical as possible, as is quite manifest in a first reading of his book on Malherbe, but he cannot help being adventurous, and the result is that his experimentation is always at once daring and deeply justified, discreet and decisive. He has, as could have been predicted, given wonderful examples of the art of the book, of the way to handle its physical components. Of course he is a first-class essayist on painting, in the tradition of Claudel and Breton, but here again he is more restrained and delicate than they.

All his works were originally collected in three volumes called *Le grand recueil* (lyres, méthodes, pièces), but a first tome was later added, *Tome premier,* in which we find his earliest publications, the ones he may consider youthful pieces (though they are not); and it's there that we find what is today his best-known collection: *Le parti pris des choses (Taking the Side of Things).* Subsequently, a fifth volume has appeared, called *Nouveau recueil.* There are also a radio-script called *Le savon,* a book explaining how he tried to write a book about Malherbe for a commercial series ("Ecrivains de Toujours," Éditions du Seuil) and couldn't, and a very intensive and meandering meditation about the fact of writing, *Pour un Malherbe.* Finally, I would mention *La fabrique du pré* (published in the beautiful series "Les Sentiers de la Création" by Albert Skira), one of Ponge's most interesting innovations in the art of bookmaking, which includes all the stages of manufacture of the piece in *Nouveau recueil* called "The Prairie."

Translation from the French by Ivar Ivask

French novelist, poet, and essayist **Michel Butor** *(1926–2016) was the 1981 Puterbaugh Fellow at the University of Oklahoma (see* WLT, *Spring 1982). He received many literary awards for his work, including the Prix Renaudot and the Grand Prix of the Académie Française.*

What Is Necessary for Culture
Francis Ponge

Merci beaucoup, thank you very much. I am very moved. This is a great day for me. Perhaps it is because I have been enclosed within *my* own language that I am listening now, hearing encomiums, compliments and receiving praise and an important prize, in a language that I cannot understand. I am not saying that there is a lesson to be learned here. I think that it is excellent to know many languages, but I am also convinced that *we* work amidst our ignorances.

One must work, defend oneself against too much knowledge and enclose oneself in one's language.

Now I would like to convey my emotion, my gratitude. This gratitude—how shall I put it—is very complex, because I owe this honor and this award to the University of Oklahoma and to *Books Abroad,* to the chairman of the jury, to the jury itself, naturally, and to the Neustadt family who have made it possible for this prize to become something perfectly magnificent. It is so rare to find this combination that I do not know how to express myself. It is certainly extraordinary that almost fifty years ago the University of Oklahoma decided to support a publication like *Books Abroad* and to continue supporting it. With Mr. Ivask's assumption of the editorship came the creation of this prize, which is so original and so unlike any other in the conditions of the deliberations, the jury which is renewed with each prize, and all the other very original things connected with it. This initiative is truly extraordinary, as is the family who supports it by playing the role one would expect of a truly cultured Maecenas, that is to say, of one who has a very devoted interest in activities other than sports. Naturally I am not against sports. I am very capable of liking them. I was even a high-jump champion in the French military and a semi-finalist in the 400 meters. I like sports.

It is, however, rare to find a university which dedicates itself to and gives what is necessary for culture, for something which is probably more important than sports and does not risk becoming an opiate of the young. I am not saying that sports are an opiate. But I think that one must also know "Mens sana in corpore sano." Both are good. It is in a healthy body that the mind becomes clear. Now, I have talked too much and I have spoken in a way that many people may find clumsy, but it is the clumsiness of sincere emotion. Thank you, I am too moved to say more.

Translation from the French by Jo Ann Chesnut

from "Notes toward a 'Francis Ponge in Norman,'" by Ivar Ivask
Books Abroad 48, no. 4 (Autumn 1974): 647–51

ELIZABETH BISHOP
THE 1976 LAUREATE

Elizabeth Bishop (1911–1979) was born in Worcester, Massachusetts. Her father died when she was very young, and as a result of the heartbreak, her mother was committed to an institution in 1916. Bishop never reunited with her mother and was subsequently raised by her grandparents. Though she dabbled with poetry while in school, Bishop left home to study music composition at Vassar College in 1929. After suffering a bout of stage fright, she changed her focus to English literature. Following her graduation from college, Bishop spent the rest of her life traveling, writing poetry, and teaching at various colleges around the United States. Her body of work includes the poetry collections *North & South* (1946), *A Cold Spring* (1956), and Farrar, Straus, and Giroux's "definitive edition," *Poems* (2011). In addition to the 1976 Neustadt Prize, Bishop was honored with the American Academy of Arts and Letters Award in 1950, the Pulitzer Prize for Poetry in 1956, and the National

Book Award for Poetry in 1970. From 1949 to 1950 she served as Poet
Laureate of the United States.

I find it extremely gratifying that,
after having spent most of my life
timorously pecking for subsistence
along coastlines of the world, I have
been given this recognition from so
many different countries, but also
from Norman, Oklahoma, a place so
far inland.

—Elizabeth Bishop

The Optical Magic of Elizabeth Bishop
Marie-Claire Blais

Elizabeth Bishop is my choice for the *Books Abroad* award because to me she is one of the finest living poets, well known in the United States but not sufficiently recognized internationally. The body of her work is relatively small, yet one cannot read a single line either of her poetry or prose without feeling that a real poet is speaking, one whose sense of life is as delicately and finely strung as a Stradivarius, whose eye is both an inner and an outer eye. The outer eye sees with marvelous objective precision, the vision is translated into quite simple language, and this language with the illuminated sharpness of an object under a microscope works an optical magic, slipping in and out of imagery, so that everything seen contains the vibration of meaning on meaning.

One scarcely knows how to choose an example, there are so many. In "The Armadillo," for instance, there is the baby rabbit on whose peaceful world a fire balloon falls: "So soft!—a handful of intangible ash / with fixed, ignited eyes." Bishop makes such an image stand for a whole world of violence, vulnerability, helpless terror and protest. One cannot read the poem without quivering with a sense of the pain inherent in every form of beauty. Or she can say something that seems to mean exactly what it says, such as "we are driving to the interior," in "Arrival at Santos," although we have been prepared earlier by "Oh, tourist, / is this how this country is going to answer you" for the idea that every great personal change is a country waiting to be explored in its interior.

Yet Bishop is not personal as Lowell or Plath or Berryman is personal. Everything we know about her from her poetry comes through images that transform her particular suffering or loneliness or longing into archetypal states of being. "Four Poems," for example, is a sequence about the pain of the loss of love in which there is a flow of energy between the interior and exterior landscapes, the latter imitating the shape, color and anguish of the former. Somehow Bishop performs the miracle of fusion without ever altering her exterior truth. The fourth stanza makes one think of Donne in its mingling of physical and metaphysical, in the preciseness of the last lines: "a separate peace beneath / within if never with." No poet has ever spoken more concisely of the state of loving someone who is no longer there, of willing good to crystallize out of the pain.

Much of Bishop's poetry is the result of this struggle for accommodation with what is intolerable in life. Some poets turn their struggle to rage and hate, but she has arrived at a kind of pure nostalgia that is both past and present and at the peace "beneath" and "within" (but not necessarily "with") which I consider essential to great poetry.

Montreal

Marie-Claire Blais *(b. 1939) is a French Canadian novelist, poet, and playwright. Her many honors include the Governor General's Award and two Guggenheim Fellowships.*

The Ecstasies of Elizabeth Bishop
John Ashbery

To call Elizabeth Bishop a writer's writer is to pay her an ambiguous compliment. We all know about writers' writers, though we are perhaps incapable of really defining that term. But we perhaps do feel, even as we say it admiringly, that it somehow diminishes the writer. Should he be placed so far above the mass of readers, not to mention the mass of writers? Mightn't such exaltation be harmful for him, even taking into account the fact that he himself hasn't asked for it and may not know precisely what to do with it?

To call Elizabeth Bishop a writer's writer's writer, as I once did in a review of her *Collected Poems*, is perhaps to compound the audacity of the compliment, to imply that her writing has sophistication—that somehow unfortunate state of felicity in whose toils most of us wallow from time to time even as we struggle to cast them off. Yet this is the first thing that strikes me about Miss Bishop's unique position among American poets, one might even say among American writers. That is, the extraordinarily intense loyalty her work inspires in writers of every sort—from poets like myself, sometimes considered a harebrained, homegrown surrealist whose poetry defies even the rules and logic of surrealism, and from a whole generation of young experimental poets to experimenters of a different sort and perhaps of a steadier eye, such as Robert Duncan and James Tate, and to poet-critics of undeniable authority like Marianne Moore, Randall Jarrell, Richard Wilbur and Robert Lowell. It shouldn't be a criticism leveled at Miss Bishop that her mind is capable of inspiring and delighting minds of so many different formations. We must see it as her strength, a strength whose singularity almost prevents us from seeing it.

I first read Elizabeth Bishop's book *North & South* when it was published in 1946, and I had the experience in the very first poem, "The Map," of being drawn into a world that seemed as inevitable as "the" world and as charged with the possibilities of pleasure as the contiguous, overlapping world of poetry. Here, as in so many of her poems, the very materials—ink and paper—seemed to enlarge the horizons of the poem as they simultaneously called it back to the constricting dimensions of the page, much as a collage by Schwitters or Robert Motherwell triumphs over its prosaic substance by cultivating its ordinariness and the responses it can strike in our minds, where in a sense everything is ordinary, everything happens in a perpetual present which is a collage of objects and our impressions of them. [. . .]

In the last line ("More delicate than the historians' are the map-makers' colors") of this first poem in her first collection Elizabeth Bishop has, I think, given us the nucleus from which the dazzling variety of her poetry will evolve. Like the highest kind of poetic idea, it presents itself in the form of a paradox. How could the map-makers' colors be more delicate than the historians'?

How could the infinity of nuances and tones which is finally transformed into history, a living mosaic of whatever has happened and is happening now, prove more delicate—and not in the sense of softness or suavity but in the sense of a rigorously conceived mathematical instrument—than the commercial colors of maps in an atlas, which are the product, after all, of the expediencies and limitations of a mechanical process? Precisely because they are what is given to us to see, on a given day in a given book taken down from the bookshelf from some practical motive.

As the critic David Kalstone has said, Bishop's poems "both describe and set themselves at the limits of description. . . . Details are also boundaries for Miss Bishop. . . . Whatever radiant glimpses they afford, they are also set at the vibrant limits of our descriptive powers. [The poems] show us what generates that precarious state, and what surrounds us. 'From this the poem springs,' Wallace Stevens remarks, 'that we live in a place that is not our own and, much more, not ourselves, and hard it is in spite of blazoned days.' Miss Bishop writes under that star, aware of the smallness and dignity of human observation and contrivance. She sees with such a rooted, piercing vision, so realistically because she has never taken our presence in the world as totally real."

It is this continually renewed sense of discovering the strangeness, the unreality of our reality at the very moment of becoming conscious of it as reality, that is the great subject for Elizabeth Bishop. The silhouette of Norway unexpectedly becomes the fleeing hare it resembles; the names of cities conquer mountains; Labrador is yellow on the map not by chance but because the Eskimo has oiled it so as to make it into a window for an igloo; the universe is constantly expanding into vast generalizations that seem on the point of taking fire with meaning and contracting into tiny particulars whose enormous specific gravity bombards us with meaning from another unexpected angle. [. . .]

In a group of memorable poems about Brazil, Miss Bishop, like Darwin whom she admires, has sought not so much to come to grips with the frightening, teeming discipline of nature as it can be experienced raw in the South American landscape as to let herself be permeated and perhaps ultimately ordered by the lesson of that swarming order. Speaking of what the act of writing might be, she has said: "Dreams, works of art, (some) glimpses of the always-more-successful surrealism of everyday life, unexpected moments of empathy (is it?), catch a peripheral vision of whatever it is one can never really see full-face but that seems enormously important. I can't believe we are wholly irrational—and I do admire Darwin—but reading Darwin one admires the beautiful solid case being built up out of his endless, heroic observations, almost unconscious or automatic—and then comes a sudden relaxation, a forgetful phrase, and one feels that strangeness of his undertaking, sees the lonely young man, his eye fixed on facts and minute details, sinking or sliding giddily off into the unknown. What one seems to want in art, in experiencing it, is the same thing that is necessary for its creation, a self-forgetful, perfectly useless concentration"—a formulation not unlike Gauguin's "placing oneself in front of nature and dreaming." Only out of such "perfectly useless concentration" can emerge the one thing that is useful for us: our coming to know ourselves as the necessarily inaccurate transcribers of the life that is always on the point of coming into being.

In many of her poems Bishop installs herself as an open-minded, keen-eyed, even somewhat caustic observer of the life that is about to happen, speaking in a pleasant, chatty vernacular tone which seeks in no way to diminish the enormity of it, but rather to focus on it calmly and unpoetically. In the three short prose poems spoken from the point of view of three creatures much lower on the scale of human consciousness—"Giant Toad," "Strayed Crab," "Giant Snail"—she gives us the mystery of awareness as filtered through the mystification of an elemental eye that is being steeped in it to the point of bemused utterance. [. . .]

In another poem where, as in "The Map," Miss Bishop shows a series of pictures which are sometimes illustrations in an old gazetteer (the poem is entitled "Over 2000 Illustrations and a Complete Concordance") and sometimes real scenes remembered from an actual voyage—memories and illustrations overlap inextricably here—she elaborates the dilemma of perception versus understanding in a sustained, almost painfully acute argument that is one of the summits of her poetry. "Thus should have been our travels:

/ serious, engravable," she begins. But "The Seven Wonders of the World are tired / and a touch familiar, but the other scenes, / innumerable, though equally sad and still, / are foreign." Throughout the poem, which dips freely back and forth from a steel-etched "Holy Land" to the coast of Nova Scotia to Rome to Mexico to Marrakesh, we are never sure that the landscape we are in is the real world or the "engravable" one. Finally travel, the movement on which so much of her poetry hinges, dissolves into a bewildering swarm of particulars.

> Everything only connected by "and" and "and."
> Open the book. (The gilt rubs off the edges
> of the pages and pollinates the fingertips.)
> Open the heavy book. Why couldn't we have seen
> this old Nativity while we were at it?
> —the dark ajar, the rocks breaking with light,
> an undisturbed, unbreathing flame,
> colorless, sparkless, freely fed on straw,
> and, lulled within, a family with pets,
> —and looked and looked our infant sight away.

In the almost twenty years since I first read this poem I have been unable to exhaust the ambiguities of the last line, and I am also convinced that it somehow contains the clue to Elizabeth Bishop's poetry. Just as the crumbling gilt of the books seems, disturbingly, to pollinate our fingers, endow them fleetingly with life, so is flame—freely fed on straw (in the illustration)—colorless, sparkless, unbreathing and undisturbed. It would have been nice, at this point, to have seen the nativity, and not only to have seen it but to have participated in it to the point of self-effacement—to have looked our infant sight away.

David Kalstone has glossed the line thoughtfully and pointed out the similarity to a line in another key poem in Bishop's oeuvre, "The Imaginary Iceberg," where she describes the monstrous perfection of the iceberg as "a scene a sailor'd give his eyes for," mentioning that both lines convey a mysterious yearning to stop observing, which they also guard against. "What will it mean," he asks, "to look and look our infant sight away?" Where or when is away? Is it a measureless absorption in the scene? Or on the contrary, a loss of powers, as in "to waste away"? Or a welcome relinquishment, a return to "infant" sight, keeping its Latin root of "speechless"?

It is no doubt all these things, and a perfect summation of the poet's act—the looking so intense that it becomes something like death or ecstasy, both at once perhaps. Behind the multiple disguises, sometimes funny, sometimes terrifyingly unlike anything human, that the world assumes in Elizabeth Bishop's poetry, this moment of almost-transfiguration is always being tracked to its lair, giving the work a disturbing reality unlike anything else in contemporary poetry.

Brooklyn College, CUNY

John Ashbery *(1927–2017) was the author of more than twenty books of poetry and served as a Chancellor of the Academy of American Poets. His many honors included the Pulitzer Prize, a National Book Award, and the Bollingen Prize.*

The Inland Coast of Recognition
Elizabeth Bishop

Thank you, Mrs. Neustadt, President Sharp, Mr. Ivask, and Mr. Ashbery. The night before I left Boston to come here, I had dinner at a Chinese restaurant. I thought you might be interested in hearing the fortune I found in my fortune cookie. Here it is. It says: YOUR FINANCIAL CONDITION WILL IMPROVE CONSIDERABLY.

However, I don't want to express my gratitude *only* for the "improvement" in my "financial condition," grateful as I am for that. Mr. Ivask has selected a poem called "Sandpiper" to be printed on the program today, and when I saw that poem, rather old now, I began to think: Yes, all my life I have lived and behaved very much like that sandpiper—just running along the edges of different countries and continents, "looking for something." I have always felt I couldn't *possibly* live very far inland, away from the ocean; and I *have* always lived near it, frequently in sight of it. Naturally I know, and it has been pointed out to me, that most of my poems are geographical, or about coasts, beaches and rivers running to the sea, and most of the titles of my books are geographical too: *North & South, Questions of Travel* and one to be published this year, *Geography III*.

The first time I came to Norman, Oklahoma—in 1973—it was the farthest I had ever been inland in my life. I enjoyed myself very much on that first visit, and of course I am enjoying myself on this second, and very special, visit. I find it extremely gratifying that, after having spent most of my life timorously pecking for subsistence along coastlines of the world, I have been given this recognition from so many different countries, but also from Norman, Oklahoma, a place so far inland. Thank you again.

Norman, Oklahoma
April 9, 1976

CZESŁAW MIŁOSZ
THE 1978 LAUREATE

Czesław Miłosz (1911–2004) was a poet, writer, and translator born in the village of Szetejnie in a district that today is part of Lithuania. His first book of poetry was published in 1934. After World War II, which he spent in Warsaw, Miłosz defected to Paris in 1951, and the Communist government of Poland banned his works. In 1960 he immigrated to the United States, where he began teaching at the University of California at Berkeley. It was not until the Iron Curtain fell that Miłosz was able to return to Poland, and he split the remaining years of his life between Poland and the United States. Among his very long list of works, the most well known are *Zniewolony umysł* (1953; Eng. *The Captive Mind*), *Zdobycie władzy* (1955; Eng. *The Seizure of Power*), *The Witness of Poetry* (1983), and *Nieobjęta ziemia* (1984; Eng. *The Unattainable Earth*, 1986). Miłosz's *Selected and Last Poems, 1931–2004* (Ecco Press), selected by Robert Hass and Anthony Milosz, were published in 2011. In addition to the Neustadt Prize, Miłosz received the Nobel Prize in Literature in 1980. Additionally, 2011 was named "The Miłosz Year," and many literary festivals were organized around the world in honor of Miłosz's contributions to world literature.

> The Neustadt literary prize belongs too, in my opinion, to those things which should not exist, because they are against the dark and immutable order of the world.
>
> —Czesław Miłosz

The Whispered Guilt of the Survivor
Joseph Brodsky

I have no hesitation whatsoever in stating that Czesław Miłosz is one of the greatest poets of our time, perhaps the greatest. Even if one strips his poems of the stylistic magnificence of his native Polish (which is what translation inevitably does) and reduces them to the naked subject matter, we still find ourselves confronting a severe and relentless mind of such intensity that the only parallel one is able to think of is that of the biblical characters—most likely Job. But the scope of the loss experienced by Miłosz was—not only from purely geographical considerations—somewhat larger.

Miłosz received what one might call a standard East European education, which included, among other things, what's known as the Holocaust, which he predicted in his poems of the late thirties. The wasteland he describes in his wartime (and some postwar) poetry is fairly literal: it is not the unresurrected Adonis that is missing there, but concrete millions of his countrymen. What toppled the whole enterprise was that his land, after being devastated physically, was also stolen from him and, proportionately, ruined spiritually. Out of these ashes emerged poetry which did not so much sing of outrage and grief as whisper of the guilt of the survivor. The core of the major themes of Miłosz's poetry is the unbearable realization that a human being is not able to grasp his experience, and the more that time separates him from this experience, the less become his chances to comprehend it. This realization alone extends—to say the least—our notion of the human psyche and casts quite a remorseless light on the proverbial interplay of cause and effect.

It wouldn't be fair, however, to reduce the significance of Miłosz's poetry to this theme. His, after all, is a metaphysical poetry which regards the things of this world (including language itself) as manifestations of a certain superior realm, miniaturized or magnified for the sake of our perception. The existential process for this poet is neither enigma nor explanation, but rather is symbolized by the test tube: the only thing which is unclear is what is being tested—whether it is the endurance of man in terms of applied pain, or the durability of pain itself.

Czesław Miłosz is perfectly aware that language is not a tool of cognition but rather a tool of assimilation in what appears to be a quite hostile world—unless it is employed by poetry, which alone tries to beat language at its own game and thus to bring it as close as possible to real cognizance. Short-cutting or, rather, short-circuiting the analytical process, Miłosz's poetry releases the reader from many psychological and purely linguistic traps, for it answers not the question "how to live" but "for the sake of what" to live. In a way, what this poet preaches is an awfully sober version of stoicism which does not ignore reality, however absurd and horrendous, but accepts it as a new norm which a human being has to absorb without giving up any of his fairly compromised values.

New York

Born in Leningrad, **Joseph Brodsky** *(1940–1996) was awarded the Nobel Prize in Literature in 1987. He immigrated to the United States in 1972 and taught at several universities, including Mount Holyoke, Yale, Columbia, Cambridge, and Michigan. He was named U.S. Poet Laureate in 1991.*

Against the Dark and Immutable Order of the World
Czesław Miłosz

One of the essential attributes of poetry is its ability to give affirmation to things of this world. And I think with sadness of the negation which has so strongly marked the poetry of my century and my own poetry. When our historical and individual existence is filled with horror and suffering, we tend to see the world as a tangle of dark, indifferent forces. And yet human greatness and goodness and virtue have always been intervening in that life which I lived, and my writings have some merits to the extent that they are not deprived of a feeling of gratitude.

Logically, I should not have preserved my identity as a poet faithful to his native tongue throughout thirty years of exile. I explain it by a mysterious influence of a land where I was born, Lithuania, and of a city where I went to school and to university, Wilno. My high school teachers have been present in my poetry, either invoked by name or as invisible guests. It is probable that I would not have become a poet without what I received from them. Particularly, I was shaped by seven years of Latin and by exercises in translating Latin poetry in class. If the names of those teachers are forgotten, I, for one, remain their grateful pupil.

For many years I have been meditating upon zones of silence covering many events, deeds and names of our age. To quote myself: "I would have related, had I known how, everything which a single memory can gather in praise of men." *Had I known how*—in fact, writing praise is a struggle against the main current of modern literature. But now, in the last quarter of the twentieth century, looking back to the time of war and political terror, I think less of crime and baseness and more and more of human capability of the purest love and sacrifice. Had I to live much longer, I would search for means of expressing my humble respect for so many anonymous and heroic men and women.

The Neustadt literary prize belongs too, in my opinion, to those things which should not exist, because they are against the dark and immutable order of the world. Normally, it should be given to film stars or at least authors of best sellers. In my case it goes to a poet who can be read only in translation and whose poems do not translate well because of many cultural-linguistic allusions in their very texture. It goes to an author who, measured by the market standard, is a permanent flop and is read by a very small public only. The decision of founding such a prize seems to me a wise one, not only because I am a recipient, but because it favors all those who in the game of life bet on improbability.

The endeavors of Ivar Ivask are an example of human will interceding against the normal and the usual. There is no reason for survival of such a magazine as *World Literature Today* and no reason for the University of Oklahoma's attracting the attention of literary communities all over the world, as it does, because of that periodical and an international prize. Yet the order of the world has to inscribe that fact as one of its components.

Norman, Oklahoma
April 7, 1978

JOSEF ŠKVORECKÝ
THE 1980 LAUREATE

Josef Škvorecký (1924–2012) was a Czech author and publisher. After receiving his PhD in philosophy, Škvorecký began to write novels, which were banned by the Communist government of Czechoslovakia. Many of his works espoused democratic ideals that threatened the state, but his novels helped to usher in the Prague Spring in 1968. When the Russian army invaded Czechoslovakia that same year, Škvorecký and his wife sought asylum in Canada, where the pair founded a publishing house that printed banned Czech and Slovak books. Škvorecký resided in Canada for the remainder of his life. Among his numerous published works are novels, novellas, essays, and screenplays. His novels include *Zbabělci* (1958; Eng. *The Cowards*, 1970), *Lvíče* (1969; Eng. *Miss Silver's Past*, 1974), *Tankový prapor* (1969; Eng. *The Republic of Whores*, 1992), and *Příběh inženýra lidských duší* (1977; Eng. *The Engineer of Human Souls*, 1984).

I feel that the prize granted to me honors all my literary rivals and dear friends in Czechoslovakia, people who in conditions inconceivable to writers in the West have not abandoned their trade, which is, as Hemingway once said, to tell the truth.

—Josef Škvorecký

Josef Škvorecký, the Literary King
Arnošt Lustig

Ladies and gentlemen, it is a privilege for me to speak to you briefly about the winner of the 1980 Neustadt Prize, one of the best contemporary Czech writers, Josef Škvorecký. This is a very pleasant occasion. Škvorecký, who is here today to receive the prize in person, was born in Czechoslovakia fifty-five years ago and is living now in Canada, in his new home, like many exiles from Central Europe, where the storms of wars and revolutions come sooner and last longer. Škvorecký is the author of more than a dozen books, five screenplays and some beautiful poems. He is also the author of one of the best-known books on the golden age of Czech cinema, the new film wave of the sixties, and is a broadcaster for the Voice of America to Czechoslovakia on contemporary American literature, just as he was a translator of American culture to his people while he lived in Prague. He is also our colleague, a professor of English.

Like Franz Kafka, Josef Škvorecký is a man who writes in a minor language and has become, in translation, the spokesman for the mind and soul of people in far greater numbers than the original language could have reached. I would like to discuss with you some of the reasons why Škvorecký—as the critic of the *New Yorker*, George Steiner, put it, "a novelist of the first rank"— has become a writer of world importance.

As I was looking for a key for presenting the personality and work of Josef Škvorecký, another great Czech artist came to mind: the world-famous composer Antonín Dvořák, about whom Škvorecký is currently writing a novel and who was the composer of the *Symphony from the New World*. I like this comparison not only because Dvořák lived here in America from 1892 to 1895, but also because he was so much in love with the inspiration he found in America, like African American music or the cultures of the American Indians. This was the principal approach of Dvořák. While receptive to the influences of the world and able to open his mind and soul to everything, he also was able to absorb it and then to express it in his own fashion, in a creative amalgam, the unique magic of art in his very personal way. He expressed his view of the world in a manner never used either before him or after. While his way of looking at things was universal, cultivated by the world, it was also very original. His expression was undeniably his own, and yet was Czech at the same time.

Škvorecký too is open to all the influences of the world with his entire heart and soul, and still remains undeniably original, very Czech, very personal. There is an Italian proverb which states that a man who changes the stars above his head doesn't change his nature. Perhaps he enriches his point of view. Perhaps he is able to see more stars, and from a more important point of view. And sometimes, as in the case of Škvorecký, he can report what he has seen.

Škvorecký is a writer from a country which begat and gave birth to writers like Comenius, Franz Kafka, Jaroslav Hašek, and Karel Čapek, or writers such as Vladislav Vančura, Jiří Langer, and Jiří Weil and many others—some good and some very, very good. They say that Prague is a very good place for writers, that there is something which cannot die, in spite of the fact that it—from time to time—cannot even live. And in that group of writers, Škvorecký means to Czech literature something akin to what the name Joseph Conrad means to English literature, Gunter Grass to contemporary German writing or J. D. Salinger to American letters.

In the late fifties Škvorecký became known in Prague overnight. This sounds a little as if it were a phrase made for the American public, but here we know that an overnight success is never really overnight, that it is a result of talent, hard work, and, only in the last place, luck as well. The scandal of Škvorecký was also similar to French history's case of Gustave Flaubert, who was tried because of his offense to the double standards of French society, whereby one could not behave at home as in public. But Flaubert's Emma Bovary was an innocent woman compared to Škvorecký. The literary perversions of Josef Škvorecký were of a different nature.

Nothing can match the very originality or, if you wish, the very absurdity of the literary conditions in the empire of the greatest hope on earth before it becomes the greatest disappointment. While the mighty literary establishment was roaring with official optimism and revolutionary promises, with the romance of the future based on the heroic past, Škvorecký, like a young, inexperienced boy from the countryside, came to Prague to publish his first novel. It was a personal account of the revolution, numbering 370 printed pages and bearing the title *The Cowards*. There was not a book in Prague more discussed than this one. The English television film *Death of a Princess* and the resulting Saudi Arabian protest are only a faint echo of what the Czech "sheiks" did to Škvorecký s book. The nation was divided overnight. The Politburo could not believe that a single book would do it to them.

Škvorecký wrote in his first—and, as many say even today, his best— book about eight days in the revolution against the Germans in a small Czech city, about a group of boys and girls who were quite happy that with the end of the war everything else was going to burn out, to be changed, and that they would be able to start a new life. He did not speak about the idols. He did not pay attention or even polite honor to those who were now in charge. His hero and the storyteller, in one voice, expressed his lack of understanding of the world, built and managed so absurdly by the fathers. He alone had the courage to say that he didn't understand, that he didn't know. This hero was not easy to understand. He was more complicated than the heroes of Czech literature before him. That was the crime of Josef Škvorecký.

The book was, of course, banned immediately. The fate of the young writer was up in the air. Škvorecký was described as a counterrevolutionary, as an anti-Soviet, petit-bourgeois element, as a man who, in his book, says more about himself than about his hero, about his own approaches, his own qualities. He was described as an agent of decadence, an agent provocateur, and the official press labeled him everything from a conventional to an immoral writer, a perverted author who tries to turn the clock of history backward. To be described as foreign to the spirit of people was an accusation whose equivalent in prison terms could be as much as a life sentence, if not worse. Today this is all evidence of Škvorecký's courage, of his honesty, of his democratic feeling. When he is described today in the *New York Times,* the

Washington Post or *Le Monde* as "a fearless writer, a symbol of free writing," it must be traced to his very first book, *The Cowards.*

Fortunately, Škvorecký was luckier than his book. After he had become a "non-person," the better times of the era of liberalization enabled him to publish his "Legend of Emöke," a beautiful story, so highly praised last year all over the world as one of the best novellas of our time. Some say that "Emöke" is about a chance a man gets only once in his life; others assert that it is a myth, a real legend, powerful and beautiful, that it is a book about courage, about the greatness and sacrifice of man, about his desire to be a man, about relating to a woman, which means relating to the entire world. It is a tale which imparts a feeling that man has a chance, that he may hope to change a bad life for a better one, that it is in his hands.

In all his books Škvorecký attacks the cowardice of life, the brutality of life, the smallness of life. What makes him such a good writer is his sense of tension, his awareness of the duty of a writer to write interestingly, with wit and suspense. The proof is his novel *Miss Silver's Past.* I like this book more than the others, and not only because it is a book about a lonely Jewish girl who, with the help of a man who now courts her beauty, challenges the postwar world alone, all her people killed and her family destroyed. Škvorecký was one of those writers with conscience, one who remembered Hitler's remark that what is Jewish is perverted and crippled, that the human conscience cripples the mind just as circumcision cripples the body.

Škvorecký wrote a beautiful story about Rebecca, "The Menorah." He did not look left, nor did he look right when searching for his themes. As a democrat with a writer's heart, he was always on the side of the underdog, and it was more than a statement when Škvorecký, a non-Jewish author, wrote in Prague about the Jewish children—of the approximately 15,000 living in Czechoslovakia before the war, only 100 survived. When the secretary general of an anti-Fascist organization in Czechoslovakia claimed that nobody in Prague was interested in glorifying those who went to their death without fighting, Škvorecký understood better than this official that it is somehow difficult for babies, for boys and girls without weapons, for old women to fight a German army which had defeated, in a few days, France, Poland and almost all the rest of Europe.

Škvorecký is a very creative person. It was a fitting choice that the judges voted to include him in a select field of writers such as Czesław Miłosz, Gabriel García Márquez, and Giuseppe Ungaretti. Not only is he rightly compared to those writers, but more, he has an extra sense of humor that is very Czech, unique, and is the core of what the established "sheiks" of socialist-realist literature fear most. Škvorecký not only makes us cry, but he makes us smile too. This is, in this crumbling world of ours, an essential contribution. He pays attention to the mysteries of life, and his observations of strange reality are marvelous. [. . .]

Ladies and gentlemen, I had ten reasons for nominating Josef Škvorecký for the 1980 Neustadt Prize. I was proud to do it. But I never quoted the letters of Graham Greene, and I would like to do this today.

7 October 1968

Dear Josef Škvorecký,

I have this moment finished reading *La Légende d'Emöke*. It is masterly and can stand comparison with Chekhov's *The Lady with the Dog*. *The Game in the Train* is magnificent, but perhaps the most moving phrase to me came at the end: "Cette indifférence qui est notre mère, notre salut, notre porte." Anyway it's a master work. I would be glad to have news of you. Are you going to England? I am told that Sir Gerald Barry has formed a committee to help Czech writers and intellectuals. He knows me and if you feel like communicating with him do use my name and say that I suggested it. I am dictating this letter to my secretary in England and I will ask her to add his address.

Yours ever,

/s/ Graham Greene

20 March 1974

My dear Škvorecký,

I've read the two stories you sent me and I shall now forward them on to Max Reinhardt. *The Bass Saxophone* I found superb—it made as great impression on me as a few years back *The Legend of Emöke*. *Pink Champagne* interested me less, but to make a volume it is certainly needed. Forgive a hasty line but I wanted to get a message off to you as quickly as possible and to sense my great admiration for the Saxophone.

Yours ever,

/s/ Graham Greene

I would like to add only a few comments. An award for Josef Škvorecký means an award for all of Czech literature: to that part of it which must be silent at home, and to her sister, the literature in exile. It is also proof that literature cannot be silenced. But it is not always so easy.

Literature is, unfortunately or fortunately, connected in our age with history, politics, philosophy, with everything in which man is involved. During Škvorecký's lifetime so many things have happened, and so many happened so close. A writer who comes from our country—which was given in appeasement by Chamberlain to Hitler in 1938, a country where children were listening to the news of how Mussolini was bravely defeating the barefooted Ethiopians with his tanks and how the Spanish Republic was lost because of Western indifference—the writer is up to his neck in politics. A writer in that part of the world has a taste of history involving human fate, like those children who are ill with a sickness that comes to them from their mothers' breasts without anyone's knowing it; years afterward, when they know, it is too late for a cure.

Why am I saying this? Because to listen to a writer means to know and maybe to be able to prevent. Kafka saw the penal colonies before they covered Europe like a plague. To recognize a writer sometimes takes a lifetime and sometimes centuries. Some writers, never discovered, disappear in the abyss of the forgotten, as does their work—sometimes in an abyss, sometimes in flames, sometimes in silence. The lives and works of some writers disappear so completely, it is as if they had never been alive, had never written. That is why recognition of a writer is so important—just like the conquest of a new continent, the finding of a secret treasure or the discovery of a new star.

There is an old proverb which states that a king who is not accepted by his people is not yet a king. Today Josef Škvorecký, the voice of Czech literature at home as in exile, opposed by the authorities in his native land and welcomed and loved by people abroad, is a king. Kings of literary realms are, contrary to other rulers, not dangerous to living creatures. They are threats only to the minds of those who claim the ownership of people as if it were the ownership of goods, those who—as in the dark times of history—are today trading and selling people for money, goods and political gain, especially writers. Literary kings do not kill their enemies; they do not kill people at all, with the exception of themselves.

Literary kings are, in comparison with the real kings of the world, more gentle, more silent, more generous, in spite of the fact that literary kings, like all kings, must fight from time to time. Josef Škvorecký is not one of those people who, by claiming that they are fighting the last battle of man, are ready to bury not only man but his world as well. It is a beautiful privilege to say that Josef Škvorecký is a winner today, and to know that he wins in the name of, and for, all of us. It must be marvelous to be a literary king. Thank you.

Norman, Oklahoma
May 17, 1980

The Jewish Czech writer **Arnošt Lustig** *(1926–2011) survived the Theresienstadt, Auschwitz, and Buchenwald concentration camps. After the Prague Spring (1968), he eventually immigrated to the United States, where he taught at American University in Washington, D.C., before returning to Prague after the Velvet Revolution (1989). The author of novels, short stories, plays, and screenplays, he was awarded the Karel Čapek Prize in 1996 and the Franz Kafka Prize in 2008.*

Truth-telling and Literary Freedom in Czechoslovakia
Josef Škvorecký

Twenty-two years ago, when my first novel *The Cowards* was published in Prague and a month later banned by the censor and confiscated from bookshops by the police, a well-orchestrated band of hired Communist Party critics pounced upon me, and at the very top of a long list of the sins and crimes I had allegedly committed in that novel, they placed the sin—or the crime—of individualism. It was indicative of the literary erudition of those critics that they deduced this individualism chiefly from the narrative mode I had chosen: the first-person singular. They had no notion of what is generally well known in the writers' trade, that the I-form is usually the least individualized of all forms, and that therefore the narrator is usually the least vivid character in the book.

This also presented an interesting paradox, which I am acutely aware of whenever I think back on the 1960s in Prague. At that time Czech literature was rapidly recovering from the almost mortal blow it was dealt by the imported socialist realism of the 1950s. Suddenly, against the collective background of hack writers who practiced that establishment literary method, a few magnificently individual authors began to appear. Along with the safely dead classics, people began once more to buy contemporary prose, and thus competition developed among those authors who had laid aside—or who had simply never adopted—that uniform mask of socialist realism. They were all able, at last, to show their own faces.

Yet—and here is the paradox—whenever I think of the 1950s, a decade branded by the establishment's notion of a collective *we*, it is always in terms of "I," whereas I never think of the 1960s, when individualism was flourishing, in any terms other than "we"—"we" referring to us Czech writers who, having painted our world in rosy hues for so long, desired to show the face of our native land and its people exactly as we saw them and loved them, without the pink makeup.

When I learned that I had been awarded the Neustadt Prize, that grand old notion of "we" came to mind, and my first thought was about my literary rivals from the sixties, those dear friends of mine: Václav Havel, who is now in prison and will remain there for another five years; Jiří Lederer, who once defended my *Cowards* and lost his job because of it, now just recently returned from four years in jail; Jiří Pištora, a poet who committed suicide after the Soviet divisions invaded my native land. And many others who are without work and cannot publish.

Why was I chosen? Why not one of them? Am I better than they are? And are they genuinely good in relation to the notoriety they have gained through persecution?

The cultural establishment of Czechoslovakia today is trying in every way it can to make cultivated westerners think that such writers are not good at all, but merely notorious; they would have you believe there is no such thing as a "Biafra of the spirit" in Czechoslovakia, as Aragon once wrote, or a "graveyard of culture," as Heinrich Böll has said. If you wish, the cultural attaché of the Czechoslovak Socialist Republic will willingly send you statistics that measure culture by the weight of paper used to make books and that try to overwhelm you with the number of books published by contemporary authors living in Prague.

It is extremely difficult to explain to westerners, who are separated from an understanding of the real situation by an ignorance of foreign languages that are far more widely used than Czech, just what kind of authors these people are. Nor do I claim that everyone who can publish legally in Prague today is an ordinary hack writer. But a kind of fanciful analogy occurred to me. Let us imagine that Mark Twain had written his *Huckleberry Finn* some thirty years before he did and tried to have it published in his native South. We must also imagine, however, that the southern slave-owners in the first half of the nineteenth century had a literary censorship equally as strict as today's socialist Czechoslovakia has. Mark Twain would undoubtedly have known that trying to publish, in a slave-owning society, a novel about the inhumanity of slavery would have been—as we might say today—unrealistic. But his great talent and the desire to write would remain. So instead of trying to publish that novel about the inhumanity of slavery, he would write another one instead, one, let's say, about the decline of table manners in the Deep South, about how people pick their teeth while eating and don't always hit the spittoon when they spit. No doubt it would be a very amusing, masterfully written and absolutely truthful humoresque about life in the slaveholding South.

The best novels coming out of Prague today are precisely of that type. The ones that do not get published, that are merely copied on typewriters for the *samizdat* Padlock Editions, are novels about the friendship of a poor white boy and an equally poor black slave. I flatter myself that even though my work can be published—because I live in the West—I still belong in a certain sense to those unpublished authors for whom human freedom is a more urgent literary theme than picking one's teeth. I feel that the prize granted to me honors all my literary rivals and dear friends in Czechoslovakia, people who in conditions inconceivable to writers in the West have not abandoned their trade, which is, as Hemingway once said, *to tell the truth*. The truth, that is, about Nigger Jim, and not about tobacco-chewers who can't hit a spittoon.

Norman, Oklahoma
May 17, 1980

OCTAVIO PAZ
THE 1982 LAUREATE

Octavio Paz (1914–1998) was born and raised in Mixcoac, part of present-day Mexico City. His family supported Emiliano Zapata, and after Zapata's assassination they were forced into exile in the United States. Paz was only nineteen when he published his first collection of poetry, entitled *Luna Silvestre* (1933). During his long career, Paz founded the literary journals *Barandal* (1932) and *Taller* (1938) and the magazines *Plural* (1970) and *Vuelta* (1975). In 1945 he began working as a diplomat for the Mexican government in such places as Paris, Tokyo, Geneva, and Mumbai. His travels influenced much of his work, and he published many of his books while working abroad. Paz's numerous collections of poetry include *Entre la piedra y la flor* (1941), *Piedra de sol* (1957; Eng. *Sun Stone*, 1991), and *Renga* (1972). Additionally, Paz wrote many essays, short stories, and plays, including *El laberinto de la soledad* (1950; Eng. *The Labyrinth of Solitude*, 1961), *Corriente alterna* (1967; Eng. *Alternating*

Current, 1973), and *La hija de Rappaccini* (1956). In addition to the Neustadt Prize in 1982, Paz was awarded the 1981 Miguel de Cervantes Prize and the Nobel Prize in Literature in 1990.

> Considering all this, in the convulsed and intolerant modern world we inhabit, the Neustadt Prize is an example of true civilization.
>
> —Octavio Paz

The Turning House
Octavio Paz

for Ivar and Astrid

There is a wooden house
on the plain of Oklahoma.
Each night the house turns
into an island of the Baltic Sea,
a stone that fell from a fabled sky.
Burnished by Astrid's glances,
ignited by Ivar's voice,
the stone slowly turns in the shadow:
it is a sunflower and burns.
                         A cat,
returned from Saturn,
goes through the wall and disappears
between the pages of a book.
The grass has turned into night,
the night has turned into sand,
the sand has turned into water.
                         Then
Ivar and Astrid lift up architectures
—cubes of echoes, weightless forms—
some of them called poems,
others drawings, others conversations
with friends from Málaga, Mexico
and other planets.
                    These forms
wander and have no feet,
glance and have no eyes,

speak and have no mouth.
>   The sunflower
turns and does not move,
>   the island
ignites and is extinguished,
>   the stone
flowers,
>   the night closes,
the sky opens.
>   Dawn
wets the lids of the plain.

(1982/83)

Translation from the Spanish by Ivar Ivask

Octavio Paz: The Poet as Philosopher
Manuel Durán

The poet Derek Walcott remarked recently, "The greatest writers have been at heart parochial, provincial in their rootedness. . . . Shakespeare remains a Warwickshire country boy; Joyce a minor bourgeois from Dublin, Dante's love of Florence was very intense. Hardy's place, of course, was rural Essex: 'I can understand / Borges's blind love for Buenos Aires, / How a man feels the veins of his city swell in his head' (Midsummer '81)."[1] There are many books and poems by Paz that proclaim his rootedness, his intimacy with Mexican traditions, landscapes, people. Books like *The Labyrinth of Solitude,* for instance, or *Posdata* could not have been written by anyone outside the mainstream of Mexican culture. No foreign observer could have given such books the impact and urgency they possess. Paz is not content with describing some of the deepest and most relevant aspects of Mexican psychology; he involves the reader in the system of values he describes because he is himself involved in it for better or for worse, inescapably. It is ancient Mexican culture with its circular patterns that molds a long poem such as *Sun Stone;* it is the experience of being an adolescent in and around Mexico City that imparts distinctive flavor to Paz's "Nocturno de San Ildefonso."

Yet very often at the conclusion of Paz's sustained efforts to explore his roots and the origins of his culture, a change of mood and of ideas begins to emerge. From the poet's direct and intimate experience he leads us toward a deeper knowledge of what it is to be a Mexican living and working in the present century, within a culture as tragic and fragmented as it is rich and complex. But the poet's experience allows him to express also much that belongs to our experience. His exploration of Mexican existential values permits him to open a door to an understanding of other countries and other cultures. What began as a slow, almost microscopic examination of self and of a single cultural tradition widens unexpectedly, becoming universal without sacrificing its unique characteristic.

This is a special gift, a gift few poets possess. The inescapable conclusion is that Paz belongs to a select group of poets who can expand the limits of poetry until they invade the realm of philosophy. Paz is a poetphilosopher, a philosophical poet. Such a gift has never been widespread. Among the classics, for instance, Lucretius would qualify, but not Catullus. Dante was a philosophical poet, and so were Shakespeare and Milton, Donne and Eliot. In each of these instances we find a persistent exploration of nature, of the place of human beings in nature. What is our place in the cosmos? Are we, as we often think in our pride, the masters of nature, the almost perfect creation of a protecting and loving God? Are we intruders barely tolerated? Are we, as Shakespeare claims in a somber moment, no more to the gods than flies are to wanton children, flies which they kill as a pastime? Or are we enveloped by the very same love which, as Dante explains, is the force that moves the Sun and the other stars? Philosophical poets may differ widely with respect to the answers they give to the riddles of life. What they have in common, however, is a mixture of curiosity and awe, and this is much more important than what separates them.

The philosopher-poet is always ready to travel with his mind and his body, through time and through space. Octavio Paz has traveled as widely as he has written, and as Anna Balakian has said, he "belongs to that new breed of humans, more numerous each day, who are freeing themselves of ethnic myopia and walking the earth as inhabitants of the planet, regardless of national origin or political preferences."[2]

It is entirely possible that all human beings are born poets, born philosophers, born scientists, but that circumstances and a poor education shrink or atrophy the imagination and the curiosity that would sustain such activities. Fortunately for us, Paz was a poet and a curious observer since childhood and has managed to retain a child's heart and vision. A sense of being open to the world was among his childhood's more precious gifts. Paz has said about himself:

> As a boy I lived in a place called Mixcoac, near the capital. We lived in a large house with a garden. Our family had been impoverished by the revolution and the civil war. Our house, full of antique furniture, books, and other objects, was gradually crumbling to bits. As rooms collapsed we moved the furniture into another. I remember that for a long time I lived in a spacious room with part of one of the walls missing. Some magnificent screens protected me inadequately from wind and rain. A creeper invaded my room. . . . A premonition of that surrealist exhibition where there was a bed lying in a swamp.[3]

I see in this room invaded by rain, wind and plants a symbol of the poet's career, always open to the wind coming from every direction of the compass, always exposed to the outside world and the forces of nature—a room quite the opposite of a fortress or an ivory tower. From this exposed vantage point the poet ventures forth. His goal is not only to see infinity in a grain of sand, as William Blake proposed, but at the same time to describe the texture and color of the grain of sand, to see its reflection in his eye—and ours.

Paz knows that human beings have many roots, not a single taproot, fibrous roots that connect them with many cultures, many pasts. The themes, meanings, images by which poetic imagination seeks to penetrate to the heart of reality—the permanence and mystery of human suffering, human hope, joy and wonder—reach the poet from many sources. The poet sees existence with the double vision of tragedy, the good and the evil forever mixed. He is constantly under strain, admitting dire realities and conscious of bleak possibilities. Yet he is aware that love, knowledge, art, poetry allow us to experience the unity and final identity of being.

Ultimately Paz as a poet is a master of language, yet one who recognizes that language is also our shaper and ruler. If the German philosopher Ernst Cassirer defined man as the animal who can create language and myths, we can also state that it is language, myths, poetry that have created man, that have made man into a speaking, mythmaking, poetry-writing animal. It is through language that Paz faces the world, sees the world as a unity, confronts the diversities of culture and explains their apparent oppositions and contradictions, their conjunctions and disjunctions, as different responses to the same identical questions. To understand is to see correspondences and patterns, structures of symmetry and dissymmetry, constellations of signs in space and in time—yet anything can be expressed and related through words. In Paz's manysplendored vision the poet is capable of flying through space and time, because like the magical monkey of Hindu legend, Hanumān, he has invented grammar and language.

From above, in his vertical flight, drunk with light and with love, the poet contemplates the fusion of opposites, the marriage of Heaven and Hell, the radiance of the void, the dark luminosity where life and death meet. The movements of planets, the patterns of seasons and nature, are circular, yet the circle becomes a spiral pointing toward vaster spaces where everything becomes possible, where I become the Other, where the labyrinth of mirrors fuses into a single blinding light. We learn to say "no" and "yes" at the same time, because through poetry we reach the certain knowledge that Becoming and Being are two facets of the same reality. As Paz describes it, "The spirit / Is an invention of the body / The body / An invention of the world / The world / An invention of the spirit" (*Blanco*).[4] Within this is language, poetic language, the language of myths and of passion that has made us what we are. Language is a huge shuttle going back and forth, weaving our world, and the poet is at the center of this operation. "By passion the world is bound, by passion too it is released," reads the epigraph from Buddhist tradition *(The Hevajra Tantra)* that frames what is perhaps Paz's most famous poem, *Blanco*. As a poet, Paz is the master of words. Word of passion, words of wisdom. They can create our ultimate vision; they can also erase it.

*

An English poet-philosopher, John Donne, wisely warns us that when we hear the bell toll for someone's death we should realize that it tolls for us, that someone else's death in a subtle but certain way diminishes us, partially kills us, for we are part and parcel of the fabric which this death unravels. I would like to point out a reverse situation: when a poet's work is heard, understood, applauded, it is a triumph for life, a celebration of Being, and therefore it is *our* victory, *our* glory, that is heard in the joyous pealing of the bell.

This celebration of Being is instinctively clear to the philosophical poet because he or she is often conscious of speaking, feeling, writing not only for himself or herself, but for all of us. Sympathy unites the philosophical poet to other human beings that he or she may not know and with whom he or she may superficially have little in common. A capacity for generalized feelings, visions, ideas is another feature of the philosophical poet that makes his or her voice different from the voices of other poets. The philosophical poet sees and describes a specific flower, a yellow rose or a purple iris, and at the same time there is a space in his mind, in his imagination, in his soul, where the rose and the iris come closer and closer to a perfect flower, the Platonic flower described by Mallarmé as "l'absente de tout bouquet"—the flower that is the essence of all flowers and therefore absent from any real bouquet.

Unless the description given above sounds too precious, we should agree on a few basic points. Aristotle stated that there can be no scientific description, no scientific knowledge, until and unless it is generalized description, knowledge, statement. The efforts of the pre-Socratic Greek philosophers were already moving in the same direction. Poetry is a personal statement, the most individualistic and intimate statement if we mean by *poetry* what most readers accept as its basic definition: that is to say, lyric poetry. How can any writer bridge the gap between the individual vision and the generalized overview of our world?

Octavio Paz gives us the answer in almost every one of his books. An analysis of his techniques as related to both his style and his ideas would become lengthy if applied to all his texts. It is reasonable to choose two individual texts, one old and one relatively new, one a prose book and the other a poem. The first is perhaps Paz's most celebrated and widely read book, his obvious best seller, *The Labyrinth of Solitude,* whereas the second, chosen in order to show how Paz is a consistently philosophical poet, is *Blanco,* a philosophical poem which both rivals and complements—perhaps *contradicts* would be a better word—T. S. Eliot's *The Waste Land.*

In *The Labyrinth of Solitude,* Paz approaches a difficult problem: how to define and explain the feelings of identity and lack of identity of today's Mexicans, especially of those Mexicans who are conscious of living, thinking and feeling according to a Mexican system of values. He uses the vocabulary and the stylistic resources of poetry: images, metaphors, oxymorons, conceits, all the figures of speech. Images and symbols, however, cluster around certain basic observations, which are often derived from a comparison with other sensitivities, other systems of values, whether American, west European or from the Orient. Early enough in the book Paz avows that most of what he has to say about being Mexican came to his mind during the two years he resided in the United States. In order to define what is Mexican, he had to understand and define several other cultural traditions and value systems: only then, profiled by the ways of life that are different, the geographical and temporal space where Mexican values are to appear begins to emerge.

This is so because the identity of an individual or a group assumes the "otherness" of the individuals and groups that surround them. The world is incredibly rich and complex: we can find our place in it only after acknowledging its thousand faces. As Paz puts it in his words of acceptance of the Neustadt International Prize for 1982:

> In esthetic terms, Plurality is a richness of voices, accents, manners, ideas and visions; in moral terms, Plurality signifies tolerance of diversity, renunciation of dogmatism and recognition of the unique and singular value of each work and every personality. Plurality is Universality, and Universality is the acknowledging of the admirable diversity of man and his works. . . . To acknowledge the variety of visions and sensibilities is to preserve the richness of life and thus to ensure its continuity.

Paz knows by instinct what German philosophers of the Romantic era—Fichte, Schelling, Hegel—found out through arduous reasoning and what in our own time Martin Buber has restated successfully: there is no *I* without a *Thou;* there is no individuality without an "otherness," a plurality. We know everything, we are everything and everybody if, and only if and when, we acknowledge our diversity, engage in a dialogue with everybody else, create bridges between human beings and their own past, their traditions and hopes. A dialogue between ourselves and nature, between human history and the history of the cosmos.

It goes without saying that when a poet invades the realm of philosophy, the impact is bound to be strong and enduring. Philosophers deal with questions that we all care about, but they often are clumsy and obscure in the way they state them and in the way they make their conclusions explicit. Few philosophers are forceful writers. So few, in fact, that their lack of expertise about language and communication is perhaps the major factor that has brought philosophy into disarray and ineffectiveness in our time. Plato was a first-rate writer; so were Nietzsche, Bergson, Ortega y Gasset.

A concern with language, a concern about language, is what poets and philosophers have most in common. Modern philosophy from Descartes to the present has paid constant attention to the tools that have helped us reach toward knowledge, and foremost among these tools is language, which brings us knowledge in such a grasping, intimate way that we receive both knowledge and language at the same time, closely intertwined. Young Emerson points out in his journals, "The progress of metaphysics may be found to consist in nothing else than the progressive introduction of apposite metaphors."[5]

Paz is committed to language, not only because he is a poet, but also because as a thinking man he sees in language a meeting place of space and time, essence and existence. "The word is man himself. We are made of words. They are our only reality, or at least, the only testimony of our reality," Paz assures us in *The Bow and the Lyre*. Moreover, as Paz writes in *Alternating Current,* "The problem of meaning in poetry becomes clear as soon as we notice that the meaning is not to be found outside, but rather inside the poem; it is not to be found in what the words have to say, but rather in what the words *have to say to each other*" (". . . en aquello que *se dicen entre ellas*").

It is perhaps in *Blanco,* a long poem published in 1966, that Paz reaches his highest level as a philosophical poet. *Blanco* is a text that unfolds in several ways. We can read it as a whole, from beginning to end, or we can read first the central column, which deals with the birth of words, the birth of language. To the left of this central column is another column, a poem in itself if we choose to read it as such, an erotic poem divided into four sections which stand for the four elements in the physical world. To the right of the central column we find another column, another poem, also divided into four parts: it deals with sensation, perception, imagination and understanding. Read as a whole, *Blanco* can be baffling and exasperating if we do not understand that it is the interaction of the different parts across time (the time it takes to read the poem) and space (the printed page with its white spaces surrounding the texts as silence surrounds our words) that conveys the message. Language cannot be born, Paz seems to say in this poem, unless we combine into one single unit space, time, sensuousness, passion and silence.

It is through language that we can approach the world around us, Paz seems to tell us, and each new word created by us enriches us with a new treasure—with the joy which this victory produces we find new strength to go on

and invent new words. This is the way he describes the creation of the word
sunflower:

> Survivor
> Among taciturn confusions,
>   It ascends
> On a copper stalk
>   Dissolved
> In a foliage of clarity,
>   Refuge
> Of fallen realities.
>   Asleep
> Or extinct,
>   High on its pole
> (Head on a pike)
>   A sunflower
> Already carbonized light
>   Above a glass
> Of shadow.
>   In the palm of a hand
> Fictitious,
>   Flower
> Neither seen nor thought:
>   Heard,
> It appears
>   Yellow
> Calyx of consonants and vowels
> All burning. (177–79)

Flashes of light and color, metaphors, images, synesthesia precede and follow
the word sunflower (*girasol*), helping in its birth, reinforcing its presence and
its meaning. Everything begins and ends in words. Words, on the other hand,
need us, need our senses, our passion, in order to be born. In an audacious

reverse movement similar to the flight of a boomerang, Paz compels poetic language to turn around and examine itself, examine words and sentences, in order to seize the second in which a sensation becomes a word.

As Ricardo Gullón has stated, "Paz, like André Breton, understands that the language of passion and the passion of language are on good terms with one another, that they are the recto and verso page of the same attitude. Moreover, language is where song happens. There is no song without words, even though a song can be diminished to a susurration or concealed in a number."[6] Poetry, language, passion: these are key words for anyone approaching Paz's texts. It is the way he relates and combines them that makes his message a universal one, no matter how closely related many of his poems and essays are to the Mexican soil and culture that shaped him. By approaching language through poetry and passion he deals with a universal fact—there is no culture without language, and language belongs to all of us—through feelings (sensuousness, sexual passion) that are also our common heritage. An intellectual and philosophical quest has been carried out through experiences that can be shared by all. Can there be a greater achievement for a philosopher-poet?

Yale University

Editorial note: Durán's essay is an expanded version of the encomium that he delivered at the 1982 Neustadt Prize award ceremonies on 9 June at the University of Oklahoma.

1. James Atlas, "Derek Walcott, Poet of Two Worlds," *New York Times Magazine,* 23 May 1982, 32.

2. Anna Balakian, "Focus on Octavio Paz and Severo Sarduy," *Review 72,* Fall 1972.

3. Rita Guibert, "Paz on Himself and His Writing: Selections from an Interview," in *The Perpetual Present: The Poetry and Prose of Octavio Paz,* ed. Ivar Ivask (Norman: University of Oklahoma Press, 1973), 25.

4. Octavio Paz, "Blanco," trans. Charles Tomlinson and G. Aroul, in *Configurations* (New York: New Directions, 1971), 193.

5. Quoted in "Emerson in His Journals," *New York Times Book Review,* 20 June 1982, 20.

6. Ricardo Gullón, "The Universalism of Octavio Paz," in *The Perpetual Present,* 80.

Manuel Durán *(b. 1925, Barcelona) is an emeritus professor in the Department of Spanish and Portuguese at Yale University and a longtime editorial board member of* World Literature Today. *After publishing an essay on Spanish and Spanish American writers in the "Nobel Prize Symposium" issue of* Books Abroad *(Winter 1967), the Swedish Academy invited him to take part in a symposium in Stockholm in September 1967.*

Literature as a Compass on the Navigable Sea
Octavio Paz

Dr. William S. Banowsky, President of the University of Oklahoma; Mrs. Doris Neustadt; Ladies and Gentlemen.

In all languages there are limpid words which are like air and the water of the spirit. To express such words is always marvelous and furthermore necessary, like breathing. One such word is *gracias*, thank you. Today I pronounce it with joy. Also with the awareness of being the object of a happy confusion. The truth is that I am not very certain of the value of my writings. On the other hand, I am certain of my literary passion: it was born with me and will die only when I die. This belief consoles me. The jurors were not completely mistaken in awarding me the Neustadt International Prize for 1982: they wanted to reward, in my case, if not excellence, then obstinacy. . . . I shall not say more about my feelings. I am no more than the incidental (or accidental?) cause, and so what should count, however deep my gratitude, is not my person but the significance of the Neustadt Prize. It is worth reflecting upon this for a moment.

Situated in the center of the United States and surrounded by immense plains, Oklahoma seemed destined due to geographic fate for interior activity and historical apartness. However, the relation of every society with its surrounding physical reality is one of contradiction: men who inhabit a valley climb mountains which separate them from the world, and men of the plains move along the endless expanse as if it were a navigable sea. These are opposite and reversible metaphors: the desert is a sea for the Arab, and the sea is a desert for the sailor. In each case the metaphor is a challenge and an invitation: the horizon remains at the same time a call and an obstacle. In the domain of literary communication, Oklahoma has overcome isolation and distance through a series of exemplary initiatives.

The first was the founding of the journal *Books Abroad* in 1927 by Roy Temple House. I remember how many years ago, when I was studying for the bachelor's degree and was beginning to discover literature for myself, a copy of the journal came into my hands. In those days the literary isolation of Mexico was almost absolute, to the degree that when I read those pages I felt the opening of the doors of contemporary literature in languages other than my own. For a while *Books Abroad* was my compass, and foreign literatures ceased to be for me an impenetrable forest. *Books Abroad* no longer exists, not because it has disappeared but because it has been transformed, enlarged and rejuvenated. Under the energetic and intelligent editorship of Ivar Ivask, a poet who himself is a lucid and intrepid literary explorer, the review has grown. It is now called *World Literature Today* and has become an indispensable periodical for all those who want to keep up with contemporary literature on a worldwide scale. I stress the word *worldwide*, which must be understood literally: *World Literature Today* is not dedicated only to the analysis of literature from the major European languages, but it also follows with genuine and admirable sympathy, not lacking in rigor, the development of letters in the so-called minor languages. It is no secret that these languages are often rich in notable works and original talents.

Following the example of *World Literature Today* and inspired by it, there have emerged during these last few years other activities which exhibit the same universal calling. One of these activities has been the series of symposia which are convened periodically at the University of Oklahoma honoring writers in Spanish or French. In these conferences critics from both the Americas and from Europe participate, and the papers and discussions represent, in many cases, essential contributions in the field of contemporary Hispanic and French literature.

Another manifestation, no doubt the most important to date, has been the establishment in 1969 of the Neustadt International Prize for Literature. In many countries there exist national literary prizes to single out a writer in a common language of several nations. On the other hand, there are very few literary prizes indeed which are truly *international*. Among these a place apart is occupied by the Neustadt Prize. Two characteristics lend it a unique face: the first is that each jury is composed of critics and writers belonging to different languages and literatures, which means that it constitutes an *international* body, as international as the prize itself; the second characteristic is that the jury is not permanent but instead changes from one prize to the next—that is, every two years. These two characteristics translate into two words: *Universality* and *Plurality*. Due to the first word, the prize has been awarded to poets and novelists in Italian, English, French, Polish, Spanish and Czech; due to the second word, Plurality, we find among the laureates not only writers of different languages but also of different literary and philosophical persuasions. In esthetic terms, Plurality is a richness of voices, accents, manners, ideas and visions; in moral terms, Plurality signifies tolerance of diversity, renunciation of dogmatism and recognition of the unique and singular value of each work and every personality. Plurality is Universality, and Universality is the acknowledging of the admirable diversity of man and his works. Considering all this, in the convulsed and intolerant modern world we inhabit, the Neustadt Prize is an example of true civilization. I will say even more: to acknowledge the variety of visions and sensibilities is to preserve the richness of life and thus to ensure its continuity. Hence the Neustadt Prize, in stimulating the universality and diversity of literature, defends life itself.

Norman, Oklahoma
June 9, 1982

PAAVO HAAVIKKO
THE 1984 LAUREATE

Finnish poet and playwright **Paavo Haavikko** (1931–2008) was born in Helsinki and lived there until his death. He published his first collection of poetry in 1951 at the age of twenty. After three more verse collections, two three-act plays, and two novels, Haavikko's first English-translated piece was published in 1961. Haavikko embraced the modernist movement in Finland and, through his prolific works, influenced many other genres of Finnish literature in his lifetime. Through his literary achievements, Haavikko became the leading writer of his generation and of the postwar period in Finland. Haavikko's poetry collections include *Tiet etädisyyksiin* (1951), *Talvipalatsi* (1959; Eng. *The Winter Palace*, 1967), *Kaksikymmentdja yksi* (1974; Eng. *One and Twenty*, 2007), and *Sillat: Valitut runot* (1984). His works of drama include the titles *Agricola ja kettu* (1968; Eng. *Agricola the Fox*, 1985) and *Kuningas Idhtee Ranskaan* (1974; Eng. *The King Goes Forth to France*, 1984).

It is the writer's lot to go on
working, in the dark, in motion,
free, alone, available. The value
of this work is not in immutable,
established classics; it is not in any
completed book; it is in the endless
work itself, the endless effort to
remain free and unbound.

—Paavo Haavikko

Paavo Haavikko's History of an Unknown Nation
Bo Carpelan

Already in his first collection of poetry, *The Ways to Far Away* (1951), Paavo Haavikko at the age of twenty emerged as a poet with a personal and original profile. As a matter of fact, his debut represented the final breakthrough of Finnish modernism. Ten years and five volumes later, in 1961, he was characterized as a "classic of modernism." Now, in 1984, he stands as the foremost living Finnish writer. Like every author of importance, he has created his own world of expression, not only linguistically but also in terms of ideas. This universe comprises, in addition to poetry, a good many short stories, novels, aphorisms and plays for stage and radio. To this should be added a controversial and brilliant history of Finland, *The National Line*, subtitled *Comments on the History of an Unknown Nation, 1904–1975*. This "unknown nation" is also a part of Haavikko's poetry. Internationally, however, he is best known for his librettos to operas by Aulis Sallinen (*The Horseman, The King Goes Forth to France*).

Haavikko's first books of poetry are characterized by a language of striking originality, particularly in *The Ways to Far Away* and *On Windy Nights* (1953). Outer and inner experiences are inseparable in a poetic landscape transformed by the changes of seasons and time; the intervals of meditation are a part of the whole. In the subsequent volumes there is a change in the language: it becomes dramatic, with great inner tensions. Irony and wit, warmth and coldness, proximity and distance, a striving for objectivity and simultaneously a strong personal engagement make *Birthplace* (1955), *Leaves, Pages* (1957) and especially *The Winter Palace* (1959) central works in Finnish literature of the 1950s.

In *Trees in All Their Verdure* (1966) Haavikko summarizes his themes— love, human relationships, loneliness, survival, the desire for political power— into a work of great intensity and depth. This central work in Haavikko's oeuvre is followed by longer poems such as *Fourteen Rulers* (1970), in which Michael Psellus's *Chronographia* of eleventh-century Byzantium serves as a source of themes. Many of the pieces in *Poems from a Voyage across the Sound* (1973; the "sound" here is the Bosporus) are also concerned with power and its uses. Still, Haavikko does not cut his ties to his home country, his "forest land." In the epic poem *Twenty and One* (1974) he gives his personal interpretation of the myth of the *sampo,* found in the *Kalevala.* In *Wine, Writing* (1976) he returns to universal themes in a short, composed and clear style free from decorations.

In his poetry, with great linguistic vigor, Haavikko creates a form of intense skepticism, or rather, a matter-of-fact relativism. His pessimism is never cynical; his humor is not always recognized but is as important as his clarity of vision. The inconstancy of feeling, the harsh conditions of a fragile life, hidden fears and the hidden longing for power are described in language that is close to the spoken word. In an interview in *Books from Finland* (1977) he summarizes his opinions about poetry: "I think the important thing with poetry is *not* to write it: keep it in your head, where it can live and grow What I've always aimed at, I think, is what I call normal expression, a sentence that is as clear and lucid as it can possibly be and is the best possible expression of what has to be said. In my own poetry I have always tried to conform to the rhetoric of speech. I've always been quite clear in my mind about this, ever since I was quite young. I try to shape it into speech: I try it out, and listen, until it really sounds like speech, like someone talking."

In answer to a question about the difficulties of language, Haavikko concludes: "I'm not terribly interested in language as such, but what does interest me is its power to usurp reality. What is language, after all? A set of symbols; and these symbols are apprehended as reality. Yet in fact these symbols lead a life of their own: you use them, but they dictate their own terms. They do whatever they like; or whatever the context wants them to do, or whatever some person wants them to do. They become totally divorced from reality. It's really a most frightening process. You can say anything, develop any idea, in such a way that it sounds like reality; what is even more dangerous, it can sound logical and wise. This is something that anyone who writes—anyone

who thinks, for that matter—has to reckon with. Reckoning with it is in fact
his job; it's what a writer's problems are all about: how to take these treacherous symbols and shape them into the truth."

For his views of the past, Haavikko could use a proverb attributed to
the great Finland-Swedish modernist Gunnar Björling: "History—to be written anew. Always." The variations between past and present are characteristic
both in Haavikko's poetry and in his paradoxically expressed aphorisms, with
political economy as a starting point: "Speak, Answer, Teach" (1972), "The
Human Voice" (1977) and "Time of Eternal Peace" (1981). In power he sees
destruction, especially in the form of ideological blindness and exploitation
of nature. His world of myths is interwoven with intense personal feeling and
with the same clearly constructed objectivity.

Haavikko's poetry is most striking in its cleanness and harmony and in
its absence of symbols and allegories: "The world itself, it is not an allegor-
ical creature." Clearness, vitality, intensity are for him the essential components of poetry. He also adds a word of great importance for himself and his
poetry: *hillitön*, meaning "unrestrained," "unbridled." This unbridled quality demands its own careful patterns. The task of the poet is to form the symbols of language into universal truth. This truth involves the grotesque and
the contemplative, darkness and light. Above all, it is a question of penetrating language and moving toward an unaffected spoken idiom.

And my breath, I blew it out, let it hang dumb,
so as not to pollute the spot with bawling.

But in fact I asked it back on loan to say goodbye,
and stole it, and it's what I'm carrying to the country that isn't a place
right out of this poem.
                    ("The Winter Palace XII ," trans. Herbert Lomas)

Helsinki

Bo Carpelan *(1916–2011) was a Finnish writer who wrote in Swedish. The author of poetry, novels, short stories, plays, and literary criticism, he won the Swedish Academy's Nordic Prize in 1997 and twice won the Finlandia Prize. He also translated Greek classics, works by Osip Mandelstam and Marina Tsvetayeva, and a number of Finnish writers, including Paavo Haavikko.*

Paying the Price of Freedom
Paavo Haavikko

Dr. William S. Banowsky, President of the University of Oklahoma; Mrs. Doris Neustadt; Ladies and Gentlemen.

More than a formal word of thanks is due to the University of Oklahoma for the work that has again gone into the preparation of this ceremony. Nor am I merely expressing thanks on my own behalf; I believe that all writers must appreciate the fact that there is an institution so dedicated to keeping up with the flow of world literature and to finding an author on whom to confer its award. I also believe that all writers, at least, realize that this choice must be appropriately subjective, since art is not a measurable activity like sport. And finally, thanks are due to the family who made this prize possible, the Neustadts. I believe that this prize will not be fully appreciated until decades from now.

The writer must work alone. In a small country he can do this with the reassuring knowledge that his readers are few and close at hand. A writer from a small country and a small linguistic area is at once confined and free. He cannot, indeed he need not think of anything wider than his own environment. He can even be free of popularity, for which he hardly has any use. He is left with very few excuses. He cannot be destroyed by money or fame or the lack of either. All that he is left with is the naked truth of how he sees himself, his potential—and literature.

It is easy to write when one knows that the significance of writing is in the work itself, in the examination of eternal issues. The inevitable consequence of this work is the realization that the only significant problems are those to which there are no answers or solutions. They must be examined constantly; they contain the limits of the possible and of human capacity. Only through the unanswerable questions can the world be depicted, constantly, unendingly.

Thus literature is always philosophical and always moral. It asks what is right in the final count, knowing that there is no reply. But it asks and it seeks, and it cannot be shackled by laws, social systems, technology or business.

Using all the rich patterns in the world, literature constructs a form in which the following things can be found: the question of injustice and justice, the movement of events in the world, and darkness. The reader is invited, he is given an opportunity—but he may walk past if he will. It is the writer's lot to go on working, in the dark, in motion, free, alone, available. The value of this work is not in immutable, established classics; it is not in any completed book; it is in the endless work itself, the endless effort to remain free and unbound. It is said that art brings nations closer together, since through art they come to know each other. Many work toward this end. I believe that it is much more important for art to bring a man closer to himself. If a man knows one person—himself—he is closer to others than if he knows many people by name, including himself.

The idea of art as a bridge between nations goes with the optimistic belief that everything can be solved in the long run, that problems were made to be solved. This may hold for practical problems. Real problems were not made to be solved, but rather to be borne with, lived with, in all countries and seasons, as time passes and changes the terms of life.

The writer has no expert help or institution as surety or support. He has only himself. There is no alternative. Everything else in developed societies is already so guaranteed, subsidized, secured, reliable and isolated from all reality—science is so exploited and subjected—that there is no alternative left but the individual, set adrift and free.

The writer needs a measure of attention and recognition. He must fight to obtain it. At the same time he must fight against turning or allowing himself to be turned into an institution, who must think of everything, including next year's income. And though I use the word *writer*, I do not wish to differentiate between this activity and the battle each individual must fight. This battle too lasts only one lifetime: it begins in medias res, it ends in medias res; it is final and inevitable.

The only meaningful freedom is that of the individual. Every system desires to offer every other kind of freedom except this one. Every organized society tends toward increasing organization: arranging, caring, protecting and guaranteeing. Every system, regardless of ideology, wishes to distribute the optimum amount of good to everyone. No system believes that man cannot endure so much good, and every system believes that all problems were made to be solved. Here is the source of the happiness and destruction of systems and political institutions alike.

To an outsider's eyes, America is a uniform, closed concept; it symbolizes a dream, and goals. Coming here as a European, I am aware that Europe is too incoherent for anyone to explain. There can be no comprehensive image of it, except that it is disrupted and broken. And Finland, a remote corner of Europe, is even less comprehensible. It is one of Europe's few neutral countries between East and West. Many think it is merely an all too small country in quite the wrong place to exist, if only in the light of recent European history. In the form that it does exist, it is a relic from a bygone age when there were still small, separate principalities in Europe. I am not trying to sell any conception or description of what the country is. It has been difficult enough even for European statesmen to fathom during a whole lifetime. All I can say, without resorting to a false comparison, is that in the light of historical wisdom, the Finns evidently have not had the sense to draw the correct conclusions about the price it is worth paying for freedom. This small nation has never set a price on freedom; it has merely paid, and for this reason it has received an excessive return on its absurd investment.

Lastly, I would like to express my thanks to Ivar Ivask for the enormous task he has accomplished as editor-in-chief of *World Literature Today*, bringing together on the pages of his review what has been written in seventy-two languages.

Norman, Oklahoma
May 31, 1984

Translation from the Finnish by Philip Binham

MAX FRISCH
THE 1986 LAUREATE

Max Frisch (1911–1991) was a Swiss novelist and playwright. Frisch's father suddenly passed away while he was studying at the University of Zurich, and Frisch had to abandon his studies and take up a job as a journalist, thus beginning his lifelong career as a writer. His first novel was published in 1934. In 1936 he returned to school and graduated with a degree in architecture, but he continued to write even as his studio thrived. By 1947, Frisch had filled more than one hundred notebooks with work, but his most active writing period occurred during the 1950s and '60s. Among the major themes in Frisch's writings are identity, individuality, and political commitment. This body of work includes the novels *Stiller* (1954; Eng. *I'm Not Stiller*, 1958) and *Homo faber: Ein Bericht* (1957; Eng. *Homo Faber*, 1959). Frisch also penned several plays, many of which have been included in various collections: *Andorra: Stück in zwölf Bildern* (1961; Eng. *Andorra*, 1964), *The Fire*

Raisers: A Morality without a Moral (1962), *The Great Fury of Philip Hotz* (1967), and *Man in the Holocene* (1980).

> The art of radically questioning himself—and the reader—is perhaps the most consummate, and the most permeating, in Frisch's works, right up to his last novel.
>
> —Adolf Muschg

The Radical Questioning of Max Frisch
Adolf Muschg

Indisputably, Max Frisch, now seventy-four, must be counted among the major writers of modern German and European literature. Together with Friedrich Dürrenmatt, he is the only living Swiss writer of world renown, translated into more than twenty languages, acknowledged as one of the authoritative voices of Western civilization, cultural values, and political conscience, and endowed with prestigious literary distinctions—short of the Nobel Prize, for which he has been a candidate for many years, and, of course, the Neustadt Prize, for which I should like to present him as a candidate.

Max Frisch, born on 15 May 1911 in Zürich, graduated in architecture from the Swiss Federal Institute of Technology in his hometown and worked in this profession well into the fifties. His early novels that appeared before the war show the extraordinary sensibility of a widely traveled young man in pursuit of his identity—a quest that, on a different level of psychological and artistic insight, would become something like the leitmotiv or hallmark of the one work that assured his international breakthrough in 1954, the novel *Stiller.* By every standard of judgment, this masterpiece of self-searching wit, with its literary strength and imaginative irony, opened a new chapter of German postwar literature, breaking away from both the self-indulgent, inward-looking privateness and the "threadbare" *(Kahlschlag)* style of the fifties in Germany. It was as though "feeling had returned to limbs numbed by a state of shock," as one contemporary critic put it.

Before, Frisch had already made his mark as an acute observer of the critical issues of his generation—the generation of "existentialism"—both in his famous *Tagebuch 1946–1949* and in several successful plays such as *Santa Cruz* (1944), *Nun singen sie wieder* and *Die chinesische Mauer* (1946), *Als der Krieg zu Ende war* (1948), and *Graf Öderland* (1951), the last anticipating the unrest of a youth at variance with bourgeois values that would manifest itself almost two decades later. *Biedermann und die Brandstifter,* his most successful play internationally, was widely interpreted as a parable of political weakness in the face of totalitarian subversion; it has stood the test of time by *not* lending itself to any single interpretation. *Andorra* (1961) succeeded by poignantly exposing the mechanism that turns a minority—Jewish or otherwise—into a scapegoat for collective frustration and common guilt.

Frisch's plays, including *Don Juan* (1952) or *Biographie: Ein Spiel* (1967), could be labeled moralistic in the sense that they confront the individual with choices on which hinges his personal credibility; they are pessimistic in the sense that the will to choose turns out to be less than free and very much defined by the fate—or fatality—of one's character. The art of radically questioning himself—and the reader—is perhaps the most consummate, and the most permeating, in Frisch's works, right up to his last novel, *Blaubart.* Under the guise of a highly critical observer of democracy—which has not endeared Frisch to the powers-that-be in his home country—hides a more basic concern with, and distrust of, human games, particularly the games of power and the games between man and woman. If Frisch is one of the most brilliant chroniclers of the vicissitudes of love, he is also one of the most self-critical analysts of masculinity, as in his novel *Montauk* (1975), where he takes stock of his "life as a man" with as much personal frankness as artistic discretion. His concern with playing roles has been pursued methodically and translated into a new form of novel-writing in *Mein Name sei Gantenbein* (1964), which has been a source of professional inspiration for many younger writers beyond the German-speaking world.

One of the basic concerns of Frisch's work has long been death—as an ultimate challenge to the "art of living." In a more somber and a more subtle way than in his earlier works (such as the provocative *Tagebuch 1966– 1971*), the issue governs Frisch's writing in *Triptychon,* a play in which the universe of human relations has frozen into an underworldly standstill, or in *Der Mensch erscheint im Holozän,* the diary of a quiet catastrophe: aging.

Frisch is a man of personal and public courage; he has never shied from making his voice heard in matters of common concern and has never sided with the high and the mighty. He has displayed an exceptional gift for finding the right word at the right time. Even the enemies he has made by speaking up have always been indebted to the level of his arguments and the depth of his insights. If he has become less controversial in his later years, it is because the facts have in time justified his concerns. His influence on contemporary European sensitivity—not only of fellow writers—can hardly be overstated; his works have accompanied young readers in their personal growth much like those of Hermann Hesse. The true legitimacy of the questions that Frisch raises rests with the credibility of his art in raising them—always stopping short of answers that can only be given by the reader's total honesty toward himself.

Swiss Federal Institute of Technology, Zürich

Adolf Muschg *(b. 1934) is a Swiss writer. He taught German and German literature at ETH University in Zürich and also served as president of the Akademie der Künste in Berlin. His many awards include the Herman Hesse Prize, the Georg Büchner Prize, the Grimmelhausen Prize, the Grand Prix de Littérature (Switzerland), and the Hermann Hesse Gesellschaft Prize.*

Building a School in Nicaragua
Max Frisch

Ladies and Gentlemen,

I am grateful—as I wrote in my letter some months ago—very grateful, and I have to tell you in a few words: grateful for what? . . . Your country spoiled me quite a lot: thirty-five years ago, with a Rockefeller Grant that gave me the chance to live in New York and San Francisco over one year (on a modest standard, but free to write every day or night). Some other recognitions followed, recognitions by American academies and American universities, and today this final decoration.

I think my ambivalence, in regard to your great country, has its origin not in personal frustration; my criticism is not an expression of personal resentment. That means it certainly is not what some like to call *Anti-Amerikanismus*. It only concerns my criticism of politics wherever politics becomes inhuman-inhumane. That's what it's all about, and I am grateful for your generous understanding. I also thank you for your kindness in traveling from Oklahoma to Zürich; your visit here, ladies and gentlemen, is an honor for our town. Dafür danke ich als Zürcher.

As to the money, you know my decision to support with these funds a nonmilitary organization in Nicaragua, a nonprofit organization. It is a Swiss group of younger volunteers working there for development, which means aid to the people of Nicaragua in their long and painful struggle for independence. Two of those volunteers, Maurice Demierre and Yvan Leykraz, were killed last year. Compared to the one hundred million US dollars for military equipment on the other side, my support is very modest indeed—twenty-five thousand dollars—but it is said to be sufficient for one of the projects presented by the Asociación de Trabajadores del Campo: a school in a village with sixty farm families who want their children to learn the alphabet. The place (so I have been informed) is not far from the region where the terrorists known as contras are using their US military equipment to destroy bridges, power plants, homes, et cetera, hunting down farmers with gunfire and killing civilians from time to time before escaping across the border to Honduras, where they are trained by US advisors. The name of the modest project: Escuela Santa Emilia. The construction time: six months, assuming that the contras do not launch a sudden attack. It will be a simple building for three classes: Escuela Santa Emilia.

Zürich, Switzerland
May 16, 1987

RAJA RAO
THE 1988 LAUREATE

Raja Rao (1908–2006) was born in Hassan, in what is now Karnataka in South India. Though his father taught Kannada at a Hyderabad college, Rao graduated from the University of Madras with degrees in English and history; he then traveled to France for postgraduate studies. Most of his publications were written in the English language, though some of his earliest publications were written in his native Kannada. His first stories began appearing in various magazines and journals in 1931, and he published his first book, *Kanthapura,* in 1938. Upon his return to India in 1939, Rao became involved in the emerging nationalist movement. From 1966 to 1983 he relocated to the United States and taught philosophy at the University of Texas at Austin. Rao's works of fiction include *Kanthapura* (1938), *The Serpent and the Rope* (1960), *The Cat and Shakespeare* (1965), and *The Chessmaster and His Moves* (1988). Much of his writing appeared in various periodicals, including "A Client" (*Mercure de France,* 1934),

"The Cow of the Barricades" (*Asia*, 1938), "The Policeman and the Rose" (*Illustrated Weekly of India*, 1963), "Jupiter and Mars" (*Pacific Spectator*, 1954), and "The Writer and the Word" (*Literary Criterion*, 1965).

The writer or the poet is he who seeks back the common word to its origin of silence, in order that the manifested word become light.

—Raja Rao

The Moves of the Chessmaster
Edwin Thumboo

Once in a while the Chessmaster, who, for some, arranges the universe, enters it—at times dramatically, at times through the heart of silence—to remind man of the possibilities of the Absolute, of the ways it, the unmoving, moves us through knowledge to truth. The Chessmaster is but a label for the essence beyond that complex of form, substance, space, and energy which is the basis of life. Those who have seen the light, as it were, and are therefore free to con- jugate the word because they have moved beyond it, understand the need for temporary metaphors which those still in the process of knowing mis- take for reality; for man makes language after his own image, after his own hunger, inventing a discourse, a code without which he cannot relate either with himself or with others or give meaning to the unities and the contradic- tions in the flow of his thought and his experience. The sense of the Absolute, or of the most high, if you prefer, is enshrined in God, the Infinite, Allah, Olodumare, the Lord of the Universe, Kronos, Zeus, Yahweh, and a thousand other names. We also recall Buddha, Mahavira, Zoroaster, Confucius, Lao- Tzu, Christ, Krishna, and Mohammed, who together offer an infinity of ways or a Way, Tao, with different routes.

That is the spiritual history of man, marked by recurring search for the numinous, for the Absolute, and concurrently for his true, indestructible, immortal self. It is a search that is ultimately personal, undertaken on and through different levels where inner compulsions confront and are strength- ened by the doctrine, the dogma, and the ritualistic prescription of a partic- ular religion in a particular milieu at a particular time. You pray to and/or meditate upon Christ, the Buddha, or Krishna. Saint, sinner, and sage cor- roborate and reaffirm. Moreover, both the level and the way are directed or occur in two broad traditions, dominated respectively by duality and non- duality. Religions characterized by a duality rest on the belief that God—or the Absolute, if you prefer—is external to man. He creates, is compassionate, lays down. He judges, punishes, forgives. Out of such sets of beliefs arises an ethos, a way of life governed by the sacred and the secular, a distinction that deeply influences morality and action; you render unto God and you render unto Caesar. Thus the potential of conflict, in which the overriding anxiety is whether soul or spirit, immortal and God-given, redeemed from sin, whether original or incurred, is protected from evil and therefore damnation. A state of grace for life, a state of grace for death, for without grace there is everlasting darkness instead of eternal joy in the presence of God.

In contrast, the Vedantic tradition is nondual. As embodied in the Vedas, commented upon, expanded, and given greater precision by Sankara (788–820 A.D.) and other sages-gurus-teachers, including Rao's own guide Sri Atmananda, it is the basis of all his thinking and, consequently, of all his writings. To refer to his *thinking* and to his *writing* is to posit a dichotomy, a duality almost, which is not there, for the two activities are intrinsically bound, singular and seamless, as they are in Vedanta, which, Rao asserts in *The Serpent and the Rope,* "must become real again before India can be truly free." Its creative, linguistic, stylistic, ideational, psychological, analytical, social, philosophical, metaphysical nature, power, and reach derive from the totality of resources that are Indian, tested and refined over some four thousand years. It is underpinned by two key features: the conviction of nonduality, and the capacity to note the concrete in order to move beyond it to abstractions. Axles upon which the circles of Rao's epistemology turn, both are intimately linked to lie compacted at the core of his efforts "to move from the human to abhuman" through a dialectic defined and propelled by the continuities of the Indian tradition. There are fundamental consequences as well. First, the primary and secondary notions of the numinous in nonduality, such as the pantheon of Hindu deities, would appear exotic and/or confusing to those committed to a thoroughgoing monotheism—God above man—whose strictly parceled morality is likely to misjudge the true, abstract relationship between, for example, Krishna and his Gopis. Such monotheism posits a duality, separating the numinous from the human. On the other hand, in Vedantic nonduality man contains divinity; religions of duality shut him out. This leads to Rao's distinction between what he calls the horizontal and the vertical.

> There are, it seems to me, only two possible perspectives on human understanding: the horizontal and (or) the vertical. They could also be named the anthropomorphic and the abhuman. The vertical movement is the sheer upward thrust toward the unnamable, the unutterable, the very source of wholeness. The horizontal is the human condition expressing itself as concern for man as one's neighbour—biological and social, the predicament of one who knows how to say, I and you.
>
> The vertical rises slowly, desperately, to move from the I to the non-I, as the Buddhists would say—the move towards the impersonal, the universal (though there is no universe there, so to say) reaching out to ultimate *being*—when there is just being there are no two entities, no I and you. The I then is not even all, for there is no other to say I to. It is the nobility of *sunyata,* of zero, of light. ("On Understanding")

Societies and psyches are identified accordingly: India is vertical, China horizontal in *The Chessmaster and His Moves,* in which Siva is vertical and JeanPierre horizontal, whereas Suzanne attempts the vertical but fails because she cannot go beyond horizontal gestures and excursions. Neither is birth into a vertical setting an automatic advantage—Raja Ashok is still a Turk, his self, his "I" unreleased because he is captive to the sensualities of the concrete, in contrast to Ratilal, who has left these behind. The distinction is crucial, as it helps, for instance, to clarify and reassert the centrality of the feminine principle in Rao's thinking/works. Woman is essential to man's progress up the vertical, for only with and by woman can man and woman find the Absolute. The relationship is deeply intrinsic, not poised, complementary, or balanced as in yin and yang, which represent a horizontal relationship, one not integrated. It is Savithri who makes Rama holy in *The Serpent and the Rope,* Jayalakshmi Siva in *The Chessmaster and His Moves,* and they through them.

Rao's circles of understanding enlarge as he absorbs and fills out his possession of the Indian tradition, whose thrust and amplitude are depicted in his essay "The Meaning of India," with an oblique brevity so characteristic of Rao, through a rare combination of beast fable (how diminishing a description when the hare turns out to be the Bodhisattva, the Buddha-to-be); a passage on the supreme Swan who symbolizes Truth, Consciousness, and Liberation; disquisitions on Consciousness and the true nature of sacrifice as "the purification of the instruments of perception"; quotations from sacred texts; accounts by European, Muslim, and Chinese travelers and scholars attesting to the wisdom, splendid order, and well-being of India. The passage Rao quotes from Max Muller is particularly appropriate.

> If I were asked under what sky the human mind has most fully developed some of its choicest gifts, has most deeply pondered on the greatest problems of life and has found solutions to some of them, I should point to India. And if I were to ask myself from what literature we, in Europe, may draw that corrective which is most wanted in order to make our life more perfect, more comprehensive, more universal, in fact more truly human, a life not for this life only, but a transfigured and eternal life—again I should point to India.[1]

If we replace India the macrocosm with Raja Rao the writer of novels, short stories, meditations upon the word, and Puranas with poems and Jatakas embedded in them, we have a comprehensive statement of his intentions and achievement. The enlarging circles of his understanding are paralleled by his work over fifty-five years, from the first stories published in 1933 to *The Chessmaster and His Moves,* which appeared this past April. That long odyssey commences with his discovery of India, leading to the increasingly confident projection of her and the taking of her with him as he visits or lives in and seeks to understand other societies and cultures and those who inhabit them and who are equally concerned with life. It is this breadth and depth which makes *The Chessmaster and His Moves* the most international novel we have.

*

I eschew any brief summary of Rao's individual works. Those who have read *The Serpent and the Rope, The Cat and Shakespeare,* and *The Chessmaster and His Moves* know how rapidly they defeat such attempts. The expansion and deepening of his fiction centers on the search by the self for a self capable of fulfillment in a world shaped by a tradition that is alive, inexhaustible, subtle, and on the move, a broad and complex continuum whose matrix consists of metaphysics, religion, and ritual as embodied in texts ranging from the Vedas to the emblematic tales from the *Ramayana* that carry, as appropriate to the capacity of reader or listener, religious, social, and political linguistic instruction and reaffirmation. Key texts and narratives are shared, pan-Indian, and connect with those that are regional—such as the collection of *vacanas* in Kannada—down to ones associated with the rhythms of life presided over by a village deity, a village history. The continuum is marked at one end by the most abstract, taxing metaphysics, at the other by humbler religious practices. It has the mutually reinforcing power of written and oral traditions—the retelling of episodes from the *Ramayana* or the stories of the gods by traveling narrators of *harikathas*—that instruct and nourish priest and villager.

Characters in search of self on various levels offer the major fictional foci and energies. More often than not they must contend with change arising from the pressure of events or the challenge of understanding the ethos of another culture. The young orphan Narsa in "Narsiga" (from *The Cow of the Barricades and Other Stories*), who herds sheep and goats and is abused by some but protected by the master of the ashram and whose growing awareness of the image of the Mahatma is described with deep insight and precise delicacy, belongs to the large Rao cast of characters that includes Rama *(The Serpent and the Rope)* and Comrade Kirillov, who both rise to the challenges but at an infinitely more sophisticated level and in a much broader, more universal, international context. The fictional ground between is established by characters such as Little Mother, Catherine, Savithri, Madeleine, Georges *(The Serpent and the Rope);* Moorthy, Rangamma, and Ratna *(Kanthapura);*

Ramakrishna, Pai, and Govindan Nair *(The Cat and Shakespeare)*; and Siva, Suzanne, and Jayalakshmi *(The Chessmaster and His Moves)*.

Rao's themes include the metaphysical apprehension of God, the nature of death, immortality, illusion and reality, duality and nonduality, good and evil, existence and destiny, Karma and Dharma; the quest for self-knowledge, the place of the guru, the influence of religion and social concepts and patterns and prejudices on individual and group behavior, corrupt priests; the ideal and meaning of love and marriage, the impact of tradition on the individual and collective life and the meaning of India's real and symbolic content, and the historical or contemporary meeting of East and West in religious, political, and psychological terms tested against the vertical/horizontal distinction. The list is by no means exhaustive. Neither does it suggest the way themes conflate, complement, or construct oppositions depicted through the increasing psychological authority of the characters from the early short stories, through *Kanthapura, The Serpent and the Rope,* and *The Cat and Shakespeare,* to the firm, monumental authority of *The Chessmaster and His Moves.* This listing belies Rao's achievement of bringing into the life of each character and his or her relationships the extraordinarily complex worlds they each occupy—Indian, French, Greek, Hebraic, African, Chinese—and which overlap and contain, in a single moment, the mundane and the metaphysical.

That is a major achievement, as is Rao's remarkably successful reorientation of a language and his assembling of a narrative mode to articulate life fully within the continuum of tradition and change in which life is played out against the larger movements of personality, situation, and environment.

Rao's choice of English as his linguistic medium has had implications, the chief of which are disclosed in his foreword to *Kanthapura.*

The telling has not been easy. One has to convey in a language that is not one's own the spirit that is one's own. One has to convey the various shades and omissions of a certain thought-movement that looks maltreated in an alien language . . . yet English is not really an alien language to us. It is the language of our intellectual make-up— like Sanskrit or Persian was before—but not of our emotional make-up. . . . We cannot write like the English. We should not. We cannot write only as Indians. We have grown to look at the large world as part of us. . . .

After language the next problem is that of style. The tempo of Indian life must be infused into our English expression, even as the tempo of American or Irish life has gone into the making of theirs. We, in India, think quickly, we talk quickly, and when we move we move quickly. . . . We have neither punctuation nor the treacherous "ats" and "ons" to bother us—we tell one interminable tale. Episode follows episode, and when our thoughts stop our breath stops, and we move on to another thought. This was and still is the ordinary style of our story-telling. I have tried to follow it myself in this story. (vii–viii)

The uniqueness of Raja Rao's style is its apt flexibility, demonstrated in how it incarnates the thoughts and emotions of characters ranging from relatively "simple" peasants to the Brahmin prone to disquisitions. His prose is resonant, bare, or poetic as required. His language accords with the Indian spirit, its speech, gestures, proverbs, and metaphysical thrust. Still, this rootedness in the Indian scene and the Indian tradition does not circumscribe his language. In fact, the sharp management of syntax, of sentence structure, the revealing use of its symbolic and metaphorical resources, gives both clarity and power.

Rao's basic narrative structure, particularly in *Kanthapura,* a majority of the short stories, and *The Cat and Shakespeare,* derives from Puranas, *sathala-puranas,* and *harikathas,* which between them bring together, inter alia, religious and metaphysical discourse, folklore, local legend and quasi-history, straight description, dramatic insets and well-managed digressions. In *Kanthapura* the first-person narrator (a favorite Rao device) is a villager. The style is fluid and simple, with the flow of narrative relieved by digression. The structure which carries the narrative voice is determined to a considerable extent by the status of the narrator himself or herself. Though this may seem obvious, it is considerably less so in that merging of a new language to an old environment. Consequently, in *The Serpent and the Rope,* narrated by Rama the young Brahmin, we find a combination of Indian and "Western" modes. It blends the scope of the notebook and the quest, both of which offer room for autobiographical excursions. The Indian elements derive from the Puranas, which mix religion, philosophy, history, and literature. Given its theme of the discovery of self and illumination through the apparently tangential instruction of a "guru," *The Cat and Shakespeare* reverts to the style of the *sathala-puranas.* The comedy and whimsy are deceptive because the message is fundamental, put across with subtlety and an indirection that is clarified by the concluding paragraphs.

Rao's greatest achievement, which I suspect only he can surpass, is the degree to which his works, especially *The Chessmaster,* contain the insights, emblems, mantras, metaphors, and other carriers of meaning and instruction that enable the individual to achieve, through his own meditations, a better understanding of self through Knowledge and Truth. They lead us, in Rao terms, from the human to the abhuman, to the Absolute or, if you will, from god to God to GOD, thus moving from the horizontal to the vertical. E. M. Forster felt the horizontal Chessmaster in *Howard's End.* In *A Passage to India,* the Chessmaster turns vertical. Walt Whitman had meditated upon a passage to more than India. Forster went further, beyond the doctrinaire religions, chiefly those which rested upon a dualism and which had helped define and maintain the horizontal. The vertical Chessmaster was at work through Godbole, especially in his disquisition on good and evil and his participation in the Gokul Astami rites at Mau, and through the experiences of Mrs. Moore and Adela in the Marabar Caves, and through the Punkawala in the courtroom scene.

> The Court was crowded and of course very hot, and the first person Adela noticed in it was the humblest of all who were present, a person who had no bearing officially upon the trial: the man who pulled the punkah. Almost naked, and splendidly formed, he sat on a raised platform near the back, in the middle of the central gangway, and he caught her attention as she came in, and he seemed to control the proceedings. [. . .]

Then life returned to its complexities, person after person struggled out of the room to their various purposes, and before long no one remained on the scene of the fantasy but the beautiful naked god. Unaware that anything unusual had occurred, he continued to pull the cord of his punkah, to gaze at the empty dais and the overturned special chairs, and rhythmically to agitate the clouds of descending dust. (217, 231)

Forster had made the move from the horizontal to the vertical, but the weight of his deeply entrenched liberalism prevented contact with a forceful liberating tradition such as Vedanta that could help him rise up to the vertical. He had a number of unanswered questions which related to the nature of Hinduism or whether "God is love" is the final message of India. Raja Rao goes beyond such questions in the sense that he provides answers not to the questions but to the uncertainties that lie behind them. It is there in his metaphysics, converted from and into experience, taken from and returned to life, in a language that connects emotion and spirit, a language restored, made central again in the life of man.

How does one end an encomium for a writer, a Purana-maker who insists with honesty and fervor that he is not their creator? Fortunately, Raja Rao the chessmaster provides a rescue which is a fitting conclusion. It is there in the first excerpt that Ivar Ivask so aptly chose for the printed program of this evening's Neustadt Prize ceremony and which reveals the roots of Rao's art and his deep compassion for mankind.

I write. I cannot not write. Yet he who writes does not know *that* which writes. So, does one write? If so who? Which?

Why write? Two birds, says the Ramayana (our oldest epic) were making love, when a hunter killed the male bird. The cry of the widowed bird, says the text, created the rhythm of the poem. The hero Prince Rama freed his wife Sita, abducted and imprisoned by the monster Ravana, King of Ceylon. Monkeys and bears helped in freeing Sita, seated in sorrow under the Asoka tree....

Why publish? That others may hear the cry of the bird hunted and killed whose mate is lost in sorrow. Uncovering the vocables is a poetic exercise. The precise word arises of love, that is pure intelligence. That is why in Sanskrit the word Kavi means the poet—and the sage.

Norman, Oklahoma
June 4, 1988

1. Raja Rao, "The Meaning of India," in *The First Writers Workshop Literary Reader*, ed. P. Lal (Calcutta: Writers Workshop, 1972), 40–41.

Poet, critic, academic, anthologist, and literary activist **Edwin Thumboo** *(b. 1933) is considered "one of Singapore's most distinguished poets and is widely regarded as the unofficial poet laureate of Singapore" (National Library Board). In 2006 he was awarded one of Singapore's highest honors, the Meritorious Service Medal.*

Words Manifested as Light
Raja Rao

I am a man of silence. And words emerge from that silence with light, of light, and light is sacred. One wonders that there is the word at all—*Sabda*—and one asks oneself, where did it come from? How does it arise? I have asked this question for many, many years. I've asked it of linguists, I've asked it of poets, I've asked it of scholars. The word seems to come first as an impulsion from the nowhere, and then as a prehension, and it becomes less and less esoteric—till it begins to be concrete. And the concrete becoming ever more earthy, and

the earthy communicated, as the common word, alas, seems to possess least
of that original light.

The writer or the poet is he who seeks back the common word to its origin of silence, in order that the manifested word become light. There was a
great poet of the West, the Austrian poet Rainer Maria Rilke. He said objects
come to you to be named. One of the ideas that has involved me deeply these
many years is: where does the word dissolve and become meaning? Meaning
itself, of course, is beyond the sound of the word, which comes to me only
as an image in the brain, but *that* which sees the image in the brain (says our
great sage of the sixth century, Sri Shankara) nobody has ever seen. So the
word coming of light is seen eventually by light. That is, every word we see is
seen by light, and that is its meaning. Therefore the effort of the writer, if he is
sincere, is to forget himself in the process and go back to the light from which
words come. Go back where? That is, those who read or those who hear us must
reach back to their own light. And that light I think is prayer.

My ancestors and, yes, the ancestors of some of you or of most of you
who speak the English tongue, came from the same part of the world thousands of years ago. Was it from the Caucasus or the North Pole? One is not
certain yet. They spoke a language close to my own language and close to your
language. There is in America a remarkable dictionary called the *American
Heritage Dictionary*. It offers almost a hundred pages (at the very end) of
the Indo-European roots of many of our words. Most of you are of European
origin. At least your thinking has been conditioned by European thought.
There is thus a common way of thinking, an Indo-European way of thinking,
between us, so that we are not so far from each other as we often think we are.
And beyond the Indo-European way of thinking in Asia, Africa, Polynesia, is
that same human light by which all words become meaning. Finally, there is
only one meaning, not for every word, but for all words *where* the word, any
word, from any language, dissolves into knowledge. It is only there at the dissolution of the sound of the word or of the image of the word that you say you
understand. And *here* there is neither you nor I. That is what I have been trying to achieve. That I become no one, that no one shines but It.

Many good things have been said by distinguished speakers—about me—this evening. But I want to say to you in utter honesty: I would like to be completely nameless, and just be that reality which is beyond all of us who hear me—that reality which evokes in me you, and I in each one listening to me this evening, that there be no one there but light. And it is of that reality the sages have spoken. The sage is one, someone beyond the saint. He is no one. He is the real seer. In fact, we are all sages, but we don't recognize it. That is what the Indian tradition says. In the act of seeing—that is, of the seer, the seen, and the seeing—in seeing alone is there pure light. Where this comes from, nobody can name. I once asked Dr. Oppenheimer, the scientist, who told me his hands were soiled by the atom bomb: Have you ever seen an object? And he answered: Never. If a scientist like Dr. Oppenheimer says he has never seen an object—yet I am hearing him say what he has in all honesty declared—it is that level of knowledge I would like to reach from where I truly write. It is to that root of writing I pay homage. The Neustadt Prize is thus not given to me, but to That which is far beyond me, yet in me—because I alone know I am incapable of writing what people say I have written.

Norman, Oklahoma
June 4, 1988

TOMAS TRANSTRÖMER
THE 1990 LAUREATE

Tomas Tranströmer (1931–2015) was a Swedish writer, poet, and translator whose poetry has been translated into over sixty languages. In his life, he was considered the premier postwar Scandinavian poet. He published thirteen volumes of poetry in Swedish, from *17 dikter* (1954) to *Den stora gåtan* (2004). His books of poetry in English include *New Collected Poems* (2011), *The Sorrow Gondola* (2010), *The Half-Finished Heaven* (2001), *For the Living and the Dead* (1995), *Baltics* (1975), *Windows and Stones* (1972), and *20 Poems* (1970), among others. In addition to the Neustadt Prize, Tranströmer was honored with the 1991 Swedish Academy Nordic Prize and the 2011 Nobel Prize in Literature.

The poem as it is presented is a manifestation of another, invisible poem, written in a language behind the common languages. Thus, even the original version is a translation.

—Tomas Tranströmer

Oklahoma
Tomas Tranströmer

I

The train stalled far to the south. Snow in New York,
but here we could go in shirtsleeves all night.
Yet no one was out. Only the cars
sped by in flashes of light like flying saucers.

II

"We battlegrounds are proud
of our many dead . . ."
said a voice as I awakened.

The man behind the counter said:
"I'm not trying to sell anything,
I'm not trying to sell anything,
I just want you to see something."
And he displayed the Indian axes.

The boy said:
"I know I have a prejudice,
I don't want to have it, sir.
What do you think of us?"

III

This motel is a foreign shell. With a rented car
(like a big white servant) outside the door.

Nearly devoid of memory, and without profession,
I let myself sink to my midpoint.

Translation from the Swedish by May Swenson with Leif Sjöberg

Editorial note: Tranströmer took the train from Chicago to Tulsa and drove around eastern Oklahoma in 1965. From *Windows and Stones: Selected Poems,* copyright © 1972 by the University of Pittsburgh Press, reprinted by permission of the publisher. Tony Hoagland writes about "Oklahoma" in "Tranströmer: The Power of Disarray," in *Twenty Poems That Could Save America* (Graywolf, 2015).

Tomas Tranströmer's Poetic Depth of Vision
Jaan Kaplinski

My candidate for the 1990 Neustadt International Prize for Literature is the Swedish poet Tomas Tranströmer. I consider him one of the most outstanding poets of our time, a poet whose work can say much to every one of us, especially to people living in northern Europe and North America. In his work Tranströmer has succeeded in achieving a synthesis between the modern and the traditional, between art and life. He has been able to breathe life into the most uninspiring realities of modern existence and in this way has significantly broadened the scope of our poetic vision of the world. He is thus a contemporary poet in the true sense of the word.

In our world that is often so confused by all kinds of ideologies and doctrines, Tranströmer has always remained a politically nonengaged humanist who understands he has no right to forget the sufferings of other people, be it in the West or in the East, but who knows that there are no quick and simple solutions to the grave problems of our time. Despite many pressures, he has refused to believe in political slogans and participate in mass movements, giving proof of a remarkable courage and clarity of vision. At the same time, he has worked for more than thirty years as a practicing psychologist, helping people, giving them something of his remarkable integrity and strength, and achieving a depth of vision into our human condition that he is able to express in his poems.

Tranströmer has published ten volumes of poetry in Swedish, from *17 dikter* (1954; 17 poems) to *För levande och döda* (1989; Eng. *For the Living and the Dead*, 1995). His oeuvre is not large but has been very influential in Scandinavia and even in North America. Among the English versions of his poetry in book form are the following: *Twenty Poems of Tomas Tranströmer* (1970), translated by Robert Bly; *Night Vision* (1971, US; 1972, UK), translated by Bly; *Windows and Stones* (1972), translated by May Swenson and Leif Sjöberg; *Selected Poems* (1981), translated by Robin Fulton; and *Baltics*, translated by Samuel Charters for the US edition (1975), by Robin Fulton for the UK edition (1980). A special issue of the journal *Ironwood* (1979) was dedicated to Tranströmer's verse, and many translations of his poems and articles about him have appeared in various other publications. His poems have been translated into numerous languages, including German, Spanish, Hungarian, Bulgarian, and the other Scandinavian tongues. Tranströmer has received many literary prizes at home and abroad, and in my opinion his work deserves the distinguished Neustadt Prize.

Tartu, Estonia

Jaan Kaplinski *(b. 1941, Tartu) is an Estonian poet, playwright, essayist, journalist, linguist, sociologist, and ecologist. He has translated a number of poets from French, English, Spanish, Chinese, and Swedish into Estonian, including a verse collection by Tomas Tranströmer.*

The Invisible Poem behind the Poem
Tomas Tranströmer

My warm thanks to *World Literature Today*, the unique magazine with its visionary editor, to the University of Oklahoma, and to the Neustadt family, which with rare generosity has taken on the task of lending literature a helping hand.

I want to draw attention to a fairly large group of men and women who share this prize with me, without getting one single cent: those who have translated my poems into different languages. No one mentioned, no one forgotten. Some are my personal friends; others are personally unknown to me. Some have a thorough knowledge of Swedish language and tradition, others a rudimentary one (there are remarkable examples of how far you can get with the help of intuition and a dictionary). What these people have in common is that they are experts in their own languages, and that they have translated my poems because they wanted to. This activity has brought them neither money nor fame. The motivation has been interest for the text, curiosity, commitment. It ought to be called *love*—which is the only realistic basis for poetry translation.

Let me sketch two ways of looking at a poem. You can perceive a poem as an expression of the life of the language itself, something organically grown out of the very language in which it is written—in my case, Swedish. A poem written by the Swedish language through me. Impossible to carry over into another language.

Another, and contrary, view is this: the poem as it is presented is a manifestation of another, invisible poem, written in a language behind the common languages. Thus, even the original version is a translation. A transfer into English or Malayalam is merely the invisible poem's new attempt to come into being. The important thing is what happens between the text and the reader. Does a really committed reader ask if the written version he reads is the original or a translation?

I never asked that question when I, in my teenage years, learned to read poetry—and to write it (both things happened at the same time). As a two-year-old child in a polyglot environment experiences the different tongues as one single language, I perceived, during the first enthusiastic poetry years, all poetry as Swedish. Eliot, Trakl, Éluard—they were all Swedish writers, as they appeared in priceless, imperfect, translations.

Theoretically we can, to some extent justly, look at poetry translation as an absurdity. But in practice we must believe in poetry translation, if we want to believe in World Literature. That's what we do here in Oklahoma. And I thank my translators.

Norman, Oklahoma
June 12, 1990

JOÃO CABRAL DE MELO NETO
THE 1992 LAUREATE

João Cabral de Melo Neto (1920–1999) was a Brazilian poet and diplomat. After moving to Rio de Janeiro in 1940, he published his first collection of poems, *Pedra do Sono*. In 1945 he was assigned to his first diplomatic post in Spain, where he continued to write. Most of Cabral's life was spent as a diplomat, which afforded him the opportunity to travel the world. Through all of his travels, he continued to write poetry, and at the end of his life, he had published more than fifteen collections. He is considered one of the greatest Brazilian poets of all time. Cabral's body of work includes *O Engenheiro* (1945), *O Cão sem Plumas* (1950), *A Educação pela Pedra* (1966; Eng. *Education by Stone*, 2005), and *Sevilha Andando* (1990). His most famous work, "Morte e Vida Severina," was translated into English in part by 1976 Neustadt laureate Elizabeth Bishop and reprinted in *Selected Poetry, 1937–1990* (1994), ed. Djelal Kadir. In addition to the Neustadt Prize, Cabral was honored with the 1990 Camões Prize.

It has made possible too the exercise of poetry as emotive exploration of the world of things and as rigorous construction of lucid formal structures, lucid objects of language.

—João Cabral de Melo Neto

The Rigors of Necessity
Djelal Kadir

Your Excellency Dom Austregésilo de Athayde, President of the Brazilian Academy of Letters, who has received us so warmly in this House, Distinguished Speakers who have preceded us at the podium, Esteemed Members of the Academy, Ladies and Gentlemen.

It is an incomparable privilege to have the opportunity in this solemn session of the Brazilian Academy of Letters to address to you words of praise in honor of one of your most illustrious poets, His Excellency Ambassador João Cabral de Melo Neto, twelfth laureate of the Neustadt International Prize for Literature.

With the recent and deserved recognition of the universal value of his work, the Brazilian poet João Cabral de Melo Neto takes his indisputable place in what is being defined as the literary pantheon of our century. The eleven great writers who preceded him already figure among those who have defined our literary canon in the second half of the twentieth century.

To arrive at the final outcome, our newest laureate, so ably advocated by the Brazilian writer and our admired friend and colleague Silviano Santiago, had to compete with the significant qualifications of such eminent writers as the Russian poet Bella Akhmadulina, the English novelist John Berger, the Italian poet Andrea Zanzotto, the Turkish novelist Orhan Pamuk, the Uruguayan writer Eduardo Galeano, and the Japanese novelist Kenzaburō Ōe, to mention a few of the candidates who were presented to the 1992 jury. What proved most impressive for the international jury of writers in the Cabral oeuvre was its rigorous honesty and profound humanity. Despite the scant quantity of his poetry available in English—a scarcity we shall ameliorate shortly with the publication of a collection of his poetry in translation—the quality of his work stood out, eliciting the admiration of the jurors, whose international and linguistic diversity converged upon the felicitous consensus that brings us together today in this historic place to celebrate this historic occasion.

Scarcity is one of the fundamental principles of João Cabral's poetics. In an interview with Selden Rodman in 1974, Cabral affirmed that poetry originates either in abundance or in insufficiency. As exemplary poets of overflow, he cites Walt Whitman, Paul Claudel, Pablo Neruda, Vinícius de Moraes, Allen Ginsberg. For his part, João Cabral de Melo Neto identifies himself with poets who write from a basis of dearth, citing as examples George Herbert, Stéphane Mallarmé, T. S. Eliot, Paul Valéry, Richard Wilbur, Marianne Moore, and Elizabeth Bishop—poets who write in order to compensate for a profoundly felt necessity or insufficiency.

Beginning with his earliest works, João Cabral has sought a form of writing that corresponds to what Ralph Waldo Emerson in the last century called pleonastically "our necessary poverty." For Emerson, that necessity is the very insufficiency that incites creative impetus, an impetus that is as strong as it is invisible, that is mysteriously sparse but tenaciously powerful. In this economy of sparseness, João Cabral has fashioned a poetic world, a world so spare that it excludes the very figure of the poet himself, or at least that figure as subject with the voice of a personal pronoun. When the inevitability of the lyrical subject becomes indispensable, our poet laureate turns apocryphal, as in the unforgettable poem "Dúvidas Apócrifas de Marianne Moore" (Apocryphal Doubts of Marianne Moore), where the Anglo-American poet serves the reticent Luso-American laureate as screen and even as pretext:

> I have always avoided speaking of me,
> speaking to me. I wanted to speak of things.
> But, in the selection of those things,
> might there not be a speaking of me?
>
> Might that modesty of speaking me
> not contain a confession,
> an oblique confession,
> in reverse, and ever immodest?
>
> How pure or impure is
> the thing spoken of?

Or does it always impose itself, im-
purely even, on anyone wishing to speak of it?

How is one to know, with so many things
to speak or not to speak of?
And if avoiding it altogether, is
not speaking a way of speaking of things? (trans. Kadir)

So much reticence! Nevertheless, João Cabral de Melo Neto characterizes himself as a social poet. And he is, in the strict sense of the word, since his poetry is founded in the social and human context of the geographic region that engendered him, that arid region of his native Pernambuco, which is as dry as Cabral has sought to be in the economy of his poetic language. His is a needful geography whose necessity he converts into the felt need of a poetic principle that demands of the poet a lapidary genius and the ingenuity of a stonemason and an engineer.

Shunning the rhetorical flourish and the ideological megaphone, Cabral has labored at his wordsmith's bench with quiet diligence and eloquent concision. In his remarkable terseness, he has endeavored to show rather than tell, and to show without being seen, an achievement best characterized by his own words as "song without guitar," "unceremoniously" wrought in "civil geometry." His trademark thus has been a visual poetry as opposed to a musical fanfare. And he has often reflected on the relationship between painting and the language of poetry, a language that aspires ceaselessly to become lapidary and constructivist. A number of his verse collections reflect this preoccupation with stonemasonry and engineering even in their titles. And like the builder at his task who fashions his edifice stone by stone, João Cabral has always labored with the painstaking awareness that poetry is made word for word, often letter by letter. In this sense, his poetry carries the unmistakable mark of a sculptor's chisel or a painter's brush, metaphorical instruments wielded by the poet with deliberate and measured reserve. And his decorum carries the mark of the humble rather than the haughty, deliberately linking itself with the modest but vital endeavors of the folk that engendered his poetic calling. Chores like fishing or culling beans, for example.

And this, ladies and gentlemen, is where my path happened upon João Cabral's poetic vocation a quarter of a century ago, when, having fallen fortuitously through the crevices of time and space, I found myself transported from the life of a young shepherd in the mountains of my native Cyprus to the halls of Yale University studying philosophy and literature. I discovered then in the Portuguese of this Brazilian poet that it was alright to be there, even for those who come from a life of such modest endeavors. Cabral's poetry taught me that there is a viable continuity between the most humble occupations and the loftiest preoccupations of philosophy and poetry. That was in 1966, when my second-year Portugueselanguage class allowed me the temerity to pick up a recently published volume of poems, a 111-page volume titled *A Educação pela Pedra* (Education by Stone) which had just been released in Rio de Janeiro in July of that year. That temerity and the fates would lead me to the even greater and more terrific impertinence of the moment, delivering an encomium for this great poet in his own House, directing myself to you, esteemed Academicians, in the language of my poor apprenticeship, here in the most august House of this language. I beg your most merciful indulgence for such audacity. And though it be the work of destiny, I do accept fully my responsibility in this predicament, and I do so in the spirit of the Stoic's philosophy that has its origins in the island of my birth.

Cutting my Portuguese teeth on Cabral's poetic stones, I came across something a bit more malleable in that pedagogic quarry. It was a poem entitled "Catar Feijão" (Culling Beans), and it evoked most vividly for me the gnarled hands of my grandmother culling beans, hands whose agility and uncanny intelligence I have yet to learn how to imitate. Being as instructive as any statement I know on the art of poetry, and as illustrative as any of our laureate's lessons in the poet's masonry, "Catar Feijão" could well be a manual, a vade mecum of any poet and student of poetry:

1

Culling beans is not unlike writing:
you toss the kernels into the water of the clay pot
and the words into that of a sheet of paper;

then, you toss out whatever floats.

Indeed, all words will float on the paper, ice-cold water,

its verb small and green and commonsensical:

in order to cull that bean, blow on it,

and toss out the frivolous and hollow, the chaff and the echo.

2

Now, there is a risk in that bean-culling:

the risk that among those heavy seeds any-old

kernel may enter, of stone or study-matter,

an unchewable grain, a tooth-breaker.

Not so, for culling words:

the stone gives the phrase its most vivid seed:

it obstructs flowing, floating reading,

it incites attention, luring it with risk. (trans. Kadir)

Not knowing, for lack of precedent, how well the voice of a Pernambucan poet and the inflection of a Cypriot might harmonize, the present exercise is fraught with great risk indeed. In the face of such risks, let us call these beans the pebbles of Demosthenes, those stones the stammering father of our rhetorical tradition put into his mouth when he went to declaim phrases to the sea. These are the hard-rock impediments the poet must perpetually overcome, as does the reader. For João Cabral teaches us not only how his kind of poetry is written, but also how it is to be read. And lest our reading facility ebb into the facile, we are waylaid, forced into the rigors of having to negotiate stone-hard obstructions and to absorb the necessary lesson of their difficulty. Language, of course, is poetry's greatest difficulty and also its greatest danger. And language becomes most perilous when it would yield with ease to one's facility.

João Cabral's poetic career consists in shunning the temptation to succumb to the facile and the gratuitous. That is why, I suspect, he has been averse to the musicality of poetry, preferring, instead, the sparsely pictorial and the assonantal rhyme to the jangle of consonantal sonority or the bombast of the declamatory. His is another sort of eloquence. And being a self-declared poet of need and insufficiency, Cabral has labored diligently to pare down the magnitude of need's necessity for fulfillment, not out of parsimony, but from an unmistakable sense of generosity. This is the poetic generosity that endeavors to allow the human subjects of his poetry to show forth on their own terms. In this sense, the geometrical and mathematical rigors of self-curtailment in Cabral's poetry, far from being the cold and mechanical acts of a formalism, represent the rigors of a poetry that is profoundly human and socially connected. And, as his wife, the poet Marly de Oliveira, has noted in her foreword to the second volume of his collected verse, Cabral's is an emotive poetry, a poetry laden with lucid emotion, the lucidity inherited from Paul Valéry's mathematical verse.

Our laureate is an artfully subtractive poet engaged in the labors of winnowing, culling, paring down. A poet who opts for the economy of the minimal with maximum effect. He practices a laconic art of deference in a poetry that curtails its own voice, as well as the ego of its author, yielding to the human context that links poetic vocation with daily life and worldly experience. In this self-circumscription, the poetry of João Cabral has transcended its own conscientious and deliberate limits, emerging as a universal cultural phenomenon that is admired by poets and lay readers all over the world. Because of his diligent labors and self-effacing devotion, João Cabral has been adopted by the Brazilian people as their reigning national poet, a status reconfirmed most recently by the São Paulo Prize conferred upon him by the government of that Brazilian state. For all these reasons, in March 1992 an international jury of his peers selected João Cabral de Melo Neto as the laureate of the 1992 Neustadt International Prize for Literature.

I am truly honored by this opportunity and the privilege of addressing you on the merits of João Cabral de Melo Neto's poetry, and doing so in this solemn session of the Brazilian Academy of Letters in the House of the great Machado de Assis. Thank you.

Rio de Janeiro
August 31, 1992

Translation from the Portuguese by Djelal Kadir

Djelal Kadir (b. 1946, Cyprus) is Edwin Erle Sparks Professor (emeritus) of Comparative Literature at Penn State University and served as the seventh editor (1991–1996) in the history of Books Abroad / World Literature Today.

Lucid Objects of Language
João Cabral de Melo Neto

Mr. President of the Brazilian Academy of Letters, Professor Djelal Kadir, Mr. Walter Neustadt Jr., my fellow members of the Academy, Ladies and Gentlemen,

On the occasion of being the recipient of so prestigious a prize, conferred upon a writer of the Portuguese language for the first time, I ought to explain one thing before all else: you have rewarded a Brazilian writer who, practically, has only written poetry—that is, a poet.

I do not know how it is in your northerly country, but in mine, in its colloquial usage, the word *poet* has a certain connotation between bohemian and irresponsible, contemplative and inspired, all things that have nothing to do with my way of conceiving poetry and with what I have managed to accomplish.

I regret that Miss Marianne Moore, who died, unfortunately, before receiving the laurels of your prize, cannot, like Francis Ponge and Elizabeth Bishop, laureates both of the Neustadt Prize, comfort me with her poet's counsel today upon receiving this prize as a poet. In truth, these were poets whose vision of poetry has nothing to do with that confessional lyricism that nowadays, since Romanticism, passes for everything that is considered poetry. In a way (and upon saying so I cannot help the feeling of a certain *mauvaise conscience*), what I have written until today has nothing to do with the "lyricism" that has come to be not only the quality of certain poets, but synonymous with what is expected of all poets.

In reality, starting with Romanticism, and in the name of individual expression, poets have left by the wayside the greater part of the kinds of material that previously could be treated in poetry. Historical poetry, didactic poetry, epic poetry, dramatic poetry, narrative poetry, confrontational poetry, all abandoned in favor of poetry of personal expression of states of mind. Everything has been sacrificed to lyricism, and this has been generalized and called poetry. Now, lyricism was merely one of the aspects in which poetry manifested itself. Thus, I do not know why today's critics and historians, though they find it strange, admit that poetry is a literary genre that survives in small circles. Meanwhile, those same critics and historians of today's literature do not keep from dedicating to that genre that is so minoritarian the best of their studies, even while they systematically begin with this genre their manuals and histories of literature, and this not just here but in any country. We know that lyricism was originally a genre to be sung, and thus it is not surprising that the current lyricism, postromantic, not sung, should be restricted to a small circle. The question is, wouldn't the true lyricism of our time be in what is called the popular song, produced and consumed all over the world, beyond geographic borders and language differences, in incomparably greater quantities than any other literary genre, however popular? Might not this natural necessity for lyricism that human beings feel be tended to today by that incalculable volume of works at which the very refined turn up their noses and which the erudite exclude from their studies? That is, might not that needed lyricism be today in the lyrics of popular songs? In those songs that, by virtue of the new technologies of communication, are produced and consumed in our time in quantities enormously larger than those of literatures ever reached in all countries and in all epochs?

Ladies and gentlemen, it is not because of simple aversion that I refuse to inscribe myself into that exclusive club of "lyrics" that today constitutes almost entirely the poetry written in our world. Nor is there any disdain on my part for that lyricism manifested in popular music—I think, on the contrary, that those new techniques have given lyricism a possibility of expression and communication never known before. I am merely offering a possible topic of meditation to the theoreticians of literature, and appealing to them not to seek in not-sung (or unsingable) poetry written today a quality, that of lyricism, that was never the intention of the authors to achieve or even to explore.

Poetry seems to me something much broader: it is the exploration of the materiality of words and of the possibilities of organization of verbal structures, things that have nothing to do with what is romantically called inspiration, or even intuition. In this respect, I believe that lyricism, upon finding in popular music the element that fulfills it and gives it its prestige, has liberated written and not-sung poetry and has allowed it to return to operate in territory that once belonged to it. It has made possible too the exercise of poetry as emotive exploration of the world of things and as rigorous construction of lucid formal structures, lucid objects of language. Thank you.

Rio de Janeiro
August 31, 1992

Translation from the Portuguese by Djelal Kadir

KAMAU BRATHWAITE
THE 1994 LAUREATE

Kamau Brathwaite (1930–2020), a poet, historian, literary critic, and essayist, was born in Bridgetown, the capital city of Barbados. Brathwaite spent his childhood in Barbados but would spend his adult life traveling, learning, and teaching all over the globe. He attended Harrison University in Barbados and Pembroke College in Cambridge, England, where he graduated with honors in 1953. After graduation, Brathwaite embarked on a journey to Ghana where he worked in Ghana's Ministry of Education for more than ten years. During that time, he familiarized himself with Ghanaian traditional verse and precolonial African myths, which would be influential in his own writing. He earned his PhD in philosophy from the University of Sussex in 1968, and taught at Harvard University, the University of the West Indies, and New York University. His works include the *Rights of Passage* trilogy (1967–69), *Days & Nights* (1975), *Mother*

Poem (1977), *History of the Voice: The Development of Nation Language in Anglophone Caribbean Poetry* (1984), *Sun Poem* (1982), *Middle Passages* (1992), *Dream Stories* (1994), *Born to Slow Horses* (2005), and, most recently, *The Lazarus Poems* (2017).

> The constant i wd even say consistent fabric & praxis of my work has been to connect broken islands, cracked, broken words, worlds, friendships, ancestories.
>
> —Kamau Brathwaite

The Voice of African Presence
Ngũgĩ wa Thiong'o

In May this year [1994] my wife and I called a few friends to our house in Orange, New Jersey, to celebrate the arrival of our daughter, born at the end of April. Among them was Kamau Brathwaite, who later rose to read a poem to honor the new arrival. The poem had lines that repeated the name of our daughter, Mũmbi, Mũmbi, Mũmbi, Mũmbi, almost like a religious chant. Now *Mũmbi* means "creator," and we gave our daughter the name because she is in fact my mother, Wanjik, who died in 1989 but is now reborn in Mũmbi. Her full name, then, is Mũmbi Wanjikũ, creator of my mother. Mũmbi is also the name of the original mother of all Gĩkũyũ people. In thinking about the evening afterwards, I was struck anew by Kamau Brathwaite's invocation of the name.

My thoughts took me back to 1972, when Kamau, then Edward Brathwaite, came to the Department of Literature at Nairobi University, Kenya, on a City of Nairobi Fellowship. The department was undergoing tremendous changes. We were trying to break away from the old colonial tradition that emphasized our colonial connections to Europe as primary but not our natural connections to Africa and the rest of the world. We are all familiar with the often-told stories of African children having to learn all about daffodils and snow long before they are able to name the flowers of their own lands. Rebellion against this was the basis of the 1969 Nairobi declaration calling for the abolition of the English Department as then constituted and for its restructuring along entirely new lines. By 1972 we had started breaking away from the centrality of English literature in our syllabus to a new dispensation that emphasized the centrality of the African experience at home on the continent and abroad in the Caribbean, Afro-America, and other parts of the world. We wanted a dialogue among all the literatures of the entire pan-African universe and between them and those of South America, Asia, and Europe in that order. Central to the enterprise was orature, the long tradition of verbal arts passed from mouth to ear in both their classical and contemporary expressions. Other needs arose from the new centrality. For instance, instead of inviting Shakespearean scholars from England, we now wanted scholars from the rest of Africa, from the Caribbean, and from Afro-America. That kind of academic exchange and communication would be more useful to us in cementing the new foundation of our literary and cultural studies. We were also rebelling against a tradition that taught literature as if it was divorced from its social and historical milieu. We wanted to see, explore connections between phenomena. So we hoped that we would get scholars with a sensitive awareness of the connections between literature and life. Who was going to be our first visitor? This was a crucial question, particularly in our new beginnings: suppose we brought a scholar who would come to reinforce the very traditions we were now fighting against?

I had met Edward Brathwaite in London in 1966 when I was doing research on Caribbean literature at Leeds University. It was a gathering which in fact was the formal beginning of the Caribbean Arts Movement. I did not know then that Brathwaite was its founding spirit. Even less did I know that at different but crucial moments in our literary lives we had both been influenced in a fundamental way by one of the classics of Barabajan and Caribbean literature, George Lamming's *In the Castle of My Skin.* For me, Kamau's brilliant poems in *Rights of Passage,* out in 1967 and followed by *Masks* in 1968 and *Islands* in 1969, had added to that sense of self-discovery. In this I was not alone. Those collections became part of the new syllabus. There was in fact something about their content and form that made everybody feel that they fit the historical moment, our search for a connection. And so there was really little doubt as to whom we wanted as our first scholar of what we saw as the beginnings of a new era. Brathwaite was then teaching history at the University of the West Indies' Mona Campus in Jamaica. We were very excited when he accepted our invitation, although the fellowship did not really amount to much in terms of money. As a lecturer, he proved a great teacher. He saw no barriers between geography, history, and literature. What formed the African and Caribbean sensibility could not be divorced from the landscape and the historical experience.

This to me is still one of the most remarkable elements in the life and work of Kamau Brathwaite. He is a connecting spirit. Europe, Africa, the Caribbean, and now America, all important landmarks in his life and thought, find expression in his work in their impact on one another. He explores the African presence in Africa, the Caribbean, and the world, not in its staticness but in its movement, in its changingness, in its interactions. In these interactions the African presence is not a passive element. Whether across the Sahara deserts, through the savannas and tropical forests, across the Atlantic, say, in all its continental and diasporic dimensions, it is a resisting spirit, refusing to succumb, ready to rebuild anew from the ashes of natural disasters and human degradation. In his work, taken as a whole, the physical cannot be divorced from the metaphysical or the material from the religious. In his capacity to move freely from geography to history to literature to cultural criticism, Brathwaite exemplifies a great tradition of the Caribbean intellectual, the tradition of C. L. R. James, Frantz Fanon, Walter Rodney, Aimé Césaire, George Lamming, to mention just a few who readily come to mind. What connects these names, apart from their intellectual versatility, is also their unapologetic claim to Africa as their roots. These islands have given so much to twentieth-century Africa and the world, and our students in Nairobi could now see that for themselves in the presence of the lecturer before them. It was remarkable, and Brathwaite was the talk among the students and faculty.

But it was when Edward Brathwaite performed sections from his poems that we truly appreciated what we had been sensing. The voice. We were being mesmerized by the voice of orature. We were captives of a heritage we knew so well but from which our education had been alienating us. His voice was returning us to our formative roots in *orature*. This was what had been created by our mothers and fathers, and it was there in his performance for us all to see. This orality runs through Brathwaite's entire work and is what gives it its very distinctive quality. This comes out powerfully through performance and makes us realize that, in his literary output, Brathwaite gropes for the word in its oral purity. In doing so, he is groping for the voice of the peasant, the submerged voice of the many who toil and endure.

But alas, our enthusiasm was not necessarily shared by the establishment, who thought they had already given in too much by agreeing to have a scholar who came from places other than England itself, the real home of real literature. Tension was in fact developing between, on the one hand, the students and the faculty, who understood, and on the other the administrative establishment, who could not realize whom we had in our midst and treat him accordingly.

Then something happened that I will never forget. I invited Brathwaite to my rented home in Tigoni, Limuru. The land around Tigoni and Limuru is truly beautiful. Not surprisingly, Tigoni was fairly central to Kenya's history, because it was one of the earliest bones of contention between the British colonial settlers and Kenyans. The demand for the return of the stolen lands of Tigoni to their original owners was one of the key elements in the anticolonial militancy which in the fifties erupted into the Mau Mau armed struggle. The fact that now in the seventies Tigoni was occupied by African landlords, though not the actual original owners, symbolized that Kenya was no longer exclusively a white man's country. Brathwaite was coming into an area hallowed with memories of intense struggles.

I should add that the invitations to meet Brathwaite were sent solely through word of mouth. It turned out to be a big welcome party, with the faculty and some students driving thirty kilometers from Nairobi to attend the gathering. Women led by my mother came from all the villages around. So the peasants from the villages and the men and women of letters from Nairobi, the big city, now gathered in this rural outpost to celebrate Brathwaite's presence. Ceremonial goats were slaughtered in his honor. The women performed. The voice of orality from rural Kenya. It was during the ceremony, with the women singing Gĩtiiro, a kind of dialogue in song and dance, that Edward Brathwaite was given the name of Kamau, the name of a generation that long ago had struggled with the elements to tame the land and make us into what we now were. Edward, the name of the British king under whose brief reign in the 1920s some of the Tigoni lands had been appropriated by blue-blooded aristocrats who wanted to turn Kenya into a white man's country, had now been replaced by Kamau. Naming Brathwaite became the heart of the ceremony, which was also symbolically appropriate.

The right to name ourselves, our landscape; the struggle for the means with which to name ourselves; the search, in other words, for the true voice of our collective being—is this not at the heart of Kamau Brathwaite's work from *Rights of Passage* in 1967 to the *Barabajan Poems* in 1994 and elaborated in his critical works, now collected under the suggestive title *Roots*? The right, the process, and the means to name our world are behind his notion of the Nation Language, that submerged language of the enslaved which, through evolutionary and at times revolutionary subversion of the dominating, asserts itself, often changing the character of what was supposed to be the mainstream.

It was this ceremony way back in 1972 that I was remembering when going over Kamau's invocations on Mūmbi's name in May this year. Little did Kamau know that he was actually invoking the name of my mother and that of all the peasants who welcomed him in 1972 and gave him his name, asserting through song and dance that he was being welcomed in the lands where his ancestral umbilical cord had been buried. Didn't know? That is not even true, because all his work is really an invocation of the power of the African peasantry in all its struggles in Africa, the Caribbean, and the world. He is saying that if we are to claim the twentieth and twenty-first century properly and creatively, we have to connect ourselves to that power. Acknowledgment of the past becomes the basis of strengthening the present and opening out to the future.

Kamau and I are now in the same Department of Comparative Literature at New York University, for reasons that well go back to what we were trying to do at Nairobi in the seventies and therefore what had made possible that invitation; but that is another story. Tonight, my wife and I are very touched at being asked to be part of this truly great occasion in honor of one of the most remarkable voices of the twentieth century. For we are celebrating thirty years of a continuous creative output in theater, poetry, criticism, and history, from his plays published in 1964 to his most recent production, *Barabajan Poems,* in 1994. We are celebrating a producer who through journals like *Savacou* has created forums for others. We are celebrating a teacher who has drawn from, and given back to, Africa, the Caribbean, Europe, and the US. We are celebrating a gifted individual who believes in the collective spirit as seen in his work as the founding spirit of efforts like the Caribbean Arts Movement. We are celebrating the voice of connections, because what is so remarkable about him is not that he is a great poet, historian, critic, and teacher, but that these are not separate entities in himself. They are rather expressions of a searching spirit, searching for the connective link in human life and struggles. We are also celebrating a most courageous man who has gone through personal adversities without succumbing to the death of the spirit. In congratulating Kamau for the 1994 Neustadt Prize, we wish him all the best as we eagerly wait for his many future productions. We hope he will continue to inspire us to join hands so that individually and collectively, we, to paraphrase him, can make here, on these broken grounds . . . something torn and new . . . , a communal future of wholeness.

Norman, Oklahoma
September 30, 1994

Renowned Kenyan writer, editor, and academic **Ngũgĩ wa Thiong'o** *(b. 1938) was himself a finalist for the 2008 Neustadt Prize and also successfully championed Nuruddin Farah for the prize in 1998. He is currently a distinguished professor of English and comparative literature at the University of California, Irvine.*

Newstead to Neustadt
Kamau Brathwaite

Professor Kadir, Editor of *World Literature Today* & Coordinator of this
Moment

Yr Excellencies: The Hon David Walters, Governor of Oklahoma; Yr
Excellency Rudi Webster, Ambassador of Barbados to the United States;
Yr Excellency Richard Leiton Bernal, Ambassador of Jamaica to the United
States and Mrs. Bernal (even though you are not here)

Professor Morris, Interim President of the University of Oklahoma; Jahruba,
divine musicians; Professor Harclyde Walcott, Artistic Director, the Philip
Sherlock Arts Centre, University of the West Indies, Mona, Jamaica; Mary
Brathwaite Morgan, my sister & Assistant Registrar, University of the West
Indies, Mona, Jamaica; Ngũgĩ wa Thiong'o & Njerri Ndungu

Walter Neustadt Jr. and Mrs. Neustadt and members of the Neustadt Family—

First I must acknowledge the totem honour you accord me in bringing
me here for this most prestigious of literary awards. As I keep on saying,
I had *no idea* this kind of thing was going on behind my back. You meet
in camera and unexpectedly publish me the picture you have so darkly
selected. The names of my colleague previous winners, the names of those
in consideration with me this year—the whole thing is so awesome it has me
walking, like a certain musician, on eggshells

What all this says is that there are still some places in the world where
writers & their writing are taken seriously, our work focussed and treated
w/respect—and at the end of the evening we're even handsomely *paid*
for it; presented w/this silver feather as a reminder of responsibility—

somewhere one senses also an arrow pointed at the heart of any personal
presumption—& there will be later even a subtle kind of festschrift erected
in our honour

Is ALTOGETHER TOO MUCH! But I not complainin. We complain enough about
'neglect'. Here at least & at last are dedicated people putting our poems
where their hearts are: Neustadt, *WLT*, Oklahoma!

And all this, haltering as it is, is to sincerely thank you on behalf of my muse,
my muses & on behalf of the Caribbean—for here is a person from these
small islands far south of here who has been brought all these prairie miles
of North American heartland to this crossroads of the 'Trail of Tears' for this
honour by an African brother a further 10,000 miles away (I refer to Kofi
Awoonor, my colleague-fellow poet & Neustadt advocat who unfortunately
cd not be here w/us this evening) and who now that he is here, recognizes, as
he hopes to show in the second part of this thanks-tune, that he was always
on the way here—that the Prize is the occasion, almost the xcuse—but not
the DNA of the business; that there is time & spaces shared by our three
landscapes—

Antillean, OklaHOMEan, African—
in which he recognize his poem

I'll speak about this in the second part of this Acknowledgement

What I want to end w/here is a plea for continued conversation among
ourselves. In a world of increase & increasing materialism—trailer-loads of
it along the information superhighway—we, as livicators of this special art
of vision/writing, dreamer/saying, are much reduced; in danger, some of us,
of becoming petitioners not practitioners—dependent upon grants; upon,
as Tennessee Williams long ago warned, the generosity &/or kindness of
strangers; estranged as many of us are from our villages, our oumforts, from
our own zodiacs

And almost as a desperate response of counter-insurrection, it wd seem, instead of SHARING more w/each other, we pull apart into our own script/ ure, into the precise particular bleeding of our own individual tick-hearts, into our own deconstructions, for goodness sake; so that the possible Global Village (Ogotemmellian as this may be) is on its way towards the Global Ghetto; and even as

artists (assuming that you will agree w/ me that there is a special grief, a special GIFT, a special plomb in being this) we allow Ourselves to be divided—or worse, to remain divided—by race by age by class by colour by gender by preoccupation of the stampen ground; producing therefore more heat than light, more artifice than art beat & far more argument than Sphinx

And I'm not saying this because I'm xpected to
SAY SOMETHING
on an august day in September such as this, but because the constant i wd even say consistent fabric & praxis of my work has been to connect broken islands, cracked, broken words, worlds, friendships, ancestories & I have seen the sea outside our yard bring grain by gentle grain out of its granary, cost upon coast, & then in one long sweep of light or night, take all away again A poem tree of tidalectics. A strange 12-branching history of it which I leave you wit

from Newstead to Neustadt
*
haltering the landscapes of the wind

The place i grow in—the underside of the leaf of my childhood—like the other & inner slide of the sea into which I am born—is call Newstead, the hoom & heart of that miracle village you must know by now as Mile & Quarter (MyLann Quarter) [*Barabajan Poems* 1994]. Here is open canefield caneland snuggled by the darker colour of trees, time, green waters of vegetation flowing around the islands of hills, Brevitor caves, windmills,

Great white houses (yr horses) on the horizon among more lime, more trees
& our warm sleepy cooking-smoke villages in the shallow valleys of sound.
And at the centre of this is this house of the ancestors, Newstead, which is
quietly preparing itself for the Neustadt Prize in a similar landscape of spirit
& spirits sixty years later on, on the other side of the wall

I bring you therefore a very special greeting of the most intimate recognition.
I in a sense am sent to return to myself what you both give me: speech, shafts
of canelight, a green silver feather, my ancestories coming to be born here
again: planter & slave, Ogoun & buffalo, Newstead & Neustadt spiritdances
of the native crossroads

And because this is such a special something in such an awesome silence
of such sound in which to rise this evening & celebration THANK YOU for
these thousand years brought to this brief account of visibility in this time &
in this town & w/this tongue, I wish w/yr permission & w/as much aplomb
& care as i can limp & limbo up to & pour a brief libation at the foot of the
several trees of me/mory I growing see here in these beautiful landscapes
where the umbilical chords of my voice, I suppose we will have to call it
that—book, bell, trigger, treasure of metaphor—have been placed all along
the curved tale & tails of my journey by my mother & father & sisters &
my ancestor brother & Bob'ob the Ogoun carpenter & Grannpa & Esse
& Fillmore and 'all the aunts & uncles' & Queen Victoria & the Sistine
Chapel & Oshogbo & Hounsi Twenefor & Stephen Daedalus & Stephen
Agyemann & Boukman & W B Yeats & Sycorax & Oya & Agamemnon
dead [. . .]

Norman, Oklahoma
September 30, 1994

ASSIA DJEBAR
THE 1996 LAUREATE

Assia Djebar (1936–2015) was the pen name of Fatima-Zohra Imalayen. She was born in a small coastal town in Algeria, where her father taught French. In 1955 she became the first woman to be accepted into the École Normale Supérieure in Paris, where she published her first novel in 1957. Her pen name originated with this novel, a work she feared would anger her father. Her first collection of verse was published in 1969, the same year that she would also publish her first work of drama. In 1978 she became a film director, and her work on *La nouba des femmes du Mont Chenoua* earned her the prestigious Grand Prize at the Venice Film Festival in 1979. In 2005, based on her superior body of work, Djebar was accepted into the Académie Française as its first member from the Maghreb. Djebar's body of prose includes the titles *Le Soif* (1957; Eng. *The Mischief*, 1958), *Les Alouettes Naïves* (1967), *Femmes d'Alger dans leur appartement* (1980; Eng. *The Women of Algiers in Their Apartment*, 1992), and *Vaste est la prison* (1995; Eng. *So Vast the Prison*,

1999). Her director's credits include the films *La Nouba des femmes du Mont Chenoua* (1977) and *La Zerda ou les chants de l'oubli* (1992). In addition to the Neustadt Prize, Djebar was honored with the 1998 International Prize of Palmi and the 2000 Peace Prize of the German Book Trade.

> Perhaps my books can prolong the echo of the voices of so many other women . . . those who keep as their hope the power of their dreams, the tenacity of their memory, and especially the unshaken force of their revolt.
>
> —Assia Djebar

A Letter to Assia Djebar
Barbara Frischmuth

Altaussee [Austria], 4 July 1996

Dear Assia,

Time and again I have been asked why I nominated *you* for the Neustadt Prize, but the answer to that question, considering your complex manner of writing, can only be a complex, multilayered one. I first came across you—actually I was pushed into you—when a representative of your Swiss publisher who recalled my earlier studies in Oriental languages and literatures sent me your book *Fantasia*. I leafed through it attempting to recognize Arabic expressions despite their francophone formulation. (Although my Arabic, which was always only "beginning-level," has long since trickled away in the flow of the years, I still like to play this little game.) Then I began to read, and with the very first page I fell under the spell of your "multiple fractured" language. I was greatly moved at how you constructed a monument to your father as "the giver of the language" in which you write. As indicated in the texts, he was a strict parent yet also one who took you by the hand and led you to school. My own father "fell" in Russia in 1943 (to use one of those euphemistic expressions for the various ways of dying in a war). I was two years old at the time and have no memory of him at all. But therefore I have never missed him either. Still, the way in which you speak of your Muslim father, who so lovingly planned your education, caused me to think about the father I never knew, just as if he had actually been lost to me.

And you, you who have received an inheritance from your father—namely, the French language and thereby a certain freedom—you had the courage, above all in your book *Loin de Médine* (Eng. *Far from Medina*, 1994), to speak of a very important subject, the daughters of Muslims and their rights to claim their inheritance, and for that alone you deserve every prize in the world. The clarity with which you diagnose the early splitting of Islam into the Sunni and Shi'a camps as a consequence of the denial of that inheritance should be the envy of many a Muslim theologian. They all speak of Ali; you speak of Fatima. It was a stroke of genius to give voice to the women around Mohammed and in Mohammed's day, to show who they were: warriors, poets, queens, noblewomen, and slaves, not merely Arab women from Mecca and Medina. In letting them speak, you rewrite the history of the origins of Muslim civilization and you quite rightly emphasize the fact that for young girls and women the Islamic revolution consisted in assuring them an inheritance, assuring them that they might receive from their fathers what was due them. But then Fatima, Mohammed's daughter, was robbed of this inheritance when she was not permitted to be "the scribe at his death"—that is, to serve as trustee of his spiritual inheritance. The consequences are well known, but I have never heard the cause (or at least one of the principal causes) called by name so clearly. For that you deserve full credit, Assia.

You appear not only to have examined your own inheritance in a critical light but also to have analyzed it precisely. "Thus the language that my father had been at such pains for me to learn [the French of your French-teacher father] serves as a go-between, and from now a double, contradictory sign reigns over my initiation," you state in *Fantasia,* and thus you make language itself the theme of your literature—namely, that "multiple fractured" language which you say in *Le blanc de l'Algérie* (1995; Eng. *Algerian White*, 2000) "has inscribed itself incessantly in a linguistic triangle" consisting of Berber, Arabic, and French. You speak of the "language of power" which seeks to marginalize anything considered to be "other," as French did to Arabic at first, then Arabic did in turn to French when it became the narrowly construed "national language." You add two more "languages of power": Latin, which was an obligatory course of study at my *gymnasium;* and Turkish, which I later studied voluntarily and at several universities. But I would not wish to read your books in any of these "languages of power," Assia. Perhaps the German translations—which are all quite good—are for precisely that reason the most suitable means of conveying to me, line by line, the unsettling content of your works: that fundamental conflict which I know from early on, since I too write in an "elevated or literary language" quite different from the dialect of my childhood and from the colloquial speech of my native land.

The sentence in which you so aptly define this constellation demands to be quoted: "To attempt an autobiography using French words alone is to lend oneself to the vivisector's scalpel, revealing what lies beneath the skin. The flesh flakes off and with it, seemingly, the last shreds of the unwritten language of my childhood." And in your books the scabs fall away as well, along with the hastily applied bandages meant more to cover than to heal the wounds inflicted upon your land in the course of its history.

Therefore I can only marvel that you have taken it upon yourself to deal with history, with raw and unhealed history. For your incorruptible eye, which has enabled even me, who knows Algeria only through television, to understand something of what has occurred and is occurring in that country, is also scientifically trained. One notices that, and I find that one may take note of it. But by itself that still would not yield a portrait in which I as an outsider can recognize not only Algeria but rather the entire horrifying course of the world. Likely, the fact that your account—so full of love and passion but also of revulsion—sounds so completely unpartisan or unbiased has to do with that distance which French accords to you in respect to your country and its history. From the very beginning, that account inspired trust in me, trust as a reader, which means that one may submit oneself unreservedly to your view of things without later feeling one has been deceived or misled concerning the facts of the matter.

The fact that the language of your childhood, the language in which you feel, shines forth time and again between the lines of your text, not in the form of individual words but rather in the form of perceptions which must first be "translated" or transcribed, opens up an entirely new dimension for French. I notice a similar phenomenon among Turks who write in German, the offspring of the first generation of guest workers, most of whom were very young when they first came to our country. Their German is as good as that of anyone who has spent thirteen years in a German-language school, but there is more to it than that: a barely perceptible shift or displacement, which, when it is handled in masterly fashion, endows German with a completely new charm. Your art—forgive me for tossing you into a single pot with others in this regard, but the connection is very important to me—and also the art of many of your Turkish, Persian, and Arab colleagues, whether they now write in French or in German, lies in that evocation of the inexhaustible resources of a world not narrated in the language in which it is spoken, a world in which feelings are deeply rooted and from which one must escape in order to be able to recognize it. Just how narrow the connection to this original world still is can be seen in the empty spaces it leaves behind, spaces which stand out in the written language like large gleaming specks against a background of cultural and sociohistorical networks. In somewhat more concrete terms, this touching human warmth, the all-permeating sympathy, the precise and detailed depiction of all the violence, crime, and perfidy which, despite everything, never posits hatred as the unavoidable counterpole—that is what, it seems to me, shines forth from your early language.

The astonishment which erupts from the young girl for the first time in speech persists in more restrained form, permeates all your books, and infects me too as a reader. And not only the astonishment but also the affection, an affection that demands time, time to expose everything that has been buried, to inspect it, as you have done with the countless stories and faces of the women of your land, the mothers and grandmothers who "were already dead long before the grave." You have made their voices audible and stripped away their multiple veils, directed our attention to their humanity and let them narrate their fate from their own point of view. And for all the clarity with which you have recorded this scandalous history of confinement, masking, and imposed silence, you have always retained a certain tenderness for the "others" (contrary to tradition, let me for once designate men as the "others"), as your latest book, *Le blanc de l'Algérie,* proves, for there you urge upon us, your readers, all the Algerian writers who have been killed or have died from illnesses. Instead of polemicizing, you recount how things happened, you attempt to follow your friends down to their final moments, in loving sympathy and with the intention of turning them into objects of affection transcending their deaths. At the same time, you succeed so well in capturing the sheer monstrousness of this war which re-erupts daily in your country that our eyes grow wide with horror. You also do not shy away from stealing into the minds of those who commit these atrocities, conveying their supposed arguments, rationales, and justifications, and showing the chain of violent acts that has made criminals of victims (and sometimes vice versa) to be a chain which binds the combatants to each other. I marvel at you for this as well.

In your works those young warriors who have strangled, stabbed, or shot to death your Algerian writer-colleagues and have considered themselves in the right in doing so talk among themselves in such a manner that one can imagine what goes on in their minds, even as one's outrage mounts, however senseless the deeds may appear and however perverted the logic of the arguments may be. They call themselves "God's Fools," an expression for madmen and mystics in early Islam, for those "from whom the pen had been taken away. Whose words and deeds the angel-scribes did not record, because the fools were not subject to the law and for them the duty of adhering to the law's precepts did not apply. (Go mad and let reason forsake you, said Leila to Madshnun. Then no one will harm you when you enter my village .)" Lokman Sarrakhsi was one of those fools of our Dear Lord, as were many others of whom the legends tell. But never executioners, who carried out judgments rendered by others.

That, then, is the list of themes which caused my interest in your work to become so strong; but it was not merely a matter of themes, as you yourself know only too well, not even when language itself is the theme. What attracted me to you most was your manner of treating those themes in your "fragmented language." (Incidentally, your narrative art is extremely refined, bathed in all the waters of the prose writer's art.) And I readily admit that this manner of yours stirs in me a delight that is not at all easy to allay— which means simply that I do not wish to stop reading you. I say *you* intentionally, for we are our books and ultimately write ourselves in an almost corporeal fashion, just as our language is always a physical, bodily thing, even in those moments when it appears most infused by the spirit or the intellect. It made me extremely happy, Assia, that I was at last able to make your personal acquaintance in Norman, and that we all danced together, and that Hanan al-Shaykh was present, and all the others as well. I hope that this prize makes you even more well known, and—what is likely more important—that it will afford you time, time "for the retreat of writing, in search of a language outside the languages," as you wished yourself at the end of *Le blanc de l'Algérie.*

I embrace you,

Barbara

Translation from the German by William Riggan

Barbara Frischmuth *(b. 1941) is an Austrian writer of novels, short stories, and plays as well as a translator. Two of her novels and a selection of short stories have appeared in English translation by Ariadne Press.*

Assia Djebar's Lyrical Longing and Pitiless Pen
William H. Gass

The lyricism which comes through the French to us is indeed like a painter's light and falls softly through a curtain on Assia Djebar's affecting scenes, as if we were supposed to see a woman bathing in a Pierre Bonnard or a dancer in a Degas and not a woman weeping in her kitchen, calling out to Allah for relief, the light letting us wonder what her trouble is since she has a shower and a sink—a porcelain sink and a pink marble tub, built-in cabinets to boot— good fortune could not have a broader smile—and a husband with the easy name of "he" whose feet at least come and go, go, god be praised, into the masculine monitored streets on masculine business concerning masculine affairs, into those vast spaces a male god made.

Assia Djebar makes it clear to us, who have a different history and live in a different time, what, for an Algerian woman, her apartment is—her whole small world—because even when she leaves it, she is not allowed to touch that great outdoors, ideally not even with her eyes.

In Afghanistan unveiled women have been beaten with radio antennas ripped from parked cars; adulterers will be stoned as in the good old days; surgeons are forbidden to operate upon female bodies, bodies which have been turned into sheeted ghosts more menacing than lepers; women's schools are closed; and in Iran, bicycle seats, since they resemble saddles, are denied a woman's weight. And why are saddles denied them? They may not rise so high or ride astride a stallion. The gradient of oppression is long and

steep; the climb, in those layered gowns, is difficult. In every country, someone no longer a child is swaddled, another injustice is suffered, varied tyrannies are endured.

In their apartments, even those women whose senses have been awakened by love can only carry them like bedclothes into the courtyard to be
aired. How many paces from one room to another? How many days will pass
before, at night, the cool air comes? Here escape is measured by degrees, as
though digging a tunnel: how far shall she walk before removing her veil? It
is a world where women watch women, where mothers try to tie their daughters to custom as much as the men do. A curse, a prayer, jostle for the same
breath, and both are useless. Was it better when there was no alternative to be
dreamt, to be glimpsed on television, to be encountered in some city square?

Assia Djebar, compelled by circumstances to write about the daily life of
Algerian women (her inherited subject) in a tongue which is not theirs, has,
nevertheless, with her novels and stories, her poetry, a play, and her films,
exposed the plight of her countrywomen to the wide world. With her percep-
tive, sensual, and resourceful French, which reaches us now hidden under
one more layer of foreign language, she has drawn open this curtained culture and spoken of it without shrillness, without endangering the modesty of
her models, without the pleasures of righteous indignation, but with a pen so
pitiless it spares us nothing of this massive crime, a condition which faces its
future by walking backward into the past, as Assia Djebar, a trained historian
and teacher, knows well, so that her characters include women living at the
dawn of Islam as well as those suffering from its nightfall.

To expose . . . to lay bare . . . What an extraordinary and daring accomplishment. How many layers of concealment had to be removed—seven veils?
And each one symbolic, through and through, of political, sexual, and educational enstiflement. Algerian women, their feelings held out of sight in their
veiled heads, their ears allowed to hear prayers, their eyes given them to weep
with, fists to beat upon their chests, their mouths for ritual wailing, their
Arabic softened as when women speak to women; kept in closed compounds,
weighed upon by husbands who have been arranged for them, so they may
then be fondled like a pipe stem; their entire life and outlook surrounded by

the plans of men and the cruel and stupid tyrannies of male "isms," by a land, for women, empty of openness or opportunity; followed always by death, as though they were a bone to a starved dog, by a death which will claim them when they become worn and ill and thin from bearing the children they will see sicken and die before they see their own death in the doorway.

It is difficult to know whether it would have been better for the Algerian women Assia Djebar has written of to be able to read her themselves and real- ize that one of them has portrayed, even celebrated, their plight, although to meager consequence; or to have their story sent into distant comers, so far away as Oklahoma, into an America where the awareness her work brings may only add to our despair at mankind's management of man, or perhaps encour- age a sympathy which dresses up a sense of superiority and inherent indiffer- ence the way wind reddens a cold cheek.

When men hide their women away, they are also hiding something of themselves, and the cruelties they practice are cruel to them too. If I strike a tree stump often enough with an axe, I shall make muscle, not merely fire- wood; and if I am a jailer, I grow bars, and my heart is hard as pavement, and I soon see only stone, the air is stale, and my food tastes of tin. How beautifully Assia Djebar presents these sour consequences, like a shining coin pressed painfully into a suppliant palm.

My copy of *A Sister to Scheherazade* (that wonderful double-threaded story of two women who have been quite different wives to the same man, finding the same man as different as two men, though hung from his history like wash on a line) is described on its cover as Fiction/Women's Literature. Heinemann does not mean to say simply that this book is about women, for *Madame Bovary* is about them, *Anna Karenina* is about them, *Sister Carrie* is about them, as is *The Wings of the Dove.* So does this label mean that Assia Djebar's work is by a woman, and can safely be ignored, or that it is a book written for women the way garter belts are fabricated? I do hate such sec- tions of the bookstore—those of "special interest," where literary importance is lowered to the level of the economics of politics and women's subjects are sanitized while women are insulted.

Penetration, pregnancy, pain, a new life delivered to an old death. The womb is not a prison for the child; the womb imprisons the woman. Assia Djebar's work should be placed in that section of the store most frequented by men: among books on horses, hunting, sport. Look there . . . a Delacroix depicting three women sitting at the edge of a darkness, waiting like saucers for their cups, like clothing in a dresser drawer. Ah . . . a volume about harems. Perhaps the man will put his curious nose in it like the fabled camel's into the tent.

Assia Djebar's work deserves to receive this distinguished prize because of the importance of her subject, certainly, and on account of the moral horrors it so vividly and fearlessly depicts. But let us for a moment wildly suppose that women have been liberated all over the world, and that men are being stoned for adultery, and circumcised when caught uncovered in the street, kept out of college but allowed to drink tea. Is *Women of Algiers,* in such a circumstance, now of only historical interest?

I remember a moment—it is in the story "The Woman Who Weeps"— when a woman whose husband has beaten her describes how her face felt as if it were going to fall into her hands, and that image took me to the poor creature, her head in hers, whom Malte Laurids Brigge encounters in a Paris street, and who, startled by his approach, pulls herself so sharply away that she leaves her torn face in her palms where it can be seen now from the inside; then, within a page length of "The Woman Who Weeps," the sultry weather is said to be subsiding like an overripe fruit will drop, and I'm sent off to recall Mahfouz's description of the Cairo sun setting in the middle of the afternoon into the city's smog, a sunset I've seen, passing from lemon to orange to plum. That is to say: Assia Djebar has entered the whole of this head's literature, so I shall remember her words when I turn to Mahfouz and her image when I reread Rilke. The sun, dunked in dust, but always a fruit. Feeding the soil its seed.

The Neustadt Prize, the most important international award we have, stands for this priceless connection which literature can make between distantly separated places and far-off times, between a ceremony in Oklahoma and a city in Algeria, between men who will worship women despite the damage they've done them and the guilt they bear, and the women whom the men hope will not one day feed them to the hogs.

This brief salute to a long career is being given by another writer and not an ambassador, not a politician, and did not begin therefore with the customary invocation of distinguished names and positions (undoubtedly deserving of everyone's gratitude), because that absence was meant by me to be another sign of our prizewinner's success (and the jury's good sense), for she has realized one of our deepest dreams: to write beautifully while still bothering people.

Assia Djebar is not being celebrated here because she has brought us more bad news, or exotic treats, or even her eloquent indignation, worthy as much of that may be; we are lauding her here because she has given weeping its words and longing its lyrics.

International Writers Center
Washington University, St. Louis

William H. Gass *(1924–2017) was the author of seven works of fiction, nine books of essays, and a book of conversations. A professor of philosophy and the humanities at Washington University in St. Louis, his many prizes included an American Book Award, three National Book Critics Circle Awards, and the Truman Capote Award for Literary Criticism. Knopf published* The William H. Gass Reader *in 2018.*

The Power of Solidarity in the Solitude of Exile
Assia Djebar

In Louisiana, on the 29th of March 1996, when I heard that I had been awarded the Neustadt Prize, I received the news with both joy and sadness. "I am happy, I am unhappy," I told Djelal Kadir over the telephone. "Happy for myself, unhappy for my country in the present time." I was both unhappy and happy for all my friends and colleagues who had died, for all those who had fallen: foreign priests, young women teachers and journalists, and the many anonymous dead in Algeria today. Happy that they have come with me, for as I present myself today before you, they are all around me; unhappy each time I speak of them, each time that I write of their absence . . .

The Arab poet Adonis has written: "Joy has wings but no body / Sadness has a body, but no wings!" Unlike my poet friend, I would like to thank you by offering a response that would have the wings—or the energy—of sadness, and that would give a body, a solidity, to the joy of our encounter here today.

I present myself as the fourteenth laureate of the Neustadt International Prize for Literature. Allow me to say a word about two of my most prestigious forerunners: Elizabeth Bishop, the great American poet, and Francis Ponge, the great French poet—"the master of still life in poetry," as Michel Butor described him. Following these two predecessors, I am the second woman and the second French-speaking writer to receive the Neustadt Prize. But in relation to them, my difference is double: on the one hand, I am a writer of fiction, a novelist; on the other hand, I come from a world where women are traditionally kept "in the shadows" and have been excluded from writing for much too long. For myself, I come from a South presently in tumult and in transition.

"Women in the shadows?" I, however, am not in the shadows. Far from it. I am an exception. Let us remember the names of other celebrated women writers: I think of the Senegalese author Mariama Bâ, who died too young, leaving us two poignant novels; I think of the great Iranian poet Forough Farrokhzad, who died in an accident at an even younger age, in the late 1960s; I also think of an Egyptian woman, the novelist Latifa el Zayyat, who passed away this past September 12 at the age of seventy-three and whose first novel, *La porte ouverte* (1960), opened the door for a new literature created by women of the Arabic language.

I inscribe my name in the celebrated list of Neustadt laureates, surrounded by my African sisters and those of Muslim origin: they could have been here, honored in my place tonight. I feel them at my side, now as I stand here before you: though they are invisible, they are very much present.

I mentioned that I am a writer of fiction. The Peruvian novelist Mario

Vargas Llosa has defined fiction in one of his essays as "truth through lying." He adds a remark that I would like to have written myself: "In the heart of all fiction, the flame of protest burns brightly." During the years of 1995 and 1996, not only in Algeria, where women are victimized because they embody images of modernity in movement, and in Iran, where silence weighs down on those women who resist, but also in Afghanistan these past few months, where the women who flee do so under the veils of ghosts which we find so strange, my own protest, born from this Islamic culture (a culture, however, where in Turkey, in Pakistan, and in Bangladesh, political women are often in command), my protest develops within fictions which I hope might become an "open door" for those women who live under the threat of an atavistic fundamentalism. I remain doubtful as to the "utility" or the impact of writings of the imagination in circumstances such as these. . . . I think, rather, that, in spite of me and in spite of my writings, perhaps my books can prolong the echo of the voices of so many other women—not all of whom are necessarily intellectuals or artists—those who keep as their hope the power of their dreams, the tenacity of their memory, and especially the unshaken force of their revolt.

Ladies and gentlemen, by honoring me here today, you give strength to my vulnerability, as you give the power of solidarity to the solitude of my exile. This Neustadt Prize will allow me to continue to write, to create, and to breathe, still in the grip of anxiety, but now assured of a public who listens.

"The stone sings while sleeping," the Arab poet writes. So does sadness, the sadness that literature must transform into luminescence. Ladies and gentlemen, I thank you.

Norman, Oklahoma
October 18, 1996

Translation from the French by Pamela A. Genova

NURUDDIN FARAH
THE 1998 LAUREATE

Nuruddin Farah was born in Baidoa, Somalia, in 1945 and now lives in Cape Town, South Africa. He is the author of twelve novels, which have won numerous awards and have been translated into more than twenty languages. His mother was a traditional storyteller, and his father was a merchant who later worked for the British government as an interpreter. Farah grew up in a multilingual environment and learned to speak Somali, Amharic, English, Italian, and Arabic. When he began to write, Farah chose English as the language of his works. His first novel, *From a Crooked Rib* (1970), depicts the authoritarian role of patriarchy in African society and earned him praise as a "male feminist." The publication of his second novel, *A Naked Needle* (1976), angered the dictatorial Somali regime and finally forced Farah into exile following several death threats. Farah would not return to live in Somalia again, but his lifelong pursuit has been to preserve his country through his writing. His other publications include *Gifts* (1993), *Secrets*

(1997, which won the Prix de l'Astrolabe 2000), *Crossbones* (2011), *Hiding in Plain Sight* (2014), and *North of Dawn* (2018).

Reading these books helped me to reach out, as though I was meant to touch the frontiers of this immense world.

—Nuruddin Farah

Nuruddin Farah's Crucible of the Imagination
Kwame Anthony Appiah

I know exactly why I remember so very well the first time I met Nuruddin Farah: it is because he made me laugh. Not just a wry smile or two, or a modest guffaw. He made me laugh so much that my abdominal muscles ached for days; so much, that I had to beg him to stop talking for a while, because I was doubled up, about to fall to the ground. I remember, too, what it was that he was so funny about. He was telling stories about a meeting with another great African writer, the South African author Bessie Head, whose eccentricities he was delineating with a mixture of gentleness, puzzlement, and profound respect. He was not telling stories *against* her: I remember thinking that if Bessie Head was listening somewhere, from beyond the grave, she would have understood at once that Nuruddin's stories and my laughter were a celebration of her; there was no mockery. What I *don't* remember is where we were—it must have been a conference about African writing—or when it was.

Though I remember my laughter, I don't remember the stories. But even if I did, I know I couldn't tell them as he did, catching each ebbing wave of laughter with another tale slipped in to return me to convulsions. So Nuruddin was locked away in my mind and heart forever not just as the marvelous writer I had read and heard of before I met him, but as this wonderful teller of stories.

I think of this anecdote as emblematic: for this was, as I say, a story about a woman—a crazy woman, but also a great writer. And anyone who has read any of Nuruddin's novels knows that he is always telling stories that have women at their center, and that his women are not the passive objects of his writing but central, vital subjects in the brilliantly imagined, fully realized, magical world of Nuruddin Farah. Indeed, his first novel, *From a Crooked Rib,* depicts the life of Somali women so compellingly that the Nigerian novelist Buchi Emecheta once wondered out loud if it could really have been written by a man. She must have been kept wondering ever since by so many Farah women.

In *Maps,* his 1986 novel, there is Misra, the Ethiopian maid who raises Askar, the Somali protagonist, a refugee from the 1977–78 war between Ethiopia and Somalia in his native Ogaden. Misra is not Askar's kinswoman, not even his countrywoman, and, as a foster parent to an orphan, she is and is not his mother: but her life is tied up with this young man whom she has raised, her love for him running against the loyalties to people and nation which are the source of so much bloodshed and division, but which are also at the heart of Askar's identity. In the first chapter, addressed to Askar (but perhaps, the novel's ending suggests, in a voice Askar himself is ventriloquising), Nuruddin Farah writes: "The point of you was that, in small and large ways, you determined what Misra's life would be like the moment you took it over."

What follows is a wonderful portrait of a bond between a mother and a child, told with enormous respect for her love, and for her own insistence that, despite all that is done to her because she is woman, she is glad to be a woman. We know she is glad to be a woman because she says so. When young Askar wakes one day with blood on his sheets, he responds to Misra's suggestion that he has begun to menstruate with an angry "But I am a man." Maybe, he suggests later, he is sick, should see a doctor.

> She didn't like his explanation. "It means you prefer being sick to being a woman."
> "Naturally," he said. "Who wouldn't?"
> She said, "*I* wouldn't."

But, as I say, Misra is one among a multitude. Throughout the extraordinary trilogy that he called *Variations on the Theme of an African Dictatorship*—in *Sweet and Sour Milk* (1979), which won the 1980 English-Speaking Union Literary Award, *Sardines* (1981), and *Close Sesame* (1983)—there are so many uncommon women: Margaritta, in *Sweet and Sour Milk,* who leads us into the world of clandestine resistance to Somalia's dictator, the Generalissimo (who is not named in the novel by his real-world name, Siyad Barre); or Medina, in

Sardines, "as strong-minded," Nuruddin says, "as she was unbending in her decisions," who leaves her husband, a minister in the government, to raise their child, Ubax, alone. Medina is protecting her daughter from the insistence of her mother-in-law, Idil, that Ubax be circumcised. She is a cosmopolitan, who amuses her daughter by reading her Chinua Achebe and the *Arabian Nights* in her own translations, a member of what Nuruddin calls "the privilegentsia," who speaks "four European languages quite well" and writes "in two." But she is also secretly working to end the dictatorship.

Medina is joined in *Variations on the Theme of an African Dictatorship* not only by her precocious, demanding daughter, Ubax, but also by such splendid creations as her mother Fatima bint Thabit, a Yemeni traditionalist; by Idil, her authoritarian mother-in-law; by Sagal, athlete and revolutionary; by Amina and Ebia, Sagal's friends. The trilogy of *Sweet and Sour Milk, Sardines,* and *Close Sesame* is a powerful assault on dictatorship *and* a powerful indictment of the oppression of women, and the particular forms it takes in Somalia: but it is also a celebration of women's agency.

If I seem to be belaboring a point, it is not because I find it surprising that a man should write convincingly about the lives and interests and concerns of women. Writing is always more about identification than identity: the work of the imagination is never simply to express our selves. Nor, despite what many would assume, is a man's preoccupation with the situation of women especially surprising in Africa: *Things Fall Apart,* the novel by Chinua Achebe that thrust modern African writing in English onto the world stage, is, in part, a novel about the tragedy of men who do not respect the feminine in nature, in their wives and mothers and daughters, and in themselves. Nuruddin Farah's treatment of women's lives is not remarkable because he is a man; it is remarkable because of the power of its moral and literary achievement. And the obvious centrality, in his work, of the suffering of women and their agency is, I think, a reflection of what is deepest in his political argument, which is his recognition of the intimate connection between the dynamics of power in the family—in relations between husbands and wives, brothers and sisters, parents and children, uncles and aunts and cousins, one generation and another—and the broader politics of states and nations. A society that is filled with contempt for women or children or the old, he suggests again and again, cannot have a healthy politics: and the poisonous, murderous struggles that have overtaken his own Somalia have their beginning, he seems to argue, in the struggles of family life. Farah is not the first feminist to have grasped that the personal is political; but he is, in my view, the African writer who has given this thesis its most persuasive imaginative demonstration.

It is important, therefore, that Nuruddin Farah's world is also full of intensely realized representations of love and loyalty: in *Secrets,* the most recent of his novels, there is the long love affair between Damac and Yaqat, mother and father to Kalaman, the novel's central figure, two people held together in a horrifying fatal secret that is both the tie between them and the greatest threat to their happiness. And there is the extraordinary relationship between Kalaman and his grandfather, Nonno, each of whom has named the other; theirs is a relationship that survives from the child's birth to the grandfather's death despite the same secret, which also stands between and binds them.

Equally memorable for me is the wonderful love of father, son, and grandson in *Close Sesame:* with Deeriye the grandfather, Mursal the son, and Samawade the grandson, locked together in a bond between the generations that is cruelly destroyed by the moral demands of life under dictatorship. Not only is *Close Sesame* a powerfully moving celebration of family across the generations; it has also given us, in Deeriye, the most fully realized picture that I am aware of in English of the interior life of a devout Moslem—indeed, one of the richest representations of a prayerfully devout human being I have ever read. Most Somalis are raised, as Nuruddin Farah was, as Moslems; as a result, the act of imagination here will probably not receive the same attention as the manner in which he has found his way into the minds of so many imaginary women. So, in celebrating the powers of his imagination, we should perhaps notice, too, that Nuruddin Farah, though raised as a Moslem, is not himself devout: he does not claim, even when it would advance his interests, to be so. One of Farah's many literary admirers is Salman Rushdie, who must, I suspect, be especially admiring of Nuruddin's capacity to represent respectfully an Islam that is no longer fully his own.

*

Nuruddin Farah, whom we honor today, was born in Baidoa in 1945, but moved at the age of one to what was then the British-administered Ogaden, where his father was a translator. When the British departed from the Ogaden, they left its many Somali inhabitants to the Ethiopians, creating a region of conflict that was to smolder always and burst, from time to time, into the flames of Somali-Ethiopian warfare over the next four decades. In 1963 his family moved to Mogadiscio during one of these wars, one family among a million refugees over the years driven by these conflicts from the Ogaden. He went to university in Chandigarh in India (choosing it over an offer from Wisconsin), and published that first novel, *From a Crooked Rib,* in London in 1970, at the age of twenty-five, becoming, with that work, the first Somali novelist—though, of course, by no means her first great literary figure, since he was raised within a tradition of oral literature that is among the richest in the world. The Mogadiscio in which he grew up was a densely cosmopolitan product of waves of political and cultural colonizers: Italianate architecture, Islam and Arabic civilization, the English language, all embedded within a Somali culture. Nuruddin speaks not only Somali but also Italian, Arabic, Amharic (the language of Ethiopian rule, from the days in the Ogaden), and, of course, the wonderful English in which he has written his eight novels and almost all his work.

In 1974 he left Somalia to begin a period of nomadic peregrination of a sort that would have made sense to his Somali ancestors, even if he has carried it out on a larger scale, living in Europe, North America, and Africa. In 1976 he published *A Naked Needle,* a novel that caught the unfriendly eye of Mohamed Siyad Barre, Somalia's dictator. He was planning to return home from Rome, and had called his brother to arrange to be collected at the airport, when he learned, from his brother, that Siyad Barre was angry with him. What began as a weeklong postponement of his return, to give the Generalissimo time to cool down, turned into a twenty-twoyear exile, which ended in 1996, five years after Siyad Barre's departure had plunged Somalia into the crisis from which it has still not emerged.

In the meanwhile Nuruddin has lived in Italy, Germany, Britain, the United States, Uganda, Sudan, Ethiopia, and Gambia; his latest place of residence is Kaduna, in northern Nigeria, the home of Amina, his wife. But next year they will be packing their tent again and moving to Cape Town. In 1986 he was kicked out of Gambia for accusing President Sir Dawda Jawara of being more interested in golf than governing. ("Stupid of me," was his laconic comment to an Associated Press journalist.) In Uganda, in 1990, he got on the wrong side of President Yoweri Museveni, then chairman of the Organization of African Unity, accusing him of failing to mediate the war in Somalia. "Museveni was inept," Nuruddin said with the special tact he reserves for presidents. After Museveni denounced him at a news conference, Nuruddin took the hint and moved to Ethiopia. Nuruddin Farah has been thrown out by more African countries than most people have visited; he has visited more than most people could name.

I wish I had time to tell you more about his writing: about the thoroughly original way his characters live as much in their dreams as in their waking lives; to describe how his novels are morally serious without being preachy, or how he teases you by writing of events that seem magical but also always have possible unmagical explanations; to show you the richness and power of his prose. I wish I could explain to you how a man who was deprived by exile of his people and his family has kept his people and his family—and the idea of family and people—alive in the crucible of the imagination. But these, fortunately, are things I don't have to tell you about, because you can read him for yourselves: all of them are there in *Secrets,* a work which proves that a master of the novel is still growing in his craft. Read it. I promise it will reward your reading: but I also have to warn you that you will end up having to read the rest of his work.

I know I am keeping you from the man himself, but I should like to say one more thing in closing: Nuruddin is a man with an extraordinary gift for friendship, and friendship is something that we should honor more than we do and give thanks for when we can. But Nuruddin is also, as I have been telling you, a magnificent novelist, and we should honor and be grateful for that, too. I have been struggling as to which of these gratitudes I should express in closing. But I realized today that I do not have to choose between thanking him for his novels and for his friendship. For his novels are a friend's gift: and he has given them, as a gift of friendship, to the great company of men and women now reading his novels around the world.

Norman, Oklahoma
October 29, 1998

Kwame Anthony Appiah *(b. 1954, London) is a philosopher, novelist, cultural theorist, and scholar of African and African American studies who teaches in New York University's Department of Philosophy and School of Law. Among his many awards and honors, he was elected a Fellow of the Royal Society of Literature in 2017.*

Wordsmith with a Difference
Nuruddin Farah

I was born into a difference at a time in my continent's history when the power of speech lay elsewhere, in other people's tongues. In those days, we, as colonials and as Somalia, existed more in reference to whom we were made into as colonial subjects than whom we presumed ourselves to be, or who we ought to have been. Ours was a language divested of authority. Moreover, I was born into a difference with its own specificity: of a mother and a father who were not wholly literate in Somali. I say "not wholly literate," because even though my father had mastered the rudimentaries of reading and writing in at least three languages and my mother was an oral poet, the truth is they were seldom engaged in activities I would associate with the fully literate.

At the age of four and a half, my three elder brothers and I were sent to school by our parents. I doubt that my parents could articulate what must have been a disturbing ambivalence in their minds; I doubt that they meant to pay hefty fees they could ill afford with a view to imposing philosophical discontinuities between their worldview and ours. We became literate in the foreign tongues in which we received our formal education. It would dawn on me before my tenth year, once I became aware of my potential, that there were immense benefits to being literate in foreign tongues. For not only could I read the Koran as a professional reciter might—by then I had earned the honorific "Haafizul Qur'an," a title given to those who have obtained the formidable distinction of committing the entire Scripture to memory—but I could read Dostoevsky and Victor Hugo in Arabic, or struggle my way through Bertrand Russell's *History of Western Philosophy* in English. Not that I understood much of what I read. But one thing was very obvious: I had gained access to a larger and more varied world than the one my parents ever anticipated, a world more dangerous but at the same time more rewarding than that which my age mates had known. And what a different world it was, with some of the distances made smaller, no bigger than a book, and new distances amplified. Reading these books helped me to reach out, as though I was meant to touch the frontiers of this immense world. I was touched by what I read, I was moved, I was changed too. In those faraway days, a particular piece of wisdom from the Prophet Mohammed was frequently on everyone's lips: "To acquire knowledge, one must travel very, very far, even to China, if need be." I had no idea where China was. However, I sensed it as if I were more than prepared to travel there or even beyond it. We valued knowledge for what it was worth, and were ready to seek it wherever we might. Because of our peculiar circumstances as colonial subjects and especially as Somalis, it mattered little where we found it, in foreign tongues or in books written by others and published in other lands. We got used to the inconveniences with which we associated these alien languages. We might have been the proverbial hunchback who makes do with his daily discomforts, but who continues to live his life most fully regardless.

Out of love, and because they wanted the best for us, our parents did not stand in the way of our acquisition of knowledge, well aware of the fact that we were growing into alien children, not wholly of their making. My father was instrumental in the establishment of a community school in our town. He travelled far in his search for a teacher willing to come and live in Kallafo. Of the many whom he interviewed, the one whom he liked best proved to be demanding, insisting that he be given free lodging in addition to his monthly salary, conditions which my father ultimately accepted. Once he arrived, the teacher lived in our own compound, and until he got married he was fed out of the same kitchen as ourselves, his guests more ours than his, as we had more space in our part of the compound.

Later, when a Christian missionary group established its own school, my brothers and I were all sent there. The school was run by evangelists, eager to win converts to their faith. But not if you paid a school fee, because then you were treated differently. As it turned out, it was not obligatory for us to attend the special Bible classes in the after-school hours, since our parents had the wherewithal to foot the bills. Not so the boys from poorer families, a handful of whom converted to Christianity out of convenience. We all knew who these were. One of them used to lend me his Bible, which boasted the marked passages thought to be relevant to one's redemption. From our perspective, it was as though we were doing a course in comparative religion, something I am sure our parents were aware of. As Somalis, we all had an extremely robust confidence in our faith then, and were convinced that we were equal to any challenges posed by other religions. We had no qualms in quoting to the missionaries the verse from the Koran, "To each his religion, you [keep to] yours and we to our own!" Our society was so self-confidently tolerant in those days, so accepting of the differences in character and mental acumen between ourselves and the Christian missionaries, whom we accused of taking advantage of those with no means to fight them off.

As residents of Kallafo, a town with a population of fifteen to twenty thousand, we were accommodating of others who were different from ourselves. The Lord knows there was a wide variety of other peoples from different parts of the world for a town in the backwaters of the Shebelle River in the Somali-speaking Ogaden. We had Yemeni Arabs in our midst, we had a small community of farmers originally from East Africa, a wide array of Somalis from other corners of the peninsula, plus a couple of Palestinian families, refugees really, who were on their way elsewhere for resettlement. Ours was a tolerant Islam. You lived your life as you saw fit, not according to self-appointed Mullahs threatening you with fire and brimstone if, in their opinion, you strayed from the righteousness of the faith, as they decreed it. We were who we were, self-confidently proud of who we perceived ourselves to be, in spite of our status as colonial subjects. With our minds open, our hearts likewise, we received the world, and along with it the knowledge that made the world larger and more varied too.

There is something forward-looking about knowing other languages, something outward-looking about studying the cultures of other peoples: not only do you enrich your understanding of your own culture, but it makes you appreciate yours all the more. I remember my first encounter with *A Thousand and One Nights* and how, reading it in the original, I felt suddenly whole. In fact, the more I read and got to know about other people's cultures, even if cursorily, the more confident I became about my own. I became more convinced than ever that I needed to create a universe familiar enough to Somalis, and which might inspire a sense of mission in themselves. Not that I could do much about the language in which I ought to write. When I started writing, no standardised system of spelling or of writing existed in Somali; none was established until October of 1972.

Despite this, writing in foreign tongues was as much fun as reading had been entertaining and edifying too. I felt encouraged by what I read, stories whose cunning and sophistication enabled me to get in touch with the narrative genius that is the African folktale. Literature of the written and oral variety became a mansion in which I moved with self-edifying ease, reading books in foreign tongues and listening to the oral wisdom transmitted in Somali. Meanwhile I enjoyed going from *Kalila and Dimna* to Ernest Hemingway, to Mark Twain, to Agatha Christie, to a Somali poem recited under the shade of a tree. I was elated by this multicultural encounter, the world now unitary, and now boasting of a wealth of differences, each expressive of a human need: the need to gain more knowledge about myself and about the lives of others, in order to be fulfilled.

It was easy for me to make the journey from the Arabic culture of *A Thousand and One Nights* to the translation of *Kalila and Dimna* from Sanskrit. With a bit of help from my eldest brother, who encouraged me, I was able to tackle Dostoevsky and Hugo in Arabic too. The quirkiness of my reading could be explained in part by the fact that, because of the oral nature of our society, books in any tongue were seldom available. But what a pleasure they were to me when I had them, and what a delight to lose my bearings in the multistoried mansion of a writer's imagined universe. Sadly, I admit to having become more fascinated by the written variety of literature, perhaps because, as with all new converts, I was attracted to the barely familiar in preference to the oral tradition which was everywhere around me. There was a freshness to the stories in the books every time I read them. I was a child apart, my parents two wordsmiths, in their different ways, each forging out of the smithy of their souls a creative reckoning of an oral universe. It was in deference to their efforts that I lent a new lease on life later to the tales told to me orally, tales that I worked into my own, all the more to appreciate them.

In addition to the powers associated with being literate in foreign tongues, there were economic benefits too. As a child, I lived in a part of the world where a large segment of the population do not read and write. So whenever I was short of cash, I hired out my services to an illiterate adult in need of a letter to be written. It occurred to me too that perhaps I had more power than did my father as an interpreter, whose oral rendering of what the Englishman said in Swahili had something short-lived about it. As a scribe, I had more power, giving flesh to ideas orally delivered and therefore transient, and which, by dint of being written down in another language, became more real. In written form, the letter could be read and reread, and its message could travel farther than an oral one, travel through space and time, unaltered.

There was something else. I had at my mercy grown men, my father's age, some humouring me so I might write a letter for them without pay, or at a discount. On occasion, my parents interceded on behalf of some of our relations. I was always paid the compliment of being a very lucky boy, some providing me with a chair and a table, some with a drink. Deferent silence attended my every intervention, respect for my status accompanied the order of the moment. I was lavishly pampered. I was so adept at what I set out to do that, in my eleventh year, I delivered a speech I helped write to the visiting emperor, Haile Selassie, an honour accorded to me after two grown men, both of them my teachers, felt too intimidated by the prospect of standing before His Majesty. My photographs decorated many a royal wall in Addis Ababa for a while as a result of delivering it.

I grew more confident the more I read. The more I got to know about the injustices perpetrated by men against the womenfolk, the more conscious I grew of my powers. I had not yet completed my twelfth year when an elderly man, a friend of my father's, required that I write a letter for him to his estranged wife—estranged, because he had the frequent habit of beating her. Apparently the woman had gone to another town where she had taken refuge amongst her kin, refusing to return in spite of their pleas and despite the assurances the husband had given to her elder brother, now sitting close by. The elder brother kept nodding his head, as if in agreement with the wife-beater, who was adamantly insistent that he had done no wrong. I also gathered that, in a message orally delivered to the husband and her elder brother, the woman had filed for divorce, a request neither the husband nor her elder brother was prepared to consider. "I will not divorce you," he instructed me to write, "and if you do not come back within a couple of days of receiving this letter, I will have you brought back forcibly and will beat you until all your bones are broken."

Unbeknownst to him, I did what was within my power to do: I sabotaged the intent of the man's message by a deliberate omission, supported by an intentional mishearing of his statements. In the letter I made him say that if she did not come back within a few days of receiving this letter, or if she continued raising objections against her being beaten by her legal husband, then there was nothing left for him but to divorce her, as she had requested. It was perhaps with a view to giving myself legal cover that I demanded the husband put the authority of his thumb to the bottom right-hand side of the letter.

Six months later I learnt of what had inevitably come to pass: the estranged wife, assuming that she was divorced, remarried another man of her choice, a man who was more tender toward her. The case went to court, and the letter I had written for the husband was produced. The Islamic Qadi decreed that the woman was now legally the wife of her current husband, by whom she had a son. I could not determine from the expression on my father's face if he were proud of me or ashamed. But he was clearly disturbed by "my wily ways," as he put it, forbidding me henceforth to write letters on behalf of others.

A question I've often asked myself is: are my parents continued in me? One was a translator communicating in Swahili to the Englishman and then transmitting the response in Somali. My father learnt Swahili as a child because he was brought up in Nairobi, in the very city—then a small town—in which the Englishman came to acquire the language, perhaps with the assistance of a native instructor. It is safe to assume that the colonialist's register of Swahili was different from my father's. Even so, almost all the transactions being oral, my father, and his boss the Governor, spoke as if in twinship with each other, the one employing Swahili, the other rendering it into Somali. I wonder if there was a point when my father ceased to be the Englishman's sidekick and became an agent in his own right, with a new authority to his agency?

Was there a point when my father's relationship to the truth of the Englishman's authority took on its own energy, through the agency generated by his own truth and authority as a colonial? No doubt there was a world's distance between the moment my father heard the Englishman say something in Swahili and the moment he interpreted this into Somali. Did my father, by interpreting, insinuate himself into the ideas he worked with, ideas to which he gave a new lease of life? How much, if any, did he transform these ideas? And did he take vengeance on the colonial master who originated the ideas? In short, was my father ever an anticolonialist?

Being a poet, my mother helped me gain access to hidden, creative energies within me, even in so young a child. I remember the placidity of her moods, as she paced back and forth in a bedroom with the door locked from inside. A family poet, she composed *buraanbur* lyrics in praise of the bride or bridegroom, or made up a special lullaby for one of her many children. Unlike my father, she had the self-confident vitality to reinvent the world daily by singing about it. There was a self-assuredness to all her doings. I thought she was more articulate than my father, who, patriarch that he was, talked in certainties, never doubting that he might be wrong. She was a great one to help one confront one's quotidian uncertainties.

Born into a difference: I lived in a world different from that of my parents. Not that I always had their permission to be different from them. All the same, we met, my parents and I, as though we were travellers meeting in a transit lounge. As children raised apart, we were, in essentials, journeymen of the future, hybrids of a new sort. In an effort to get closer to my mother, or perhaps to bridge a chasm, I learnt as much of the oral tradition as I possibly could. It was maybe in imitation of the poet in her that I tried my hand at making up my own lyrics in Somali to tunes borrowed from the songs that were popular in those days.

As a youth, I was as inventive as children who speak the correct language to the correct parent, to each parent his or her own, in a world with its own value systems, where the calendars are not the same, where people do not worship the same deities. For me, as a child, the most prominent distances were those between temperaments, my mother's and my father's. I am alluding to the fact that language, and what uses we make of it, is the longest distance between two persons, the one a poet, sensitive, committed to ideas larger than herself, the other despondently despotic, a patriarch willing to submit the world to the authority of his whim. My mother once described another man who was equally deficient in sensibilities as rather like a three-legged stool with one leg missing. She demonstrated what she meant, her head exaggeratedly tilted to one side, one of her arms bent at the elbow, hanging down as though broken.

She was interested in what I wrote, my mother was, often requesting that I tell her the stories as I developed them in my head. Generous to me, she accommodated my eccentricities and provided me with as much space as I required. (We spoke once of how she might have become a major poet if she hadn't spent all her time looking after her numerous children.) Interested in where the story was headed, she put me right when I got the spirit of the tale wrong. Not my father. He would've been happier, he told me, if I had become a clerk at the bank and brought home all my earnings. And yet it was he who had sought out "knowledge" in the shape of teachers, he who had helped establish the first school in our town. My mother died sixteen years after we last met, whilst I was still in exile. But my father and I met more recently in a hospital in Mombasa, Kenya, where he was recovering from an injury to his head. I found him intolerant of my views. We had a set-to about my choice of dress, of habits, of friends. He was at his friendliest when showing me off to his cronies, when he chose to be praiseful of my achievements as a writer.

On my way to the airport, I called on him to make peace with him, and to say my farewell. The two of us alone, I reminded him of how I had been impressed with his contributions in terms of our secular education, which hadn't until then been available in our town; how, in fact, it was he who had made it possible for me to become a writer. He looked restless, a man wanting to get something off his chest. And he spoke regretfully about "knowledge." Pronouncing the Somali word for knowledge, *aqoon*, as though it were synonymous with venom, he accused me of betraying all his aspirations, and of being treacherous to his and everyone's expectations of me. I do not know why, but I reminded him of the dialogue between Knowledge and Everyman in the English morality play *Everyman*, when Knowledge says, "Everyman, I will go with thee and be thy guide, In thy most need to go by thy side." Maybe I hoped he would be supportive of my efforts as a writer the way my mother had been. Would he not agree, I wondered, that I had continued where he and my mother left off as a professional interpreter, and a poet, considering that I turned out to be a wordsmith with a difference.

He said, "No one trusts subversives."

I said I was not sure what he meant.

In his reply he quoted a Somali folktale in which a boy, born to a single mother, reaches the mature age of nine before uttering a word. The woman prays daily, appealing to God to make her son speak. At the age of ten, he does so. To his mother, he says, "Shall we fornicate, Mother, you and I?" Shocked, the mother then prays to the Almighty to make him mute once again.

I asked myself if, in the opinion of my father, I was subversive, because I wrote in foreign tongues, or because, in my writings, I challenged the authoritarian tendencies of Somali tradition? I could say, in self-defence (but did not), that writing in cosmopolitan settings, in foreign tongues, is, to my mind, more forward-looking, ultimately more outward-looking, than much of the writing done in the indigenous languages in Africa and elsewhere; that a great body of these literatures is remarkable for its nationalistic bent, and its jingoism too; and that much of Somali oral poetry and prose is reactionary, inward-looking in a clannish sort of way.

Instead I said, "I was born into a difference, born into a world not of my own making. I wish the two of us would be sufficiently tolerant of each other so as to celebrate our differences. It is time we got to know ourselves better, time we celebrated the differences in our worldviews."

Norman, Oklahoma
October 29, 1998

DAVID MALOUF
THE 2000 LAUREATE

David Malouf was born in Queensland, Australia, in 1934 and became a full-time writer in 1978. He has published poetry, novels, short stories, essays, opera librettos, and a play and has been widely translated. His first two published books were collections of poetry. His first novel, *Johnno* (1975), is the semi-autobiographical tale of a young man growing up in Brisbane during the Second World War. His second novel, *An Imaginary Life* (1978), is a fictional account of the exiled Roman poet Ovid. Later novels include *Child's Play with Eustace & The Prowler* (1982), *Fly Away Peter* (1982), *Harland's Half Acre* (1985), *The Great World* (1990)—which won the Commonwealth Writers Prize (overall winner, best book) and the Prix Femina Étranger (France)—and the acclaimed *Remembering Babylon* (1993), which was shortlisted for the Booker Prize for Fiction, won the first International IMPAC Dublin Literary Award in 1996, and the Commonwealth Writers Prize (South East Asia and South Pacific Region, best book). *The Conversations at Curlow Creek* (1996) followed. His collections of short stories include *Antipodes* (1985), *Dream Stuff* (2000), and *Every Move You Make* (2006). Recent publications are *Ransom* (2009), a novel inspired by a part of Homer's *Iliad,* and *Earth Hour* (2014), a poetry collection. He was shortlisted for the Man Booker International Prize in 2011. His most recent volume of poetry is *An Open Book* (2018).

> It's a tribute to all forms of making, from the grandest to the most domestic and humble, as the sign of our human need to come home to the world we live in, to make a home of whatever things, small or large, that we have added to it.
>
> —David Malouf

David Malouf's Music of Human Loss and Love
Ihab Hassan

In the finest writers, the evidence may overflow the work. It moves in a gesture, fills a pause. Or it may guide you on a walk, such as David Malouf invited us— Sally Hassan and me—to take around Cremorne Point, in Sydney. Think of a winter day, the sky blue, strung with pale clouds, barely a chill in the air. The path wound through trees, shrubs, flowers, rocks tumbling down toward the waters of Jackson Harbour on one side, the creamy houses of Cremorne rising on the other. And as we walked, we talked of Australian history, Aboriginal misery, the new immigrants, the fabulous wines of Oz. But David Malouf kept noticing, stopping, pointing: here was a ghost gum, here an angophora, there some primitive ferns, and look at that little yellow wattle. Then he stooped, touching with tenderness a tiny pink flower, pink shading into magenta, flickering in the grass. "I don't know the name of this one," he said sadly.

And right there I saw a glimmer of his gift: wakefulness and precision of feeling, blended in wonder, and a delicacy that can surprise the mystery of creation itself. It was this elusive quality, inward with his poetic sensibility, a quality akin to love, that first drew me to the work of David Malouf. It was the same quality that prompted me to nominate him for the Neustadt International Prize for Literature before I had ever met the man. There may have been some extrinsic factor in my beguilement, which I am certain owed nothing to our common Arab background—his, Lebanese Christian; mine, Egyptian Moslem. That extrinsic factor may have been the Antipodes, crying for just recognition.

Consider this: English, the world's largest second language, has become many dialects, many Englishes, expressing now diverse cultures, creeds, climes. Australian English, like Indian or Nigerian or American English, has its own tang and timbre—a sound full of wry coloratura. Modern Australian writers, from Patrick White and Les Murray to David Malouf, convince us how live that language is, and how it promises to fill the ears of the world with new cadences, fresh feelings.

The language rises from the continent Down Under, and from its now polyglot throat. Home of the most ancient, continuous culture, dating back some fifty thousand years, Australia enters the world's awareness through two bloody gates: the genocide of Aborigines and the incarceration of the Anglo-Irish poor. From this dreadful origin has come one of the most vital, decent, and humorous multicultural societies. Immigrants from Southern Europe, the Middle East, and above all Asia have deeply enriched the old Anglo-Celtic and Aboriginal strains. Australia, which Malouf once described as a "raft," "a new float of lives in busy interaction," is dreaming its future, as it once dreamt its primordial past, with zest and only a modicum of turbulence.

But the revival of a continent—a strange continent at that, full of wombats, bandicoots, emus, wallabies, where swans are black, Christmas comes in heat waves, and trees shed their bark instead of their leaves—that revival is not a function of history or politics or even myth alone. The revival draws on the roots of that obscure energy we call, in dumb amazement, the human spirit. It is this energy that David Malouf taps in his oeuvre, comprising some twenty prizewinning volumes of fiction, poetry, drama, essays, memoirs, and libretti.

The work, compellingly universal in appeal, carries the signature of a truly original temperament. Its master themes are easy enough to discern: history, nature, love, art, memory, the frailties of identity, and, above all, the spirit's unappeased quest, on the highways and darker byways of existence, for reconciliation in the heart of being. Far more difficult to convey here are the sensuous splendor, technical ingenuity, aching insight, and luminous wisdom of that work.

Luminous, indeed, in its delicacy, like that little pink and magenta flower, but musical too, in another fold of mind. The music issues, of course, from Malouf's personal voice. But it rises also, farther away, from the center of compassion, a music of human loss in a universe wherein nothing is ever lost, a counterpoint of forms, drawn to dissolution, yet ever re-creating their patterns in the imagination. "I have always felt," Malouf wrote in the preface to his libretto for *Jane Eyre*, "that in any action that presents itself as a subject of opera there should be an element that for its fullest expression demands music rather than simply tolerating it." That demand for music, music of different and sometimes inaudible kinds, is what the work of David Malouf makes on us, makes and supremely satisfies.

University of Wisconsin–Milwaukee

Ihab Hassan *(1925–2015) was an Egyptian-born literary theorist and writer. The recipient of two Guggenheim Fellowships and three Senior Fulbright Lectureships, he was Vilas Research Professor (emeritus) at the University of Wisconsin–Milwaukee.*

A Writing Life
David Malouf

An award like the Neustadt, which is given for a body of work, is bound to draw attention to just that, to the sort of whole a writer's work makes. It's a question that can scarcely arise of course till the body of work is actually there, till one after another, novel, story, poem, has been added to the rest, relates itself to the rest, and subtly changes it; what emerges then is likely to be as surprising to the writer as it is obvious to his readers and commentators, since he never consciously planned it—how could he, following his instincts and working piecemeal in the dark? How could he know, beginning tentatively as we all do, what would lie up ahead? What is revealed at last, if the writer has been working at any depth and exploring to the full all that is in him, all that he knows and does not know that he knows till it appears on the page before him, is nothing less than his own consciousness, soaked through with the experience of a particular temperament in a particular place and time. I want to say something here of how the books that make up my body of work got themselves written; something too of the extent to which they are, like all things created in this way, the expression of an idiosyncratic reading of the world, of nature, of men and women, of life's events and accidents, and at the same time products of the particular world I came out of, mid- to late twentieth-century Australia.

I began as a poet and had already published three collections of verse, and got myself some reputation as a poet, before I produced a piece of fiction I felt in any way pleased with. In fact, I had been trying my hand at fiction from the start, stories, a novel, but a convincing prose voice, a narrative tone that might be as rich and straightforward as the one I had struck in poetry, eluded me. So, for a long time I published only poems. Later, when the works of fiction did come, and followed one another quickly, I found that ideas—a phrase, an image—this might, if followed up and allowed to develop, have become a poem, tended to be absorbed in whatever fiction I was engaged on, though I continued to write poetry and still do. Novels are voracious. They demand the whole of your attention. There's a hard little voice in them that insists *Don't go away, this is for me*. Part of the joy of novel writing is this sense you have, for the "duration" so to speak, that the whole universe has turned in the direction of what you are writing, that every stray thought that comes to you, everything you read in the newspaper or see in the street, every conversation you overhear, is a message from the book, which has, by a kind of magnetism, drawn the whole world into its sphere.

My first novel was called *Johnno*. When I wrote it, in 1972, after nearly ten years of failed beginnings, I was already in my late thirties. It wasn't published—I still wasn't sure that I wanted it to be seen—till three years later.

It was about growing up in my hometown, Brisbane, a place that for some reason had never till then got itself into a book—or not anyway in a form that had brought it alive in people's minds and stuck. I wanted to put it on the map; to make it, in all its particularity, a place that would exist powerfully in the lives of readers in the same way that Dickens's London does, or Dostoevsky's Petersburg. That is, as a place fully imagined, since I had already grasped something paradoxical, which is that places become real in a reader's mind not as embodiments of observation and fact but through invention, as imaginary places that bear the names of real ones, and if they are created with sufficient immediacy and glow, will in the end replace the real one; or perhaps I should say live as its more lively and convincing double. What I wanted to do was to create a fictional Brisbane that the reader, wherever he happened to be from, would enter as if he were returning to the place he had grown up in, and whose weather, light, architecture, and verbal habits and social tensions had shaped him as they had my two central characters. Of those two characters, one was destroyed by the place, the other saved by his need, his writer's need, to re-create and objectify it to the point where he could at last see what it was, then wrestle with it and understand or forgive.

That first novel was in the first person, though I should add—I had learned a thing or two from all those failed drafts—that the narrator was not myself. For one thing, he knew more than I had ever done, or than I knew, in fact, till the half-autobiographical experience I was dealing with had been shaped by the needs of fiction and set down. What I mean to stress, in saying this, is that everything in the book, characters, events, places, even what remained of my own experience, had been, as they must be of course, relived in imagination: imagined. Even the most realistic books—and *Johnno* is meant to at least *look* realistic—books that are set in real verifiable places and deal with actual events, can live in the reader's mind only to the extent that they are works of imagination and engage the reader's imagination.

Second novels, as most writers will tell you, are the real test. It is with the second novel that a writer begins to stake out his territory, establish that he is there for the long haul, and begins to perceive in the first outlines of an emerging body of work the obsessive preoccupations and odd ways of thinking and feeling that he must follow if his writing is to be coherent and whole.

I solved this problem of the second novel, without quite knowing as yet that it was a problem, by leaping as far from *Johnno* as possible, to the very limits of my imagination. The book I wrote, *An Imaginary Life*, part prose poem, part speculative essay, part dramatic monologue, was about the Roman poet Ovid in exile and made the fairly outrageous claim for an Australian book in the 1970s that an Australian writer could take up a non-Australian subject and write about a non-Australian place without ceasing to be either Australian or himself. But how, if the work sprang from any deep place in him, could it not express what he was and what had shaped him? Early Australian commentators tended to see *An Imaginary Life* as what they called a European book. It was European readers who pointed out that so many of the subjects it took up, all the anxieties it expressed, the optimism it breathed, spoke to them at least of the new world and of a sensibility that was unmistakably antipodean.

But the point I want to make here is this: that what I had done in these two very different books, and without as yet quite seeing it, was to map out the limits of my world as a writer. I tend to see my work at this distance in spatial rather than chronological terms, and for me the interesting thing about *An Imaginary Life* is that it seems to have got itself written out of sequence. It ought to have been my last book, an old man's summing up, a late meditation on death, on continuity and change, the possibility of transformation, along with all those other topics that come up in a book that is open enough, lyrical enough, to be discursively rich in topics: the power of language as a means of structuring, interpreting, remaking experience; the need to remap the world so that wherever you happen to be is the centre; the interplay of civilisation and wildness, animal and human, body and soul; the moves by which we embrace accident and reread it as fate—all topics I would return to and deal with in new ways later. So, as I say, a last book that in my case happened to come second, and, in appearing so early, opened up the whole view backward, or rather ahead. My succeeding books, *Fly Away Peter*, *Harland's Half Acre*, *The Great World*, *Remembering Babylon*, have in some ways been a matter of "filling in" the ground between the realism of my first book and the distant but, as it has appeared, connected *non*realism of the second.

Two comments about being a writer whose immediate world and material happen to be Australian.

The first has to do with nature; not that grand category of creation we all belong to, and whose chain of connectedness has been an important element in my writing, but nature as it embodies itself, in a particular place, as land, landscape, weather, space, light, and which not only forms a background to the dramas and occasions we call history but also significantly shapes them, and shapes as well the psyche of those who live with the opportunities and limitations they present.

We tend to forget that in most places what we call nature is something *made*, a landscape shaped by centuries of industry and use that deeply humanises it and gives back, by reflection, a happy sense of human presence and power, of an idealised vision made real. In Australia what we mostly have before us is *un*made nature, a landscape that gives back no comfortable and reassuring vision of the centrality of humans and their works. This makes Australian attitudes to nature, and Australian writing about it, very different from the ones that appear in other forms of English. Nature in Australian poetry and fiction is seldom the source of moral reflections on order and industry. It does not offer itself as an emblematic language of feeling, or, as the Duke in *As You Like It* suggests, as material for sermons. What the vastness of Australian spaces evokes is anxiety. This is a landscape that has no need of human presence or a shaping mind or hand to complete it. It is already complete—which seems to be how the aboriginal world has always seen it; the land, for them, is something to be known, protected, revered, but not, as is our way, to be changed and "improved." For those of us who come to it with a European culture behind us, of making, of making use, it is a challenging and forbidding presence, and its beauty, its resistance, its hostility as some have seen it, raises questions about man's place in the scheme of things that do not arise, or not so sharply, elsewhere.

This leads me to the second point I want to make about the world as the Australian writer encounters it.

That largely unmade landscape is also, from our non-aboriginal point of view, very largely uninterpreted. It has not yet had laid down over it, as in England or France or other places with a long history of settlement and culture, that network of myths and legends and folk stories that make a landscape glow in the mind, that fund of associations and references which gives it meaning and depth. The work has begun, of course, but the network is still open. It is still full of interesting spaces and gaps. The meanings are not yet definitive. This puts the Australian writer in a position that is unusual, maybe at this point unique.

In one way we stand, like other contemporary writers, at the end of a tradition, the tradition that goes back, through the language we work in, English, to the Greeks and beyond; we live within that tradition with the same sense of "lateness" as Thomas Bernhard, or Thomas Pynchon, or Italo Calvino, or Georges Perec. But when it comes to the world that immediately surrounds us, we also stand, in a curious telescoping of time, at the beginning—in the position, say, of Hesiod, with the real making still to do.

Not all Australian writers feel this: daily life in Australia is varied and complex enough for a writer to ignore the sort of things I have been speaking of and write urban novels of the immediate present, just as in London or New York. That I *have* felt it, and in the sort of personal way that shapes all of one's thinking and feeling, is clear from the books themselves, which would be very different if I had not. In these matters we all do what we need to do, what our particular sort of writing demands.

A good many of my novels deal with verifiable moments in Australian history, not with known events but with that underside of events which is where most of us experience them, and in many cases go on experiencing them as pain or loss. I would want to call this an interior history, and what interests me is that in the ordinary way of things, so much of this, in Australia, goes unexpressed: unwritten about but also unspoken.

When Australia was still a small nation of just under four million, at the time of the First World War, we lost sixty-two thousand men at Gallipoli and in the trenches in France. I grew up in the shadow of that loss, which struck every small town and virtually every family in Australia, but did not produce, as it did in England, say, or in Germany and France, a reparative literature— poems, novels, plays—through which the deep horrors of that experience could be remade and taken in and come to terms with. The men who had directly suffered did not write about it, and, except in an offhand way, did not speak about it either. But until such things *are* spoken about, and, most of all, have been taken inside and lived through in the imagination, reexperienced as meaning rather than muddle, individual lives, and the larger life of the community, cannot recover and be healed. When a significant body of writing about the First World War did appear at last in Australia, it was in poems and fiction produced nearly forty years after the event by my generation; I did it myself in *Fly Away Peter*. It's a matter, as always, of the writer's dealing with what touches him personally—these things cannot be taken up coldly or out of duty—but by doing so, he also provides a kind of healing for the world he comes out of, whose sorrows and losses he shares with the rest.

One other thing I would like to add, which is where the two aspects of the Australian scene that I have been outlining, the land and the history, come together. This is the process by which, as settlers and latecomers, we have begun to come into full possession of the place.

Of course we already possess it in fact, through occupation or conquest, and that possession is legitimised by law. But there is only one way that we can truly possess the land (I wrote a novel, *Harland's Half Acre*, about this): that is by taking it into ourselves, interiorising and reimagining it as native people have done. This too is a work for poetry, and for the kind of fiction that dares to take on what it is too often left for poetry alone to do.

I want to end with a short poem that speaks of the business of making in all its forms; of what it means to us; what we are seeking when we set out there in the world some artefact, some made thing, that was not previously part of nature but is now, so that nature is changed, enlarged by its presence. It's a tribute to all forms of making, from the grandest to the most domestic and humble, as the sign of our human need to come home to the world we live in, to make a home of whatever things, small or large, that we have added to it.

Making

That a man should wonder
what he might find
at day's end beyond darkness:
something made
that was not there till he made it,

a thing unique
as all that our eyes

are schooled to. At its hour
at the masthead, Canopus,
a moon if it is writ

in the calendar, and this,
which nature had not thought
to add but once
there cannot do without
and whether of breath

made, or stone, egg-white,
earth, old sticks, odd clippings,
to be as the child lost
in his own story seeks it,
a home, another home.

Norman, Oklahoma
October 20, 2000

ÁLVARO MUTIS
THE 2002 LAUREATE

Álvaro Mutis (1923–2013) was a Colombian poet, novelist, and essayist. Though he was born in Colombia, he lived in Brussels until he was eleven years old. His first collection of poetry was published in 1948, and his first short stories appeared in 1978. Mutis is best known for his award-winning novellas, published in the United States in two collections, *Maqroll* and *The Adventures of Maqroll*. His body of work includes *La Nieve del Almirante* (1986; Eng. *The Snow of the Admiral*, 1995), *Ilona llega con la lluvia* (1987; Eng. *Ilona Comes with the Rain*, 1995), *La última escala del Tramp Steamer* (1989; Eng. *The Tramp Steamer's Last Port of Call*, 1995), and *Abdul Bashur, soñador de navíos* (1991; Eng. *Abdul Bashur, Dreamer of Ships*, 1995). His most famous book is *Empresas y Tribulaciones de Maqroll el Gaviero* (Eng. *The Adventures and Misadventures of Maqroll*), consisting of seven novellas.

All that I have written is destined to celebrate and perpetuate that corner of the *tierra caliente* from which emanates the very substance of my dreams, my nostalgias, my terrors, and my fortunes.

—Álvaro Mutis

The Passionate Fire of Álvaro Mutis
Juan Gustavo Cobo Borda

Who among today's Spanish-language writers is capable of engaging in dialogue, with poised enthusiasm, with authors as diverse as the Italian Giuseppe Ungaretti, the Frenchman Francis Ponge, the Pole Czesław Miłosz, or the Brazilian João Cabral de Melo Neto, as well as with those who have been or are presently the author's close friends, such as Octavio Paz and Gabriel García Márquez?

The Colombian Álvaro Mutis (b. 1923) is, without doubt, a contemporary writer who possesses a cultural background sufficiently broad and universal to transcend languages and borders. This cosmopolitanism allows him to moderate a compelling debate where poetry and its interplay with the destiny of humankind in this tenuous world succeed in bringing together participants from all walks of life. His work has been translated into approximately twenty languages, including English, French, German, Italian, Portuguese, Japanese, Greek, Hebrew, Turkish, Polish, Dutch, Swedish, and Danish. Such international acclaim fits seamlessly within the ideal of a world community of literature that the Neustadt Prize endeavors to foster and recognize.

Mutis's poetry, short stories, novels, and essays reflect a convergence of historical influences, beginning with the Bible, extending to the cultures of Islam and Byzantium, and finally arriving at such seminal figures in Latin American history as Simón Bolívar—all of which embody and illuminate the complex relationship between Europe and America. A universal dialogue of cultures that comes alive in Mutis's essays and commentary reflects his intimate understanding of Russian literature, French history, and the development of the novel in the United States, without ever distorting or underestimating the pivotal role of Spain in the formation of Latin America.

Mutis represents a rare combination of the cosmopolitan and the universal on the one hand and Latin America's unique local flavor on the other. Like

Jorge Luis Borges, Mutis is capable of appreciating, understanding, and evaluating through his literary creations the various nations that a broad world offers us as readers.

There is yet another argument for championing Mutis's work for the Neustadt Prize: the central figure who brings everything together, endowing it with unique character, is a protagonist named Maqroll el Gaviero (Maqroll the Lookout). Marginalized, out of place, adrift on the rough seas of an indifferent world, his adventures are both pilgrimages and farces, undertaken with lucid and penetrating fatalism.

Such despair, intuitive and stripped of all self-delusion, goes hand in hand with a sober and sublime respect for the illusions to which human beings cling so fiercely, giving rise to one of the most perfect creations of twentieth-century Latin American literature. Maqroll becomes, for readers the world over, a compelling and indispensable being.

Mutis's fiction takes place within the evocative framework of the tropics, a burning landscape where splendor commingles with the limits of human endurance and where the fragility of memory and the devastating force of untamed nature devour both the creations and the cherished beliefs of humankind. Along with violence and desire, these elements combine to produce a passionate search for those traits that lead to the stubborn obsession of individuals to make their lives—in the midst of precarious and conflicting societies—more secure and enduring. Here, too, a most ancient awareness confronts a world in perpetual crisis and renewal. From this backdrop have sprung the vibrant pages of *La Nieve del Almirante* (1986), *Ilona llega con la lluvia* (1987), *Un bel morir* (1989), *La última escala del Tramp Steamer* (1989), *Amirbar* (1990), and *Abdul Bashur, soñador de navíos* (1991), and also the stories and testimonials found in *La mansión de Araucaíma* (1973) and *Diario de Lecumberri* (1959).

With refined literary acumen, Mutis succeeds in creating a saga deeply rooted in verse, as found in the *Summa de Maqroll el Gaviero,* where the plot never departs from the epic and universal aspects of poetry. On the contrary, his fiction offers a sagacious parable not only of the Colombia and the coffee-growing lands of the author's childhood, but also of a land that resonates throughout all Latin America. He shows to what extent his country has been changed and how its passionately held core values have been destroyed by harsh and painful realities. Nevertheless, Mutis always penetrates beyond those tragedies in an unambiguous attempt to pose vital questions that force his protagonists to confront their own transcendental existence. From his exile in Mexico he has succeeded in crafting tangible and compelling images of his homeland and of Latin American reality in general. Mutis uses these images as a foundation for the construction of a unique world that manages to subsist due to its internal consistency and its faithfulness to the obsessions that have haunted the author since 1948, when he published his first collection of poetry, *La Balanza* (The scales). His characters are forged from a passionate fire originating in a long coexistence with the author himself.

Although his protagonists create a stage where European and Western influences contend with the hybridization and metamorphosis they undergo upon arriving in the New World, Mutis's work is never a simple essay about identity. It is a literary journey in which the reader discovers and confronts his- or herself.

The utopia that Mutis ultimately proposes is that of an infinite and open reading process similar to the one Joseph Conrad defined when referring to Marcel Proust: one in which analysis has become the creator. A literary journey where a single, definitive reading of a work is all but impossible, thus allowing the text to accompany us through the successive changes in our own lives without becoming irrelevant. By honoring and recognizing Álvaro Mutis, the jurors of the Neustadt International Prize for Literature will be honoring one of the great creative literary minds of our time and, consequently, reaffirming the Neustadt Prize's own criteria for literary excellence.

Bogotá, Colombia

Translation from the Spanish by David Draper Clark

Juan Gustavo Cobo Borda *(b. 1948, Bogotá), a distinguished poet and critic, was elected to permanent membership in the Academia Colombiana de la*

Lengua in 1993, pursued a career in government service beginning in the mid-1970s, and has been a member of WLT's editorial board since 2001.

Álvaro Mutis on Himself
Álvaro Mutis

I was born in Bogotá on August 25, 1923, the feast day of Saint Louis, king of France. I cannot deny the influence of my patron saint on my devotion to monarchies. I completed early studies in Brussels, then returned to Colombia for periods that were at first vacations, and, later—as they became more and more extended—I lived on a coffee and sugar plantation that my maternal grandfather had founded. It was called "Coello" and was located in the foothills of the Central Highlands. All that I have written is destined to celebrate and perpetuate that corner of the *tierra caliente* from which emanates the very substance of my dreams, my nostalgias, my terrors, and my fortunes. There is not a single line of my work that is not connected, in a secret or explicit way, to the limitless world that for me is that corner of the region of Tolima in Colombia.

In a final attempt to earn my high school diploma, I enrolled in the Colegio Mayor de Nuestra Señora del Rosario in Bogotá. My professor of Spanish literature was the noted Colombian poet Eduardo Carranza, and two blocks from the school were the pool halls of the Café Europa and the Café Paris. Carranza's classes were for me an unforgettable and passionate initiation to poetry. Billiards and poetry took precedence over my acquiring that much-sought-after diploma.

Alternating his poems with my own, Carlos Patiño and I published a chapbook titled *La Balanza* (The scales), which we distributed ourselves among our bookseller friends on April 8, 1948. The following day, our publication went out of print as the result of a fire. On April 9 the "Bogotazo" occurred when the downtown of the city was set ablaze by the enraged supporters of presidential candidate Jorge Eliécer Gaitán, who was assassinated that day in the capital. In 1953—after publishing some poems, the first in the journal *La Razón* at the hands of Alberto Zalamea, and others in the Sunday supplement to *El Espectador*, thanks to Eduardo Zalamea Borda—my verse collection *Los elementos del desastre* (The elements of the disaster) appeared in the collection "Poets of Spain and America" published by Losada, directed by Rafael Alberti and Guillermo de la Torre in Buenos Aires.

In 1956 I traveled to Mexico, where I reside today. Octavio Paz, who had written some laudatory reviews of my poetry, opened doors for me in literary supplements and magazines. Paz himself presented my work in a generous essay on my book *Reseña de los Hospitales de Ultramar* (A report on the overseas hospitals), published in 1958 as a supplement to number 56 of the magazine *Mito*, directed in Colombia by Jorge Gaitán Durán. In 1959 *Diario de Lecumberri* (Diary of Lecumberri) came out, published by the Universidad Veracruzana in its Fiction series. In 1964 Ediciones Era, also in Mexico, published a collection of poems, all written in Mexico, entitled *Los trabajos perdidos* (Wasted efforts). Two works appearing simultaneously in 1973 were *Summa de Maqroll el Gaviero*, which brought together all my poetry up to that date, published by Barral Editores of Barcelona, and *La Mansión de Araucaíma* (The mansion of Araucaíma), released by Sudamericana in Buenos Aires, which collected all my short stories. In 1978 Seix Barral of Barcelona produced a new expanded edition of the collection that included the short story "El último rostro" (The last face seen).

In 1982 Mexico's Fondo de Cultura Económica brought out a book of poems entitled *Caravansary* in its Tierra Firme collection. In 1984 the same publisher produced another volume of poetry, *Los emisarios* (The emissaries), in the same series, and in 1985 Cátedra of Madrid released *Crónica Regia y Alabanza del Reino* (Royal account and praise of the realm), poems dedicated to King Phillip II, his family, and court. In these last works I explore—not without difficulties, vacillations, and flashes of doubt—a new way of telling the same old thing, that which will remain the same and which, for me, is the only thing worth telling: that the ghosts from my avid and scattered readings during childhood at the Coello plantation visit me with invariable frequency—ghosts born in large part in the corners of the history of the Western world and in the golden decadence of Byzantium, engulfed, always, by the warm mists of the coffee plantations.

In 1987, and with the same purpose of recapturing vast periods from my past, I published *Un Homenaje y siete Nocturnos* (An homage and seven nocturnes), brought out by El Equilibrista of Mexico and Pamiela of Pamplona. Subsequently, I resolved to try my hand at the short story by expanding some of the prose pieces I had written on Maqroll el Gaviero (Maqroll the Lookout), a character who, beginning with the first poems I wrote, has visited me sporadically. Out of this enterprise was born *Empresas y tribulaciones de Maqroll el Gaviero*, which includes the following novellas: *La Nieve del Almirante* (1986; Eng. *The Snow of the Admiral*, 1995), *Ilona llega con la lluvia* (1987; Eng. *Ilona Comes with the Rain*, 1995), *Un bel morir* (1989; Eng. *Un Bel Morir*, 1995), *La última escala del Tramp Steamer* (1989; Eng. *The Tramp Steamer's Last Port of Call*, 1995), *Amirbar* (1990; Eng. *Amirbar*, 1995), *Abdul Bashur, soñador de navíos* (1991; Eng. *Abdul Bashur, Dreamer of Ships*, 1995), and *Tríptico de mar y tierra* (1993; Eng. *Triptych on Sea and Land*, 1995). After being published separately, in Spain as well as in Latin America, the works were released as two volumes with the publishing house Siruela in 1993 and in a single volume with Alfaguara in 1995.[1]

In 1988 Mexico's Fondo de Cultura Económica published short stories and essays under the title *La muerte del Estratega* (The death of the strategist), and in 1990 it brought out *Summa de Maqroll el Gaviero*, which collected all my poetry up to that time. The volume was reprinted in Spain by Visor in 1992.

Of my prose works, there are translations into English, French, German, Italian, Portuguese, Danish, Swedish, Polish, Greek, Dutch, and Turkish. Of my poetry, complete translations exist in French, Italian, and Romanian, and there are anthologized versions in Chinese, Russian, English, Greek, and German.

I have never taken part in politics; I have never voted, and the last event in the political realm that truly concerned me or had anything to do with me in a clear and honest way was the fall of Constantinople at the hands of the Turks on May 29, 1453, nor have I failed to recognize that I still have not gotten over the trip to Canossa by the Salic King Henry IV in January 1077 to pay homage to the Sovereign Pontiff Gregory VII—a trip of such ill-fated consequences for the Christian West. Hence, I am a defender of the Holy Roman Empire, monarchic, and legitimist.

Norman, Oklahoma
October 18, 2002

Translation from the Spanish by David Draper Clark

Editorial note: First published as "Mutis por Mutis," in *Caminos y encuentros de Maqroll el Gaviero: Escritos sobre Álvaro Mutis*, ed. Javier Ruíz Portella (Barcelona: Áltera, 2001), 19–23.

1. In English, all seven novellas are available in *The Adventures and Misadventures of Maqroll*, trans. Edith Grossman (New York Review Books, 2002).

ADAM ZAGAJEWSKI
THE 2004 LAUREATE

Adam Zagajewski (b. 1945) was born in the city of Lwów (now Lvov, Ukraine) but was forced to leave almost immediately thereafter when the Red Army occupied the area. After studying philosophy at Jagiellonian University in Kraków, Zagajewski emigrated to Paris, where he would remain until 2002. He began writing poetry in the 1970s and helped lead the movement that would come to be known as the Polish New Wave. He built his career around teaching at various universities throughout the world, including the University of Houston and the University of Chicago in the United States. Much of Zagajewski's body of work has been translated into English, including the poetry collections *Tremor* (1985), *Canvas* (1991), *Mysticism for Beginners* (1997), *World Without End: New and Selected Poems* (2002), *A Defense of Ardor* (2004), *Eternal Enemies* (2008), *Unseen Hand* (2011), *Slight Exaggeration* (2017), and *Asymmetry*

(2018). He also wrote a memoir, published in 2000, entitled *Another Beauty*. In addition to his Neustadt honor, Zagajewski was also named a Guggenheim Fellow in 1992.

Poetry must be written, continued, risked, tried, revised, erased, and tried again as long as we breathe and love, doubt and believe.

—Adam Zagajewski

Enchantment and Despair in the Poetry of Adam Zagajewski

Bogdana Carpenter

The leading poet of his generation, Adam Zagajewski continues the best tradition of Polish postwar poetry—established by such writers as Czesław Miłosz, Zbigniew Herbert, and Wisława Szymborska—in verse marked by intellectuality, historical awareness, a strong ethical stance, and formal sophistication. At the same time, Zagajewski has found his own distinct voice, not to be confused with any of his illustrious predecessors. In his poetry, he manages to combine tradition and innovation, participation in a poetic community, and staunch individualism. The fabric of Zagajewski's poetry is made of disparate elements: reality and dreams, the keen observation of reality and imagination, artistry and spirituality, erudition and spontaneity of emotions. In his poetry culture and nature share equal space.

Zagajewski's biography, as well as his poetry, are marked by polarities: allegiance to his native city and a sense of displacement caused by exile; solidarity with his generation and a sense of solitude; a dark vision of the world and tender sensitivity to its beauty, despair, and joy. These geographic, historical, and philosophical polarities define the space within which he moves as a poet. They explain his acute awareness of twentieth-century history, combined with a willingness to forget it in favor of an ahistorical, existential dimension.

Born in Lwów in 1945, Adam Zagajewski left his native city as an infant after its occupation by the victorious Red Army and subsequent integration into the Soviet Union. He lived first in Gliwice, a depressing Silesian city that before World War II belonged to Germany, but as a result of shifting frontiers became part of Poland after 1945. At the age of eighteen he moved to Kraków, where he studied philosophy at the Jagiellonian University. In the 1980s and 1990s he lived in Paris, but he returned to Kraków in July 2002. Each winter he teaches creative writing at the University of Houston. Zagajewski's life follows a twentieth-century paradigm of exile—a life lived outside the place to which we belong by birth and culture. As in so many other writers, exile resulted in a sense of displacement: "If people are divided into the settled, the emigrants and the homeless, then I certainly belong to the third category," he confesses.

Zagajewski's poetic career started in the 1970s when he formed part of a movement known as the New Wave or the Generation '68; this group called for poetry of social and political commitment. The principal target was the language of official communist propaganda, cleverly paraphrased in poetry to reveal its vacuity and falseness. From the beginning, the group was united more by its political goals than by its poetics. Zagajewski was one of the first to break away. He wrote an essay entitled "Solidarity and Solitude"; its title summarizes well his position, midway between commitment to collective causes and self-introspection. Or, as he puts it in a poem, "I take a seat in between. . . . I am alone but not lonely."

Philosophically, Zagajewski's poetry moves between two worlds, "one serene, the other insane." The world experienced by the senses is one of beauty and splendor, but the world known from history is one of suffering, death, and destruction. Although Zagajewski did not experience war directly, "the iron grip" of the twentieth century is the source of his pessimism and dark vision. By temperament, Zagajewski is a *homo aestheticus*, sensitive to beauty in all its manifestations—people, nature, art, music: "Only in the beauty created / by others is there consolation." The dark specter of history remains in the background and is rarely mentioned by name. In one of the poems, for example, its destructive power is evoked by such sharp objects as scissors, penknives, pruning shears, and razor blades. The foreground of Zagajewski's poetry is luminous, filled with buckets of raspberries and gentle hills; it is the world at peace where one can hear birds grow quiet and listen with rapture to Gregorian chants.

Behind soft air, wet leaves, and scarlet sunsets, however, lurk crematoria and razed cities: "Where starlings sing now, a branch / of Auschwitz had been built." A generation younger than Tadeusz Różewicz, Zbigniew Herbert, and Wisława Szymborska—the pleiad of Polish poets referred to by Miłosz as "poets of ruins"—Zagajewski's historical awareness stems less from memory than knowledge and imagination. This is why in his poetry enchantment and despair, a glimmering surface and dark interior, honey and soot walk hand in hand, and it is from the clash of these opposite emotions that the spark comes in his lines. "A poem grows on contradictions but it can't cover it," he writes in one of his poems.

Nevertheless, Zagajewski never turns to cynicism or nihilism; despite everything, he is a poet of affirmation who believes that "not every thunderbolt kills" and that "incidental dreams vanish at dawn / and the great ones keep growing." Art transforms pain into beauty. It is Zagajewski's great gift to know how to translate both ugliness and splendor into the brilliance of a poetic word: "I was in that strait where / suffering changes into song." His is a poetry of striking metaphors: beautiful, intricate, but at the same time apt and precise. They become instruments of cognition as well as moments of epiphany, when passive contemplation is transformed into the creative act of forging a new reality: "shining moments plucked from my imagination like a thorn drawn from an athlete's narrow foot."

This Neustadt ceremony carries with it a special poignancy and symbolism: Adam Zagajewski is the second Polish poet to win the Neustadt Prize. The first—and until today the only other Polish writer to receive it—was Czesław Miłosz in 1978. Miłosz who, according to Joseph Brodsky, was one of the greatest poets of the twentieth century, died on August 14, 2004. Awarding the prestigious Neustadt International Prize for Literature to Adam Zagajewski, the most gifted poetic heir of Miłosz, is like passing on a baton, providing reassurance that Polish poetry is alive and doing well.

Norman, Oklahoma
October 1, 2004

Bogdana Carpenter *is emeritus professor of Polish and comparative literature at the University of Michigan and an esteemed translator of Polish literature. A native of Poland, she grew up, as did Adam Zagajewski, in the city of Gliwice. She was a student of Czesław Miłosz at the University of California at Berkeley, where she earned a PhD in comparative literature.*

Poetry for Beginners
Adam Zagajewski

Let me express my gratitude for this prize, the Neustadt International Prize for Literature, which I've known about since 1978, when Czesław Miłosz received it. I remember regarding with awe his Neustadt photograph representing a handsome poet in a tuxedo, smiling and proud. Miłosz was in the 1970s a poet for the happy few, a secret and—within the Soviet-dominated part of Europe—prohibited poet whom we in Kraków read avidly, the way one studies a sacred text. We read his work in informal seminars, in private apartments, for he was banned from the university then.

Norman, Oklahoma, may not be Paris, and yet you display here a generosity that is mostly lacking in the old, traditional centers. It seems also—I've learned all this after the news about the prize reached me in Kraków—that you've invented an ingenious and completely transparent system for your international jury's debate and vote.

Thank you for this beautiful prize; when I look at the list of its winners I can't believe my eyes. I find on this list the great names of contemporary literature, starting with Giuseppe Ungaretti. Then comes Gabriel García Márquez, Elizabeth Bishop, Octavio Paz, and many others. Could you imagine a room filled with all these giants? The roar of laughter, friendly exchanges, but also brilliant, malicious remarks? Norman, Oklahoma, has established itself as one of the undeclared capitals of modernity.

I want to thank the Neustadt family for their kindness and for their interest in the art of writing, and *World Literature Today* for its zeal and tenacity in covering so many different linguistic realms of fiction and poetry. My gratitude goes also to Bogdana Carpenter who, unbeknownst to me, championed my work in front of the other jurors. Given the time difference between Oklahoma and Poland, I can easily claim that she fought for me as I was sleeping in Kraków under the gray October sky. Thank you, Clare Cavanagh, the magic translator of my poems and essays. And, last but not least, thank you, Maya—for everything.

Standing here in front of you, I'm thinking of Joseph Brodsky, who came to Norman to present and praise Miłosz's work for the Neustadt. I'm also thinking of my great compatriot, my mentor and friend, Zbigniew Herbert, whose name appeared several times during the Neustadt Prize deliberations and who, almost always unlucky in the external circumstances of his existence, was never chosen the winner of the prize—of course, he would have deserved this award in such an obvious way that even saying this seems to me futile.

I look at you, dear audience; I see many juvenile faces, and I realize that some young, very young poets, poet-candidates, so far unknown to the world and yet great in their daydreams and potential promises, have gathered in this room. This makes me think of poetry itself, poetry that is greater than any of us can comprehend.

Here we are, in this beautiful modern hall within the Sam Noble Oklahoma Museum of Natural History; we find ourselves in the company of dinosaurs and other dignified beasts, illiterate yet intriguing, once danger-ous, now posthumously domesticated. And yet there's a different, silent, and invisible company that doesn't need any special building to be permanently present in our lives (well, a good library is a useful thing)—the dead poets' society: Homer and Sappho, Virgil and Keats, Emily Dickinson and Adam Mickiewicz, Antonio Machado and Anna Swir. The fact that we, the living ones, still write poems verges on impudence. After all these masterpieces! After all this perfection! After all these dramatic events, after Shelley's drown-ing death, after Keats's agony in Rome, after Goethe's long and laborious life, after Mickiewicz's expedition to Turkey, after Georg Trakl's anguish in a mili-tary hospital in Kraków! Can we match the legendary realm, can we fancy our-selves poets in a way comparable to theirs?

We respond to this question through our deeds, through the action of writing. We know that to answer it directly would be impertinent, not neces-sary, but we also recognize that imagination has to struggle with the dragon of time afresh each day. Time brings about new things, good and bad; we must ascertain them. Time kills people and civilizations; we must save them, to remember them in poetry. We understand that the ongoing war between imagination and time (alas, a war that will never be won) cannot end, that we cannot turn, all of us, into historians of poetry and content ourselves with reading old poets. Poetry must be written, continued, risked, tried, revised, erased, and tried again as long as we breathe and love, doubt and believe. We always remember, of course, that we write our poems in the gigantic shadow of the dead and that we should be humble, at least in those long hours when we do not compose. (Being too humble in the very moment of creation would not be very wise.)

We need to go on, paying the price, sometimes, of being not only imperfect but even, who knows, arrogant and ridiculous.

An award like yours, the Neustadt Prize, with its silver feather lost by a silver eagle somewhere in the silver imaginary mountains, helps a lot. It helps to forget, if only for a brief moment of a ceremony like this one, the immense risk involved in writing poetry today. Poetry, according to Friedrich Hölderlin, this bard of loneliness, is the most innocent of all occupations. That is very true, and yet innocence is perhaps the most daring thing in the entire world.

Norman, Oklahoma
October 1, 2004

Claribel Alegría (1924–2018) is often considered the most important contemporary Central American writer. She was born in Estelí, Nicaragua, but spent most of her youth in the Santa Ana region of western El Salvador because of her father's political exile. In 1943 she came to the United States to study at George Washington University, where she received her bachelor's degree in philosophy and letters. She would not return to her country of origin until 1979, after the Sandinista National Liberation Front took control of the government. Influenced by the political climate of Central America, Alegría's poetry focused on the human condition in the region. Alegría's numerous books of poetry include *Anillo de silencio* (1948), *Acuario* (1956), *Huésped de mi tiempo* (1961), *Sobrevivo* (1978), *Mujer del río /Woman of the River* (1989), *Saudade* (1999; Eng. *Sorrow*, 1999), and *Soltando amarras* (2002; Eng. *Casting Off*, 2003). Her two major poetry anthologies in Spanish include *Una vida en poemas*, ed.

Conny Villafranca F. (2003), and *Esto soy: Antología poética de Claribel Alegría*, ed. Luis Alvarenga (2004). Posthumously, her work was included in *Ghost Fishing: An Eco-Justice Poetry Anthology* (2018).

> Quite often I have used my poetry as a sword, and I have brandished it against my internal and external demons.
>
> —Claribel Alegría

Knowing Claribel Alegría
Daisy Zamora

Which Claribel Alegría should I speak of today? The fiction writer, the chronicler of history, the storyteller, the political activist, the translator, or the poet? After years of reading her work (a vast literary landscape that includes poetry, fiction, historical testimony, translations, and anthologies) and having the privilege of knowing her personally for many years, I can say with some authority that a rare, extraordinary symbiosis exists between Claribel Alegría and her writing—that is, between her life and her words.

Nicaraguan poet José Coronel Urtecho once said that either to read her work and get to know her afterward, or to know her first and then read her work, is like being a witness to a miracle. One realizes in either case that Claribel and her writing are one and the same, and that unusual, miraculous fact provokes a sense of bewilderment, a feeling that such a range of accomplishment should be impossible, at the very least an illusion, and that is because the quality of a writer being one with his or her own writing is rare indeed. But for Claribel Alegría, the ethics of her work, the energy and beauty of her words, stand for herself, for her acts as a person, for the way her life matches her words. That being the case, I will center my remarks on the particular symbiosis between Claribel Alegría and her poetry.

At first glance, her poetry can be superficially judged as being simple because of its brief lines and language, which give it a fast, pulsating quality, a mercurial rhythm (even when the poet herself reads it aloud) that sounds almost like the singing of a nightingale. But such apparent simplicity is a mirage. On closer examination, an attentive reading reveals a powerful, accurate distillation of language, line by line, until it achieves, like a nightingale, a maximum capacity of complex expression. The exact weight that the poet extracts from the apparent simplicity of each word, and the complexity it really contains and expresses, gives the work perfect balance. Each poem has within itself a compass that guides it on the right path, in such a way that it never digresses, never gets lost, or misses its own route toward harmony and lucidity.

The same may be said of Claribel as a person, as a human being. Whoever reads her poetry can easily imagine how she is, and in the event that the reader happens to meet her, he or she becomes a witness to the miracle I mentioned before, amazed by the evidence of how similar the poet and her poetry are, how both share the same substance.

In 1989 José Coronel Urtecho, whom I mentioned before and who is one of our most important Nicaraguan poets (founder of the Vanguardia movement, one of its main leaders, whose seminal work has influenced several generations of writers in Nicaragua), wrote an extraordinary book called *Líneas para un boceto de Claribel Alegría* (Lines for a sketch of Claribel Alegría). In that book, he writes that Claribel's poetry is like something "sifted" through her being, after having gone completely "through" her. One never knows where the borders between herself and her words converge, the zone or line where light and shadow meet or melt, because the poet and her imagination and her words blend into one reality. Word by word, line by line, poem by poem, Claribel is her poetry, and her poetry is her. Coronel Urtecho also wrote that every time he read Claribel's poems, he was amazed all over again by how she can be such a great poet even in her shortest poems, because each of her words is loaded with so much life and meaning. He said that all her poems are miraculous.

Claribel's unusual and extraordinary ability to be one and the same with her poetry springs from an authentic and profound sense of humanity. She has the capacity to imagine, to visualize the "other," to move toward the other, toward the human. She has within herself a deep sense of her own dignity as a human being as well as of the dignity of others, which also includes a compassionate understanding for the world as a whole. This is the basic and authentic quality of a true humanist, and one finds this quality present throughout her entire body of work.

Sergio Ramírez, a most important Nicaraguan writer and former vice president of Nicaragua, has called her "the mythical Claribel Alegría" who was surrounded from early childhood by many great figures of Latin American literature, like Salvador Salazar Arrué (Salarrué), José Vasconcelos, and Joaquín García Monge. Later on, she studied with the Spanish poet Juan Ramon Jiménez, who took her to meet Ezra Pound, by then locked up in St. Elizabeth's Hospital. Still later, Miguel Ángel Asturias visited her in Santa Ana in El Salvador. In Santiago, Chile, she met Augusto Monterroso, and went with Asturias to Isla Negra to meet Pablo Neruda. There are also the long friendships she and her husband, Darwin J. (Bud) Flakoll, had with Robert Graves, Juan Rulfo, Julio Cortázar, and many writers of the Latin American "boom," of whom Claribel and Bud were the early editors and translators, years before many of them became famous. Together, they edited the anthology *New Voices of Hispanic America* published by Beacon Press in Boston, in 1962, which included Julio Cortázar, Augusto Monterroso, Juan Rulfo, Blanca Varela, Juan José Arreola, Ernesto Cardenal, Augusto Roa Bastos, and others. Therefore, says Sergio Ramírez, Claribel was born for literature, which is a substantial part of her existence, of her life.

I could talk almost endlessly of Claribel Alegría's impressive body of work, but she never speaks of herself because she is always and forever too curious about others and of the world that surrounds her. She is so interested and engaged in learning more about life and about all of us, her fellow human beings, that she forgets to talk about herself. But when she enters a room, or wherever she goes, her presence is felt immediately. I can only explain it in this way: When she appears, it is as if a rose is placed in a room. If I brought a rose to this room and put it on this table, its presence, even though quiet and silent, would change the whole mood of the room. Even if we wanted to ignore it, we wouldn't be able to, because that rose, with its beauty, its form, its color, and its fragrance, would make us all pay attention to it, although it would not be saying: Hey, here I am, look at me!

Claribel Alegría is that rose.

Norman, Oklahoma
September 29, 2006

*Daisy Zamora (b. 1950, Managua) is a prominent Nicaraguan poet, essay-
ist, translator, and advocate for human rights and feminist issues. Her bilin-
gual collection* The Violent Foam: New and Selected Poems *was published by
Curbstone in 2002.*

The Sword of Poetry
Claribel Alegría

First and foremost, I would like to express my appreciation for this important and unexpected prize in the name of my husband, Darwin "Bud" Flakoll,
who passed away some years ago. I am profoundly grateful for this award
and to the Neustadt family; the prestigious magazine *World Literature Today*;
its executive director, Robert Con Davis-Undiano; its editor in chief, David
Draper Clark; to the members of the jury who bestowed upon me this prize,
and—last but not least—to Nicaraguan poet Daisy Zamora, who nominated
me for the award. It is a very great honor to be here, with you, to accept this
prize. In all modesty, I confess that I never dreamed of receiving it, and I hope
not to disillusion you.

Throughout my life, I have made incursions into many literary genres,
but ever since my childhood, poetry has been and continues to be my passion.
From before I knew how to read, my parents had me memorize poems by
Rubén Darío, the great Nicaraguan poet who founded the modernist movement that transformed the Spanish language and whose work I recited with
pleasure to whoever was naïve enough to ask me to do so. The rhythm of
Darío's poems fascinated me. Often—and even alone—I would recite his work
out loud. Understanding the meaning of his verse didn't matter, for the music
of his poems was the most important thing. It was like the voice of the wind,
the pounding of rain on windows, or the eternal roar of the ocean waves. As

I grew older, I became more and more enamored of words. I wanted to know the meaning of each one of them and to memorize the dictionary.

Words are sensual. They seduce us and spark our imagination, but they also express intelligence and logic in constructing towers of ideals and culture. The Bible tells us that "In the beginning was the Word, and the Word was with God, and the Word was God." The word is our sword, our strength, the magic force that is given to things in order to name them. Having already entered into adolescence, I wanted to express myself through words. I evoked them, was delighted by them, but at times I also came to hate them, to come to blows with them when they didn't respond to me. As a poet, I like to invent and conjure up words, watch them fly, remain in flight, and many times fall and rise again bruised and wounded. There are words that reveal and others that conceal and still others that steal our sleep. Words are often empty, and we know not what to do with them, and they make us want to throw them to the floor and stomp on them to see what might emerge.

From very early on, I was quite fond of reading poetry. It is a habit of mine. At night, whenever possible, I read at least one poem before going to sleep. There have been good and bad influences on me as a poet. I have written many imitations of whatever I might be reading at any given time. I learned numerous tricks, some of which are quite useful and still serve me well. The Bible has greatly influenced me: the Book of Job, the Psalms, Ecclesiastes, the Song of Solomon. And poetry, as Percy Shelley observed, is like a great river into which thousands of tributaries flow. In essence, all poets contribute to writing the great endless poem.

The poet celebrates humankind, the universe, and the creator of the universe. It is impossible for one to remain indifferent to the turbulence that our planet and its inhabitants suffer through: war, hunger, earthquakes, misery, racism, violence, xenophobia, deforestation, AIDS, and childhood affliction, among others. In the region from which I come, Central America, we love poetry, and at times we use it to denounce what is happening around us. There are many fine testimonial poems. The poet, especially where I'm from, cannot and should not remain in an ivory tower.

To be a female poet was very difficult for me as an adolescent. I began writing relatively early. At the age of fourteen, after reading *Letters to a Young Poet*, by Rainer Maria Rilke, I knew that this vocation was for me. My parents never voiced opposition to the idea, but I used to write virtually in hiding. Except for my parents, I showed my poetry only to my literature professor; to Salarrué (Salvador Salazar Arrué), a great Salvadoran short-story writer; and to Alberto Guerra, a Nicaraguan/Salvadoran poet. If my women friends had been aware that I was writing poetry, they would have made fun of me, and no young man would want to approach me, not even to dance. Among my generation in Central America, women of the leisure class had the option of marrying or controlling their husband's purse strings or of remaining chaste and virtuous, baking cakes for their nieces and nephews.

Just a few years ago, one could easily identify the women in all of Latin America who stood out in literature. Names like Gabriela Mistral, Alfonsina Storni, Juana de Ibarború, Delmira Agustini, Claudia Lars, not to mention the greatest of them all, Sor Juana Inés de la Cruz, who, five hundred years ago, took off her feminist gloves when she wrote, "Stupid men, who, without cause, accuse women," words proclaimed rather shockingly. I suspect that Sor Juana opted to become a nun in order to have the opportunity to receive an education, without which she would have been veiled in silence.

In my particular case, after finishing secondary school, I had to spend two years learning to sew, cook fine cuisine, and play "Für Elise" on the piano before I could rebel. My father in no way wanted me to travel abroad to study or to attend the university in El Salvador. He said that there were hardly any women there and that I would be the object of disrespect. Finally, with the complicity of my mother, along with threats of my own, I succeeded in convincing my parents to allow me to travel to the United States to continue my studies. In spite of the fact that my father was *machista*, he never opposed my pursuing a career as a poet. On the contrary, I believe deep down that he was pleased that I did, for he loved poetry.

Soon before traveling to the United States, my parents invited me and my younger sister to gather in the living room. There, my father showed an upright Steinway piano to my sister, who had great musical talent, and told her, "This is your instrument. Take advantage of it." In turn, he brought me a wooden case with a felt-lined interior that housed a Parker fountain pen: "This is your instrument. Use it as a sword," he instructed. My father was intuitive. I'm sure he feared his own words, but he had to speak them to me, nevertheless. Quite often I have used my poetry as a sword, and I have brandished it against my internal and external demons.

Norman, Oklahoma
September 29, 2006

Translation from the Spanish by David Draper Clark

Patricia Grace (b. 1937) is the author of seven novels, five short-story collections, and several children's books. In 2006 she received the New Zealand Prime Minister's Award for Literary Achievement. Awards for her work include the Deutz Medal for Fiction for the novel *Tu* at the Montana New Zealand Book Awards in 2005, the New Zealand Fiction Award for *Potiki* in 1987, the Children's Picture Book of the Year for *The Kuia and the Spider* in 1982, and the Hubert Church Prose Award for the Best First Book for *Waiariki* in 1976. She was also awarded Frankfurt's LiBeraturpreis in 1994 for *Potiki*, which has been translated into several languages. *Dogside Story* was longlisted for the Booker Prize and won the Kiriyama Pacific Rim Fiction Prize in 2001. Her latest novel, *Chappy*, was a finalist in the Ockham New Zealand Awards for fiction and winner of Nga Kupu Ora Award 2016. Her children's book *Whiti Te Ra* was also a Nga Kupu Ora Award winner in 2015. Her novel *Cousins* is in the process of being made into a feature film.

Grace was a recipient of the Distinguished Companion of the New Zealand Order of Merit (DCNZM) in 2007. She has received honorary doctorates in literature from Victoria University of Wellington in 1989 and the World Indigenous Nations University in 2016.

It is what we know—the touchables, reachables, the experiences and thoughts that we have, that are central to the work of a writer—the things that surprise, excite, hurt, or move us in some way.

—Patricia Grace

Patricia Grace, Storyteller of the People
Joy Harjo

Oketv semvnvckosen pom pvlhoyes. Momen pom vlakeckat heretos.
A beautiful day has been loaned to us. Your arrival makes it great.

Hopiyen vlvkeckat mvto cekices. Cem vtotketv vcake tomekv,
    ecerakkueces.
From far you have come, and we say thank you. Your great work we
    value.

Ceme porakkuececkat, matvpomen ece rakkueces.
You honor us, and we honor you.

Vnokeckv sulken cemoces.
We have lots of love/respect for you.

E te rangatira, tena koe. Nga mihi aroha. Ka nui te aroha kei
    waenganui i a tatou.
Greetings to you, esteemed leader. Greetings of love. There is much
    love between us all [gathered here].

We were all created by a story. Each and every one of us walked, swam, flew, crawled, or otherwise emerged from the story. It is a terrible and magnificent being, this story. Each of us has a part. Each thought, dream, word, and action of every one of us continues to feed the story. We have to tend the story to encourage it. It will in turn take care of us as we spiral through the sky.

Every once in a while a storyteller emerges who brings forth provocative, compassionate, and beautiful tales, the exact story-food the people need to carry them through tough, transformative times. Patricia Grace of the

Māori people is one of these storytellers given to the people of Aotearoa, and now to the world as she is honored as the twentieth laureate of the Neustadt International Prize for Literature.

What distinguishes Grace's storytelling in the novel, short story, and children's book form is her ability to reach back to the ancestors and the oldest knowledge and to pull it forward and weave it together with forward-seeing vision, to create what is needed to bring the living story forward. She uses the tools of grace, humor, humbleness, and wisdom to make the design. The design is not extravagant or show-off; it is exactly cut and crafted to fit the shape of Māori culture and ideals. In Patricia Grace's stories everyone has a voice. In her stories, there is no separation between the land, the water, the sky, and the will of the people. Those relationships are honored.

If we have gathered the materials to make a structure with rapt attention and songs and have followed a protocol of respect, then as we construct the story it will want to come and fill that place; it will endure and inspire. And we will endure and be inspired. Grace's stories make a shining and enduring place formed of the brilliant weave of Māori oral storytelling and contained within the shape of contemporary Western forms. We are welcomed in, and when we get up to leave, we have been well fed, we have made friends and family, and we are bound to understanding and knowledge of one another. We become each other in the moment of the story. We understand that we have all been colonized, challenged by the immense story we struggle within. We are attempting to reconstruct ourselves with the broken parts. Patricia Grace's stories lead us back toward wholeness, to a renewal of integrity. This is the power of story. This is the power of Patricia Grace's gift to the Māori people, to indigenous people and the world.

Last year as I prepared to present Patricia Grace's legacy to an esteemed panel of jurors from all over the world, I called together an informal meeting of Pacific Islander writers in Hawai'i. We sat at a table in Manoa, over home-cooked food and refreshing drinks. I had researched everything I could through books and the Internet and wanted to know what Grace's own people, what other writers from the Pacific had to say about her and her writing. I heard many things that afternoon. I was told of her extensive help in mentoring young writers, that she writes from within a Māori community, that she always went beyond as she published a substantial and continual solid body of literature and raised her seven children. We talked about how there's a Māori level and an English literal level and how each story contains a storehouse of wisdom and knowing. "It's about time an indigenous person finds their way into these kinds of circles," said one. "She's an ambassador for Māori women. Her novel *Cousins* restored women to the story of history. "Her range of Māori voices is unparalleled. . . . She has exposed the Māori world to the rest of the world, showing that Māori people are as diverse as any other." All the stories at the table as we talked about Patricia Grace kept spiraling back to respect, love, and accomplishment in these times of immense difficulty in our indigenous communities.

Finally, as I got up to leave, everyone wished me well in the presentation but agreed that, with such competition of world-renowned writers, Grace wouldn't have much of a chance. "We know her and love her in the Pacific," they said. "She's one of our treasures. She isn't known far outside the Pacific. At least the jurors will come to read her and her work might find a way through them." We now know the ending to this story and are here to celebrate. I must acknowledge the panel of jurors who were enthusiastically supportive of Grace. I did not have to do much convincing at all.

Joining me in celebration here tonight with their words are a few of Grace's Māori colleagues:

Kia ora taatou.

I send my greetings and my family's *aroha* to Patricia Grace for her Neustadt laureateship. The distinguished jury chose eminently well. Patricia Grace has mentored and encouraged many younger writers through her work with the Māori writers' organization Te Ha (which means "the breath") and through the example she has set being an ambassador for Māori writing and culture internationally. I have always looked up to her with admiration for this generosity, given all that she has achieved in literature. Her children's books have represented to New Zealand children all their wonderful possibilities from a Ma⁻ori perspective and have become classics in our nation's literature. Her novels similarly engage Ma⁻ori artistic potential and bring us to the same literary table as New Zealand's most successful women writers, Janet Frame and Katherine Mansfield, and all of our brothers and sisters who are renowned for their literary prowess from our Pacific region and elsewhere. Patricia is our first Neustadt laureate, and also the first Ma⁻ori woman to publish a literary collection. I thank you for choosing so wisely this author who is of our country's community of writers and of her tribal people. She is a national *taonga*, that is, highly prized by those who respect great writing. Patricia is our *rangatira*, our leader. She is an important, compassionate voice, an immensely patient and nuanced voice, who shares Ma⁻ori values and thus furthers our community. *Arohanui* to you, Patricia. Your writing brings *Mauri Ora*, the well-being of life's energy, to us all.

Robert Sullivan, Poet
Nga Puhi, Ngati Raukawa,
Kai Tahu, Galway Irish

Pat's work is such an inspiration to all indigenous people, to indigenous women, and especially, to Māori. We are very proud of her and gratified to see her honored by this very distinguished organization for her considerable contribution to the world of literature. Without writers such as Patricia Grace the world would know little, or nothing, of the enormous struggle Māori and other indigenous people all over the world have had—and continue to have—to survive and, hopefully, to thrive. Patricia Grace gives us a voice, she tells our stories, she shows in very human and personal ways the damaging effects of colonization and how we continue to exist and to prosper in spite of those. Her stories remind us that we are connected—to our past from which we draw wisdom and courage, and to others in similar situations around the world. As a Māori woman and a teacher of literature, I am especially grateful that Patricia Grace continues to write us into the wider world picture, adding our experiences to those of human beings everywhere.

Reina Whaitiri
Kaitahu, Aotearoa / New Zealand

Mvto Mvto, Patricia Grace, for taking care of your gift and sharing with us.

Norman, Oklahoma
September 19, 2008

Joy Harjo *(Mvskoke) has published eight books of poetry, a memoir, and a play. The recipient of many awards and fellowships, she is a Chancellor of the Academy of American Poets and was named the twenty-third U.S. Poet Laureate in 2019. She lives in Tulsa, Oklahoma.*

The World Is Where You Are
Patricia Grace

By way of further introducing myself to you, I would like to tell you briefly about the place in New Zealand where I live, and from there to lead into some thoughts about the work of a fiction writer and a little of what the process may involve.

I come from a place in New Zealand called Hongoeka Bay, which is right by the sea and is situated thirty kilometers from the capital city of Wellington on the North Island. There are about twenty-seven houses in this small settlement, and because we are by the sea we like to spend our leisure time fishing—either from small boats or from the rocks on the shore. We can gather shellfish there when the weather is calm and the tide is low. Or even when the tides are not so good, if you're the owner of a wetsuit (and if you're much younger than what I am), you can go diving in much deeper water. When the weather's rough and the waves are high, the surfers among us pick up their boards and go surfing.

It's a stony, rocky, and quite rugged coastline but a good place for walking or for family picnics. There's always plenty of driftwood about that we can gather, make a fire, and cook our fish or shellfish or maybe a few sausages.

It's the beginning of spring in Aotearoa, New Zealand, at the moment, and after quite a harsh winter we're all looking forward to better weather so we can get to the water.

The land we live on, the settlement that I am speaking of, is on ancestral land that has been handed down to us through generations, from our ancestors. It is a remnant of land of three interrelated tribal or family groups. Because of it being ancestral land, it means that everyone in our community is related to me or is married to a relative of mine. Some are closely related. For example, we have a son and daughter and their families living there. My brother lives in front of me. Several of my first cousins are close by. Others are more distantly related through common ancestry.

So when I was a child staying there I was among grandparents and other elders as well as aunts, uncles, and cousins. And this was like having several grandparents, many mothers and fathers, and many brothers and sisters. Now living there as an older person I still have my same cousins around me, and our children and their children have grown up together. When Māori people speak of family we include extended family, those related through genealogy. Even those no longer living are considered to be still part of the family.

There are a range of occupations and professions in our community. Among us are builders, drivers, artists, office workers, public servants, health professionals, and teachers. My husband and I both trained as teachers. I left teaching in 1984 to become a full-time writer, and my husband, Waiariki, continued a career in education.

As part of our community we have a carved and decorated ancestral meeting house. Ours is not an old house. It is a house we built ourselves—raising finances, using our own voluntary labor and our own artists. It was a task that took about fifteen years. The house was dedicated and opened in 1997.

This is where we get together for meetings, for cultural and spiritual events, for teaching and learning, and for all sorts of social occasions such as birthday celebrations and weddings. This is where we carry out traditional rituals and ceremonies—especially so when someone dies. Along with the building of the meeting house has come the building and growing of ourselves, especially in the learning and use of the Māori language, our arts and traditions.

Adjacent to the meeting house is a kitchen and dining room facility, so when we welcome visitors, whether they have come to pay respects to the dead or for any of many reasons, they are able to be accommodated—to sleep in the meeting house and to have meals, which we prepare for them, in the dining room. Sometimes we host twenty people, sometimes a hundred or more. This can be a lot of work, but what I like about it is that all generations work together on all that needs doing to make our visitors feel welcome and comfortable.

Because I live a family / extended family / community life, I suppose it is not surprising that this is evident in the writing that I do. Exploring intergenerational relationships interests me greatly. In the writing of my novel *Potiki* I have drawn very much on the place where I live, in its setting and the type of community it is. Although the characters are all created characters, the issues surrounding land, which give foundation to the story, are ones that Māori communities live with every day.

The issues faced by the family in *Baby No-Eyes* are firmly based in reality. The characters in the stories "Valley" and "It Used to Be Green Once" lived in communities similar to the one I have described.

What I am doing, then, is writing about what I know.

It is what we know—the touchables, reachables, the experiences and thoughts that we have, that are central to the work of a writer—the things that surprise, excite, hurt, or move us in some way.

I am often asked why I became a writer, and I don't really know the answer to that. But as a child I did like the written word. I loved to read though

I didn't have many books at all. I could read by the time I went to school. But I didn't have writer role models, didn't know anyone who wrote. Except that my mother wrote letters now and again, I didn't see anyone writing.

Sometimes when people ask me why I became a writer, I tell them that it is because my parents worked in a stationery factory. My father used to bring home paper for us to write and draw on. I sometimes think that may be the true reason I became a writer—that fact that we had the raw material.

My parents both left school during the depression of the 1930s to work in a stationery factory, and that is where they met. Although my parents were not role models as far as actual writing went, they did share stories with us. Quite often these were family anecdotes or snippets about their own childhoods. But sometimes they were even less than that. They were just little one-liners that they would leave us with, that were funny or amazing in some way, and memorable.

For example, my mother told us about a great-great-grandfather who had two sets of teeth—two rows top and two rows bottom—and that they were very useful to him when climbing ship's rigging. Or my father would say, "You know your Uncle Jack rode on a whale."

Now the imagination could do wonders with unexplained morsels like that. Less can be more. I realize now that the Uncle Jack who rode on a whale may have done so when the poor dead animal was being towed ashore by a whaling boat. But in those days, what I imagined was that this fabled uncle spent his days riding the oceans of the world on the back of a whale, having all kinds of adventures.

If I was wanting to give advice to young writers (and there are many of you here today—you are writers because you do write), for those who wish to develop the craft of writing, I would say: Write every day. Read every day. Write what you know and push the boundaries of what you know.

You will want to explore how words work—how words can be made to work. You will want to be aware of the job that words, sentences, and paragraphs can do.

It is important for a writer to understand who he/she is and to understand that she/he is unique with a unique set of experiences, and that it is the everyday experiences which are important.

In the past, when workshopping with young writers, I've had things said to me such as, "Oh, I don't have anything to write about, my life is too dull, too boring." I have to persuade them that writing is about everyday things.

I know that many of you have read my story called "Beans." It's a good illustration of what I'm talking about because it's simply the story of a young boy going to play rugby on a Saturday morning and going home again. He is a boy who loves life. He draws the world in around him through sights, sounds, smell, and taste. He stands on his own two feet and doesn't need to be entertained. When I wrote the story I was living in a place similar to the one in the story. The story was based on one of our sons. I was writing a familiar, everyday event.

You can write about eating breakfast, a good day, a bad day, a sad day, a broken shoe, an embarrassment, a relationship. There is something happening to us every moment of our lives. None of us lives on a little antiseptic spot with nothing happening to us, around us, or inside of us.

Everything is food for someone who wants to write. To each ordinary day we bring our own individuality, our own style, our own creativity. It is good to remember that even though there is a big wide, world out there, the whole world is not out there.

The world is where you are. *Your* world is where you are.

Norman, Oklahoma
September 19, 2008

DUO DUO
THE 2010 LAUREATE

Duo Duo 多多 (b. 1951) is the pen name of Li Shizheng. He started writing poetry in the early 1970s as a youth during the isolated, midnight hours of the Cultural Revolution, and many of his early poems critiqued the Cultural Revolution from an insider's point of view in a highly sophisticated, original style. Often considered part of the "Misty" school of contemporary Chinese poetry, he nevertheless kept a cautious distance from any literary trends or labeling. After witnessing the 1989 Tiananmen Square massacre, Duo Duo left China and did not return for more than a decade. Upon his return to China in 2004, the literary community received him with honor and praise. Duo Duo currently resides on Hainan Island and teaches at Hainan University in China. Collections of his English translations include *Looking Out from Death: From the Cultural Revolution to Tiananmen Square* (1989) and *The Boy Who Catches Wasps* (2002). *Snow Plain*, published in 2010, is a collection of translated short stories.

Perhaps pondering words is also
a form of seeking justice. If a
monologue can invite a chorus,
then perhaps it can speak for others
as well. Poetry is self-sufficient in
its uselessness, and therefore it is
contemptuous of power.

—Duo Duo

Duo Duo: Master of Wishful Thinking
Mai Mang

Duo Duo is a great lone traveler crossing borders of nation, language, and history as well as a resolute seer of some of the most basic, universal human values that have often been shadowed in our troubled modern time: creativity, nature, love, dreams, and wishful thinking.

Born in 1951, Duo Duo's poetry career began in the early 1970s in Beijing during the isolated, midnight hours of the Cultural Revolution. As a lone, disillusioned Red Guard youth, he was inspired by his clandestine reading of Baudelaire and other Western authors. His very first poems immediately strike one with unusually intense and abstract yet vivid visions, such as in the beginning lines of the short poem "Untitled" (1972): "The sound of singing eclipses the blood stench of revolution / August is stretched like a cruel bow." Or, in "Untitled" (1974): "The blood of one class has drained away / The archers of another class are still loosing their arrows." Or, in "To the Sun" (1973), whereas the entire poem sounds like a reformulated ode to the omnipresence and omnipotence of the sun, an orthodox reference to the "great helmsman" Chairman Mao at that time, the last line underscores, or exposes, the paradoxical fate of the sun itself: "You create, rising in the East / You are unfree, like a universally circulating coin!" These powerful, bare-boned epiphanies all critiqued the Cultural Revolution from an insider's point of view and in a highly sophisticated, dialectical, and original style. In Duo Duo's 1976 poem "Instructions," he further summarizes his and his contemporaries' artistic deeds conducted in the underground of the Cultural Revolution and delivers a sober conclusion: "What they have experienced— is only the tragedy of birth."

Through such negative visions, Duo Duo gained his own historical subjectivity and individual agency. He paid a high price for these insights. An abandoned, bad-blooded bastard child of revolution and modernism, Duo

Duo from the very onset of his career foresees a life that is exiled from but also imprisoned by history: "From that superstitious moment on / The motherland was led away by another father" ("Blessings," 1973); "Ah moonlight, hinting at the clearly seen exile . . ." ("Night," 1973). In "Marguerite's Travels with Me" (1974), Duo Duo reveals the ultimate existential gap faced by the lyrical protagonist torn between a real China and an imaginary West. The poem's first part starts with lines "Like you promised the Sun / Get crazy, Marguerite," echoing Baudelaire's famous "Invitation to the Voyage," and inviting a certain Marguerite to a spontaneous, freewheeling rhapsody of cosmopolitan travel. But such a fantastic voyage only ends up, in the second part, in pledging this imaginary "Ah, noble Marguerite / Ignorant Marguerite" to take an alternate, heavyhearted, utterly sobering visit to the impoverished Chinese countryside that had been hopelessly stuck in the mire of a failed revolutionary utopia. The idealized, romantic bond between Marguerite and "me" thus has to be rendered as an impossible cul-de-sac. Duo Duo's early poetry hence generates meaningful and nuanced reflections on history and revolution as well as on modernity and modernism, sketching a Sisyphean fate imposed upon individuals from within and without the borders of nation and history.

Duo Duo's poems of the 1980s continued but also expanded on his poetic experimentation. In particular, Duo Duo proves himself to be a great innovator of linguistic forms and poetic craft whose liberating power is always inspiring and sublime. Constantly, Duo Duo bets on "wishful thinking": "If the making of language comes from the kitchen / The heart is the bedroom. They say: / If the heart is the bedroom / Wishful thinking is the bedroom's master" ("Language Is Made In the Kitchen," 1984). Meanwhile, Duo Duo increasingly focuses on the theme of the northern landscapes of China, intending to invoke and restore an abundant correspondence between nature and ancient human spirit against the ensnarement of modern history and its rigid, harsh noise that lacks any human or natural breath. This elemental tendency is shown in his poem "Northern Voices" (1985), whose ending lines remind one of Laozi, the ancient Taoist philosopher's teaching that "the greatest utterance is silence": "All languages / Shall be shattered by the wordless voice."

But it would be a grave mistake to say that Duo Duo is a poet who has renounced hope and the prospect of human communication. While cleansing and reforming a polluted, ossified language, Duo Duo seeks to speak, nevertheless, through a different medium, and pays tribute to its great power and awe. Another poem in this "North" sequence, "Northern Sea" (1984), depicts a vast, almost eschatological, panoramic scene of solitude, alienation, and desolateness. And yet the same poem closes with an ultimate affirmation of human love, even if such love may be merely a phantom evoked from the past: "But from a large basket lifted up high / I see all those who have loved me / Closely, closely, closely—huddled together . . ."

In a most dramatic fashion, Duo Duo left China on precisely June 4, 1989, after witnessing the incidents of Tiananmen Square at first hand. During the ensuing fifteen years, Duo Duo lived in exile and traveled throughout western Europe, North America, and many other parts of the world, seeming to literally fulfill the dark prophecies of his own early poetry written during the Cultural Revolution. In poems written shortly after he settled in the West, such as "Rivers of Amsterdam" (1989), "In England" (1989–90), and "Watching the Sea" (1989–90), Duo Duo conjures his lyrical power and wrestles most bravely and indigenously with that giant beast called "exile." While cursed with a nightmarish and claustrophobic history, Duo Duo, this lone, exiled traveler and one of the "Nails far removed from the motherland" ("Map," 1990), actually succeeds in opening up a great, alien expanse of space for his poetry and creating a post-exilic and post-historical universe of deprivation and ineffability. And, as in his 1993 poem "Just Like It Used to Be," he presents an utterly defiant, haughty, and insuppressible "burst of a furious growth" and "ubiquitous powers of persuasion" that "No arrangement whatsoever can reproduce." Against the gravity of nihilism and desert of exile, this shamanistic, steadfast reaffirmation of "like it used to be" crystallizes a positive, primitive, and badly needed universal message: a persistent, heroic reclamation of the possibility of human speech and power of memory rising above differences of human tongues.

Among the esteemed so-called Misty poets of his generation, Duo Duo was nearly the last to emerge aboveground. His only book of poetry officially published in China prior to his exile was a thin volume, *Salute* (1988). However, his stature was universally revered, as evidenced by the fact he was awarded the first (and, until this day, only) Today Poetry Prize in 1988. The prize was presented to him by none other than Bei Dao himself, the other leading Misty poet and co-founder of the legendary samizdat literary journal *Today*. The award statement reads: "Since the early 1970s, Duo Duo's solitary and tireless exploration of the art of poetry has always inspired and influenced many of his contemporaries." Between 1989 and 2004, while sojourning in the West, Duo Duo kept up a strong output of poetry and prose writing and was invited to numerous international poetry readings and literary events. Duo Duo returned to China in 2004 to assume a professorship at Hainan University. Since his return, he has been steadily "rediscovered" by a younger generation of Chinese writers and poets. Duo Duo is an extremely fastidious craftsman of poetry as well as dedicated servant of the Muse. He does not publish his work regularly or professionally, as do most of his Western counterparts. Instead, he prefers to date his finished poems and let them sit in manuscript for extended periods, sometimes more than a decade, before he is willing to allow them to come to light, a habit that may have been directly derived from his experience of writing clandestinely during the Cultural Revolution. Such inclination to marginality and anonymity, on the other hand, like a Cain's mark, has haunted Duo Duo and kept him, almost criminally, from the recognition he truly deserves.

Duo Duo is one of the most original, penetrating, inspiring, and unforgettable voices ever heard in contemporary Chinese poetry. He is also, as Eliot Weinberger put it, "one of the mountains in the topographical map of contemporary world poetry." Duo Duo's contribution to both contemporary Chinese and world poetry is astounding and will be, in a definitive term, everlasting. Duo Duo is not an easy poet, whose obsessive, sometimes schizophrenic pursuit "to preserve / That which orders the stripes on the tiger's back / His madness!" ("The Winter Night Woman," 1985) poses great intellectual and aesthetic challenges to both his readers and his translators in other languages, who may not be readily familiar with the gigantic scope and difficulty of his odyssey beyond borders. Even the most able translations available today may not always do adequate justice to the brilliance of his Chinese originals. But it is precisely in this sense that I believe the 2010 Neustadt Prize belongs to Duo Duo, this marvelous, bold, persistent, if underappreciated Chinese genius of poetry. The Neustadt Prize will provide a perfect venue and forum for the world to listen to Duo Duo's distinctive voice issued from the dark depths of an alternate, labyrinth-like world that we used to live in but often tend to leave in oblivion.

New London, Connecticut

Author note: Of the poems cited in this nomination statement, I would like to acknowledge translations from the following three pioneering books on Duo Duo in the English-speaking world: Gregory Lee and John Cayley's *Looking Out from Death: From the Cultural Revolution to Tiananmen Square* (1989), Maghiel van Crevel's *Language Shattered: Contemporary Chinese Poetry and Duoduo* (1996), and Gregory Lee's *The Boy Who Catches Wasps* (2002). At some places I have modified them or have used my own translations from *Contemporary Chinese Literature: From the Cultural Revolution to the Future* (2007).

Mai Mang *(Yibing Huang 麦芒), born in Changde, Hunan, in 1967, established himself as a poet in the 1980s and received his BA, MA, and PhD in Chinese literature from Beijing University and a second PhD in comparative literature from UCLA. He is currently an associate professor of Chinese at Connecticut College.*

This Is the Reason We Persevere
Duo Duo

Ladies and Gentlemen:

Tonight, in front of everyone here, I wish to keep my tone low, so that the word *gratitude* can be heard more clearly. This is a word that must be said, and should have been said a long time ago.

Upon hearing the verses of Baudelaire, Lorca, Tsvetaeva, and Ehrenburg for the first time, a generation of Chinese poets was already grateful—for the transmission of creativity from hand to hand during those stark years. Words, in the hands of their receivers, had directly become destiny.

Poetry hit us with its power of immediacy, and I believed that from that point of impact, the power would be transmitted back out from us.

Since then, my borders have been only two rows of trees.

Even as I speak, remnants of the 1970s still resound, and contain every echo of the reshaping of one's character. One country, one voice—the poet expels himself from all that. Thus begins writing, thus begins exile. A position approaches me on its own. I am only one man; I establish myself on that. I am only a man.

I am not speaking about history, but about man, whose appearance in this word *history* has long been debated. In this word, life is led away by poetry, to search for, as Sylvia Plath said, "a country far away as health."

I am speaking about writing, that difficult étude.

In the process, what must be spoken meets what cannot be said. Each word is a catalyst, requiring the writer to break out forcefully from another story, from the primitive camp where history, society, and politics converge, to touch upon that "what" and that "who." At that touch, one finds the unlimited boundaries of man, concealed by words.

At this point, half of each word has been written, the half that can be understood. Grammar is still pondering the other half. Each word is not only a sign. Inside each word there is an orphan's brain. No words can be younger, but inside the word *suffering* are all the secrets of being human.

Perhaps pondering words is also a form of seeking justice. If a monologue can invite a chorus, then perhaps it can speak for others as well. Poetry is self-sufficient in its uselessness, and therefore it is contemptuous of power.

At the very least, the ideal of poetry demands this: even as the poet is still catching up, it has already revealed its most dignified aspect. It allows light to be cast on the scales, which light must shine and move upon. Light therefore arrives where man himself can arrive, so as to recognize love anew.

What illuminates us is hesitancy, so action is always condemning; darkness becomes more complete, to the point that it has sealed up all its remaining cracks, without knowing that light in fact originates from within itself. And that is what words must penetrate through.

The present is thereby even more hidden, the hierarchy cannot speak this rule—a spell that has been written down.

When the road has already become an unstressed word, even when tracing its genealogy, what returns are only the echoes of this particular civilization. So we stop here, we stop at the place where we think we can go back and experience the whole journey, on a quest for that word which has been enclosed in ore along with a swooning, ancient past—a sealed-up riddle that is only testing its listener.

In a poet's listening, at the limits of his honesty, at the ends of logic, a "what" will be opened, that "what"—the present moment. From its deepest roots, a word will burst out from the riddle. Perhaps this word is what has been revealed by hints: an approaching, an encountering, a dialogue.

The road is only in the present, and we use the echoes as milestones.

What I am speaking about is how a poet's experience is brought into words.

After experiencing the cacophony of revolution, subversion, experimentation, and deconstruction, what can the poet still hear? Inside this word that has burst out from the riddle—*silence*—is our common condition: on the level of a completely material world, on a human physical level, we are allowing a dysfunctional intelligence to peck at and eat away the landscape; it is a continuation of slogans; a sustainable violence is using memory as fuel, and what has been replenished is the echo of our condition, because the exile of words begins here.

But from the discursive space created by the poetic canon, what constantly echoes is the speech that has never been separated from silence: there is only memory, no forgetting, because there are no mountains, only peaks. . . .

The pantheon of classical Chinese poets is emerging, bringing mountain ranges, rivers, weight, and pressure along in their words and between their lines, to be with us not only where language breaks but also at geological fault lines, waiting for us to pick up where they left off—another season in this meadow of life. In another story, in the same allegory, the way we return to the sound of the fresco is the way the light creates our horizon.

At this point, we need the voice of an all-encompassing story to speak.

To speak of East–West, West–East, to speak of this common stage on which we all appear—the earth, the advancing starry skies and dwellings—our allies in writing, our readers—our grasslands under the sea . . .

Nature already has no other water or ink, the danger has been found, poetry has fallen to the periphery, and this periphery comes close to home. Poetry takes this periphery as a blessing and continues to offer rituals for the sick rivers, to offer readable landscapes for the heart.

This is the reason we persevere.

Norman, Oklahoma
October 22, 2010

Translation from the Chinese by Mai Mang

ROHINTON MISTRY
THE 2012 LAUREATE

Born in Bombay, **Rohinton Mistry** (b. 1952) has lived in Canada since 1975. He is the author of three novels, all of which have been shortlisted for the Booker Prize, and a collection of short stories, *Tales from Firozsha Baag*. His first novel, *Such a Long Journey*, won the Governor General's Award, the Commonwealth Writers Prize for Best Book, and the SmithBooks / Books in Canada First Novel Award. It was made into an acclaimed feature film in 1998. *A Fine Balance* was winner of the Giller Prize, the Commonwealth Writers Prize for Best Book, the Los Angeles Times Fiction Prize, the Royal Society of Literature's Winifred Holtby Award, and Denmark's ALOA Prize. It was shortlisted for the International IMPAC Dublin Literary Award, the Irish Times International Fiction Prize, and the Prix Femina. In 2002 *A Fine Balance* was selected for Oprah's Book Club. *Family Matters* won the Kiriyama Pacific Rim Book Prize for Fiction and the Canadian Authors Association Fiction Award. It was shortlisted for the International IMPAC

Dublin Literary Award and the James Tait Black Memorial Prize. Mistry was awarded the Trudeau Fellows Prize in 2004 and a Guggenheim Fellowship in 2005. Elected Fellow of the Royal Society of Literature in 2009, he was a finalist for the 2011 Man Booker International Prize. At the 2014 Times of India Mumbai Literature Festival, he was presented with its Lifetime Achievement Award. In 2016 he was appointed to the Order of Canada. His work has been published in more than thirty-five languages.

Remembering is a benediction: in time, the answer began to crystallize. In the space between the two, where the paradox resides, the idea of home could be built, anew, with memory and imagination, scaffolded by language.

—Rohinton Mistry

Rohinton Mistry's Omniscient Gaze
Samrat Upadhyay

I was in graduate school at Ohio University in the late 1980s, an aspiring writer from Nepal, when I read Rohinton Mistry's *Swimming Lessons and Other Stories from Firozsha Baag*. Those years I didn't have authors in English from my own country I could turn to, so it was mostly Indian writers whose work I was devouring. I'd already felt the heady jolt of Salman Rushdie's *Midnight's Children*, as many writers of my generation had. There were also others I was reading: Anita Desai, Bharati Mukherjee, Amitav Ghosh. And now here was Rohinton Mistry, and I knew that I had encountered someone who could teach me a thing or two about, as Raja Rao (the 1988 Neustadt winner) put it decades ago, "how to convey in a language that is not one's own the spirit that is one's own."

In a story called "Squatter" in *Swimming Lessons*, a young Indian who has immigrated to Canada finds that he is able to adapt to the Western way of life in everything, except one: in the bathroom he finds himself unable to sit on the commode and has to squat, desi-style. Even after living in Toronto for ten years, this character is "depressed and miserable, perched on top of the toilet, crouching on his haunches, feet planted firmly for balance upon the white plastic oval of the toilet seat." But our hero doesn't give up trying. "Each morning he seated himself to push and grunt," Mistry writes, "grunt and push, squirming and writhing unavailingly on the white plastic oval. Exhausted, he then hopped up, expert at balancing now, and completed the movement quite effortlessly."

For days I couldn't stop laughing at the picture of this young man's predicament. Yet it was not only funny, it was also the truth. With that one image, Mistry had captured for me a perennial problem of the migrant: how to adapt to one's new culture without giving up one's fundamental identity—that of a squatter!

Mistry is not a writer of linguistic riffs, he is not enamored by language for its own sake—and thank god for that. He's a writer who's interested in telling stories . . . stories about the human heart and the human mind and of how we all struggle in this world, whether we are migrants or bank workers, beggars or college students, tailors or pavement artists. An old-fashioned storyteller, Mistry is adept at revealing not only our flaws but also our virtues, our ability for human connection and kindness. Who can forget, for example, the bond that Gustad Noble and Tehmul-lungra form in *Such a Long Journey*? And what about the troubled yet moving relationship that forms among the four main characters in *A Fine Balance*: the prim Dina, the hounded tailors Isvar and Omprakash, and the endearing Maneck?

Mistry is a connoisseur of small details. The description of Crawford Market in *Such a Long Journey*, for example, is a welcome assault on the senses: "It was a dirty, smelly, overcrowded place," Mistry writes, "where the floors were slippery with animal ooze and vegetable waste, where the cavernous hall of meat was dark and foreboding, with huge wicked-looking meat hooks hanging from the ceiling . . . and the butchers trying various tacks to snare a customer, now importuning or wheedling, then boasting of the excellence of their meat while issuing dire warnings about the taintedness of their rivals', and always at the top of the voices."

Yet the sum of the little details in Mistry's novels accrue to something larger, an omniscient gaze that recalls Dickens and Tolstoy. It's not only individual lives that Mistry paints with such meticulousness; it's how he stretches his canvas to embrace the wider world that makes his work comparable to the contemporary giants of literature. Gustad Noble's struggles in *Such a Long Journey* are inextricably tied to the headaches of the nation under Indira Gandhi. In *A Fine Balance*, not only the city of Bombay but the whole of India ripples outward from the cramped shop where our tailors and their friends toil all day.

This is a largeness of the spirit, a merging of the individual consciousness with that of the collective yearning for love and belonging, and, simply, a decent, dignified life. In Mistry's hands, the form of the novel itself expands, and it ends up making us, the readers and the participants of his journey, filled with wonder at the beauty and spaciousness of this world.

Bloomington, Indiana

Samrat Upadhyay *is the author of several award-winning novels and story collections. He is the Martha C. Kraft Professor of Humanities and teaches creative writing at Indiana University.*

The Road from There to Here
Rohinton Mistry

A few months before I was to leave Bombay for Toronto, a friend asked to borrow my copy of *A Hard Day's Night*. It was 1975, and the Beatles had long since recorded their last studio album, but my friend—I'll call him Harish— working his way backward, was now enthralled by their earlier work.

He was constantly trying to find hidden meanings in songs, parsing, analyzing the lyric as though it were Wittgenstein or Schopenhauer. When B. B. King moaned that his woman had done him wrong, Harish was happy to spend an afternoon in the St. Xavier's College canteen debating, over endless cups of tea, what it was that the bluesman and his guitar were actually saying. With his ever-present flicker of a smile, Harish was agreeable company; the mischief he sought to provoke, the arguments he instigated were always welcome, as was his readiness for laughter.

Borrowing and lending within our circle of friends was rampant, second nature to us, learned long ago in kindergarten with rubber balls and painted wooden toys. And later, books and records, too, were considered common property, more or less. We traded, bartered, borrowed, and lent with a reckless disregard for Polonius's advice; otherwise, childhood and youth would have been bleak places.

When I gave Harish the Beatles LP, his request had barely registered. In 1975, India, in grave turmoil, had gripped everyone's attention. People were filling the streets in the hundreds of thousands, marching daily against misrule and corruption. Newspapers wrote, before censorship silenced them, about goon squads and torture, police brutality and custodial deaths, the disappearance of dissidents and union leaders, and about bodies found, bloodied, and broken, beside suburban railway tracks. The prime minister's response to all this, the unleashing of a State of Emergency, was barely a month away.

Changes in my personal life, though less drastic, were no less unsettling. My Canadian immigration visa had arrived. The convulsions that racked the country I observed detachedly, as I got ready to go. After all, my lower-middle-class life, like countless others, had been spent preparing for this moment, with encouragement from parents, friends, teachers, and counselors. The picture painted could have been titled *India: The Sinking Ship*: no prospects, no future in this place of ignorance and disease and poverty, where, instead of the rule of law, there was the law of bribery, where government would forever remain in corrupt or incompetent hands, where the only solution was to settle in the West, to make a better life for oneself, and where one would actually fit in much better, thanks to one's upbringing.

It strikes me now as odd that in the endless talk about what would be gained by migration, no one ever wondered if something might be lost. The stark choice, between clinging to the sinking ship or booking passage on the luxurious ocean liner, left little room for hesitation and deliberation. These were the generations who had borrowed, or borrowed from, the culture of the colonizer, that imperial lender who had made the loan seem a gift: seductive, pain-free, tantalizing. And, in time, the borrowers came to believe it was their birthright, their own culture, flowery frocks and Enid Blyton and Marmite and all, vastly superior to the native one which had been quietly expunged from their lives.

And where did it begin for me, the journey from there to here? The question is difficult; and perhaps this is oversimplification, but my father's record collection is as good a place to start as any.

In many ways, my long and winding road from Bombay to Toronto was merely an extension of the one that had led me to the LP of *A Hard Day's Night* from my father's 78 rpms. His eclectic collection of shellac pressings included things such as Gilbert and Sullivan operettas, Mozart's *Jupiter* Symphony, Brahms's *Hungarian Dances*, George Formby's "Blackpool Prom," a medley of English pub songs like "Down at the Old Bull and Bush," and so on, with Tin Pan Alley and Broadway also represented in the stack of records.

And though I never heard Ravi Shankar's sitar till many years later, when I saw the documentary where he performs with George Harrison in the *Concert for Bangladesh*, as a child I could sing all the words to "Don't Fence Me In": "Oh give me land lots of land under starry skies above, don't fence me in, let me ride through the wide-open country that I love, don't fence me in . . ."

The Gene Autry record was a serviceable soundtrack and theme song for the westerns I was reading then, the comics and novels, including the Lone Ranger series by Francis Striker. Cowboy was the career I had settled on. Those books were my operations manuals, consulted to make a list of required equipment: spurs, chaps, saddle, a white Stetson, bowie knife, belt and holsters for six-shooters. The job description seemed irresistible: riding the range, fighting cattle-rustlers and Injuns, lassoing the two-legged varmints and presenting them bound and helpless to the sheriff, and then, after sunset, building a fire to sit around and sing what else but "Don't Fence Me In," before falling asleep under the starlit sky. In short, the perfect life. I had decided that as soon as I was old enough I would leave Bombay on an Air India flight bound for the Wild West, where I would team up with the cowboys, wear a white hat, and ride a white horse. It never occurred to me that one look at this skinny subcontinental Indian boy and the white hats would relegate me to the losing side.

From time to time, I still marvel at the reach of that mythology and propaganda, halfway around the world, and the inadequacy of an education which kept me from making even the most superficial connection with, or feeling

DISPATCHES FROM THE REPUBLIC OF LETTERS

the slightest empathy for, the misnomered Indians of the Americas—subjugated, exploited, dispossessed, annihilated. Ignorance was not only bliss, it had fenced me in completely.

The gramophone that spun my father's 78s was his proudest possession, made in England by the Garrard Engineering and Manufacturing Company. My brothers and I were discouraged from playing it. This seemed unfair to us, who were always taught to share. Aware of the contradiction, our father would explain that the records were fragile, easily broken; besides, gramophones were dangerous for children because of the risk of electric shocks; and mishandling might blow the main fuse, plunging our flat into darkness, or even the entire block of flats. This convinced me, for it was a period during my childhood when I was scared of the dark, and of shadows, especially the shadows of foliage that played on the windowpane beside my bed, monster claws trying to break through the glass.

Every now and again, a brittle 78 would indeed shatter, and we would mourn its shellac shards for days. Electricity, too, sometimes corroborated my father's explanations by making the tone-arm deliver a nasty jolt. And fuse boxes and connections did go faulty, the wiring under perpetual siege from rats. But there is no doubt that my father guarded the gramophone fiercely, the cherished symbol of things he had wanted in his life: art, theater, ballet, the symphony—wanted for his family, in abundance, and could afford in meager portions only. The supply was scant, the price of admission mostly beyond reach.

When the Bolshoi Ballet came to Bombay in the 1960s, though, my father managed to get tickets for us all at Shanmukhanda Hall, a huge cavern of a place. Our seats were in the last row of the balcony. The dancers, in a performance of *La Dame aux Camélias*, would have been specks on the stage were it not for the binoculars loaned to us by our gentle upstairs neighbor. A veterinary surgeon, he was the principal of the Bombay Veterinary College. His duties included officiating at the Bombay Turf Club. The binoculars were the ones he used on Sunday afternoons to observe thousands of pounds of horseflesh fly around the Mahalaxmi Racecourse. At the ballet his bulky glasses captured the pirouettes and *pas de deux* as efficiently as the gallop and the canter. And I was certain that the people around us, peering through their dainty little opera glasses, could not see half as much as I with my big binoculars.

The Bolshoi Ballet was one of the rare moments when my father must have felt like a bona fide consumer of culture. But, over the years, as I pieced things together, I understood more. My father had started violin lessons at a young age—four or five, I think; and he had become rather good at the instrument by the time he was in university. Then everything changed. His father's illness, which sent their large and prosperous bookshop into decline, led to bankruptcy and the seizure of the books and bricks and mortar by the creditors. He had to give up his violin lessons, give up university, and, armed only with his BA in history and economics, find work to support the family.

So, years later, my father continued to carry the burden of yearnings created by the imperial lender, while the gramophone shouldered the weight of his dreams. He treated it with the same reverence that he showed his bookcase. Everything he did concerning the Garrard—dusting the rosewood cabinet, cleaning the tone-arm, selecting a record, switching on the turntable—had an air of ritual, as though in a temple. If the needle went blunt, he would select a new one from a small, enamelled metal box lined with tinfoil, and, for a while, the music would sound brighter, clearer. Those were the best days, the new-needle days; they made the future seem more hopeful.

I liked sitting close to the gramophone. With my cheek against the cabinet I could breathe in the warm fragrance of polished wood, feel the hum and vibration of the turntable, and imagine the music becoming a part of me. And I loved to watch the record spin because the grooves in the shiny shellac appeared to create an endless spiral which almost induced a trance, almost made visible the passage of time; and suddenly, eternity was not an idea that evaded grasping, but music that played forever.

My earliest memory of the gramophone is connected with a set of nursery-rhyme records, from the time I started kindergarten at Villa Theresa School. Thanks to the gramophone, I was already familiar with much of the kindergarten syllabus the nuns taught us: "Here We Go Round the Mulberry Bush," "Jack Sprat," "Oranges and Lemons," "A Frog He Would a-Wooing Go."

Time passed, and other records in my father's collection began to interest me. All grown up in the second standard and tired of nursery rhymes, I would ask my father to play selections from *The Maid of the Mountains* or *No, No, Nanette*. But, as master of ceremonies, he had to give equal time to my younger siblings. My requests would have to wait in line. To show my impatience, or just to show off, I would start singing something else: "He's up each mornin' bright and early, to wake up all the neighborhood, to bring to every boy and girlie, his happy serenade on wood . . ."

Then I would be asked to shut up. But before long I would start again, with another song: "A boy from Texas, a girl from Tennessee, he was so lonely in New York and so was she. The boy said howdy, the girl said hi y'all, he could have kissed her when he heard that southern drawl . . ."

Sometimes, we divagated into the realm of Indian music. There was a Hindi record called *Haji Malang Baba*, about a Sufi saint, whose shrine, halfway up a mountain in a suburb of Bombay, was visited by pilgrims of all races and religions—by Hindus, Muslims, Sikhs, Christians, Parsis—because Haji Malang granted all prayers and boons, in all languages. As for Hindi film music, a song from the blockbuster *Mother India* was my mother's favorite: "Na mai bhagwan hoon, na mai shaitaan hoon, array duniya jo chaahey samjay, mai to insaan hoon" (Neither am I a god, nor am I a devil, the world may think what it wants to, I'm just plain human). My mother's childhood influences had been of a more ecumenical nature; she endeavored to embrace everything, and encouraged us to do the same.

The nursery rhymes were on seven-inch records, the other songs on ten-inch. And every gramophone recital ended with something classical, like Rachmaninoff or Tchaikovsky, on twelve-inch shellac. This was fitting, I used to think, the increase in size as one moved from children's music to music for big people.

The consumption of gramophone needles also kept increasing. My father was constantly replenishing them, regarding them to be necessities like milk and bread. The years went by, inflation continued to climb, and the economy, as it always has, continued to baffle the economists without dampening their enthusiasm for pontificating. Prices rose, wages languished, and, for the middle- and lower-middle classes, turned necessities into luxuries that they could no longer afford.

My father took to using a dark, menacing file to resharpen the blunted gramophone needles. This, in my eyes, profaned the sacred ritual; I hated the rasping sound that tore things out of their happy sequence.

But at least the music played on. Bing Crosby would croon for us, "Darling, je vous aime beaucoup, je ne sais pas what to do, you know you've completely stolen my heart . . ." After that, Caruso might sing Schubert's "Ave Maria," followed, perhaps, by Nelson Eddy's paeans of love for Rose Marie ringing out across the Canadian wilderness, in the middle of Bombay: "Oh Rose Marie I love you, I'm always dreaming of you . . ." Then Jeanette MacDonald would respond in kind with the "Indian Love Call," and our run-down flat would fill with joy and yearning and confusion.

Though I adored the old Garrard, I longed, now, for a modern record player that could play LPs and 45 rpms. Now I wanted to listen to the latest hits, be able to borrow them from my friends at St. Xavier's so I could take part in all the vital discussions and debate the important questions of the day: was "Eleanor Rigby" superior to "Yesterday"? If you could be any one of the Beatles, which one would you be? And why?

To my envy, neighbors in an adjacent flat bought a hi-fi soon after *The Sound of Music* came to Bombay. They already had a dog, the other object of my envy, and it became too much to bear. The soundtrack would pour out their window every afternoon when their seven-year-old daughter came home from school. The song about the lonely goatherd was her favorite, receiving lots of extra play.

Everyone had seen the film, and we listened with pleasure, the first few times. But the LP continued to be played over and over. By the end of the week, it seemed that Maria and the Captain with seven children had moved into our little three-room flat, to yodel their way through the rest of our lives.

In the end, the Von Trapp family was an auspicious presence, for when the film had finished its year-long run at the Regal, things improved financially at home. My father found freelance work to supplement his full-time job, and the result was a modern multispeed turntable. Manufactured in India

by HMV, it looked like a cheap little suitcase, but to us it was an elegant suf-
ficiency, capable of miracles: if, once upon a time, the Word was made flesh,
then here, in our humble flat, the Vinyl was, at long last, made music.

And the denizens of this creation, this new world spinning at 33⅓ or
45 revolutions per minute—Cliff Richard, Elvis Presley, Herman's Hermits,
the Rolling Stones, and many more—we welcomed them all, and all of their
music, the good, the mediocre, the appalling, as though it had sprung from
the soil of our South Bombay neighborhood. We held this truth to be self-evi-
dent, that everything with a "Made Somewhere in the West" tag was automat-
ically superior. Through the years of high school, there were pointy shoes,
tight pants, Elvis's sideburns, and Cliff's white fishnet T-shirt from the movie
Summer Holiday, making short work of anything Indian in our lives that had
survived the onslaught of the 78s, and so skilfully, we were forever oblivious
of that sleight of hand. By the time we discovered Jethro Tull, Pink Floyd, and
Crosby, Stills, Nash, and Young, our fate was sealed.

Resistance was impossible when the generations, old and young, were
fifth-columnists contributing to the success of the multipronged campaign
of infiltration, occupation, and conquest of imagination and language, begun
so long ago. Nursery rhymes and Enid Blyton's Noddy books in kindergarten were merely the first salvo. The libraries at St. Xavier's High School and
College came next, the very heart of the battlefield. And the British Council,
the United States Information Services, the Max Mueller Bhavan all championed the cause by bringing up the rear, where books, films, music descended
in a blizzard which, the cynics among us claimed, was thick enough to conceal entire cells of MI6 and CIA agents. The spies and spooks maintained
a suitable invisibility, while we, the recipients of international generosity, entertained our newfound scepticism about the loving, sharing ways of
superpowers, even as we revelled in Edward Elgar, Aaron Copland, Vaughan
Williams, Mahalia Jackson, Benjamin Britten, Pete Seeger, Bob Dylan, and
much, much more.

These foreign libraries were always deliciously air-conditioned. To step
inside, out of the Bombay heat and humidity, was like entering Scotty's trans-
porter on *Star Trek*, to be beamed instantly to a fantastic new planet, whence

we returned cooled and refreshed, cradling our treasures of books and records. My friend Harish used to joke that if the LPs were not returned on time, the US cavalry would ride in to rescue them from the clutches of the Indians.

But borrowing finally requires reimbursement: the lender always comes calling. And the original loan, the one masquerading as the colonizer's gift, would be repaid in emigrant sons and daughters who had been raised to believe their ancient country was futureless, its ways inferior, and the only solution was to settle abroad to make a better life.

So now it was time to leave the sinking ship and head for the promised land. But it was hard, for in that vessel were people and places and things one cared about. To cope, there was self-deception and inconsistency, best served up wrapped in platitudes: that some day, in the not-too-distant future, we would all reunite, in the land of milk and honey; or, that one's own sojourn in the foreign land would last a few years at best, till one returned home, redeemed by wealth and success.

Such were the tricks to thwart emotions, to sort twenty-three years of life to fit into one suitcase—maximum weight: twenty kilos. The most precious among things to be left behind were never even considered, impossible to convey in any case. Things like the fragrance in the air, every June, of the approaching monsoon; and before the rains, the flamboyant gulmohar trees, blooming across Bombay in a scarlet blaze; or the taste of sweet translucent targolay, fruit of the palmyra palm; and the evening breeze off the Arabian Sea, like silk upon the skin.

Instead, one fretted about the easily replaceable, such as the small collection of LPs. Not surprisingly, it was as absurdly eclectic as my father's 78s. Excluded by the baggage allowance was Rodgers and Hammerstein's *Oklahoma!* and Bizet's *Carmen*. There was no room for Harry Belafonte, Jim Reeves, James Taylor, or Richie Havens. Not even for *Mary Poppins*, Joni Mitchell, Joe Cocker, or Leon Russell.

And there was the Beatles album, still with my friend Harish. I wanted it in its slot, before I left Bombay. On the verge of exchanging my life, my country for one that I had never seen and knew almost nothing about, I was fixated on getting that record back.

With departure less than a week away, I finally reminded him. He was not done with it, he said. It would have been churlish to press harder, and we parted, as usual, with a joke, a laugh, he wishing me *bon voyage*, as though I were off on a short holiday.

Pursuit of the LP continued in my first letters from Toronto. Perhaps I should have taken a page from Harish's book and looked instead for the hidden meaning. But homesickness was an ailment of the less sophisticated, more suited to the emblematic peasant who leaves his drought-stricken village for work in the city, believing, season after season, that he will soon be home. I, of course, having read all the right books, knew I could not go home again. But at least my LP would return to where it belonged.

And so the long-playing album kept spinning, round and round in my head, like the 78s I used to watch as a child on the old gramophone. I remembered, again, how my father would stand beside his beloved Garrard and sing along with the record, conducting the music, encouraging us to sing along too. What pleasure those hours had brought to his careworn life. I promised myself that one day I would copy all his old shellac pressings onto audio cassettes and bring them to Toronto—in an act of homage, I told myself, clutching at a source of comfort, trying to assuage a sense of loss.

But there was something else I remembered: years ago, just before the age of vinyl had dawned in our home, my father had suddenly lost interest in his gramophone. The ritual had been abandoned. And it had saddened me, like the time when he had decided he would no longer accompany us on Sunday mornings to play cricket. I also remembered how much I had missed the joy and optimism which my father, with his music, could spread through the flat, with his confidence that everything would be all right in the end. And I remembered a thousand other things.

But remembering brings with it a benediction; it brings understanding. My father, I now felt, had made his peace with the hand that life had dealt him. Gradually, he had freed himself from the false burdens foisted on him by history. The place of refuge that he had created, he needed no longer. And his abandoned shelter would be useless to anyone who tried to take it over or to replicate it.

One could not go home again—that much I knew. But all those memories of youth and childhood, running endlessly through my mind, now taught
me the corollary, that one could never leave home either. So the question persisted: how to make sense of the contradiction in these two?

But remembering is a benediction: in time, the answer began to crystallize. In the space between the two, where the paradox resides, the idea of
home could be built, anew, with memory and imagination, scaffolded by language. The LP did not matter.

Sometimes, a delinquent loan is a blessing realized.

Norman, Oklahoma
September 28, 2012

MIA COUTO
THE 2014 LAUREATE

Mia Couto was born in 1955 in Beira, Sofala Province, Mozambique. He lived in Beira until he was seventeen, when he went to Lourenço Marques to study medicine. He interrupted his medical studies to start a journalistic career. On his own initiative, he returned to the university to study biology, and he currently works as a biologist in Mozambique. He has published more than thirty books that have been translated and edited in thirty different countries. His books cover many genres, ranging from romance to poetry, from short stories to children's books. He has received dozens of awards in his career, including (twice) the National Prize for Literature and the Camões Prize. In 2016 he was a finalist for one of the most prestigious international awards, the Man Booker Prize. His novel *Terra Sonâmbula* was considered by an international jury meeting in Zimbabwe as one of the ten best African books of the twentieth century. He is a member of the

Brazilian Academy of Letters. With his wife, Patrícia Silva, he has three children, all of whom live and work in Maputo.

In that very familiar and domestic moment, the very essence of what is literature was present: a chance to migrate from ourselves, a chance to become others inside ourselves, a chance to re-enchant the world.

—Mia Couto

Giving Birth to a New Land
Gabriella Ghermandi

When I was invited to be part of this most distinguished panel, the first thought that came to mind was that I would nominate an African woman writer. But then my heart spoke up and posed a question: What does being a writer mean to me? A writer is not simply a person who knows how to shape and mold words to tell a story, but who, in doing so, helps us view its limits and dream of a way of going beyond them, to where the dream takes on the power of the vision. Someone who is able to communicate not only with his/ her "local" world but also with the "global" one, and who can express all this in words, in stories, in narratives. This being the case, there was only one possible candidate for me. Only him. Mia Couto, a writer from Mozambique, the author of *Sleepwalking Land*.

Condensing Mia Couto's work into a few pages is very difficult. I will therefore try to give you a short overview, hoping that I will be able to expand on it in person when we meet. In order to talk to you about Mia Couto and about his fascinating use of the written language, I must first say something about Mozambican history that is at the heart of Couto's construction of the self and, therefore, of his artistry, of the way he uses words. This history of Mozambique I am referring to is linked to five hundred years of Portuguese colonization. A colonization that, like all forced relationships and governments, coerced the country into a forced relationship between the center and the periphery. In this case, the center was the power—white, Portuguese—of the written language, and the periphery was black submission and oral culture. A fixed and hegemonic relationship.

In 1975, after the 1974 fall of the dictatorship in Portugal, the Frelimo Party (the Mozambique Liberation Front) gained independence from Portugal. Unfortunately, though, the belief system shaped by five hundred years of colonization did not disappear along with the colonizers. It remained in people's minds. After liberation, within the ruling Frelimo Party, certain centrifugal forces arose in opposition to the leadership. Frelimo was not able to change pace. It did not know how to accommodate the dissenting voices within the party. Finding itself in difficulty, it decided to resort to the familiar: it reestablished a fixed relationship between center and periphery, basically identical to the one enforced during colonial times.

The same thing happened within Renamo, the opposition party. This party was initially illegal because of its ties to Ian Smith's Rhodesia and to the belief system of South African Apartheid. When, many years later, it became legal and assumed the role of opposition party, it could not divest itself of the center-periphery model. Even if it put forward values that were different from the hegemonic model, it could not avoid duplicating its structure.

Therefore, it continued to produce identities that were absolutist, mono-chromatic, at odds with the richly diverse and multilayered society.

Even the cultural aspects were still based on colonial models. There was a certain stasis in the idea that writing equates with emancipation and should, in a short period of time, completely supplant the oral culture of the peoples of Mozambique: yet another aspect of the fixed relationship between center and periphery. A relationship that, once more, signified exclusion by creating a stereotype of emancipation as a static idea outside the country's cultural context.

These were the years that gave birth to Mia Couto's writing, a writing born expressly as a form of struggle against the center-periphery duality. A struggle that aims at breaking down the stereotypical idea of emancipation seen as the progressive increase in alphabetization and the gradual fading out of oral culture. This is the first target of his writing. Language, reports the writer, is one of the first traps in forced relationships. Language paints the landscape for our minds, it values and devalues, excludes and includes. Bearing in mind that Portuguese in Mozambique was the language of exclu-sion, it was therefore necessary to turn it upside down, forcing it to open up a dialogue with the excluded part that needed to be awarded equal importance.

In order to direct his writing and, as a result, his readers, towards this consideration, Mia Couto redesigns the Portuguese language. With the precise intent to confuse the reader and force him to abandon the by-now-automatic frames of reading and therefore of thought, Couto invents a "different" Portuguese language (*what follows is an attempt to give you an approximate taste in English of what Couto does with the Portuguese language*).

He adds prefixes where they don't exist: "redie"; he substitutes similar prefixes: "unashamed" for "disashamed"; he creates new words to produce new semantic and aesthetic meanings: "groanentia" ("groan" + dementia); he makes new words spring from onomatopoeic words of the oral culture ("my heart boomboomed"), or from Bantu meanings attributed to Portuguese words ("mammas"—used for many women in the family, not just the mother); he changes idiomatic expressions: "my word, my business" to "his/her word, our business." A recolonialized Portuguese language, capable of allowing room for the oral culture of the Mozambique peoples, pluralistic, symbolic, tied to its prelinguistic identity and to its prelinguistic form of communication.

A recolonization that springs from his deep knowledge of Portuguese—so deep a knowledge that it allows him to manipulate the language at will—and from his profound knowledge of the cultures of Mozambique. All of Mia Couto's writing is steeped in images from the oral culture of the peoples of Mozambique that intersect with written Portuguese. The result is a "frontier" language, in which "frontiers" refer to a marginalized territory that has an unmarked, indefinable border. This new language-tongue, in constant flux, is the message from the writer to the peoples of Mozambique: the various groups, the different parties must be involved in a dialogue in order to find a fluid identity, a shifting balance.

This is what is indispensable for Mozambique in order to have a possible future.

Sleepwalking Land is situated at the center of this message. The novel begins with two figures that appear in a Mozambique devastated by a long civil war. They are an old man and a child: Tuahir and Muidinga. They have escaped from one of the many refugee camps. They are fleeing from the war the only way they can: on foot. They are only looking for a quiet haven. A burned-out bus full of corpses, once cleansed of the death that had transformed it into a metal coffin, will do. So the *machimbombo* (the bus) becomes their lair: "If the bandits come, we'll act like we are dead. Pretend we died along with the bus."

Near the wreck there is a bag and inside, among other things, some notebooks, the pages filled with writing. The child knows how to read, and he begins to give voice to the letters in Kindzu's notebooks. And so the narrative begins, alternating between the present, that is the story of Tuahir, and Muidinga and the past, that is Kindzu's diary. Two furrows in the same hell.

Old Tuahir had met and saved Muidinga from certain death by taking responsibility for him. The child had completely lost his memory and Tuahir decided to call him Muidinga. The little one often asks him to tell him the story of how they met, truly a second birth for him, as when the old man renamed him after he had decided to "adopt" him. The child demands to hear the story of what are now his origins with the same obstinacy of one who demands his childhood, denied to him by history. His determined fight to fulfill this need has the force of a primeval instinct, of a survival instinct: "Conte, tio. Se é uma estória me conte, nem importa se é verdade" (Tell me, Uncle. If it is a story, it doesn't matter whether it is true or not).

It is a caring relationship between the two of them, a mutual caregiving, their roles sometimes reversing. Not only does the adult take care of the child, restoring to him a past and therefore a future, but the opposite also happens: the child, the only one who can read and write, reads him the stories in Kindu's notebooks, found near a burned corpse inside a bus, on a country road.

The child is the symbol of the new Mozambique, born of independence, the Mozambique that looks to the future, the Mozambique of the written world. A lost child who does not know his origins nor where he was born, who does not even remember his name. He knows he has a family somewhere and wants to find them, and he asks Tuahir to accompany him. Tuahir, symbol of the old Mozambique, who cannot read or write but knows how to tell stories following an ancient tradition. Stories capable of healing, of helping the child to remain rooted in life, in the land, in order to reach his goal.

Conversely, the old man is nourished by Kindzu's written diary through Muidinga's readings. A diary that ends at the conclusion of their journey. The pages they were leafing through turn into leaves when they return to the earth.

A final message built on the ambiguous Portuguese word *folha* that means both a sheet of paper and the leaf of a tree. Therefore the return to the earth as birthplace, as a last dwelling place, but also forging transformation for new growth.

Some critics have called Mia Couto "the smuggler writer," a sort of Robin Hood of words who steals meanings to make them available in every tongue, forcing apparently separate worlds to communicate. If, on one hand, Mia Couto's work is a message to his native land, for a complete decolonization that cannot ignore language, and consequently the mind and its tendency to stasis, on the other hand, he addresses the whole world seeking to resonate with each and every individual.

Constantly breaking the static nature of the written language and of linguistic codes, and, as a result, of a fixed identity (so as to become open to other cultures that exist in today's world) is a way of freeing oneself from the idea that growth takes place only when one of our identities is chosen as the superior one. Knowing how to pair the linearity of written language with the plurality of oral culture (that also has origins in the prelinguistic world, in the invisible, in symbology), keeping one's mind open to the languages of the soul, of nature, of the oral tradition and making these languages available to the rational self, allows man to follow the path of a particular bilingualism that puts into communication two worlds usually separate or subordinate. Mia Couto defines such a capacity as a "bilingualism," capable of giving birth to a new man, the nation-man who lives in an "unbalanced" balance in endless movement, dancing with its times, with its local and global context. A man who looks to the future while leaning on the past. A past that is so deep as to be timeless.

Bologna, Italy

Gabriella Ghermandi *is an Ethiopian-Italian performer, novelist, and short-story writer. Her stories have been published in several collections and journals, and her first novel,* Queen of Flowers and Pearls, *was published in 2007.*

Re-enchanting the World
Mia Couto

Dear friends,

It is a great honor to receive this award. I am saying this not just as a simple formality. It is a deeper feeling. The importance of this award goes far beyond the work of a particular writer. What we are celebrating here, in Oklahoma, year after year, is more than literature. With the Neustadt Prize we all praise the cultural diversity of our world and the cultural diversity of each one of us. That is crucial in a moment where personal and national identities are constructed like fortresses, as protection against the threats of those who are presented to us as aliens.

This prize is important for the relations between our worlds, which seem to be situated not only on different continents but on different planets. Despite all diplomatic and political efforts, a considerable reciprocal ignorance still prevails between Mozambique and the United States of America. We tend to assume this remoteness as natural, given the physical location of our countries. However, we must nowadays question what is presented as "normal" and "natural." There are, indeed, other reasons that lead to our mutual lack of knowledge. And those reasons have nothing to do with geography.

We have a common struggle for freedom, democracy, and independence. We share a past and a present of resistance against injustice and discrimination. But in the quest to affirm the uniqueness of our nations we have created, without knowing, a reductive and simplistic vision of the other, and of ourselves. We suffer from a narrow and stereotyped vision of a multicolor reality. We are only able to recognize one cultural dimension of reality. We have fallen into the temptation of the "Single Story" against which the Nigerian writer Chimamanda Adichie so eloquently warned us.

The Neustadt Prize has the merit of promoting dialogue between cultures and creating bridges where there is distance and, worse than that, mere indifference.

It's good to know that literature can help build neighborhoods in a world which imagines that the proximity between cultures is totally resolved by technological solutions.

Dear friends,

I am the second son of a Portuguese couple forced to emigrate, trying to escape from the fascist regime in Portugal. Each night, my mother and my father told me stories. They thought they were getting us to sleep. In fact, they were producing a second and eternal birth.

What fascinated me was not exactly the content of those tales. As a matter of fact, I can't remember a single one of those stories. What I remember, first of all, is having my parents just for me, next to my bed, next to my dreams. More than anything I remember the passion that they found in the invention of those stories. That intense pleasure had a reason: using words, they could travel and visit their missing homeland. They could erase time and distance.

In that very familiar and domestic moment, the very essence of what is literature was present: a chance to migrate from ourselves, a chance to become others inside ourselves, a chance to re-enchant the world. Literature is not only a way to affirm our existence. It is a permission to disappear and to allow the presence of those who seem to be absent.

We Africans come from a long and painful narrative to affirm our nations and our singular identity. I am afraid that, although historically necessary, part of the nationalist discourse has become a burden that prevents us from being plural, available to be others and to travel inside other lives. That availability is the essence of literature. And the essence of our humanity.

I come from a nation that is regarded as one of the poorest in the world. I don't know how poverty is measured, but many of the African languages spoken in my country do not have specific words for saying "poor." To designate a poor person, one uses the term *chissiwana*. This word means "orphan." A poor person is someone who lives without family and without friends. He is someone who has lost the ties of solidarity.

This other poverty, born of solitude, is more widespread than one might think. Never before has our world been so small, so simultaneous, so instantaneous. But this speed has not solved our solitude. Never before have there been so many roads. And never before have we made so few visits. What could bind us together would be the desire to tell and to listen to stories.

There are many hidden dimensions of the art of writing. A few years ago I experienced an episode that showed me a different meaning of what I do as writer.

It happened in 2008, in northern Mozambique in a coastal village called Palma. It's a remote region, without water, without electricity, in the middle of the savannah. I had finished my day's work as a biologist, and I was in the shadow of my tent, when a peasant came and called me. *Come here*, he said. *Come and see a man who's been killed.* I went into the darkness, and I followed the old man along a path in the middle of the bush. *How did he die?* I asked. And the man replied: *He was killed by a lion. That lion is still nearby. And he's going to come back to fetch the rest of the body.* I returned hastily to the tent, with no wish to see whatever he had to show me.

I closed the zipper of the tent, knowing how inadequate this gesture was as protection. A short distance from me lay a corpse ripped up by a lion, and a wild beast roamed nearby like a murderous shadow. During my professional life, I have worked for many years in regions where there are still dangerous animals. But I didn't know how to deal with a situation like that. I remember that the first thing I did was to switch on my small flashlight and begin writing in my notebook. I was not describing what was going on, because I didn't know, nor did I want to know what was happening. The truth is that until daybreak, I was busy writing in order not to be overcome with fear.

That fear was a primitive feeling, a memory of another time, in which our fragility was more evident. I am an urban man, born and raised in modernity. I had no defense against a fear that was more ancient than humanity itself. I gradually realized that the wild creatures were not lions but the monsters that have dwelt within us for centuries.

Only later did I understand; I wasn't really taking shelter in the tent.

I was taking shelter in fiction. I was creating a story like someone making a house not just to live in but to erase reality. Without knowing it, I was beginning to write a novel called *Confession of the Lioness*.

But another one of my novels served as the basis for the choice of this prize, the novel *Terra sonâmbula (Sleepwalking Land)*. This book speaks of a dramatic moment in the history of Mozambique. For sixteen years we suffered a civil war, which killed the economy and crippled the country.

Those sixteen years of conflict left a million dead out of a population of eighteen million. In its intention, violence is opposed to the art of telling stories: that intention is to dehumanize us, a dehumanization achieved in various ways. We were living in a kind of absolute solitude: isolated from hope, incapable of turning the present into a treasure trove of stories. We were all alone, the dead and the living. Without a past, without a future, without stories. The present was only worthwhile insofar as it was born to be forgotten.

Terra sonâmbula was the only book I found painful to write, because it was written during the war, at a time when I was also besieged by despair. For months I spent sleepless nights visited by friends and colleagues who had been killed during the conflict. It was as if they came knocking on the door of my insomnia, asking to live in stories, even if they were lies, or just a way for me to fall asleep.

I remember that once, after one of these sleepless nights, I came out of the building of the biology station where I was working and sat on the beach. And I realized that there, very close to the breaking waves, was a whale which had decided to come and die on the beach. Then I saw people arriving hastily at the beach. In an instant they rushed together at the dying animal to hack chunks from it, ripped to pieces with the greed of a hunger of centuries. It had not yet died, and its bones were already shining in the sun. Little by little, I came to think of my country as one of those whales coming to die in agony on the beach. Death had not yet come, and yet the knives were already stealing chunks of it, each person trying to take as much as possible for himself. As if that were the last animal, the final opportunity to grab a meal. I went back to my room weighed down by an incurable sadness. On that early morning I wrote the final chapter of my novel. Two months later, when I was delivering the text to my publisher, the news arrived of the peace agreement.

When the peace agreement was signed in 1992, we thought that revenge and the settling of scores would be inevitable. But it didn't happen like that. People decided on a kind of collective amnesia. The reminders of violence were cast into a pit of oblivion. We know that this oblivion was false. A war is impossible to forget. But we wanted the war to forget us.

Mozambique's experience showed how literature can play an active role in the construction of peace. Fiction and poetry do not cause the guns to fall silent. But they can reconcile us with the past, no matter how painful it might be. Fiction and poetry can help reconquer our inner tranquility and promote reconciliation with others. By means of stories, these others were freed from the condition of demons. I can say with pride that poets and writers have helped to rehumanize my country.

Unfortunately, it is not so much stories that unite humanity. What unites us today, in all countries, on all continents, is above all fear. The same feeling of abandonment and insecurity brings us together everywhere. There are no great or small powers that are safe from fear. We live the same anguish faced with the other transformed into an enemy. We all live in a small tent surrounded by the threat, real or imaginary, of a beast in the dark wanting to devour us.

The fear that rules us is, in large measure, nourished by the profound ignorance we have of one another. Literature can be a response against the invitation to fabricate fear and mistrust. Literature and storytelling confirm us as relatives and neighbors in our infinite diversity.

Dear friends,

It is very gratifying to know that the next laureate is an African as well. We know that the Neustadt Prize is not limited by the author's geographical origin; the only issue is the quality of his or her work. This means that Africans are imposing themselves on the international scene without recourse to any paternalistic criteria. In truth, for some years now, we African writers are freeing ourselves from a literature dominated by a desire to affirm our identity. Formerly, we felt a historic and psychological need to demonstrate that we were as able as others. This period of affirmation made sense after centuries of cultural and historical denial. But today we are more free to act without fulfilling our function as the Other.

A new generation of Africans is more and more free to act as universal writers. They feel free to write about any subject, in the language they choose. Our new literature is now less afraid of the accusation of not being faithful to genuineness, or not respecting the so-called "tradition." We are producing a literature that is free from having to show its Africanness as a kind of passport to be accepted.

Many of our young writers are using literature to denounce the arrogance, corruption, and nepotism of some current political leaders. But more than that, they are busy producing good literature. And they know that there are as many Africas as there are writers, and all of them are reinventing continents that lie inside their very selves. This is not a quest that is exclusively ours, as Africans. There isn't a writer in the world who doesn't have to seek out his or her own identity among multiple and elusive identities. In every continent, each person is a nation made up of different nations.

Dear friends,

The Neustadt Prize is announced as follows (and I quote): "This is the first international literary award of its scope to originate in the United States and is one of the very few international prizes for which poets, novelists, and playwrights are equally eligible."

I would like to thank the Neustadt family, the University of Oklahoma, and *World Literature Today* for the open and all-embracing conception of this initiative. The format of this celebration reveals a concern not to reduce the event to an award ceremony alone. In this way, justice is done to the principle that what is important are books and not so much their authors.

One of the merits of this prize is that it is guided by criteria devoted exclusively to literary quality. I present myself to you not as a representative of a place, of an ideology, of a religion. But I will never forget those who give meaning to my writing, the anonymous people of my country. Some of those

Mozambicans—who are, together with me, author of my books—do not know how to write. Many don't even speak Portuguese. But they are guardians, in their everyday lives, of a magical, poetical dimension to the world that illuminates my writing and gives delight to my existence.

It would be an injustice not to mention here the people who have given my presence here their support: The first of these people is Gabriella Ghermandi, the member of the panel that proposed me as a candidate. Without her, I would not be here. I would not be here if it weren't for my longtime translator, David Brookshaw. A translator is a co-author and should appear on the covers of books, and his presence in this ceremony is totally justified. Accompanying me is my wife, Patricia, who is my primary inspiration and my first reader. Present with us is my daughter, Luciana, and she represents here my other children, Madyo and Rita. No prize can prove stronger than the delight we have in seeing ourselves born in our own children. To them I owe this feeling of lived eternity.

I shall end by reading a poem I wrote some years ago. I remembered these verses when I discovered that the emblem for this prize was an eagle's feather. This symbolic representation is a metaphor for writing that seeks to have the lightness of wings. I shall ask David Brookshaw to read this poem, in his own translation.

In Some Other Life I Was a Bird

I preserve the memory
of landscapes spread wide
and escarpments skimmed in flight.
A cloud and its careless trace of white
connect me to the soil.
I live with the heartbeat
of a bird's wing
and plunge like lightning
hungering for earth.

I preserve the plume
that remains in my heart
as a man preserves his name
over the span of time.
In some other life I was a bird
in some other bird I was life.

Norman, Oklahoma
October 24, 2014

Translation from the Portuguese by Paul Fauvet

DUBRAVKA UGREŠIĆ
THE 2016 LAUREATE

Over the past three decades, **Dubravka Ugrešić** (b. 1949) has established herself as one of Europe's most distinctive novelists and essayists. From her early postmodernist excursions, to her elegiac reckonings in fiction and the essay with the disintegration of her Yugoslav homeland and the fall of the Berlin Wall, to her more recent writings on popular and literary culture, Ugrešić's work is marked by a rare combination of irony, polemic, and compassion. Following degrees in comparative and Russian literature, Ugrešić worked for many years at the University of Zagreb's Institute for Theory of Literature, successfully pursuing parallel careers as both a writer and as a scholar. In 1991, when war broke out in the former Yugoslavia, Ugrešić took a firm antiwar stance and became a target for nationalist journalists, politicians, and fellow writers. Subjected to ostracism and persistent media harassment, she left Croatia in 1993. Her books have been translated into over twenty languages. She has taught at a number of American and European universities and is the winner of several major literary prizes. Her recent books include the novel *Fox* and the book of essays *American Fictionary*, both published in 2018. Her latest book, *The Age of Skin,* appeared in autumn 2019. She lives in Amsterdam.

> We should invest all our energies in supporting people who are prepared to invest in literature, not in literature as a way to sustain literacy but as a vital, essential creative activity, people who will preserve the intellectual, the artistic, the spiritual capital.
>
> —Dubravka Ugrešić

Along a Path to Transnational Literature
Alison Anderson

In 1997 I was offered a job to teach English to adults in Croatia. Of course I had been following the events that had torn Yugoslavia apart between 1991 and 1995; and just as I was learning what I could about the newly independent country of Croatia, Dubravka had already left it behind, in 1993, to go into exile first in Berlin and then Amsterdam. The irony is that I ordered two of Dubravka's early books, to learn more about a country that, in fact, no longer existed, and where she no longer lived nor could feel at home. But these two books were a good introduction nevertheless: *Steffie Speck in the Jaws of Life* and *Fording the Stream of Consciousness* are both works of fiction and belong to a tradition of playful satire and black humor that was prevalent all through eastern Europe during the communist era. As a student of Russian I had read both the classics and the Soviet-era satirical work that followed, so there was something that felt wonderfully familiar about her fiction and new at the same time. Were it not for the accident of history, so to speak, Dubravka might have gone on writing novels in this satirical vein, poking fun at her fellow writers, or lovesick women, or life in the little republic of Croatia when it was part of the Socialist Federal Republic of Yugoslavia.

It is significant that the breakup of the country drove her into exile only four years after the fall of the Berlin Wall; it is also significant that the once-"dissident" writers of the Soviet bloc suddenly found themselves in a literary context that was utterly changed—they had freedom of expression at last, yes, but not necessarily the freedom to publish or be read; market forces suddenly determined everything that was published throughout the former Eastern bloc. The breakup of Yugoslavia meant not only the transition to a capitalist culture but also a severing of ties among the former republics that at times bordered on the absurd, as new dictionaries were created for each republic's "language"—no longer known as Serbo-Croatian but as Bosnian-Croatian-Serbian (and sometimes Montenegrin).

Now Dubravka found herself living in western Europe but writing in Croatian, living in, as she calls it, a literary out-of-nation zone. Who would read her? Who was her audience? Whom was she writing for? Back then, perhaps only a few dissenting Croats or fellow exiles, unhappy with the nationalistic regime of the 1990s; her Yugoslav audience had virtually vanished. Would the Germans, the Dutch read her in translation? Could she find a place as a European writer? These were some of the questions I asked myself as I began to learn both about Dubravka's biography and about life in Croatia in the late 1990s.

After the year I spent in Zagreb, I returned to the US and was heartened to see that Dubravka's books were appearing regularly in English: *Have a Nice Day*, *The Culture of Lies*, *The Museum of Unconditional Surrender*, *Thank You for Not Reading*, *Ministry of Pain*, *Nobody's Home*, etc. I realized too that she had found a new voice—the voice of exile, one might call it—and that the bubbly, sardonic novels of her youth had given way, for the most part, to incisive, often heartfelt and angry, but always ironic and cautionary essays about life in post-Yugoslavia, in Europe, and in the wider world. Her works appeared not only in English but in many countries, in translation, and she has, so fortunately for us, found her place, at latest count, in twenty-seven languages.

I would like to focus briefly on her novel from 1997, *The Museum of Unconditional Surrender*, because it is the pivotal work written from her first exile in Berlin, and it is also a work that echoes and reflects the events of the late 1980s and '90s in Europe. Before 1989 Berlin was a divided city, the very heart of the tension between western and eastern Europe; then, after the fall of the Wall it became the home not only to many refugees from the war in the Balkans but also to a host of economic migrants from eastern Europe in search of a better life. Russians, Poles, Hungarians, Romanians, and let's not forget East Germans all came in search of a new life in the open city of Berlin. Dubravka's novel brings that transitional, transitioning city to life with its migrants, refugees, lost souls, artists, exiles—there are Bosnians and Russians but also Brits and Indians; we also meet Americans and Portuguese as the narrator travels for her work. There are chapter headings in German, notably *Wo bin ich?*—"Where am I?"—and this refers not only to the narrator's or an immigrant's bewilderment in the situation of exile and a new language but also leads to the question *Wer bin ich?*—"Who am I?"—the question of identity totally turned on its ear, particularly for the former Yugoslavs, but even for the other ordinary migrants. Could a Russian now say he was German, or European? Was he still Russian? What is identity? How much of it is necessarily bound up in geographical location or place of birth; how much of it will be influenced by politics?

For that period of time in Berlin, Dubravka witnessed the distress of these immigrants and chronicled it, offsetting the passages set in Berlin with memories of her childhood, her mother and grandmother, and the dual loss of youth and home. *The Museum of Unconditional Surrender* is a novel that is deeply rooted in European history but has become uprooted from its "Croatian" context or tradition—other than the fact that it was written in Croatian—to move into, I would say, a category of its own. If one must categorize a book, the way clueless booksellers sometimes do, we could say this book belongs to the literature of exile. But there are no shelves in bookstores for "exile"; you will find Nabokov under American literature, Brodsky under Russian, Joseph Conrad among the classics, etc.

Unlike many other works of European literature, Dubravka's oeuvre is pan-European, in the sense that it deals with many different countries, and people from many different backgrounds and nationalities. Let me explain by providing a contrast. To name two of the most salient examples of contemporary European literature currently enjoying both critical and popular success in the US, there is, first of all, Karl Ove Knausgaard's *My Struggle*, then Elena Ferrante's Neapolitan Quartet. The first is very clearly set primarily in Norway, and its hero is very typically Norwegian in many respects, albeit his wife is Swedish and they live in Sweden; Ferrante's novels are even more bound to their location and its inhabitants—you could even say that Naples is a character throughout the novels. Granted, these are works of "fiction," so to speak, whereas Dubravka is now writing principally nonfiction, but all her books feature a rich variety of characters and places, usually quite specifically described, but with an intent to reveal the universal nature of the dilemma or situation in which these passing protagonists find themselves.

I have been thinking, since I was first invited to speak on this panel, of how I would situate Dubravka "in the context of contemporary European literature," and my conclusion is, to be honest, that I cannot. If I think of the novels I have translated from French over the last decade, most of them are very ethnocentric, very much part of a French tradition, or certainly taking for granted that they belong to the realm of "French literature," often catering to a French readership or, in any case, assuming that the primary readership will be French. There is no such easy assumption available for Dubravka's work; in fact, she said herself in a recent interview: "I have passionately propagated the notion of transnational literature . . . a literary territory for those writers who refuse to belong to their national literatures" (*Music & Literature*). Again, if we turn to her biography, her geographical history, it becomes very clear why this is. Very early on in the conflict, Dubravka was expected to take sides and could not, would not. She chronicled her outrage and disgust at her countrymen in *The Culture of Lies;* she continues to target Croatia—now a member of the European Union—for its lack of transparency, its corruption, its multiple shortcomings. She has seen through the tawdry nationalism of flag-waving; she is appalled by the population's fairly recent protests against the International Criminal Tribunal for the Former Yugoslavia regarding the war crimes trials of men whom Croatians refer to as "heroes." She has been a direct victim of that particular nationalism, but nationalism, as we hardly need reminding, is on the rise everywhere.

The work of Dubravka Ugrešić stands apart from any specific European literature precisely because she comes from a European literary tradition that gave her the tools to gaze coldly on the dangers of classifying and codifying, of pinning labels, the dangers of conformity and submission to a nation or an ideology. Nor is globalization the answer, as a reaction to nationalism; she illustrates this in *Karaoke Culture*, which describes a universal culture of dumbing down, conformity, and laziness. Dubravka's work belongs, rather, to its own "transnational" category, a literature that defies and crosses borders wherever there are readers who are open to the outside world, who are not afraid of the other, the foreigner, readers who do not want to go through life building walls to remain in a comfortable, blinkered, nationalistic homeland. She writes for those who, like herself, defend supranational values—freedom of speech, empathy, justice, and integrity.

Buchillon, Switzerland

Alison Anderson *is a novelist and translator. Her most recent novel,* The Summer Guest, *based on an episode in the life of Anton Chekhov, was published in 2016. She lives in Switzerland.*

A Girl in Litland
Dubravka Ugrešić

The first two books I wrote were for children. When I published my first book I was twenty-one. I soon gave up on writing children's literature when I realized that I didn't have the very particular god-given talent that only the exceptional writers for children possess. I still believe that the career of the children's author—with the gift of a Lewis Carroll—is the most joyous career a writer could wish for, and it is, at the same time, a "natural" choice: writing for children means living in an extended childhood. I say this because adults work at jobs that are useful, while children work at tasks that have no practical application. Literature, too, is a nonuseful task. It has no price tag, there can be no compensation for it—just as a child's drawing has no price tag—nor can it be manipulated, though many people are hard at work at precisely that, "manipulating" literature. Even writers, after all, do not hesitate to manipulate.

At a historical turning point for the cultural community it was decided that literature, this useless task, should be granted a more serious standing. The status of modern literature began at the moment when it became a subject of study at universities, and this happened only several hundred years ago. Any standing is vulnerable to change. In other words, a vast amount of time is needed to build a pyramid, even more to maintain it, but only a few short moments to tear it down. In this sense literature, as a system of knowledge devised and built by hardworking people over the centuries, is a fragile creation. Those who work at literature should keep this in mind. Perhaps it would be apt here to think back to Ray Bradbury's cult novel *Fahrenheit 451* as well as to the many postapocalyptic science-fiction movies. There are no books to be seen in the latter. At least I haven't seen one. And besides, when the time comes for everybody to start writing books—and that moment, thanks to technology, is upon us—there will no longer be literature. This is because literature is a system that requires arbitration. The arbiters used to be "people of good literary taste": theoreticians, critics, literature professors, translators, editors, and, don't forget, the attendant mediocrities: the censors, the salespeople, the "Salieris," the ideologues of various stripes—from religious to political. Today the market has anointed itself as arbiter, as have the readers. The market is allied with the "majority reader." Authors are no freer as a result—along with politicians and entrepreneurs, today authors are expected to *please* the consumer, to *lobby, blog, vlog, post, tweet*, to be *liked*, to spread with diligence to their digital fan base who will support them and buy their books.

I was born into a world in which the first technological wonder was the radio. I remember waking up at night and turning the big dial to move the red line across to the stations inscribed on the display while I listened to languages I didn't understand. Our radio was called a Nikola Tesla, and it had a green eye that glowed in the dark. I was born a few years after the close of the Second World War in a small country, poor and ravaged by war, where there was a pressing need to manufacture goods that were more utilitarian than those from a toy factory. That's why I got my first "real" doll when I was already too big to play with dolls. In my early childhood, what I found sensational had nothing to do with toys but with books, the radio, and Hollywood movies for grown-ups: the text, sound, and image gave me the illusion of flight from my provincial little town into the grand, thrilling world. I envisioned the world with the help of books, and the role played by interactivity—to use contemporary jargon—was huge. The field of the imagination is more circumscribed today; the cultural industry has satisfied every need we could only have dreamt of before. Here are our "prechewed" products (*Anna Karenina for Beginners*), or streamlined, readapted, and commercialized versions of original works (*Anna Karenina and the Zombies*), or experiments such as the use of hologram books. The new media today are filling the space of the imagination to its last inch: they are taking the soul, time, and money of their "consumers" and leaving nothing behind.

In my childhood and even in my student days, publishing was not yet referred to as an *industry*, nor was there a literary marketplace, and the borders between children's literature and writing for adults were not so sharply drawn. There were no psychologists hovering over the process of consumption; with passion we read whatever we could get our hands on. Thanks to the media and the marketplace, our taste today is standardized. The powerful industry nourishes every consumer capillary of the world. In the very poorest quarters of Kolkata where people inhabit space the size of a matchbox, they may be impoverished, but miniature screens (television and otherwise) glow day and night from their makeshift abodes.

In the bygone days of Yugoslav publishing there used to be an unpopular penalty known as *the pulp tax*. Those who chose to satisfy the more "pedestrian" tastes of the readership had to pay a special tax for the pulp fiction they published. If the tax for pulp were to be levied at a global level, this would amass a vast store of money, which could be used for publishing both high-quality and inexpensive books for a free and fine education, for teachers, for artists, for the creative folk. All this can be imagined, of course, but the only thing that defies the imagination is the decision of who would evaluate what fiction is pulp and what isn't. And it bears mentioning that the terms *pulp fiction* and *kitsch* have faded from the parlance. Some thirty years ago kitsch was still a subject for discussion and a focus of research among theoreticians of art and literature. Then the powerful global market elbowed the concept of *kitsch* out of its vocabulary. Anything that separates the "wheat from the chaff" is undesirable in a global marketplace that works to sell everything, and sell as much of it as possible.

There are key tags to be found in the vocabulary of the brilliant sociologist Zygmunt Bauman that have relevance not only for our age but for the culture industry, including that of literature right now. One of them is *waste*. Our industrially hyperactive civilization generates, among other things, waste. With the most popular commands of *copy and paste* there appears the need for a command to *save*. Our digital age is shaping the mind-set and physicality of the digital human. Our fingers are growing thinner, longer, and more adept, but we're keeping ophthalmologists busy as we constantly adjust the lenses in our eyeglasses. Our language, too, is changing. Now, not just children but adults rely on abbreviations and emoticons. Our emotions, too, have changed, as have our sensors for reception, our codes, our ways of communicating, and, foremost, our sense of time. We feel we're immersed in an all-accessible, domineering NOW. In this sense a feeling of cultural discontinuity has crept into older specimens of the human race, such as myself, despite the all-accessible search engines that can connect us, in seconds, to bygone times. In parallel to the emancipating and powerful sense of control through digital devices such as the smartphone, a *liquid fear*, as Baumann would put it, has come to dwell in people, a neurosis of insecurity (perhaps this being our need to leave millions of selfies in cyberspace to confirm that we lived).

The story "Who Am I?" was born out of a sense not only of security but of literary plenty thirty-three years ago, at a time when I was as happy as a mouse nesting in a wheel of cheese. My wheel of cheese was the library, a university job, the certainty that literature was autonomous and that the only thing worth dedicating myself to was literature. The short story that has been staged by the students from the OU Helmerich School of Drama, directed by Judith Pender, came about out of a powerful feeling of literary well-being, of continuity. I was intrigued by the idea of a defamiliarized reading within a profound familiarization with world literature.

Internet literature, the fan fiction I explored while writing my essay

"Karaoke Culture," is today guided by a similar principle, but the canon is different. These are not classic works of the literary canon but belong to a new, contemporary canon of millions of readers and viewers: *Harry Potter, Twilight Saga, Hunger Games,* and others like them.

Because of all this, and perhaps because of my unjustified feeling that the system of literature as we know it is on the way out—what with digital civilization taking over Gutenberg civilization—we should invest all our energies in supporting people who are prepared to invest in literature, not in literature as a way to sustain literacy but as a vital, essential creative activity, people who will preserve the intellectual, the artistic, the spiritual capital. I couldn't have dreamed that one day a student theater in Norman, Oklahoma, would be putting on the first-ever staging of my story, written thirty-three years ago. Literary continuity, therefore, does exist, and the fact that it describes an unexpected geographical trajectory only heightens the excitement.

The literary landscape that has greeted me in Norman has touched me so deeply that I, briefly, forgot the ruling political constellations. I forgot the processes underway in all the nooks and crannies of Europe, I forgot the people who are stubbornly taking us back to some distant century, the people who ban books or burn them, the moral and intellectual censors, the brutal rewriters of history, the latter-day inquisitors; I forgot for a moment the landscapes in which the infamous swastika has been cropping up with increasing frequency—as it does in the opening scenes of Bob Fosse's classic film *Cabaret*—and the rivers of refugees whose number, they say, is even greater than that of the Second World War.

A continuity of literary evaluation does, nevertheless, exist. The knowledge of what is good literature has not been lost for good. This is a moment to recall Vladimir Nabokov and his words, which belong to the realm of sorely needed literary evaluation:

> There are three points of view from which a writer can be considered: he may be considered as a storyteller, as a teacher, and as an enchanter. A major writer combines all three—storyteller, teacher, enchanter—but it is the enchanter in him that predominates and

makes him a major writer. . . . To the storyteller we turn for entertainment, for mental excitement of the simplest kind, for emotional participation, for the pleasure of traveling in some remote region in space or time. A slightly different though not necessarily higher mind looks for the teacher in the writer. Propagandist, moralist, prophet—this is the rising sequence. We may go to the teacher not only for moral education but also for direct knowledge, for simple facts. . . . Finally, and above all, a great writer is always a great enchanter, and it is here that we come to the really exciting part when we try to grasp the individual magic of his genius and to study the style, the imagery, the pattern of his novels or poems.

We are met here at the Neustadt Festival, a literary festival for celebrating the enchanter, whoever he or she may be. We have gathered to celebrate all those who have been, who are, and who will be our past, present, and future—enchanters . . .

Norman, Oklahoma
October 28, 2016

Translation from the Croatian by Ellen Elias-Bursać

EDWIDGE DANTICAT
THE 2018 LAUREATE

Edwidge Danticat is the author of several books, including *Breath, Eyes, Memory*, an Oprah Book Club selection; *Krik? Krak!*, a National Book Award finalist; *The Farming of Bones*, an American Book Award winner; and the novels-in-stories *The Dew Breaker* and *Claire of the Sea Light;* as well as *The Art of Death*, a National Books Critics Circle finalist. She is also the editor of *The Butterfly's Way: Voices from the Haitian Dyaspora in the United States, The Beacon Best of 2000, Haiti Noir, Haiti Noir 2,* and *Best American Essays 2011.* She has written seven books for young adults and children—*Anacaona Golden Flower, Behind the Mountains, Eight Days, The Last Mapou, Mama's Nightingale, Untwine,* and *My Mommy Medicine*—as well as a travel narrative, *After the Dance: A Walk through Carnival in Jacmel,* and two collections of essays, *Create Dangerously* and *The Art of Death.* Her memoir, *Brother, I'm Dying*, was a 2007 finalist for the National Book Award and a 2008 winner of the National Book Critics

Circle Award for autobiography. She is a 2009 MacArthur Fellow. Her most recent book, *Everything Inside,* a collection of stories, was published in 2019.

Writing that story had reinforced for me the idea that the page— my writing home—has to also be free from death because creating anything, be it words, images, song, and dance, means that we believe in immortality.

—Edwidge Danticat

Bearing the Unforgivable
Achy Obejas

Thank you to the Neustadt Prize committee, Neustadt sisters and family, the University of Oklahoma, the incredible writers who served with me on the jury last year.

It is my great honor to introduce Edwidge Danticat. As you've no doubt experienced by now, Edwidge is a woman of exceptional poise and elegance, uncommon intelligence, and unusual wisdom.

You can see in her eyes—those very deep, endless pools—that there is inside her an immeasurable reservoir of kindness and an extensive capacity for forgiveness. This last quality, I think, is what singularly marks her work: a fierce forgiveness, a forgiveness that comes not from a fear of the hereafter or acceptance of any inevitability but rather from a kind of recognition, an acknowledgment of our capacity to fall into the temptations of violence, of selfishness, of irrationality, and still, somehow, also be able to nourish and love.

Sometimes we do terrible things for very good reasons; sometimes we do beautiful things for terrible reasons. But that we may be able to do these terrible things does not necessarily make us so terrible as to be exempt from redemption.

The worlds Edwidge writes about are complicated, and their inhabitants operate with complicated intentions and ethics, complicated moralities and spiritual paths. But they are also common, as common as you and me, as common as the daily tragedies of children separated from their mothers, and as common as the petty corruptions we've come to accept in our politicians.

And yet—Edwidge's work does not ask us to forgive. It isn't righteous; it does not make that argument. It does something much more profound: it asks us to consider our own capacity for the unforgivable, our ability to bear the unforgivable, and the measure of our own powers of forgiveness. Because that's how forgiveness is so often framed in her stories: as a kind of power. A very unsentimental, very divested power.

Forgiveness, not as forgetting, but as an awakening.

Forgiveness as foresight.

Forgiveness as essential, as essential as the air we breathe, and as essential as love.

There are many things I love about Edwidge and about her work—its tight discipline, the sheer beauty of her words, the sublime architecture of her sentences, the way it disturbs us and makes us question our day-to-day lives, the way it makes us wonder about the unknown burdens our neighbor may be carrying, the secret lives around us we may never fully know—but to me this powerful force for forgiveness is what brings me back to her over and over: we are imperfect, we are unfathomable, and without recognition and forgiveness, how could we possibly go on?

I've been reading Edwidge since her first book, almost twenty-five years ago, *Breath Eyes Memory*. I read her latest, *The Art of Dying*, as if it was a prayer, and this much I know: with each book, Edwidge's work gets stronger, more confident, more sage. With each new book, her already very personal and independent path grows longer and wider and makes room not just for more of her stories but also for those of so many others, for so many of us who are women, women of color, women of the Caribbean, island people, mothers and daughters, immigrants, wanderers, exiles. With each new book, her voice is ever clearer, ever more a clarion call. Each new story, each new word, brings a different kind of awe.

I feel an enormous sense of gratitude to Edwidge Danticat.

I'm honored to be here introducing her.

Norman, Oklahoma
October 11, 2018

Achy Obejas *is the author of the critically acclaimed* Tower of the Antilles *and a noted translator of works by Rita Indiana, Junot Díaz, Wendy Guerra, Megan Maxwell, and many others. A native of Havana, she is currently based in the San Francisco Bay area.*

All Geography Is Within Me:
Writing Beginnings, Life, Death, Freedom, and Salt
Edwidge Danticat

1

This past June I was in Haiti in part for the opening of a library in a southern town called Fond-des-Blancs. Fond-des-Blancs, which literally means "The Fountain of the Whites," is mostly known for being home to a large number of people of Polish lineage, the descendants of soldiers from a Polish regiment that switched alliances from the French armies they were fighting alongside in nineteenth-century Haiti to join the Haitians in their battle for independence from France in 1804. The mutinous Polish soldiers who ended up settling in Fond-des-Blancs were the only whites and foreigners who were granted Haitian citizenship after Haiti became the first black republic in the Western hemisphere in 1804.

The library we were there to celebrate had been started by a nonprofit called Haiti Projects, which was run by an acquaintance of mine whose mother is American and whose father is Haitian. The opening-week program included writing workshops and conversations with writers. I took part in a conversation and writing workshop with the Haitian novelist and short-story writer Kettly Mars. Our moderator, a Haiti-based educator named Jean-Marie Théodat, asked each of us to read both the beginning and the end of one of our short stories, then explain to the group of twenty-five or so eager teenagers why we had chosen to begin and end that story the way we had.

If you have ever spoken to a group of teenagers, you know how intimidating it already is to explain anything to them, but this was a bit extra-intimidating for me. It is much easier to explain or elaborate on an ending than a beginning. For endings, you can always say that it ended *this* way because it had begun *that* way. Or it ended that way because something popped up in the middle that led me there. Beginnings have a much bigger burden and are often less clear.

In the beginning was the Word, the Good Book tells us. And perhaps the Word—or the Words—was, were . . .

Once Upon a Time,

Il était une fois or

Te gèn yon fwa or

Krik? Krak!

I feel the same dilemma right now while trying to trace the geography, or cartography, both internal and external, that has brought me from my own beginnings to this moment.

Once upon a time, a little girl was born in Haiti during the middle part of a dynastic thirty-year dictatorship. Her parents were poor, though maybe not as poor as others. My parents didn't get very far in school because their parents could not afford it. My mother was a seamstress. My father, a shoe salesman and a tailor.

When I was two years old, my father left Haiti and moved to the United States to look for work. Two years later, my mother joined him and left me and my younger brother, Bob, in the care of my aunt and uncle in Port-au-Prince.

One of my earliest childhood memories is of being torn away from my mother. On the day my mother left, I wrapped my arms around her legs before she headed for the plane. She leaned down and tearfully unballed my fists so that my uncle could peel me off her. As my brother dropped to the floor, bawling, my mother hurried away, her tear-soaked face buried in her hands. She couldn't bear to look back.

If my life were the short story I was asked to explain the beginning of in that writing workshop with the teenagers in Fond-des-Blancs, this might have been my chosen beginning, the most dramatic one I can remember. After all, as the French-Algerian writer Albert Camus wrote, a person's art is "nothing but this slow trek to rediscover, through the detours of art, those two or three great and simple images in whose presence his heart first opened."

Since I was too young to remember my father leaving Haiti for the

United States, my mother's departure was one of the first images in whose presence both my heart and my art first opened, an art and a heart that suddenly expanded beyond geographical confines and also made me realize that one can love from both near and far.

In Haitian Creole when someone is said to be *"lòt bò dlo,"* on the other side of the water, it can either mean that they've traveled abroad or that they have died. My parents were already *lòt bò dlo*, on the other side of the waters from me, before I fully even knew what that meant. My desire to make sense of this separation, this *lòt bò dlo*-ness, is one of the things that brought me to the internal geography of words and how they can bridge distances.

One way I used to communicate with my parents was through letters. We spoke on the phone once a week while sitting in a telephone booth, where we had a standing appointment every Sunday afternoon, but we also communicated through cassettes that we sent back and forth with people who were traveling between New York and Port-au-Prince. We wrote letters too. Every month my father would send us a half-page letter composed in stilted French to offer news of his and my mother's health as well as details on how to spend the money he and my mother wired for my and my brother's food, lodging, and school expenses.

When my parents' letters and cassettes found their way to me from Brooklyn to Port-au-Prince, I again realized how words—both written and spoken—can transcend geography and time. My mother could tell me stories—once upon a time—in my mind. And I knew, because she later told me this, that she was imagining every day of my life, then whatever indispensable thing I needed to know, only she could tell me. The way she imagined my life in her absence was sometimes better and sometimes worse than what was actually happening to me at ages four, five, six, seven, eight, nine, ten, eleven and twelve, but we were constantly alive in each other's imagination. And because my mother did not write letters and because I did not ever want to forget the things I wished my mother were telling me, the stories I wish she were telling me, I tried to write them down in a small notebook I made from folded sheets of paper bound together by thread. In that notebook, I also sketched a series of stick figures, which were so closely drawn that they almost bumped each other off the page. But mostly I wrote stories, which I later found myself elaborating on. Stories like one of the first prose poems I would write years later and call "Legends."

"Legends" is about a desire, a hunger, I had developed both in my parents' absence and, much later, to tell stories. "Legends" is about a little girl who is dreaming of telling her immigrant mother a story. It's also about a mother who works in a sweatshop in the United States while dreaming of telling stories to her daughter back home in Haiti.

> Once, upon an endless night,
> I dreamed of telling you a story,
> Of pleating you a tale out of my breath
> And carving it into your flesh with my hair.

I imagined that my parents wanted to tell me stories because they were worried that I would forget not just them but the geographies within both me and them. I imagined they wanted to tell me what in Creole we call *lejann*, stories about night women, women with wings of flames who want to draw you out of your bed. Stories about three-legged horses rising at full speed to either snatch or rescue children who had lost their way.

I also imagined that they wanted to tell me what it was like to work in a sweatshop where they might or might not pay you at the end of the week because you're undocumented. Or how the immigration police might come and raid your workplace at anytime and take you to a detention center to await your deportation. I imagined that they wanted me to know even before I stepped foot in the United States that the streets were not littered with gold.

> Once, while cradling someone else's child in my arms,
> Standing at a kitchen stove,
> Stirring a soup for the child's hunger,
> I dreamed of telling you a story.
> A story that rains with salt.

I am telling you to open your mouth,
And catch as much of the salt as you can.
The salt sizzles on your tongue.
And suddenly you understand
That this story is all I know,
And that this story is all I have.

I often tell people about this salt by way of a question I am asked quite often. *Who taught you to write?* I always say that my best writing teachers were the storytellers of my childhood, who were not readers at all—and some not even literate—but who carried stories like treasures inside of them. In my mother's absence, my aunts and grandmothers told me stories. They told me stories in the evenings in the countryside, or when the lights went out in the city, or while they were doing my hair, or while I was doing their hair. This too is another possible beginning. These stories that were told to me in such intimacy by women like the ones the great writer Paule Marshall called kitchen poets. The kitchen poets in my life are also the *poto mitan*, the middle pillars of my beginning as a writer, because they taught me that no story is mine alone, that a story lives and breathes and grows only when it is shared.

2

I moved to the United States in 1981 at age twelve to join my parents soon after cases of acquired immunodeficiency syndrome (AIDS) were first discovered in the United States. The Centers for Disease Control named four groups at "high risk" for the disease: intravenous drug users, homosexuals, hemophiliacs, and Haitians. Haitians were the only ones solely identified by nationality, in part because of twenty or so Haitian patients who'd shown up at Jackson Memorial Hospital in Miami. Suddenly, every Haitian was suspected of having AIDS. At the public junior high school where my parents enrolled me, some of the non-Haitian students would regularly shove and hit me and the other Haitian kids, telling us that we had dirty blood. My English as a Second Language class was excluded from a school trip to the Statue of Liberty out of fear that our sharing a school bus with the other kids might prove dangerous to them.

But I also had a wonderful teacher at this junior high school, a Haitian exile named Raymond Dusseck. Mr. Dusseck was part of my beginning in the United States. Mr. Dusseck built science, math, and ESL lessons around games and songs to help us begin speaking in our new tongue. He taught us English songs that were full of stories, starting with the African American national anthem. I remember being enchanted by James Weldon Johnson's beautiful lyrics:

> Lift every voice and sing,
> Till earth and heaven ring,
> Ring with the harmonies of Liberty . . .
> Let us march on till victory is won.

I was eventually mainstreamed from ESL to a regular English class, where my English teacher, an African American woman named Mrs. Wright, asked me to write an essay about my first Thanksgiving. I wrote that I was looking forward to eating the "golden" turkey, which I thought was rather original. Later I would be horrified by my cliché, but she told me I had a great writing voice. Lift every voice, indeed.

In high school, I had a history teacher named Mr. Casey who taught an elective black history class during our lunch period. I wrote an essay for that class about wanting to be a writer, and Mr. Casey loaned me a book called *Black Women Writers (1950–1980): A Critical Evaluation*, which was edited by the African American poet, writer, and dramatist Mari Evans. It was in that book that I discovered, among others, Paule Marshall, Alice Walker, Audre Lorde, June Jordan, Gayle Jones, Sonia Sanchez, Gloria Naylor, Nikki Giovanni, Toni Morrison, and Zora Neale Hurston, who would become some of the great literary loves of my life.

They were not only part of my new beginning as a writer, but they, along with the great Haitian writers I began reading in New York, writers like Marie Vieux Chauvet, Jacques Roumain, Jacques Stephen Alexis, J. J. Dominique, Ida Faubert, and Dany Laferrière, gave me a place to stand.

"Give me a place to stand," the Greek mathematician Archimedes is believed to have said, "and I will move the earth." But how can we move the earth when all seems to be against it? I asked myself then and ask myself that now. Can words, language change some of the worst conditions we face, especially in situations that seem insurmountable?

The day that Donald Trump was sworn in as president of the United States, I went to hear the Alabama-based poet Ashley M. Jones read from her book *Magic City Gospel* at my local bookstore in Miami, a city that is home to one of the largest foreign-born populations in the United States. In his inaugural speech, Trump had repeatedly invoked "the people" and said, "And this, the United States of America, is your country," but it was hard to believe that he meant to include my black and brown neighbors, friends, and family, many of whom came to America as immigrants. Trump's speech was dark, rancorous. Political language, like poetry, is rarely uttered without intention. Afterward, I wanted to fall into a poet's carefully crafted, insightful, and at times elegiac words.

At the bookstore, I listened as Ashley M. Jones read a poem called "In the beginning there was sound":

After I was born,
I cried for three months straight . . .
Alive, I said.
Pain, I said.

Later that same week, some writer friends and I, along with dozens of others, rallied in front of Miami International Airport to protest Trump's executive order barring all refugees, particularly those from seven predominantly Muslim countries. At the airport rally, we carried signs, like mine, that said "No Human Being Is Illegal." A woman held one that read "Immigrants Are America's Ghostwriters." Another woman had simply scribbled on a piece of cardboard the word "No."

Throughout the rally, my thoughts kept returning to the late Gwendolyn Brooks and some lines from her ode to the singer, actor, and activist Paul Robeson:

> we are each other's
> harvest:
> we are each other's
> business:
> we are each other's
> magnitude and bond.

Once again, I was seeking a new beginning in words.

How far do we have to go through to provoke new beginnings? Does it take the image of children in cages, cell-phone videos of policemen and women shooting black men, women, and children in the back?

What does the artist do to move the world? I want to say we can begin by bearing witness. Not everyone is comfortable with the term *witness*. But no matter what term we use, it means, to me, being as Henry James said, "one of those on whom nothing is lost."

In a 1984 *New York Times* interview, James Baldwin had the following exchange with the writer Julius Lester:

> "Witness is a word I've heard you use often to describe yourself. What are you witness to?" Lester asked.
>
> Baldwin answering in the simplest terms said, "Witness to whence I came, where I am. Witness to what I've seen and the possibilities that I think I see."

Witness is not just where I began but also where I want to end up as a writer. This is the kind of writer I would like to be. Sometimes we cannot fully move the world, but it can move us with its vastness, its expanse, its limitless-ness, its geography or geographies, its beginnings and endings, its injustices, and *lòt bò dlo*-ness.

A few weeks ago, a friend I was talking to about this week told me that I should talk about love. I started considering all the things I could possibly have to say about love, but then I realized that, without sounding too lofty here, that every word I put down on paper is in some way an act of love. And I'm sure that I am not the only writer for whom this is true.

I also started thinking about what James Baldwin wrote about love in *The Fire Next Time*. In that essay, he talks to us about the geography of love that is potentially within us all. "Love takes off the masks that we fear we can-not live without and know we cannot live within," Baldwin wrote. "I use the word 'love' here not merely in the personal sense but as a state of being, or a state of grace—not in the infantile American sense of being made happy but in the tough and universal sense of quest and daring and growth." Yes, that kind of love is also part of my beginning.

So along with this particular kind of love, I decided instead to also talk about the geographies within me, starting with my beginnings.

3

After Zora Neale Hurston's mother, Lucy, died and she was forced to leave her home and travel to places previously unknown to her, she wrote in her autobiography, *Dust Tracks on a Road*, that she realized that she was suddenly forced into "the beginning of things" and that "all that geography was within me. It only needed time to reveal it."

All that geography was within me. It only needed time to reveal it. I love this line so much that sometimes I misquote it as "All geography is within me. It only needs to reveal itself."

When, after graduating from high school in Brooklyn, I had yet another beginning and became a student at Zora Neale Hurston's alma mater, Barnard College, I felt as though her ghost was shadowing me. This new and unex-pected geography—Barnard and Zora—was now within me too, along with all the others from my past and the possibility of other geographies in the future. Like reading and writing, this type of geography can take you away and bring you back, internally and spiritually, back to the source, back to the ground from which you had been wrestled away.

Zora's ghost was also shadowing me in the car in March 2014 after my mother had been told by her doctor that she had terminal ovarian cancer. At a red light, where I stopped for too long, my mother spoke up for the first time since we'd heard the news and warned, "Don't suddenly become a zombie." My mother was telling me not to lose my good sense, to keep my head on my shoulders, but it popped up in my mind that a motherless Zora had gone to Haiti to study zombies.

When we got home from the doctor's that day, my mother made us each a small cup of coffee that she sprinkled with salt. According to Haitian folklore, one way zombies can be liberated from their living death is by eating salt. People who suddenly receive terrible news are also given salt, in coffee for example, to help ward off the *sezisman*, the shock, so that we are able to pick ourselves up and keep moving.

This salt is for me the source of all forceful beginnings and the source of all freedom. We are here because in some way we were given the salt. For some of us that salt is *words*. For others, it is *paint*. For others, it is *music*. For others, it is God. For some it is simply the ability to survive.

When I first came to this country, I remember being shocked that salt was powdery white. In my household in Haiti, we would often buy rock salt in the market, and it often looked like little crystals or small pebbles, which were unevenly shaped and had dark streaks either on the surface or inside. You always had to wash the crystals before putting them in food, and even after you washed them they looked more gray than white. This is the salt I imagined those seeking their liberation wanting to be fed.

This type of salt shows up in another part of "Legends":

And what was that Sleeping Beauty,
If not a zombie?
And what was it that gave her freedom

From the sleeping sickness,

If not the taste of salt on the prince's lips?

Let no one tell you that it was the man's breath itself.

Everyone knows—or Manman knows—that it was the salt.

It is always the salt that wakes the dead.

And brings the children home.

This home for me is first and foremost the page. And the page is both full of death and free of it. Full of death because a trail of bodies from the Middle Passage lies behind me in the sea that made the first kind of salt I ever knew.

"The sea is salt," Zora Neale Hurston wrote.

"The sea is History," Derek Walcott wrote.

The sea has been part of both our beginnings and our endings.

The story whose beginning I chose to explain to the teenagers at the library in Fond-des-Blancs is from my 1995 short-story collection *Krik? Krak!* and is called "Children of the Sea." It is about a group of Haitian refugees who are trying to reach the United States by boat, like so many refugees and migrants have been trying to reach so many shores, lately including European shores.

I began the story the way I did, I told them, with lines borrowed from a Haitian proverb: "Dèyè mòn gen mòn." Behind the mountains are more mountains. The story begins with "They say behind the mountains are more mountains. Now I know it's true." I began it this way because that story had reminded me that some people's potential new beginnings can also lead to their end. Writing that story had reinforced for me the idea that the page—my writing home—has to also be free from death because creating anything, be it words, images, song, and dance, means that we believe in immortality, that we believe we can survive, even on the other side of the waters, even *lòt bò dlo*.

You never know a person until you've eaten salt together, Toni Cade Bambara writes in *The Salt Eaters*. And this week we have all had the privilege of eating salt together, by yes, breaking bread together, but also with the words we have spoken, the songs we have sung, the ways that we have moved our bodies through these dances that have come to us, both ancestral memory and more recently acquired knowledge. And for this I do not have enough words to say thank you. So, I will offer my gratitude in the voices of those who came before me, with all my honor and respect (Onè, Respè).

Mèsi anpil, anpil.

Thank you.

Norman, Oklahoma
October 11, 2018

Acknowledgments

As the editor of this anthology, I am indebted, first and foremost, to the Neustadt family. Serving as the editor in chief of *World Literature Today* is in itself an honor, and helping facilitate the visits of writers from around the world to the University of Oklahoma is one of the great pleasures of the work we are entrusted to carry out. Since I arrived on campus in 2000, I've always looked forward to the annual Neustadt Festival as one of the highlights of the fall social calendar, especially the culminating banquets that are replete with august traditions and a sense of literary history in the making. Until he passed away in 2010, it was always Walter Neustadt Jr. who, with great charm and modesty, presided over the family's role in presenting the Neustadt Prize to that year's laureate, with his wife, Dolores, at his side. Since then, their daughters—Nancy, Susan, and Kathy—have lifted the torch of the family's philanthropic ideals even higher. Their counsel and friendship have made us all more faithful stewards of the mission we are privileged to sustain.

My thanks as well to my predecessors as editors, in particular Roy Temple House (fellow Nebraskan), Robert Vlach, Bernice Duncan, Ivar Ivask, and William Riggan, who each brought editorial acumen and erudition to the "misery and splendor" of running a literary journal. We're fortunate, indeed, that Ms. Duncan was finally able to persuade Dr. Ivask to pick up stakes and move to the Southern Plains, with the result that what many perceived to be a literary backwater became a cosmopolis of culture.

Special thanks to Dr. Riggan, whose deep institutional knowledge proved invaluable as I delved into the early history of the Neustadt Prize, as did the many photocopies of articles and rare correspondence that he provided.

To my current colleagues at *WLT*—RC Davis-Undiano, Jen Blair, Kay Blunck, Michelle Johnson, Terri Stubblefield, and Rob Vollmar—the pleasure of working together to help make Norman, Oklahoma, "one of the undeclared capitals" of literary modernity will forever be one of the highlights of my professional career as well as a true personal privilege. Dr. Davis-Undiano, in particular, gave me the support and encouragement to undertake this book project, with enthusiasm and wise counsel along the way.

Without the editorial assistance of Adrienne Crezo, Patrick Ortez, and Grey Simon, it would have been impossible to finish my work on this project in timely fashion.

During my tenure at *WLT*, President David L. Boren, President Joseph Harroz Jr., Provost Nancy L. Mergler, and Provost Kyle Harper have given *WLT* unflagging support as we approach the milestone of one hundred years of continuous publication.

To our colleagues in Monnet Hall—the curator and staff of OU's renowned Western History Collections—I'm indebted for having been given unrestricted access to the *Books Abroad* and *World Literature Today* archives. Librarian Jacquelyn Slater Reese, in particular, helped facilitate my research in OU's rich institutional archives.

Thanks as well to Lynette Lobban, director of publications for the OU Foundation, for providing a copy of Boyd Gunning's September 25, 1969, letter to Doris Westheimer Neustadt, which helped me connect the dots between the early history of the Neustadt family's legendary generosity to the university with Walter Neustadt Jr.'s 1972 decision to endow the Neustadt Prize in perpetuity. She also graciously offered feedback on the penultimate draft of my introduction, as did Dr. Riggan.

My thanks to all the living laureates who granted permission to reprint their acceptance speeches, and I owe a debt to many of the past jurors as well.

I'm also grateful to the following literary agents for their kind assistance in helping secure reprint rights: Andrew Nurnberg Associates, literary agent for Assia Djebar; Nicole Aragi, literary agent for Nuruddin Farah and Edwidge Danticat; and Jane Novak, literary agent for David Malouf.

Yinan Wang's illustrations of all the past laureates—a continuation of work she first undertook while a student intern at *WLT*—provided an elegant aesthetic touch to the anthology, as did Jen Blair's guiding art direction and cover design.

I'm also grateful to David Shook for immediately offering to publish this volume when I first approached him about it in December 2018. While it's been a privilege to witness his meteoric rise from all-star *WLT* intern to international cultural impresario, David has also been an inspiration as a fellow poet, translator, and editor.

To Will Evans, executive director and publisher of Deep Vellum, whose infectious enthusiasm for publishing an elegant hardcover trade edition inspired me to imagine an audience for the book beyond the circle of those who already knew about the prize.

Finally, my eternal thanks goes to my wife, Alba, and to our three daughters for their support and wings of love that lift me up and inspire me more than any book will ever do.

—*Daniel Simon*

The 1969 Charter

Announcement of the Establishment of the *Books Abroad*
International Prize for Literature

PREAMBLE

Since its inception, *Books Abroad* has manifested a lively concern for the annual choices made by the Swedish Academy for that most respected of writing awards, the Nobel Prize for Literature. Under the original editorial aegis of Roy Temple House, we find in the quarterly such critical symposia as "Prodding the Nobel Prize Committee" (1932), "Nominations for the Nobel Prize for Literature" (1935), and *"Books Abroad's* Super-Nobel Election" (1940). The second editor, Ernst Erich Noth, sponsored an exchange of ideas entitled "What's Wrong with the Nobel Prize?" (1951), and the late Robert Vlach convened the most comprehensive discussion of all, the "Nobel Prize Symposium" of 1967. As guest editor of the last named issue, Professor Herbert Howarth (University of Pennsylvania) even sketched some possible guidelines for the Swedish Academy to consider, such as ". . . not to the *best-wishing* maker but to the best maker-even if the best maker appears to wish ill." He recommended that poets and dramatists be considered on a par with novelists; that the Prize should not necessarily crown a life's work, but should upon occasion direct attention to an important life work *in progress;* finally, that authors from the less-known literatures should not be regarded as the least eligible.

In spite of such critical scrutiny, in *Books Abroad* as in other journals throughout the world, no other important international literary prize has been established. To date, there is no competition to the criteria set up by the Swedish Academy, with its attendant perquisites of professional status and monetary compensation. We propose therefore that *Books Abroad,* as the oldest international literary review in the English language, sponsor the establishment of a new award to be known as the *Books Abroad* International Prize for Literature.

I

In the beginning, the Prize is to be awarded in alternate years, later perhaps annually. The choice will be announced in February-fittingly, it is felt, since *Books Abroad* began publication with the Winter issue of 1927. The first award is to be made in 1970, the amount to be $10,000 or more, contingent upon support from certain foundations and private donors who will be approached. The award will be presented at the University of Oklahoma in Norman approximately thirty days after the announcement of the choice.

II

Candidates for the Prize will be reviewed by an international Board of Selection which will meet for a three-day weekend conference in February of the year in which the Prize is to be offered. The Board will meet at the University of Oklahoma in Norman, which sponsors the publication of *Books Abroad*. In addition to the Editor of the quarterly, who will be the only permanent member, the Board is to include eleven members to be chosen by the Editor in consultation with the Editorial Board of *Books Abroad*. With the exception of the Editor, the Board of Selection will be composed of new members for each year that the Prize is to be offered. The following Board is suggested for the Prize of 1970:

1. *J. P. Clark* (Nigeria)
2. *Heinrich Böll* (Germany)
3. *Frank Kermode* (England)
4. *Richard Wilbur* (USA)
5. *Gaëtan Picon* (France)
6. *Jan Kott* (Poland)
7. *Piero Bigongiari* (Italy)
8. *Mario Vargas Llosa* (Peru)
9. *A. K. Ramanujan* (India/USA)

10. *Andrei Voznesensky* (USSR)

11. *René Wellek* (USA)

III

Eligibility. Each Board member is invited to present to the jury a maximum of three names to be considered for the Prize. The final choice shall be made by balloting, the winner to be decided by a majority vote (seven votes or more). No writer shall be eligible whose work is not currently available or cannot be presented to the Board in a major Western language.

Candidates may also be suggested by the public at large to the Editor of *Books Abroad,* but without any guarantee that they will necessarily be presented to the Board for consideration.

IV

In years in which the Prize is awarded, *Books Abroad* will devote one of its issues to a critical symposium on the work of the recipient. The University of Oklahoma Press will also consider the publication of a book by or on the laureate chosen for the International Prize.

V

Since *Books Abroad* is only the international forum charged with administering the Prize, the University of Oklahoma will seek contributions from foundations, publishers, and individuals in order to make the award financially worthwhile and representative of American concern for genuine achievement in world literature.

PEN International Congress
Menton, France
September 15, 1969

Books Abroad 43, no. 4 (Autumn 1969): 483–84

About the Neustadt Family

The Neustadt family's major support of the University of Oklahoma has been crucial to the institution's development. From the gift to the university of land for Max Westheimer Airpark to the addition of the Neustadt Wing of the Bizzell Memorial Library, sponsorship of the Neustadt International Prize for Literature, and establishment of the Neustadt Professorship in Comparative Literature, through three generations of active, visionary leadership, the Neustadt family has promoted excellence in higher education.

The Neustadt family endowed what was then known as the Books Abroad International Prize for Literature in 1972. **Walter Neustadt Jr.** (1919–2010) had received his master's degree from OU in 1941 and was a member of the Board of Regents and a trustee of the OU Foundation when President Paul F. Sharp announced the $200,000 gift on May 17, 1972. The award received its present name, the Neustadt International Prize for Literature, in 1976. In 1992 Walter received the Oklahoma Governor's Arts Award for his support of literature and the arts in the state and an honorary Doctor of Humane Letters degree from OU in 2005.

With the NSK Neustadt Prize for Children's Literature, a new generation of the Neustadt family has dedicated itself to advancing the cause of literary excellence at the University of Oklahoma. The letters "NSK" stand for Nancy, Susan, and Kathy, the children of Walter and Dolores Neustadt and the benefactors of the prize. The three sisters decided to encourage the improvement of writing for children by honoring an accomplished contemporary writer or illustrator of children's literature every other year. All three were honored with Regents' Alumni Awards in 2011 for their dedication and service to the university.

Nancy Barcelo lives in Watertown, Massachusetts, with her husband, Scott. She is a retired hospice volunteer director and was involved in all aspects of hospice for twenty-five years. She has always loved books and received a BA in English from Skidmore College. She received a master's degree as a reading specialist from Lesley College in Cambridge, Massachusetts. Nancy's husband, Scott, is a lifelong scholar of Eastern religion and philosophy and received a master of divinity degree from Harvard University. Sam Barcelo received his MBA degree at Boston University with an emphasis on the nonprofit sector, and Emma Barcelo graduated from Colorado College and has developed political digital media aimed for millennials.

Susan Neustadt Schwartz cofounded Equest, a therapeutic horseback-riding program, in 1981 and continues to serve on its board of directors. She also helped start a therapeutic horseback riding program in a women's prison in Canada in 2010. She served on the Shelton School and Evaluation Center's board of directors from 2006 to 2014 and the Fairhill School board of directors from 1982 to 1986. She graduated from the University of Oklahoma with a BFA and went on to receive her master's degree in education from Southern Methodist University. Before starting Equest, she taught at Fairhill School for twelve years and tutored children at Shelton and Saint Philip's School. Her awards include the volunteer of the year award from the international organization PATH, the Professional Association for Therapeutic Horsemanship, and the Woman of Distinction Award from Lake Forest Academy in Chicago. She has two daughters, Elizabeth and Kate, and fostered two boys, Aaron and Elijah, whose parents died when they were very young.

Kathy Neustadt lives in Denver and is a freelance field producer for ABC News. Before television, she worked in radio broadcasting in the mountains of Colorado for five years before going to work at KCNC-TV in Denver as a news writer. Kathy works extensively in not-for-profits in the Denver area. She is on the board of trustees at the Rose Community Foundation in Denver, current board chair of the Mizel Arts and Culture Center, and the former chair and longtime board member of the Staenberg-Loup Jewish Community

Center. In 2012 Kathy endowed what is now the Neustadt JAAMM Festival, which features Jewish authors, speakers, music, and film at the JCC every fall. She attended the University of Oklahoma and graduated from the University of Denver with a degree in mass communications. She loves to ski and hike in the Rockies and has two children, Tess and Josh Hankin.

After the announcement of the endowment of the Books Abroad Prize by the Neustadt family at the University of Oklahoma, May 17, 1972. *Seated from left:* Doris Westheimer Neustadt, Walter Neustadt Jr., and Nancy Davies, president of the OU Board of Regents. *Standing from left:* University of Oklahoma president Paul F. Sharp, Dolores Neustadt, Marilyn Neustadt, and Allan Neustadt.

The Neustadt Silver Eagle Feather
Mike Dirham

Like the laurel leaf from the sacred tree of Apollo, woven into a garland to crown the poet, the hero, the laureate, so the eagle feather signified success for the original Americans. In many cultures the eagle has been associated with the life of the spirit, with the transcendent experience, and among North American Plains tribes the eagle symbolized the Great Powers themselves.

Catching the eagle for its feathers was a holy task accompanied by prayer and fasting, and when the eagle came, it was received as a gift from those Powers it represented. It was accepted as a reward for human effort both physical and spiritual. The feather of the eagle was worn with great reverence and humility and respect.

Two traditions come together here. Two traditions—the eagle feather of the American Indian and the quill of the poet—are united in this prize. It is an appropriate fusion of meanings for an award to honor the highest achievements in the literature of the world.

Books Abroad 47, no. 3 (Summer 1973): 443

Mike Dirham *(1941–2018), former art director of* Books Abroad / World Literature Today, *designed the Neustadt silver feather.*

Laureates by Country and Their Nominating Jurors
1970–2018

A complete list of past jurors and their respective nominees can be found on the Neustadt Prize website (neustadtprize.org).

Year	Laureate	Country	Juror(s)
1970	Giuseppe Ungaretti	Italy	Piero Bigongiari (Italy)
1972	Gabriel García Márquez	Colombia	Thor Vilhjálmsson (Iceland)
1974	Francis Ponge	France	Michel Butor (France)
1976	Elizabeth Bishop	United States	John Ashbery (US) and Marie-Claire Blais (Canada)
1978	Czesław Miłosz	Poland / United States	Joseph Brodsky (USSR/US)
1980	Josef Škvorecký	Czechoslovakia / Canada	Arnošt Lustig (Czechoslovakia/US)
1982	Octavio Paz	Mexico	Manuel Durán (Spain/US)
1984	Paavo Haavikko	Finland	Bo Carpelan (Finland)
1986	Max Frisch	Switzerland	Adolf Muschg (Switzerland)
1988	Raja Rao	India	Edwin Thumboo (Singapore)
1990	Tomas Tranströmer	Sweden	Jaan Kaplinski (Estonia)
1992	João Cabral de Melo Neto	Brazil	Silviano Santiago (Brazil)
1994	Kamau Brathwaite	Barbados	Kofi Awoonor (Ghana)
1996	Assia Djebar	Algeria	Barbara Frischmuth (Austria)
1998	Nuruddin Farah	Somalia	Ngũgĩ wa Thiong'o (Kenya/US)
2000	David Malouf	Australia	Ihab Hassan (Egypt/US)
2002	Álvaro Mutis	Colombia	Juan Gustavo Cobo Borda (Colombia)
2004	Adam Zagajewski	Poland	Bogdana Carpenter (Poland/US)
2006	Claribel Alegría	Nicaragua / El Salvador	Daisy Zamora (Nicaragua/US)
2008	Patricia Grace	New Zealand	Joy Harjo (US)
2010	Duo Duo	China	Mai Mang (China/US)
2012	Rohinton Mistry	India / Canada	Samrat Upadhyay (Nepal/US)
2014	Mia Couto	Mozambique	Gabriella Ghermandi (Ethiopia/Italy)
2016	Dubravka Ugrešić	Croatia / The Netherlands	Alison Anderson (US/Switzerland)
2018	Edwidge Danticat	Haiti / United States	Achy Obejas (Cuba/US)

Recommended Reading

Historic correspondence about past Neustadt juries, press releases, and the like can be found in the World Literature Today / Books Abroad *archives in the Western History Collections at the University of Oklahoma, Norman.*

LAUREATES' ACCEPTANCE SPEECHES / LECTURES

Claribel Alegría, "The Sword of Poetry," trans. David Draper Clark, *World Literature Today* 81, no. 3 (May 2007): 30–32.

Elizabeth Bishop, "Laureate's Words of Acceptance," *World Literature Today* 51, no. 1 (Winter 1977): 12.

Kamau Brathwaite, "Newstead to Neustadt," *World Literature Today* 68, no. 4 (Autumn 1994): 653–60.

João Cabral de Melo Neto, "Laureate's Acceptance Speech," trans. Djelal Kadir, *World Literature Today* 66, no. 4 (Autumn 1992): 603–6.

Mia Couto, "Re-enchanting the World: The 2014 Neustadt Prize Lecture," trans. Paul Fauvet, *World Literature Today* 89, no. 1 (January 2015): 50–53.

Edwidge Danticat, "All Geography Is Within Me: Writing Beginnings, Life, Death, Freedom, and Salt," *World Literature Today* 93, no. 1 (Winter 2019): 59–65.

Assia Djebar, "Neustadt Prize Acceptance Speech," trans. Pamela A. Genova, *World Literature Today* 70, no. 4 (Autumn 1996): 783–84.

Duo Duo, "This Is the Reason We Persevere: The 2010 Neustadt Prize Lecture," trans. Mai Mang, *World Literature Today* 85, no. 2 (March 2011): 46–47.

Nuruddin Farah, "Celebrating Differences: The 1998 Neustadt Lecture," *World Literature Today* 72, no. 4 (Autumn 1998): 709–12. Reprinted by permission of Nuruddin Farah and Aragi, Inc.

Max Frisch, "Neustadt Prize Acceptance Speech," *World Literature Today* 62, no. 1 (Winter 1988): 11–13.

Gabriel García Márquez. *See* Ivar Ivask, "Allegro Barbaro."

Patricia Grace, "The World Is Where You Are: The 2008 Neustadt Lecture," *World Literature Today* 83, no. 3 (May 2009): 28–31.

Paavo Haavikko, "Laureate's Acceptance," trans. Philip Binham, *World Literature Today* 58, no. 4 (Autumn 1984): 500–501.

Ivar Ivask, "Allegro Barbaro, or Gabriel García Márquez in Oklahoma," *Books Abroad* 47, no. 3 (Summer 1973): 439–40.

———, "Homage to Giuseppe Ungaretti: The Old Captain's Last Voyage," *Books Abroad* 44, no. 4 (Autumn 1970): 543–51.

———, "Notes toward a 'Francis Ponge in Norman,'" *Books Abroad* 48, no. 4 (Autumn 1974): 647–51.

David Malouf, "A Writing Life: The 2000 Neustadt Lecture," *World Literature Today* 74, no. 4 (Autumn 2000): 701–5.

Czesław Miłosz, "Laureate's Words of Acceptance," *World Literature Today* 52, no. 3 (Summer 1978): 368–71.

Rohinton Mistry, "'The Road from There to Here': The 2012 Neustadt Prize Lecture," *World Literature Today* 87, no. 1 (January 2013): 44–50.

Álvaro Mutis, "Álvaro Mutis on Himself," trans. David Draper Clark, *World Literature Today* 77, no. 2 (July 2003): 9–11.

Octavio Paz, "Laureate's Words of Acceptance," *World Literature Today* 56, no. 4 (Autumn 1982): 595–96.

———, "The Turning House" [poem], trans. Ivar Ivask, *World Literature Today* 57, no. 3 (Summer 1983): 386.

Francis Ponge. *See* Ivar Ivask, "Notes toward a 'Francis Ponge in Norman.'"

Raja Rao, "Laureate's Words of Acceptance," *World Literature Today* 62, no. 4 (Autumn 1988): 534–35.

Josef Škvorecký, "Laureate's Words of Acceptance," *World Literature Today* 54, no. 4 (Autumn 1980): 501–4.

Tomas Tranströmer, "Laureate's Words of Acceptance," *World Literature Today* 64, no. 4 (Autumn 1990): 552–53.

———, "Oklahoma" [poem], *World Literature Today* 64, no. 3 (Summer 1990), 436.

Dubravka Ugrešić, "A Girl in Litland: The 2016 Neustadt Prize Lecture," trans. Ellen Elias-Bursać, *World Literature Today* 91, no. 1 (January 2017): 58–60.

Giuseppe Ungaretti. *See* Ivar Ivask, "Homage to Giuseppe Ungaretti."

Adam Zagajewski, "Poetry for Beginners: The 2004 Neustadt Lecture," trans. Clare Cavanagh, *World Literature Today* 79, no. 2 (May 2005): 10–13.

JURORS' ENCOMIA / NOMINATING STATEMENTS

N.B. *No formal nominating statement from Piero Bigongiari appears in the archives, only his letters to Ivar Ivask presenting the names of his two nominees: Giuseppe Ungaretti and René Char.*

Alison Anderson, "Dubravka Ugrešić and Contemporary European Literature: Along a Path to Transnational Literature," *World Literature Today* 91, no. 1 (January 2017): 61–63.

Kwame Anthony Appiah, "For Nuruddin Farah," *World Literature Today* 72, no. 4 (Autumn 1998): 703–5.

John Ashbery, "Second Presentation of Elizabeth Bishop," *World Literature Today* 51, no. 1 (Winter 1977): 8–11.

Kofi N. Awoonor, letter to Djelal Kadir nominating Kamau Brathwaite for the 1994 Neustadt Prize, September 9, 1993, *World Literature Today* archives, box 125, Western History Collections, University of Oklahoma, Norman.

Marie-Claire Blais, "Presentation of Elizabeth Bishop to the Jury," *World Literature Today* 51, no. 1 (Winter 1977): 7.

Joseph Brodsky, "Presentation of Czesław Miłosz to the Jury," *World Literature Today* 52, no. 3 (Summer 1978): 364.

Michel Butor, "Francis Ponge: Presentation to the Jury," trans. Ivar Ivask, *Books Abroad* 48, no. 4 (Autumn 1974): 658.

Bo Carpelan, "Presentation of Paavo Haavikko to the Jury," *World Literature Today* 58, no. 4 (Autumn 1984): 497–98.

Bogdana Carpenter, "A Tribute to Adam Zagajewski," *World Literature Today* 79, no. 2 (May 2005): 14–15.

Juan Gustavo Cobo Borda, "Nominating Statement for Álvaro Mutis," trans. David Draper Clark, *World Literature Today* 77, no. 2 (July 2003): 6–8.

Manuel Durán, "Octavio Paz: The Poet as Philosopher," *World Literature Today* 56, no. 4 (Autumn 1982): 591–94.

Barbara Frischmuth, "A Letter to Assia Djebar," trans. William Riggan, *World Literature Today* 70, no. 4 (Autumn 1996): 778–80.

Gabriella Ghermandi, "Nominating Statement for Mia Couto" [2014], previously unpublished.

Joy Harjo, "In Honor of Patricia Grace," *World Literature Today* 83, no. 3 (May 2009): 34–36.

Ihab Hassan, "Encomium: David Malouf," *World Literature Today* 74, no. 4 (Autumn 2000): 710–12.

Djelal Kadir, "The Rigors of Necessity: Encomium for João Cabral De Melo Neto," *World Literature Today* 66, no. 4 (Autumn 1992): 599–602. [for Silviano Santiago]

Jaan Kaplinski, "Presentation to the Jury," *World Literature Today* 64, no. 4 (Autumn 1990): 552.

Arnošt Lustig, "Encomium for Josef Škvorecký," *World Literature Today* 54, no. 4 (Autumn 1980): 505–8.

Mai Mang, "Duo Duo: Master of Wishful Thinking," *World Literature Today* 85, no. 2 (March 2011): 48–50.

Adolf Muschg, "Presentation of Max Frisch to the 1986 Neustadt Prize Jury," *World Literature Today* 60, no. 4 (Autumn 1986): 543–47.

Ngũgĩ wa Thiong'o, "Kamau Brathwaite: The Voice of African Presence," *World Literature Today* 68, no. 4 (Autumn 1994): 677–82.

——, "Nuruddin Farah: A Statement of Nomination to the 1998 Neustadt Jury," *World Literature Today* 72, no. 4 (Autumn 1998): 716.

Achy Obejas, "Bearing the Unforgivable: A Tribute to Edwidge Danticat," *World Literature Today* 93, no. 1 (Winter 2019): 66–67.

Luciano Rebay, "Encomium for Giuseppe Ungaretti," *Books Abroad* 44, no. 4 (Autumn 1970): 551–56.

Silviano Santiago, "João Cabral de Melo Neto" [1992 Neustadt Prize nominating statement], trans. Djelal Kadir, *World Literature Today* archives, box 126, Western History Collections, University of Oklahoma, Norman.

Edwin Thumboo, "Encomium for Raja Rao," *World Literature Today* 62, no. 4 (Autumn 1988): 530–33.

Samrat Upadhyay, "Rohinton Mistry's Omniscient Gaze," *World Literature Today* 87, no. 1 (January 2013): 51–52.

Thor Vilhjálmsson, "Presentation of Gabriel García Márquez," *Books Abroad* 47, no. 1 (Winter 1973): 10–11.

Daisy Zamora, "Knowing Claribel Alegría," *World Literature Today* 81, no. 3 (May 2007): 44–45.

ABOUT THE HISTORY OF THE PRIZE

Mike Dirham, "The Neustadt Silver Eagle Feather," *Books Abroad* 47, no. 3 (Summer 1973): 443.

David Draper Clark, "*Books Abroad / World Literature Today:* Past, Present and Future," *Publishing Research Quarterly* 18, no. 1 (Spring 2002): 38–45.

Ivar Ivask, "Announcement of the Establishment of the *Books Abroad* International Prize for Literature," *Books Abroad* 43, no. 4 (Autumn 1969): 483–84.

———, "The *Books Abroad* / Neustadt International Prize for Literature 1972: A Progress Report," *Books Abroad* 46, no. 3 (Summer 1972): 426.

———, "Giuseppe Ungaretti: Laureate of Our First International Prize for Literature," *Books Abroad* 44, no. 2 (1970): 191–94.

———, "Revised Charter of the *Books Abroad* International Prize for Literature," *Books Abroad* 46, no. 2 (Spring 1972): 253–54.

———, "World Literature Today, or Books Abroad II and Geography III," *World Literature Today* 51, no. 1 (Winter 1977): 4–6.

Walter Neustadt Jr., "Address at the Banquet Honoring the 1972 Jury of the *Books Abroad* / Neustadt International Prize for Literature," *Books Abroad* 47, no. 3 (Summer 1973): 441–42.

William Riggan, "A Conversation between William Riggan and Janette Turner Hospital," in *Dictionary of Literary Biography Yearbook: 2002*, edited by Matthew J. Bruccoli and George Garrett (Gale, 2003), 171–84.

———, "The Nobel Connection," *Sooner Magazine*, Spring 1981, 16–20.

———, "The Nobel Prize in Literature: History and Overview," in *The Nobel Prize Winners: Literature, 1901–1926*, ed. Frank N. Magill (Englewood Cliffs, NJ: Salem Press, 1987), 1–26.

———, "The Swedish Academy and the Nobel Prize in Literature: History and Procedure," *World Literature Today* 55, no. 3 (Summer 1981): 399–405.

WHAT OTHERS HAVE SAID ABOUT THE NEUSTADT (AND THE NOBEL)

Patrick Healy, "Oklahoma's Coveted Literature Prize," *Chronicle of Higher Education*, January 10, 1997, B8–9.

Herbert Howarth, "A Petition to the Swedish Academy," *Books Abroad* 41, no. 1 (Winter 1967): 4–7.

Ivar Ivask, "Greek Poet Odysseus Elytis, Nobel 1979, and Czech Novelist Josef Škvorecký, Neustadt 1980," *World Literature Today* 54, no. 2 (Spring 1980): 189–95.

Olof Lagercrantz, "A Literary Prize in Oklahoma," *Books Abroad* 48, no. 3 (Summer 1974): 445–46.

William Marling, "The Neustadt Prize and the Framing Effect," *World Literature Today* 90, nos. 3–4 (May 2016): 42–45.

Edwin McDowell, "The Oklahoma 'Nobel,'" *New York Times*, February 26, 1982.

"Nobel Prize Symposium," *Books Abroad* 41, no. 1 (Winter 1967).

"Nobel Prize Symposium II: Choices and Omissions, 1967–1987," *World Literature Today* 62, no. 2 (Spring 1988), 197–241.

Barbara Palmer, "Oklahoma's Nobel: OU's Neustadt Prize for Literature Shines in the Shadow of the Nobel," *Oklahoma Today*, January–February 1999, 40–43.

Chad W. Post, "The American Nobel: Oklahoma's Neustadt Prize," *World Literature Today* 91, no. 1 (January 2017): 64–65.

Maarten Van Delden, "Claribel Alegría, the Neustadt Prize, and the World Republic of Letters," *World Literature Today* 81, no. 3 (May 2007): 45–48.

Lawrence Van Gelder, "Footlights," *New York Times*, February 26, 1998.

MORE ABOUT *WORLD LITERATURE TODAY*

Genova, Pamela Antonia, ed. *Twayne Companion to Contemporary World Literature: From the Editors of* World Literature Today. New York: Twayne, 2003.

www.worldlit.org

Contributors' Index